"This is a 'tour de force', rich in its depth of analysis of an international context. Its conclusions will challenge makers and is essential reading. It is economic geograph

"Regional and urban policies matter for countries' economic performance: this is a fundamental link often overlooked in the design of pro-growth policy packages. Taking the case of the UK economy, Professor Philip McCann makes in this book a splendid demonstration of how the system of regions and cities contributes to aggregate productivity and growth. His analysis, backed by a rich body of academic literature and empirical evidence, shows how well-tailored policies to regional differences and assets could mobilise a currently untapped growth (and wellbeing) potential existing in UK regions and cities."

— *Joaquim Oliveira Martins, Head of the OECD Regional Policy Division and Associate Professor, University Paris-Dauphine*

The UK Regional–National Economic Problem

In recent years, the United Kingdom has become a more and more divided society with inequality between the regions as marked as it has ever been. In a landmark analysis of the current state of Britain's regional development, Philip McCann utilises current statistics, examines historical trends and makes pertinent international comparisons to assess the state of the nation.

The UK Regional–National Economic Problem brings attention to the highly centralised, top-down governance structure that the UK deploys, and demonstrates that it is less than ideally placed to rectify these inequalities. The 'north-south' divide in the UK has never been greater and the rising inequalities are evident in almost all aspects of the economy including productivity, incomes, employment status and wealth. Whilst the traditional economic dominance of London and its hinterland has continued along with relative resilience in the South West of England and Scotland, in contrast the Midlands, the North of England, Northern Ireland and Wales lag behind by most measures of prosperity. This inequality is greatly limiting national economic performance and the fact that Britain has a below average standard of living in European terms has been ignored. The UK's economic governance inequality is unlikely to be rebalanced by the current governance and connectivity trends, although this definitive study suggests that some areas of improvement are possible if they are well implemented.

This pivotal analysis is essential reading for postgraduate students in economics and urban studies as well as researchers and policy-makers in local and central government.

Philip McCann holds the University of Groningen Endowed Chair of Economic Geography at the University of Groningen, the Netherlands, and is also the Tagliaferri Visiting Fellow in the Department of Land Economy at the University of Cambridge, UK.

Regions and Cities

Series Editor in Chief
Susan M. Christopherson, *Cornell University, USA*

Editors

Maryann Feldman, *University of Georgia, USA*
Gernot Grabher, *HafenCity University Hamburg, Germany*
Ron Martin, *University of Cambridge, UK*
Martin Perry, *Massey University, New Zealand*
Kieran P. Donaghy, *Cornell University, USA*

In today's globalised, knowledge-driven and networked world, regions and cities have assumed heightened significance as the interconnected nodes of economic, social and cultural production, and as sites of new modes of economic and territorial governance and policy experimentation. This book series brings together incisive and critically engaged international and interdisciplinary research on this resurgence of regions and cities, and should be of interest to geographers, economists, sociologists, political scientists and cultural scholars, as well as to policy makers involved in regional and urban development.

For more information on the Regional Studies Association visit www.regionalstudies.org

There is a **30% discount** available to RSA members on books in the **Regions and Cities** series, and other subject related Taylor and Francis books and e-books including Routledge titles. To order just e-mail alex.robinson@tandf.co.uk, or phone on +44 (0) 20 7017 6924 and declare your RSA membership. You can also visit www.routledge.com and use the discount code: **RSA0901**

The UK Regional–National Economic Problem

Geography, globalisation and governance

Philip McCann

Routledge
Taylor & Francis Group

LONDON AND NEW YORK

First published 2016
by Routledge
2 Park Square, Milton Park, Abingdon, Oxfordshire OX14 4RN

and by Routledge
711 Third Avenue, New York, NY 10017

First issued in paperback 2017

Routledge is an imprint of the Taylor & Francis Group, an informa business

British Library Cataloguing in Publication Data
A catalogue record for this book is available from the British Library

Library of Congress Cataloguing in Publication Data
A catalog record for this book has been requested

ISBN 13: 978-1-138-89508-9 (pbk)
ISBN 13: 978-1-138-64723-7 (hbk)

Typeset in Times New Roman
by Out of House Publishing

To Raquel, Mark Alexander and All of My Family

Contents

Figures

Tables

Preface

In order to examine and address the issues being investigated and discussed in this book the approach adopted here heavily relies on both an international comparative perspective and also a long-run perspective, as well as on detailed evidence and discussions regarding internal UK-specific issues. This international comparative approach reflects the intellectual approach to the questioning about UK issues which I have adopted over many years as a result of my own professional experience. In addition to working as an academic for over a decade within the UK I have also spent much more than half of my academic career teaching in universities in a range of other countries including USA, New Zealand, Japan, Thailand and The Netherlands, while also working with various high-level international organisations and government bodies. During these overseas periods I have found myself asking questions about the UK economy in the light of my observations of the experience of other countries. On so many levels when it comes to urban and regional issues the UK is such a puzzling case. Internal debates within the UK public policy arena are so heavily dominated by internal political narratives that they tend either to totally ignore potential lessons from other countries, or instead they immediately lean towards supposed US lessons for the UK case. However, as will become clear in this book, there is far more to be gained by considering the UK issues in a much wider international context. Throughout the book I have therefore followed a broadly OECD type of evidence-based approach, which sets the analytical arguments regarding the UK in the context of the international empirical evidence from many different countries. This type of approach throws a great deal of doubt on the standard internal UK debates and narratives, and opens an analysis of the UK internal regional economy-governance mismatches into a much broader and deeper light. The data, evidence, insights and arguments employed in this book are derived from some 2000 different sources of material ranging over 50 years. However, in order to make the book equally accessible to policy-makers, researchers and wider interested parties, the book contains no econometrics and no mathematics, but instead has many tables and figures to help with the narrative and exposition. For many years I also have collected first editions of classic publications in regional science, urban economics, economic geography, regional planning, economic history and other areas of economics and social sciences, and this material has proved to be totally invaluable in constructing the arguments marshalled here. Reading the original texts has allowed me to develop an understanding of how the thinking on these issues has itself evolved, and to put the current evidence and debates on UK regional, urban and governance issues in a much broader international context, as well as in a much longer historical perspective.

In terms of the regional and geographical nomenclature to be used throughout this book I have had to make several decisions as regional definitions have changed somewhat over time. The terminology I use to describe Scotland, Wales and Northern Ireland are the three 'devolved regions' or 'devolved administrations'. I am aware that the governance administrations have not always been devolved during the last five decades but this proves to be the most parsimonious terminology I can find. Similarly, the 12 large regions of the UK which are constructed for statistical purposes were the 12 Government Office regions, and these include the three devolved regions, although the Government Offices no longer exist as such. For accuracy I therefore use the terminology of the OECD-TL2/EU-NUTS1 regions for these large regions, as these are the OECD-wide and EU-wide benchmarks for statistical purposes. For small regions I use the terminology of the OECD-TL3/EU-NUTS3 regions and in Chapter 4 I also refer to the EU-NUTS2 regions.

I am very grateful to the following experts who each read different parts of the manuscript and provided extremely constructive feedback on numerous points: David Bailey, Aston University; Richard Barkham, CBRE, London; Michael Batty, University College London; Tony Champion, University of Newcastle; Bernard Fingleton, University of Cambridge; Richard Harris, University of Durham; Paul Hildreth, University College London and University of Salford; Simona Iammarino, London School of Economics; Martin Jones, University of Sheffield; Vassilis Monastiriotis, London School of Economics; Gianmarco Ottaviano, London School of Economics; Bob Rowthorne, University of Cambridge; Mark Shucksmith, University of Newcastle.

Chapters 2 and 3 greatly benefited from data provided by Lewis Dijkstra from the European Commission and Monica Brezzi from the OECD Paris as well as the calculations undertaken for me by Enrique Garcilazo from the OECD Paris. Chapter 4 benefited from the real estate investment calculations undertaken by Colin Lizieri of the University of Cambridge; from the trade data and calculations provided by Mark Thissen from PBL Netherlands; and from the WIOD input-output and global value-chain calculations undertaken for me by Gaaitzen de Vries and Bart Los at the University of Groningen. I am also very grateful to Tony Champion of the University of Newcastle and Alessandra Faggian of Ohio State University, USA, who provided me with, or helped me source data for Chapter 5 and Sarah Jewell from the University of Reading, Maria Abreu from the University of Cambridge, Heather Dickey from the University of Aberdeen, Theodoros Soukos from the University of

Nijmegen and Vasiliki Tsafka-Tsotskou from the University of Groningen, all of whom provided me with detailed data and calculations for the material presented in Chapter 1 and in Chapter 5.

In addition various other people have kindly provided me with material or suggested additional reading material for me to consider, and here I am grateful to: Richard Barkham, CBRE, London; Michael Batty, University College London; Ed Cox, Institute for Public Policy Research North; Stephen Gibbons, London School of Economics; Ian Gordon, London School of Economics; Arthur Grimes, Motu Economic and Public Policy Research and University of Auckland, New Zealand; Oliver Harvey, Deutsche Bank, London; Adrian Healy, Cardiff University; Paul Hildreth, University College London and University of Salford; Martin Jones, University of Sheffield; Colin Lizieri, University of Cambridge; Colin Mason, University of Glasgow; Joseph McCann; Kevin Morgan, Cardiff University; Raquel Ortega-Argilés, University of Groningen, Netherlands; Mark Partridge, Ohio State University, USA; Andrés Rodriguez-Pose, London School of Economics; Stephen Roper, Warwick Business School; Bob Rowthorne, University of Cambridge; Koen Samelink, University of Groningen, Netherlands; Richard Shearmur, McGill University Canada; Mark Shucksmith, University of Newcastle; Jon Wyss and Sue Wyss.

I am very grateful to Rob Langham and Elanor Best at Taylor & Francis and Sally Hardy at the Regional Studies Association for their continuing support to this book project, and also to Penny Harper and Rebecca Willford for their excellent editorial work on the manuscript.

The material in this book is very detailed, wide-ranging and in parts very dense, but this simply reflects the complexity of the issues being examined and is necessary in order to do justice to the issues being examined. I have therefore also constructed a short synopsis of the whole book in order to provide the reader with a brief roadmap of the basic arguments contained in the book.

Finally, the views expressed in this book are entirely my own and reflect my personal understanding of these issues as a scholar and policy adviser. The arguments offered in this book are the result of many years of research and reflection on these matters and are also the result of discussions with numerous scholars and policy analysts in many countries over many years. As such, the views expressed here do not reflect the views of any sub-national, national or international organisation, but rather my own understanding and conclusions as a long-time urban and regional economist.

Book synopsis

Chapter 1 introduces the basic problem being examined in the book, namely the UK's large interregional economic inequalities which co-exist with a national governance system which is highly centralised and top-down. The UK economy is internally not only diverging but it is now disconnecting, decoupling and dislocating into two or possibly three quite separate economies. One economy is broadly London plus its hinterland regions, including the South West, which are amongst the most successful economies in Europe. A second economy is comprised of the English regions of the North and Midlands plus the two smaller devolved regions of Wales and Northern Ireland. While London and its hinterland regions perform strongly almost half of the UK population now live in regions and cities whose productivity is similar to, or even below, that of the poorer regions of the former East Germany and weaker than many regions even in the Czech Republic, Poland, Hungary and Slovakia. Meanwhile, Scotland has also taken something of a different course and is now more prosperous than many of the regions of England or the other devolved regions. At the same time, the overly centralised UK government system has not only failed to respond to this dislocating and decoupling for many years but in some ways has acted so as to exacerbate this. As such, while parts of the UK have experienced growing productivity and prosperity many other parts have failed to enjoy these benefits such that the UK as a whole is only a very modest economic performer by OECD or EU standards. The UK is currently only the 13th or 14th richest country in Europe. The weak long run productivity performance of the UK is largely a result of the fact that productivity benefits do not spread across the country but remain largely localised in the south generating large interregional inequalities. Meanwhile in economic terms the highly centralised and top-down UK governance system is really only appropriate for governing a country which is relatively homogenous internally, which the UK clearly is not. The mismatch between the UK's imbalanced internal economic geography and its overly centralised governance system is the UK's regional–national economic problem. Moreover, it is a fundamental and deep-seated problem which will not go away with a few minor policy changes.

Efforts to consider the origins or possible solutions to these problems are also often hampered by the UK media. The disconnection between the UK's internal interregional economic realities and its top-down centralised governance system has been exacerbated by the fact that large sections of the UK media and political circles appear to be largely unaware of where the UK as a whole actually sits in international rankings in terms of economic prosperity, and this greatly limits the learning of possible lessons from the experience of other countries, and in particular those that do not have English as their official language. Much of the reason for this is that the UK media and political circles are dominated by the day to day experience of London and its hinterland, and as such, the media and political circles frame discussions of these issues entirely with a London-specific backdrop, one which is not even approximately reflective of the UK as a whole. However, recently concern has been raised by commentators across the political spectrum regarding the current trajectory of the UK economy, and in particular the apparent dislocation of London and its hinterland from the rest of the country. This has led to fundamental questions being raised in many quarters regarding the suitability and efficacy of the UK's governance system and these issues have recently been thrown into sharp relief by the Scottish independence referendum. Calls for greater devolution are growing across the devolved regions and also the English regions, and in particular at the level of the large cities, as greater numbers of people doubt the ability or effectiveness of the UK's centralised governance system to respond to these issues.

The UK's interregional inequalities are not a new phenomenon. Rather, it is the growing scale of these inequalities which is so remarkable and unusual by OECD and EU standards. For the last three decades, however, these issues were largely ignored or swept under the carpet on the assumption that a successful London would act as the motor or prosperity-engine for the whole country. Yet, as Chapters 2 and 3 demonstrate this simply has not happened, and the beneficial linkages between London and its hinterland and the rest of the UK are extremely weak. As Chapter 2 demonstrates the UK is not only now one of the most interregionally unequal countries in the OECD on a range of different economic, health and wellbeing indicators but that there is a very specific core-periphery logic to these inequalities. The UK has 'gone south' in the sense that the core of the UK economy based in and around London has largely decoupled from the rest of the UK. Indeed, OECD-wide comparisons suggest that the rest of the UK has not benefited from the prosperity of the southern and eastern regions of England. While productivity is strong in London and its hinterlands it is consistently weak outside of this arena. Moreover, the productivity growth in these non-core regions has under-performed relative to all of the OECD comparator regions, suggesting that the prosperity of London has had no generally beneficial effects for the rest of the UK. This finding is also mirrored when we look at the UK's major cities. As Chapter 3 also demonstrates, the UK's productivity problems are not primarily related to urban issues. Urban economic explanations related to city productivity-scale advantages, agglomeration-related spillovers and city-size distributions only provide a limited and weak explanation of the UK's experience because urban economic issues are subsumed by the broader regional economic issues in ways which are not apparent in most other countries. As such, the UK's interregional decoupling and dislocating is not fundamentally an urban issue but a regional issue, although as Chapter 4 explains, the major catalyst for this decoupling is not simply related to internal economic issues.

As Chapter 4 examines, the role played by modern globalisation in reconfiguring and reorienting the whole UK economy as well as the economic trajectories of its individual regions is crucial. As well as accelerating a general southward economic drift, the impacts of modern globalisation on the London economy are simply of different orders of magnitude on numerous levels to anywhere else in the UK. The internal decoupling of the UK has been primarily triggered by the differential shocks associated with globalisation on different parts of the UK, while the weaknesses of the linkages between London and the rest of the economy have failed to ameliorate these differences. From this analysis it also becomes clear how large is the influence of the EU on the UK economy. The scale of the demand linkages between Europe and the UK is far greater than most people understand while the scale of the linkages between the rest of the world and the UK is far smaller than most people understand. The scale of the demand impacts of the EU Single Market on the UK is equivalent to half of the London economy, two-thirds of the economy of the South East, and larger than the economy of any other UK region. At the same time, the rest of the UK is relatively much more dependent on trade with Europe than is London, which is rather more global in its economic orientation. Understanding these economic relationships is critical because the governance relationship between the UK and Europe is intricately connected with the governance relationship between Scotland and the UK, as well as the governance relationships between the UK regions and the rest of the UK. The patterns of international economic linkages are interrelated with the patterns of governance linkages, and changes to the former will change the latter.

Modern globalisation has exacerbated the UK's long-standing interregional inequalities to a remarkable degree. Having said this, however, it is still not entirely clear why this has happened to such a degree in the UK, particularly when examined in the light of the experience of other more prosperous countries. As such, there are still various debates and arguments regarding specific aspects of the UK's interregional experience and in Chapter 5 we therefore examine many of the issues which have been put forward as possible explanations as to why the UK's experience has been as it has. Two currently popular explanations concern the UK's spatial distribution of education and also the potential role played by interregional migration in the spatial 'sorting' of human capital which may favour higher income regions. A detailed long-run examination of the data on these issues provides very little if any support for either of these interrelated explanations. The UK's interregional educational differences are very small and have been so for several decades, and moreover they have also narrowed over recent decades in response to numerous national educational policy interventions. At the same time, the internal interregional migration flows within the UK have remained both tiny and also remarkably stable over four decades. Indeed, this is also the case for by far the most mobile cohort, namely young university graduates, whose migration behaviour has barely changed over decades. Indeed, as UK higher education has expanded, if anything, labour mobility amongst the tertiary-educated graduates cohort has become more localised over time, rather than more dispersed. Human capital and spatial 'sorting' explanations provide few clues as to the UK's interregional experiences. Similarly, potential explanations associated with regional or interregional knowledge spillovers, as well as interregional financial and fiscal linkages again provide few if any real clues as to the UK experience. Indeed, the scale of the UK's interregional transfers is largely an outcome of the interregional inequalities rather than a cause, while financial issues again simply point to the operation of different and largely segmented UK markets with London markets operating rather differently to the rest of the UK.

Meanwhile, explanations based on the constraining role played by the UK's land use planning system also provide no real clues as to the UK's experience. Although the planning system was originally socially progressive in its conception, it has become nothing short of a national disaster on many levels, constraining more than 80 per cent of the UK population to live in some of the most densely populated urban areas in the western world and inhabiting the smallest and most expensive houses in the western world. At the same time some 15 per cent of the UK population enjoy very low density living in rural areas. The combined effects of these density distortions mean that increasing numbers of especially young people are effectively barred from home ownership, but fundamentally reforming the system is almost impossible as there are too many institutional blockages. However, the distortionary price and wealth-related effects associated with the land use planning system are again as much as anything an outcome rather than a cause of the UK's interregional inequalities, although there are now grounds for thinking that in the future it may also become a catalyst for generating further interregional inequalities. The adverse effects of the planning system are real but they are not the cause of the UK's interregional inequalities, and neither is system reform necessarily a solution.

Similarly, explanations based on the UK's rather strange city-size distribution again also provide few clues as to the UK's interregional experience. A historical analysis of UK city sizes in the context of the material presented in Chapter 2 again suggests that what is observed in terms of UK city sizes again appears to be largely an outcome rather than a cause of the UK's interregional inequalities, with London's overwhelming dominance primarily a result of its global city status in the era of modern globalisation. Indeed, one of the key manifestations of this global city type dominance is international immigration, and on this dimension London has benefited more than any other city in the world, with enormous international human capital injections. London has greatly gained from international migration in terms of the role that immigration has played in enhancing London's human capital, in a manner which has no parallel elsewhere in the UK and almost no parallel elsewhere in the world. This is the aspect of the assumed human capital 'sorting' process which overwhelmingly favours London, although this is not an internal UK interregional 'sorting' phenomenon but rather an international one, and one which is also largely unaffected by domestic changes to education policies. This again points to the differential effects of globalisation on the different parts of the UK as being the catalyst for the UK's internal decoupling, building on long-standing inequalities, but greatly exacerbating them.

The realities of the UK's internal economic disconnection, dislocation and decoupling mean that the UK's domestic policy agenda concerning regional and urban matters is shifting rapidly according to two major themes, namely facilitating increased governance devolution and also the fostering of improved interregional connectivity. This rather hybrid policy agenda has arisen in part as a result of numerous high-profile reports and commissions all of which have tended to point to similar sets of weaknesses in the UK economy, as well as similar types of policy recommendations. However, as Chapter 6 demonstrates, the UK policy debates are not fundamentally UK-specific but rather part of a much wider set of analytical and policy-related debates taking place internationally. These policy debates relate to three fundamental analytical problems, namely the problem of the optimal currency area, the problem of the optimal size of a nation, and the problem of place-based versus space-blind economic development policy. The current UK policy debates cannot be properly understood without recourse to these fundamental analytical discussions, the insights of which provide the rationale for these policy trends. However, there are of course particular aspects of these discussions which are specific to the UK, and most notably these include both the high levels of national top-down governance centralisation and also the current challenges to the system being raised by the Scottish devolution agenda, the increasing devolution pressures in the other devolved regions, as well as the growing city-region devolution agenda.

Chapter 7 builds on the insights derived from the three underlying analytical problems outlined in Chapter 6 in order to provide powerful grounds for assessing the opportunities and challenges associated with the current UK policy trajectory. International evidence on national-regional governance systems allows us to throw light on the wider UK governance challenges associated with simultaneous shifts towards both greater devolution in the devolved regions along with a more wide-ranging city-region devolution agenda within England. The opportunities associated with more local decision-making and greater regional autonomy relate to the increased mobilisation of local actors, institutions and local knowledge, as well as enhanced legitimacy and accountability at the regional or city-region levels. At the same time, however, the dangers in the current trajectory relate to the development of a highly unbalanced governance system, with many decisions being made at the wrong spatial level. Functional urban regions are appropriate spatial units for policy decisions relating to the provision of many types of public services, but not for all such decisions, and the wider inter-urban regional scale is very important for many types of policy decisions relating to economic development, as is clear from fully functioning federal governance systems. This is the arena in which the trajectory of the current UK policy agenda is largely lacking, and attempts to address these issues as they relate to, for example, advanced transport infrastructure, are currently largely under-rehearsed. Exactly, how the current policy agenda is therefore meant to enhance the productivity of the UK's weaker regions is still unclear. As such, the underlying mismatch between the UK's governance system and its economic geography – which is the UK's regional–national economic problem – will not be fully resolved by the current policy trajectory. Given that the UK is already in reality moving to a quasi-federal structure much more fundamental governance reforms will be required in the long run to address these underlying economic weaknesses. However, if it is well implemented, the current policy agenda may go some way to responding to particular aspects of this mismatch. Yet, whether the much-needed and more fundamental governance reforms will indeed be forthcoming in the future is a rather different matter.

1 The UK regional–national economic problem

1.1 Introduction to the UK regional–national economic problem

The UK is a deeply uneven country on two broad dimensions, namely the geographic dimension and the governance dimension. The effects of modern globalisation, and in particular the links between automation, out-sourcing, off-shoring and the 'hollowing out' of many middle-skills jobs, mean that while globally we have observed a broad international convergence between countries' incomes, within advanced economies we increasingly observe a greater polarisation and divergence of incomes (Bourguignon 2015; Atkinson 2015a, 2015b; Galbraith 2012). In other words falling inequalities internationally are widely associated with increasing intra-national inequalities (McCann 2008; Goos *et al.* 2009; Iammarino and McCann 2013). However, intra-national inequalities also challenge good governance (Galbraith 2012; Berg 2015). Yet, the extent to which these inequalities are also both geographical and regional in nature is almost unique in the case of the UK. In most other advanced economies these changing employment, skills and income distributions are dispersed much more evenly across the country, whereas in the UK they appear to be more heavily biased towards certain regions than in almost any other advanced economy. Moreover, although they pre-dated the 2008 global financial crisis by several decades, these divergence trends have accelerated in the years immediately before and after (Williams 2011) the crisis. Being characterised by these long-standing interregional divergence processes the economic geography of the UK nowadays increasingly reflects the patterns typically observed in developing or former-transition economies rather than in other advanced economies. As we will see in this book, these interregional inequalities also challenge good governance.

As well as interregional inequalities part of the reason is that the UK also simultaneously exhibits one of the most highly centralised governance systems in the industrialised world (Cheshire *et al.* 2014; Coy 2014; RSA 2014; HoC 2014; Adonis 2014; RSA 2015; Diamond and Carr-West 2015). After more than 70 years of increasing centralisation (Diamond and Carr-West 2015)[1] central government in London rather than sub-national government dominates almost all arenas of policy-design, policy-making and policy interventions to a scale that is almost unknown elsewhere amongst the advanced economies. According to the UK Prime Minister David Cameron "This country has been too London-centric for far too long"[2] and

> Over the last century Britain has become one of the most centralised countries in the developed world ... I am convinced that if we have more local discretion – more decisions made and money spent at the local level – we'll get better outcomes.[3]

and largely the same point is made by the previous UK Prime Minister Gordon Brown throughout his recent book (Brown 2014) and by the Chancellor of the Exchequer George Osborne.[4] At the same time, however, the UK has an also varied and increasingly unequal regional governance system which in many ways is completely out of step with the economic geography realities of today's UK economy and which works well neither in theory nor in practice. A governance system which in the past appeared to be reasonably well-suited to responding to both national and regional challenges now appears to be increasingly incapable of such responses, in some sense reflecting the regional divergences and in other senses exaggerating them (Bogdanor 2015a).

It is this stark mismatch between the UK's interregional economic geography and the UK's regional governance system that is at the heart of the UK's regional economic problem. Moreover, the scale of this misalignment between the economic geography and the governance system is now so great that most simple policy, academic and constitutional 'solutions' offered as remedies for resolving the "over-centralised state and the south-centric economy that are two of Britain's biggest problems"[5] wholly fail to address the fundamental nature of the problem, which is the *combination* of these two problems.

In order to understand why this mismatch is such a fundamental problem there are two major features that we need to be aware of, namely the role of interregional inequality, and the role of appropriate governance systems, in the functioning and performance of a modern economy. These complex issues are discussed in great detail in the various chapters of this book, but at this stage we can highlight the broad outlines of some key themes central to the overall arguments in the book.

In terms of income inequality, there is now a growing body of evidence emerging from very high-level sources such as the IMF and OECD which demonstrates that growth in internal income inequality is not beneficial for long-run national economic growth (Berg and Ostry 2011; OECD 2014a, 2015a; *The Economist* 2014a) and neither is inequality beneficial for urban (Royuela *et al.* 2014) or regional (de Dominicis 2014) economic growth.[6] In particular, in the case of the UK the adverse effects of growing income inequality since the 1980s on the economy's long-run performance since 1990 have been the third worst in the OECD (OECD 2014a). Whereas previous growth models tended to focus almost entirely on aggregate productivity growth with little concern for distributional issues, nowadays environmental sustainability and social cohesion are increasingly understood as being essential elements for ensuring strong growth in the long term. In particular, greater income inequality limits the opportunities and thereby inhibits the ability of the lower middle classes to engage and participate in growth-enhancing activities such as education and entrepreneurship, and this subsequently reduces social mobility (OECD 2014a). While higher social class households are largely unaffected by rising income inequality its adverse impacts are felt almost entirely by the lower 40 per cent of the income spectrum, and these adverse impacts on such a broad group reduce the long-run lost potential of the economy (OECD 2014a). At the same time, there is no evidence that redistributive measures promoting access to skills-training, education and welfare via taxes and transfers hamper long-run growth, as these provide social investments for enhancing and widening opportunities.

The awareness that growth is a more multi-dimensional phenomenon than was appreciated in the past has been emerging over the last decade (Stiglitz *et al.* 2009). Indeed, this shift in thinking towards a more multi-dimensional understanding of growth and development reflects something of a worldwide shift away from the more narrow and largely sectoral approaches popular in previous decades which tended to focus almost entirely on investments in human, physical and research capital with little regard for social or environmental sustainability. These new and broader lines of international[7] thinking which pre-dated the 2008 global financial crisis (Stiglitz 2002; Krugman 2003, Porrit 2005) have of course also been bolstered by the painful experience of the 2008 global economic crisis (Roubini and Mihm 2010) and subsequently have underpinned a range of very high-level international reports and commissions examining the nature of growth and development (Stiglitz *et al.* 2009; OECD 2009a; World Bank 2008, 2010a, 2010b). As with previous research, these shifts in thinking have not produced a simple and complete analysis of growth. Rather, what these shifts in thinking all share is a growing consensus that successful long-term development needs to be environmentally aware,[8] broad-based and socially inclusive (World Bank 2008, 2010a, 2010b; NIC 2012; OECD-Ford Foundation 2014) in order to be long-lasting (OECD 2014a, 2015a; Berg and Ostry 2011; Ezcurra 2007; *The Economist* 2014a; Florida 2010; Sachs 2011; Stiglitz 2012, 2015; Piketty 2014), and rising income inequality (Stiglitz 2012; Piketty 2014) is evidence that the current growth trajectory is moving against these desired societal trends (Dorling 2011).

From a policy perspective, these shifts in thinking also imply that in order to be effective policies must be built on a broadly based political consensus. In other words, as well as enhancing economic drivers modern policy approaches to growth and development must also connect with the broader dimensions of social and environmental sustainability, because each of these features plays an important role in fostering the economic, social and civic engagement aspects underpinning the different dimensions of wellbeing (OECD 2011a).[9] As a result, recent policy frameworks such as the 2009 OECD "Global Standard"

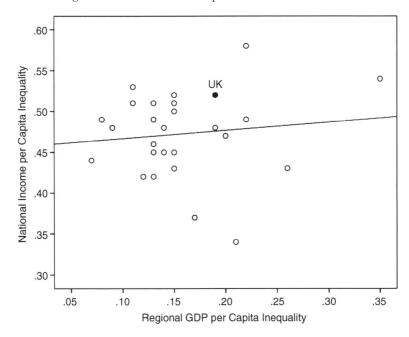

Figure 1.1 National income inequality (pre taxes and transfers) and interregional
inequality in GDP per capita across OECD and BRIICS countries
Sources: OECD (2013, 2014c); OECD Database.

growth strategy (OECD 2009a) of 'stronger, cleaner and fairer growth',[10] the
Europe 2020 Strategy of 'smart, sustainable and inclusive' growth (European
Commission 2010), and the US growth strategy of 'sustainable communities,
innovation clusters, revitalizing neighborhoods'[11] all aim to better translate
these dimensions into a broader agenda and framework for policy-makers.
Yet, changing policy frameworks are themselves unlikely to solve these problems in the near future, and in reality reflect a changing set of emphases and
priorities for current and future decision-making. In contrast, today's internal
domestic income inequality is a result of complex social, economic and historical forces as well as political decisions taken over many previous years
regarding the role, the scale and the use of the state's fiscal resources. As has
also been mentioned above, over recent years the forces of modern globalisation are also increasingly influencing internal income disparities in many different countries. For our purposes here, however, an important observation is
that internal national income inequality is also associated with interregional
inequality.

Figures 1.1 and 1.2 show the scatterplots across the OECD and BRIICS[12]
countries in 2010 of the relationships between the Gini index of interregional GDP per capita – calculated at the OECD-TL3 level – and the Gini
index of domestic income inequality, prior to and post taxes and transfers,

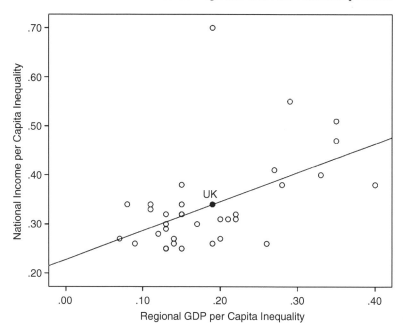

Figure 1.2 National income inequality (post taxes and transfers) and interregional inequality in GDP per capita across OECD and BRIICS countries

Sources: OECD (2013, 2014c); OECD Database.

respectively. In general countries in the lower left part of the scatterplots exhibit low income inequality and low interregional inequality in GDP per capita while those in the upper right hand part of the scatterplots exhibit high income inequality and high interregional inequality in GDP per capita. Countries in the lower right part of the scatterplots exhibit high interregional inequality in GDP per capita but low income inequality while those in the upper left part of the scatterplots exhibit high national income inequality but low interregional inequality in GDP per capita.

As we see from Figure 1.1 and 1.2 there is a correlation between the level of national interregional inequalities in GDP per capita and also the national levels of income inequality, measured either before or after taxes and transfers. We know that the differences between the pre and post transfers and taxes inequalities are a result of the extent to which the national tax systems are redistributive, and across the OECD these systems differ significantly. Yet, even allowing for these differences, the general pattern remains clear that interregional inequality in GDP per capita is associated with higher national income inequality. As such, some levels of income inequality appear to be largely independent of spatial or regional issues, while higher levels of inequality do appear to be related to spatial, geographical and regional issues.

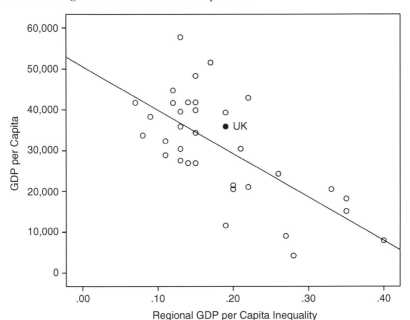

Figure 1.3 National GDP per capita and interregional inequality in GDP per capita
across OECD and BRIICS countries

Sources: OECD (2013, 2014c); OECD Database.

In both cases the position of the UK in the scatterplots is significant. In
each of the two scatterplots the UK is at the upper right extreme of the scatterplot of the rich OECD countries with only one of the countries to the right
of the UK exhibiting a higher GDP per capita than the UK. All of the other
countries to the right of the UK are poorer countries than the UK, comprising the BRIICS countries plus Latin American countries, along with the
former transition economies in Europe. In contrast, the countries to the left
of the UK in the scatterplots are primarily the group of richer OECD economies, with 12 of the countries to the left of the UK exhibiting higher GDP
per capita than the UK.

One often used response to these types of observations is that the national
and interregional inequality scores of the UK are primarily due to the great
success of the London economy, a genuine 'global city' which provides an
enormous boon to the overall UK economy and which must not be jeopard-
ised. As we will see in Chapters 2, 3 and 4, the evidence for this position is very
much weaker than is typically understood. Yet, doubt about the veracity of
this argument immediately emerges from Figure 1.3.

Figure 1.3 displays the scatterplot of the relationship between national
GDP per capita and interregional inequality in GDP per capita. This relationship is downward sloping such that scatterplot points in the upper left

hand side of the figure are countries with high GDP and low interregional variations in GDP per capita while those in the bottom right of the figure represent countries with low GDP per capita and high interregional inequalities in GDP per capita. As we see in Figure 1.3, the scatterplot point of only one of the 14 OECD countries with equal or higher GDP per capita than the UK and for which interregional data are available, is located to the right of the UK. All of the other countries to the right of the UK exhibit lower GDP per capita than the UK.

At this stage we make no claims here regarding the mechanisms or directions of causality regarding the relationships between interregional inequalities, national inequalities or national levels of GDP per capita, nor the reasons for the particular position of the UK in these OECD-BRIICS scatterplots. It is simply sufficient at this stage to point out that as a general cross-country pattern there is a positive relationship between interregional inequality in GDP per capita and national income inequality and also a negative relationship between interregional inequality in GDP per capita and national GDP per capita. Yet, one of the issues which emerges immediately from both the observation that interregional inequality, national inequality and national productivity are correlated with each other in differing ways and also that our understanding of growth and development is shifting to a broader and multi-dimensional appreciation, is that the role of place and geography is not neutral. Greater interregional differences imply greater national differences and clues as to much of what is happening nationally are therefore also to be found in what is happening locally. Moreover, this is not simply an aggregation or scaling issue, but rather an essential point about the economic role played by cities and regions in driving national growth. As such, nowadays local and regional elements quickly enter into national growth and policy discussions (OECD 2011b, 2014b) and one of the most obvious policy challenges to be faced is the fact that the trade-offs and complementarities between the different stronger (smart), cleaner (sustainable) and fairer (inclusive) growth dimensions differ between regions and localities (OECD 2009a, 2009b, 2011b, 2014b; Moretti 2012; Hughes 2012). Moreover, while trade-offs tend to arise naturally in contrast complementarities often have to be constructed (Braga de Macedo and Oliviera-Martins 2008, 2010; Braga de Macedo *et al.* 2013), and as such these differences pose major challenges for local, regional and urban policy, aiming to foster stronger and more resilient growth (Zolli and Healy 2012). In particular, the institutional and policy-setting frameworks need to be adaptable to these differing circumstances, and emerging evidence from numerous sources suggests that appropriate and well-functioning governance systems are essential for fostering growth both locally and nationally (OECD 2011a, 2012, 2014b).

These issues would appear to be particularly pertinent in the case of the UK. In Figs 1.1 and 1.2 we see that the UK is at the upper end of each of the dimensions of the OECD inequality scatterplot distributions. As we will see in Chapter 2, in the UK the interregional inequalities have increased markedly since the early 1990s, as have national income inequalities. Indeed, across the whole of the OECD's 34 countries as well as the EU28 (Armstrong and Ebell 2015), the UK is now one of the most unequal countries according to interregional inequalities, as well as both forms of income inequality. Furthermore, as Chapter 3 argues, the performance of the UK's large cities also largely depends on which region they are located in. As such, in terms of economic geography, the UK's regional and urban challenges are largely synonymous with each other. Moreover, to the extent that UK long-run growth performance has been significantly and adversely affected by rising internal income inequality, the UK's rising interregional inequality is likely to be a fundamental part of this story. Indeed, understanding the interregional inequality story is the major objective of the first five chapters of this book.

The second major issue to be discussed concerns the questions of institutions and governance. While market mechanisms are central to our understanding of the processing re-shaping economic geography (World Bank 2009), at the same time contemporary thinking about economic development (Rodrik 2007) also emphasises that well-functioning and appropriate governance systems are essential for fostering economic growth. Indeed, modern regional economic development approaches (Pike *et al.* 2010; OECD 2011b; Barca *et al.* 2012; Storper 2013; McCann and Ortega-Argilés 2013) follow exactly the same logic. However, in the particular case of the UK there are growing intellectual grounds for arguing that the current UK governance system may not be particularly appropriate, well-suited or well-functioning for responding to the realities and challenges thrown up by today's UK economic geography, characterised as it is by significant and growing interregional inequalities (Armstrong and Ebell 2015). Moreover, and in some ways even more important than the growing intellectual arguments are the recently shifting public perceptions. A broadly based alignment of public perceptions is essential for underpinning the salience, credibility and legitimacy (Cash *et al.* 2003) requirements of national governance and institutional systems and when these perceptions begin to shift or fracture the salience and legitimacy of the current workings of government begin to weaken. The various devolution and independence debates being played out within the UK suggest that there is now also a growing groundswell of public opinion in the popular press and the world of politics that national, regional and local governance and the links between these three governance levels (*The Economist* 2014b) may not be ideally suited to the UK's interregional and economic geography realities. Understanding the causes of the UK's interregional inequalities and also the links between these inequalities and the UK's different types of regional and national governance systems is therefore imperative if we are to improve the future functioning and performance of the UK economy. Therefore, the major theme examined by the second part of the book comprising three chapters concerns the question of how UK governance can be better shaped to respond to the UK's current economic geography realities and the intellectual ideas and insights driving these debates. These arguments depend partly on internal discussions and experiences and also on insights from other countries. However, this is not so straightforward, because of the pattern of internal UK political discourses.

A problem here is that UK internal political and popular debates tend to pay very little heed to the possible lessons derived from other countries, and where they do so, they tend to overly emphasise insights from the USA or other rich Commonwealth countries such as Australia, Canada or New Zealand which have similar legal and land market systems to the UK. This is particularly the case when discussing issues heavily shaped by modern globalisation such as inequality and governance. As much as anything this myopia is likely to be related to our poor foreign-language skills which limit our exposure and awareness of developments taking place in other more appropriate comparator countries. In addition, UK academic debates also tend to be heavily dominated and in some cases over-dominated by US-oriented debates. The UK interregional inequalities are so large and over such short distances that these 'Anglo-Saxon' comparisons offer rather little in terms of useful insights. Moreover, these other 'Anglo-Saxon' countries all tend to be very different to the UK in terms of governance systems, most notably having separate political and economic capitals, and in all but one case functioning as a federal state with a written constitution. In contrast, the UK is in many ways both a very strange as well as a unique polity and more fruitful insights can be gained by observations from a broader range of comparator cases than the usual set of other English-speaking countries which are typically alluded to. Most of these alternative comparator cases are in Europe or East Asia but there is often a reluctance in the UK media to engage seriously with the lessons and insights from these countries. In part, this is due to a lack of awareness of the potential for learning that the UK can enjoy by considering these cases, and to some extent this is also driven by a lack of appreciation of the lead that some of these countries have over the UK in various specific matters. The reasons for this lack of awareness and appreciation are likely to be found in a mix of linguistic limitations and cultural perceptions, but whatever the reasons, the point is that they inhibit UK learning from other more appropriate cases. We will return to these issues shortly at the end of this chapter.

In terms of governance, the United Kingdom nation-state is comprised of four nations: England, Scotland, Wales and Northern Ireland, each with different governance systems, and all of which are embodied in different ways within the overall UK governance system. Each of the four member nations of the unified UK state displays different levels and forms of autonomy relating in each case to different issues. While on cultural grounds, and to differing extents also political grounds, these four operate as countries or partially autonomous regions, in purely economic grounds they each operate as open regions within the unitary national state. Yet, to some extent this situation is already beginning to change in a rather ad hoc manner into something of a quasi-federal state (Bogdanor 2015b).

The recent debates and the 2014 vote on Scottish independence, plus the ensuing Smith Commission[13] recommendations regarding the devolving of income tax powers to Scotland have subsequently spurred a wider debate regarding devolution and decentralisation amongst not only the four constituent nations of the UK, but also amongst the cities and regions of England (*The Economist* 2014c, 2014d, 2014e; Brown 2014; Mount 2014; Gallagher 2014; *The Guardian* 2014a; *The Spectator* 2014). As we will see in Chapter 6, these debates and various policy actions and governance reforms long pre-date the Scottish independence referendum,[14] but the Scottish vote has given a major impetus to these debates. These debates are particularly pertinent in the case of the UK because UK local government has a very limited role by international standards (OECD 2013), with the vast majority of its funding and policy priorities and implementation frameworks being decided centrally. At the same time, the three devolved regions of Scotland, Wales and Northern Ireland display differing degrees of autonomy from the Westminster government. However, within England in particular, the highly centralised and largely top-down and 'one-size-fits-all' governance system is wholly at odds with the economic geography of the UK. In terms of economic geography the current reality of the UK economy is one of almost unprecedented inequality and these inequalities are most marked in the case of England. Moreover, the UK as a whole, and within the UK England in particular, is not only a largely unitary state, but one which is more centralised than almost any other large state anywhere else in the world (Cheshire *et al.* 2014; Coy 2014; RSA 2014). The business cycles and patterns of economic shocks across UK regions are today less correlated than those between countries across the European Union with the London economy in particular becoming increasingly disconnected from the rest of the UK (Deutsche Bank 2013). In other words, the internal workings of the UK interregional economic system are in many ways actually less cohesive and integrated than the wider EU economy. Indeed, at the level of the 12 UK OECD-TL2/EU-NUTS1 large statistical regions the scale of UK interregional differences in GDP per capita is comparable to the international GDP per capita differences across 17 European countries and across 22 OECD countries. At the lower level of the OECD-TL3/EU-NUTS3 regions of the UK, the interregional GDP per capita differences within the UK are comparable to those across 22 European countries and 27 OECD countries.

One outcome of these inequalities is that the UK does not resemble anything like an optimal currency area and as we will see in detail in Chapter 6 these increasing UK interregional inequalities pose fundamental questions regarding the economic governance of the unified UK state. While on the one hand the various parts of the English economy increasingly appear to co-exist without any real economic interactions taking place with other parts of the same country, at the same time on the other hand, the English governance system in particular, is based on the assumption that England is economically a cohesive whole, which it is clearly not. Given the economic governance difficulties faced by the Eurozone since the 2008 global economic crisis, the fact that the UK nowadays is actually less of an optimal currency area than the EU itself challenges the notion that the UK's highly centralised government system is indeed the most appropriate governance structure for managing the UK economy for the benefit of all parts of the UK.

In order to describe the current interregional realities of the UK's economic geography *The Economist* (2013f) uses the distinction between the two codes of the sport of rugby, namely rugby union and rugby league, as a useful metaphor for this type of co-existence and separation. These two codes of rugby and all of their associated fan-bases and commercial support largely co-exist with little or no interactions between them. In England Rugby League is played almost entirely in towns scattered along what is known as the 'M62 Corridor', and this broadly describes an area which is oriented east-west and which links the northern cities of Liverpool, Manchester, Leeds and Hull. Traditionally from the late nineteenth century, throughout the twentieth century and into the early twenty-first century, this was perceived of primarily as being a game for miners, steelworkers and factory workers, and indeed the towns which excel in these sports largely reflected this economic history. In England, Rugby Union in contrast was largely a game associated with private and grammar schools and elite universities and almost all of the major rugby union clubs are located south of an imaginary line linking the River Severn in the south west of England with The Wash on the northern edge of East Anglia. To an external observer with little detailed knowledge of these games both codes of rugby appear to be very similar to each other and to substantiate this point there are many high-profile players and coaches who have successfully switched between the two codes at various points in their careers. More recently, however, such switches have tended to be uni-directional and away from Rugby League and towards Rugby Union as increasing moneys pour into Rugby Union. To the vast majority of people deeply embedded within each individual code of rugby, including supporters and club members, however, the two codes of rugby largely co-exist, with little interaction, mutual awareness, or other forms of linkages between them at the same time as one of the codes is becoming increasingly wealthy relative to the other.[15] As much as anything, the reason is that the societal context within which the two sports are played reflect very different social, cultural, geographical and industrial histories (Collins 1998), and these different contexts remain deeply entrenched on many levels. Indeed, this rugby metaphor provides a surprisingly good analogy of the current economic geography realities within England, which as we will see in Chapters 2–5, reflect a deeply and increasingly divided nation. Similar metaphors can increasingly be provided nowadays also by professional football.[16] If we add to these English economic geography realities also the diverse economic experiences of the three devolved regions of Wales, Scotland and Northern Ireland (Cambridge Econometrics 2013) plus the high levels of international openness displayed by the UK economy as a whole, then the overall picture becomes both extremely complex and interesting. On a regional level people's experiences of the economic and social realities are simply so different in the UK that nowadays regional as well as local communities perceive also their needs in totally different ways.[17] This will have profound long-run implications for the governance of the UK as many of the social and cultural national institutions underpinning the national polity increasingly give way to diverging regional interests. In terms of the public consciousness, the most obvious case, of course, is that of Scotland. Yet, as we will see in the coming chapters, the issues raised in this book do not fundamentally change if at some point in the future Scotland chooses to become independent from the rest of the UK. Many of the important issues arising out of the Scottish case are also at least as applicable in the case of other UK regions, if not more so. Indeed, on many levels many of these issues would become even more starkly delineated in the event of Scotland becoming fully independent.

The fact that in economic terms at least many UK regions appear to co-exist while displaying little or no economic cohesion between the different parts of the country therefore raises three fundamental governance questions. First, how are public resources to be allocated? Should they be targeted at the more prosperous parts of the UK or at the weaker parts of the UK and why? Overman (2013) refers to these challenges in his 'jam-spreading' analogy which argues that resources – i.e. 'jam' – should not be spread too thinly on political grounds and instead focused on potentially successful cities in order to generate scale effects. This analogy has also since been picked up by front-line political circles with Boris Johnson's 'jam and Ryvita' argument that by concentrating resources – i.e. jam – in London eventually much greater economic benefits will spread out across the country – i.e. across the Ryvita – according to some sort of spatial 'trickle down' or interregional 'spread' (Richardson 1978) effect.[18] The Overman (2013) use of the analogy raises important issues regarding resource concentration and policy prioritisation which we begin to discuss in detail from Chapter 6 onwards whereas the Johnson version of the analogy is incorrect. While 'trickle down' ideas at the national level have been firmly refuted by the OECD (2014a) and IMF (Berg and Ostry 2011) on the basis of all of the available international evidence as well as the intellectual arguments (Stiglitz *et al.* 2009; OECD 2009b, 2009c), as we will see in Chapters 2 and 3 especially as well as Chapters 4 and 5 of this book, all of the available interregional evidence from the UK also refutes the contention that widespread and beneficial economic spatial spread effects from London to other regions are evident in the UK. The evidence suggests that there are no real spread effects at all. To use the same metaphor, it appears that the 'jam' is either too viscous or the surface of the 'Ryvita' far too rough or porous for any economic benefits to spread to the rest of the country.

Second, as we will see in Chapter 6, if the UK is not even approximately an optimal currency area, then should the UK state be broken up into smaller constituent parts or should its governance system be largely reconfigured to reflect local and regional differences and to better cope with asymmetric economic shocks? Third, and following on directly from the first question, would

smaller national or regional polities be more successful in managing economic conditions in the modern era of globalisation than the current highly
centralised UK state?

In the UK these are clearly not merely abstract philosophical questions, as
evidenced by the recent Scottish vote on independence, although this is a discussion which actually goes much deeper and wider than just the Scottish case.
Obviously, many of the independence, autonomy and devolution arguments
within the four constituent nations of the UK reflect deeply held cultural and
philosophical convictions (*The Times* 2014; *The Guardian* 2014b) and also
some well-considered economic arguments. However, in the aftermath of the
Scottish independence vote, what were previously just the domain of academics working on either constitutional issues or regional development issues
these wider discussions about regional autonomy and devolution have now
taken centre-stage within many UK domestic political debates and a complex continuum of regional–national–international governance and constitutional interrelationships are starting to be uncovered which previously have
been largely below the surface. The governance and political aspects of the
city-region devolution debates in England are closely related with the devolution debates in the devolved administrations of the three devolved regions
of the UK, while the governance issues facing the three devolved regions are
closely interrelated with the relationships between the UK and the EU in ways
which are markedly different from those evident within England (Bogdanor
2015b; Emmott 2015). Indeed, not only are they related, but they are closely
interrelated in myriad and complex ways.[19] At the same time, as we will see
in Chapter 6, all of these governance debates are also intrinsically linked to
economic geography and in particular to the UK's distorted and highly unequal economic geography (Morgan 2002, 2006, 2007). Yet, while these issues
for decades were almost purely contained within academic circles, now that
they have emerged in the popular press and mainstream political media these
debates now go well beyond questions about the UK's internal economic
geography, and also variously include wider discussions regarding the UK's
place within Europe, its role in the global economy, and also the dominant
and what is perceived as an increasingly disconnected role of London within
the UK economic and political arenas (O'Brien 2012a, 2012b).[20] Rather than
providing clarity, however, the rather unfortunate result of these various
discourses is that many of the current independence and separatist debates
within the four constituent nations of the UK now reflect a rather confused
mixture and conflation of anti-globalisation and mercantilist trade narratives
pitting 'us' against 'them' with populist narratives railing against 'metropolitan elites' (Little 2014) and 'London rule' or 'Whitehall rule' (Brown 2014,
p. 184). In particular, to many observers much of the support for independence parties in all four constituent nations of the UK is either a reaction to, or
builds upon, the perceived self-seeking dominance of the London economy
(Little 2014; *Financial Times* 2014a; White 2014), a region which appears to
benefit greatly from globalisation, which is perceived to drive up inequality

(Small 2014) by sucking in resources from the rest of the country (*Financial Times* 2014b; Coy 2014; *The Scotsman* 2014; White 2014)[21] and whose political and business elites including immigrant billionaires (*Standpoint* 2015),[22] multi-millionaires (Knight Frank 2015) and overseas property investors (Deutsche Bank 2014) all appear to be increasingly decoupled from the experience of much of the rest of the UK (O'Brien 2012a, 2012b), including even those in other prosperous areas.[23]

There is obviously debate and disagreement amongst different commentators about the veracity of these London characterisations[24] although as we will see in the coming chapters it is clear that some of these perceptions are not entirely without substance, and it would be a mistake to see these perceptions as deriving solely from the smaller and populist political parties. Indeed, both the wider public[25] as well as mainstream political parties also share many of these concerns and aspire to address these issues. According to the UK Prime Minister David Cameron our

> economy has become more and more unbalanced, with our fortunes hitched to a few industries in one corner of the country, while we let other sectors like manufacturing slide ... We will help to rebalance our economy, ensuring that success and prosperity are spread more evenly across regions and industries ... Today our economy is heavily reliant on just a few industries and a few regions – particularly London and the South East. This really matters. An economy with such a narrow foundation for growth is fundamentally unstable and wasteful – because we are not making use of the talent out there in all parts of the United Kingdom ... And it doesn't mean ignoring London ... but it does mean having a plan to breathe economic life into the towns and cities outside the M25.
>
> (Cameron 2010).

These themes are also echoed by the Scottish Government's First Minister Nicola Sturgeon who argued that

> London has a centrifugal pull on talent, investment and business from the rest of Europe and the world. That brings benefits to the broader UK economy. But as we know, that same centrifugal pull is felt by the rest of us across the UK, often to our detriment. The challenge for us all is how to balance this in our best interests – not by engaging in a race to the bottom, but by using our powers to create long-term comparative advantage and genuine economic value.[26]

As we will see in Chapters 2 and 3, the economic dominance of the London economy within the UK state is now relatively greater than it has been at any time since the very early years of the twentieth century. Moreover, as we will also see in Chapters 4 and 5, much of this ascendancy is indeed related to globalisation, in which evolving global value-chains and cross-border economic integration re-shape the relationships between the local, regional, multinational and global contexts. Today there are increasing tensions between the existence of individual nation-states, their ability to maintain democratic governance, and ongoing and increasing globalisation processes (Rodrik 2011). Yet, a resolution of these tensions does not imply a wholesale move towards greater protectionism and isolation, a movement which would be heavily counter-productive. Rather, it requires more nuanced and varied forms of multinationalism (Rodrik 2011) As such, some of the independence and devolution narratives currently circulating in the UK media and political circles ignore many of today's most fundamental economic mechanisms, and as such, many of the policy 'solutions' they propose are entirely unsuitable for addressing the long-term economic challenges that the UK faces. Therefore, developing a much deeper understanding of the relationships between the UK national state, its constituent nations, regions and cities, and the differential impacts of globalisation on each of these polities and spaces, is essential before we are able to point towards possible policy approaches or solutions.

Addressing these types of questions also involves dealing with public perceptions, many of which are based on little or no knowledge of the available evidence or data. Many currently crucial political decisions are being made with very little recourse to any real analysis of the likely impacts of these decisions. Problems involving mismatches of perceptions are particularly acute when regional and urban challenges are discussed in the popular media in the context of UK governance and institutional issues. For example, while the issues raised by the 'West Lothian question' have re-emerged with a vengeance in Westminster in political circles in the wake of the 2014 Scottish independence referendum, outside of the three devolved regions there currently appears to be little appetite for devolution amongst the English. Devolution and regional and city governance[27] issues of themselves tend to be far down the list of priorities of most English voters (Kellner 2014; *The Observer* 2014), while inequality, unemployment and the overall economic situation are all very high on the list of voters' priorities. Yet, while in the minds of today's voters these economic and social issues may seem to be largely divorced from questions of governance and local autonomy, as we will see throughout this book these issues are all very closely interrelated. Indeed, many policy-makers, private sector actors and civil society representatives already know this, and it is at the level of cities and regions rather than at national government levels that these various different parties most frequently interact with each other in order to bring about change (OECD 2014b). Not surprisingly, therefore, the pressure for greater governance decentralisation, devolution and reform within England at the regional and city levels is emerging from city and local governance authorities themselves.

Numerous actors within the UK government arena are nowadays increasingly well aware of the serious inadequacies and misalignments of the current national governance situation and the imperative for mobilising actors at the regional and city levels in order to drive growth. These arguments have been highlighted in ten major UK reports (Heseltine 2012; IPPR 2012, 2014; CBI 2012; RSA 2014, 2015; Adonis 2014; HoC 2014; ICLGF 2014, 2015) plus various more city-specific and metropolitan area reports (MIER 2009; PWC and Demos 2012; ResPublica 2014, 2015) as well as reports addressing the governance issues facing non-metropolitan and rural areas (NMC 2014, 2015; LGA 2015; Diamond and Carr-West 2015), and all of these reports which are set against the backdrop of a range of high-level international reports (Barca 2009; OECD 2009b, 2009c, 2011b, 2012, 2014b) echoing these same types of themes. Moreover, in the UK setting, these issues also link to many of the issues raised in earlier reports specifically addressing the challenges facing UK cities and urban areas (Scottish Executive 2002; ODPM 2004, 2006a, 2006b; DCLG 2011). These various reports all argue broadly that in the context of heterogeneous cities and regions and in today's economy, in order to best foster growth and development we need multi-level governance arrangements including wide-ranging local autonomy and decision-making powers implemented at the right spatial and local levels. Top-down and highly centralised governance systems can rarely provide such an environment. In small economies top-down centralised governance systems may be appropriate but in large and highly diverse economies such as the UK this is very unlikely to be the case. As this book will repeatedly argue and demonstrate on the basis of both UK domestic data as well as international comparisons, it is actually within England itself than the mismatches between economic development and governance are the most acute and so there is the need for major governance reform at the regional levels as well as at the level of the devolved administrations. Moreover, as we will see later on, any political movement towards 'English votes for English laws'[28] will have little or no effect whatsoever on these economic-institutional mismatches and because the problems are more fundamental and of much greater orders of magnitude than these largely philosophical-political arguments.

While some independence and devolution arguments are indeed well-founded on economic and social grounds, where this is not the case, however, it is likely that most of the rather spurious independence and devolution arguments are in a reality a result of a breakdown of public trust in central government and reaction to the perceived failures of central government. Indeed, in the aftermath of the 2008 global financial crisis, in many countries the levels of public trust in governments are now at very low levels (OECD 2013; European Union 2014a). The limited ability of national governments to respond effectively to the impacts of the 2008 global economic crisis has reduced the public's belief that national governments can deliver on their promises. Yet, until recently this was not the case. Perceptions of governments during the 'great moderation' between the mid-1990s and 2008 remained relatively sanguine as inflation was kept low by processes of globalisation which allowed for massive increases in the global supply of low wage labour, while misguided 'financial innovation' (Padoan 2012) combined

with benign monetary policy contributed to excessive risk-taking and inflation in asset prices. The UK, and the London economy in particular, was
a principal exponent of this pattern. Yet, the aftermath of the 2008 global
economic crisis led to a rude awakening in the fields of economics, finance,
political science and international relations in that so much of the previously
accepted analytical wisdom was found wanting (Padoan 2012). The fact
that problems originating in just 3 per cent of US domestic real estate assets
(Padoan 2012) could have wreaked such havoc across so many nations and
for so long, has underscored the limitations of many previously accepted analytical frameworks and also the limited power of these frameworks in assisting national governments in the face of major and adverse global market
movements (Wolf 2014a; Krugman 2014). Yet, in many cases this declining
public trust in government and political institutions has moved beyond mere
scepticism and increasingly is reflected in outright hostility towards political
process and systems. Unfortunately, however, the adverse role which political
decision-making – which is overwhelmingly based on domestic discourses –
can also play in thwarting possible realistic responses, is also becoming
increasingly evident in many countries.

In the European contexts, some of these independence discourses and
narratives are pro-European but anti-central government at the national
level, while others are primarily anti-European and pro-national government. Moreover, many of these different narratives are often rather contradictory with each other, drawing as they do from ideas and inspiration from
quite different ends of the political spectrum, depending on the underlying
agenda of the parties in question. However, what these independence and
devolution narratives and discourses all share in common is a belief that the
national institutional status quo is no longer appropriate for dealing with the
twenty-first-century economic realities. In particular, they all share the idea
that national central government is too remote and unaccountable from the
public which elects it, and these beliefs are largely held in common, irrespective of whether the independence being sought is from either Westminster or
Brussels as is the case in the UK versions of these narratives (*The Economist*
2015a), or from Ottawa, Madrid, Rome, Paris, Stockholm, or the institutions
of the European Union.[29]

In the case of regional devolution or independence narratives, they naturally draw some of their leading themes from a similar pool of ideas as do
the national independence narratives. However, there are also many aspects
of the regional devolution or independence debates which differ greatly from
those operating purely at the national level. Yet, although many of the currently popular regional independence or devolution narratives differ markedly from each other, they do raise fundamental concerns regarding the
governance of regions, countries, groups of regions and groups of countries,
in the modern era of globalisation. These concerns are actually very timely, in
that differences in government and governance performance across countries
have been very marked in the aftermath of the crisis and the role played by

sub-national governance in these responses has become increasingly apparent (OECD 2013, 2014b; European Union 2014a). In particular, the relationships between sub-national and national government are increasingly seen as being key to the effectiveness of responses to the crisis. Either the breakdown of central-regional governance relationships or the absence of strong and meaningful national-local governance relationships are increasingly understood as limiting the economic resilience of the national state in the face of adverse global market movements.

The experience of the UK with its highly centralised governance systems and limited local governance roles increasingly appears to be at odds with the economic realities of the UK. From an academic perspective, therefore, the enormous mismatch between the current economic geography of the UK and its governance systems and structures throws up many fundamental analytical questions and challenges regarding the wider relationships between geography and governance. The reason is that although the various political narratives questioning the performance of central government are largely cultural, philosophical and political in nature, as we will see in Chapter 6, common to all of these narratives are two underlying theoretical economic problems which are central to these political economy discussions in the UK and elsewhere. These are first the 'optimal currency area' or 'optimal currency region' (Mundell 1961) problem and second the 'optimal size of a nation' problem (Alesina and Spolaore 2005). What is important about these underlying theoretical economic arguments is that they do raise important questions regarding the suitability of the governance system of the UK in the current context, one which is characterised by almost unprecedented interregional differences. Indeed, the questions and challenges posed by these theoretical arguments regarding the role of the UK's institutions and governance arrangements in shaping development relate not only to the specifics of the UK but more generally to broader worldwide discussions. The fact that the UK is such a patchwork of governance systems overlaying extreme interregional inequalities means that any answers and insights which can be gleaned from an analysis of the current UK context are also likely to lead to more general insights which will be applicable in many other national and international contexts.

1.2   The UK shift from 'regional' narratives to 'local', 'urban' and 'city' discourses

The current and future discussions regarding governance issues in the UK are heavily shaped by nomenclature and terminology employed because the specific language used itself fundamentally frames the political debates. In the case of issues concerning the economic geography and governance of the UK there has been a major shift in recent years, and in particular since the Coalition government came to power in 2010, away from using the nomenclature of 'local' and 'regional' and instead in favouring the terminology of 'local', 'city' and 'urban' in official documents (BIS 2010; HM Government 2010, 2011; GOS

2013) and public discourses. The greater inclusion of 'urban' and 'city' in current terminology is very welcome as this potentially allows for a more nuanced and focused debate regarding the role of, and challenges faced by, our major centres of population, as well as increased awareness of the potential for community involvement in governance issues. However, whereas prior to 2010 terms such as 'region', 'regions' or 'regional' dominated UK official publications (DTI 1998, 1999; DCLG 2008; HM Treasury 2001, 2003; HMT, DTI and ODPM 2003) dealing with matters related to the UK's internal economic geography and governance challenges, since 2010 these terms have almost disappeared entirely from the nomenclature of current official publications and political discourses. By late 2014 and early 2015 some regional and interregional terminology had again started to return implicitly into government and public discussions in the form of the expanded HS2 debates (DfT 2014a, 2014b) and also a 'Northern Powerhouse' narrative (HM Government and Transport for the North 2015),[30] somewhat echoing the prior 'Northern Way'[31] narratives which had emerged a decade earlier before disappearing by 2010.

As will be seen throughout this book, the recent widespread removal of the nomenclature of 'region', 'regions' or 'regional' from many public policy discourses is very unfortunate and there are two reasons for this. First, the majority of 'local' neighbourhood issues operating within UK 'urban' areas relating to house price hedonic effects and the social segregation or mixing of neighbourhoods are not particularly different from those evident across the majority of the advanced OECD economies. While there may be a few specific features operating in the UK which are noticeable such as the role of the UK land use planning system, there are also many other countries with similar types of systems, and as discussed in Chapter 5, although the system has profound and often deleterious economic effects the operation of the system itself explains little regarding the issues raised in this book. In marked contrast, as will be argued throughout this book and in particular in Chapters 2–4, when it comes to economic geography it is the interregional situation within the UK that makes the UK case almost unique, and as such requires a great deal of analysis to understand why the UK is apparently so different to the vast majority of other OECD countries. Not only has there been a long-standing 'north–south' divide in the UK which has been articulated by economists and geographers (Fothergill and Gudgin 1982; Baker and Billinge 2004), but this divide has increased dramatically in the last two decades. In economic terms the UK is characterised by an incredibly strong core-periphery spatial structure whereby the 'core' was traditionally defined as the regions located to the south of an imaginary line drawn between the River Severn and The Wash and the periphery being those regions located to the north of this line (Balchin 1990; Baker and Billinge 2004; Dorling 2010).[32] In economic and wellbeing terms this basic divide now holds stronger than ever, except for the fact that an additional imaginary line demarcating the economic 'core' from the 'periphery' nowadays also exists, which is the line describing the border between northern English regions and Scotland. As we will see in

Chapters 2–4, unlike in earlier decades, Scotland is nowadays increasingly part of the 'core' along with the three southern English regions; while the northern and midlands English regions plus Wales and Northern Ireland make up an economic periphery which is becoming increasingly decoupled and dislocated from the core regions. This tripartite decoupling is also reflected on social and political levels as well fundamentally on economic grounds.[33] Obviously this does not mean that all problem areas are in northern regions and all prosperous areas are in southern regions (*The Economist* 2014g). Nor does it mean that every town or city north of the imaginary Severn–Wash line and south of the Scottish border exhibits lower income and wealth than towns located south of the Severn–Wash line or north of the Scotland–England border. Indeed, southern regions include some of the poorest local neighbourhoods, almost all of which are in London, while northern regions do include some of the most affluent local neighbourhoods. Of the poorest 50 UK neighbourhoods according to child deprivation figures, some 32 are located outside of the southern and eastern regions of England and of the 18 which are located in southern regions, all are in London. At the same time, the southern regions of England contain 31 of the top 50 least deprived UK neighbourhoods.[34] The result of this complex picture is that London contains some of the richest and poorest neighbourhoods in the UK (Dorling 2013a), while Cheshire is richer than Cornwall, Harrogate is wealthier than Hastings. Lowestoft[35] has lower incomes than Lancaster, East Kilbride is poorer than Knutsford, and Hackney has more deprivation than Hexham. Indeed, Cornwall is one of the poorest counties of the UK. As such, extending our imaginary Severn–Wash line back through the River Tamar may better capture some additional variations.

Yet, even allowing for these types of variations and exceptions, as we will see in Chapters 2 and 3 the general pattern described by the Severn–Wash line and the England–Scotland border is remarkably consistent at the broad interregional level and at also the urban level (Dorling 2013b). Moreover, this is an explicit spatial pattern which is evident in the context of a country which exhibits a largely monocentric type of spatial structure in that there is a regional coincidence of the centres of government, commerce and also trade routes. The confluence of these three dimensions in the same regions is almost unique amongst OECD countries and this is an explicitly spatial and regional feature. Therefore, an over-emphasis on 'local' and 'urban' and a widespread exclusion of the term 'regional' from the UK public discourses removes most of the explicitly spatial and geographical underpinnings of the economic challenges faced by the UK. As we see in Chapter 3, in order to understand what is taking place in large UK cities it is essential to discuss each city in the context of the region in which it is located. In the UK urban issues are fundamentally regional issues in a manner which is not the case in many other OECD countries, whereas the reverse does not hold to the same extent. UK regional issues are not necessarily urban issues to the same extent as they are in other OECD countries, and unlike regional issues, UK urban issues are not particularly different to those evident in many other countries. Again, this of course is not to say that all urban (*The Economist* 2014g) or sub-urban (Dorling 2013a) areas in the south of England are prosperous nor that all of those in northern areas are poor. However, the correlation between urban issues and regional issues is so strong in the UK case, defined by an extraordinarily strong centre-periphery arrangement whose spatial structures are also closely related to governance structures, that to remove 'regional' from public debates is to miss most of the issue.

Second, it is the interregional situation which is now primarily putting so much pressure on the UK governance system, and not local neighbourhood or even urban issues. While economic issues are increasingly global in nature, and as we will see in Chapter 4 particularly those operating at the regional level, in contrast UK politics is becoming increasingly regional and local, with some of the UK's most powerful political actors leveraging off sub-national regional power bases, purportedly defending the region or city against central government or international institutions (*Prospect* 2015). Therefore, regrettably, removing 'region' and 'regional' from the nomenclature of public debate limits the ability of public debate to accurately and effectively respond to the realities of the UK economic geography and the associated governance challenges being faced by the UK, which by OECD standards are now on an almost unprecedented scale and complexity. A much more fruitful way forward would be to have 'local', 'urban' and 'regional' terminology all as regular parts of the nomenclature of UK public discourses relating to the economic geography and governance challenges we face today. This is because nomenclature used in public discourses affects both the geography of perceptions and the perceptions of geography. When it comes to regional issues and their associated governance challenges, within the UK political debates many of the perceptions regarding both the underlying mechanisms and also the lessons which can be learned from both domestic observations and international observations are not only highly questionable, but also they tend to inhibit the search for improved and potentially workable governance solutions. As far back as 1983, Britain's foremost social historian Asa Briggs bemoaned the scale of UK interregional disparities and argued that solutions for these could not be found with either purely local or national policies. The intermediate regional level is a crucial part of the UK social and economic story and institutional and governance issues will need to respond at this level as well as at the urban and local levels in order to be effective (Briggs 1983).

1.3 A problem of the geography of perceptions

As mentioned above, one of the difficulties in having a discussion about UK interregional and governance issues, and particularly in the context of the challenges associated with modern globalisation, is that UK internal debates tend to pay very little heed to lessons from other countries. The willingness and desire to learn from the policy experiences of other countries ought to be greater when it is understood that other countries exhibit significant advantages in particular policy arenas than we do. However, in the case of the UK this willingness tends to be very limited, and part of this is because there is such a widespread lack of awareness of the relative positioning of the UK economy on so many dimensions. Policy ideas and initiatives emerge primarily in domestic political economy debates which themselves are heavily influenced and shaped by the debates and discourses operating in the public media. Yet, ideas and experiences from other countries ought to partly shape these debates where it is clear that the domestic situation is weaker than elsewhere. However, many of the narratives operating in today's UK popular and tabloid press, and in particular Eurosceptic narratives, tend to frame discussions about the UK's current international economic challenges as though we were living sometime in the 1950s rather than the twenty-first century. In other words discussions start from an implicit assumption that the UK is fundamentally a dynamic and strong economy surrounded and, if anything, largely held back by weaker and largely sclerotic polities.[36] Thi s was indeed true during the 1950s when the UK was the sixth richest country in the world and richer than all other European economies except for Switzerland, with UK productivity premia of between 10 per cent and 40 per cent above other western and northern European economies (Broadberry and Klein 2011). Yet, today's reality is totally different with the UK lagging behind almost all other advanced economies in terms of productivity levels and growth, as we will see in detail below. As such, claims that the UK might be the most prosperous economy by 2030 are likely to be pure fantasy (Wolf 2015) given the current dire productivity performance of the UK, the severity of the UK demand contractions in the aftermath of the 2008 crisis (Krugman 2015a) and many of the budget-related changes being introduced.[37] Therefore, before we can begin to put any flesh on a skeleton outline of the issues to be faced ahead in the rest of this book regarding the UK interregional economic and governance challenges, it is important to try to set out the broad economic and policy context and background in which these debates take place in order to assess the extent to which the UK may fruitfully learn lessons from other countries. This also requires us to reconsider some of the fundamental long-run national and international changes undergone by the UK economy and to accurately position the current UK in wider global trends.

Obviously the UK is a member of the group of approximately 40 or so countries which by global standards are regarded as the rich and advanced economies. Yet within this group the UK is currently ranked between the 25th and 28th richest country in the world, depending on whether we use IMF, World Bank, OECD or CIA data. Multifactor productivity growth in the UK between 1985 and 2007 more than matched the majority of advanced OECD economies, but the reversal of productivity growth experienced by the UK in the aftermath of the 2008 global financial crisis was amongst the most severe of any industrialised economy,[38] with UK growth 2009–2012 ranked 25th in the OECD and far below both the EU and OECD averages.[39] As such, today the UK exhibits: only just above average GDP per capita scores when compared against the 28 countries of the European Union, including those in Eastern and Southern Europe; below average GDP per capita per hour scores and also GDP per worker scores in comparison to the Eurozone; below average GDP per capita scores and also GDP per worker productivity scores in comparison to the EU-15; and below average GDP per capita productivity scores when compared with the 34 OECD countries (OECD 2014c). The only EU-15 countries which were part of the EU by 1995 with lower GDP per capita than the UK are Italy, Spain, Portugal and Greece. Indeed, overall GDP per capita levels for the UK are currently only between 5 per cent and 10 per cent above Italy and Spain, respectively (OECD 2014c) and are actually some 3.7 per cent below the average for the 34 OECD countries (OECD 2014c). Moreover, today the UK's GDP per worker levels today are actually below those of Italy and Spain (OECD 2014c; Dolphin and Hatfield 2015). In fact, without Greater London's productivity premium, which as we will see in the next chapter is currently more than 77 percentage points above the UK average, the overall GDP per capita of the UK would be more than 4 per cent below Italy (including the Mezzogiourno) and equal with Spain. This is the reality that most UK public debates either largely ignore or are largely unaware of. As of today the UK is the 13th or 14th richest country in Europe,[40] the 10th or 11th richest country in the EU, and the most unequal western and northern European country in terms of income inequalities. While most economic discussions in the popular media automatically compare the UK with our northern and western European countries or with North American competitors, in reality without the productivity premium of London all of our most appropriate economic comparisons would be with southern European and Mediterranean countries. The productivity and prosperity benefits of the core regions of the UK largely fail to spill over or translate to the UK's non-core regions, and the aggregate effect of this is poor overall national productivity performance. This failure to diffuse productivity gains throughout the national economy and the inhibiting effect that this has on overall growth is a major part of the UK regional (and national) economic problem.

These realities are reflected in a variety of other statistics. In terms of innovation, the overall UK innovation systems appear reasonably strong by global standards.[41] However, the UK is still not regarded as an innovation leader and instead is described as an 'innovation follower' whose innovation system is only ranked 7th in the EU (European Union 2014b). The level of proficiency of the UK secondary school population in mathematics, reading and science skills ranks 16th in the OECD at almost exactly the OECD average levels and only 12th in Europe (OECD 2014d). In terms of the percentage of the UK population who are working in private and public sector research roles the UK ranks 13th in Europe and 11th in the EU, just very slightly above the overall EU-28 average.[42] Meanwhile, in terms of the proportion of R&D

personnel and researchers within the business sector the UK ranks only 20th in the OECD, 15th in Europe and 13th in the EU, and actually below the overall EU-28 average.[43] Similarly, both the UK's gross domestic expenditure on R&D and also the business expenditure on R&D are now below the average for both the OECD[44] and the EU-28 (OECD 2014e) and both have fallen from slightly above the EU-28 average in 2000 (OECD 2014e). Of the R&D which is undertaken in the UK, the UK exhibits the second lowest share of R&D which is domestically financed of any advanced economy (OECD 2014e). Even more surprisingly to many observers is the fact that, although the UK now has relatively the 5th highest number of university graduates in the OECD and attracts the second highest number and proportion of foreign students in the OECD,[45] at the same time UK expenditure on higher education relative to GDP ranks only 22nd in the OECD and the level of university R&D as a percentage of GDP is lower in the UK than the EU-27 average and only fractionally above the OECD average (OECD 2014e).[46] Moreover, even adjusting for different industrial structures and the greater role played by the service sector in the UK than in many other economies, the broad picture does not significantly alter (Hughes and Mina 2012).[47] The overall effects of these low R&D and skills-related scores are that, as with the UK productivity data, the only EU-15 countries[48] with relative lower scores for the number of researchers in the business sector than the UK are Italy, Spain, Portugal and Greece, and this is also the case for the gross and business R&D expenditure shares (OECD 2014e). In other words, these UK patterns and rankings regarding R&D and skills are also almost exactly repeated in terms of the UK's GDP per capita relative to its competitor countries.

Other manifestations of the UK's poor productivity performance are reflected by the fact that today the UK does not contain a single company in the world's top 100 global innovators (Thomson Reuters 2014) and only two in the world's top 50 R&D investors, which is the same number as Sweden and Switzerland (European Union 2014c). For comparison purposes the USA has 19 companies, Japan has 9, Germany has 8 companies, France has 2 companies and Italy has 1 such company in the global top 50 R&D investors (European Union 2014c). Amongst the major corporate R&D investors the total UK corporate R&D expenditure is currently 86 per cent of that of France and only 41 per cent of that of Germany (European Union 2014c). In terms of the attractiveness for international R&D-related investments the UK is perceived to be only two-thirds as attractive as France, half as attractive as The Netherlands, less than one-third as attractive as Germany, and even ranks slightly below Poland (European Union 2014d). Overall, what we see is that on a broad range of criteria related to skills, technology and productivity, the UK is just an average performer in comparison to both the EU and the OECD, and weaker on many productivity-related aspects than the majority of the world's and also Europe's advanced economies.

In part the domestic and popular misperceptions which view the UK as fundamentally a dynamic and strong economy surrounded by sclerotic and less dynamic countries are a natural result of the UK's island status and former Empire history, which still heavily colour many domestic cultural and political narratives. More importantly, however, the overwhelming majority of opinion-formers within the UK media and political circles – including the press, think-tanks, consultancies, political advisory bodies, world-class research centres, and heritage institutions – live and work in London or its surroundings. This is also an inevitable result of the UK having such a centralised state in which the largest city is also the seat of government and the dominant centre of business. As such, this provides a context in which national public debates and opinions are likely to be heavily shaped by the experience of the capital city.[49] The day-to-day experience of the vast majority of highly influential people is shaped and moulded by being resident in the highly prosperous regions of London and the South East whose productivity, wealth and disposable incomes in comparison to the rest of Europe are indeed reflective of the 1950s relationships between the UK and the rest of Europe. Unfortunately, as we will see in Chapters 2 and 3, these relationships do not hold even approximately, for more than half of the UK population.

As such, many of the political and cultural narratives currently dominating UK media and political circles reflect problems of the geography of perceptions as much as anything else. Moreover, these problems of the geography of perceptions are both domestic problems – in that they tend to ignore most of the UK's internal geographical inequalities – and also international problems – in that they tend to ignore the geographical patterns of productivity surrounding the UK. As such, in reality these backward-looking types of narratives are wholly unreasonable for a serious discussion about the UK's internal and external interregional relationships in that they frame such debates in settings which are totally unrealistic and unreflective of the current international and global economic settings. Realism is essential and accuracy is paramount if we are to have a meaningful discussion of these complex and important issues. Moreover, we haven't even begun to discuss why the UK's economy is positioned where it is today and why it is so profoundly different to where it was in the early twentieth century.

For our purposes here, what is important is to position the UK correctly in terms of economic performance in order to identify the extent to which observations and lessons from other countries may be instructive for re-imagining and re-visioning the UK economic and governance system. Most countries which are more successful and richer than the UK have much lower levels of interregional inequality. As we have already seen, while the UK exhibits a very high degree of interregional as well as national inequality, if this was associated with very strong economic performance then in some quarters or circles this may be perceived as providing some sort of defence or justification for this phenomenon along the lines of the schema trotted out in the 2009 World Development Report (World Bank 2009; Barca *et al.* 2012). However, as we have already seen, the poor overall performance of the UK economy suggests that the UK interregional inequalities are not a result of any natural or automatic trade-off between interregional inequality and economic performance, but rather reflect deep-seated structural problems within the UK economic system. Moreover, these economic and structural problems are now increasingly spilling over into political problems. Indeed, insights from the most extreme case of interregional inequality, namely Thailand, suggest that regional spillovers are not simply economic and monetary in nature, and negative governance externalities are far more intractable once they reach a certain threshold. While the UK is as yet nowhere near the Thailand experience it is certainly no longer natural to assume that if things continue to progress as they are that the largely unitary and top-down UK state is viable in the long run. Other countries have much to teach us and those which probably have the most to teach us are generally geographically very close to us.

1.4   International benchmarking of the modern UK economic context

From a policy perspective, in order to make any headway in deepening our understanding of the current UK interregional inequalities and their likely evolutions over the coming decades requires that we set these discussions against the backdrop of profound structural change within the UK economy during the last century, and in particular, over five decades. From this vantage point, it is well known that for much of the nineteenth century the UK displayed the highest levels of GDP per capita for any country, and it was only in the last decades of the century that both Australia and New Zealand overtook the UK (Maddison 2006). During the first decade of the twentieth century US GDP per capita also overtook that of the UK (Broadberry and Klein 2011; Maddison 2006) and as we will see in Chapter 2 this was a period of significant UK interregional inequalities. In the first decade following the First World War both Switzerland and Canada overtook the UK, although the UK and Switzerland also continued to leapfrog over each other throughout the 1930s.

In the post-war years between the 1950s and early 1970s the UK economy grew at its fastest rate for any comparable period in the previous century or centuries (Briggs 1983). However, even during these years the growth rate of the UK was typically only 50–60 per cent of the growth rate of other European economies (Briggs 1983), and this remained the case even as the UK higher education system was doubling in size during the 1960s following the recommendations of the 1963 Robbins Report (Briggs 1983). In the post Second World War era Switzerland's GDP per capita emerged as being systematically higher than that of the UK (Broadberry and Klein 2011) and from the 1950s onwards the GDP per capita of other countries also began to exceed that of the UK. By 1973, at the time of the UK's accession to the EEC Common Market, GDP per capita in the other EEC economies of Belgium, France, West Germany,[50] Denmark, The Netherlands and Luxembourg had also overtaken the UK GDP per capita levels, as had the non-EEC country of Sweden (Broadberry and Klein 2011). This was also a period of declining UK interregional inequalities. As we will see in Chapter 4, during this post-war era the UK increasingly shifted away from its former Empire and Commonwealth trading partners in favour of greater trade and economic integration with other European economies, culminating with the UK's entry into the EEC Common Market in 1973. This changed the UK's internal economic geography (Overman and Winters 2005, 2011) in favour of the southern and eastern regions. In the wake of the first oil price shock of 1974, the mid-1970s to early 1980s was a period characterised by numerous industrial disputes and a breakdown of the previously benign industrial relations between workers and management in many parts of the UK economy, being replaced instead by widespread adversarial relationships.

UK manufacturing also suffered an especially harsh period during the monetarist high interest rate regime of the early 1980s following the second oil price shock of 1981. The decade was characterised by numerous examples of long-standing and successful British manufacturing and engineering companies either entering liquidation or being bought out by foreign buyers (Comfort 2012). In marked contrast, since the 1980s employment in economies such as the UK is increasingly accounted for by service industries. Yet, the relative size of the shift away from manufacturing and towards a service-dominated economy has been greater in the case of the UK than almost all of its major international competitors (Comfort 2012). The rise of London-centred international financial services as a perceived cornerstone of the future UK economy has been widely discussed in numerous arenas (Casson and McCann 1999), along with the rise of other types of business and commercial services. As we will see in Chapter 4 these domestic structural shifts away from manufacturing and in favour of service industries have also been reflected in shifts in the composition of UK exports and imports. However, there is significant heterogeneity of the performance of service industries. Services such as finance, business services and personal services exhibit low-productivity growth but increasing employment shares, while distribution services exhibit constant employment shares and rapid productivity growth (Jorgensen and Timmer 2011). Since the 1980s national and international productivity growth has been driven far more by activities such as logistics, manufacturing and information technology than by personal, business or financial services (Jorgensen and Timmer 2011). As such, although service industries account for the lion's share of employment activities, many of them contribute very little to aggregate productivity growth (Jorgensen and Timmer 2011). Ironically, these low-productivity-enhancing sectors are the very sectors on which the UK economy has been expected to base its future prosperity.

During the 1970s and 1980s the associated adverse regional shocks associated with these structural changes were asymmetric in that they were heavily oriented towards those regions which were outside of the southern regions of England while the southern regions were relatively more oriented to the emerging service industries (Leunig and Overman 2008). UK manufacturing was increasingly seen in many political circles as being out-dated and UK manufacturing in particular as being especially so (Comfort 2012). However, as we will see in Chapter 2 the GDP per capita differences between UK regions remained largely constant during this period. Instead, the emerging differences in regional fortunes were manifested primarily in terms of greatly differing regional unemployment rates, and as a result, it was during this period that discussions about the 'north–south' divide started to emerge with a vengeance on both economic (Fothergill and Gudgin 1982; Harrison and Hart 1993) and also political economy grounds (Brown 1989).

Market deregulation continued apace throughout the 1980s and early 1990s and as we will see in Chapters 2–4, all aspects of the UK economy were affected in numerous and diverse ways by the shocks associated with modern globalisation which emerged from the early 1990s onwards. By 1990, the EU economies of Finland and Austria had also overtaken the UK in terms of GDP per capita, as had the non-EU economy of Norway, and by 2000, the list also included Ireland (Broadberry and Klein 2011). Although by the early 1990s the former West Germany had out-performed the UK in terms of GDP per capita for almost three decades and was more than 12 per cent richer per capita than the UK by 1990 (Broadberry and Klein 2011), not surprisingly the GDP per capita of the reunified Germany fell below that of the UK from the 1990 date of reunification.[51] However, by 2008 even the reunified Germany also exhibited higher per capita GDP than the UK, and has continued to do so ever since (OECD 2014c). Indeed, even allowing for the enormous resources involved in upgrading the former East Germany, the reunified Germany today exhibits a GDP per capita advantage over the UK which is almost exactly the advantage that West Germany displayed over the UK in 1990 (Broadberry and Klein 2011). In the wake of the 2008 crisis, the UK has made remarkably little long-term economic progress in comparison to its peer economies. In fact, the only country since the end of the Second World War that was previously richer than the UK and which the UK has subsequently overtaken in terms of GDP per capita is New Zealand, which the UK surpassed in the late 1980s (McCann 2009; Maddison 2006). Moreover, even in this case, although the productivity gap that the UK had over New Zealand reached some 20 per cent at the turn of the millennium (McCann 2009), in the wake of the 2008 crisis the gap had been almost closed again by 2012 (OECD 2014c).

It was from the early 1990s onwards that increasing UK interregional disparities really began to emerge. Between 1999 and 2007 the UK economy experienced almost a decade-long growth surge with annual productivity growth averaging 2.3 per cent (Wolf 2014b), which was faster than any other large OECD economy (Maddison 2006; OECD 2014c) and this allowed the UK to almost regain parity in terms of GDP per capita with both Canada and Australia in 2004 (OECD 2014c). As UK growth started to slow after 2004 both of these countries maintained a small productivity lead over the UK, but this gap widened significantly after the 2008 crisis. Indeed, following the

2008 global economic crisis the decade-long period of fast UK growth came to an abrupt end. Indeed, the UK has since faced amongst the most severe declines and medium- or long-term losses of economic potential of any major OECD economy (Ball 2014; Bank of England 2014; *The Economist* 2014f, 2014g, 2014h) with output per hour falling at a trend rate of 2.2 per cent per annum between the first quarter of 2008 and the third quarter of 2014 (Wolf 2014b). Yet, unlike many southern European economies, although the UK has experienced dramatic losses of productivity since 2008 it has only experienced limited associated increases in unemployment, which have since been falling (Wolf 2014b; *The Economist* 2015b). Taken together these observations lead to what is variously described as the UK 'productivity puzzle' (Bank of England 2014) or the UK 'productivity mystery' (Pessoa and Van Reenen 2014). Both the UK service industries and the UK production industries have faced severe productivity declines greater than in almost any other major OECD economy (Wolf 2014b). Most analyses of these issues focus on sectoral and firm-level analyses and examine the effects of factor substitution and labour market dynamics (Riley *et al.* 2015; Bryson and Forth 2015; Dolphin and Hatfield 2015). In particular, while UK productivity growth prior to the 2008 crisis was driven by the professional services, manufacturing, banking, retail and information and communication sectors, since the crisis the worst affected sectors have been professional services, telecommunications and computing, banking and finance, and manufacturing.[52] In other words, most of the same sectors which spearheaded productivity growth prior to the crisis have since spearheaded the productivity declines. There have been very recent productivity improvements in both the medium- and high-technology transport-manufacturing sectors as well as in low-technology sectors such as the administration and support sector, while the worst performing sectors are still finance and insurance and chemicals and pharmaceuticals.[53] Labour hoarding was apparent in manufacturing in the wake of the crisis as firms were concerned about losing skills, but this cannot explain ongoing productivity weaknesses (Berkeley *et al.* 2011). The increasing role of part-time work also cannot explain these productivity declines because they also are apparent in the output per hour data (Wolf 2014b). Moreover, neither can wage declines in the financial markets be the sole reason because the declining productivity effects are also very apparent in many areas of manufacturing (Wolf 2014b), although some areas of manufacturing such as automobiles are displaying strong productivity recovery well beyond pre-crisis levels (SMMT 2015). Nor can weaknesses in the UK's credit system be the major culprit as the financial system is recovering (Wolf 2014b). Rather, one of the best guesses as to the reasons for this apparent 'productivity puzzle' (Bank of England 2014) is related to the highly deregulated nature of the UK labour market and the rising costs of business capital costs (in spite of almost zero base rates) which have encouraged firms to substitute labour for new capital investment (Pessoa and Van Reenen 2014). This argument suggests that during the Great Recession the UK economy has absorbed much of the adverse shock effects of the crisis over recent years in terms of falling productivity and real wages rather than primarily in terms of rising unemployment (Bank of England 2014), as has been the case in countries located on the southern and eastern fringes of Europe. Yet, even after the shock-absorbing effect of a more than a 25 per cent post-crisis devaluation[54] of Sterling between mid-2008 and early 2009 the UK's export performance has barely improved at all and effectively no 'rebalancing' (Hunt 2013) of any form has taken place since.[55] As such, the fact that the UK's productivity performance remains poor even in the upturn of 2014 weakens the rather optimistic arguments in certain quarters that the UK will soon emerge again as a relatively strong dynamic economy (Wolf 2014b).

Indeed, the scale of the UK productivity 'puzzle' or 'mystery' can be underlined by the fact that although it is widely understood that in the aftermath of the 2008 global economic crisis Spain, Ireland and Italy suffered some of the worst economic declines amongst all of the advanced economies, in reality during the post-crisis period 2008–2012 all three countries experienced stronger GDP per capita growth than did the UK during the same period (OECD 2014c), as did even Japan (Wolf 2014b). Today the UK exhibits GDP per capita per hour levels which are 11 per cent below the Eurozone average and only just equal to the EU-28 average, including the central and eastern European countries (OECD 2014c), while GDP per worker levels are currently ranked only 13th in the EU. Indeed, some 207 million people within the EU, or 47 per cent of the population of the rest of the EU, now live in countries which are richer than the UK. This figure for the whole of Europe rises to some 221 million people or 49 per cent, if we also include the EFTA countries. By western and northern European standards as well as EU-15 standards the UK is a relatively low achiever. As we have already seen, overall GDP per capita levels for the UK are currently only between 5 per cent and 10 per cent above Italy and Spain, respectively (OECD 2014c) and are actually some 3.7 per cent below the average for the 34 OECD countries (OECD 2014c), while UK GDP per worker levels today are below those of Italy and Spain. GDP per hour worked in the UK is lower than in Italy and almost 25 per cent lower than in France.[56] Although in part lower worker productivity partly reflects a trade-off between productivity and employment (Wolf 2014b) the UK today exhibits both worker productivity and total GDP per capita which is still at least 15–30 per cent below that of other northern European economies and North American economies with similar levels of unemployment to the UK. Moreover, there are no signs as yet that the picture is changing as the UK's current performance is the worst relative to our competitors since records began in 1991.[57] In reality, the UK as a whole is a far poorer country and a much weaker economy than is reflected in many of the London-centric narratives circulating in the national popular press.

There are of course some grounds for optimism. Although between 2007 and 2012/13 the UK under-performed relative to both the Eurozone and the OECD as a whole (OECD 2015b), after a six-year period of little or no growth in 2014 the UK economy posted GDP growth of somewhere between 2.5 per cent and 3 per cent and again for the first time passed its pre-crisis levels of nominal output in early 2014, reaching some 2.1 per cent above the pre-crisis levels by the third quarter of 2014 (Wolf 2014b). During the same year UK wage growth for those already in work contracts for more than one year also began to outpace the growth in living costs for the first time in six years, with future expectations of productivity employment growth improving across all UK regions.[58] However, real wages for those on short-term or recent contracts continued to fall,[59] with the poorest households facing the fastest cost of living rises.[60] Poverty amongst working households is now on a greater scale than those households which are out of work or retired (*New Statesman* 2014) due to the scale of under-employment rather than just unemployment. Indeed, even allowing for recent improvements,[61] the observed patterns and trends in wage and productivity performance mean that many observers doubt whether we will again return to the type of economy buoyancy enjoyed between 1997 and 2007. Instead they argue that we may well have entered a period of 'secular stagnation' (*The Economist* 2014h; Coutts and Gudgin 2015) characterised by long periods of slow growth (Krugman 2014), low innovation and investment and poor productivity performance (Wolf 2014b), all of which are exacerbated by rising income inequalities (Summers 2013) and adverse demographic change. Of particular concern is the decline of the working age population relative to the retired population (*The Economist* 2014g). The sharp downward shift of the UK's productivity performance since 2008 has also led to downward revisions to the long-run growth expectations of the UK economy and to heavily downward-adjusted expectations regarding the medium-term fiscal position of the UK (Adam *et al.* 2012; Amior *et al.* 2013). These downward growth expectations also underpin the wide-ranging fiscal retrenchment which the UK is undergoing between 2010 and 2020. These current discussions regarding the UK's 'productivity mystery' or 'productivity puzzle' are very important for helping to understand both the current behaviour and likely future prospects of the UK economy.

For the purposes of this book, however, a much deeper, more wide-ranging and a far more long-standing productivity 'puzzle' or 'mystery' is why the productivity and prosperity benefits in one part of the UK so consistently fail to spill over or transmit to other parts of the UK in a manner which is almost unique amongst advanced economies. As we will see in Chapters 2 and 3, when compared with OECD and EU comparator regions and cities it is abundantly clear that the long-run productivity gains achieved in the core regions of the UK have simply failed to transmit to the non-core regions of the UK over more than four decades. Given that the non-core regions account for almost half of the UK population, the overall effect is that UK national productivity growth is consistently weak, and the UK as a whole is a much poorer country and much more unequal country than public and media debates assume. The result of this is that today within Europe the UK is the only large country with EU-NUTS2 regions in all five quintiles of

GDP per capita and at the level of EU-NUTS3 regions the degree of inter-regional inequality is even greater (Armstrong and Ebell 2015). Moreover, this situation is worsening in the aftermath of the 2008 crisis because the private sector 'credit crunch' (Parkinson *et al.* 2009) and the subsequent public sector cutbacks associated with the UK national fiscal consolidation are adversely affecting economically disadvantaged regions relatively even more severely than more prosperous regions (Oxford Economics 2008; Parkinson *et al.* 2009; Beatty and Fothergill 2013; Ward 2013a, 2013b; SPERI 2015)[62] while potentially offsetting and corrective policy schemes have in reality to some extent also favoured the more prosperous regions (Pike *et al.* 2013, 2015). Yet, rather than being a recent or current issue,[63] as will become clear in Chapter 2 the evolution of these UK interregional productivity disparities is a long-run phenomenon over four decades, and not simply a result of the 2008 crisis.

Yet, exactly why the productivity and prosperity benefits in the core regions so consistently fail to spill over to other non-core parts of the UK is a puzzle and a mystery, and a key point of discussion in Chapters 4 and 5 of this book. As we will see over the years there have been many suggested explanations. However, the currently widening UK interregional inequalities cannot be solely or even primarily the result of three decades of structural shifts from manufacturing to modern service industries. In terms of sectoral shifts, by value-added the UK still contains the ninth largest manufacturing industry in the world, although this is down from the UK's 1990 ranking of fifth since being overtaken by France, Italy, China, Brazil and South Korea (MGI 2012). Yet, many of today's UK manufacturing sectors are still highly productive, most notably the UK automobile industry (SMMT 2015). Similarly, as we have already seen, many service industries contribute very little to productivity growth and the UK is no exception in this regard (Dolphin and Hatfield 2015). In terms of regional shifts, countries with relatively much smaller service industry bases and larger manufacturing sectors than the UK such as Germany, Japan, Korea, The Netherlands, Sweden, Austria and Finland all experience much smaller interregional inequalities than the UK and all of these countries have also fared much better than the UK in the aftermath of the 2008 crisis.[64] Moreover, their observed interregional inequalities are not particularly characterised by spatial distinction between manufacturing and service industries. Other explanations, beyond overly simple sectoral explanations, need to be sought to understand both the poor productivity performance of the UK and the current interregional inequalities.

Today, although in total size the UK economy is the third largest in the EU the UK ranks only 10th or 11th in terms of productivity and per capita incomes. However, as we have already seen, it exhibits: only just above average productivity scores when compared against the 28 countries of the European Union, including those in Eastern Europe; below average productivity per worker per hour scores in comparison to the Eurozone; below average productivity scores in comparison to the EU-15; and below average productivity scores when compared with the 34 OECD countries (OECD 2014c). As we see, today the UK's productivity performance is only marginally higher than in Italy or Spain and the current productivity gap between countries such as The Netherlands, Germany, Austria and the Scandinavian economies is approximately the same as the productivity gap between the UK and the Czech Republic (OECD 2014c). The same is true for Australia and Canada (OECD 2014c). More starkly, the current productivity gap between the USA and the UK is only marginally greater than the current productivity gap between the UK and Turkey (OECD 2014c).

These observations suggest that the UK economy as a whole is a far weaker and less productive economy than much of the London-centric press appear to be aware of or to acknowledge. Indeed the UK's productivity performance was barely mentioned in the 2015 general election debates in the UK media.[65] What is more remarkable is how little any of the economic and policy changes experienced by the UK over four decades have altered the relative performance of the UK economy. The 1970s was a difficult decade for the UK economy (Briggs 1983) and this was followed in the 1980s with major changes in many areas of the economy. The difficult industrial relations and inflationary experience of the 1970s along with the deregulation and privatisation agenda of the 1980s and early 1990s tend to lead to highly polarised views and memories even many years later (Marr 2007), and people who experienced these years still tend to hold firm views as to the justification, efficacy and outcomes of government policies. Yet, in comparison to other northern and western European economies and also in comparison to the USA, the relative levels of UK productivity in 2000 were almost exactly the same as they were in both 1990 and 1973, the year the UK joined the Common Market (Broadberry and Klein 2011). In fact, in each case they fell by only a fraction of one percentage point. As we have already seen during the years following the millennium the UK economy grew in comparison to most of our European and OECD competitors, but most of these relative gains have since been wiped out in the aftermath of the 2008 global economic crisis. Again, as we have already seen, the UK economy is now relatively weaker than it was in 1970, 1990 or 2000. Importantly, however, even prior to the 2008 global financial crisis, relative to our main European and OECD competitor countries the UK had hardly advanced any further than its position in 1970 or 1990, and adjusting for labour quality the UK has since declined even further in real terms since 2008 (Krugman 2015b).

For many people these data might appear rather puzzling, as they do not correspond to their preconceptions, leading to something of a conundrum. In particular, claims that the changes wrought during the 1980s redefined the UK as a leading competitive economy appear to be totally unfounded. As such, people who view the widespread economic changes implemented wrought during the 1980s and early 1990s as being both transformational and positive for the UK economy, and London in particular, might question how it could be that these changes have had such little aggregate impacts on the UK economy? Similarly, beliefs that the long-run economic performance of the UK was undermined by these 1980s changes are also unfounded. In particular, those with personal experiences of the 1980s deindustrialisation (Rowthorne and Wells 1987) might wonder why the adverse effects in aggregate were so much less than they might have expected?

As will be explained throughout in this book, many of the clues providing answers to this conundrum are related to where we are in regional terms. The transformation of the UK economy since the late 1980s and early 1990s has benefited almost exactly one-half of UK economy while for the other half of the economy there is no real evidence of any specific benefits related to these changes. That this is the case is evident both at the regional level and at the urban level, but most importantly, which urban areas display which outcomes depends on which regions the cities are located in. London in particular has benefited from the effects of modern globalisation to a greater extent than most other cities in the world, an experience unparalleled elsewhere in the UK. Although London and the rest of the UK may exhibit some level of demographic convergence[66] regarding patterns of ethnic diversity and composition this is one of the very few areas of social or economic convergence between the capital and the rest of the UK. As such, the strong economic performance of one-half of the UK since the late 1980s is counter-balanced by a much weaker performance on the part of the other half of the UK economy. The combination of these two trends pulling in different directions is that the UK has barely moved forward at all in comparison to competitor countries over the last 40 years, as confirmed by the international data.

As already mentioned above, when discussing economic issues in an international context, many commentators and opinion-formers in the UK's popular press and political circles are heavily, and probably overly, swayed by their daily experience of the success of London and its surroundings, which gives rise to a problem of the geography of (erroneous) perceptions. These misleading and erroneous perceptions are reflected by frequent popular press discussions regarding London's performance relative to New York or Hong Kong in a manner in which the performance of London is taken to reflect the performance of the UK (which it is not), and London's supposed pre-eminence in European cities (even though Paris is as large and richer and seven other European cities are also richer than London). In reality many of these commentators and opinion-formers are largely unaware of how weak are the UK's productivity levels and how narrow the economic gaps are between the UK and countries such as Italy and Spain and how large they are between the UK and the other northern European economies. In other words, discussions linking London and New York or Hong Kong are of little use in analysing UK economic issues because the London regional economy does not even remotely represent or reflect the UK economy as a whole. As we will see in Chapters 2–4, an over-emphasis within the London-centric UK media and political circles on the role played by London in the UK economy tends to be very misleading and to paint a very distorted picture from what happens in the UK as a whole.

What becomes very clear in Chapters 2 and 3 is that the vast majority of the UK's poor productivity performance and productivity puzzle (Bank of England 2014) or mystery in the aftermath of the 2008 global economic crisis is contained in the 'non-core' regions outside of London and the south of England, with the possible exception also of Scotland. Moreover, to the extent that in the UK poor regional economic performance is also closely associated with poor urban productivity performance, as we will also see in Chapter 3, the UK cities facing severe productivity problems are those cities located in these same non-core regions. The regional dimension of the weak UK productivity performance has been strangely absent in the recent official government publications of HM Treasury, BIS the Department for Business, Innovation and Skills, and other various influential publications (Aghion *et al.* 2013)[67] discussing the UK's productivity, innovation and competitiveness. Yet a moment's thought serves to illustrate the issue. While there are frequent discussions in the press regarding the current UK productivity 'puzzle' or 'mystery', few commentators are heard bemoaning the poor productivity performance of London and its hinterland regions. The reason, as most people understand, is that these regions do not exhibit serious underlying productivity problems, because as we will see in Chapter 4, London has been in the vanguard of the transformations wrought by modern globalisation. As such, much of the UK productivity problem is not fundamentally a UK 'national' problem, but rather a *regional* problem, experienced by all but one of those regions which faced severe de-industrialisation in the 1980s. It is only a national problem to the extent that the aggregated national productivity performance is weakened. Similarly, as we will also see in the forthcoming chapters, the buoyant performance of the London economy and to a lesser extent its hinterland regions is also not a 'national' success story, but rather a *regional* success story. It is only a national success to the extent that the national productivity is strengthened, although the available evidence in Chapters 2, 3 and 5 suggests that few if any of the benefits of the 1990s resurgence of London have spread beyond the southern regions of England. As such, the combined effects of this dividing and decoupling, whereby one-half of the UK experiences economic buoyancy and one-half of the UK experiences economic sluggishness, are that the aggregate long-run national effect is almost zero, when compared to our main European and OECD competitors.

As we will see throughout this book the UK economy is increasingly dislocating, dividing and decoupling into two largely separate economies and one's perceptions regarding how changes of the 1980s and 1990s have impacted on the UK and its role in the world depend almost entirely on where one is geographically located within the UK. This issue regarding perceptions is also critical concerning internal UK debates. The Scottish independence and devolution agendas have now put the issues of the UK's internal governance on a different footing from previously and now governance devolution and decentralisation in city regions as well as the devolved administrations reflect mainstream political discourses. Moreover, these various different devolutionary pressures are also likely to lead to changes in the nature of, if not the role of, the state. Again, how one views these issues is also likely to be largely shaped by where one is located. On the one hand, there is evidence that England and Wales are decoupling from Scotland in terms of their mutual perceptions of the benefits of union.[68] At the same time, perceptions of the centralisation of the UK state and its role in favouring the London economy over many years differ according to whether one is located in London and the 'south' or in 'the north'.[69] Yet, while there now appears to be no doubt that major changes to the UK internal governance arrangements are in the process, exactly what role these changes will play in re-shaping the long-run economic geography of the UK also depends on the actual forms and scale of the diverse devolution arrangements, and on exactly how the agreed governance changes relate to the underlying economic fundamentals.

On these important and current issues there is now a great deal of commentary and debate in the popular press and the media. However, in comparison to the popular and political narratives, there is surprisingly little by way of any systematic assessment of these issues, little real analysis of the actual wide-ranging evidence regarding these matters, and no overall framework for shaping the discourses. Yet, there is an enormous amount of evidence on these matters which is nowadays publicly available, but much of it is either ignored or under-utilised, and public debates therefore tend to over-emphasise the ideas of a small number of high-profile and popular publications or of a few specific and high-profile sources of commentary and opinion. The obvious danger here is that major policy decisions become overly dependent on narrow narratives and on political discourses which are too tightly framed. As this book will consistently argue, however, the UK interregional issues are fundamentally economic issues, not political or constitutional issues, although they do have profound political and constitutional implications, as is now becoming clearly evident. Therefore, the explicit intention of this book is to provide a much-needed and systematic analysis of the nature, causes and consequences of the UK's interregional inequalities and imbalances and to do this in a way which underpins a robust framing for these discussions in the popular and political discourses.

1.5   Conclusions

This chapter has outlined the case that the UK does indeed face a serious regional and national economic problem relating to the scale of the UK's interregional imbalances and the apparent inability of the government system to respond in a manner which reflects the wishes and needs of local communities. The UK is increasingly dislocating and decoupling internally and this puts immense strain both on the legitimacy and effectiveness of the UK's governance systems, as well as limiting the overall productivity growth of the country as a whole. The Scottish independence referendum has thrown these issues into sharp relief and the allied governance and devolution trends in other parts of the UK also reflect growing tensions and strains within the UK's governance system. Yet, the issues are so fundamental and wide-ranging that even if Scotland eventually does choose to leave the union, as we will see throughout this book, the overall arguments here barely change at all.

Notes

1 "Time for a Civic Surge", *The Economist*, 6 June 2015; "Spreading their Wings: English Cities", *The Economist*, 6 June 2015.
2 Quoted in Stark *et al.* (2013).
3 See www.bbc.com/news/uk-30520065.
4 We all know that the old model of trying to run everything in our country from the centre of London is broken. It's led to an unbalanced economy, it's made people feel remote from the decisions that affect their lives. It's not good for our prosperity, it's not good for our democracy.

 George Osborne announcing on 14 May 2015 that a bill for English city devolution is to be included in the first Queen's Speech of the new Parliament following the 2015 UK general election. See "George Osborne Outlines City Devolution Plan for England", www.bbc.com/news/uk-politics-32726171.
5 "Bagehot: Not Just a Hatchet Man", *The Economist*, 14 March 2015.
6 These analyses run counter to much of the previous orthodoxy which had assumed that inequality was necessary for growth, instead arguing that the evidence does not support this contention. However, some commentors have questioned the veracity of these analyses arguing that they do not necessarily imply that inequality is bad for growth. However, this is a slightly different argument to saying that inequality is necessary for growth. See: Giles, C., 2015, "Inequality is Unjust – It is Not Bad for Growth", *Financial Times*, 19 August.
7 As reflected in the 2014 Richard Dimbleby Lecture entitled "A New Multilateralism for the Twenty First Century" given by the Managing Director of the IMF Christine Lagarde on 3 February 2014. See: www.imf.org/external/np/speeches/2014/020314. htm and in National Intelligence Council (NIC 2012) report.
8 http://report.mitigation2014.org/spm/ipcc_wg3_ar5_summary-for-policymakers_ approved.pdf.
9 See also: "Monitoring Economic Performance, Quality of Life and Sustainability" jointly produced by the French 'Conseil d'analyse économique' and the German Council of Economic Experts, December 2010. Available at: www.cae.gouv.fr/ IMG/pdf/095_ANG.pdf.
10 See: www.oecd.org/document/10/0,3746,en_2649_201185_42393354_1_1_1_1,00. html.
11 See: www.whitehouse.gov/sites/default/files/omb/assets/memoranda_2010/m10- 21.pdf; www.whitehouse.gov/blog/2010/06/30/place-based-investments; www.eda. gov/pdf/CEDS_Flyer_Wht_Backround.pdf; http://yosemite.epa.gov/opa/adm- press.nsf/0/75E1F57EB6D0FCEC8525788CA0063A5CB.
12 Brazil, Russia, India, Indonesia, China and South Africa.
13 www.smith-commission.scot/wp-content/uploads/2014/11/The_Smith_ Commission_Report-1.pdf.
14 Indeed, the idea that different parts of the UK might be governed in different ways by different people goes back to the 1880s (King 2015).

15 These realities whereby some professional players and coaches switch between codes but supporters and club members inhabit quite different social networks, also largely hold in other countries where both codes of rugby are played, such as Australia, New Zealand, France and Samoa.

16 Neville, G., "The North is Being Cut Adrift in English Football – and I Fear the Damage May be Permanent", *The Daily Telegraph*, 25 September 2015.

17 "This General Election Will be Fought Along Regional Lines", *Financial Times*, 4 January 2015.

18 In Part 1 of the Evan Davis BBC television programme *Mind the Gap: London vs the Rest* which was broadcast on Monday 3 March 2014, BBC2 at 21.00–22.00.

19 "Bagehot: This House is Falling", *The Economist*, 18 July 2015.

20 "Disunited Kingdom: London in a World of Its Own", *Financial Times*, 2nd March 2015. See also Simon Jenkins, "London Must Stop Sucking up Cash from the Rest of Britain", *The Guardian*, 23 December 2015.

21 Tony Travers of LSE is widely quoted in many outlets as saying "London is the dark star of the economy, inexorably sucking in resources, people and energy. Nobody quite knows how to control it" and this quote has been repeated by Alex Salmond, the then leader of the Scottish National Party (Coy 2014; *The Scotsman* 2014). "London Draining Life Out of Rest of Country – Vince Cable", 19 December 2014 www.bbc.com/news/uk-politics-25444981; "Vince Cable: London 'is Sucking Life Out of the Rest of the Country", *The Independent*, 19 December 2014; "London 'Draining Life' from Rest of UK Economy", *CBS News Moneywatch*, 19 March 2014; Prowle, M., "Scottish Independence: The London Problem", 12 June 2014, see: http://opinion.publicfinance.co.uk/2014/scottish-independence-the-london-problem.

22 See: "The Super Rich and Us" broadcast on BBC2 on 8 January 2014 at 21.00.

23 "Why is UKIP So Popular in South East England?", 9 January 2015, www.bbc.com/news/uk-england-30745787; "The End of the British Establishment", *Financial Times*, 24 February 2015.

24 www.britishfuture.org/blog/the-myth-of-planet-london/; http://blogs.spectator.co.uk/alex-massie/2012/04/planet-london-and-planet-edinburgh/; www.ft.com/cms/s/2/81d96998-3aa0-11e4-bd08-00144feabdc0.html#axzz3JPq0SADG; www.theguardian.com/news/datablog/2014/oct/10/london-uk-inequality-productivity-premium.

25 "New Poll Finds That Most People Feel the Economy, Politics and Media Are Too London-Centric", *Centre for Cities*, 13 May 2014.

26 Sturgeon, N., 2014, Speech to Scotland's Business Sector, SSE Business Offices, Glasgow, 1 December 2014, as quoted in Martin *et al.* (2015).

27 "Greater Manchester Mayor: What Do Local People Think?" BBC News, 3 November 2014, www.bbc.com/news/uk-england-manchester-29879148.

28 See: "Bagehot: England's Sensible Slumber", *The Economist*, 20 June 2015.

29 www.businessinsider.com/map-of-separatist-movements-in-europe-2014-9

30 www.bbc.com/news/uk-politics-32726171;www.bbc.com/news/magazine-32720462.

31 http://webarchive.nationalarchives.gov.uk/20100202100434/www.thenorthernway.co.uk/document.asp?id=766.

32 The line wavers in and out of Gloucestershire, Warwickshire, Leicestershire and Lincolnshire (Colley 2014). Indeed, Dorling (2010) argues on the basis of a wide range of socio-economic and health-related data (Dorling 2013b, 2013c) that instead of approaching The Wash the north-eastern part of the line actually travels slightly north of the city of Lincoln and turns east to the coast just south of the town of Grimsby.

33 www.theguardian.com/commentisfree/2015/mar/29/three-new-tribes-of-voters-will-dominate-this-election.

34 In terms of child poverty "Two Schools Worlds Apart in Lancashire", BBC News, 1st April 2015, and "The Great Constituency Swap", Danny Dorling and Simon Szreter, Prospect, 6 March 2015. See: bbc.com/news/uk-31905037.

35 See: *Panorama* "What Britain Wants: Something to Hope For", broadcast on BBC1 at 20.30 on Monday 23 March 2015.

36 http://www.telegraph.co.uk/news/worldnews/europe/eu/11184605/Explainer-Why-must-Britain-pay-1.7bn-to-the-European-Union-and-can-we-stop-it-happening.html.

37 www.theguardian.com/commentisfree/2015/jul/12/osborne-budget-homes-business.

38 OECD (2013); OECD Productivity Statistics, www.oecd.org/statistics/productivity.

39 OECD (2013), *OECD Science, Technology and Industry Scoreboard: Innovation for Growth*, Organisation for Economic Cooperation and Development, Paris.

40 Not including the European microstates such as Andorra, the Channel islands, Monaco and Lichtenstein, most of which are tax havens and not surprisingly also richer than the UK.

41 www.innovationsindikator.de/fileadmin/user_upload/Dokumente/Presse/Innovationsindikator_2014_English-Extract_241014.pdf.

42 OECD (2013); *OECD Science, Technology and Industry Scoreboard: Innovation for Growth*, Organisation for Economic Cooperation and Development, Paris.

43 http://ec.europa.eu/euraxess/pdf/research_policies/Researchers%20Report%20 2014_FINAL%20REPORT.pdf.

44 OECD (2013); *OECD Science, Technology and Industry Scoreboard: Innovation for Growth*, Organisation for Economic Cooperation and Development, Paris.

45 OECD (2013); *Education at a Glance*, Organisation for Economic Development and Cooperation, Paris.

46 In relative terms therefore the UK university system performs strongly, particularly given its lower inputs. See "On Pound-for-Pound Basis, UK is a Knockout Performer", *Times Higher Education*, 21 May 2015.

47 OECD (2013); *OECD Science, Technology and Industry Scoreboard 2013*, Organisation for Economic Development and Cooperation, Paris.

48 Which were part of the EU by 1995.

49 Amongst the other 'Anglo-Saxon' capitalist economies the UK is almost unique in this regard, with the USA, Canada and Australia all being federal systems with separate government and commercial capitals, while the centralised but tiny economy of New Zealand also has separate business and government capitals. Only Ireland is akin to the UK, and again is a tiny economy relative to the UK.

50 Part of the difficulty of assessing the long-run performance of the UK economy relative to other comparators, and in particular European comparators, is because of changing boundaries and borders, and estimates need to adjust for these changes. Broadberry and Klein (2011) provide estimates for the period 1870–2000 which explicitly control for these changes.

51 The former country of West Germany with some 63 million people was merged in 1990 with the former East Germany, a country whose population of 16 million was one-quarter of that of West Germany but whose GDP per capita in 1990 was also only one-third of that of West Germany (Broadberry and Klein 2011). The reunification involved enormous fiscal transfers over more than two decades from the western to the eastern German regions.

52 www.ft.com/cms/s/0/3e0082a8-e502-11e4-bb4b-00144feab7de.html#axzz3g WhIW03a.

53 *The Economist*, "Under the Bonnet", 30 May 2015.

54 www.x-rates.com/average/?from=GBP&to=USD&amount=1&year=2009.

55 www.birminghampost.co.uk/business/business-opinion/march-makers-goes-reverse-9696685.

56 "Bargain Basement", *The Economist*, 14 March 2015.
57 www.thetimes.co.uk/tto/business/economics/article4561736.ece?CMP=OTH-gnws-standard-2015_09_18; www.theguardian.com/business/2015/sep/18/uks-poor-productivity-figures-show-challenge-for-government?CMP=Share_iOSApp_Other.
58 www.bbc.com/news/business-30568093. See also: www.highfliers.co.uk/download/GMReview14.pdf.
59 www.bbc.com/news/business-30117284 and www.bbc.com/news/business-30512657.
60 www.bbc.com/news/business-30477699.
61 www.bbc.com/news/business-34410030.
62 "Council Cuts: Who Will Lose Out the Most?" BBC News, 18 December, www.bbc.com/news/uk-politics-30537288; "Poorest Council Areas 'Hit Hardest by Cuts', say MPs", BBC News, 28 January, www.bbc.com/news/uk-politics-31012671.
63 "Recovery Likely to Widen Wealth Gap Between London and Regions", *Financial Times*, 19th January 2014; "Two-Speed Britain as London Soars Away", *The Observer*, 11 May 2013.
64 www.birminghampost.co.uk/business/business-opinion/march-makers-goes-reverse-9696685.
65 "Osborne Faces Up to Productivity Challenge", BBC News, 20 May 2015, www.bbc.com/news/business-32820716.
66 Cunliffe, J., "Britain's Future Looks Like This: Look at the Capital and You'll See Britain's Future – Better Educated, Less White and Increasingly Liberal", *Prospect*, 18 June 2015.
67 In the submissions to the LSE Growth Commission various matters were raised regarding the effects of land use restrictions and the impacts of various urban and neighbourhood issues, but there was no explicit UK-wide regional dimension to the Commission's discussions or its conclusions. See Cheshire *et al.* (2012).
68 While the Scottish independence movement has gained so much ground over recent years a willingness to pay in order to maintain the union is even lower in England and Wales than in Scotland. See: "Our Opinion Poll: Scotland is Another Country. What the English Think About Their Northern Neighbours", *The Economist*, 2 May 2015.
69 "Time for a Civic Surge", *The Economist*, 6 June 2015.

References

Adam, S., Brewer, M., Browne, J., Crawford, R., Emerson, C., Fitzsimons, E., Goodwin, A., Jin, W., Johnson, P., Joyce, R., Miller, H., Phillips, D., Roger, D., Slater, A., Stoye, G. and Tetlow, G., 2012, *The IFS Green Budget February 2012*, Institute for Fiscal Studies, London.

Adonis, A., 2014, *Mending the Fractured Economy: Smarter State, Better Jobs*, Final Report of the Adonis Review, An Independent Review for the Labour Party Supported by the Policy Network, London, www.policy-network.net.

Aghion, P., Besley, T., Browne, J., Caselli, F., Lambert, R., Lomax, R., Pissarides, C., Stern, N. and Van Reenen, J., 2013, *Investing for Prosperity: Skills, Infrastructure and Innovation*, Report of the LSE Growth Commission in Partnership with the Institute for Government, Centre for Economic Performance, London.

Alesina A., and Spolaore, E., 2005, *The Size of Nations*, MIT Press, Cambridge, MA.

Amior, M., Crawford, R., and Tetlow, G, 2013, "The UK's Public Finances in the Long Run: The IFS Model", *IFS Working Paper W13/29*, Institute for Fiscal Studies, London.

Armstrong, A., and Ebell, M., 2015, "The Economics of UK Constitutional Change: Introduction", *National Institute Economic Review*, 233, R1–R4.

Atkinson, A.B., 2015a, *Inequality: What Can be Done?*, Harvard University Press, Cambridge, MA.

Atkinson, A.B., 2015b, "What Can Be Done About Inequality?", *Juncture*, 22.1, 32–41.

Baker, A.R.H., and Billinge, M., 2004, (eds.), *Geographies of England: The North-South Divide, Material and Imagined*, Cambridge University Press, Cambridge.

Balchin, P.N., 1990, *Regional Policy in Britain: The North-South Divide*, Paul Chapman Publishing, London.

Ball, L.M., 2014, "Long-Term Damage from the Great Recession in OECD Countries", *NBER Working Paper 20185*, Cambridge, MA.

Bank of England, 2014, "The UK Productivity Puzzle", *Bank of England Quarterly Bulletin Q2*, 114–128, June.

Barca, F., 2009, *An Agenda for A Reformed Cohesion Policy: A Place-Based Approach to Meeting European Union Challenges and Expectations*, Independent Report Prepared at the Request of the European Commissioner for Regional Policy, Danuta Hübner, European Commission, Brussels.

Barca, F., McCann, P. and Rodriguez-Pose, A., 2012, "The Case for Regional Development Intervention: Place-Based versus Place-Neutral Approaches", *Journal of Regional Science*, 52.1, 134–152.

Beatty, C., and Fothergill, S., 2013, *Hitting the Poorest Places Hardest: The Local and Regional Impacts of Welfare Reform*, Centre for Regional Economic and Social Research, Sheffield Hallam University, Sheffield.

Berg, A.G., and Ostry, J.D., 2011, "Inequality and Unsustainable Growth: Two Sides of the Same Coin", *IMF Staff Discussion Note, SDN/11/08*, International Monetary Fund, Washington DC.

Berg, J., 2015, (ed.), *Labour Markets, Institutions and Inequality: Building Just Societies in the 21st Century*, Edward Elgar, Cheltenham.

Berkeley, N., Jarvis, D. and Begley, J., 2011, "The Impact of the Recession on Businesses", in Bailey, D., and Chapain, C., (eds.), *Local and Regional Responses to the Downturn*, Routledge, London.

BIS, 2010, *Understanding Local Growth*, Department for Business, Innovation and Skills, and Department for Communities and Local Government, BIS Economics Paper No. 7, October, London.

Bogdanor, V., 2015a, "This General Election Will be Fought Along Regional Lines", *Financial Times*, 4 January.

Bogdanor, V., 2015b, "Now Rewrite the Rules: Britain Must Have a New Constitution", *Prospect*, June.

Bourguignon, F., 2015, *The Globalization of Inequality*, Translated by Scott-Railton, S., Princeton University Press, Princeton, NJ.

Braga de Macedo, J., and Oliviera-Martins, J., 2008, "Growth, Reform Indicators and Policy Complementarities", *Economics of Transition*, 16, 141–164.

Braga de Macedo, J., and Oliviera-Martins, J., 2010, "Policy Complementarities and Growth", 1–37, *OECD/CESifo/Ifo Workshop Regulation: Political Economy, Measurement and Effects on Performance*, 29–30 January, Munich.

Braga de Macedo, J., Oliviera-Martins, J. and Rocha, B., 2013, "Are Complementary Reforms a 'Luxury' for Developing Countries", *Journal of Comparative Economics*, 42.2, 417–435.

Briggs, A., 1983, *A Social History of England*, Book Club Associates, London.

Broadberry, S., and Klein, A., 2011, "Aggregate and Per Capita GDP in Europe, 1870–2000: Continental, Regional and National Data with Changing Boundaries", Working Paper, Department of Economics, University of Warwick.

Brown, G., 1989, *Where There's Greed: Margaret Thatcher and the Betrayal of Britain's Future*, Mainstream, London.

Brown, G., 2014, *My Scotland, Our Britain: A Future Worth Sharing*, Simon and Schuster, London.

Bryson, A., and Forth, J., 2015, *The UK's Productivity Puzzle*, NIESR Discussion Paper No. 448, National Institute of Economic and Social Research, London.

Cambridge Econometrics, 2013, *Economic Prospects for the Nations and Regions of the UK*, Cambridge, May.

Cameron, D., 2010, "Transforming the British Economy: Coalition Strategy for Economic Growth", A Transcript of a Speech Given by the UK Prime Minister David Cameron on 28 May 2010 on the economy. See: https://www.gov.uk/government/speeches/transforming-the-british-economy-coalition-strategy-for-economic-growth.

Cash, D.W., Clark, W.C., Alcock, F., Dickson, N.M., Echley, N., Guston, D.H., Jäger, J. and Mitchell, R.B., 2003, "Knowledge Systems for Sustainable Development", *Proceedings of the National Academy of Sciences*, 100.14, 8086–8091.

Casson, M.C., and McCann, P., 1999, "Globalisation, Competition, and the Corporation: The UK Experience", in Whitman M., (ed.), *The Evolving Corporation: Global Imperatives and National Responses*, Group of Thirty, Washington DC.

CBI, 2012, *The UK's Growth Landscape: Harnessing Private-Sector Potential Across the Country*, Confederation of British Industry, London.

Cheshire, P.C., Leunig., T., Nathan, M. and Overman, H.G., 2012, *Links Between Planning and Economic Performance: Evidence Note for LSE Growth Commission*, paper submitted to the LSE Growth Commission, June.

Cheshire, P.C., Nathan, M. and Overman, H.G., 2014, *Urban Economics and Urban Policy: Challenging Conventional Wisdom*, Edward Elgar, Cheltenham.

Colley, L., 2014, *Acts of Union and Disunion: What Has Held the UK Together – and What's Dividing It?*, Profile Books, London.

Collins, T., 1998, *Rugby's Great Split: Class, Culture, and the Origins of Rugby League Football*, Routledge, London.

Comfort, N., 2012, *Surrender: How British Industry Gave Up the Ghost 1952–2012*, Biteback Publishing, London.

Coutts, K., and Gudgin, G., 2015, *The Macroeconomic Impact of Liberal Economic Policies in the UK*, Centre for Business Research, Judge Business School, University of Cambridge, Cambridge.

Coy, P., 2014, "Can an Independent Scotland, Free of London's Dominance, Survive?", *Bloomberg Business*, www.bloomberg.com, 11 September.

DCLG, 2008, *Why Place Matters and Implications for the Role of Central, Regional and Local Government*, Economic Paper 2, Department for Communities and Local Government, London.

DCLG, 2011, *Updating the Evidence Base on English Cities: Final Report*, Department for Communities and Local Government, London.

de Dominicis, L., 2014, "Inequality and Growth in European Regions: Towards a Place-Based Approach", *Spatial Economic Analysis*, 9, 120–141.

Deutsche Bank, 2013, *London and the UK: In for a Penny, In for the Pound*, Deutsche Bank Markets Research Special Report, London, 27 November.

Deutsche Bank, 2014, *UK Housing: London vs The Rest*, Deutsche Bank Research, London, 18 July.

DfT, 2014a, *HS2 Plus: A Report by David Higgins*, Department for Transport, London, October.

DfT, 2014b, *Rebalancing Britain: From HS2 Towards a National Transport Strategy*, Department for Transport, London, October.

Diamond, P., and Carr-West, J., 2015, *Devolution: A Roadmap*, Local Government Information Unit, London.

Dolphin, T., and Hatfield, I., 2015, *The Missing Pieces: Solving Britain's Productivity Puzzle*, Institute for Public Policy Research, London.

Dorling, D., 2010, "Persistent North-South Divides", Coe, N.C., and Jones, A., (eds.), *The Economic Geography of the UK*, Sage, London.

Dorling, D., 2011, *Injustice: Why Social Inequality Persists*, Policy Press, Bristol.

Dorling, D., 2013a, *The 32 Stops*, Penguin Books, London.

Dorling, D., 2013b, *The Population of the UK, 2nd Edition*, Sage, London.

Dorling, D., 2013c, *Unequal Health: The Scandal of Our Times*, Policy Press, Bristol.

DTI, 1998, *Regional Competitiveness Indicators*, Department for Trade and Industry, London, February.

DTI, 1999, *Regional Competitiveness Indicators*, Department for Trade and Industry, London, February.

Emmott, B., 2015, "The British Question", *Prospect*, June.

European Commission, 2010, *Europe 2020: A European Strategy for Smart, Sustainable and Inclusive Growth*, [COM (2010) 2020] 3.3.2010, Brussels.

European Union, 2014a, *Investment for Jobs and Growth – Promoting Development and Good Governance in EU Regions and Cities: Sixth Report on Economic, Social and Territorial Cohesion*, Publications Office, Brussels.

European Union, 2014b, *Innovation Union Scoreboard 2014*, Publications Office, Brussels.

European Union, 2014c, *EU R&D Scoreboard: The 2014 EU Industrial R&D Investment Scoreboard*, Publications Office, Brussels.

European Union, 2014d, *EU R&D Survey: The 2014 EU Survey of Industrial R&D Investment Trends*, Publications Office, Brussels.

Ezcurra, R., 2007, "Is Income Inequality Harmful for Growth? Evidence from the European Union", *Urban Studies*, 44.10, 1953–1971.

Financial Times, 2014a, "Why Capital Cities Can Be Unloved", 27 May.

Financial Times, 2014b, "Recovery Likely to Widen Wealth Gap Between London and the Regions", 19 January.

Florida, R., 2010, *The Great Reset: New Ways of Living and Working Drive Post-Crash Prosperity*, Random House Canada, Toronto.

Fothergill, S., and Gudgin, G., 1982, *Unequal Growth: Urban and Regional Employment in the United Kingdom*, Heinemann, London.

Galbraith, J.K., 2012, *Inequality and Instability: A Study of the World Economy Just Before the Crisis*, Oxford University Press, Oxford.

Gallagher, J., 2014, "The English Question: It's Time for the UK to Give England More of a Voice – and This is How to Do It", *Prospect*, November.

Goos, M., Manning, A. and Salomons, A., 2009, "Job Polarization in Europe", *American Economic Review*, 99.2, 58–63.

GOS, 2013, *The Competitiveness and Evolving Geography of British Manufacturing: Where is Manufacturing Tied Locally and How Might This Change?*, Bryson, J.R., Clark, J., Mulhall, R., Future of Manufacturing Project: Evidence Paper 3, Foresight, Government Office for Science, London.

Harrison, R., and Hart, M., 1993, (eds.), *Spatial Policy in a Divided Nation*, Routledge, London.

Heseltine, M., 2012, *No Stone Unturned*, Independent Report Submitted to HM Government, Department for Business, Innovation and Skills, London.

HM Government, 2010, *Local Growth: Realising Every Place's Potential*, London, 28 October.

HM Government, 2011, *Unlocking Growth in Cities*, London, December.

HM Government and Transport for the North, 2015, *The Northern Powerhouse: One Agenda, One Economy, One North*, Department for Transport, London, March.

HM Treasury, 2001, *Productivity in the UK: 3 The Regional Dimension*, HM Treasury, London.

HM Treasury, 2003, *Productivity in the UK: 4 The Regional Dimension*, HM Treasury, London.

HMT, DTI and ODPM, 2003, *A Modern Regional Policy for the United Kingdom*, HM Treasury, Department of Trade and Industry and Office of the Deputy Prime Minister, London.

HoC, 2014, *Devolution in England: The Case for Local Government*, HC503 Incorporating 1018, Session 2013–2014, House of Commons Communities and Local Government Committee, The Stationery Office, London.

Hughes, A., 2012, "Choosing Races and Placing Bets: UK National Innovation Policy and the Globalisation of Innovation Systems", in Greenaway, D., (ed.), *The UK in a Global World. How Can the UK Focus on Steps in Global Value Chains That Really Add Value?*, BIS e-book, CEPR and Department for Business, Innovation and Skills. See: www.cepr.org/pubs/books/cepr/BIS_eBook.pdf.

Hughes, A., and Mina, A., 2012, *The UK R&D Landscape: Enhancing Value Task Force*, UK-Innovation Research Centre and Council for Industry and Higher Education, Cambridge and London.

Hunt, T., 2013, (ed.), *Rebalancing the British Economy*, Civitas, London.

Iammarino, S., and McCann, P., 2013, *Multinationals and Economic Geography: Location, Technology, and Innovation*, Edward Elgar, Cheltenham.

ICLGF, 2014, *Public Money, Local Choice*, Interim Report of the Independent Commission of Local Government Finance, Local Government Association and CIPFA The Chartered Institute of Public Finance and Accountancy, London, 30 October.

ICLGF, 2015, *Financing English Devolution*, Final Report of the Independent Commission of Local Government Finance, Local Government Association and CIPFA The Chartered Institute of Public Finance and Accountancy, London, 18 February.

IPPR, 2012, *Northern Prosperity is National Prosperity: A Strategy for Revitalising the UK Economy*, Institute for Public Policy Research North, Newcastle, November.

IPPR, 2014, *Decentralisation Decade: A Plan for Economic Prosperity, Public Service Transformation and Democratic Renewal in England*, Institute for Public Policy Research North, Newcastle, September.

Jorgensen, D.W., and Timmer, M.P., 2011, "Structural Change in Advanced Nations: A New Set of Stylised Facts", *Scandinavian Journal of Economics*, 113.1, 1–29.

Kellner, P., 2014, "English Questions", *Prospect*, November.

King, A., 2015, *Who Governs Britain?*, Pelican Books, London.

Knight Frank, 2015, *The Wealth Report 2015: The Global Perspective on Prime Property and Wealth*, London.

Krugman, P., 2003, *The Great Unraveling: Losing Our Way in the New Century*, Norton, New York.

Krugman, P., 2014, "Why Weren't Alarm Bells Ringing?", *The New York Review*, 23 October.

Krugman, P., 2015a, "That Old Time Economics", *New York Times*, 16 April.

Krugman, P., 2015b, "Seriously Bad Ideas", *New York Times*, 13–14 June.

Leunig, T., and Overman, H.G., 2008, "Spatial Patterns of Development and the British Housing Market", *Oxford Review of Economic Policy*, 24.1, 59–78.

LGA, 2015, *English Devolution: Local Solutions for a Successful Nation*, Local Government Association.

Little, R., 2014, "Ukip is a Party for People who Hate London: That's Why Labour Should be Scared", *The Spectator*, 8 November.

McCann, P., 2008, "Globalization and Economic Geography: The World is Curved, Not Flat", *Cambridge Journal of Regions, Economy and Society*, 1.3, 351–370.

McCann, P., 2009, "Economic Geography, Globalisation and New Zealand's Productivity Paradox", *New Zealand Economic Papers*, 43.3, 279–314.

McCann, P., and Ortega-Argilés, R., 2013, "Modern Regional Innovation Policy", *Cambridge Journal of Regions, Economy and Society*, 6.2, 187–216.

Maddison, A., 2006, *The World Economy. Volume 1: A Millennial Perspective; Volume 2: A Historical Perspective*, Organisation for Economic Cooperation and Development, Paris.

Marr, A., 2007, *A History of Modern Britain*, Macmillan, Basingstoke.

Martin, R., Pike, A., Tyler, P. and Gardiner, B., 2015, *Spatially Rebalancing the UK Economy: The Need for a New Policy Model*, Regional Studies Association, March.

MIER, 2009, *Manchester Independent Economic Review*, www.manchester-review.org.uk/index.html.

MGI, 2012, *Manufacturing the Future: The Next Era of Global Growth and Innovation*, McKinsey Global Institute.

Moretti, E., 2012, *The New Geography of Jobs*, Houghton Mifflin Harcourt, New York.

Morgan, K., 2002, "English Question: Regional Perspectives on a Fractured Nation", *Regional Studies*, 36.7, 797–810.

Morgan, K, 2006, "Devolution and Development: Territorial Justice and the North-South Divide", *Publius: The Journal of Federalism*, 36.1, 189–206.

Morgan, K., 2007, "The Polycentric State: New Spaces of Empowerment and Engagement?", *Regional Studies*, 41.9, 1237–1251.

Mount, F., 2014, "It's Never Been So Easy For the Rich to Get Richer", *London Evening Standard*, 24 April.

Mundell, R.A., 1961, "A Theory of Optimal Currency Areas", *American Economic Review*, 51.4, 657–664.

New Statesman, 2014, "The Wealth and Poverty of Our Nation", 19 December.

NIC, 2012, *Alternative Worlds 2030: Global Trends 2030*, National Intelligence Council, Office of the Director of National Intelligence, Washington DC.

NMC, 2014, *The Future of Prosperity and Public Services in Non-Metropolitan England; Interim Report*, Independent Commission on Economic Growth and the Future of Public Services in Non-Metropolitan England, March.

NMC, 2015, *Devolution to Non-Metropolitan England; Seven Steps to Growth and Prosperity: Final Report of the Non-Metropolitan Commission*, Independent Commission on Economic Growth and the Future of Public Services in Non-Metropolitan England, March.

O'Brien, N., 2012a, "Planet London", *The Spectator*, 12 April.

O'Brien, N., 2012b, "The Great Divide: National Politics No Longer Has Anything to Say to the North of England. The Results are Frightening", *The Spectator*, 1 December.

ODPM, 2004, *Competitive European Cities: Where Do the Core Cities Stand?*, Office of the Deputy Prime Minister, London.

ODPM, 2006a, *State of the English Cities Report: A Research Study Volume 1*, Office of the Deputy Prime Minister, London.

ODPM, 2006b, *State of the English Cities Report: A Research Study Volume 2*, Office of the Deputy Prime Minister, London.

OECD, 2009a, *OECD "Global Charter"/"Legal Standard" An Inventory of Possible Policy Actions*, ILO International Labor Organization, the IMF International Monetary Fund, the OECD Organisation for Economic Cooperation and Development, the World Bank and the World Trade Organization, Organisation for Economic Cooperation and Development, Paris.

OECD, 2009b, *How Regions Grow*, Organisation for Economic Growth and Development, Paris.

OECD, 2009c, *Regions Matter: Economic Recovery, Innovation and Sustainable Growth*, Organisation for Economic Growth and Development, Paris.

OECD, 2011a, *How's Life?*, Organisation for Economic Cooperation and Development, Paris.

OECD, 2011b, *OECD Regional Outlook 2011*, Organisation for Economic Cooperation and Development, Paris.

OECD, 2012, *Promoting Growth in All Regions*, Organisation for Economic Cooperation and Development, Paris.

OECD, 2013, *Regions at a Glance 2013*, Organisation for Economic Cooperation and Development, Paris.

OECD, 2014a, *Focus on Inequality and Growth: Does Inequality Hurt Economic Growth?*, Organisation for Economic Cooperation and Development, Paris.

OECD, 2014b, *OECD Regional Outlook 2014: Regions and Cities Where People Meet*, Organisation for Economic Cooperation and Development, Paris.

OECD, 2014c, *OECD Factbook 2014: Economic, Environmental and Social Statistics*, Organisation for Economic Cooperation and Development, Paris.

OECD, 2014d, *PISA 2012 Results: What Students Know and Can Do (Volume I, Revised Edition, February 2014): Student Performance in Mathematics, Reading and Science*, Organisation for Economic Cooperation and Development, Paris.

OECD, 2014e, *Main Science and Technology Indicators, Vol. 2013/2*, Organisation for Economic Cooperation and Development, Paris.

OECD, 2015a, *In It Together: Why Less Inequality Benefits All*, Organisation for Economic Cooperation and Development, Paris.

OECD, 2015b, *Financing SMEs and Entrepreneurs: An OECD Scoreboard*, Organisation for Economic Cooperation and Development, Paris.

OECD-Ford Foundation, 2014, *Changing the Conversation on Growth: Going Inclusive, Background Note*, OECD-Ford Foundation Workshop, 27 February, Ford Foundation, New York.

Overman, H.G., 2013, "The Economic Future of British Cities", *Centrepiece*, Summer.

Overman, H.G., and Winters, L.A., 2005, "The Port Geography of UK International Trade", *Environment and Planning A*, 37.10, 1751–1768.

Overman, H.G., and Winters, L.A., 2011, "Trade and Economic Geography: The Impact of EEC Accession on the UK", *The Manchester School*, 79.5, 994–1017.

Oxford Economics, 2008, "Regional Winners and Losers in UK Public Finances", Economic Outlook, Oxford.

Padoan, P.C., 2012, "The Evolving Paradigm", in *OECD Yearbook 2012: Better Policies for Better Lives*, Organisation for Economic Development and Coordination, Paris.

Parkinson, M., Ball, M., Blake, N., and Key, T., 2009, *The Credit Crunch and Regeneration: Impact and Implications: An Independent Report to the Department of Communities and Local Government*, London.

Pessoa, J.P., and Van Reenen, J., 2014, "The Great British Jobs and Productivity Mystery", *Vox EU*, 28 June.

Pike, A., Rodriguez-Pose, A. and Tomaney, J., 2010, (eds.), *Handbook of Local and Regional Development*, Routledge, Abingdon.

Pike, A., Marlow, D., McCarthy, A., O'Brien, P. and Tomaney, J., 2013, *Local Institutions and Local Economic Growth: The State of the Local Enterprise Partnerships in England – A National Survey*, SERC Discussion Paper 150, Spatial Economics Research Centre, London, November.

Pike, A., Marlow, D., McCarthy, A., O'Brien, P. and Tomaney, J., 2015, "Local Institutions and Local Economic Development: The Local Enterprise Partnerships (LEPs) in England, 2010-", *Cambridge Journal of Regions, Economy and Society*, Forthcoming.

Piketty, T., 2014, *Capital in the Twenty-First Century*, Translated from French by Arthur Goldhammer, Harvard University Press, Cambridge, MA.

Porrit, J., 2005, *Capitalism: As If The World Matters*, Earthscan, London.

Prospect, 2015, "The Big Ideas of 2015: Politics Goes Local as Economics Goes Global", January.

PWC and Demos, 2012, *Good Growth for Cities*, Price Waterhouse Coopers, London.

ResPublica, 2014, *Devo-Max Devo-Manc: Place-Based Public Services*, London, September.

ResPublica, 2015, *Restoring Britain's City States: Devolution, Public Service Reform and Local Economic Growth*, London, February.

Richardson, H.W., 1978, *Regional Economics*, University of Illinois Press, Urban-Champaign.

Riley, R., Bondibene, C.R. and Young, G., 2015, *The UK Productivity Puzzle 2008–2013: Evidence from British Business*, NIESR Discussion Paper No. 450, National Institute of Economic and Social Research, London.

Rodrik, D., 2007, *One Economics Many Recipes: Globalization, Institutions and Economic Growth*, Princeton University Press, Princeton, NJ.

Rodrik, D., 2011, *The Globalization Paradox: Why Global Markets, States and Democracy Can't Coexist*, Oxford University Press, Oxford.

Roubini, N., and Mihm, S., 2010, *Crisis Economics: A Crash Course in the Future of Finance*, Penguin, New York.

Rowthorne, R.E., and Wells, J.R., 1987, *De-Industrialization and Foreign Trade*, Cambridge University Press, Cambridge.

Royuela, V., Ramos, R. and Veneri, P., 2014, "Income Inequality, Urban Size and Economic Growth in OECD Regions", Working Paper, Regional Development Policy Division, Organisation for Economic Cooperation and Development, Paris.

RSA, 2014, *Unleashing Metro Growth: Final Recommendations of the City Growth Commission*, Royal Society of Arts, London.

RSA, 2015, *Devo Met: Charting a Path Ahead*, Royal Society of Arts, London, March.

Sachs, J., 2011, *The Price of Civilization: Economics and Ethics After The Fall*, Bodley Head, Random House, London.

Scottish Executive, 2002, *Review of Scotland's Cities: The Analysis*, Scottish Executive, Edinburgh.

Small, M., 2014, "Red Star or Dark Star?", *BellaCaledonia*, 23 January, www.bellacaledonia.org.uk.

SMMT, 2015, *Sustainability Report 2015*, Society of Motor Manufacturers and Traders, London.

SPERI, 2015, *Public and Private Sector Employment Across the UK Since the Financial Crisis*, Sheffield Political Economy Research Institute, University of Sheffield, Sheffield, February.

Standpoint, 2015, "Whittle's London", January/February.

Stark, P., Gordon, C. and Powell, D., 2013, *Rebalancing Our Cultural Capital: A Contribution to the Debate on National Policy for the Arts and Culture in England*, www.theroccreport.co.uk.

Stiglitz, J.E., 2002, *Globalization and Its Discontents*, Penguin, London.

Stiglitz, J.E., 2012, *The Price of Inequality*, Penguin, London.

Stiglitz, J.E., 2015, *The Great Divide*, Penguin, London.

Stiglitz, J.E., Sen, A. and Fitoussi, J-P., 2009, *Report by the Commission on the Measurement of Economic and Social Progress*, www.stiglitz-sen-fitoussi.fr/en/index.htm.

Storper, M., 2013, *Keys to the City: How Economics, Institutions, Social Interaction, and Politics Shape Development*, Princeton University Press, Princeton, NJ.

Summers, L.H., 2013, "Economic Possibilities for Our Children: The 2013 Martin Feldstein Lecture", *NBER Reporter*, 4, National Bureau of Economic Research, Cambridge, MA, www.nber.org/reporter.

The Economist, 2014a, "Free Exchange: Inequality is Bad for Growth", 1 March.

The Economist, 2014b, "No More Parachuting In", 13 December.

The Economist, 2014c, "Now for the English Question", 27 September.

The Economist, 2014d, "Metropolitan Revolutions: Power Surge", 28 June.

The Economist, 2014e, "Decentralisation: Let Them Fly", 8 November.

The Economist, 2013f, "A Sticky Pitch for the Tories", 30 November.

The Economist, 2014g, "The Trials of Life in Tilbury", 16 August.

The Economist, 2014h, "Free Exchange: Wasted Potential", 14 June.

The Economist, 2014i, "Free Exchange: No Country for Young People", 22 November.

The Economist, 2015a, "The Great Fracturing", 21 February.

The Economist, 2015b, "When What Comes Down Doesn't Go Up", 2 May.

The Guardian, 2014a, "What Will the Scottish Referendum Mean for Leeds, Manchester or Bristol?", 29 May.

The Guardian, 2014b, "This Time There'll Be No Collapse in Ukip Support", 27 May.

The Observer, 2014, "Opinium/Observer Poll: What Young People Are Thinking", 28 December.

The Scotsman, 2014, "Alex Salmond: London is 'Dark Star of the Economy'", 4 March.

The Spectator, 2014, "Devolution vs Democracy", 8 November.

The Times, 2014, "The Map of Politics has Been Redrawn with Very Different Kinds of Discontent", 30 June.

Thomson Reuters, 2014, *Thomson Reuters 2014 Top 100 Global Innovators: Honoring the World Leaders in Innovation*. http://top100innovators.com/.

Ward, M., 2013a, *Rebalancing the Economy: Prospects for the North: Report of the 'Fair Deal for the North' Inquiry Undertaken by the Smith Institute*, The Smith Institute, London.

Ward, M., 2013b, *Public Services North: Time for a New Deal?*, The Smith Institute, London.

Williams, P., 2011, "The Credit Crunch in the UK: Understanding the Impact on Housing Markets, Policies and Households", in Forrest, R., and Yip, N-M., (eds.), *Housing Markets and the Global Financial Crisis: The Uneven Impact on Households*, Edward Elgar, Cheltenham.

White, M., 2014, "Salmond Makes Good Case for Scottish Independence but I am Not Convinced", Politics Blog, *The Guardian*, 5 March.

Wolf, M., 2014a, *The Shifts and the Shocks: What We've Learned and Still Have to Learn from the Financial Crisis*, Penguin, London.

Wolf, M., 2014b, "Hope for the Best on Productivity, but Prepare for the Worst", *Financial Times*, 14 November.

Wolf, M., 2015, "UK Recovery Conceals Dire Productivity Growth", *The Irish Times*, 29 April.

World Bank, 2008, *Growth Report: Strategies for Sustained Growth and Inclusive Development*, World Bank, Commission on Growth and Development, Washington DC.

World Bank, 2009, *World Development Report 2009: Reshaping Economic Geography*, Washington DC.

World Bank, 2010a, *Post-Crisis Growth in Developing Countries: A Special Report of the Commission on Growth and Development on the Implications of the 2008 Financial Crisis*, Commission on Growth and Development, Washington DC.

World Bank, 2010b, *Globalization and Growth: Implications for a Post-Crisis World*, Commission on Growth and Development, Spence, M., and Leipziger, D., (eds.), Washington DC.

Zolli, A., and Healy, A.N., 2012, *Resilience*, Headline Publishing, London.

2 The economic performance of UK regions

2.1 Introduction

This chapter examines the inequalities in economic performance between UK regions. The chapter begins by examining how UK interregional inequalities have evolved over the twentieth century, and in particular since the 1980s through to the present day. Many changes have taken place over recent decades. In particular, what we observe in the context of the experience of other OECD economies is that the UK regional inequalities are both real and also very significant by the standards of other advanced economies. Moreover, they have become far more marked over recent years, with the existing core-periphery structure becoming magnified. Part of a possible explanation as to why this is the case could be that the strong performance of London has benefited the wider UK, even though such regional inequalities have become more pronounced. However, a comparison of UK regional performance in the context of the wider experience of OECD regions suggests that this is not the case. The performance of London and its hinterland regions appears not to have benefited the rest of the UK.[1]

2.2 Inequalities in the productivity performance of UK regions

The material used in the first part of this chapter is primarily derived from the OECD regional database, which provides the most comprehensive cross-country regional data sets available. The data in the OECD regional data sets are constructed according to Territorial Levels, by which TL1 is national administration level, TL2 is the first tier of data analysis below that of the national level and TL3 is the second tier below the national level. In each country these levels are partly related to tiers of governance or to tiers of statistical aggregation and in the case of most European countries including the UK they are consistent with the Eurostat NUTS classification scheme (Eurostat 2007). In Europe TL2 is largely equivalent to the Eurostat NUTS1 classification and TL3 is largely equivalent to the NUTS3 spatial units, although there are exceptions relating to countries such as Belgium, The Netherlands and Greece where they are NUTS2 regions, and Germany, where they are spatial planning regions. For the UK the OECD-TL2 classification is the same as the NUTS1 classification of the 12 large statistical regions of the UK with an average size of 5.27 million people in 2012. The OECD-TL3 classification is the same as the 139 UK NUTS3 regions, and allowing for some exceptions at the large city level largely follows the UK local government areas, with an average population of just over 455,000 people (OECD 2013a).

In terms of regional economic development it is immediately clear from inter-regional comparisons of Gross Domestic Product per capita (GDP/capita) that the UK is a highly unequal country. This is the case irrespective of whether we consider regional productivity variations in terms of the Gini index of per capita GDP inequality (OECD 2013a) or in terms of absolute GDP per capita variations.

2.2.1 Measures of Interregional Inequality in Economic Performance

When interregional productivity variations at the OECD-TL2/EU-NUTS1 level are considered in terms of the absolute scale of the variation, the UK absolute interregional variations are greater than those evident in any other OECD country, except for the case of a few extraction-industry regions in Mexico and Canada. However, even here, if the oil and gas outputs ascribed to the Mexican region of Campeche and the Canadian region of Northwest Territories are excluded in the same way that North Sea Oil revenues are excluded from UK regional accounts, then the UK absolute productivity variations are greater than in any OECD economy. When these absolute interregional differences are normalised with respect to the national average productivity levels, what we see is that when measured at the level of OECD-TL2/EU-NUTS1 of larger regions, the current UK interregional variations across the 12 large statistical regions are now of the order of 106 per cent of the UK average GDP per capita level. Again, at the OECD-TL2 level these inequalities are only surpassed by Mexico, Canada, Turkey and Chile. In the case of Mexico, Canada and Chile some very high regional productivity levels are observed in a small number of regions dominated by extraction industries, so if we ignore such cases, then the interregional productivity variations in the UK are greater than in any other OECD country at these spatial scales. When the interregional GDP per capita inequalities at the OECD-TL2/EU-NUTS1 level are computed using a Gini index measure of interregional inequality the UK is one of the most unequal countries in Western Europe (OECD 2011a). At this level, the only large western European economies[2] exhibiting greater interregional inequalities than the UK are Italy and Germany and their indices of inequality have been falling over the last two decades while those of the UK have been rising (OECD 2011a).

At the EU-NUTS2 level, the UK is the only large country in Europe with regions in all five quintiles of the GDP per capita range (Armstrong and Ebell 2015), while the absolute scale of these interregional GDP per capita inequalities are even more marked when measured at the smaller regions defined by the OECD-TL3/EU-NUTS3 level (Armstrong and Ebell 2015). At this scale, the range of UK interregional productivity differences, defined in terms of GDP per capita, is much greater than is observed for any other OECD country (OECD 2013a). However, in order to make allowance for the possible geographical effects of different levels of national development, if the absolute interregional variations measured at the OECD-TL3/EU-NUTS3 level are normalised with respect to the national average GDP per capita levels, we see that the normalised interregional productivity variations in the UK are of the order of 525 per cent of the UK average GDP per capita. As such, they are not only by far the highest in the OECD, but they are also almost twice as large as what is observed in any other advanced OECD economy (OECD 2013a).

If interregional inequalities at the NUTS3 level are calculated using the standard deviation of regional GDP figures normalised relative to the country level as an index of dispersion, then the UK emerges as the second most unequal country in Europe, behind only Slovakia (London Economics 2013). Moreover, in the years immediately following the 2008 global economic crisis the rise in UK interregional disparities at this spatial scale was the third highest in Europe, on top of the fact that the UK was already one of the most unequal countries (London Economics 2013).

If on the other hand, we employ a Gini index of inequality at this smaller region OECD-TL3/EU-NUTS3 level, in 2010 the Gini index for the UK TL3 regions showed that the UK was the most unequal country within the EU-15 western European economies after Ireland (OECD 2013a), with UK interregional inequalities being equivalent to that of Poland or Hungary (OECD 2013a). Similarly, if inequalities are calculated using a Coefficient of Variation at the NUTS3 level, we see that Portugal is also slightly more unequal than the UK (Monastiriotis 2014). However, both the Gini index of interregional productivity inequality and the interregional Coefficient of Variation for the UK have increased by almost a half since 1995, at a time when the levels of interregional inequality have actually been falling in many rich European economies (Monastiriotis 2014). In 1995 the UK index of per capita GDP interregional inequality was almost identical to that of Germany and only slightly higher than France in the same year, but this gap has since widened enormously, such that the levels of interregional inequality in France and Germany are still lower today than they were in the UK in 1995 (OECD 2013a). The levels of interregional inequality at the OECD-TL3/EU-NUTS3 level in the UK are now some 50 per cent higher than in similar-sized economies such as France and Germany, a third higher than Italy and almost twice as high as Spain. Moreover, the UK levels of interregional inequality at this level are some 50 per cent higher than in countries with governance-centralisation structures which are similar to England such as New Zealand and The Netherlands, and more than twice as high as countries with somewhat larger geographical areas such as Sweden, Finland and Japan.

Similarly, if we consider gross value-added per worker (GVA/worker) we see that the UK interregional variations in absolute GVA per worker at the TL2 level are again greater than in any other economy, except for the case of Chile and Mexico. In the case of Mexico the extreme variation is due to the fact that largely offshore oil revenues are included in the regional accounts for Campeche[3] while in Chile extreme variations are due to the small population extraction-industry region of Antofagasta. Excluding Campeche and Antofagasta, then again it is the case that the UK interregional variations in GVA per worker are the largest in the OECD. As before, if we normalise these variations in GVA per worker with respect to the national levels, then the variations in regional GVA per worker in the UK are only surpassed by those in Mexico, Chile and Turkey. If we ignore these three developing economies which are at quite different development levels and trajectories to a country such as the UK, at the TL2 levels the interregional variations in GVA per worker are greater in the UK than in any other advanced OECD economy. In the UK the absolute variations in GVA per worker at the OECD-TL2 level amount to some 95 per cent of total UK average GVA per worker, whereas the equivalent figure in Germany is 58 per cent, France 54 per cent and Italy 28 per cent. If we observe only the regions which prior to German reunification were part of the former West Germany, the figure for Germany is 41 per cent.

If we consider the interregional variations in income per household, the interregional variations in income per household are much smaller in all countries than for GDP per capita or for GVA per worker because of the impacts of progressive taxes such as income and housing taxes. At the same time, cross-country comparisons are affected by the fact that there are differing average taxation levels across countries. By European standards, the UK is a relatively low tax economy with the fourth lowest overall taxation levels in the EU (OECD 2014a) and the second lowest tax rates on the average worker (OECD 2014a). The result of this is that the absolute income per household interregional variations in the UK are almost exactly the same as those which exist in both Italy and Canada, and greater than those which exist anywhere else in Europe. If we normalise these interregional household income variations with respect to the average national income per household, the inequalities levels in UK are smaller than in Italy, a relatively higher tax economy, and greater than those in Canada, a relatively lower tax economy.

What becomes very clear is that in terms of productivity and household income, the interregional variations in the UK are amongst the most severe in the whole of the rich OECD countries, irrespective of whether we define regions at the OECD-TL2/EU-NUTS1 or at the OECD-TL3/EU-NUTS3 levels. The UK was already a very unequal economy back in the 1970s and 1980s when discussions regarding the 'north–south' divide (Fothergill and Gudgin 1982; Briggs 1983; Goddard and Champion 1983; Martin 1988) again began to emerge for the first time since the interwar era (Briggs 1983), but these inequalities in economic vitality and living standards have subsequently increased dramatically since the mid-1990s. The UK is currently a highly unequal economy interregionally and one which is more reminiscent of central and eastern European economies or developing countries at the bottom of the OECD productivity league tables than northern and western European countries or countries at the top of the OECD productivity rankings.

2.2.2   *The UK Regional Performance Trends Over Many Decades*

These current inequalities in the UK interregional system and their re-emergence during the last four decades need to be considered in the light of the long-running changes in the GDP per capita of the different UK regional economies. UK interregional inequalities declined from the 1860s onwards with poorer regions catching up with the richer South East of England (Geary and Stark 2015a). This convergence trend was interrupted by the First World War and divergence characterised the 1920s with inequalities rising to their highest levels between 1929 and 1931 at the onset of the Depression (Crafts 2005; Scott 2007; Gardiner *et al.* 2013; Geary and Stark 2015b). By this stage GDP per capita in London was 144 per cent of the average for Great Britain while that of the Rest of the South East was 114 per cent (Geary and Stark 2015b). In contrast, all of the other nine regions of Great Britain exhibited GDP per capita levels below the average of Great Britain and six of these regions exhibited GDP per capita below 90 per cent of the average for Great Britain (Geary and Stark 2015b). Prior to the last decade of the twentieth century, the years spanning the 1920s and 1930s were those that saw the highest levels of interregional inequality in Britain (Geary and Stark 2015b). These interregional inequalities were also very closely tied up with social class-related inequalities (Briggs 1983).

However, the interregional convergence trends started to re-emerge again in the early 1930s (Crafts 2005; Geary and Stark 2015b). This was presumably due in part to the adverse wage and wealth effects of the Depression on high-income asset holders, as has also been the case recently in the wake of the 2008 global financial crisis. In the immediate post-war years of the late 1940s and early 1950s these interregional convergence trends were spurred on as the UK economy underwent a radical restructuring associated with the nationalisation of many sectors, the establishment of the welfare state and the introduction of a comprehensive land use planning system. All of these domestic and internal changes also took place under the umbrella of the trans-national changes heralded by the Bretton-Woods system (Casson and McCann 1999) which served to limit the international transmission mechanisms that had magnified the adverse impacts of financial shocks during the 1930s. UK interregional inequalities in GDP per capita gradually declined throughout the post-war era from the 1940s right through to the 1970s reaching their lowest levels in the mid-1970s. At this point, between the mid-1970s and the early 1980s the economies of the South East, East and South West typically exhibited GDP per capita levels of some 106 per cent, 96 per cent[4] and 93 per cent of the UK average, respectively (CSO 1990). Meanwhile, the economies of the West Midlands, East Midlands, North West, Yorkshire and Humberside and the North East typically exhibited values ranging between 91 per cent and 98 per cent of the UK average (CSO 1990). During this same period spanning the mid-1970s to the early 1980s the economies of Scotland, Wales and Northern Ireland typically exhibited productivity levels of the order of 95% per cent, 85 per cent and 78 per cent of the UK average, respectively (CSO 1990). At this time all regions except Wales and Northern Ireland exhibited GDP per capita levels above 90 per cent of the UK average (Geary and Stark 2015b).

The transition from the mid-1980s to the 1990s was the period when inter-regional inequalities again began to slowly emerge (Townroe and Martin 1992). During the second half of the 1980s and the early 1990s the economies of the South East, East and South West typically exhibited GDP per capita levels of some 113 per cent, 100 per cent[5] and 94 per cent of the UK average (CSO 1990, 1992; ONS 1997). Meanwhile, during the second half of the 1980s the economies of the West Midlands, East Midlands, North West, Yorkshire and Humberside and the North East typically exhibited values ranging between 88 per cent and 94 per cent of the UK average (CSO 1990, 1992; ONS 2001). During this same period the economies of Scotland, Wales and Northern Ireland typically exhibited productivity levels of the order of 93 per cent, 84 per cent and 76 per cent of the UK average, respectively (CSO 1990, 1992). As such, relative to the period between the mid-1970s and the mid-1980s the second half of the 1980s saw a decline on the part of English regions outside of the south and east, a rise in the performance of the southern and eastern regions of England, and a largely stable situation for the three devolved regions.

The decade of the 1990s witnessed major changes. During the first half of this decade the GDP per capita of the South East and Eastern[6] regions was generally some 108 per cent and 112 per cent of the UK average while that of the South West was of the order of 92 per cent of the UK average (ONS 1997, 2000, 2001). In contrast, during the 1990s the regions in the Midlands and the North of England exhibited falling relative productivity levels. At the start of the decade these regions typically exhibit GDP per capita levels ranging between 84 per cent and 92 per cent of the UK average (ONS 2000, 2001), whereas by the end of the decade relative productivity levels of these regions had fallen in most cases by some 3–6 percentage points.[7] By the end of the 1990s the Midlands and northern regions of England typically exhibited GDP per capita values of between 77 per cent and 91 per cent of the UK average (ONS 2000). Meanwhile, in terms of the devolved regions, during the 1990s, Wales also lost more than 7 percentage points of its relative per capita GDP performance, falling to 77 per cent of the UK average by the end of the decade. In contrast both Northern Ireland and Scotland saw improvements during this decade of the order of 3–5 percentage points, with the growth in Scotland occurring mainly in the first few years of the 1990s (CSO 1995;

ONS 1996, 1997) while that in Northern Ireland was rather more gradual and spread out across the decade (ONS 1997, 1998, 1999). By the turn of the millennium UK interregional inequality had again reached levels equivalent to those which pertained in the 1930s (Geary and Stark 2015b).

In the years following the millennium and before the onset of the global financial crisis the OECD regional database[8] shows that inequality continued to rise between 2001 and 2008. The regions in the English midlands experienced falls in relative per capita GDP of 3–4 percentage points levels declining from between 92 and 95 per cent of the UK average at the turn of the millennium to some 82–91 per cent of the UK average immediately prior to the crisis. Meanwhile, the three northern English regions experienced falls of 4–6 percentage points during this period, with per capita GDP levels of the order of 81–87 per cent of the UK average on the eve of the crisis (ONS 2008). During this period Wales suffered the most severe losses of some 7 percentage points resulting in per capita GDP levels of 71 per cent in 2007, while Scotland declined by some 3 percentage points.[9] In contrast, Northern Ireland improved by 4 percentage points (ONS 2008), presumably in part a result of the vastly improved political situation post-1998.

If we now also consider the effect of the Greater London region on the UK interregional variations we see that during the first three decades of the twentieth century the productivity of London relative to the rest of Great Britain rose steadily from 134 per cent of the Great Britain average at the start of the century to a peak of 144 per cent in the early 1930s (Geary and Stark 2015b). This was also the time in which the population of London reached its highest point in the twentieth century, and coincided with a period in which the 15 largest cities in the world were located in the 8 largest and richest economies (McCann and Acs 2011). During these early years of the twentieth century there appeared to be a fairly simple correspondence between urbanisation, industrialisation and globalisation (Iammarino and McCann 2013), with the productivity growth of the most powerful nation-state and empire-system economies focused on their largest cities.

During the three decades of the immediate post-war era the GDP per capita advantages of London over the rest of Great Britain varied between around 138 per cent and 145 per cent (Geary and Stark 2015b), but by the mid-1970s the London productivity premium had fallen by some 15 percentage points as the Greater London population shrank to its lowest level of the twentieth century. Between the mid-1970s and the early 1990s the GDP per capita of the London economy remained generally of the order of 124–128 per cent of the UK average (CSO 1990) and it remained largely stable within this range during these years even as London experienced transformations such as the 1986 'Big Bang' (Casson and McCann 1999). There were, of course fluctuations during this period, with London's productivity premium growing in the mid-1980s and then falling after the 1987 crash, and again a similar pattern is observed between 1988 and the aftermath of the 1992 currency crisis (Martin *et al.* 2015). However, it was really only during the middle years of 1990s that the GDP per capita of the London region rose rapidly from something of the order of 130 per cent of the UK average (ONS 2000) to something of the order of 140 per cent of the UK average (ONS 2000). By the late 1990s the GDP per capita premium of the London economy had risen to well over 150 per cent of the UK average (ONS 2008) and during the years following the millennium it was typically of the order of 160 per cent of the UK average. By this time London's most recognisable and in many ways the most important activities were in the high-wage financial services sector, the second most spatially concentrated sector after extraction industries, followed by other high-wage business and information services and real estate services sectors, all of which are also highly geographically concentrated (ONS 2012a). In 2007 and 2008, on the eve of the onset of the global financial crisis in late 2008, the GDP per capita of the London region was 74 per cent above the UK average (OECD regional database). In the year immediately following the crisis the GDP per capita gap between London and the UK as a whole narrowed by one percentage point as London initially bore the brunt of the adverse financial market shocks but then the gap between London and the rest of the UK increased rapidly again. By 2011 the gap had risen to 76.7 per cent, its highest level ever, and more than 30 percentage points above its previous high points in 1931 and 1961 (Geary and Stark 2015b). London now has the highest GDP per capita of any OECD-TLC2/EU-NUTS1 regions outside of Luxembourg.[10]

Meanwhile in terms of gross value-added per worker, during the mid-1990s worker productivity in London was typically some 25 per cent higher than the average for the UK as a whole. By the turn of the millennium this had risen to 66 per cent, and by 2008 at the outbreak of the global financial crisis London's GVA per worker was 71 per cent higher than the UK average. In the year following the onset of the crisis the GVA per worker gap between London and the UK as a whole narrowed by three percentage points but then again regained its pre-crisis levels. As such, the differences in GVA per worker between London and the UK as a whole are very slightly less than the equivalent differences between GDP per capita. London now has the highest GVA per worker of any OECD-TLC2/EU-NUTS1 region in Europe and the fourth highest in the whole of the OECD.

As well as different measures of productivity, the advantages of London in terms of disposable household incomes are also very clear. In the mid-1990s the gap between the disposable incomes of London households and the UK average was 20 per cent. By the turn of the millennium this gap was just under 26 per cent, and by the eve of the onset of the global economic crisis in late 2008 the gap in household incomes between London and the UK as a whole was almost 29 per cent. Today London has the highest disposable household income of any OECD-TLC2/EU-NUTS1 region in Europe.

The effects of these various regional performance changes over the last three decades means that the UK's Gini index of interregional inequality has increased markedly since the early 1980s at the OECD-TL2/EU-NUTS1 level apart from a brief period in the early 1990s after which it increased rapidly before slowing down during the 2000s (OECD 2011a). The period of the most rapid growth in interregional inequality in GDP per capita was the early to mid-1990s, after which the inequality has increased albeit at a much slower pace. If we look at the OECD-TL3/EU-NUTS2 level figures and compare the Gini index of the GDP per capita figures for 1995 (OECD 2013a), 2001 (OECD 2005), 2003 (OECD 2007), 2005 (OECD 2009a) and 2010 (OECD 2013a), we see that broadly the same picture emerges of rising UK interregional inequality in terms of GDP per capita, with the most rapid rises taking place during the 1990s followed by a period of continuously rising inequality although at a slower rate.

In terms of absolute interregional differences in productivity, during the 1970s and 1980s the maximum difference between London and the other 11 large statistical UK regions was typically of the order of 48–50 per cent of the value of the UK average productivity levels (CSO 1990) with Northern Ireland exhibiting the lowest score every year. However, given the complexities associated with the political situation in Northern Ireland during this period, if instead we consider only the 11 large regions of Great Britain, we see that the maximum interregional variations between London and the rest of Great Britain were typically some 44 per cent of UK average productivity levels (CSO 1990). Meanwhile, the differences between London and the large industrial regions of the North and Midlands of England were typically around one-third of the UK average productivity levels (CSO 1990). By the 1990s the differences in the per capita GDP levels between London and the weakest UK regions were of the order of 50 per cent of UK average productivity (ONS 2000, 2001). Meanwhile during this decade the gap between London and the large industrial regions of the north and midlands of England rose during this period from typically something of the order of 32–37 per cent of UK average productivity to something of the order of 36–43 per cent (ONS 2001). At the turn of the millennium the maximum productivity gap between London and the weakest UK regions had reached 97 per cent of average UK productivity levels.

These trends have since continued during the early years of the twenty-first century and by the time we reached the eve of the global financial crisis the inequalities had progressed even further. By 2008 the maximum GDP per capita difference between London and the rest of the UK regions was over 105 per cent of UK average productivity and the typical difference between London and the large industrial regions of the midlands and north of England was typically over 90 per cent of UK average GDP per capita. Today, in the period following the global financial crisis, the maximum GDP per capita difference between London and other UK regions is 106 per cent of UK average per capita GDP and the typical gap between London and the large industrial regions of the midlands and northern England is now of the order of 95 per cent of UK average GDP per capita.

This pattern of ongoing interregional inequalities in productivity is also largely mirrored in terms of the patterns of household disposable income. During the 1980s the differences in personal disposable income between London and the rest of the UK was typically of the order of 24 per cent, while that of the South East was 9 per cent, followed by the South West and East Anglia having the next highest relative scores which were typically very close to the UK average score (CSO 1990, 1992). Industrial regions in the midlands and north of England typically exhibited personal disposable income scores of between 90 per cent and 97 per cent of the UK average, as did Scotland (CSO 1990, 1992). Meanwhile, during the 1980s, the maximum gap between the personal disposable incomes of the South East and other UK regions was some 38 per cent of UK average personal disposable income (CSO 1990, 1992).

In the 1990s a slightly different pattern emerged. During the early years of the 1990s (ONS 1999, 2000, 2001) disposable incomes per head declined by 5 percentage points relative to the UK average, in the wake of the financial crises of 1987 and 1993 (Casson and McCann 1999). During the mid-1990s onwards per capita household disposable incomes in London remained more or less constantly at around 20 per cent above the UK average (ONS 2000, 2001). Personal disposable household incomes in the South East region remained at some 11–12 per cent above the UK average for most of the 1990s while the equivalent figure for the East rose steadily during the decade to something of the order of 7–8 per cent (ONS 2000, 2001). These various changes, and in particular those affecting London, also slightly reduced the maximum gap during this period between London and other UK regions to around 35 per cent of average disposable income per head (ONS 2001). Meanwhile, the household disposable incomes per head in the industrial regions of the midlands and north of England during much of the 1990s remained at 5–10 per cent below the UK average disposable incomes per head, with the levels in Scotland remaining around 3–5 per cent below the UK average during this period.

By the end of the 1990s the gaps in disposable household income per head started to re-emerge (ONS 2008). As we see from the OECD regional database, the London disposable household income premium was again some 25 per cent above the UK average by the turn of the millennium (and similar to the 1980s premia) and it remained of the order of 23–28 per cent for most of the years between the millennium and the advent of the economic crisis in 2008. By 2008, just as the crisis broke, personal disposable household incomes per head in London were 29 per cent above the UK average, the highest values they had ever attained in the post-war period. In 2008, the maximum gap in personal household disposable incomes per head between London and the rest of the UK was of the order of 45 per cent of UK average disposable household incomes per head, again the largest it has ever been in the post-war era. Moreover, by 2008 the typical gap in personal disposable household income per head between London and the large industrial regions of the midlands and north of England was now over 40 per cent of the UK average household disposable income per head. Meanwhile, the personal household disposable incomes per head in the South East rose to over 15 per cent above the UK average at the turn of the millennium and in the following years fell back slightly to just over 12 per cent on the even of the economic crisis. Similarly, the relative scores for the disposable household income per head in the East of England fell during this period from a high of 8 per cent just prior to the millennium to around 5 per cent on the eve of the economic crisis.

Scotland and the South West of England are today the two UK regions whose disposable household incomes per head almost exactly mirror the UK national average. In the case of the South West, the regional disposable incomes per head have very closely reflected the UK average since the 1980s (CSO 1990, 1992; ONS 2000, 2001, 2008). As such, the South West is relatively weak in terms of GDP per capita (and much more similar to the industrial regions of the English north and midlands) but relatively resilient in terms of disposable income per household much like the southern and eastern regions.

The relative position of Scotland is rather different. Scottish disposable household incomes have remained relatively stable at around 95 per cent of the UK average between 1995 (ONS 2008) and 2005. As such, during this period they were typically some 3–5 percentage points above the equivalent scores for the large industrial regions in the midlands and north of England (ONS 2008). Since then the scores for Scotland have actually increased by between 2–3 percentage points while those in most other regions outside of the south and east of England have fallen by one or two percentage points. Scotland now exhibits disposable household income per capita levels which are some 10–11 per cent higher than most of the large industrial regions in the midlands and the north of England and the other devolved regions. Although because of the Barnett formula[11] Scotland benefits from higher per capita inward fiscal transfers than other regions, in recent years the costs of these transfers may have been largely cancelled out by the implicit Scottish oil-related revenue transfers to the UK central government (CEBR 2012). However, there is significant disagreement about these matters, and particularly with regard to the long-term impacts of future revenue streams from oil-related activities and also overseas-owned activities within Scottish industry (Deutsche Bank 2014; Scottish Government 2014; Phillips 2013; Phillips and Tetlow 2013, 2014; McLaren *et al.* 2013, 2014).

The various long-running changes described here can be observed by comparing the economic performance indices for the 12 NUTS1 large statistical regions for the years 1995, 2008 and 2011, each of which has been normalised with respect to the UK average of 100 for each respective year and indicator. As we see in Tables 2.1, 2.2 and 2.3, over the last two decades the weaker group of regions in the north and midlands of England plus Wales and Northern Ireland have progressively slipped further behind London and the South East, while Scotland, the South West and the East have largely maintained their relative positions in terms of disposable income if not GDP per capita. This

Table 2.1 1995 regional economic performance indices

1995 Indices	GDP per Capita	GVA per Worker	Disposable Household Income per Capita
North East	81.1	95.6	87.8
North West	88.2	94.5	92.3
Yorks and Humber	87.2	89.7	91.1
East Midlands	91.7	93.4	92.4
West Midlands	90.6	91.5	93.4
East	93.7	94.9	106.3
London	149.9	123.3	119.9
South East	100.6	99.0	109.4
South West	89.8	87.3	100.8
Wales	81.7	92.7	90.9
Scotland	96.4	97.1	96.3
Northern Ireland	77.5	88.1	89.2
United Kingdom	100	100	100

Source: OECD Regional Database.

Table 2.2 2008 regional economic performance indices

2008 Indices	GDP per Capita	GVA per Worker	Disposable Household Income per Capita
North East	73.2	77.1	83.9
North West	84.3	88.5	89.7
Yorks and Humber	81.5	82.3	87.6
East Midlands	79.4	77.9	91.5
West Midlands	80.9	84.9	88.6
East	90.9	88.1	104.7
London	174.5	171.1	128.8
South East	104.4	99.1	112.3
South West	86.6	84.2	98.7
Wales	69.2	74.4	87.7
Scotland	93.9	91.4	97.2
Northern Ireland	77.5	84.1	90.7
United Kingdom	100	100	100

Source: OECD Regional Database.

has been a long-run and continuing trend which has not been altered by the effects of the 2008 global economic crisis. Although the arrival of the crisis in the UK began in the London capital markets, both London and the South East, along with Scotland, have actually increased their relative economic position in comparison with other UK regions in the aftermath of the crisis (BIS 2012).

As a whole, the regions exhibiting both strong productivity and disposable household income scores comprise the regions in the south and east of

Table 2.3 2011 regional economic performance indices

2011 Indices	GDP per Capita	GVA per Worker	Disposable Household Income per Capita
North East	72.3	76.9	84.5
North West	84.4	88.6	90.2
Yorks and Humber	79.7	82.1	86.2
East Midlands	81.4	79.9	90.7
West Midlands	81.6	86.9	89.4
East	89.5	87.5	103.7
London	176.7	169.2	128.3
South East	105.2	100.7	112.8
South West	87.1	87.1	99.9
Wales	70.8	74.9	87.9
Scotland	92.9	89.7	97.5
Northern Ireland	74.0	82.0	86.9
United Kingdom	100	100	100

Source: OECD Regional Database.

England and in 2012 these accounted for some 22 million people and there-fore just under 36 per cent of the UK population. Meanwhile, the regions in the English midlands and north along with Wales and Northern Ireland which exhibit both weak productivity scores and also low disposable house-hold income levels account for over 29 million people and therefore over 47 per cent of the UK population. The two additional cases which do not cor-respond to either of these road patterns are Scotland and the South West region. Scotland's disposable household income per capita relative to the UK average is markedly higher than its GDP per capita score relative to the UK average. This is likely to be partly due to the impacts of North Sea oil, the GDP of which is treated as being offshore in UK accounts whereas many of the oil-related incomes are paid to workers and firms based in Scotland. At the same time, Scotland receives different and rather beneficial tax and benefit treatment in comparison to the rest of the UK[12] due to the workings of the Barnett formula (Phillips and Tetlow 2013, 2014). In contrast, the disposable household income per capita in the South West when measured against the UK average is much higher than its relative GDP per capita score. This is likely to reflect the fact that many households in the South West are older and rela-tively wealthy in-migrants from other parts of the UK seeking a more favour-able climate and natural amenities. Moreover, if Cornwall, one of the UK's poorest counties, is removed from the South West region, then the South West appears even more affluent on every indicator. As such, both Scotland and the South West are rather specific cases whose workings cannot so easily be gen-eralised to other regions. Indeed, as London Economics (2013) make clear, the strong performance of Scotland means that at the NUTS1 and NUTS2 scales, as a whole our observations mean that UK inequalities are actually the most evident at the level of north versus southern England rather than north

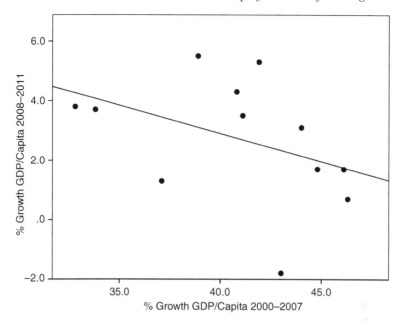

Figure 2.1 Percentage growth in GDP per capita for UK OECD-TL2/EU NUTS1
regions 2000–2007 and 2008–2011

versus south of the UK (London Economics 2013). Moreover, these interregional productivity and income differences are also reflected in interregional differences in wealth distributions (ONS 2013a). Local productivity and productivity growth is capitalised into local housing prices, and housing asset growth is the main means of wealth accumulation for the majority of UK households (SMCPC 2014). Not surprisingly, therefore, the southern regions of England, and in particular London, account for the largest numbers of high net wealth households, with higher proportions of lower wealth households resident in regions outside of southern England (ONS 2013a, 2013b).

During the most recent years the trends described above have continued. In the years since the 2008 global economic crisis the downturn in London was less severe and shorter than in other regions and this was followed by a more marked recovery (ONS 2013c). In contrast, some of the regions in the north and midlands of England which had experienced relatively strong growth in the years following the turn of the millennium suffered severe contractions. As we see in Figure 2.1, the effects of these differing regional experiences is that some regions which grew relatively slowly prior to the crisis remained relatively resilient in the aftermath of the crisis, while other regions experienced strong growth followed by severe contractions. A third group experienced relatively strong growth followed by continued and ongoing resilience. The differing regional experiences pre and post the 2008 economic crisis and the resulting spatially unbalanced growth (Gardiner *et al.* 2013) had some clear impacts, the most marked of which is that in the very recent years London has continued to grow relative to the rest of the UK (ONS 2013c). London had increased its share of UK economic output defined in terms of gross value-added, from 20.7 per cent to 21.9 per cent between 2007 and 2011 (ONS 2013c) and further still to a value of 22.8 per cent by 2012 (Harari 2014). Indeed, in the years between 2001 and 2011 the only other regions which have increased their shares of UK output (GVA) are the South East and Scotland (ONS 2013c) with the South East accounting for 14.9 per cent of UK output by 2012 (Harari 2014). In contrast, the regions whose UK output shares declined the most between 2001 and 2011 were the North West and the West Midlands (ONS 2013a). By 2012 all UK regions experienced increases in annual output with the South East rising the quickest, except for the East Midlands which still faced contraction (Harari 2014), although by the end of 2014 the situation was slightly more fluid with both the North West and East Midlands growing at similar rates to Scotland and the South East, with London again spearheading growth (RBS/NatWest 2014).

The outcome of these various changes means that by 2011, the combined gross value-added of London, the South East and the Eastern regions together accounted for 45.2 per cent of UK total output (GVA), while the rest of England's regions accounted for 40.6 per cent, and the three devolved regions together accounted for some 14.2 per cent (ONS 2013c). Between 2001 and 2011 the combined share of UK output accounted for by the three devolved regions had remained constant since 2001 whereas the combined share of London, South East and East had risen by 2.1 per cent since 2001, an exact mirror image of the declines faced by the rest of the English regions (ONS 2013c). By 2012 just London and the South East accounted for 38 per cent of total UK output. This was more than the combined output of the five midland and northern English regions at 32 per cent (Harari 2014), even though these other five English regions contained 50 per cent more people than the two southern regions. These differing regional output and productivity levels are also reflected in wages, with London, the South East, Scotland and the Eastern region exhibiting the highest earnings (ONS 2013c).

2.3   International comparisons and regional benchmarks for UK regions

As we have already seen, the Gini indices of interregional inequality calculated on the basis of GDP per capita suggest that in many ways the interregional economic geography of the UK is more akin to what is typically observed in the former transition economies of Central and Eastern Europe than what is normally observed within the richer OECD economies of Western and Northern Europe, North America and Australasia (OECD 2013a). Obviously, in part, the very high UK interregional productivity variations are very much due to the extreme effects associated with the London economy, an issue to which we will return shortly. However, even if we exclude the case of London, then by identifying the most appropriate comparator regions in other countries which most closely correspond to various UK regions, it is possible to present a much clearer picture of the scale of the inequalities within the UK, which remain amongst the highest of any advanced OECD country.

Excluding London, at the level of the 12 OECD-TL2/EU-NUTS1 large statistical regions of the UK, in terms of GDP per capita and GVA per worker the regions in the south and east of England plus Scotland most closely resemble regions in the former West Germany, Northern Italy, along with parts of France, the Low Countries and the Nordic Economies. In marked contrast, in terms of GDP per capita and GVA per worker, the regions in the north and midlands of England along with Northern Ireland and Wales most closely resemble the regions located in the former East Germany (Thuringia, Mecklenburg-Vorpommern, Saxony, Brandenberg and Saxony-Anhalt) excluding Berlin which not surprisingly is richer, along with many of the poorer and largely rural and low-population Spanish and French regions, and also the regions located in the northern part of Italy's Mezzogiorno, such as Umbria, Marche or Abruzzo. Similarly, these UK regions display GDP per capita and GVA per worker scores of typically between 5 per cent and 30 per cent lower than the two US states widely seen as facing intractable long-term development problems, namely West Virginia and Mississippi. Most strikingly, these UK regions exhibit GDP per capita scores which are only some 10–20 per cent higher than many of the regions in the former transition economies of Czech Republic, Slovakia, Hungary and Slovenia and also some of the regions in Portugal and Greece, the two weakest economies in western Europe, and in some cases are actually somewhat lower than these regions. As such, almost half of the UK population now live in regions whose economic performance is comparable to the poorer parts of the former East Germany.

In terms of disposable household income, again at the level of the 12 OECD-TL2/EU-NUTS1 large statistical regions of the UK, the regions in the north and midlands of England along with Northern Ireland and Wales most closely resemble the regions located in the former East Germany and also the poorer and smaller-population French and Spanish rural regions, along with the regions located in the northern part of Italy's Mezzogiorno. In addition, these UK regions also display disposable household income levels which are typically only 10–20 per cent higher than those in the more prosperous regions of the former transition economies of the Czech Republic, Slovakia and Slovenia and those in Greece and Portugal, western Europe's weakest economies.

In the UK the favourable impacts of the relatively lower tax burden and less progressive tax structures in comparison to many other European economies along with specific fiscal provisions for Scotland associated with the Barnett formula, mean that the wealthier regions in the south and east of England along with Scotland most closely resemble the very richest regions in Germany, Austria and Norway, and now out-perform most of the other OECD regions with similar GDP per capita and GVA per worker scores. As such, at the higher end of the UK regional income distribution, the effect of the differing tax regimes across countries is that the wealthier UK regions now exhibit disposable household income scores equivalent to regions in other countries which exhibit higher productivity scores. In contrast, the poorer UK regions exhibit disposable household income levels which are similar to those in regions in other countries which exhibit similar productivity levels. In terms of disposable household income, therefore, the burden and structure of the UK tax system appears to have no beneficial effect on the household income of the UK's weaker regions in the midlands and north of England along with Wales and Northern Ireland, but a markedly favourable effect on its richer regions in the south and east of England along with Scotland.

As already mentioned, the economically weaker UK regions in the midlands and north of England along with Wales and Northern Ireland, currently account for just under 30 million people and over 47 per cent of the total UK population. Yet when we compare these regions with those regions in the former East Germany (not including Berlin) whose productivity and per capita disposable incomes are both comparable to these weaker UK regions, we see that these East German regions account for under 13 million people and therefore only just over 15 per cent of the total German population. In contrast, some 85 per cent of the German population lives in much richer and more productive regions, whereas in the UK the figure is 36 per cent. This largely explains not only why aggregate GDP per capita is nowadays some 17 per cent higher in Germany than in the UK.

All in all, however, what becomes clear is that in terms of variations in regional productivity and income, the UK is an extremely unequal economy when compared with most other economies of a similar size and level of development. Yet, even after excluding the extreme case of London, the comparator cases which most closely resemble different UK regions demonstrate that the UK interregional inequalities are still very stark and probably far more marked than most people are aware of. Although interregional differences in economic performance are sometimes discussed in the UK political arenas, the fact that much of the UK resembles East Germany and the Northern Mezzogiorno while the southern parts of England and Scotland more closely resemble the richest parts of Norway, Germany and Austria is likely to come as a surprise to many people. In the post-war period the regions of Eastern Germany have suffered four and a half decades of communism plus a traumatic post-unification economic transition process while the Mezzogiorno regions have suffered from severe governance and institutional problems (Putnam 1993; Ginsborg 2001). Yet, the observation of today's economic performance indicators suggests that in economic terms the severity of the experiences of the German and Italian regions appears to have been similar to the severity of the experience undergone by many UK regions during the last half century or more.

2.4   The productivity growth performance of different types of UK regions

The modern era of globalisation began in earnest at the end of the 1980s and the beginning of the 1990s (McCann 2008, 2009; McCann and Acs 2011; Iammarino and McCann 2013). The currently popular arguments regarding the role of agglomeration economies (MGI 2011) might lead us to assume that UK economic growth in the modern era of globalisation has been driven by cities, and similarly that the growth responses to the 2008 global financial crisis are likely to have been led by primarily urban regions. From Table 2.3 we know that the growth role of London is very significant. Moreover, the proportion of UK economic growth 1995–2010 accounted for by the 10 per cent largest GDP OECD-TL3/EU-NUTS3 regions (51 per cent) is one of the highest amongst the rich OECD economies (OECD 2013a) and much higher than the share of national output accounted for by these same regions (39.6 per cent). However, although London plays a large role in driving UK economic growth the role of other urban areas is less clear-cut. In reality, the experience of the UK is far less straightforward than simple agglomeration arguments imply and we will deal with the explicitly urban issues in much more detail in the following chapter. However, at this stage it is important to outline the role played by different types of UK regions in the growth experience of the UK.

The OECD Regional Typology groups the 139 OECD-TL3/EU-NUTS3 regions into three categories, namely 87 primarily urban (PU) regions, 41 intermediate (IN) regions and 11 primarily rural (PR) regions, accounting for 70 per cent, 28 per cent and 2 per cent of the 2012 UK population, respectively (OECD 2013a). There are no primarily rural (PR) regions in England, and all 11 of these are located in Scotland, Wales or Northern Ireland.

Out of these 139 regions, only 29 have GDP per capita scores higher than the UK national average and of these 25 (86 per cent) are primarily urban (PU) regions with the remaining four being intermediate (IN) regions. Of those 110 regions with lower productivity than the national UK average 62 (56 per cent) are primarily urban PU regions with 37 (34 per cent) being intermediate (IN) regions. Meanwhile, rather than the national average if instead we consider the regional average productivity, then there are 49 regions at the OECD-TL3/EU-NUTS3 level with higher GDP per capita scores than is exhibited by the respective OECD-TL2/EU-NUTS1 region in which they are located. Of these 49 regions, 39 are primarily urban (PU) regions, with 9 being intermediate (IN) regions and one being a primarily rural (PR) region. On the other hand, there are 90 OECD-TL3/EU-NUTS3 regions whose GDP per capita scores are less than the respective score for the OECD-TL2/EU-NUTS1 region in which they are located. Of these 90 TL3 regions, some 44 (49 per cent) are primarily urban (PU) regions with 32 (36 per cent) being intermediate (IN) regions and 10 being primarily rural (PR) regions. As such, 10 out of 11 primarily rural (PR) regions at the OECD-TL3/EU-NUTS3 level display productivity levels lower than for their own OECD-TL2/EU-NUTS1 region in which they are located. This is not surprising, in that we know from urban economic theory (McCann 2013) that rural areas on average are likely to have lower productivity than urban areas. While productivity in UK agriculture in the 1970s was relatively strong by European standards and agricultural wages grew faster than in any other UK sector during the 1970s as a result of the introduction of the CAP Common Agricultural Policy (Briggs 1983), since the early 1980s productivity in UK agriculture has generally declined in comparison to other EU countries. Although productivity in EU agriculture has still increased steadily since the 1980s, UK agriculture now exhibits amongst the lowest productivity by western EU standards and England, the UK's most productive land (*The Economist* 2015a) generates only a half of the agricultural productivity of the US, The Netherlands, Denmark, Germany, Flanders or Australia (DEFRA 2014; HM Government 2014) and only generates marginally higher incomes than the average for the whole of the EU-27 countries including the central and eastern European economies (DEFRA *et al.* 2014). Moreover, in spite of its critics (Rickard 2012) the low levels of UK agricultural productivity relative to other EU countries cannot be blamed on the CAP per se (*The Economist* 2015a). The UK agriculture is characterised by a sector with a long tail whereby just one-third of agricultural enterprises account for 92 per cent of total agricultural output (HM Government 2014) and where agricultural productivity growth since 1990 is one of the lowest in the industrialised world (*The Economist* 2015a). The long-run downward trends in UK agricultural performance relative to other countries therefore reinforce the low-productivity tendency of many of the UK's predominantly rural areas, which on average generate productivity levels which are only just over 40 per cent of UK average productivity (DEFRA *et al.* 2014; Webber *et al.* 2009; Curry and Webber 2012). Moreover, on various indicators of production and service quality even rural regions also display a strong north–south orientation (Ricketts *et al.* 2006). Yet, as a whole this poor productivity performance only produces a relatively small drag effect on the UK economy because agriculture contributes no more than 0.64 per cent of UK GVA (gross value-added) and 1.5 per cent of total UK employment (DEFRA *et al.* 2014; ONS 2008). Rural areas (16 per cent) and intermediate areas (12 per cent) consisting of significant rural environments account for more than a quarter of England's output (DEFRA 2015) which demonstrates that most jobs even in these rural regions are outside of agriculture in sectors such as logistics and distribution, tourism, real estate and business services (DEFRA 2015). Of more concern, however, given their share and spatial distribution of population, is the fact that many of the UK's urban areas also exhibit relatively low productivity. Although London clearly leads the UK productivity rankings, within England the intermediate areas (IN) which combine urban with rural environments actually out-perform the other major primarily urban (PU) areas, with predominantly rural (PR) areas exhibiting the lowest levels of productivity (DEFRA 2015).

The growth rates in GDP of the three types of regions at the OECD-TL3/EU-NUTS3 level are depicted in Figure 2.2 with Figure 2.2a based on yearly

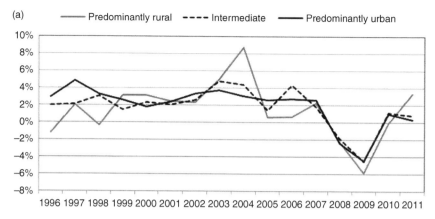

Figure 2.2a OECD regional typology of UK regions: yearly growth rates in GDP among TL3 regions, 1995–2011

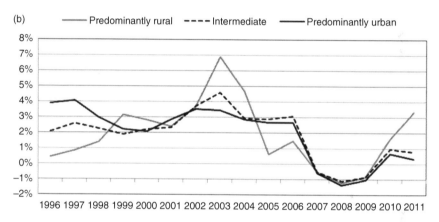

Figure 2.2b OECD regional typology of UK regions: two-year moving average growth rates in GDP among TL3 regions, 1995–2011

growth rates and Figure 2.2b based on smoothed two-year moving average growth rates.

As we see from Figure 2.2 during the 1990s the GDP growth rates of the UK's primarily urban (PU) regions tended to be systematically higher than for the intermediate (IN) regions and in many cases also out-performed the growth rates for the primarily rural (PR) regions. After the millennium, however, from around 2002 onwards we observe a change in regime, whereby the GDP growth of primarily urban (PU) regions starts to under-perform relative to intermediate (IN) regions. The extent of the change becomes particularly noticeable in the aftermath of the global economic crisis when the GDP growth rates in primarily urban (PU) regions clearly under-perform relative to intermediate (IN) regions which in turn are out-performed by the primarily rural (PR) regions.

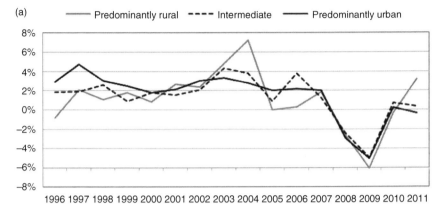

Figure 2.3a OECD regional typology of UK regions: yearly growth rates in GDP per capita among OECD-TL3 regions, 1995–2011

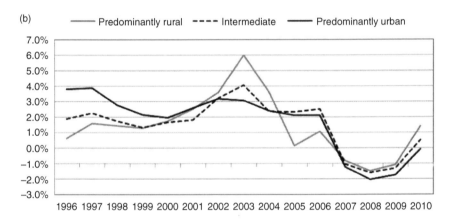

Figure 2.3b OECD regional typology of UK regions: two-year moving average growth rates in GDP per capita among OECD-TL3 regions, 1995–2011

This regime change and also its timing are not unique or specific to the UK and have been observed across the whole of Europe (Dijkstra *et al.* 2013). As such, at first glance some UK-based commentators familiar with the problems associated with the UK's restrictive land use planning system may assume that this regime change must be associated with the effects of this system which limits urban expansion and thereby encourages firm decentralisation and worker commuting across the green belt. However, this same pattern is also observed across Europe and across a wide range of countries (Dijkstra *et al.* 2013, 2015) including those with weak, lax and permissive land use planning systems as well as those with restrictive systems. As such, these changes are likely to relate more to technology-led changes in work practices and shifting preferences regarding work-life balances than the impacts

Table 2.4 OECD regional typology of UK regions: annual
average growth rates in GDP among TL3 regions,
1995–2011

	1995–2007	*2007–2011*
PR	2.24%	−1.34%
IN	2.62%	−1.16%
PU	2.80%	−1.43%

of restrictive land use planning systems. However, we will return in detail to these issues later in this book.

Notwithstanding the regime change, overall during the period 1995–2007 as we see in Table 2.4 the primarily urban (PU) regions still exhibited the higher average annual GDP growth rates, followed by the intermediate (IN) regions and then the primarily rural (PR) regions. As we have already seen, after the global economic crisis the picture changes dramatically with the primarily urban (PU) regions suffering the most severe adverse growth shocks.

As we see in Figure 2.3 the picture for GDP growth according to the different types of region depicted in Figure 2.2 is also largely reflected in terms of growth in GDP per capita according to these different types of regions. Productivity growth during the 1990s was very much dominated by primarily urban (PU) regions whereas after the millennium the observed regime change favoured intermediate (IN) regions over primarily urban (PU) regions. In the aftermath of the global economic crisis the primarily urban (PU) areas performed the worst of the three types of regions with primarily rural (PR) regions out-performing intermediate (IN) regions. The adverse effects on GDP per capita of the global economic crisis are clearly seen in Table 2.5 with the primarily urban (PU) areas facing by far the most severe shocks.

As we see in Figure 2.4 a similar but slightly different type of pattern is revealed when we observe gross value-added (GVA) per worker. Again the primarily urban (PU) regions dominated the growth rates GVA per worker throughout the 1990s until just after the millennium when the performance of intermediate (IN) regions surpassed that of the primarily urban (PU) regions. Again, this situation became more marked in the aftermath of the global economic crisis.

The only difference between observed growth patterns of GDP per capita and GVA per worker over time and according to different types of regions relates to the small number of primarily rural (PR) regions. As we see in Figure 2.4 and in Table 2.6, in the aftermath of the global economic crisis, while the primarily rural (PR) regions lead the intermediate (IN) regions in terms of growth of both GDP and GDP per capita, in the case of GVA per worker the primarily rural (PR) regions lagged both the intermediate (IN) regions and primarily urban (PU).

The reasons for these differences relate to demographic and labour market issues. As we will see in the following sections, the reason is that although the growth in GVA per worker was relatively low in primarily rural (PR) regions,

Table 2.5 OECD regional typology of UK regions: annual
average growth rates in GDP per capita among TL3
regions, 1995–2011

	1995–2007	*2007–2011*
PR	2.00%	−1.60%
IN	2.02%	−1.65%
PU	2.34%	−2.12%

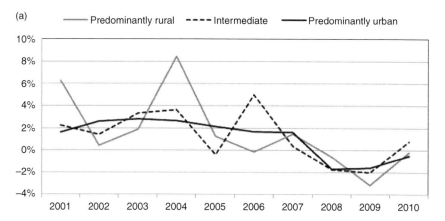

Figure 2.4a OECD regional typology of UK regions: yearly growth rates in GVA per
worker among OECD-TL3 regions, 2000–2010

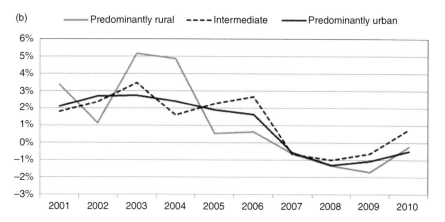

Figure 2.4b OECD regional typology of UK regions: two-year moving average
growth rates in GVA per worker among OECD-TL3 regions, 2000–2010

the population and employment growth in these regions was relatively even
lower. In contrast, the population and employment growth in primarily urban
(PU) and intermediate (IN) regions was faster than the relatively higher levels
of growth in GVA per worker.

Table 2.6 OECD regional typology of UK regions: annual average growth rates in GVA per worker among TL3 regions, 1995–2011

	2000–2007	*2007–2010*
PR	1.18%	−1.45%
IN	1.32%	−1.07%
PU	1.82%	−1.34%

2.5 Regional demographic and labour market performance in the UK

Between 1961 and 1971 the UK population grew annually at a rate of 0.6 per cent leading to an increase of 3 million people during this decade. Annual population growth shrank to less than 0.1 per cent between 1971 and 1981 such that the population grew by less than half a million people, or 0.8 per cent of the total population, during this decade (CSO 1990). The annual population growth rate rose to 0.2 per cent during the 1980s when the population grew by just over 1.5 million (CSO 1992) or some 2.6 per cent of the population. This rate of population of growth continued into the 1990s, with the UK population again growing by just over a million and a half people between 1991 and 1999 (ONS 2001). However, from Table 2.7 it is clear that while the UK population growth started again to increase around the millennium the major surge in population growth was from 2005 onwards. As we will see in Chapter 4, the UK population increases from the 1990s onwards are largely related to migration and these increases are largely in line with the worldwide increases in international migration, driven by a mixture of globalisation, refugees fleeing from political crises, and also EU integration processes spurred on by the establishment of the EU Single Market at the turn of 1991/1992. The more recent population and employment increases since 2005 onwards are largely associated with both the 2004 eastwards expansion of the European Union (Wadsworth 2014) as well as large increases in in-migration from South and East Asia (OECD 2012), although the immigration resulting from the eastward expansion of the EU is actually rather limited in comparison to immigration from outside of Europe (Barrell *et al.* 2010).[13] These more recent flows are slightly different to those in the previous decade in which immigration was largely characterised by in-migration from northern European economies plus Australia, New Zealand and South Africa (OECD 2008).

These population increases which are primarily associated with immigration into the UK have reversed many of the long-term demographic trends exhibited by some of the weaker UK regions and further exacerbated the demographic trends exhibited by the stronger UK regions. Between the early 1970s and the years around the millennium the regions of the North East, the North West and Scotland continually lost population (ONS 2001). The

Table 2.7 UK regional populations (000s) and per cent of national total

	1988	1995	2004	2008	2012
North East	2,581.8 (4.5)	2,585.7 (4.5)	2,540.7 (4.3)	2,565.5 (4.2)	2,618.0 (4.1)
North West	6,851.8 (12.0)	6,833.4 (11.8)	6,808.8 (11.4)	6,868.9 (11.2)	7,033.5 (11.1)
Yorkshire and Humber	4,912.8 (8.6)	4,960.3 (8.6)	5,048.1 (8.5)	5,199.6 (8.5)	5,336.2 (8.4)
East Midlands	3,970.2 (7.0)	4,081.7 (7.0)	4,272.8 (7.2)	4,413.2 (7.2)	4,545.2 (7.2)
West Midlands	5,206.5 (9.1)	5,253.1 (9.1)	5,316.5 (8.9)	5,393.4 (8.8)	5,564.4 (8.8)
East	5,080.5 (8.9)	5,191.8 (9.0)	5,484.4 (9.2)	5,683.0 (9.3)	5,907.8 (9.3)
London	6,805.6*	6,893.3 (11.9)	7,396.4 (12.4)	7,635.3 (12.5)	8,136.3 (12.9)
South East	7,678.9*	7,737.3 (13.3)	8,097.3 (13.6)	8,332.0 (13.6)	8,665.9 (13.7)
South West	4,633.8 (8.1)	4,769.5 (8.2)	5,021.3 (8.4)	5,194.4 (8.5)	5,330.8 (8.4)
Wales	2,857.0 (5.0)	2,888.0 (5.0)	2,936.1 (4.9)	2,983.1 (4.9)	3,035.0 (4.8)
Scotland	5,094.0 (8.9)	5,136.6 (8.9)	5,067.9 (8.5)	5,156.2 (8.4)	5,268.2 (8.3)
N Ireland	1,578.1 (2.8)	1,645.3 (2.8)	1,706.7 (2.9)	1,767.3 (2.9)	1,814.8 (2.9)
UK	57,065.5 (100.)	57,976,0 (100)	59,697.2 (100)	61,192.1 (100)	63,256.1 (100)

Sources: CSO (1990); OECD Regional Database.
* 1991 figures (ONS 1997).

population of the North East region shrank to its lowest level in 2002 but by 2010 it had recovered its 1995 population level and by 2012 it had reached 99 per cent of its 1981 population level (ONS 2008). The population of the North West region reached its lowest level in 2001 but by 2006 it had recovered its 1995 population level and by 2011 had again reached its 1981 population level (ONS 2008). Similarly, Scotland's population shrank to its lowest level in 2003 but by 2008 it had recovered its 1995 population level and by 2009 had recovered its 1981 population level (ONS 2008). The population growth in the years between 2001 and 2006 for the regions of the North East, the North West and Scotland was 0.6 per cent, 1.2 per cent and 1 per cent, respectively (ONS 2008). Meanwhile, during the 1970s London lost 9.6 per cent of its population from level of 7.53 million in 1971 to 6.8 million in 1981 (ONS 1997) but this process was reversed in the 1980s during which London then experienced a population increase of 0.4 per cent to 6.89 million by 1991 (ONS 1997, 2001). Between 1991 and 2001 London's population grew by 7.2 per cent (ONS 2008) and by 2.6 per cent between 2001 and 2006 (ONS 2008). At the same time, all of the other UK regions have also experienced population growth since the 1970s with the fastest population growth rates being in the South East, East, East Midlands and the South West (ONS 2008).

As we see in Table 2.8 the population growth rates in London, the East and the South East regions 1995–2012 are 18 per cent, 13.8 per cent and 12 per cent, respectively. The East Midlands, the South West and Northern Ireland are the other three regions whose population growth has exceeded the overall UK population growth rate over this period. As we also see in Table 2.7, the major share of the population growth in all UK regions has been since 2004. In the eight years between 2004 and 2012 UK population grew by 68 per cent of the total population increase experienced between 1995 and 2012. Population growth in the recent years has been particularly marked in the more rapidly growing regions in the south and east of England, while the population declines in the northern regions of England and Scotland were reversed. Much of this increase has been driven by immigration, and while all UK regions have experienced population growth since the mid-1990s, the patterns of population growth being biased towards the southern and eastern regions of England have been reinforced by immigration. As of 2014 almost 3.2 million, or 39 per cent, of London's inhabitants are forecast to have been born abroad, a figure which is approximately 200,000 more than at the time of the 2011 census, while the foreign*born population of the South East is forecast to be more than 1.1 million, or just under 13 per cent.[14] From the 2011 UK census the foreign-born population shares of the rest of the UK regions were as follows: East (11 per cent), South West (8 per cent), East Midlands (10 per cent), West Midlands (11 per cent), North West (8 per cent), Yorkshire and Humberside (9 per cent), North East (5 per cent), Wales (5 per cent), Scotland (6 per cent) and Northern Ireland (6 per cent). Between 2011 and 2014 these various percentage figures are forecast to have increased by 1 percentage point.[15]

Table 2.8 UK regional population changes 1995–2012, 2004–2012

	Population Change 1995–2012 (000s)	% Change in Population 1995–2012	Population Change 2004–2012 (000s)	% Change in Population 2004–2012	Ratio of Population Change 2004–2012/1995–2012
North East	32.3	1.2	77.3	3.0	2.39
North West	200.1	2.9	224.7	3.3	1.12
Yorkshire and Humberside	375.9	7.6	288.1	5.7	0.77
East Midlands	463.5	11.4	272.4	6.3	0.59
West Midlands	311.2	5.9	247.9	4.7	0.79
East	716.0	13.8	423.4	7.7	0.59
London	1,242.9	18.0	739.9	10.0	0.60
South East	928.6	12.0	568.8	7.0	0.61
South West	561.3	11.7	309.4	6.2	0.55
Wales	146.9	5.1	98.9	3.3	0.67
Scotland	131.6	2.6	200.3	3.9	1.52
NI	169.5	10.3	108.1	6.3	0.64
UK	5,280.1	9.1	3,588.9	6.0	0.68

Source: OECD Regional Database.

At the same time, however, the vast majority of international migrants are of working age (16–65). As such, as we see in Table 2.9 the growth in the UK population has therefore also been associated with an increase in the UK working age population which is relatively greater than the overall population increase.

As we see in Table 2.9, the regions of London, the East and the South East exhibit the largest working age population growth rates 1995–2012, with only London (18 per cent) and the East (13.8 per cent) exhibiting growth rates higher than the overall UK growth rates. London already had the highest share of its population of working age in 1995 but the gap between London and next highest share region, Scotland, had increased further by 2012. What is also noticeable is that the reversals in the long-run population declines faced by the regions of northern England and Scotland have been associated with increases in their working age populations. The share of the working age population in these regions has risen between 1995 and 2012 as it has in all UK regions except for the Eastern region which has declined very slightly and the South East and West Midlands whose share has remained constant.

If instead of population trends we now consider long-run trends in unemployment, we are able to get a sense of the ability of the region to gainfully absorb cohorts of workers into economic activities. The national unemployment rates in the UK increased from just over 4 per cent in the mid-1970s to over 11.2 per cent in 1986 (CSO 1990). However, these changes masked significant interregional variations. During the mid-1970s the inter-regional variations in unemployment rates across Great Britain were less than two percentage points ranging from 3.1per cent in the South East in 1976 to 5.1 per cent in the North West and Scotland and 5.3 per cent in the North and Wales, respectively. By 1986 the unemployment rates in the North, North West, Yorkshire and Humberside and West Midland had reached 15.4 per cent, 13.8 per cent, 12.6 per cent and 12.6 per cent respectively, while those for Scotland and Wales were 13.4 per cent and 13.9 per cent, respectively (CSO 1990). Meanwhile, unemployment rates in the South East and East Anglia were 8.1 per cent and 8.3 per cent, respectively (CSO 1990).

During this period the highest regional unemployment rates in the UK were in Northern Ireland, standing at 7.1 per cent in 1976 and rising to 17.4 per cent in 1986. However, the complexities associated with the political situation at the time mean that it is difficult to compare the situation in Northern Ireland with the other UK regions in Great Britain.

National UK unemployment rates fell steadily from the second half of the 1980s onwards until they reached 5.8 per cent in 1990 after which they increased again from 1991 reaching 10.3 per cent by 1993 (CSO 1995; ONS 1996) during the period of the pound-EMS currency crisis. After 1993 the national unemployment rate of the UK fell steadily throughout the rest of the 1990s reaching close to 5 per cent by the turn of the millennium (ONS 2001). It then continued to fall to its lowest level of 4.6 per cent by 2004 (OECD

Table 2.9 UK regional working age population changes 1995–2012

	Working Age Population 2012 (000s)	Change in Working Age Population 1995–2012	% Change in Working Age Population 1995–2012	% Regional Population of Working Age 1995	% Regional Population of Working Age 2012
North East	1,724,399	32,312	1.2	64.6	65.6
North West	4,601,766	200,054	2.9	64.1	65.4
Y & H	3,511,959	375,892	7.6	64.3	65.8
East Mids	2,966,451	463,516	11.4	64.8	65.3
West Mids	3,582,350	311,250	5.9	64.4	64.4
East	3,802,270	715,990	13.8	64.7	64.4
London	5,687,684	1,242,984	18.0	67.0	69.9
South East	5,596,214	928,638	12.0	64.6	64.6
South West	3,386,863	561,341	11.7	63.1	63.5
Wales	1,942,610	146,975	5.1	63.1	64.0
Scotland	3,517,500	131,647	2.6	65.6	66.8
NI	1,186,055	169,506	10.3	63.4	65.4
UK	41,506,121	5,280,105	12.7	64.7	65.6

Source: OECD Regional Database.

2014b; ONS 2008) after which again it rose slightly to 5.28 per cent by 2007 on the eve of the global financial crisis (ONS 2008). As such, in the years directly following the turn of the millennium the aggregate UK economy moved close to full employment levels after which they only increased very slightly in the years immediately prior to the crisis as immigration surged. On the eve of the financial crisis the UK economy as a whole exhibited very low unemployment rates even while immigration was increasing rapidly.

Again, these national trends mask significant interregional variations. The unemployment rate of the Northern region never fell below 10 per cent between the mid-1980s and the mid-1990s (ONS 1996) while that of the other regions in the north and midlands of England plus Wales and Scotland still remained between 8.3 per cent and 9 per cent from the mid-1980s up to 1995 (ONS 1999). In the late 1990s unemployment in these regions fell to between 5.2 per cent and 9.2 per cent as the national economy prospered (ONS 2001), and this downward trend continued after the millennium until 2007 on the eve of the global financial crisis, by which time the unemployment rates in these regions ranged between 4.6 per cent in Scotland though to 7.1 per cent in the West Midlands (ONS 2008). In contrast, by 1989 the unemployment rate in the South East was only 3.8 per cent and in 1990 was 4.2 per cent (ONS 1996). It rose to a maximum of 8.5 per cent in 1993 after which again it fell continually to 2.94 per cent in 2001. Between the millennium and 2007 on the eve of the global financial crisis it remained between 3.8 per cent and 4.7 per cent, standing at 4.3 per cent in 2007 on the eve of the global financial crisis. Similarly, during the 1990s and 2000s the unemployment rates in the East and South West regions typically varied by less than one percentage point from the unemployment rate of the South East (ONS 1999, 2004, 2008).

A slightly different case is that of London. At the beginning of the 1980s unemployment in London stood at 5.4 per cent rising to 9.1 per cent in 1986 after which it fell to 5 per cent in 1990 (ONS 1996). The London economy bore the brunt of the 1992–1993 currency crisis such that by 1995 unemployment in the London region stood at 11.5 per cent (ONS 1999). The London unemployment rate then fell steadily to 7.1 per cent in 2000 (ONS 2001) rising slightly to 7.5 per cent in 2007/2008 on the eve of the global financial crisis (ONS 2008). As we see in Table 2.10, in the years between the millennium and the global financial crisis, unemployment rates in London slowly converged with those of the weaker regions in the north and midlands of England, Wales and Northern Ireland.

As a whole, in the years preceding the 2008 global financial crisis the UK economy was operating at very low levels of unemployment and very high levels of employment and at levels not seen for more three decades. Moreover, this was the case even as immigration was surging and regional populations were growing rapidly. However, these trends went quickly into reverse in the aftermath of the global financial crisis which broke during the third quarter of 2008. Within a year of the crisis regional unemployment spiked sharply as the contagion effects of toxic financial linkages spread rapidly from the real

Table 2.10 UK regional ILO unemployment rates

	1999	2004	2007	2009	2011	2013
North East	10.04	5.35	6.2	9.2	10.77	10.06
North West	6.18	4.28	5.81	8.34	8.53	8.05
Y & H	6.58	4.25	5.56	8.51	9.42	8.77
East Mids	5.23	3.99	5.25	7.1	7.93	7.29
West Mids	6.86	5.38	6.27	9.66	8.99	9.06
East	4.19	3.85	4.66	6.17	6.53	6.03
London	7.63	6.43	6.73	8.91	9.57	8.44
South East	3.67	3.66	4.4	5.8	5.96	5.81
South West	4.78	3.15	3.87	6.14	6.41	6.18
Wales	7.09	4.5	5.27	8.07	8.63	7.66
Scotland	7.34	5.86	4.75	6.9	7.92	7.14
NI	7.2	4.65	4.43	6.52	7.21	7.57
UK	6.0	4.6	5.28	7.55	8.02	7.5

Source: OECD Regional Database.

estate sector infecting the balance sheets of the wider real economy. In particular, the London region now suffered a sharp jump in its unemployment rate as it was very much in the 'eye of the storm' of the financial crisis due to being so specialised in international financial services. As such, although London exhibits much higher worker productivity, a much higher working age population share, and also a much higher population growth than all other regions, at the same time the unemployment rate in London continues to be at similar levels to those pertaining in some of the economically weaker regions of the midlands and northern England. Yet, it has long been argued that there is no simple dichotomy between 'employed' and 'unemployed', but rather a spectrum of labour market possibilities between 'complete employment' and 'complete non-employment' in between which are unemployment and inactivity, both of which can be partial in nature and either voluntary or involuntary (Green and Owen 1998) depending on the context and institutional set-up of the labour market. Following this type of logic allows us to take a more nuanced look at the nature of the interface between employment and unemployment by considering 'involuntary non-standard employment' (Green and Livanos 2015), which includes all involuntary part-time working and involuntary temporary working, along with underemployment relative to education and skills (Rafferty *et al.* 2013). These approaches clearly demonstrate that today there is a strong core-periphery pattern within the UK on each of these dimensions (Green and Livanos 2015; Rafferty *et al.* 2013) which is little different from what was observed in earlier decades (Green and Owen 1998). Workers in London are systematically less likely to experience involuntary non-standard employment arrangements or underemployment relative to education and skills than workers in other regions, with the more geographically peripheral and weaker regional economies exhibiting much

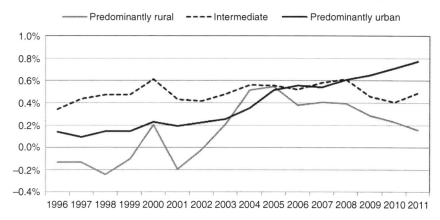

Figure 2.5 OECD regional typology of UK regions: yearly growth rates in population among OECD-TL3 regions, 1995–2011

higher levels of each of these types of working arrangements (Green and Livanos 2015; Rafferty *et al.* 2013).

Again, we can consider these demographic and labour market issues according to different types of regions at a smaller OECD-TL3/EU-NUTS3 region level according to different types of regions. In terms of population growth rates, as we see in Figure 2.5, from the mid-1990s through to the early years after the turn of the millennium population growth was the fastest in UK intermediate (IN) regions followed by primarily urban (PU) regions. In contrast, from 2005 onwards this pattern was reversed and the population growth in primarily urban (PU) regions surged, most probably in response to the increasing influx of workers from eastern European economies. These trends continued in the aftermath of the global financial crisis with the population growth of primarily urban (PU) areas increasing even further, while that of other types of regions slightly slowed. The result is that between the millennium and 2010 rural and intermediate areas grew faster than urban areas although from 2011 onwards the growth rates between urban and rural areas had converged (DEFRA 2015). The result of these changes is that, as we see in Table 2.11, during all of the period between the mid-1990s and 2012

Table 2.11 Population growth rates for OECD-TL3 UK regions by period

	1995–2007	*2007–2011*
PR	0.5%	0.3%
IN	0.5%	0.4%
PU	0.3%	0.7%

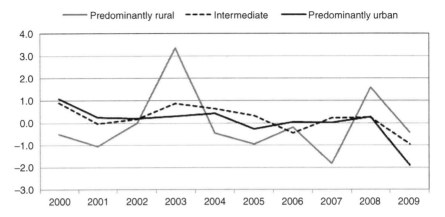

Figure 2.6 OECD regional typology of UK regions: percentage point change in
employment rate among OECD-TL3 regions, 2000–2010

Table 2.12 Average annual percentage point change in employment
for OECD-TL3 UK regions by period

	1999–2008	*2008–2010*
PR	0.01	−0.44
IN	0.33	−0.94
PU	0.25	−1.90

the population growth rates in primarily rural (PR) regions have been lagging
behind other types of regions. None of the overall categories of UK regions
as a whole have experienced population decline.

These rapid population growth rates over recent years have also been associated with rising numbers of workers seeking employment. As we see in
Figure 2.6 and Table 2.12 during the years immediately following the turn of
the millennium employment rates only increased slowly each year and slightly
below the population growth rates. The employment growth rates in intermediate (IN) regions were only marginally higher than those in primarily urban
(PU) regions. Meanwhile those in primarily rural (PR) regions were rather
more volatile prior to and post the crisis.

In the aftermath of the global economic crisis employment growth went
into reverse in all types of regions. These reversals were most marked in primarily urban (PU) regions followed by intermediate (IN) regions, while those
in primarily rural (PR) regions were slightly less marked.

Figure 2.7 depicts the percentage point change in the regional unemployment rate from the turn of the millennium and through to the aftermath of
the global financial crisis. As we see for the first few years of the twenty-first
century the change in the unemployment rate in all types of regions varied

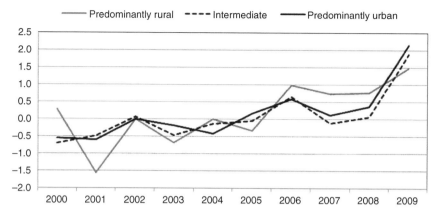

Figure 2.7 OECD regional typology of UK regions: percentage point change in unemployment rate among OECD-TL3 regions, 2000–2010

Table 2.13 Annual average percentage point change in unemployment rates for UK OECD-TL3 regions by period

	1999–2008	*2008–2010*
PR	−0.07	1.49
IN	−0.13	1.89
PU	−0.06	2.15

very little from zero and only started to increase from 2005 onwards. It is likely that this increase was associated with greater competition for jobs, and particularly at the lower end of the skills spectrum, from immigrant workers from eastern European economies. The result of the markedly rising populations from 2004 onwards combined with relatively flat employment growth led to slowly rising unemployment in all types of regions during the years 2005–2008. However, as we see in Figure 2.7 and Table 2.13, during 2009 the ongoing rapid population growth combined with the sudden sharp contractions in employment meant that unemployment accelerated rapidly in all types of regions and most notably so in primarily urban (PU) regions followed by intermediate (IN) regions.

Table 2.13 shows that during the period 1999–2008 intermediate (IN) regions exhibited the fastest falls in unemployment followed by the primarily urban (PU) regions. However, in the aftermath of the global financial crisis the unemployment rates increased in all types of regions, and as we see in Table 2.13 these increases were particularly marked in the primarily urban (PU) regions and in the intermediate regions, those same regions which had absorbed large inflows of labour in the years prior to the crisis.

Yet, nationally, the growth in UK unemployment rates since 2008 has been lower than in many other economies and UK interregional dispersion of unemployment at both the OECD-TL2/EU-NUTS1 levels and the OECD-TL3/EU-NUTS3 levels are very low by OECD standards (OECD 2013a). Meanwhile productivity levels and growth rates have also been lower than in most other OECD economies. As we see here, however, much of this poor productivity performance has a very strong regional dimension to it. While the London economy, and to a smaller extent the South East economy, have emerged largely unscathed from the crisis, even though London was central to the global transmission mechanisms of the crisis, the other UK regions which are economically weaker have suffered disproportionately in the aftermath of the crisis. Yet, while adverse regional shocks of the 1970s and 1980s were manifested in these regions primarily in terms of rising unemployment and falling employment today the major impacts of these adverse shocks are evident in terms of lagging productivity growth.

2.6   Regional wellbeing, quality of life and income inequalities

In the UK discussions regarding the 'wellbeing' of individuals and households can be traced back to the early 1950s amid concern for the relative effects of market forces and the state on people's livelihoods and as a way of shifting the emphasis of political economy debates away from the negative connotations associated with 'welfare' (Briggs 1983). Many of these debates subsequently remained largely dormant from the 1960s to the 1990s, yet, it is nowadays increasingly accepted that while they are crucial, traditional measures of societal progress such as GDP alone paint an incomplete picture of people quality of life (Layard 2005; OECD 2011b, 2013b; ONS 2012b; *The Economist* 2014). While broader approaches encompassing both self-reported measures of happiness (Layard 2005) and objective measures of quality of life are not without their critics (Johns and Ormerod 2007), following recent trends (Stiglitz *et al.* 2009), in 2010 the UK government policy initiated an agenda for measuring wellbeing across various dimensions (ONS 2012b, 2012c). Importantly, wellbeing and quality of life issues are also related to perceptions, values and expectations, and people's sense of their ability to influence their own futures, as well as their actual income and wealth conditions (ONS 2012b).[16] There is now a very large literature on these issues (OECD 2011b, 2013b) and according to the UN the UK currently ranks as the 21st country in terms of the global happiness index,[17] a ranking which is similar to its productivity ranking, although recent evidence suggests that we are becoming happier.[18] What is important for our purposes, however, is that these issues also have very strong local and regional dimensions (Demos 2011) because so much of our daily and family lives are played out in very small spatial arenas (ONS 2012d; OECD 2014a). Regional wellbeing and quality of life comprises different dimensions relating not only to local incomes and employment, but also to local health conditions, local security, local civic engagement, the local

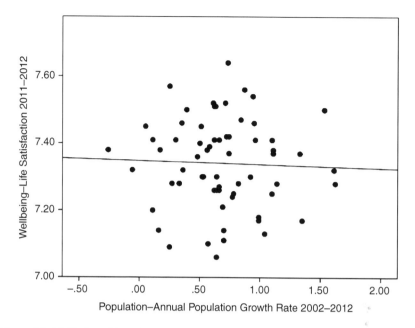

Figure 2.8 Wellbeing–life satisfaction and population growth in small regions

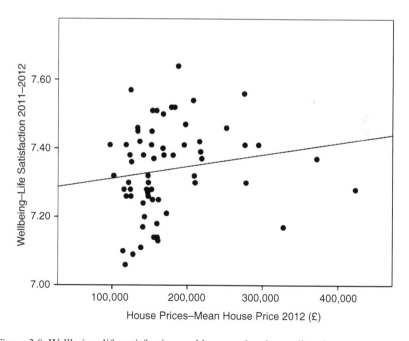

Figure 2.9 Wellbeing–life satisfaction and house prices in small regions

living (natural and built) environment, cultural and heritage assets (Stark *et al.* 2014), access to local amenities and services (OECD 2014a) and people's perceived ability to influence local governance and decision-making regarding the improvement of their local living conditions (ONS 2012d). Early results from the new UK wellbeing measurement initiatives provide some interesting insights regarding regional variations in wellbeing and quality of life (ONS 2012d, 2012e). Overall life satisfaction is highest in London (ONS 2012e) although people in London also experience the highest levels of anxiety (ONS 2012e), presumably due to work-related stress. Meanwhile, and perhaps not surprisingly, people in less densely populated UK regions are happier with the levels of quiet local living conditions and with the local provision of green spaces (ONS 2012d). Quality of life, environmental amenities and household wealth are generally all higher in UK rural areas than in urban areas (OECD 2011c). Yet, unlike many other parts of the OECD, the vast majority of rural dwellers in England live within a 30 minute drive of an urban area of at least 50,000 inhabitants (OECD 2011c), which is why they are classed by the OECD as intermediate areas, and the high quality of life in these places accounts for the fact that they exhibit faster population growth than other types of UK areas (OECD 2011c).[19] However, many quality of life-related amenities are not simply natural-environmental. Indeed, UK cultural and heritage-related assets and funding streams, including those from the National Lottery, are overwhelmingly biased towards London in almost every arena of culture and the arts (Stark *et al.* 2013, 2014; HoC 2014).[20] If the attraction of high-quality human capital is also related to the consumption of highly income-elastic human-produced amenities (McCann 2013) then the spatial allocation of these funding streams will also shape patterns of high-quality labour mobility in favour of London.

As well as at the scale of large regions, there are also major wellbeing and quality of life variations even at a very local level within each UK region (ONS 2012e).[21] If we examine UK wellbeing at the small spatial scale of OECD-TL3/EU-NUTS3 regions using the Centre for Cities data sets[22] we see from Figure 2.8 that there is very little if any systematic relationship between self-reported wellbeing and population growth. Significant popula-tion growth, which in the case of UK regions is often closely related to inter-national immigration as well as interregional migration, is taking place both in regions with high and low wellbeing and life satisfaction rankings, and the same is also true for regions experiencing low population growth. Population growth appears to be related to the effects on migration of employment demand rather than quality of life reasons. Yet, hedonic models also suggest that quality of life benefits and any induced migration will be capitalised into house prices. Indeed, as we see from Figure 2.9, those regions with higher house prices also tend to be the ones with higher self-reported wellbeing and life satisfaction scores. Similar findings arise from amenity-valuation models based on the relationship between housing cost-earning differentials and vari-ous natural and built-environment attributes (Gibbons *et al.* 2011). Indeed, if we also consider the fact that for most people housing equity is the most important form of saving and is increasingly used later in life to allow migration for amenity reasons or the funding of health-care, then accrued housing equity will be an even more important index of lifetime amenity-consumption benefits.[23] These various considerations all suggest that economic demand and quality of life effects are likely to be highly correlated across UK regions, resulting in a general south–north and west–east pattern (Gibbons *et al.* 2011).[24] Overall wellbeing and quality of life impacts come together to determine life expectancy, and on this measure at the small area level, the overall north–south regional differences are more marked than ever, and increasing (Bennett *et al.* 2015).[25]

However, a difficulty here is that wellbeing, quality of life and life satisfaction are comprised of many different dimensions and aggregate indices relating to house prices and population growth hide many of the potentially different mechanisms which operate to promote or hinder local wellbeing. For example, high local house prices are often beneficial to long-standing home owners as they generate potentially higher long-term equity gains, whereas for renters high prices reduce their quality of life by increasing their costs of living. Population growth may have similar conflicting effects, depending on the different cohorts, income and interest groups involved and the location. Indeed, population changes are mediated in part by migration behaviour and the interactions between wellbeing and migration are complex, given that the underlying motivations and mechanisms driving migration are varied and may be primarily employment related, wage related, career expectations related, amenity related or service provision related. The observed interactions between wellbeing and migration patterns and the resulting relationship between local living costs and local earnings differ depending on the dominant underlying migration motives (McCann 2013) and plots of these relationships across regions (Overman and Gibbons 2011) therefore reflect complex interactions between these different mechanisms in different places. For example, while London and the southern regions of England generally score highly on quality of life after adjusting for different living costs (Gibbons *et al.* 2011), the high local costs of living[26] mean that some of the low-income groups in London may fare amongst the least well-off groups in the UK. As we have already noted in the previous chapter, some 18 of the poorest 50 UK neighbourhoods according to child deprivation figures are located in London.[27] Therefore, if we consider the differences between after-tax wages and housing costs it is clear that money goes much further in some northern locations such as Huddersfield,[28] Barnsley, Burnley or Wolverhampton than in London boroughs (Overman and Gibbons 2011) due to the much lower costs of living. As such, if we treat the residual monetary surplus after living costs are accounted for as an index of wellbeing, then we might expect to observe the widespread migration of lower income groups away from London and into these types of areas. However, this is not what we typically observe, because as we will see in Chapter 5, the after-tax wage-income on which such calculations would be made also depends heavily on employment expectations, house price growth expectations and also equity gain via capital repayments on nominal housing mortgage values. These all favour southern regions. Following a Harris–Todaro type of framework, the expected long-term wages of these economically weaker areas are very much lower than the nominal after-tax wages earned due to the local risks associated with facing periods lacking stable employment. Even allowing for the personal, social and cultural factors which inhibit mobility (Gibbons *et al.* 2011) these risks are taken into account by potential low-income migrants and on this basis there appear to be very few perceived advantages associated with leaving London and moving to Huddersfield. Indeed, the only people who will tend to make such moves from the more prosperous to these economically weaker areas are those who originally came from such areas and following a migration life-cycle process (Fielding 2012) are moving back after several years working in the London economy. The people who move back are either those who have built a sufficiently successfully career in London to assuage doubts regarding their long-run local employment stability or those unable to maintain stable employment in London and who therefore prefer to return home at no perceived employment disadvantage. The low-income workers in London facing very high costs of living and who are originally from London are very rarely amongst the in-migrants to places such as Wolverhampton, Barnsley or Burnley, and their lack of such mobility is likely to be due mainly to employment-risk-related reasons (Hughes and McCormick 1985, 1987) over and above simply the adjusted living costs when being in employment. In contrast, where people do leave London these movements tend to be dominated by higher income groups moving into the other southern regions of England or to outside of the UK, primarily for amenity-related reasons.

These different migration motivations also tend to reflect different social and income cohorts exhibiting broadly different classes of housing tenures. As we will discuss in much more detail in Chapter 5, the differences in housing status also tend to demarcate differing interest groups regarding perceived wealth-generation opportunities and these differences also lead to differing incentives regarding residential mobility and housing supply debates. These differing incentives can in turn lead to tensions regarding the political economy of the city and the neighbourhood. These tensions and potential conflicting interests reflect the fact that regions and cities embody and encapsulate complex social spaces and social systems and there is no guarantee that regional or urban prosperity implies prosperity for all local citizens. Indeed, poverty is not automatically reduced for all citizens as regions and cities become more economically buoyant because such buoyancy may be associated with rising costs of living (Lee *et al.* 2014). In particular, rising living costs and the operation of the housing markets tend to lead to greater levels of social and spatial segregation both between regional neighbourhoods and also within cities. There are differing views as to the desirability of such segregation (Cheshire 2009; Bolt and van Kempen 2013; *The Economist* 2015b) and also its relationships to urban scale (Gordon and Monastiriotis 2006), but the key point is that employment growth is in general the strongest defence against poverty. That is, of course, unless the jobs which are created locally are either low paid or accrue primarily to people living elsewhere (Gordon and Kaplanis 2014), in which case the potentially beneficial impacts of employment growth on local poverty reduction may be minimal (Lee *et al.* 2014).

The UK exhibits wellbeing levels which are just above the average for the EU-28 (ONS 2014), and as such closely reflect the UK's GDP per capita ranking within the EU-28. Importantly again, the countries which are below the UK in the EU wellbeing rankings are largely former transition economies. In order to try to decompose the various different dimensions of wellbeing we can exploit the new OECD regional wellbeing data set[29] which standardises and compares all of the available regional data on wellbeing-related issues now emerging from OECD countries. As well as decomposing the various dimensions of local wellbeing, this data set also allows us to get a sense of how UK regions rank internationally in terms of wellbeing and quality of life (OECD 2014a).

Table 2.14 shows the rankings of the UK OECD-TL2/EU-NUTS1 large statistical regions in comparison to 300 regions across the OECD for which comparable data are available. In terms of people's access to a wide variety of services (OECD 2014a) the UK ranks fifth out of the 34 OECD countries and all UK regions are ranked in the top one-third of OECD regions. This is due in part to the densely populated geography of the UK which facilitates accessibility. At the same time, within the UK the spatial distribution of UK service provision is also very uneven, ranking 18th out of 33 countries in the OECD, which implies that in terms of variations in the scale and quality of service provision across the UK the inequalities are relatively marked by OECD standards. In particular, the southern and eastern regions of England all score in the top 5 per cent of OECD regions in terms of access to services along with Northern Ireland, whereas the rest of the regions of Great Britain range between the top 13 per cent and the top 20 per cent of OECD regions, except for the North East.

The interregional inequality in UK service accessibility and provision primarily favours regions in the south and east of England, and although this reflects a pattern of interregional inequality in one particular dimension of UK wellbeing, this general pattern is also seen to apply to other measures of wellbeing such as regional education levels, regional levels of civic engagement, regional disposable income levels and regional environmental amenities (Gibbons *et al.* 2011).

The UK's overall education level ranking of 15th place out of 34 OECD countries puts the UK just above the OECD average for education. This is also reflected in the individual UK regional rankings, none of which fall within the top 39 per cent, except for London which displays a markedly higher score, although one which is still not especially high by OECD standards. On the other hand, when we consider the UK's interregional inequalities

Table 2.14 UK regional and national indices of quality of life 2010

OECD % Ranking (out of 300 regions)	Access to Services	Disposable Income	Civic Engagement	Education
North East	Top 31%	Top 49%	Bottom 31%	Top 49%
North West	Top 13%	Top 42%	Bottom 37%	Top 49%
Yorkshire and Humberside	Top 17%	Top 46%	Bottom 39%	Bottom 49%
East Midlands	Top 6%	Top 42%	Bottom 48%	Top 50%
West Midlands	Top 20%	Top 43%	Bottom 44%	Bottom 47%
Eastern	Top 5%	Top 26%	Bottom 49%	Top 49%
London	Top 5%	Top 15%	Bottom 43%	Top 24%
South East	Top 5%	Top 20%	Top 50%	Top 40%
South West	Top 5%	Top 29%	Top 46%	Top 42%
Wales	Top 18%	Top 45%	Bottom 44%	Top 47%
Scotland	Top 15%	Top 32%	Bottom 42%	Top 40%
Northern Ireland	Top 5%	Top 45%	Bottom 22%	Bottom 29%
UK Rank Number (out of 34 OECD countries)	5	9	23	15
UK Regional Inequalities Rank Number (out of 33 OECD countries)	18	25	17	12

Sources: OECD Wellbeing Datasets.

in education, we see from Table 2.14 that the UK ranks 12th amongst the 34 OECD economies, which just outside the top third of OECD countries. This regional inequality in education ranking is slightly better than the overall UK ranking and suggests that UK regional education variations are relatively low by OECD standards. As we will see in Chapter 5, the fact that UK interregional educational inequalities are so significantly lower than the UK's interregional income inequalities calls into question some of the arguments which posit that the interregional and income inequality is due primarily to differences in education and skills.

When we consider civic engagement the picture is rather different again. As a whole the UK ranks only 23rd out of 34 OECD countries in terms of general levels of civic engagement, putting it in the bottom third of OECD countries, below almost all of the richer advanced OECD economies. Only two UK regions, namely the South East and the South West, rank in the top half of OECD regions. Although the UK ranking for interregional inequalities in civic engagement is slightly better at 17th than its overall ranking of 23rd, it still remains the case that the regions in the south and east of England perform relatively better than other UK regions, a pattern which is also reflected in the other wellbeing indicators.

As we see in Table 2.14, the UK's relatively high ranking of 9th in disposable income is markedly higher than its ranking of 17th in the OECD rankings of GDP per capita (OECD 2014b), and this is largely due to the fact that UK taxes are relatively low in comparison to many of the relatively richer and more productive OECD economies. Yet, the Gini index ranking of the UK's interregional inequalities in household disposable income at the OECD-TL2 level is only 21st out of the 34 OECD economies (OECD 2013a). The UK is one of the six OECD countries in which households in the richest regions have disposable incomes more than 40 per cent higher than the national median income (OECD 2013a). Again, the UK's skewed interregional pattern heavily favours the regions in the south and east of England plus in this case also Scotland (Gibbons *et al.* 2011), as we have already seen in Table 2.3. In terms of quality of life these patterns at the large regional scale are also reflected even more sharply at the smaller regional level both in urban areas[30] and also in rural areas.[31] Moreover, the one characteristic of those countries with greater interregional household income inequalities than the UK is that they all have lower tax and government expenditure shares than the UK. This is due to the fact that the larger taxation and government expenditure shares act as a stronger partial stabiliser for interregional inequalities in GDP per capita. In cases where the tax and government expenditure shares are smaller, then the potential redistributive roles facilitated by the state are weaker.

In terms of societal cohesion and governance issues at the local, regional and national levels, this issue of wide income inequalities both between regions and within regions represents one of the most important governance challenges facing the UK. All societies have a tolerance for income inequality, because wage variations provide incentives for competition and innovation between individuals. However, modern globalisation has increased income inequalities between skills groups (Goos *et al.* 2009) and this is now becoming a major concern in many national and international arenas (OECD 2009b), particularly in the aftermath of the 2008 global financial crisis. The reason is that such inequalities erode the incentives for investing in education (OECD 2014c) or for widespread civic engagement, both of which are necessary for societal cohesion and good governance (OECD 2009b).

The rising UK income inequality between the mid-1970s and the mid-1990s was primarily a result of within-region inequality rather than between-region inequality (Dickey 2001, 2007). Indeed, there is some evidence that in the early 1990s the between-region inequality index actually fell slightly, although this is likely to have been a result of the greater recessionary impacts on financial services in London and the South East in the aftermath of the 1997 stock market crash and the 1992 exit from the ERM. Moreover, international immigration and emigration have slightly increased UK income inequality (Dickey 2014). On the other hand, between 1991 and 2005 UK interregional mobility, driven both by domestic movements and international movements, have had different effects on the broad regions of the UK. The Greater London, Scotland and the northern English regions have all seen increased income inequality associated with mobility whereas Wales has experienced falling income inequality (Dickey 2014).

By 2010–2011 UK income inequality was lower than it had been at any time since the turn of the millennium, although it was still much higher than it was before the dramatic widening of inequality which began in the late 1980s and early 1990s (Cribb *et al.* 2013). This is because UK income inequality fell in the aftermath of the 2008 global economic crisis as highest income groups faced falling real incomes. Yet, at the same time as this was the case, UK earnings inequality rose during the same period (Cribb *et al.* 2013). There are two reasons for observing falling income inequality at the same time as rising earnings inequality. First, earnings make up a larger share of overall income for high-income earners at the top of the income distribution than at the bottom, such that falls in high earnings had a greater impact on indices of inequality than falls in low earnings, while second, any real increases in incomes from benefits and tax credits have favoured low earnings households (Cribb *et al.* 2013).

High income inequalities can become especially problematic at the local and regional levels in that public governance and policy-making may become severely hampered by local income inequalities. The reason is that rising local income inequalities are likely to lead to declining societal cohesion, and this will become most evident in the local context. If we consider the regional dimensions of income inequality, as we see in Table 2.15, for the UK as a whole, the 2010 Gini index of inequality before taxes and transfers is 0.517 and after taxes and transfers is 0.338.[32] In terms of poverty rates calculated at the upper limits of 60 per cent or 50 per cent of the national median disposable income, the 2010 UK poverty rate after taxes and transfers is 0.170 at the

Table 2.15 UK regional income inequality 2010

	Gini Index of Inequality After Taxes and Transfers	Gini Index of Inequality Before Taxes and Transfers	Poverty Rate After Taxes and Transfers 60% Line	Poverty Rate After Taxes and Transfers 50% Line
North East	0.296	0.522	0.201	0.108
North West	0.302	0.510	0.190	0.099
Yorks and Humb	0.310	0.513	0.205	0.111
East Midlands	0.306	0.487	0.177	0.103
West Midlands	0.307	0.487	0.208	0.117
Eastern	0.349	0.501	0.134	0.075
London	0.405	0.555	0.163	0.100
South East	0.349	0.489	0.123	0.072
South West	0.296	0.471	0.146	0.083
Wales	0.303	0.509	0.198	0.111
Scotland	0.324	0.503	0.167	0.102
N Ireland	0.302	0.510	0.225	0.130
UK	0.338	0.517	0.170	0.097

Source: OECD Regional Database.

60 per cent cut-off and 0.097 at the 50 per cent cut-off.[33] Not surprisingly, the most unequal region both before and after adjusting for taxes and benefits is Greater London, due to the presence of a large minority of very highly paid workers living alongside large groups of low-paid workers. The wages of the low-paid workers have not risen in line with other workers, and in the case of London this appears to be largely due to immigration (Gordon and Kaplanis 2014). The majority of people living in London exhibit wages which reflect middle-class earnings and living standards. However, the increasingly polarised nature of employment and income distribution is most marked in London, primarily due to the presence of large cohorts of very highly waged workers, although the degrees of inequality are significantly reduced by the operation of the UK tax and benefits system.

From Table 2.15 it is clear that the North East also exhibits levels of inequality which are above the UK average prior to the operation of the tax and benefits system, and most other northern English regions along with the devolved UK regions also exhibit similar levels of income inequality. The lowest inequality levels prior to the effects of tax and benefit transfers are the regions in the midlands and south of England. However, after the operation of the tax and benefits transfer system the picture is rather different. Apart from London, the only other regions with Gini indices of inequality which are higher than the UK average after taxes and benefit transfers are the South East and the East, and this is due to largely the same story as in the case of London in whereby this reflects the presence of significant cohorts of very high earners. All other UK regions now exhibit relatively lower levels of inequality after the operation of the tax and benefits system. The reason for this change in regional patterns of inequality pre and post the application of the tax and benefits system is that the devolved regions and those in northern England exhibit higher cohorts of low-paid workers, unemployed workers, and also much lower numbers of very highly paid workers. In other words, even though in many of these regions the regional Gini indices of inequality are quite similar to London, the difference is that the regional distribution of income patterns are centred around much lower average income levels.

That this is the case is reflected by the fact that in these other regions there are much higher proportions of people below the poverty lines. From Table 2.15 we see that after the application of the tax and benefits transfer system, if we take the threshold of 60 per cent of the UK regional median income (Cribb *et al.* 2013), we see that all of the regions in southern and eastern England along with Scotland exhibit poverty levels below the UK average, while all of the regions in the midlands and north of England along with Wales and Northern Ireland exhibit levels which are higher than the UK average. Moreover, this is not simply a result of the fact that both incomes and living costs are higher in more prosperous regions and lower in weaker regions, because these regional poverty thresholds are adjusted to the local regional income levels. This pattern mirrors the general interregional patterns of inequality described above using other indices, and reflects the fact that these poorer regions contain large numbers of people on very low earnings even by the relatively lower income levels of these regions (Plunkett *et al.* 2014; SMCPC 2014). If we consider a 50 per cent cut-off level, the picture remains largely the same, except for the fact that now London and Scotland both exhibit indices above the UK average, reflecting the fact that they also contain pockets of the very lowest paid workers, with London workers adversely affected by the high local costs of living (IPPR-RF 2013). While the 1980s poverty debates tended to focs on inner city neighbourhoods, city centre urban regeneration processes and the complexities of spatial restructuring mean that today some 57 per cent of those in poverty in England and Wales live in suburbs and in small urban areas, and these numbers are rising (Hunter 2014). In the UK poverty is a much more spatially diffuse phenomenon at the regional level than it is purely an urban phenomenon.

An expected return to real earnings growth between 2015 and 2020 and further cuts to benefits and tax credits associated with the remaining 40 per cent of fiscal consolidation to be undertaken (SMCPC 2014) arc likely to lead to a reversal of the trends towards a narrowing of income inequality trends which have been evident in the years following the 2008 crisis and to a further widening of aggregate income inequality in the coming years (Cribb *et al.* 2013). Moreover, this increasing income inequality is likely to have strong spatial implications (ONS 2012f). In terms of low pay and fragile employment security, the decade following the 2008 global financial crisis appears to have been characterised by a widening gap between the more prosperous and the least prosperous OECD-TL2/EU-NUTS1 large statistical large UK regions, and most notably between London and the rest of the country. These general patterns are also reflected at the more local OECD-TL3/EU-NUTS3 levels, although the variability here is higher both between regions and within the large statistical regions (MacInnes *et al.* 2014; Ballas *et al.* 2005; Dorling *et al.* 2007; Dorling and Thomas 2004, 2007). Most of the available evidence suggests that this gap is likely to widen further in the coming years (Plunkett *et al.* 2014; SMCPC 2014), exacerbated by regionally differing wealth effects and the effects of public sector retrenchment (ONS 2013a, 2013b).

2.7 The impacts of the London economy on the rest of the UK regions

It is clear that there are significant long-standing and growing interregional economic inequalities in the UK centred around the relationship between the performance of the London regional economy and other UK regions. Since 2011 almost one-third of new jobs created in the UK have been created in London.[34] As such, when questions or concerns are raised about these high and rising inequalities a common response to this is simply to say that this is an inevitable and natural outcome of economic geography forces related to the working of 'big hubs' and that as a whole the UK economy *including the other UK regions* benefits from the growth of London.[35] However, this response typically tends to be rather more by way of an assertion than analysis. There have been several attempts to outline the effects of the London economy on the wider UK economy (CLC 2004, 2009; 2011, 2012; CEBR 2012c) but these tend to focus on the current share of UK output (ONS 2013d) and employment activity accounted for by the London regional economy, the likely net interregional fiscal transfers emanating from the London regional economy to other regions (CLC 2009; CEBR 2012c), and also the possible employment multipliers generated by London (CLC 2004, 2009). Unsurprisingly, the general picture painted by these reports is that the London economy plays a powerful and beneficial role in the overall UK economy via demand effects, supply-side effects, globalisation effects and fiscal effects. Demand effects arise from the fact that London is a large market providing strong purchasing linkages for other UK regions to supply as well as employment demand for people in hinterland regions (CLC 2004) and beyond (CLC 2009). In terms of supply effects, London provides specialist supplies of key innovation-related activities, high-level skills, key education and training opportunities, and a location for highly skilled professionals to find gainful employment within the UK rather than migrating out of the country (CLC 2004). In addition, there is a unique role which is assumed to be played by London's financial markets, which have been argued to provide UK firms with wider access to finance and at lower prices than otherwise would be the case (CLC 2004). Yet, the key beneficial role of London in terms of the wider UK economy is that it is an important global 'hub' containing world-class transport, labour-market, tourism, heritage, culture, sport, business-networking, education, and headquarter-function assets and activities. It is this global hub role of London which is seen as being the dominant and UK-wide benefit of London economy. In addition, as a large and powerful economy London naturally generates very substantial tax revenues which translate into net fiscal transfers to all other UK regions except for the South East (CEBR 2012), thereby benefiting these other regions in terms of public expenditure. It has to be noted that this interregional net fiscal contribution largely disappeared in the wake of the global financial crisis as the UK Exchequer's public finances contracted largely in part due to the contraction of the London economy (CLC 2011, 2012). As well as these potentially beneficial linkages between London and the rest of the UK, there are also potential downsides. For example, financial services in other UK cities and regions are primarily domestically oriented, and as such are only weakly and indirectly linked to London's global financial markets (CLC 2004), with the possible exception of Edinburgh. As such, the arguments relating to easier access to finance on the part of UK firms across the country is rather difficult to substantiate. In addition, housing constraints and also speculative inflows from overseas of real estate capital puts upward pressure on the UK's inflationary pressures, which also translate into macroeconomic effects via the influences on monetary policy.

A problem with all of these arguments, however, is that they can often be just as easily applied to many different spatial structures in many different countries, including those which are far more polycentric and less dominated by a single city, such as is the case for the USA, Australia, Canada, Germany and The Netherlands. As such, it is not exactly clear how these linkage-types of arguments link to the spatial structure of the UK economy or the specific role played by London's extreme relative dominance. In addition, these types of linkage analyses and arguments do not provide any answers to the question of what is the scale of the long-run impact across the whole of the UK of London's dominant growth trajectory and whether the rest of the UK's other regions have indeed benefited from London's expansion in comparison to a more spatially balanced pattern of growth.

What we do know is the long-run post-war productivity premium of London did not increase from its typical values of 24–27 per cent above the UK average during the 1980s, and it was really only in the 1990s that the productivity performance of the London economy began to surge. The 1980s and 1990s were decades characterised by some major institutional and infrastructure changes in the London economy including: the 1984 'Big Bang' deregulation in the London financial markets; the start of the Canary Wharf London Docklands development in 1988 much of which was largely completed by 1993; the completion of the London orbital motorway the M25 in 1986; the beginning of the construction of Channel Tunnel which was finally opened in 1993; and the public inquiry during 1995–1999 that finally approved the construction of Heathrow Terminal 5 in 2001, which itself opened in 2008. Yet, interestingly, there were no changes in the productivity premium of

London during the decade of the 1980s itself, which suggests that the 'Big Bang' alone had little or no immediate economic impact. The productivity surges in the London regional economy only really took place from the early 1990s onwards.

The wider economic effects of London on the more distant UK regions, however, and especially those regions which are economically weaker, is a moot point. As we will see in Chapter 4 there are various arguments which suggest that London may have had a positive effect on these regions, while on the other hand there are also arguments which suggest that London's success may have had an adverse effect on these regions. At this stage we will leave these debates open, and simply assess the impacts on the basis of some simple assumptions.

It is possible to provide an assessment of the likely effects of the growth of the Greater London regional economy on other UK regions by adopting a counter-factual type of analysis. Obviously, it is not possible to obtain highly accurate and detailed estimates regarding the effects of the expansion and productivity growth of London on the wider UK regions because there is no fully calibrated general equilibrium interregional model calibrated using decades of data. However, it is possible by means of a counter-factual approach to relatively quickly arrive at reasonable estimates of the impact of London's growth on other UK regions. To do this we can use the various pieces of information at our disposal regarding the relative contribution to the UK economy over time of the various UK regions and to consider what might have taken place under alternative scenarios. We can then assess these alternative counter-factual scenarios in the light of the appropriate international comparisons of the productivity performance of London and other more distant UK regions over several decades.

We can start the counter-factual scenario exercise by assuming three hypothetical alternative possibilities. The first hypothetical scenario – a neutral scenario – is that the growth of London has had no real effect on the long-run performance of other more distant UK regions. The second possibility – a positive scenario – is the expansion has had a net positive effect on the other UK regions (Coyle and Rosewell 2014) and that over the years these other UK regions have performed better than they would have done if London had not been so successful. The third scenario – a negative scenario – is that the expansion of London has had a net negative effect on the other UK regions and these other UK regions would have performed better if London had not been so successful.

In order to get a sense of the likely realism of any particular hypothetical counter-factual scenario in comparison with the other two counter-factual scenarios, we can consider the experience of other comparator OECD regions which closely resemble the experience of the various UK regions in order to assess what might have happened to these various UK regions under different circumstances. The sample of comparator regions against which we will benchmark our UK regions are those whose GDP per capita in 1995 was within a plus or minus 10 per cent range of UK regions, giving a range of US$18,150–US$24,899 in 1995. This provides a sample of 49 comparator regions in 14 other OECD countries against which we can benchmark the performance of these 7 non-core UK regions.

We know that over two or three decades a whole series of different influences will have affected the growth of the seven UK regions, including technological change, labour-market deregulation, industrial restructuring, macroeconomic effects, developments in education and training systems, along with all of the institutional and (information) technological issues associated with modern globalisation, as discussed in detail in Chapter 4. Moreover, we know that many of these influences will also have affected these 49 other benchmark OECD regions in varying ways, so in order to assess whether our first hypothetical counter-factual scenario is realistic, we need to identify whether in comparison to other OECD benchmark regions there is any evidence these UK regions have benefited from the growth of London in addition to these other potential influences.

As we see in Table 2.16, for the economically weaker UK regions which are not geographically close to London, comprising the North East, North West, Yorkshire and Humberside, East Midlands, West Midlands, Wales and Northern Ireland, we can consider their GDP per capita scores in 1995 and 2011 relative to comparison regions. These dates are the earliest and most recent dates at which fully comprehensive international comparisons can be made using the OECD Regional Database. The details of these 49 OECD comparator TL2 regions whose performance is summarised in Table 2.16 are given in the Appendix in Table A2.1.

In comparison to these international comparator regions, if the growth of London had indeed provided growth benefits to these other UK regions which would otherwise not have been available to them then we might expect to observe that their growth in GDP per capita would be superior on average when benchmarked against these 49 comparator regions in the 14 other countries. Yet, what is immediately clear from Table 2.16 is that GDP per capita growth performance of these UK regions is not markedly higher than their foreign OECD counterparts. On the contrary, whether GDP per capita growth is measured in absolute terms or in terms of relative to national performance, this particular group of seven UK regions has under-performed. Moreover, we can also repeat the exercise by comparing these regions against those 83 OECD-TL2 regions with similar productivity scores in 2011, as detailed in Table A2.2 in the Appendix. Again, as we see in Table 2.17 the results hardly change at all.

These comparative results suggest therefore that this group of seven economically weaker UK regions has not benefited from the growth success of London, and if anything the evidence points in the opposite direction, suggesting that London's success may have had some slight adverse effects on these regions. In other words, the positive growth effects on the UK economy of the London regional economy 1995–2011 appear not to have been accompanied

Table 2.16 The performance of 1995 UK and OECD-TL2 comparator regions

OECD-TL2 Region	GDP per Capita 1995 (2000 constant prices)	GDP per Capita 2011 (2000–constant prices)	Regional % Change in GDP per Capita 1995–2011	National % Change in GDP per Capita 1995–2011	Difference between Regional and National % Change
North East	20,014	23,870	19.2	33.7	−14.5
North West	21,776	27,862	27.9	33.7	−5.8
Yorks and Humberside	21,520	26,334	22.4	33.7	−11.3
East Midlands	22,636	26,872	18.7	33.7	−15.0
West Midlands	22,365	26,916	20.3	33.7	−13.4
Wales	20,166	23,379	15.9	33.7	−17.8
Northern Ireland	19,143	24,429	27.6	33.7	−6.1
Average for 7 UK regions			21.7		−12.0
Average for 49 TL2 Comparable OECD regions			25.59		−2.98

Source: OECD Regional Database.

The GDP per capita scores of these regions in both 1995 in 2011 are given in 2005 constant prices.

Table 2.17 The growth performance of 2011 OECD-TL2 comparator regions

OECD-TL2 Region	GDP per Capita 1995 (2005 US$ constant prices PPP)	GDP per Capita 2011 (2005 US$ constant prices PPP)	Regional % Change in GDP per Capita 1995–2011	National % Change in GDP per Capita 1995–2011	Percentage Point Difference between Regional and National % Change
North East	20,014	23,870	19.2	33.7	−14.5
North West	21,776	27,862	27.9	33.7	−5.8
Yorks and Humberside	21,520	26,334	22.4	33.7	−11.3
East Midlands	22,636	26,872	18.7	33.7	−15.0
West Midlands	22,365	26,916	20.3	33.7	−13.4
Wales	20,166	23,379	15.9	33.7	−17.8
Northern Ireland	19,143	24,429	27.6	33.7	−6.1
Average for 7 OECD-TL2 UK regions			**21.7**		**−12.0**
Average for 71 OECD-TL2 2011 Comparable OECD regions (1995–2011)			**32.54**		**0.0732**
Average for all 83 OECD-TL2 2011 Comparable OECD regions (including those with varying start dates for data comparability)			**29.03**		**−0.971**
Average for 77 OECD-TL2 2011 Comparable OECD regions excluding all very rapidly growing Polish and Korean regions			**23.17**		**−2.806**

Source: OECD Regional Database.

Table 2.18 2011 regional shares of total UK Output 1995, 2008 and 2011

2011 Indices	*1995 Regional Share of UK GDP*	*2008 Regional Share of UK GDP*	*2011 Regional Share of UK GDP*
North East	3.64	3.15	3.03
North West	10.4	9.44	9.39
Yorkshire and Humberside	7.49	6.92	6.96
East Midlands	6.42	5.73	6.43
West Midlands	8.24	7.12	7.14
East	8.43	8.45	8.39
London	17.8	21.8	22.3
South East	13.4	14.2	14.4
South West	7.36	7.36	7.37
Scotland	8.57	7.89	7.78
Wales	4.09	3.39	3.41
Northern Ireland	2.17	2.25	2.13
United Kingdom	100	100	100

Source: OECD Regional Database.

by significant additional induced GDP per capita growth effects in these other UK regions, because otherwise these regions would have out-performed those other EU regions with similar productivity scores in 1995. In terms of GDP per capita, this finding of no identifiable positive growth effect suggests that our first hypothetical counter-factual neutral scenario, namely that the success of the Greater London regions has had little or no positive effect on the rest of the UK regions, may in reality actually be very accurate. Alternatively, the fact that these regions have under-performed relative to all of the comparator groups of regions could also be interpreted as supporting our third hypothetical negative scenario whereby London may have had an adverse effect on the economic performance of these regions. However, with no a priori grounds on which to base such a hypothetical argument at this stage we assume that the neutral scenario is the most likely scenario reflected by the data.

The combination of regional demographic changes and regional productivity changes which have taken place over the last two decades has led to changes in the contribution of each region to national output. As we see in Table 2.18, the contribution of the London economy to overall UK Gross Domestic Product has increased markedly since the mid-1990s. The Greater London economy now accounts for more than 22 per cent of UK output. The South East has also slowly increased its share of UK output since the mid-1990s while the shares for the South West, the East, the East Midlands and Northern Ireland have all remained largely unchanged. In contrast, the contributions to UK national output associated with all other UK regions have fallen by between 0.5 and 1 percentage points during this period.

Using this information, in conjunction with the other evidence derived above, we can therefore begin to calculate the likely overall effect of London on the UK economy by assuming the first hypothetical counter-factual scenario in which London has no discernible positive effect on other more distant UK regions. Under this neutral scenario, all other UK regions would have performed at the same aggregate output and GDP per capita levels as they currently do and their performance is therefore largely independent of the performance of London, and instead has been driven by 30 years of technological change, market deregulation and global institutional changes. Under this neutral scenario, any under-performance observed in these regions relative to all comparator groups of regions would be ascribed to endogenous factors purely within the regions and not related to external factors.

Following this logic, we know that the OECD-TL2/EU-NUTS1 definition of the London region accounts for some 12.6 per cent of the UK population in 2011 and we also know from Table 2.3 that the 2011 London region relative productivity premium was 76.7 per cent above the UK average. As such, on these definitions the region of London currently accounts for some 22.3 per cent of the total UK economic output, as we see in Table 2.18. Under this scenario, we can consider what would have happened if the London region were today to continue to exhibit a productivity premium of some 24 per cent relative to the UK average as was typical in the 1980s, rather than the 76.7 per cent premium that we do observe. Under this scenario, the GDP per capita of the UK economy as a whole would be 6.7 per cent less than it is now, ceteris paribus. On the other hand, if today the London economy were to exhibit a productivity premium of 49.9 per cent as it did in 1995 rather than one of 76.6 per cent, this implies, ceteris paribus, that the UK economy would be just under 3.37 per cent smaller than it is now. As such, following the first hypothetical counter-factual scenario and therefore assuming that the other UK regions would have grown to the same levels as they have done, this rather crude and simplistic 'back-of-the-envelope' calculation suggests that the relatively more rapid economic growth of the London region during the last three decades since the mid-1980s has increased UK aggregate GDP per capita by 6.7 per cent over this period, a value which is similar to the growth effects on the UK of the EU Single Market. Similarly, according to this approach, the growth of the London economy over the last two decades since 1995 has increased UK aggregate GDP per capita by 3.37 per cent, about half the effect of the EU Single Market over a similar period. Moreover, these estimates are *maximum* estimates, given the fact that the observed data could also be interpreted as pointing somewhat to our third negative counter-factual scenario.

Therefore, on the basis of this simple calculation based on the first hypothetical counter-factual scenario, half of the long-term beneficial effects of London's growth on the UK economy would be a result of London's productivity growth between the mid-1980s and the mid-1990s, while half would be due to London's growth since the mid-1990s. As we will see in Chapter 4, these orders of magnitude regarding the impacts of London's growth on the wider UK economy since the mid-1980s are also consistent with the growth effects of the EU Single Market on the UK economy since the early 1990s while the impacts of London's growth on the UK economy since the mid-1990s are approximately half of the impacts of the EU Single Market over a similar period.

Following a similar logic it may also be possible to argue that much of the productivity growth of the South East region is also likely to have been directly due to London's growth and therefore these wider effects also need to be considered. If we make the most extreme assumption that all of the productivity growth of the South East is directly due to London's growth, then we can repeat the exercise above here again by assuming that the growth of all other UK regions including London would have taken place largely irrespective of the performance of the South East region, and we can then multiply the growth in the relative per capita GDP premium in the South East between 1995 and 2001 by the population share of the region. This gives a value of 0.59 per cent, which if added to the 3.37 per cent derived above suggests that the total GDP per capita effect on the overall UK economy today due to the combined productivity growth of London and the South East is likely to be less than 4 per cent. Again, and as indicated above, if we adopt the first hypothetical counter-factual scenario, the effects on the overall UK economy of London's growth 1995–2011 are found to be markedly less than the estimated effects discussed in Chapter 4 of the EU Single Market on the UK economy during more or less the same period.

The three decades of growth of the London regional economy since the mid-1980s are only likely to have increased UK GDP per capita by some 6–7 per cent, and by half of this amount since 1995. To many casual observers, these London–UK national productivity effects are likely to be much less than most people would assume. The popular press, many politicians and not a few academic commentators are frequently espousing the important growth effects of London for the UK as a whole, and these perceptions are likely to have been heavily swayed by direct day-to-day experience of London's success on the part of many of the authors of these texts. Yet, these relatively simple calculations above present a rather different picture which suggests that the overall impact of London's growth since the 1980s accounts for only 3.33 per cent since the mid-1990s and only 6.67 per cent since the mid-1980s. Moreover, the evidence from the other UK regions and their OECD comparators suggests that in general, the growth effects of London appear to be largely confined to London and its immediate hinterland. London's growth appears to have contributed far less to increasing the overall UK GDP per capita growth over many years than many people assume or assert. In particular, it appears to have contributed little or nothing to the growth of the economically weaker UK regions which are not geographically close to London, but which are home to half of the UK population.

2.8   Conclusions

The OECD-wide evidence presented here suggests that the performance inequalities in the UK's regions are very serious. Prosperity, growth and wellbeing in the UK is increasingly being concentrated in the south of England and in Scotland at the same time as many of the UK's regions are becoming increasingly dislocated and decoupled from the success of these buoyant regions. Moreover, the evidence suggests that the aggregate growth effects of the London region economy on the UK as a whole are much less than is assumed by many people. Part of the reason for this is that little or no growth benefits appear to spill over from the London regional economy to many of the UK's regions. As such, the London region and its adjacent regions along with Scotland increasingly appear to act largely as islands of prosperity, providing real benefits for their inhabitants but not the inhabitants of most other UK regions. The estimates here, however, are based on the first hypothetical counter-factual scenario, namely that London has had little or no discernible positive effect on the performance of these other UK regions, and obviously these 'back-of-the-envelope' calculations depend on hypothetical scenarios whose ceteris paribus assumptions can be challenged. Yet, the OECD-wide evidence suggests that not only are these estimates relating to the overall UK aggregate GDP per capita increases associated with London's growth provided above likely to be realistic, if anything they are likely to be rather generous over-estimates.

Having said this, at the same time the strong performance of the London regional economy boosts UK national output and growth figures. At present, as we see in Table A3.5, productivity per employee in the UK is now almost exactly at the average level for the 28 countries of the European Union, and below that of the Eurozone economies. Yet, without the observed productivity growth in the London region over the last three decades the UK as a whole would nowadays exhibit a lower GDP per capita in purchasing power parity terms than Italy and one which is more or less equivalent to those of Spain or New Zealand (OECD 2014a). As such, these figures therefore serve to highlight the role played by the London economy in maintaining the overall GDP per capita scores of the UK economy at levels which are at the lower end of the richer northern European economies rather than at the upper end of the weaker southern European economies.

Nowadays, many commentators emphasise the role played by cities in driving productivity and economic growth, and as such, tend to downplay the role of regional issues. In particular, one criticism is that regions per se often have little real economic rationale and that economic mechanisms tend to be concentrated and organised according to the logic of functional urban regions (FURS) rather than at any regional level. The data we have employed here relate to the OECD-TL2/EU-NUTS1 large statistical regions of the UK and also the local government OECD-TL3/EU-NUTS3 Local Government areas. As such, these analyses are also open to this critique. In the following chapter we will then continue our investigation by focusing on urban areas at different levels. As we will see, many of the conclusions outlined here are not only largely repeated when conducting our analysis at the level of UK cities rather than UK regions, but in many ways they are actually magnified.

Appendix 2.1

The growth performance of UK and OECD comparator OECD-TL2 regions 1995–2011 on the basis of their 1995 productivity performance

Table A2.1 The growth performance of 1995 OECD-TL2 comparator regions

OECD-TL2 Region	GDP per Capita 1995 (2005 US$ constant prices PPP)	GDP per Capita 2011 (2005 US$ constant prices PPP)	Regional % Change in GDP per Capita 1995–2011	National % Change in GDP per Capita 1995–2011	Percentage Point Difference between Regional and National % Change
North East	20,014	23,870	19.2	33.7	−14.5
North West	21,776	27,862	27.9	33.7	−5.8
Yorks and Humberside	21,520	26,334	22.4	33.7	−11.3
East Midlands	22,636	26,872	18.7	33.7	−15.0
West Midlands	22,365	26,916	20.3	33.7	−13.4
Wales	20,166	23,379	15.9	33.7	−17.8
Northern Ireland	19,143	24,429	27.6	33.7	−6.1
Average for 7 OECD-TL2 UK regions			**21.7**		**−12.0**
Abruzzo (Italy)	22,007	23,311	5.9	7.4	−1.5
Athens (Greece)	19,255	29,475	53.0	25.0	18.0
Aquitaine (France)	22,764	26,367	15.8	19.3	−3.5
Aragon (Spain)	22,648	30,026	32.5	24.9	7.6
Auverne (France)	23,827	24,050	0.9	19.3	−18.4
Brandenburg (Germany)	18,492	24,642	33.2	24.3	−8.9
Brittany (France))	21,305	24,684	15.9	19.3	−3.4
Burgundy (France)	22,647	24,925	10.0	19.3	−9.3

(Continued)

Table A2.1 Continued

OECD-TL2 Region	GDP per Capita 1995 (2005 US$ constant prices PPP)	GDP per Capita 2011 (2005 US$ constant prices PPP)	Regional % Change in GDP per Capita 1995–2011	National % Change in GDP per Capita 1995–2011	Percentage Point Difference between Regional and National % Change
Canary Islands (Spain)	20,400	22,982	12.6	24.9	−12.3
Carinthia (Austria)	23,930	30,789	28.7	31.7	−3.0
Castille e Léon	20,153	26,326	30.6	24.9	5.7
Central Norrland (Sweden)	24,396	32,198	31.9	41.8	−9.9
Champagne-Ardennes (France)	23,479	25,451	8.4	19.3	−10.9
Corsica (France)	18,523	25,145	35.8	19.3	16.5
East Middle Sweden (Sweden)	21,701	30,100	38.7	41.8	−3.1
Eastern and Northern Finland	18,936	26,342	39.1	46.4	−7.3
Franche-Comté (France)	24,421	23,827	−2.75	19.3	−22.1
Iceland	24,803	33,587	35.4	35.4	0
Languedoc-Roussilon	19,869	23,130	16.4	19.3	−2.9
La Rioja (Spain)	24,062	30,230	25.6	24.9	0.7
Limousin (France)	20,726	22,850	10.2	19.3	−9.1
Lisbon (Portugal)	24,272	30,106	24.0	23.4	0.7
Lower Austria (Austria)	22,933	29,797	29.9	31.7	−1.8
Lower Normandy (France)	21,629	23,302	7.7	19.3	−11.6
Mecklenburg-Voorpommern (Germany)	18,348	23,595	28.6	24.3	−4.3
Melila (Spain)	18,928	21,409	13.1	24.9	−11.8
Mississippi (USA)	24,928	29,200	17.1	26.3	−9.2
Molise (Italy)	19,164	20,870	8.9	7.4	1.5
Montana (USA)	24,608	34,786	41.4	26.3	15.1
New Brunswick (Canada)	22,121	29,726	34.3	30.4	3.9
Nova Scotia (Canada)	20,969	28,989	38.2	30.4	7.8
Nord Pas de Calais (France)	20,170	24,288	20.4	19.3	1.1
North Middle Sweden	22,606	29,405	30.0	41.8	−11.8

Picardy (France)	21,752	22,925	5.4	19.3	-13.9
Poitou-Charentes (France)	21,195	24,011	13.3	19.3	-6.0
Quebec (Canada)	24,933	37,837	51.7	30.4 (>1996)	21.3
Sardinia (Italy)	18,255	20.542	12.5	7.5	5.0
Saxony (Germany)	18,749	25,108	33.9	24.3	9.6
South Australia	23,681	31,832	34.4	42.5	-8.1
Tasmania (Australia)	20,809	27,108	30.2	42.5	-12.3
South Sweden	22,719	29,835	31.3	41.8	-10.5
Southern Finland (Finland)	22,250	28,238	26.9	46.4	-19.5
Styria (Austria)	24,076	31,365	30.3	31.7	-1.4
Upper Norrland (Sweden)	23,015	34,926	51.7	41.8	9.9
Valencia (Spain)	20,042	23,538	17.4	24.9	-7.5
Wallonia (Belgium)	19,564	24,185	23.6	44.3	-20.7
West Virginia (USA)	24,223	31,760	31.1	26.3	4.8
West Sweden	23,536	32,957	40.0	41.8	-1.8
Western Finland	19,553	29,056	48.6	46.4	2.2
Average for 49 OECD-TL2 1995 Comparable OECD regions			**25.59**		**-2.98**

Source: OECD Regional Database.Note: data for Canada are 1996–2011.

Appendix 2.2

The growth performance of UK and OECD comparator OECD-TL2 regions 1995–2011 on the basis of their 2011 productivity performance

Table A2.2 The growth performance of OECD-TL2 comparator regions 1995–2011

OECD-TL2 Region	GDP per Capita 1995 (2005 US$ constant prices PPP)	GDP per Capita 2011 (2005 US$ constant prices PPP)	Regional % Change in GDP per Capita 1995–2011	National % Change in GDP per Capita 1995–2011	Percentage Point Difference between Regional and National % Change
North East	20,014	23,870	19.2	33.7	−14.5
North West	21,776	27,862	27.9	33.7	−5.8
Yorks and Humberside	21,520	26,334	22.4	33.7	−11.3
East Midlands	22,636	26,872	18.7	33.7	−15.0
West Midlands	22,365	26,916	20.3	33.7	−13.4
Wales	20,166	23,379	15.9	33.7	−17.8
Northern Ireland	19,143	24,429	27.6	33.7	−6.1
Average for 7 OECD-TL2 UK regions			**21.7**	**33.7**	**−12.0**
Abruzzo (Italy)	22,007	23,311	5.9	7.4	−1.5
Athens (Greece)	19,255	29,475	53.0	25.0	18.0
Algarve (Portugal)	19,326	21,190	9.64	23.4	−13.75
Alsace (France)	26,451	27,958	5.69	19.3	−13.6
Aquitaine (France)	22,764	26,367	15.8	19.3	−3.5
Aragon (Spain)	22,648	30,026	32.5	24.9	7.6
Asturias (Spain)	18,494	25,236	36.4	24.9	11.6
Auverne (France)	23,827	24,050	0.9	19.3	−18.4

Region					
Balearic Islands (Spain)	25,675	28,279	10.1	24.9	−14.76
Brandenburg (Germany)	18,492	24,642	33.2	24.3	−8.9
Brittany (France)	21,305	24,684	15.9	19.3	−3.4
Border, Midland and Western (Ireland)	17,316 (1996)	24,076	39.0 (1996–2011)	66.8 (1996–2001)	−27.77
Burgenland (Austria)	17.988	24,331	35.2	31.7	3.56
Burgundy (France)	22,647	24,925	10.0	19.3	−9.3
Canary Islands (Spain)	20,400	22,982	12.6	24.9	−12.3
Cantabria (Spain)	19,551	26,128	33.6	24.9	8.74
Capital Region (Korea)	16,580	26,489	59.8	78.1	−18.34
Carinthia (Austria)	23,930	30,789	28.7	31.7	−3.0
Castille e Léon (Spain)	20,153	26,326	30.6	24.9	5.7
Central Bohemia (Czech Republic)	13,918	21,695	55.9	53.3	2.57
Central Hungary (Hungary)	16,739	28,254	68.8	47.4	21.39
Central Norrland (Sweden)	24,396	32,198	31.9	41.8	−9.9
Centre (France)	23,539	25,069	6.49	19.3	−12.81
Champagne-Ardennes (France)	23,479	25,451	8.4	19.3	−10.9
Chugoku (Japan)	27,899 (2001)	30,121	7.96 (2001–2011)	6.9 (2001–2011)	1.06
Corsica (France)	18,523	25,145	35.8	19.3	16.5
East Middle Sweden (Sweden)	21,701	30,100	38.7	41.8	−3.1
Eastern and Northern Finland	18,936	26,342	39.1	46.4	−7.3
Franche-Comté (France)	24,421	23,827	−2.75	19.3	−22.1
Galicia (Spain)	17,125	24,231	41.5	24.9	16.59
Gangwon (Korea)	13,799	22,428	62.5	78.1	−15.57
Gyeonbuk (Korea)	13,741	25,783	87.6	78.1	9.5
Hedmark+Oppland (Norway)	31,628 (1997)	26,078	−17.54 (1997–2011)	13.3 (1997–2011)	−30.84
Hokkaido (Japan)	26,365 (2001)	27,440	4.07 (2001–2011)	6.9 (2001–2011)	−2.83
Jeju (Korea)	13,622	22,635	66.2	78.1	−11.94
Jeolla (Korea)	14,247	27,655	94.1	78.1	16.01
Kansai (Japan)	28,846 (2001)	30,268	4.92 (2001–2011)	6.9 (2001–2011)	−1.98
Kyushu-Okinawa (Japan)	23,834 (2001)	26,851	12.7 (2001–2011)	6.9 (2001–2011)	5.75

(Continued)

Table A2.2 Continued

OECD-TL2 Region	GDP per Capita 1995 (2005 US$ constant prices PPP)	GDP per Capita 2011 (2005 US$ constant prices PPP)	Regional % Change in GDP per Capita 1995–2011	National % Change in GDP per Capita 1995–2011	Percentage Point Difference between Regional and National % Change
Languedoc-Roussilon (France)	19,869	23,130	16.4	19.3	−2.9
La Rioja (Spain)	24,062	30,230	25.6	24.9	0.7
Liguria (Italy)	24,953	28,316	13.5	7.4	6.07
Limousin (France)	20,726	22,850	10.2	19.3	−9.1
Lisbon (Portugal)	24,272	30,106	24.0	23.4	0.7
Lorraine (France)	21,940	23,003	4.85	19.3	−14.46
Lower Austria (Austria)	22,933	29,797	29.9	31.7	−1.8
Lower Normandy (France)	21,629	23,302	7.7	19.3	−11.6
Madeira (Portugal)	14,863	25,641	72.5	23.4	49.11
Mazovia (Poland)	11,507	29,389	255.4	99.6	155.8
Mecklenburg-Voorpommern (Germany)	18,348	23,595	28.6	24.3	−4.3
Midi-Pyrénées (France)	22,515	26,224	16.5	19.3	−2.83
Mississippi (USA)	24,928	29,200	17.1	26.3	−9.2
New Brunswick (Canada)	22,121	29,726	34.3	30.4	3.9
North Island (New Zealand)	20,788 (2000)	25,070	20.6 (2000–2011)	19.1 (2000–2011)	1.5
Nova Scotia (Canada)	20,969	28,989	38.2	30.4	7.8
Nord Pas de Calais (France)	20,170	24,288	20.4	19.3	1.1
North Middle Sweden	22,606	29,405	30.0	41.8	−11.8
Pays de la Loire (France)	22,593	26,620	17.8	19.3	−1.48
Picardy (France)	21,752	22,925	5.4	19.3	−13.9
Piedmont (Italy)	28,740	29,413	2.34	7.4	−5.06
Poitou-Charentes (France)	21,195	24,011	13.3	19.3	−6.0
Provence-Alpes-Côte d'Azur (France)	23,577	28,661	21.6	19.3	2.26
Rhône-Alpes (France)	25,602	30,102	17.6	19.3	−1.73
Saxony (Germany)	18,749	25,108	33.9	24.3	9.6
Saxony-Anhalt (Germany)	17,194	24,078	40.0	24.3	15.7

Region					
Shikoku (Japan)	25,817 (2001)	27,707	7.32 (2001–2011)	6.9 (2001–2011)	0.42
Schleswig-Holstein (Germany)	26,874	29,089	8.24	24.3	−16.06
South Eastern Norway (Norway)	34,476 (1997)	28,849	−19.32 (1997–2011)	13.3 (1997–2011)	−32.62
South Island (New Zealand)	17,965 (2000)	23,795	32.5 (2000–2011)	19.1 (2000–2011)	13.35
Tasmania (Australia)	20,809	27,108	30.2	42.5	−12.3
Thuringia (Germany)	17,073	23,738	39.0	24.3	14.7
South East (Czech Republic)	14,425	21,812	51.2	53.3	−2.1
South Sweden	22,719	29,835	31.3	41.8	−10.5
Southern Finland (Finland)	22,250	28,238	26.9	46.4	−19.5
Styria (Austria)	24,076	31,365	30.3	31.7	−1.4
Tohoku (Japan)	25,448 (2001)	27,233	7.01 (2001–2011)	6.9 (2001–2011)	0.11
Tuscany (Italy)	26,898	29,417	9.36	7.4	1.96
Umbria (Italy)	25,003	24,717	−1.14	7.4	−8.54
Valencia (Spain)	20,042	23,538	17.4	24.9	−7.5
Wallonia (Belgium)	19,564	24,185	23.6	44.3	−20.7
West Sweden	23,536	32,957	40.0	41.8	−1.8
Western Finland	19,553	29,056	48.6	46.4	2.2
Western Slovenia (Slovenia)	19,142	29,841	55.9	57.5	−1.6
Zealand (Denmark)	22,735 (1997)	22,753	0.01 (1997–2011)	11.9 (1997–2011)	−11.98
Average for 71 OECD-TL2 2011 Comparable OECD regions (1995–2011)			**32.54**		**0.0732**
Average for all 83 OECD-TL2 2011 Comparable OECD regions (including those with varying start dates for data comparability)			**29.03**		**−0.971**
Average for 77 OECD-TL2 2011 Comparable OECD regions excluding all very rapidly-growing Polish and Korean regions			**23.17**		**−2.806**

Source: OECD Regional Database.
Note data for Canada are 1996–2011.

Notes

1 Unless otherwise stated, the data in this chapter are all derived from the OECD Regional Statistics Database. www.oecd.org/gov/regional-policy/regionalstatistic-sandindicators.htm.
2 The indices for Norway and Finland are higher than the UK but only if the extremely sparsely populated Arctic regions are included in the calculation.
3 No GVA per worker data are available for the Northwest Territories in Canada.
4 The large statistical regions here refers to East Anglia.
5 Ibid.
6 The 1990s definition of East is now different to the former East Anglia region and now includes areas previously incorporated in the 1980s definition of the South East region. Similarly, the 1980s definition of the North disappeared as the area of Cumbria was transferred away from the North East and included in the North West region. These regional definitional changes from Standard Statistical Regions into Government Office Regions were associated with the reorganisation of local government in England which came into effect on 1 April 1997 (ONS 1997).
7 http://stats.oecd.org/Index.aspx?datasetcode=REG_DEMO_TL2.
8 Ibid.
9 Ibid.
10 No regional data are available for Switzerland.
11 www.prospectmagazine.co.uk/opinions/dont-abandon-the-barnett-formula;https://pure.strath.ac.uk/portal/en/publications/the-barnett-allocation-mechanism(24469744-da3c-44ad-aeb0-82152882546f).html.
12 See: "Daily Question: How Much Does Scotland Pay in Tax and How Much Does it Spend?", www.bbc.com/news/uk-scotland-28879267 See also: http://www.resolutionfoundation.org/media/press-releases/scotland-has-overturned-english-pay-premium/.
13 www.bbc.com/news/uk-30113687.
14 www.bbc.com/news/uk-31748422.
15 www.migrationobservatory.ox.ac.uk/number-foreign-born-local-area-district; www.bbc.com/news/uk-31748422.
16 In general UK residents tend to exhibit higher levels of happiness and trust in government than the detailed decompositions of wellbeing would suggest. While the overall UK indices of both happiness and trust in government levels are ranked in the top 20 per cent of OECD countries, most of the detailed wellbeing indices described here are ranked relatively much lower by OECD standards. See www.bbc.com/news/business-24822394; www.bbc.com/news/uk-24635183.
17 http://worldhappiness.report/.
18 O'Donnell, G., 2015, "General Election: We're Happier Than You Think", *Prospect*, 14 April.
19 Some 20 per cent of the English population live in rural areas of whom 6.7 per cent, or one-third, live in villages and hamlets of fewer than 500 people, while another third of the population live in villages of between 500 and 2500 (OECD 2011c). As such, two-thirds of the English rural population of some 11 million people live in villages of fewer than 2500 people (OECD 2011c).
20 For example, per licence-fee payer BBC funding in the northern regions of England (including the investments in Salford media centre) amounts to £80, in Wales the investments amount to £122, in the Midlands the investments amount to £12.40, and in London amount to £757. See: "Fairer BBC Funding for Regions in Green Paper", *Birmingham Post*, 23 July 2015.
21 www.neighbourhood.statistics.gov.uk/HTMLDocs/dvc124/wrapper.html.
22 www.citiesoutlook.org/.
23 Note that this does not require any assumptions regarding the expectations of migrants regarding long-term equity accrual or the explicit incorporation of

long-term housing equity gains in short-term migration decisions (Gibbons *et al.* 2011). In the same way that no-one in the 1980s could have foreseen the forthcoming global transformations of the 1990s onwards and their impacts on London and the Southern and Eastern regions of England (or on parts of eastern Scotland), no-one could have foreseen the scale of associated housing equity surges in these regions. While as we will see in Chapter 5 there were some commentators who in the late 1980s were already raising concerns about the impacts of land use planning controls on housing and land prices in the South East, the scale of the inter-regional imbalances today is of a different order of magnitude from the 1980s.

24 A notable exception to the general pattern of findings outlined here from many different lines of research derives from postcode-based analyses carried by the CEBR (Centre for Economics and Business Research) for the Royal Mail which finds that many postcodes in northern England are the most 'desirable' places to live on the basis of a work-life balance, in that good schools, green spaces, affordable housing and shorter average commuting times are relatively more accessible and attainable in these locations. However, this 'affordability' approach is at odds with both the hedonic and user costs of capital arguments outlined above (Gibbons *et al.* 2011) in that both employment-related and amenity-related benefits are also incorporated into housing costs simultaneously. This survey therefore fails to distinguish between the endogenous and exogenous influences on housing costs and is best interpreted simply as a quality-of-life index for those who have long-term stable employment and yet who are not and never will be property-owners. Of course those with long-term stable employment are the most likely group to be home owners. As such, these survey results only refer to a small sub-group of the population who are in the lower echelons of the income distribution. Wealthy people seeking high amenities in general do not move to the towns ranked as the highest on this survey. See: www.royalmail-group.com/bebington-ch63-postcode-most-desirable-place-live-and-work-england; "Most Desirable Postcodes in the UK Revealed", BBC News, see: www.bbc.com/news/uk-32016713; www.cebr.com/reports/which-postcode-is-best/.

25 "Early Deaths: Regional Variations 'Shocking' – Hunt", see: www.bbc.com/news/health-22844227; "North-South Health Divide 'Is Widest for 40 Years' ", BBC News, 16 February 2011; Newton *et al.* (2015); see: www.bbc.com/news/health-12464427; www.theguardian.com/society/2015/sep/14/health-life-expectancy-england-regional-differences-poorest-richest.

26 See: *A Minimum Income Standard for London*, 2015, Trust for London and University of Loughborough Report, www.trustforlondon.org.uk/wp-content/uploads/2015/05/MIS-London-full-report.pdf.

27 In terms of child poverty "Two Schools Worlds Apart in Lancashire", BBC News 1st April 2015, and "The Great Constituency Swap", Danny Dorling and Simon Szreter, *Prospect*, 6 March 2015. See: bbc.com/news/uk-31905037. In the UK there is also a strong urban dimension to poor health. See: "The Fat of the Land", *The Economist*, 19 December 2015.

28 See comments by Professor Carol Propper in the BBC Radio 4 Current Affairs Documentary Programme *Analysis: Regions* presented by Alison Wolf at 20.30–21.00 on 3 June 2013.

29 www.oecdregionalwellbeing.org/region.html.

30 www.bbc.com/news/uk-england-30560011; www.bbc.com/news/uk-25474188.

31 www.lloydsbankinggroup.com/globalassets/documents/media/press-releases/halifax/2013/2903_rural.pdf.

32 For comparison purposes, the Gini index for inequality before taxes and transfers in the USA is 0.516 and after taxes and transfers is 0.389. The equivalent figures for Switzerland are 0.419 and 0.298, for Sweden are 0.435 and 0.273, for Spain are 0.490 and 0.329, for The Netherlands are 0.427 and 0.286, for Japan are 0.488 and 0.336, for Italy are 0.342 and 0.322, for Germany are 0.466 and 0.286, for France are 0.505 and 0.303, for Canada are 0.438 and 0.316 and for Australia are 0.469 and 0.334.

33 For comparison purposes, the equivalent 60 per cent and 50 per cent cut-off figures for Switzerland are 0.163 and 0.095, for Sweden are 0.174 and 0.097, for Spain are 0.214 and 0.150, for The Netherlands are 0.137 and 0.077, for Japan are 0.221 and 0.160, for Italy are 0.201 and 0.130, for Germany are 0.153 and 0.088, for France are 0.144 and 0.079, for Canada are 0.190 and 0.117 and for Australia are 0.217 and 0.146.

34 http://data.london.gov.uk/dataset/workforce-jobs/resource/5cc2f5d3-63ba-4a62-8 82b-7a3745c9bdce; https://londondatastore-upload.s3.amazonaws.com/dataset/ workforce-jobs/Workforce-jobs-ons.xls.

35 See the 'jam and Ryvita' analogy of Boris Johnson contained in Part 1 of the Evan Davis BBC television programme *Mind the Gap: London vs the Rest* which appears to pick up on an earlier analogy by Overman (2013) and which was broadcast on Monday 3 March 2014 BBC2 at 21.00–22.00. The analogy was intended to demonstrate that pouring increasingly more resources into London in the long run generates more UK-wide benefits which eventually spread out across the whole country in comparison to conditions under which resources are spread evenly and thinly across the UK. Indeed, this type of implicit assumption or explicit assertion, which as we see here is totally unsubstantiated, dominates much of the narrative of both Part 1 and Part 2 of the two-part television programme *Mind the Gap: London vs the Rest*, the second part of which was broadcast on BBC2 on Monday 10 March 2014 at 21.00–22.00. Moreover, this unsubstantiated assertion was again repeated by Boris Johnson on *The Andrew Marr Show* broadcast on BBC1 on Sunday 12 October 2014 at 09.00–10.00 who again claimed that London provides enormous economic benefits for the rest of the UK economy. The problem with this first argument is that the evidence simply does not support it. An alternative type of rhetoric typical in the London popular press is to accept that although the evidence regarding the growing UK interregional inequalities suggests that much of the rest of the UK economy does not in fact benefit from London's growth, it is still imperative that we must not implement any public policies which might favour other regions and thereby reduce London's productivity premium. See: www.theguardian.com/ news/datablog/2014/oct/10/london-uk-inequality-productivity-premium. This approach argues that *national* UK public policy should strive at all costs to maintain London's performance. The problem with this second argument is that the conclusion regarding the need to continually prioritise London cannot in any way be derived from the evidence on interregional inequality. The links between the former and the latter are very complex and are the subject of this book and, as such, most of these arguments are largely normative and subjective.

References

Armstrong, A., and Ebell, M., 2015, "The Economics of UK Constitutional Change: Introduction", *National Institute Economic Review*, 233, R1–R4.

Ballas, D., Rossiter, D., Thomas, B., Clarke, G. and Dorling, D., 2005, *Geography Matters: Simulating the Local Impacts of National Policies*, Joseph Rowntree Foundation, York.

Bank of England, 2014, "The UK Productivity Puzzle", *Bank of England Quarterly Bulletin Q2*, 114–128, June.

Barrell, R., Fitzgerald, J. and Riley, R., 2010, "EU Enlargement and Migration: Assessing the Macroeconomic Impacts", *Journal of Common Market Studies*, 48.2, 373–395.

Bennett, J.E., Li, G., Foreman, K., Best, N., Kontis, V., Pearson, C., Hambly, P. and Ezzati, M., 2015, "The Future of Life Expectancy and Life Expectancy Inequalities in England and Wales: Bayesian Spatiotemporal Forecasting", *The Lancet*, http://doi.org/10.1016/S0140-6736(15)60296-3.

BIS, 2012, *Commentary on Regional Economic Performance Indicators*, Department for Business, Innovation and Skills, London, September.

Bolt, G., and van Kempen, R., 2013, "Introduction Special Issue: Mixing Neighbourhoods: Success or Failure", *Cities*, 35, 391–396.

Briggs, A., 1983, *A Social History of England*, Book Club Associates, London.

Casson, M.C., and McCann, P., 1999, "Globalisation, Competition, and the Corporation: The UK Experience", in Whitman M., (ed.), 1999, *The Evolving Corporation: Global Imperatives and National Responses*, Group of Thirty, Washington DC.

CEBR, 2012, "One Pound in Five Earned in London Subsidises the Rest of the UK – Northern Ireland, Wales and North East Receive More Than a Fifth of Their Income as Subsidies from Outside of the Region", *News Release*, 13 February, Centre for Economics and Business Research, London, www.cebr.org.

Cheshire, P.C., 2009, "Policies for Mixed Communities: Faith-Based Displacement Activity?", *International Regional Science Review*, 32.3, 343–375.

CLC, 2004, *London's Linkages with the Rest of the UK Economy*, City of London Corporation, London.

CLC, 2009, *London's Place in the UK Economy, 2009–2010*, City of London Corporation, London.

CLC, 2011, *London's Competitive Place in the UK and Global Economies*, City of London Corporation, London.

CLC, 2012, *London's Finances and Revenues*, City of London Corporation, London.

Coyle, D., and Rosewell, B., 2014, "Investing in City Regions: How Does London Interact with the UK System of Cities and What Are the Implications of this Relationship", *Future of Cities Essay*, Foresight: Government Office for Science, London.

Crafts, N.F.R., 2005, "Regional GDP in Britain, 1871–1911: Some Estimates", *Scottish Journal of Political Economy*, 52.1, 54–64.

Cribb, J., Hood, A., Joyce, R. and Phillips, D., 2013, *Living Standards, Poverty and Inequality in the UK: 2013*, IFS Report R81, Institute for Fiscal Studies and the Joseph Rowntree Foundation, London.

CSO, 1990, *Regional Trends 25*, Central Statistical Office, ISSN 0261-1783, London.

CSO, 1992, *Regional Trends 27*, Central Statistical Office, ISSN 0261-1783, London.

CSO, 1995, *Regional Trends 30*, Central Statistical Office, HMSO, ISSN 0261-1783, London.

Curry, N., and Webber, D.J., 2012, "Economic Performance in Rural England", *Regional Studies*, 46.3, 279–291.

DEFRA, 2014, *Rural Development Programme in England: Draft Programme Published Alongside Strategic Environmental Assessment of the Programme*, March. See https://consult.defra.gov.uk/communications/consultation-on-the-strategic-environmental-assess/supporting_documents/Rural%20Development%20Programme%20for%20England%20draft%20Programme%20March%202014.pdf. See also: https://www.gov.uk/government/uploads/system/uploads/attachment_data/file/86100/Rural_Economy_Growth_Review.pdf.

DEFRA, 2015, *Statistical Digest of Rural England*, Department for Environment, Food and Rural Affairs, London, April.

DEFRA, DARD (NI), DRAH (WA) and RERAD (Scottish Government), 2014, *Agriculture in the United Kingdom 2013*, Department for Environment, Food and Rural Affairs, Department of Agriculture and Rural Development (Northern Ireland), Welsh Assembly Department for Rural Affairs and Heritage, Scottish Government Rural and Environment Research and Analysis Directorate, London.

Demos, 2011, *Good Growth: A Demos and PWC Report on Economic Wellbeing*, London.

Deutsche Bank, 2014, *Scotland: Wrong Turn*, London, 12 September.

Dickey, K., 2001, "Regional Earnings Inequality in Great Britain: A Decomposition Analysis", *Regional Studies*, 35.7, 605–612.

Dickey, H., 2007, "Regional Earnings Inequalities in Great Britain: Evidence from Quantile Regressions", *Journal of Regional Science*, 47.4, 775–806.

Dickey, H., 2014, "The Impact of Migration on Regional Wage Inequality: A Semiparametric Approach", *Journal of Regional Science*, 54.5, 893–915.

Dijkstra, L., Garcilazo, E. and McCann, P., 2013, "The Economic Performance of European Cities and City-Regions: Myths and Realities", *European Planning Studies*, 21.3, 334–354.

Dijkstra, L., Garcilazo, E., and McCann, P., 2015, "The Effects of the Global Financial Crisis on European Regions and Cities", *Journal of Economic Geography*, 15.5, 935–949.

Dorling, D., and Thomas, B., 2004, *People and Places: A 2001 Census Atlas of the UK*, Polity Press, Bristol.

Dorling, D., and Thomas, B., 2007, *Identity in Britain: A Cradle-to-Grave Atlas*, Polity Press, Bristol.

Dorling, D., Rigby, J., Wheeler, B., Ballas, D., Thomas, B., Fahmy, E., Gordon, D., and Lupton, R., 2007, *Poverty, Wealth and Place in Britain 1968 to 2005*, Joseph Rowntree Foundation, York.

Eurostat, 2007, *Regions in the European Union: Nomenclature of Territorial Units for Statistics*, Official Publications of the European Communities, Luxembourg.

Fielding, A.J., (Tony), 2012, *Migration in Britain: Paradoxes of the Present, Prospects for the Future*, Edward Elgar, Cheltenham.

Fothergill, S., and Gudgin, G., 1982, *Unequal Growth: Urban and Regional Employment Change in the UK*, Heinemann, London.

Gardiner, B., Martin, R., Sunley, P. and Tyler, P., 2013, "Spatially Unbalanced Growth in the British Economy", *Journal of Economic Geography*, 889–928.

Geary, F., and Stark, T., 2015a, "Regional GDP in the UK, 1861–1911: New Estimates", *Economic History Review*, 68.1, 123–144.

Geary, F., and Stark, T., 2015b, "What Happened to Regional Inequality in Britain in the Twentieth Century?", *Economic History Review*, Forthcoming, DOI: 10.1111/her.12114.

Gibbons, S., Overman, H.G. and Resende, G., 2011, *Real Earnings Disparities in Britain*, SERC Discussion Paper 65, Spatial Economics Research Centre, London.

Ginsborg, P., 2001, *Italy and Discontents 1980–2001: Family, Civil Society, State*, Penguin, London.

Goddard, J.B, and Champion, A.G., 1983, (eds.), *The Urban and Regional Transformation of Britain*, Methuen, London.

Goos, M., Manning, A. and Salomons, A., 2009, "Job Polarization in Europe", *American Economic Review*, 99.2, 58–63.

Gordon, I.R., and Kaplanis, I., 2014, "Accounting for Big City Growth in Low Paid Occupations: Immigration and/or Service Class Consumption", *Economic Geography*, 90.1, 67–90.

Gordon, I.R., and Monastiriotis, V., 2006, "Urban Size, Spatial Segregation and Inequality in Educational Outcomes", *Urban Studies*, 43.1, 213–236.

Green, A.E., and Livanos, I., 2015, "Involuntary Non-Standard Employment and the Economic Crisis: Regional Insights from the UK", *Regional Studies*, 49.7, 1223–1235.

Green, A.E., and Owen, D., 1998, *Where are the Jobless? Changing Unemployment and Non-Employment in Cities and Regions*, Policy Press and Joseph Rowntree Foundation, Bristol.

Harari, D., 2014, "Regional Economic Output Statistics", *Standard Note SN/EP/5795, Economic Policy and Statistics*, House of Commons Library, London.

HoC, 2014, *The Work of the Arts Council, Third Report of Session 2014–15*, House of Commons Select Committee on Culture, Media and Sport, London, 28 October.

Hughes, G., and McCormick, B., 1985, "Migration Intentions in the UK: Which Households Want to Migrate and Which Succeed?", *Economic Journal*, 95, 113–123.

Hughes, G., and McCormick, B., 1987, "Housing Markets, Unemployment and Labour Market Flexibility in the UK", *European Economic Review*, 31, 615–645.

HM Government, 2014, *United Kingdom Partnership Agreement Official Proposal: Part 1 Sections 1 and 2*, 13 August. See: https://www.gov.uk/government/uploads/system/uploads/attachment_data/file/306987/bis-14-755a-draft-united-kingdom-partnership-agreement-official-proposal-part-one.pdf.

Hunter, P., 2014, *Poverty in Suburbia: A Smith Institute Study into the Growth of Poverty in the Suburbs of England and Wales*, Smith Institute, London.

Iammarino, S., and McCann, P., 2013, *Multinationals and Economic Geography: Location, Technology, and Innovation*, Edward Elgar, Cheltenham.

IPPR-RF, 2013, *Beyond the Bottom Line: The Challenges and Opportunities of a Living Wage*, Lawton, K., and Pennycook, M., Institute for Public Policy Research and the Resolution Foundation, London.

Johns, H., and Ormerod, P., 2007, *Happiness, Economics and Public Policy*, Institute of Economic Affairs, London.

Layard, R., 2005, *Happiness: Lessons from a New Science*, Allen Lane, Penguin, London.

Lee, N., Sissons, P., Hughes, C., Green, A., Atfield, G., Adam, D. and Rodriguez-Pose, A., 2014, *Cities, Growth and Poverty: A Review of the Evidence*, Joseph Rowntree Foundation and the Work Foundation Alliance, York.

London Economics, 2013, "Regional Disparities in GDP per Capita in the EU after the Financial Crisis", *Noteworthy Statistics Briefing*, 28 May. See: www.londonecon.co.uk.

McCann, P., 2008, "Globalization and Economic Geography: The World is Curved, Not Flat", *Cambridge Journal of Regions, Economy and Society*, 1.3, 351–370.

McCann, P., 2009, "Economic Geography, Globalisation and New Zealand's Productivity Paradox", *New Zealand Economic Papers*, 43.3, 279–314.

McCann, P., 2013, *Modern Urban and Regional Economics*, Oxford University Press, Oxford.

McCann, P., and Acs, Z.J., 2011, "Globalisation: Countries, Cities and Multinationals", *Regional Studies*, 45.1, 17–32.

MacInnes, T., Aldridge, H., Bushe, S., Tinson, A. and Barry Horne, T., 2014, *Monitoring Poverty and Social Exclusion 2014*, Joseph Rowntree Foundation and New Policy Institute, York.

McLaren, J., Armstrong, J. and Gibb, K., 2013, *Measuring an Independent Scotland's Performance*, Centre for Public Policy Research Briefing Paper, University of Glasgow, 23 April.

McLaren, J., Armstrong, J. and Gibb, K., 2014, *Analysis of Scotland's Past and Future Fiscal Position: Incorporating GERS 2014 and the 2014 UK Budget*, CPPR Briefing Note, Centre for Public Policy Research, University of Glasgow, March.

Martin, R., 1988, "The Political Economy of Britain's North South Divide", *Transactions of the Institute of British Geographers*, 13, 389–418.

Martin, R., Pike, A., Tyler, P. and Gardiner, B., 2015, *Spatially Rebalancing the UK Economy: The Need for a New Policy Model*, Regional Studies Association, March.

MGI, 2011, *Urban World: Mapping the Economic Power of Cities*, McKinsey Global Institute.

Monastiriotis, V., 2014, "Regional Growth and National Development: Transition in Central and Eastern Europe and the Regional Kuznets Curve in the East and the West", *Spatial Economic Analysis*, 9.2, 142–161.

Newton, J.N., *et al.*, 2015, "Changes in Health in England, with Analysis by Regions and Areas of Deprivation, 1990–2013; A Systematic Analysis for the Global Burden of Disease Study 2013", *The Lancet*. See: www.thelancet.com/pdfs/journals/lancet/PIIS0140-6736(15)00195-6.pdf.

OECD, 2005, *OECD Regions at a Glance*, Organisation for Economic Development and Cooperation, Paris.

OECD, 2007, *OECD Regions at a Glance*, Organisation for Economic Development and Cooperation, Paris.

OECD, 2008, *International Migration Outlook*, Organisation for Economic Cooperation and Development, Paris.

OECD, 2009a, *OECD Regions at a Glance 2009*, Organisation for Economic Development and Cooperation, Paris.

OECD, 2009b, *OECD "Global Charter"/"Legal Standard" An Inventory of Possible Policy Actions*, ILO International Labor Organization, the IMF International Monetary Fund, the OECD Organisation for Economic Cooperation and Development, the World Bank and the World Trade Organization, Organisation for Economic Cooperation and Development, Paris.

OECD, 2011a, *OECD Regional Outlook 2011: Building Resilient Regions for Stronger Economies*, Organisation for Economic Development and Cooperation, Paris.

OECD, 2011b, *How's Life? Measuring Well-Being*, Organisation for Economic Cooperation and Development, Paris.

OECD, 2011c, *England: United Kingdom: OECD Rural Policy Reviews*, Organisation for Economic Cooperation and Development, Paris.

OECD, 2012, *International Migration Outlook 2012*, Organisation for Economic Cooperation and Development, Paris.

OECD, 2013a, *OECD Regions at a Glance 2013*, Organisation for Economic Development and Cooperation, Paris.

OECD, 2013b, *How's Life? 2013: Measuring Well-Being*, Organisation for Economic Cooperation and Development, Paris.

OECD, 2014a, *How's Life in Your Region? Measuring Regional and Local Well-Being for Policy-Making*, Organisation for Economic Cooperation and Development, Paris.

OECD, 2014b, *OECD Factbook 2014: Economic, Environmental and Social Statistics*, Organisation for Economic Growth and Development, Paris.

OECD, 2014c, "Focus on Inequality and Growth: Does Income Inequality Hurt Economic Growth?", Organisation for Economic Development and Cooperation, Paris.

ONS, 1996, *Regional Trends 31*, Office for National Statistics, HMSO, ISSN 0261-1783, London.

ONS, 1996, *Regional Trends 31*, Office for National Statistics, The Stationery Office, ISSN 013-0400, London.

ONS, 1997, *Regional Trends 32*, Office for National Statistics, The Stationery Office, ISSN 0261-1783, London.

ONS, 1998, *Regional Trends 33*, Office for National Statistics, The Stationery Office, ISSN 0261-1783, London.

ONS, 1999, *Regional Trends 34*, Office for National Statistics, The Stationery Office, ISSN 0261-1783, London.

ONS, 2000, *Regional Trends 35*, Office for National Statistics, The Stationery Office, ISSN 0261-1783, London.

ONS, 2001, *Regional Trends 36*, Office for National Statistics, The Stationery Office, ISSN 0261-1783, London.

ONS, 2004, *Regional Trends 38*, Office for National Statistics, The Stationery Office, ISSN 0261-1783, London.

ONS, 2008, *Regional Trends 40*, Office for National Statistics, ISSN 0261-1783, Palgrave Macmillan, Basingstoke.

ONS, 2012a, "The Geographical Concentration of Industries", Office for National Statistics, London, 20 July.

ONS, 2012b, "Measuring National Well-being: Life in the UK, 2012", Office for National Statistics, London, 20 November.

ONS, 2012c, "Measuring National Well-being: Summary of Proposed Domains and Measures", Office for National Statistics, London, 24 July.

ONS, 2012d, "Measuring National Well-being – Where we Live – 2012", Office for National Statistics, London, 24 July.

ONS, 2012e, "First ONS Annual Experimental Subjective Well-being Results", Office for National Statistics, London, 24 July.

ONS, 2012f, "Household Disposable Income Across the UK", Office for National Statistics, London, 13 July.

ONS, 2013a, "The Impact of Age and Location on Total Household Wealth", Office for National Statistics, London, 4 June.

ONS, 2013b, "Total Household Wealth by Region and Age Group", Office for National Statistics, London, 4 June.

ONS, 2013c, "Regional Economic Indicators, March 2013", Office for National Statistics, London, 4 June.

ONS, 2013d, "London's Economy has Out-Performed Other Regions Since 2007", Office for National Statistics, London, 13 March.

ONS, 2014, *Measuring National Well-being: European Comparisons*, Office for National Statistics, London, 18 June.

Overman, H.G., 2013, "The Economic Future of British Cities", *Centrepiece*, Summer.

Overman, H.G., and Gibbons, S., 2011, "Unequal Britain: How Real Are Regional Disparities?", *Centrepiece*, Autumn.

Phillips, D., 2013, *Government Spending on Benefits and State Pensions in Scotland: Current Patterns and Future Issues*, IFS Briefing Note BN139, Institute for Fiscal Studies, London.

Phillips, D., and Tetlow, G., 2013, *Taxation, Government Spending and the Public Finances of Scotland: Updating the Medium Term Outlook*, IFS Briefing Note BN148, Institute for Fiscal Studies, London.

Phillips, D., and Tetlow, G., 2014, *Policies for an Independent Scotland? Putting the Independence White Paper in its Fiscal Context*, IFS Briefing Note BN149, Institute for Fiscal Studies, London.

Plunkett, J., Hurrell, A. and Whittaker, M., 2014, *The State of Living Standards: The Resolution Foundation's Annual Audit of Living Standards in Britain*, Resolution Foundation, London.

Putnam, R, 1993, *Making Democracy Work: Civic Traditions in Modern Italy*, Princeton University Press, Princeton, NJ.

Rafferty, A., Rees, J., Sensier, M. and Harding, A., 2013, "Growth and Recession: Underemployment and the Labour Market in the North of England", *Applied Spatial Analysis and Policy*, 6.2, 143–163.

RBS/NatWest, 2014, *Regional Growth Tracker Q4 2014*, Royal Bank of Scotland and National Westminster Bank, London.

Rickard, S., 2012, "Liberating Farming from the CAP", *IEA Discussion Paper No. 37*, Institute of Economic Affairs, London.

Ricketts, J., Ilbery, B. and Kneafsey, M., 2006, "Distribution of Local Food Activity in England and Wales: An Index of Food Relocalization", *Regional Studies*, 40.3, 289–301.

Scott, P., 2007, *Triumph of the South: A Regional Economic History of Early Twentieth Century Britain*, Ashgate, Aldershot.

Scottish Government, 2014, *Outlook for Scotland's Public Finances and the Opportunities of Independence*, May.

SMCPC, 2014, *State of the Nation 2014: Social Mobility and Child Poverty in Great Britain*, Report Presented to Parliament Pursuant to Section 8B(6) of the Child Poverty Act 2010, Social Mobility and Child Poverty Commission, The Stationery Office, London, October.

Stiglitz, J.E., Sen, A. and Fitoussi, J-P., 2009, *Report by the Commission on the Measurement of Economic and Social Progress*, see: www.stiglitz-sen-fitoussi.fr/en/index.htm.

Stark, P., Gordon, C. and Powell, D., 2013, *Rebalancing Our Cultural Capital: A Contribution to the Debate on National Policy for the Arts and Culture in England*, www.theroccreport.co.uk.

Stark, P., Gordon, C., Powell, D. and Trow, S., 2014, *The PLACE Report: Policy for Lottery, the Arts and Community in England*, 25 April, www.theplacereport.co.uk.

The Economist, 2014, "Free Exchange: Joy to the World", 20 December.

The Economist, 2015a, "Dig for Victory!", 7 February.

The Economist, 2015b, "The Paradox of the Ghetto", 31 January.

Townroe, P., and Martin, R., 1992, (eds.), *Regional Development in the 1990s: The British Isles in Transition*, Jessica Kingsley, London.

Wadsworth, J., 2014, *Immigration, the European Union and the UK Labour Market*, Centre for Economic Policy Research, London.

Webber, D.J., Curry, N. and Plumridge, A., 2009, "Business Productivity and Area Productivity in Rural England", *Regional Studies*, 43.5, 661–675.

3 Debates regarding the economic role of cities

The UK experience in the light of international comparisons

3.1 Introduction

The economic role played by cities has emerged centre-stage of many current economic growth debates (OECD 2006; MGI 2011, 2012a, 2012b, 2013; PWC 2012; World Bank 2009) and this has never been more so in the case of the UK. A textbook approach suggests that in general large cities exhibit higher productivity than smaller cities, density and city-size are highly correlated and associated with productivity, city-size distributions exhibit regularities, and the recent experience of the modern era of globalisation favours big cities (Glaeser 2011; McCann 2013). While on the one hand this increasing focus on the economic role played by cities in the UK is very welcome on many levels, at the same time, some of the arguments and explanations variously offered in the academic, public-policy and popular press arenas have been less accurate, realistic or representative than might have been expected or desired. Many such discussions have tended to borrow 'off-the-shelf' types of stylised narratives from other arenas including the North American and Asian contexts with little consideration for their relevance in the UK context. Guaranteeing that our discussions of the UK context take place on the most solid grounding possible is imperative in order to ensure that our prognoses and prescriptions are as realistic as possible.

In order to do this it is again useful to consider the nature and performance of UK cities in a comparative perspective at both the domestic and international levels, as was the case with our analysis of the UK regions. In particular the OECD and European context provides powerful comparators which are highly relevant to the UK case. This allows us to then consider what insights can usefully be derived for UK cities from the international narratives currently popular in academic and policy circles, and to distinguish these from those issues that realistically are specific to the UK context. Therefore, in order to identify the extent to which the UK's cities reflect our simple textbook-type arguments and to consider how the UK experience relates to that of other countries, a straightforward way to organise this discussion is to examine the issues regarding the UK's levels of urbanisation, the relationships between city size and productivity, the nature of city-size distributions, and also to consider the effects of the 2008 global financial crisis on the UK's cities, in the light of the experience of a range of other countries.

3.2   Introduction to urban economic issues

During much of the post-war era, outside of the regional science and regional studies communities these discussions of urban economic issues were largely at the margin of economic thinking, and it is only during the last two and half decades that these issues have become increasingly central in debates regarding growth and development (World Bank 2009). In part this shift is a result of the impact of a series of key and seminal analytical publications, most notably by Krugman (1991a, 1991b), Porter (1990), Scott (1988) and Glaeser *et al.* (1992), all of which were published within a very short time frame of each other and which opened up these issues to a wide-ranging and influential audience. At the same time, however, there has also emerged a greater empirical awareness of the importance of these issues, largely as a result of the greater availability of data and the computer and GIS systems available to analyse these data. Third, and for the first time in economic history, as of 2008 more than half of the global population are urban residents (UNFPA 2007). Yet, while there is a much-needed and very welcome renewal of interest in these urban issues, at the same time it is important that a carefully nuanced approach is adopted when applying these insights to a country such as the UK. This is more pertinent in the case of many advanced economies, in which simple stories of ever-greater urbanisation and a growing importance of the role of cities in the economy are often not at all representative of the actual realities on the ground. Moreover, the need for careful consideration and nuancing is especially so in terms of discussions regarding the UK which displays many features not at all reflective of many of the currently popular narratives.

Many of the broader global discussion relate to countries which are currently experiencing large-scale population movements from rural to urban areas, as is typical in the BRIICS economies along with many other smaller newly emerging and newly industrialising countries (MGI 2011, 2012a, 2013; World Bank 2009). Indeed, similar processes are also under way in central and eastern European countries (European Union 2014).[1] These population movements reflect not only transitions to greater levels of urbanisation but also to higher levels of industrialisation. Yet, many of the more advanced OECD economies are not experiencing such shifts, and the UK is one such country. The spatial transformation of countries such as the UK reflects a quite different growth and development trajectory to those in many other parts of the world, and the appropriate cases against which to compare or benchmark the UK experience are rather different from those motivating discussions of these global trends. In order to address these various issues, it is useful to begin by very briefly reviewing some of the conventional wisdom regarding urban features as discussed in textbooks, and then to consider how these issues play out in the UK context in comparison to Europe, the USA and other parts of the industrialised world.

Agglomeration arguments suggest that urban areas will generally exhibit higher productivity than non-urban areas, and that in turn, large cities will generally exhibit higher productivity than smaller cities (Ciccone and Hall 1996). The various pieces of evidence on this point suggest that the range of urban scale advantages typically exhibit elasticities of between 0.02 and 0.08 with a mid-point of the order of 0.04–0.05 (Rosenthal and Strange 2004; de Melo *et al.* 2009; Duranton 2011; Brakman and van Marrewijk 2013; Bettencourt 2013; Bettencourt and West 2011, 2014; Glaeser 2014; Ahrend *et al.* 2014), and that urban density advantages exhibit very similar orders of magnitude (Duranton 2011; Brakman and van Marrewijk 2013; Ahrend *et al.* 2014) with European estimates being in the upper range (Brakman *et al.* 2009). These numbers imply that a doubling of city size is associated with a 4–5 per cent increase in productivity, and the evidence on European cities partly reflects these general patterns although with some differences. However, higher productivity levels associated with urban size do not imply that larger and more productive cities grow faster than smaller or less productive cities (OECD 2009a, 2009b, 2014), because this would also imply that all growth is explosive and everyone would eventually live in the same city.[2] As such, the links between urban productivity levels and urban productivity growth are issues to be examined in each case, and as we will see in the various chapters of this book, these relationships are contingent on many other factors. For example, some arguments suggest that urban growth is also associated with the diversity of sectors (Glaeser *et al.* 1992) and firm types (Duranton and Puga 2001) within a city, as well as the human capital (Berry and Glaeser 2007; Faggian and McCann 2009) and skills-sorting effects (Combes *et al.* 2008) operating between and within cities. At the same time, the ways in which these scale-related and structural aspects of cities allow them to respond to diverse economic shocks is also argued to lead to the emergence of systems of cities whose size distribution properties tend to correspond to something close to Zipf's Law. There have been several attempts to provide theoretical and statistical foundations for Zipf's Law (Duranton 2006, 2007; Gabaix 1999a, 1999b) as has also been the case with the questions regarding city-sectoral structure. In general, however, the evidence on these various urban growth issues is still rather mixed and depends on the data and estimation method employed (de Groot *et al.* 2009; Beaudry and Schiffauerova 2009) and the scale of aggregation adopted (Mameli *et al.* 2014). Yet, although the evidence on these structural issues is rather inconclusive, there is general agreement that cities are associated with higher productivity than non-urban areas. Moreover, many observers equate this observation with an assumption that cities are also associated with higher economic growth and these types of assumptions also currently dominate many narratives in the popular press[3] and policy circles, although in reality the relationship between urban productivity levels and economic growth is a much more complex matter. Indeed, the international evidence on this issue is very mixed and in Chapter 5 we will discuss these various matters in much more detail in the light of the urban and regional empirical evidence arising from the UK. At this point, however, this very brief sketch provides us with enough of a conceptual background in which to commence our empirical investigation of the performance of the UK's cities.

3.3   The economic performance of the UK's cities: OECD and EU evidence

In order to investigate the economic performance of the UK's cities in the following sections we employ the OECD urban data set (OECD 2012) which is based on a new standardised definition of 'urban' defined according to contiguous development patterns and commuting behaviour. The analysis in this chapter focuses primarily on the performance of the large UK cities and urban areas since the millennium, while historical analyses reaching further back are discussed in Chapter 5. In this OECD definition, urban areas can be split into 'cities' and 'towns and suburbs' while 'cities' can be further differentiated by the size of their urban centre, with 'metropolitan urban areas' being the larger cities and their commuting zones with a total of over 500,000 inhabitants. This OECD (2012) methodology, which is based on observations of dense commuting patterns as well as contiguity of the built environment, is more advanced than other urban classification systems such as the United Nations (2012) estimates and provides estimates of urban economic characteristics which can also allow for polycentric as well as monocentric-type urban structures. In our analysis here we will focus on the metropolitan areas of over 500,000 and in the later parts of the chapter we will also make use of the Eurostat metropolitan region data set which complements the OECD data set, and which allows us to examine a wider group of urban regions with populations above 250,000. On the basis of the OECD metropolitan urban area definition the UK is ranked as the ninth highest country in the OECD in terms of its share of the total population resident in cities of over 500,000 (OECD 2014)

Following the OECD 2012 definition of 'urban' we see in Table 3.1 that the 2010 population of London economy was 11,793,530, and this accounted for 19 per cent of the total UK population. Meanwhile the total 2010 population of the 14 next largest UK cities amounted to 13,480,937, which represents 21.73 per cent of the UK 2010 population. As such, in population terms the London economy accounted for 87.5 per cent of the total 2010 population of all of the UK's other cities of over 500,000 people. The only other advanced OECD country with a more skewed urban population pattern towards the largest city is Korea,[4] while that of France, in which Paris has 86.6 per cent of the population of the next largest 14 French cities, has an almost identical pattern to that of the UK. As of 2012 the total population of the UK's next 14 largest cities had increased to 13,700,726 while London had increased to

Table 3.1 UK city population (OECD 2012 'urban' definition)

City	2000	2004	2008	2010	2012
London	10,491,206	10.979,005	11,509,970	11,793,530	12,090,254
Manchester	1,694,458	1,739,830	1,802,638	1,841,199	1,855,530
Birmingham	1,742,448	1,792,821	1,851,478	1,884,199	1,919,346
Leeds	1,117,468	1,131,827	1,153,060	1,166,267	1,181,206
Glasgow	927,952	931,256	940,693	947,809	956,593
Liverpool	925,818	920,304	925,871	933,127	943,613
Sheffield	837,321	845,640	865,548	880,237	898,347
Newcastle	1,012,051	1,020,740	1,038,273	1,050,561	1,065,336
Edinburgh	673,741	689,390	712,749	727,620	744,798
Nottingham	777,652	798,828	822,653	835,625	849,372
Leicester	594,440	619,137	646,244	660,817	676,119
Bristol	719,067	745,811	777,485	795,481	815,137
Cardiff	594,891	610,814	629,868	640,632	652,280
Bradford	488,443	502,809	525,428	540,172	557,445
Portsmouth*	540,687	554,272	569,184	577,191	585,604
UK	58,785,246	59,435,480	61,192,125	62,026,962	63,256,141

Source: OECD Metropolitan Database.
* includes Southampton.

Table 3.2 UK city population growth 2000–2012 (OECD 2012 'urban' definition)

City	% Population Change 2004–2012	% Population Change 2008–2012	% Population Change 2000–2012	Average Annual % Growth Rate in Population 2000–2012
London	10.1	5.0	15.2	1.189
Manchester	6.6	2.9	9.5	0.794
Birmingham	7.1	3.6	10.2	0.809
Leeds	4.3	2.4	5.7	0.463
Glasgow	2.7	1.7	3.1	0.254
Liverpool	2.5	1.9	1.9	0.159
Sheffield	6.2	3.8	7.2	0.588
Newcastle	4.4	2.6	5.3	0.429
Edinburgh	8.0	4.5	10.5	0.839
Nottingham	6.3	3.2	9.2	0.738
Leicester	9.2	4.6	13.7	1.079
Bristol	9.3	4.8	13.3	1.05
Cardiff	6.8	3.6	9.6	0.77
Bradford	10.9	6.1	14.1	1.107
Portsmouth	5.7	2.9	8.3	0.667
UK	6.4	3.3	7.6	0.613

Source: OECD Metropolitan Database.

12,090,254, such that London has increased further to some 88.2 per cent of the population of the 14 next largest cities.

In terms of city population changes, using these new more advanced OECD urban calculations we see in Table 3.2 that the populations of the 15 largest UK cities have all increased since the millennium. In terms of annual growth rates, 10 of the top 15 cities of the UK have grown faster during the period 2000–2012 than the UK national average. On an annualised basis we see that London has grown at the fastest rate of any UK city since the millennium with a population growth rate which is almost twice that of the national average. In population terms other fast-growing cities relative to the UK national average are Bradford, Leicester, Bristol, Manchester, Edinburgh, Birmingham, Nottingham, Cardiff and Portsmouth. The cities whose population growth lags the national average are Leeds, Liverpool, Sheffield, Newcastle and Glasgow. Relatively faster population growth is therefore mainly oriented to cities in the south and midlands of the country while slower population growth is more focused on the UK's more northerly cities.

When comparing population growth rates, part of the problem is simply a matter of scale. In absolute terms the population changes in London are of a different order of magnitude to all other UK urban areas. If we plot the absolute population changes for each urban area during the period 2000–2007 against the urban area population changes during the period 2008–2010 we

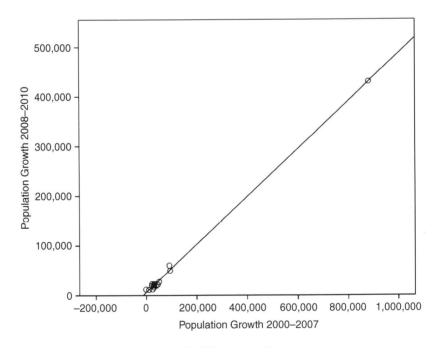

Figure 3.1 Population growth and the UK metropolitan urban areas

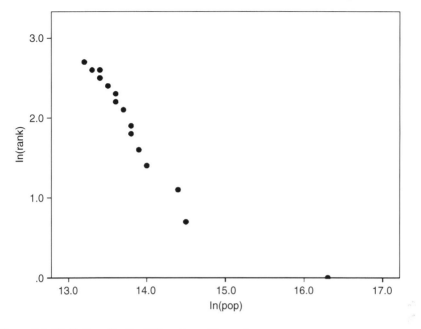

Figure 3.2 Zipf's Law for the UK metropolitan urban areas

see in Figure 3.1 that the population changes of London totally dominate all of the other cities. These population changes for each city during the decade following the millennium, allied with the existing urban population distribution of the UK at the millennium, also means that the UK urban distribution is far from what might be expected according to Zipf's Law. Figure 3.2 plots the natural log of the rank of the urban area against the natural log of the population size for the 15 largest UK urban areas in 2012. As we see in Figure 3.2, given the size of London, the lower parts of the urban distribution corresponding to the smaller of the large cities appear to conform to the requisite Zipf's Law slope parameters, whereas as we move up the urban distribution the city sizes all increasingly diverge from a Zipf's Law-type size distribution. If there is any genuine underlying economic rationale for a Zipf's Law construction, then according to this argument, the eight largest cities after London are too small. These cities are Birmingham, Manchester, Leeds, Newcastle, Glasgow, Liverpool, Sheffield and Nottingham.

In terms of population density, the UK is one of the most densely populated large economies, and amongst the OECD countries is only surpassed by Japan, Korea, Israel, Belgium and The Netherlands. Similarly, the 15 large UK cities of over 500,000 people are also very densely populated by OECD standards with, as we see in Table 3.3, 8 such cities displaying densities of over 1000 persons per square kilometre, while 5 more display population densities of the order of 600–900 persons per square kilometre. Many of the other

Table 3.3 UK city population density (OECD 2012 'urban' definition) per square km

City	2000	2004	2008	2012
London	1515.88	1586.36	1663.08	1746.93
Manchester	1180.8	1212.42	1256.19	1313.95
Birmingham	1198.27	1232.91	1273.25	1319.92
Leeds	647.43	655.75	668.05	684.36
Glasgow	1084.26	1088.12	1099.15	1117.72
Liverpool	1663.17	1653.26	1663.82	1695.13
Sheffield	754.43	759.10	779.86	809.41
Newcastle	352.25	355.28	361.38	370.80
Edinburgh	526.53	538.76	557.01	582.06
Nottingham	700.12	719.18	735.04	764.69
Leicester	540.79	563.26	587.92	615.10
Bristol	890.70	915.01	963.06	1009.70
Cardiff	807.32	828.93	854.79	885.21
Bradford	1101.01	1133.39	1184.38	1256.55
Portsmouth	1261.51	1293.21	1328.00	1366.31
UK	241.10	246.18	251.66	260.84

Source: OECD Metropolitan Database.

OECD cities of similar sizes to these large UK cities generally exhibit similar or lower population densities than the UK's major cities.[5] Meanwhile, many of Europe's metropolitan areas tend to be more densely populated than those in North America or Australasia.

The UK metropolitan areas are generally amongst the top third most densely populated metropolitan areas in the OECD (OECD 2013) and furthermore they are also becoming more densely populated at the second fastest rate of any OECD country (OECD 2013). On the other hand, although in aggregate London's population density is high, when compared with other European capital cities, the central city population densities in London are actually relatively low at every spatial distance away from the city centre up to a 15 km radius with cities such as Madrid, Athens, Stockholm, Vienna and Paris all exhibiting much higher city-centre densities. Indeed, the centre-city population densities of London are far more typical of much smaller cities such as Berlin, Brussels, Amsterdam, Budapest and Lisbon (European Union 2014).[6]

In terms of changes to urban population densities we see from Table 3.4 that all of the UK's large cities have experienced ongoing density increases between 2000 and 2012. In most cases these urban population densities started to increase more rapidly in the period after 2004 as the UK population itself started to increase more rapidly in response to increasing immigration trends. In addition, widespread urban regeneration and gentrification were operating in many cities, most likely spurred on by the expansion of the UK higher education system. The population density growth was particularly

Table 3.4 Growth in UK city population density (OECD 2012 'urban' definition)

City	% Population Density Change 2000–2004	% Population Density Change 2004–2008	% Population Density Change 2008–2012	% Population Density Change 2008–2012
London	4.64	4.83	5.04	15.5
Manchester	2.68	4.83	4.59	11.3
Birmingham	2.89	3.27	3.66	10.2
Leeds	1.28	1.87	2.44	5.70
Glasgow	0.35	1.01	1.68	3.08
Liverpool	−0.59	0.63	1.88	1.92
Sheffield	0.61	2.73	3.78	7.28
Newcastle	0.86	1.71	2.6	5.26
Edinburgh	2.32	3.38	4.50	10.5
Nottingham	2.72	2.20	4.03	9.22
Leicester	4.15	4.37	4.62	13.7
Bristol	2.72	5.25	4.84	13.4
Cardiff	2.67	3.11	3.56	9.64
Bradford	2.94	4.49	6.09	14.1
Portsmouth	2.51	2.69	2.88	8.3
UK	2.1	2.2	3.6	8.19

Source: OECD Metropolitan Database.

marked in the case of London, the city which also exhibited the highest population density rates. London's population density growth was followed by Bradford, Leicester,[7] Bristol, Manchester, Edinburgh, Birmingham, Cardiff, Nottingham and Portsmouth, all of which experienced population density growth rates higher than the UK average over the period 2000–2012. In contrast, the cities of Sheffield, Newcastle, Glasgow and Liverpool all experienced population density growth rates which were lower than the UK average.

In Table 3.5 we see that the total output of the London economy is US$548,778.03 in 2000 prices, and this accounts for 27.8 per cent of UK 2010 output. Meanwhile, the total output of the next 14 largest UK cities is US$415,672,000 in 2000 prices, which represents 21 per cent of the 2010 UK national output. In other words, the total output of the UK's 14 next largest cities is only 73.8 per cent of the output of London alone. Moreover, the relative dominance of London over all of the UK's other large cities as a group has increased slightly since the 2008 economic crisis by 1.15 percentage points, or the equivalent of the economy of Sheffield. The only other city whose share of national output has increased markedly since the economic crisis is Bristol whose share increased by 0.7 of a percentage point. As with the case of population distributions, the only advanced OECD country whose urban output pattern is more skewed towards the dominant city than the UK is Korea while again that of France is almost identical to the UK. The total output of the 14 next largest French cities is 69 per cent of the output of Paris.

These figures highlighting the enormous dominance of the London economy also have implications for the national growth contribution of metropolitan

Table 3.5 UK city GDP (OECD 2012 'urban' definition)

City Economic Performance	GDP 2000 Millions (% of UK GDP)	GDP 2008 Millions (% of UK GDP)	GDP 2010 Millions (% of UK GDP)
London	435,983.44 (26.0)	562,487.26 (27.65)	548,778.03 (27.8)
Manchester	59,972.85*	60,843.07 (2.99)	59,653.08 (3.02)
Birmingham	54,503.93*	55,044.05 (2.70)	53,266.64 (2.70)
Leeds	40,071.59*	40,637.10 (1.99)	37,894.33 (1.92)
Glasgow	29,694.60	36,734.59 (1.80)	34,877.81 (1.77)
Liverpool	23,147.04	25,869.94 (1.27)	24,953.73 (1,26)
Sheffield	19,047.35	22,857.25 (1.12)	22,432.87 (1.14)
Newcastle	22,536.18	26,849.30 (1.32)	26,215.76 (1.32)
Edinburgh	24,825.22	32,456.42 (1.59)	31.564.29 (1.60)
Nottingham	21,394.06	25,112.90 (1.23)	23,826.28 (1.20)
Leicester	16,956.01	20,138.90 (0.09)	19,255.58 (0.10)
Bristol	24,314.87	30,092.62 (1.47)	30,421.51 (1.54)
Cardiff	16,090.63	19,328.69 (0.10)	18,600.24 (0.09)
Bradford	12,086.44	13,167.50 (0.06)	13,148.73 (0.07)
Portsmouth	14,931.22	19,473.80 (0.10)	19,561.90 (0.10)
UK	1,734,098	2,116,466 (100)	2,040,348 (100)

Source: OECD Metropolitan Database. All figures in US$ 2005 PPP prices.
* Initial data refer to 2005 figures not 2000 data.

areas. In the case of the UK the metropolitan areas contributed 57 per cent of national economic growth between 2000 and 2010, and this share was some 16–17 percentage points above the 2010 employment and population shares of the UK's metropolitan areas. In other words, this implies that UK metropolitan areas accounted for more than 40 per cent more economic growth during this period than would have been expected simply on the basis of their populations. Yet, while this may appear to be a high figure pointing to the pre-eminent role of cities in growth, the equivalent values for France, Ireland, Denmark, Belgium and even Greece are even higher (OECD 2013). Moreover, of the 57 per cent of UK economic growth which is accounted for by metropolitan areas between 2000 and 2010, some 38 per cent was due to a London effect alone (OECD 2013). In other words, all of the UK's metropolitan areas outside of the capital together accounted for only 19 per cent of national economic growth 2000–2010. This represents half of London's output growth contribution during this same period. In other words, in the UK London alone accounted for two-thirds of the growth contribution of metropolitan areas to the national economy 2000–2010. Clues as to why this is the case can be gleaned from Table 3.6.

The changes in the respective cities' shares of UK national output are driven by very different growth experiences between the UK's cities since the millennium, and in particular there are marked differences in growth patterns prior to, and subsequent to, the 2008 economic crisis. Table 3.6 shows that during the period 2000–2008 all of the UK's large cities increased their

Table 3.6 Growth in UK city GDP (OECD 2012 'urban' definition)

City	% Change in GDP 2000–2008	% Change in GDP 2008–2010	% Change in GDP 2000–2010	Difference between City and UK GDP Change 2000–2008	Difference between City and UK GDP Change 2008–2010	Difference between City and UK GDP Change 2000–2010
London	29.0	−2.4	25.8	+7.0	+1.19	+8.2
Manchester	1.5*	−1.96	−0.53*	−20.5*	+1.63	−17.1*
Birmingham	0.09*	−3.2	−2.27*	−21.9*	+0.39	−19.9*
Leeds	1.4*	−6.75	−5.43*	−20.6*	−3.16	−23.0*
Glasgow	23.7	−5.05	17.5	+1.7	−1.46	−0.1
Liverpool	11.8	−3.5	7.8	−10.2	+0.09	−9.8
Sheffield	20.0	−1.85	17.8	−2.0	+1.74	0.2
Newcastle	19.1	−2.36	16.3	−2.9	+1.23	−1.3
Edinburgh	30.7	−2.75	27.1	+8.7	+0.84	+9.5
Nottingham	17.4	−5.12	11.3	−4.6	−1.53	−6.3
Leicester	18.8	−4.38	13.6	−3.2	−0.79	−4.0
Bristol	23.8	1.1	25.1	+1.8	+4.69	+7.5
Cardiff	20.1	−3.78	15.6	−1.5	−0.19	−2.0
Bradford	8.9	−0.14	8.8	−13.1	+3.45	−8.8
Portsmouth	30.4	0.04	31.0	+8.4	+3.99	+13.4
UK	22.0	−3.59	17.6			

Source: OECD Metropolitan Database.

* Initial data refer to 2005 figures rather than 2000 figures. However, as we see in the detailed data explanations in Table 3.9, these figures for 2005–2010 are likely to be very accurate reflections of the changes evident in 2000–2010.

economic output in real terms. However, when measured against UK national performance the picture is rather different. As we see in Table 3.6, when compared with the UK national performance 2000–2008 the cities which grew faster than the UK economy were Edinburgh, London, Portsmouth, Bristol and Glasgow. In contrast, in the aftermath of the 2008 global economic crisis, only the cities of Cardiff, Leicester, Nottingham, Glasgow and Leeds contracted faster than the UK average. Yet, many of the cities which had contracted by less than the UK in the immediate post-crisis period such as Liverpool and Bradford, had barely grown during the pre-crisis decade. The combination of these changing fortunes means while the UK economy grew by 17.6 per cent overall in real terms between 2000 and 2010, the large cities located in the south of England along with Scotland have all grown by between a quarter and a third, thereby significantly out-performing the UK economy during the first decade of the twenty-first century. In marked contrast, between 2000 and 2010 the output of the cities in the midland and northern regions of England along with Wales have all grown at a slower rate than the UK national economy.

If we consider the relationship between urban area output growth during the pre-crisis period and during the post-crisis period, as we see from Figure 3.3 there is some level of correlation between these two periods. Broadly speaking, those cities exhibiting strong output growth in the pre-crisis period also tended to exhibit lower output declines in the post-crisis period.

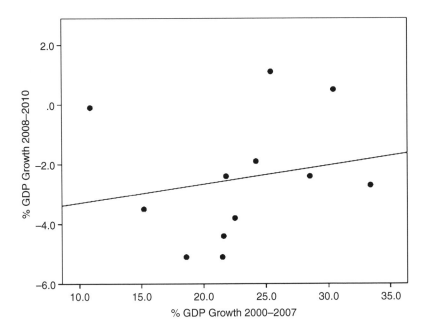

Figure 3.3 GDP growth in the UK metropolitan urban areas

In other words, post-crisis output resilience appears to be related to pre-crisis dynamism.

As we have seen in Tables 3.1 and 3.2 urban population growth since the millennium has tended to be greater in the cities of the south and midlands of the UK, and weaker in the northern regions of the UK. Meanwhile, as we see in Tables 3.5 and 3.6 urban output growth has also tended to be stronger in the cities of the south and weaker in the cities of the midland and northern regions of the UK. The combination of a growing economy since the millennium, UK population growth which accelerated after 2004 and which was primarily oriented towards cities, and then a period of declining output in all of the UK's cities in the aftermath of the 2008 economic crisis, means that GDP per capita of the UK's cities has increased since the millennium but then has subsequently fallen back to varying degrees since 2008, as indicated in Table 3.7 and Table 3.8.

In Table 3.7 we also see that the simple core-periphery model of regional productivity described in Chapter 2 is almost exactly replicated here for the UK cities. As we see in Table 3.7, 5 of the UK's largest 15 cities exhibit GDP per capita scores higher than the UK average while 8 of these urban areas exhibit GDP per capita scores below the UK average. All of the major metropolitan urban areas in southern England plus Scotland exhibit a productivity performance which is higher than the UK average while all of those cities located in the other UK regions exhibit productivity levels which are below the UK average. In other words, as with the findings in Chapter 2, the cities with GDP per capita scores higher than the UK average are all located in the south of England and Scotland. Meanwhile, all of the cities whose GDP per capita scores are below the UK average are located in the midlands and northern regions of England plus Wales.

Meanwhile, we also see from Table 3.8 that 11 of the UK's largest 15 urban areas exhibit GDP per capita scores which are above the average GDP per capita score for the region in which the city is located, as might be expected from urban economic theory. In contrast, we see that the cities of London, Liverpool, Bradford and Portsmouth all exhibit GDP per capita scores which are below those of the regions in which they are located. Yet, London is an exception here because the OECD-TL2/EU-NUTS1 large statistical region of 'Greater London' does not include large parts of the surrounding commuter hinterland, all of which is included in the OECD (2012) 'urban' definition. However, this is not the case with the other cities and regions, in that all of the other OECD-TL2/EU-NUTS1 regions are much bigger than the OECD (2012) definitions of the 'urban' areas contained within them. The GDP per capita of Portsmouth is below that of the South East regional average but above the UK average, while the GDP per capita scores of both Liverpool and Bradford are below both their own local regional average as well as the UK national average.

Not surprisingly, the GDP per capita of London is much higher than for any other city, with Edinburgh being the next most productive city at some

Table 3.7 UK city GDP per capita (OECD 2012 'urban' definition)

Metropolitan Area Economic Performance	City GDP per Capita 2000	City GDP per Capita 2008	City GDP per Capita 2010	GDP per Capita 2010 of Region	Index of City GDP per Capita 2010 relative to UK GDP per Capita
London	41,557	48,870	46,532	57,082	141.5
Manchester	34,195*	33,752	32,395	28,377	98.5
Birmingham	30,168*	29,730	28,270	26,873	85.9
Leeds	35,259*	35,243	32,491	26,485	98.8
Glasgow	32,000	39,051	36,798	30,172	111.9
Liverpool	25,002	27,941	26,742	28,377	81.3
Sheffield	22,747	26,408	25,485	26,485	77.5
Newcastle	22,268	25,860	24,954	23,637	75.9
Edinburgh	36,846	45,537	43,380	30,172	131.9
Nottingham	27,511	30,527	28,513	26,539	86.7
Leicester	28,524	31,163	29,139	26,539	88.6
Bristol	33,814	38,705	38,243	29,360	116.3
Cardiff	27,048	30,687	29,034	22,782	88.3
Bradford	24,745	25,060	24,341	26,485	74.0
Portsmouth	27,615	34,214	33,892	34,903	103.0
UK	29,499	34,587	32,894	32,894	32,894

Source: OECD Metropolitan Database. All figures in US$ 2005 PPP prices.
* Initial data refer to 2005 not 2000 data.

Table 3.8 UK city relative GDP per capita (OECD 2012 'urban' definition)

Metropolitan Area	GDP per Capita 2000	GDP per Capita 2008	GDP per Capita 2010	GDP per Capita of Urban Area Relative to Region 2000	GDP per Capita of Urban Area Relative to Region 2008	GDP per Capita of Urban Area Relative to Region 2010[a]
London	140.9	147.0	141.5	84.0	84.2	81.5
Manchester	103.7*	101.5	98.5	117.4*	120.4	114.2
Birmingham	92.4*	89.4	85.9	106.5*	110.5	105.2
Leeds	105.0*	106.0	98.7	127.3*	130.1	122.6
Glasgow	108.5	117.5	111.9	121.1	125.1	121.9
Liverpool	84.8	84.1	81.3	94.9	99.7	94.2
Sheffield	77.1	79.5	77.5	96.0	93.7	84.7
Newcastle	75.5	77.8	75.9	107.7	106.3	105.5
Edinburgh	124.9	137.0	131.9	139.5	145.9	143.8
Nottingham	93.3	91.8	86.7	114.1	115.6	107.4
Leicester	96.7	93.8	88.6	118.3	118.1	109.7
Bristol	114.6	116.4	116.3	131.4	134.4	130.3
Cardiff	91.7	92.3	88.3	129.8	133.4	127.4
Bradford	83.8	75.4	74.0	104.4	92.5	91.9
Portsmouth	93.6	102.9	103.0	85.2	98.6	97.1
UK	100	100	100			

Source: OECD Metropolitan Database. All figures in US$ 2005 PPP prices.

* Indices refer to 2005 not 2000 data.

[a] If we observe the OECD-TL3/EU-NUTS3 local government areas then we see that all of the UK's local government areas encompassing the central business districts of each of the UK's major cities exhibit GDP per capita levels which are higher than their respective regions, except for the cases of Bradford and Portsmouth. However, these city-centre local government areas generally fail to capture the full economic structure of the wider urban area, and they are often surrounded by urban local government areas whose GDP per capita levels are far lower, and in many cases well below the regional average. The OECD metropolitan urban area and the Eurostat metropolitan urban region estimates have all been developed precisely in order to overcome the measurement problems associated with governance-area fragmentation.

10 percentage points below London. Bristol and Glasgow are a further 15 and 20 percentage points below Edinburgh, respectively. Apart from Portsmouth, the rest of the UK's large cities exhibit productivity levels below the national average. The economically weakest cities of Bradford, Sheffield, Newcastle and Liverpool all display GDP per capita levels which are 20–25 per cent below the UK average and some 50–65 percentage points below the figures for Edinburgh and London, respectively.

As we see in Table 3.8, currently ten of the UK's largest cities exhibit productivity levels which are higher than the regions in which they are located. In contrast, as we also see in Table 3.8, Liverpool, Bradford, Sheffield, Portsmouth and London all exhibit productivity levels below the average for the region in which they are located. In the case of London, the reason is that the London metropolitan area is much larger than the Greater London region, as this also includes lower productivity hinterland areas of commuting.

Relative to the UK national average GDP per capita, the levels of city GDP per capita have changed noticeably in some of these cities since the millennium. As we see in Table 3.8 the cities whose GDP per capita scores relative to the UK average increased during the period 2000–2010 were London, Glasgow, Edinburgh, Bristol, Portsmouth plus Newcastle and Sheffield. In contrast, all of the rest of the large cities located in the midlands and northern regions of England plus Wales have all experienced falls in their GDP per capita relative to the UK average. Yet, in reality, as we see in Table 3.8 and 3.9, the increases in the GDP per capita scores for Sheffield and Newcastle relative to the UK average are largely negligible, to the extent that their relative positions are more or less unchanged over a ten-year period. Meanwhile, the reason why the relative increase for London is also very low is because it is the GDP per capita changes in the London economy, heavily weighted by the size of the London economy, which largely have driven the changes in the overall UK per capita GDP scores.

While most of the cities located outside of the south of England or Scotland have seen their productivity performance decline relative to the UK average between 2000 and 2010, in addition, even in comparison to the regions in which they are located, most of these cities have also seen falls in their relative productivity. These trends have had different features at different points. In Table 3.8 we see that relative to their own regions, 11 of these cities had increased their productivity premium between 2000 and 2008, but these productivity premia also then fell in the aftermath of the global financial crisis. By 2010 ten of these cities exhibited lower productivity premia relative to their own regions than they did in 2000. In contrast Glasgow, Edinburgh and Portsmouth increased their productivity premia over their respective regions during this period. As such, many of the UK's urban productivity advantages have been declining over recent years even relative to the cities' own hinterland regions.

Once again, if we consider the relationship between the growth in urban GDP per capita during the pre-crisis period and also the post-crisis period we

Table 3.9 Changes in UK city GDP per capita (OECD 2012 'urban' definition)

City	% Change in GDP per Capita 2000–2008	% Change in GDP per Capita 2008–2010	% Change in GDP per Capita 2000–2010	Percentage Point Difference between Urban and UK% Growth in GDP per Capita 2000–2010
London	17.6	−4.78	12.0	+0.5
Manchester†	−4.63*	−4.02	−8.47* (−9.5†)	(−21.0†)
Birmingham†	−5.76*	−4.91	−10.4* (−10.1†)	(−21.6†)
Leeds†	−1.71*	−7.81	−7.80* (−12.6†)	(−24.1†)
Glasgow	22.0	−5.76	15.0	+3.5
Liverpool	11.7	−4.29	6.95	−4.55
Sheffield	16.1	−3.49	12.0	+0.5
Newcastle	16.1	−3.50	12.1	+0.6
Edinburgh	23.6	−4.73	17.7	+6.2
Nottingham	11.0	−6.59	3.64	−7.86
Leicester	9.25	−6.49	2.15	−9.35
Bristol	14.5	−1.19	13.1	+1.6
Cardiff	13.5	−5.39	7.34	−4.16
Bradford	1.27	−2.87	−1.63	−13.1
Portsmouth	23.9	−0.0.94	22.7	+11.2
UK	17.2	−4.89	11.5	

Source: OECD Metropolitan Database. All figures in US$ 200% PPP prices.
* For Manchester, Birmingham and Leeds the 2000–2010 GDP and GDP per capita growth rates are calculated on the original 2005 data from the OECD Metropolitan Area.
† These figures are calculated using the Eurostat Metropolitan Region database. For Manchester, Birmingham and Leeds the 2000–2010 GDP and GDP per capita growth rates are calculated on the original 2005 data from the OECD Metropolitan Area database. However, it is likely that these estimates very closely reflect the 2000–2010 growth. The reason is that these 2005–2010 OECD estimates also very closely reflect the 2001–2011 growth changes calculated using the Eurostat Metropolitan Region data set. According to the Eurostat figures, as we see in Table A3.3 the output of the Manchester metropolitan region fell from 56,441.10 million Euros (in current prices) in 2001 to 55,590.80 million Euros in 2011, while population increased from 2,515,914 to 2,682,537 during the same period. As such, GDP per capita fell by 7.8 percentage points between 2001 and 2011. This is very close to the −8.47 percentage point fall for the OECD Manchester metropolitan area. Meanwhile, according to the Eurostat metropolitan region definition the output of the Birmingham–West Midlands economy fell by 10.1 percentage points between 2001 and 2011. This is very close to the −10.4 percentage point OECD metropolitan area figure reported here. Meanwhile, according to the OECD the population of the Birmingham metropolitan area also grew by some 9.5 per cent during the same period. This would suggest that the Birmingham GDP per capita had fallen by 19.9 percentage points between 2001 and 2011. Finally, according to the Eurostat metropolitan region definition the output of the Leeds economy fell by 12.6 percentage points between 2001 and 2011. Meanwhile, the OECD metropolitan area figures show that the population of Leeds remained almost exactly the same between 2000 and 2011 and the Eurostat population figures for Leeds metropolitan region (1,068,000) are very close to the OECD figures. As such, the Eurostat metropolitan region output estimate for Leeds is likely to be a very accurate proxy for the OECD metropolitan area of Leeds.

see a similar set of relationships as we observed for the urban output, even allowing for the differential urban population changes described above. As we see in Table 3.9, those cities experiencing strong GDP per capita growth in the pre-crisis era also tended to exhibit lower GDP per capita declines in the post-crisis era. Again, in terms of GDP per capita a city exhibiting pre-crisis dynamism is more likely to be relatively resilient in the post-crisis era. The geography of metropolitan urban area growth during the period 2000–2010 is heavily weighed in favour of the south of England and Scotland and against the midlands and northern regions of England and Wales. The geographical patterns of urban performance appear to closely mirror those of the regional patterns described in the previous chapter.

As with urban area output changes, in the case of urban area GDP per capita changes we also see in Figure 3.4 that there is some level of correlation between pre-crisis dynamism and post-crisis resilience. The urban areas which exhibited strong GDP per capita growth in the pre-crisis era also exhibited either higher growth or lower declines in the post-crisis period. Again, pre-crisis urban economic dynamism is related to post-crisis economic resilience.

As we have already seen, our population data suggest that many of the UK's cities are too small according to a Zipf's Law-type argument, and this might suggest that such cities ought to expand or be allowed or encouraged to expand. However, a problem with this type of logic is that urban expansion

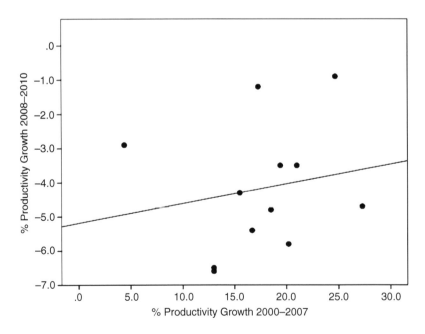

Figure 3.4 GDP per capita growth in the UK metropolitan urban areas

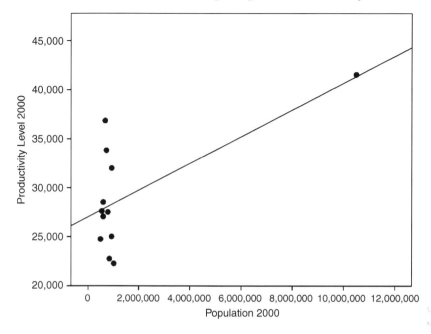

Figure 3.5 Productivity-scale relationships in the UK metropolitan urban areas
            in 2000

requires that these cities exhibit sufficient productivity premia and associated
wage premia to attract firms, investment and people into these cities in order
to drive these expansions. Yet, in the case of the UK urban system the relationship between productivity and scale appears to be rather different from
what one might expect from textbook-type descriptions.

As we see in Figure 3.5 and Figure 3.6 on first inspection there appears
a weak link between productivity and city size in the UK urban system,
although this link is totally dominated by the case of London. However, if
London is removed from the sample any such relationship between urban
scale and productivity largely disappears. Moreover, this is true irrespective of whether we consider 2000 or 2010 data. The lack of any systematic
relationship between productivity and city-scale in the UK has also been
observed.

In a similar vein to the productivity-scale types of relationships, as we have
seen above, we know from urban economic theory and widespread empirical
evidence from around the world that urban productivity is generally associated with both urban scale and urban density. As such, we might expect that
either the largest UK cities or the most densely populated UK cities are likely
to exhibit the highest productivity premia. In the case of urban density, as
we see in Figure 3.7 and Figure 3.8 there initially appears to be something
of a link between urban population density and urban productivity. Again,

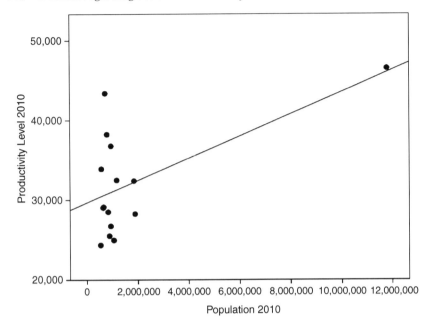

Figure 3.6 Productivity-scale relationships in the UK metropolitan urban areas
          in 2010

however, if London is removed from Figure 3.7 and Figure 3.8 it becomes
clear that there is no such relationship.

The lack of any clear relationship between urban scale and urban productivity or between urban density and urban productivity amongst the 14 largest cities after London, poses significant theoretical challenges in translating
the textbook lessons from urban economics to the UK urban system. Simple
recommendations that many of the UK's next largest cities after London
should be allowed or encouraged to expand in population some two or three
times their current size appear rather problematic because these cities do not
exhibit the requisite productivity premia or associated wage premia required
to induce such expansions. As we have seen, while all but 2 of these 15 largest
cities exhibit productivity levels which are higher than the regions in which
they are located, only 5 actually exhibit productivity levels higher than the
UK average, and all of these cities are located just in the south of England or
in Scotland. Indeed, from all of the evidence provided here regarding urban
population, population density, urban GDP and GDP per capita, the overall
picture suggest that since the millennium the large cities located in the south
of England along with those located in Scotland have grown faster than the
overall UK average, while those located in the midlands and northern regions
of England along with Wales have grown slower than the national average. As
such, the city patterns described here from the OECD urban database of large

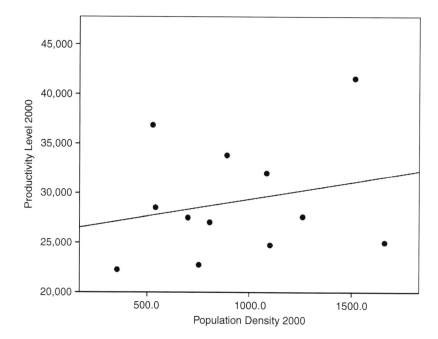

Figure 3.7 Productivity-density relationships in the UK metropolitan urban areas in 2000

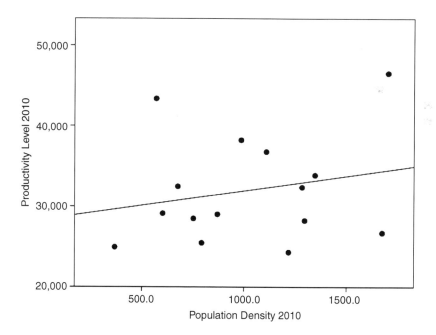

Figure 3.8 Productivity-density relationships in the UK metropolitan urban areas in 2010

cities of over 500,000 people closely reflect the regional patterns described in the previous chapter.

One potential caveat with the evidence provided so far is that it is based only on a sample of 15 cities which together account for just under 41 per cent of the UK population. We know that some 74 per cent of the UK population live in urban areas, and therefore by restricting our analysis to just these 15 largest metropolitan areas of over 500,000 people we are potentially ignoring the information available from almost half of the UK's urban areas. As such, it could be argued that we may be missing, or at least only crudely capturing, some of the key features of the UK's urban system. Therefore, in order to respond to this potential criticism we are able to make use of a larger and more detailed data set constructed by the European Commission and Eurostat in conjunction with the OECD. The Eurostat 'metropolitan region' data set[8] is constructed according to exactly the same principles as the OECD urban data set, except for the fact that the Eurostat definitions include all cities of over 250,000 and these are also adjusted to fit as closely to groupings of NUTS3 areas as possible. As such, the definition of a 'metropolitan region' employed by the European Commission and Eurostat[9] is almost exactly consistent with the new OECD definition of 'metropolitan urban' area, except for the variations associated with allowing for the geographical definitions of the relevant EU-NUTS3 areas. This EU metropolitan region data set provides us with detailed information on the 35 largest UK metropolitan regions all with

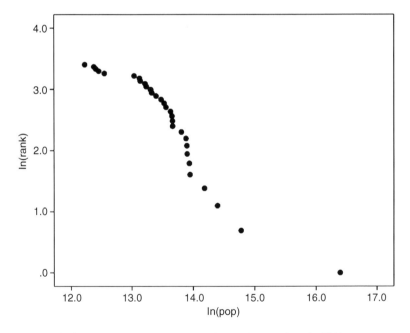

Figure 3.9 Zipf's Law and the UK metropolitan urban regions in 2010

populations over 250,000, and in aggregate account for 42,822,926 people in 2012, or some 67.7 per cent of the total UK population.

Using these Eurostat metropolitan region data we can again trace out the population distributions of the UK's urban areas. As we see in Figure 3.9 the metropolitan region data again confirm that the upper echelons of the UK's urban system do not correspond closely to Zipf's Law whereas the lower echelons of the urban system appear to do so. The London metropolitan region has a population which is larger than the combined population of the UK's next largest eight metropolitan regions, and as we see in Table A3.2, in terms of gross value-added (GVA) the London metropolitan region economy is larger than the next 18 metropolitan regions combined.

We know that these city population and output distributions change slowly over time as the performance of cities varies according to different shocks and conditions. From Figure 3.10 we see that in absolute scale terms the patterns of population growth in the UK's metropolitan regions are again dominated by London, the orders of magnitude of which dwarf all other UK metropolitan regions.

As well as population changes, we can also consider the relationship between the changes in the output performance of the metropolitan regions in the period prior to, and post, the economic crisis. As we see in Figure 3.11, using these data suggests that there is a slightly negative relationship between the growth in GDP of the metropolitan regions prior to, and post, the 2008

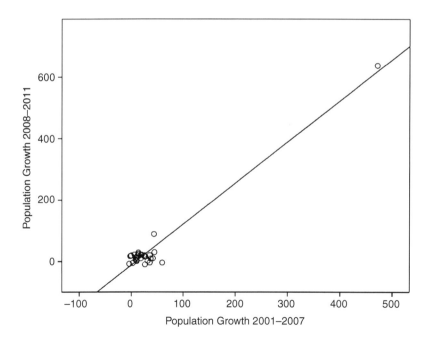

Figure 3.10 Population growth in the UK metropolitan urban regions in 2010

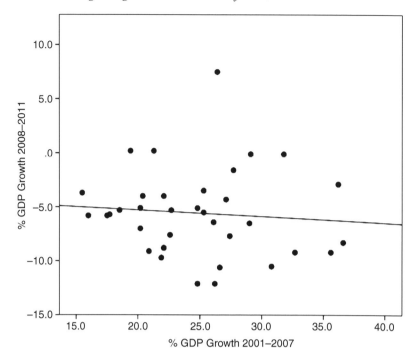

Figure 3.11 GDP growth in the UK metropolitan urban regions

global economic crisis. As such, it appears that many of the metropolitan regions which grew strongly in the earlier period have since struggled in the aftermath of the crisis. Given our OECD urban area results, this might suggest that any negative effects have been more marked on the smaller metro regions than on the larger ones, as has also been the case across many parts of Europe (European Union 2013a). Yet, the observed patterns for the UK demonstrate that the relationship is in reality very weak, and a wide range of possible outcomes is clearly evident.

Allowing for population changes as well as output changes, we can consider the productivity performance of the UK's metropolitan regions. If we consider productivity growth in the periods prior to, and post, the 2008 crisis, we see from Figure 3.12 that there is again a weakly negative relationship. This suggests that in terms of output growth, some of the metropolitan regions which performed well immediately prior to the crisis have been badly affected since the crisis.

The metropolitan region data on output and productivity levels before and after the 2008 global economic crisis suggest that many of the UK's metropolitan regions are very vulnerable to adverse shocks and lack resilience (Fingleton *et al.* 2012). Indeed, further direct evidence for this is available from the metropolitan region data set. The most recent data for 2011 show

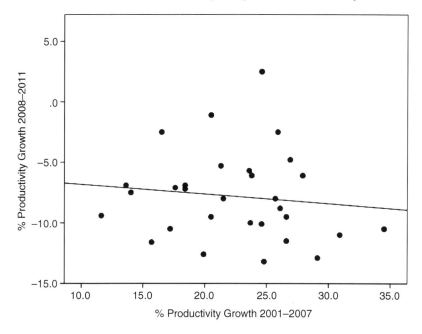

Figure 3.12 Productivity growth in the UK metropolitan urban regions

that the overall productivity for the UK as a whole in 2011 was exactly equal to the EU average, so this conveniently provides a direct set of very useful domestic and international benchmarks. From these data we can also see that in 2011 the 35 metropolitan regions of the UK exhibited an average productivity level which was 105 per cent of the UK and EU average. Meanwhile, the average productivity level for the non-metropolitan regions was 88 per cent of the UK and EU average. These non-metro regions represent all of the small town and rural parts of the UK. However, while the metro-region and non-metro region figures might suggests that metropolitan regions are typically more productive than non-metro areas, just as textbook descriptions would suggest, in actual fact in the UK only 7 out of these 35 metropolitan regions exhibit worker productivity levels which are higher than the UK or EU average,[10] and only 5 exhibit productivity levels which are above the average for the UK's metropolitan regions.[11] Most noticeably, 20 of the 35 metropolitan regions exhibit worker productivity levels below the non-metro average, while the remaining 8 exhibit productivity levels below the UK average but above the non-metro average. As such, 80 per cent of the UK's metropolitan regions of over 250,000 people under-perform relative to the national average. Obviously, the average productivity levels for the metropolitan regions are heavily skewed by the small number of major metropolitan regions whose productivity levels are very high, and of course, most importantly here, is the case of London.[12] Yet, some 57 per cent of the UK's metropolitan regions under-perform in terms of productivity in comparison to the UK's non-metropolitan regions.

These results are in part due to the severe effects of the 2008 crisis on the UK's metropolitan urban regions. As we see in Table A3.3, in current prices only 1 out of 35 of the UK's metropolitan regions, namely Aberdeen, in 2011 was producing at an output level which is higher than it was in 2007. In the period immediately prior to the 2008 global financial crisis, some two-thirds of UK metropolitan regions of over 250,000 exhibited productivity levels which were above the UK average productivity levels for non-metropolitan regions, while only a third of such metropolitan regions exhibited productivity levels below the non-metropolitan average (Dijkstra *et al.* 2013). Now we see that the shares have changed dramatically. As we see in Table A3.4 some 20 out of 35 metropolitan regions, or rather 57 per cent of the UK's metropolitan regions, exhibit GVA per worker levels which are below the average for the UK's non-metropolitan regions. Even using current prices the GDP per capita scores of 26 out of 35, or rather 74.2 per cent, of the UK's metropolitan regions, now exhibit lower scores than they did in 2001. The reason are partly that the output of the cities has grown much slower since 2001 than their populations, but more importantly the cumulative rise in prices over the decade has been far higher than the increases in output. The dramatic downward shift in the fortunes of the UK's metropolitan urban regions means that the adverse impacts of the crisis on urban productivity have been more severe in the UK than in almost any other EU economy (European Union 2013a). Yet, at the same time, these downward shocks are not only the result of the 2008 crisis. Many of the UK's cities had experienced little or no productivity growth in the years following the millennium. As outlined in the previous chapter, this was reflected in the rapidly declining growth fortunes of primarily urban regions in the early years of the twenty-first century.

As we see in Figure 3.13 and Figure 3.14 in the case of UK metropolitan regions there is little or no relationship between urban scale and urban productivity. We have already observed this result using the OECD data for the 15 largest metropolitan urban areas with populations over 500,000 and we see exactly the same results here using the metro region data for those 35 metropolitan regions with populations over 250,000.

Recent work from the OECD (Ahrend *et al.* 2014) shows that immediately prior to the onset of the global financial crisis, the UK relationship between urban scale and productivity was little different from zero, except for the case of London whose productivity performance was much larger than would be expected simply on the basis of scale, and this was also the case with some of London's satellite cities. This situation is clearly depicted in Figures 3.5, 3.6 and Figures 3.13 and 3.14. The data suggest that there must be strong agglomeration-type effects operating in London, although whether these are specifically agglomeration mechanisms or also a mix of other effects will be discussed in the following chapters. Yet, across a wide range of UK city sizes there appear to be basically no agglomeration effects which are associated

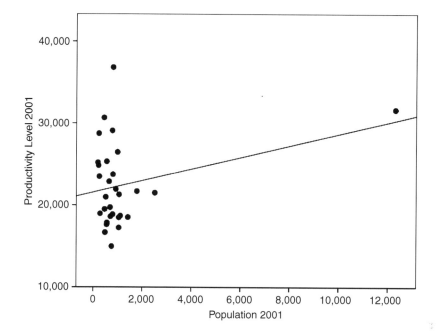

Figure 3.13 Productivity-scale relationships in the UK metropolitan urban regions 2001

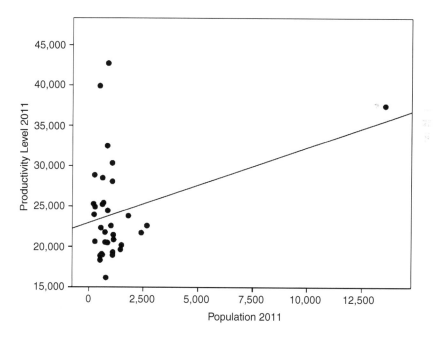

Figure 3.14 Productivity-scale relationships in the UK metropolitan urban regions 2011

with urban scale (Ahrend *et al.* 2014; OECD 2015). Indeed, the analysis presented here confirms that this is the case for the 14 next largest metropolitan urban areas after London, and for the majority of the 35 metropolitan urban regions. Nor do the scale-distribution arguments associated with Zipf's Law appear to provide many clues as to the UK's lack of apparent agglomeration economies. Arguing that many of the UK's largest cities need to become larger would only be persuasive if such as scale-productivity relationships were clearly evident, as indeed they are in many other countries. However, the OECD and Eurostat evidence presented here suggests that there is no such relationship in the UK, thereby largely undermining the city-size distribution arguments. As such, neither the UK urban system as a whole nor many of the UK's largest cities conform to many of the standard textbook type of descriptions of urban productivity premia. This raises the question as to whether the UK's cities under-perform in economic terms, or whether there is something else about the UK's city-size distribution which is problematic.

3.4   OECD and EU comparisons of UK urban economic performance

A useful way of beginning to address these questions regarding the performance of the UK's cities is by comparing the performance of the UK's cities with those in other countries. A similar approach was adopted for assessing the performance of the UK's regions in the previous chapter. Yet, identifying good comparator countries and cities against which to benchmark the performance of the UK's cities and regions is not so straightforward and requires some consideration. When discussing urban and regional issues it is often tempting in academic circles to compare countries such as the UK with the experience of the USA (MGI 2012b). Yet, in terms of urban scale and growth, amongst the OECD advanced economies the USA is part of a group which also comprises Japan and Korea and to some degree also Canada, Australia and New Zealand, all of whose urban features are rather different from many of the other European OECD economies, including the UK (McCann and Acs 2011). The UK, in contrast, shares far more with other western European countries in terms of most of its urban features, such as the typical sizes of the cities, the distances and geographical spacing between the cities, the city population densities, the urban-rural productivity premia, the urban responses to the 2008 economic crisis, and also the ages of many of the cities. In other words, automatic comparisons with the other 'Anglo-Saxon' or 'Western Offshoot' (Maddison 2006) economies of North America or Australasia need to be complemented with other comparisons from Europe. The approach we will adopt here, therefore, is to compare the performance of the UK's cities with those comparator cities across the OECD as a whole and then also to consider their performance with respect to other European cities. This way we are able to build up both a comprehensive and a nuanced picture of the performance and characteristics of the UK's major urban areas.

We do know that urbanisation and industrialisation are closely related phenomena and that as a whole the advanced industrial economies exhibit urbanisation levels of some 78 per cent (United Nations 2012). However, within this large and diverse group there are noticeable variations. On the basis of standard administrative data, North America, Japan, Korea and Australasia all exhibit urbanisation levels approaching 80 per cent (MGI 2011; UN-Habitat 2012) while Europe as a whole exhibits urbanisation levels of 72.6 per cent (UN-Habitat 2012). Yet, western Europe exhibits high urbanisation rates, with 77 per cent of the EU-15 population being urban residents (MGI 2013), a level which is almost exactly the same as the North American and Australasian economies. The high levels of urbanisation in western Europe, parts of Asia and Australasia approaching some 80 per cent of the population reflect the fact that in earlier periods the advanced OECD economies have all experienced significant rural-urban migration flows associated with shifts away from an economy dominated by primary sector activities to an economy dominated by secondary-sector and then on to tertiary-sector activities, the latter two of which are overwhelmingly urban activities (MGI 2013). These United Nations urbanisation estimates are calculated on the basis of national statistical population registers which are then broken down by administrative area definitions. However, these types of data often face problems in that commuting patterns and contiguous urban development do not always closely follow governance structures. Moreover, governance structures and definitions vary greatly across countries. Therefore, in order to overcome these limitations we are able to employ the OECD (2012) 'urban' data discussed in detail here. These data allow us to compare the features and performance of cities within the UK on a standardised and common basis and they also allow for international performance comparisons with urban areas in other countries.

These more recent and advanced OECD figures used here tell a somewhat different story to the United Nations or MGI (2011, 2013) data. In particular, according to these definitions the North American economy is rather less urbanised than has been previously understood, with the share of the US and Canadian populations who are 'urban' dwellers being 69 per cent and 73 per cent respectively (OECD 2013), while that of the OECD as a whole is 68 per cent, ranging from 87 per cent in Korea to 38 per cent in Slovakia (OECD 2013). The highest levels of urbanisation are in the UK and The Netherlands at 74 per cent, followed by Spain (69 per cent), France (65 per cent), Germany (64 per cent) and Belgium (59 per cent), with the rest of the western European economies exhibiting urbanisation rates of between 48 per cent in Norway and 58 per cent in Austria (OECD 2013). According to these definitions, apart from Korea the only other OECD countries with higher urbanisation rates than the UK are Luxembourg, Turkey and Japan.[13] As such, the UK is already an extremely highly urbanised society by the standards of the OECD, the European Union and the global economy.

These features are reflected in the foregoing sections which all point to the UK being a very highly urbanised economy with a large proportion of its population living in cities whose population densities are high by OECD standards. As we saw in Tables 3.1 and 3.4 the 2010 share of the UK's national population living in the UK's metropolitan areas of 500,000 or over was just under 41 per cent, while these same cities accounted for 48.8 per cent of UK output (OECD 2013). Meanwhile, amongst OECD countries the average contribution of metropolitan areas to national output is over 57 per cent, while for employment and population it is just below 50 per cent. As such, the UK's shares regarding the contribution of large metropolitan areas to national output and national employment are each case some 9 percentage points below the OECD averages and actually much closer to the OECD median values.

For the OECD as a whole the average figure for the growth contribution of metropolitan areas during this period is 60 per cent and this is higher than the 2010 OECD average metropolitan area output, employment and population shares of 57 per cent, 49 per cent and 48 per cent, respectively. These differences reflect the fact that between 2000 and 2010 larger cities have increased their relative contributions to overall OECD growth (OECD 2013). A similar pattern is also observable for the UK. The contribution of UK metropolitan areas to aggregate UK economic growth between 2000 and 2010 was 57 per cent, and this figure was noticeably higher than the respective 2010 output, employment and population shares for the UK, which were just under 50 per cent and some 40 per cent (OECD 2013).[14] For comparison purposes (OECD 2013) the equivalent figures for the contribution of metropolitan areas to national economic growth in Japan, Korea, USA and Canada are 75 per cent, 66 per cent, 63 per cent and 54 per cent respectively. Amongst the European economies the only countries with higher shares than the UK are Greece (80 per cent), France (74 per cent), Hungary (72 per cent), Estonia (65 per cent), Denmark (62 per cent) and Ireland (58 per cent). In all of the other European economies the contribution to national economic growth which was accounted for by large metropolitan areas during 2000–2010 was lower than the 57 per cent share evident in the UK, with the lowest values being in Slovakia with 35 per cent and The Netherlands with 38 per cent (OECD 2013).

In terms of the national growth contribution of the dominant city, during the period 2000–2010 London accounted for 38 per cent of the UK's overall economic growth, with 19 per cent of national economic growth accounted for by the remaining metropolitan areas. In other words, London alone accounted for two-thirds of the total growth contribution of the UK's metropolitan areas (OECD 2014) between 2000 and 2010.[15] Meanwhile, as we have already seen from the OECD urban data set, the 2010 share of UK output accounted for by London was 27.8 per cent, while the combined share of UK output of the next 14 largest UK metropolitan areas was 21 per cent. In other words London accounted for 57 per cent of the 2010 output of the UK's 15 largest metropolitan areas. This means that the contribution of the London metropolitan area economy to overall UK economic growth between 2000 and 2010 was some 10 percentage points higher than would be expected purely on the basis of its output share. In contrast, the contribution to overall UK economic growth 2000–2010 accounted for by the next 14 largest UK metropolitan areas was some 2 percentage points below what would have been expected on the basis of their output share. Many of the UK's cities have clearly under-performed as drivers in the years following the millennium.

Similarly, in terms of employment-generation activities, we see that while the average OECD employment-creation share of large metropolitan areas between 2000 and 2012 was 56 per cent, the equivalent figure for the UK was 48 per cent (OECD 2013). As such, the UK's large cities appear to have played much less of an employment-generation role over recent years than has been the case in most other OECD economies. At the same time, although the inter-urban variation in both UK urban employment growth rates and also UK urban unemployment rates is just above the OECD average, the rate of increase in UK urban unemployment in the aftermath of the 2008 global financial crisis was slightly below the OECD average (OECD 2013). As such, both in terms of output changes and also employment changes, as a group the UK's large cities are somewhat less instrumental in national economic performance than is the case in many other OECD countries. We know that London is a very strong and growing economy which we see from Table A4.1 has marginally out-performed the UK economy in terms of GDP per capita growth between 2000 and 2010. However, it appears that many of the UK's cities are under-performing. The evidence on the earlier sections suggests that these under-performing cities are all located in the midlands and northern regions of England along with Wales. In order to examine whether these UK cities really are under-performing we are able to conduct a similar benchmarking exercise to that which was undertaken in the previous chapter for the case of UK regions, whereby in this case UK metropolitan areas can be compared with appropriate OECD comparator metropolitan areas.

In order to do this we examine the productivity growth performance of the UK's ten large metropolitan areas of over 500,000 which are located in the midlands and northern regions of England along with Wales. All of these cities exhibit productivity levels which are below the UK average and have under-performed in terms of GDP per capita growth between 2000 and 2010 in comparison to London. In contrast, the five large UK metropolitan areas located in the south of England and Scotland exhibit GDP per capita levels above the UK average. Moreover, they have all out-performed the UK economy in terms of GDP per capita growth 2000–2010 and four of these cities have also out-performed London in this regard. As with the regional benchmarking exercise undertaken in the previous chapter, our aim here at this stage is to identify how the group of ten economically weaker UK cities perform relative to other similar cities across the OECD, in order to assess the extent to which they have indirectly benefited from spillovers associated with the growth of the five more prosperous cities in the south of England and in Scotland. In order to identify appropriate comparator cities for these ten cities we identify all of those OECD metropolitan areas which displayed GDP

per capita scores in 2000 within the range displayed by the ten UK metropolitan areas at the same time period. The list of comparator cities for 2000
includes many cities from France, Southern Europe and Japan along with the
four poorest large metropolitan areas within the USA and the three poorest
metropolitan areas in Canada. We then calculate the average GDP per capita
growth rates of the ten UK metropolitan areas during the period 2000–2010
and also we calculate the difference between each of these rates and the UK
aggregate GDP per capita growth rate during the same period. We then repeat
exactly the same exercises for each of the 69 comparator metropolitan areas
across the OECD.

As we see in Table 3.10 and also in detail in the Appendix in Table A3.1
the average GDP per capita growth performance of the ten UK metropolitan
areas which are not located in the south of England or in Scotland stands at
1.04 per cent and relative to the overall UK growth in GDP per capita stands
at −10.5 per cent. These UK cities have clearly heavily under-performed relative to their OECD comparators whose average GDP per capita growth
during the period 2000–2010 was 12.3 per cent, and some +3.41 per cent
relative to their national economies. During this period the UK was actually one of the fastest growing advanced OECD economies, so our results
may be somewhat affected by the inclusion of the three slowest growing
large OECD economies, namely Japan, Italy and France. If we remove the
27 Japanese cities in the sample, we see that the average growth in GDP per
capita of the metropolitan areas in Europe and North America was 14.35
per cent and some +3.71 per cent relative to national growth. As such, the
under-performance of the UK's cities becomes even more noticeable. Even
though the Japanese economy was largely flat during this period, in terms
of absolute growth of GDP per capita the comparator group of Japanese
cities markedly out-performed the UK cities by almost 9 percentage points
and by more than 13 percentage points in terms of GDP per capita growth
relative to the national economy. Similarly, the cities of France also markedly
out-performed these UK cities on both criteria. Indeed, in terms of the absolute growth of GDP per capita the performance of these particular UK cities is actually more similar to the experience of Italian cities than any other
country, although the Italian cities perform stronger relative to their national
economy. Indeed, whatever is the index against which these metropolitan
areas are benchmarked, it is a fact that all of the UK's large cities located in
the midland and northern regions of England or in Wales, have performed
very poorly by OECD standards.

In marked contrast, if we exclude the case of London which we discuss in
detail in Chapter 4, the productivity growth performance of the UK's other
four large metropolitan areas of over 500,000 that are located either in the
south of England or in Scotland, is seen to be very strong. These metropolitan areas exhibit GDP per capita levels above the UK average and have also
out-performed both the UK economy and London in terms of GDP per capita growth 2000–2010. Indeed, the growth of Portsmouth has been so strong

Table 3.10 UK-OECD metropolitan urban area productivity growth comparisons for ten UK cities

City	GDP per Capita 2000	GDP per Capita 2010	% Change in GDP per Capita 2000–2010	Percentage Point Difference between Urban and National % Growth in GDP per Capita 2000–2010
Manchester	35,795[†]	32,395	−9.5[†]	−21.0[†]
Birmingham	31,466[†]	28,270	−10.1[†]	−21.6[†]
Leeds	37,175[†]	32,491	−12.6[†]	−24.1[†]
Liverpool	25,002	26,742	6.95	−4.55
Sheffield	22,747	25,485	12.0	+0.5
Newcastle	22,268	24,954	12.1	+0.6
Nottingham	27,511	28,513	3.64	−7.86
Leicester	28,524	29,139	2.15	−9.35
Cardiff	27,048	29,034	7.34	−4.16
Bradford	24,745	24,341	−1.63	−13.1
Average for 10 UK Cities			**1.04**	**−10.5**
Average for 72 OECD Cities			**12.96**	**3.82**
Average for 45 European and North American Cities			**15.28**	**4.35**
Average for 11 French Cities			**+5.84**	**+1.36**
Average for 3 Italian Cities			**+0.26**	**+2.42**
Average for 27 Japanese Cities			**+9.87**	**+2.96**

Source: OECD Metropolitan Database. All figures in US$ 2005 PPP prices.
[†] The values are imputed by using the 2010 values and the growth rates calculated by comparing the OECD metropolitan area output and population estimates with the Eurostat metropolitan region estimates.

that it has moved from being part of the group of economically weaker cities whose productivity levels were below the UK average in 2000 to being part of the group of economically stronger cities whose productivity levels are above the 2010 UK average. In these circumstances, in order to benchmark the relative performance of these more prosperous cities, the most appropriate comparison group are those OECD cities whose productivity performance in 2010 is within the same range as this group of four relatively prosperous UK cities. Table A3.2 in the Appendix provides the details of the group of 89 comparator OECD metropolitan areas which includes many cities from North America, western Germany and other northern European economies. As such, in terms of geographical distribution this is a very different comparison group to the group of comparator cities for the ten economically weaker

Table 3.11 UK-OECD metropolitan urban area productivity growth comparisons for four UK cities

City	GDP per Capita 2000	GDP per Capita 2010	% Change in % Growth in GDP per Capita 2000–2010	Percentage Point Difference between Urban and National % Growth in GDP per Capita 2000–2010
Bristol	33,814.50	38,242.91	13.09	1.59
Portsmouth	27,615.27	33,891.56	22.72	11.22
Glasgow	32,000.14	37,572.01	17.41	5.91
Edinburgh	36,846.84	45,166.39	22.57	11.07
Average for 4 UK Cities			**18.94**	**7.45**
Average for 89 OECD Cities			**11.80**	**0.782**
Average for 47 Non-USA OECD Comparator Cities			**17.81**	**4.235**
Average for 42 USA Comparator Cities			**5.064**	**−3.083**

Source: OECD Metropolitan Database. All figures in US$ 2005 PPP prices.

UK metropolitan areas described above which as we see from Table A3.1 comprised mainly cities from southern Europe, France and Japan.

As we see in Table 3.11, the GDP per capita growth performance of the four relatively prosperous UK metropolitan areas located in the south of England or in Scotland has been relatively stronger than the average for their comparison group, irrespective of whether their performance is measured in absolute terms of relative to the national growth performance and irrespective of whether or not the many US cities are included in the comparison group. The economic performance of this group of four UK cities is clearly in marked contrast to the performance of the other group of ten UK cities located in the midlands and north of England plus Wales.

Our OECD-wide metropolitan area benchmarking analysis therefore produces almost exactly the same results as our OECD-wide regional benchmarking exercise presented in the previous chapter, albeit with somewhat even starker results. As with the case of UK regions, when we examine metropolitan area performance there is no evidence whatsoever that the strong growth performance of either London or the prosperous large cities in the south of England and Scotland, has provided any benefits whatsoever to the UK's other large metropolitan areas located in the midland and northern regions of England and Wales. Again, the evidence, if anything, points in the other direction.

These OECD-wide data along with the Eurostat data clearly suggest that in the case of many of the UK's large urban areas, the expected textbook-type links between cities, urban scale, productivity and economic growth appear to be either very weak or non-existent, except in a few specific cases. Moreover, there appear to be few or no wider positive spillover or linkage effects associated with urban prosperity, other than within certain UK regions. As such, the evidence suggests that the success of London and other cities in the south of England and Scotland appears to have had no positive growth effects whatsoever on cities in other parts of the UK. Indeed, without any discussion about causality at this stage, it is clear from the benchmarking exercises presented in this chapter and in the previous chapter that if anything, the success of cities and regions in the south of England and in Scotland may actually have hampered the growth performance of the cities and regions in the midlands and north of England, Wales and Northern Ireland.

Given that the UK is such an urbanised and densely populated country these observations therefore pose something of a puzzle and raise many questions. Do these metropolitan area productivity growth figures represent the under-performance of the UK's cities or are they a reflection of a different UK urban structure, relative to other countries? Why is it the case that urban output is below typical OECD values when the UK is so urbanised? Why do UK's urban responses to the crisis appear to be weaker than in many other countries?

Answering these questions *prima facie* is slightly problematic because these average OECD-wide values are heavily dependent on the data from Japan, Korea, Mexico and the United States, which as a group contain very large numbers of very large cities in comparison to most other OECD countries. If we therefore also focus just on the European economies which are much closer in terms of many urban characteristics to the UK we see that the contribution of large metropolitan areas to national output, employment and population is lower in the UK than in Belgium, Greece, France and Austria, while it is higher in the UK than the rest of the European economies (OECD 2013). As such, when benchmarking the UK against other European cities the structure of the UK urban system appears to be less unusual than is the case when we compare the UK with the OECD as a whole.

These much closer European comparisons can also be very instructive for assessing the performance of the UK's cities because many features of European cities do reflect standard textbook-type discussions. For example, Europe's cities tend to exhibit higher levels of tertiary-educated human capital (European Commission 2007), higher activity rates (ESPON 2013) and higher levels of a range of different knowledge indicators (European Union 2011) than are typically observed in small towns, suburbs and non-urban areas. In particular, these knowledge-related advantages appear to be especially associated with capital cities, with Europe's capital cities dominating the top positions in the productivity rankings (Eurostat 2013). However, while these features are typically observed across all of Europe, there are many ways in which the UK still appears as something of an outlier. For example, higher education attainment rates in the UK are lower in major cities than in other areas, and similarly the number of patents per capita is lower in the UK's major cities than in other areas (European Union 2011). Although the latter result is driven primarily by the effects of Oxford and Cambridge, even so, the overall knowledge-related indicators do not point in favour of widespread agglomeration effects operating in the UK's major cities, and amongst the EU's economies, the UK appears to be unique in this regard. Similarly, the overall level of satisfaction with the quality of life in UK large cities is mediocre by European standards, with no UK city even in the top 25 per cent of the rankings (European Union 2013b).

As we see in the Appendix in Table A3.4, the result is that more than half of the UK's metropolitan regions currently exhibit productivity levels which are below the average productivity levels for the UK's non-metropolitan regions (European Union 2013a). Indeed, this represents the highest share of under-performing urban regions for any country within the EU (European Union 2013a). The other European economies which also have a high share of under-performing cities are Germany, Spain, France, Italy and Poland in which approximately one-third of the metropolitan regions in each of these countries exhibit productivity levels below their respective non-metropolitan averages (Dijkstra *et al.* 2013). Yet, on the other hand, in the case of both Germany and Spain (Ahrend *et al.* 2014) along with France (European Union 2013a) the urban scale-productivity relationships described in textbooks are much stronger than is the case in the UK urban system (Ahrend *et al.* 2014). As such, the stronger and more positive scale-agglomeration relationships evident in these countries appear to act as more of a counterweight to their under-performing metropolitan regions. Moreover, a majority of metropolitan regions in both Poland and Germany are experiencing GDP per capita growth above their national average, while half of French and Italian metropolitan regions perform well relative to their national economies. In contrast, the fall in productivity associated with the economic crisis has adversely affected the UK's metropolitan regions to a greater extent than any other European economy. On the other hand, in terms of employment falls, the adverse effects of the crisis on the UK's metropolitan regions has been somewhat less severe than other countries such as Spain, Portugal, Ireland and various countries in central and eastern Europe.

If we consider the effects of the 2008 global financial crisis, we see that in the aftermath of the global financial crisis the decline in GDP per head between 2007 and 2010 in the UK's metropolitan regions was more severe than in any other EU economy except for Greece and Ireland, while the productivity decline in non-metropolitan regions was only greater than the UK in the case of Ireland (European Union 2013a). Some 40 per cent of the UK's metropolitan regions exhibited productivity declines more severe than the national output decline while a third of the UK's metropolitan regions exhibited productivity declines more severe than the average for non-metropolitan regions (European Union 2013a). Cities with lower skills tended to be more adversely affected than those with higher skills base, although the degree of sectoral diversity or specialisation was not a major issue (Lee 2014). Rather, it was the particular sectors which a city was specialised in which was more important, with those cities which were relatively specialised in financial services, manufacturing and construction being particularly vulnerable (Lee 2014). Moreover, the adverse effects of the crisis on unemployment was relatively greater in cities in the midlands and northern regions of England and Wales, relative to those in the southern regions of England plus Scotland (Lee 2014), reflecting familiar patterns already described above. Interestingly, the existing level of unemployment was not a good indicator of resilience in the immediate aftermath of the crisis (Lee 2014). Yet, although the crisis appears to have exacerbated existing inequalities, the current UK patterns are not simply a result of the crisis. During the years 2000–2008 immediately prior to the global financial crisis, more than half of the UK's metropolitan regions of over 250,000 had experienced declines in productivity and also more than half had experienced declines in population (Dijkstra *et al.* 2013). As such, it appears that the aggregate economic growth contribution of UK metropolitan areas since the millennium was in reality accounted for by less than half of the metropolitan regions whose growth performance more than compensated for the declining growth contribution of the other half of the UK's metropolitan areas. Severe structural weaknesses in the UK's urban system were already becoming very evident, but were largely masked by the generally buoyant economic conditions at the national level.

The pattern of the post-crisis productivity shocks across the UK's metropolitan regions looks very similar to those which are evident in Spain and very different to those observed in France, Germany or even Italy (European Union 2013a). Yet, although in aggregate the overall productivity decline in all types of the UK's regions was extremely severe, on average the productivity decline in the major metropolitan regions between 2007 and 2010 was actually slightly less than in the non-metropolitan regions (European Union 2013a). In these terms the UK case is also slightly different to most other EU economies, in which the performance of the country's cities has tended to reflect and magnify the national effects. In particular, in all of the EU economies which experienced productivity growth during the years 2007–2010 immediately following the crisis the major metropolitan regions were very much in the vanguard of this national growth. Conversely, the major metropolitan regions tended to be the areas most adversely affected in most of the countries experiencing severe output contractions (European Union 2013a). In contrast, in the case of the UK, there is a very strong geographical logic to these urban shocks. As we have seen, the large cities whose productivity has remained relatively resilient are all located in the southern regions of England and in Scotland, while those whose productivity has severely declined are all located outside of these regions. In terms of the geography of urban productivity change, the starkly simple urban and regional picture in the UK in the aftermath of the 2008 crisis was indeed rather different to many other European economies. In some ways this also mirrors the fact that it was rather different during the years immediately preceding the crisis.

If we consider employment and employment growth rather than output and output growth we see a slightly different picture. During the years prior to the 2008 global financial crisis most OECD economies exhibited high activity and participation rates and low levels of unemployment (OECD 2014). In contrast, in the aftermath of the crisis unemployment rose rapidly in many countries, and in particular in countries located on the southern or eastern fringes of the EU. For those countries experiencing rising unemployment during the years 2007–2010 the employment falls tended to be greater in non-metropolitan regions than in the metropolitan regions; conversely for those countries experiencing employment growth the job creation tended to be focused on metropolitan regions (European Union 2013a). As such, while the positive relationships between the output and employment performance of cities and national performance is similar for Europe's growing economies, in Europe's declining economies this relationship generally differs, with metropolitan areas typically accounting for greater productivity declines and lower employment declines than non-metropolitan areas (European Union 2013a). As we have already seen, in the case of the UK, an economy which has faced amongst the most severe declines and loss of economic potential of any major OECD economy (Ball 2014; Bank of England 2014; *The Economist* 2014), the role played by metropolitan regions has therefore been slightly different to most other European economies. More than half of the UK's metropolitan regions have faced more severe employment declines than the national average and one-half have also faced more severe employment declines than the non-metropolitan average (European Union 2013a). At the same time, one-third of the UK's metropolitan regions have exhibited employment growth during the period 2007–2010, and the combined effect of these different urban employment changes is that metropolitan regions in aggregate have experienced lower employment declines than non-metropolitan regions (European Union 2013a). As such, for more than half of the UK's metropolitan regions the picture looks very similar to other declining European economies, whereas for a third of UK metropolitan regions the picture looks rather different. In terms of the pattern of employment shocks across metropolitan regions between 2007 and 2010, the overall picture in the UK most closely corresponds to that which is observed in France and The Netherlands, although the scale of the employment contractions in the UK was much greater (European Union 2013a).

When it comes to national employment changes, as a group the UK's large cities appear to be somewhat less of a bellwether of national economic performance than is the case in many other countries, but when it comes to national output changes, a majority of the UK's large cities are central to the explanations. Much of the UK's productivity collapse in the wake of the 2008 crisis is actually focused on cities outside of the south of England and Scotland. The adverse shock effects are heavily concentrated in cities in the midlands and northern regions of England and Wales, and as such, this is rather less of a 'puzzle' than it appears to be. The UK's productivity problem is a regional and urban problem. However, this is not simply something which has appeared after the crisis. The seeds of the problem were being sown in the decade prior to the crisis, although strong national growth, and in particular strong growth in London, the south of England and Scotland, together largely masked the underlying growth problems emerging elsewhere.

3.5   Conclusions

As we have seen in this chapter, many of the conclusions at the regional level outlined in the previous chapter are not only largely repeated when conducting our analysis at the level of UK cities rather than UK regions, but in many ways they are actually magnified. UK urban performance corresponds only weakly to a textbook-type model, and in order to make sense of the performance of UK cities also requires understanding of the regional context in which those cities are situated. When compared against OECD cities on a common basis, the under-performance of the UK's large cities which are located in the midlands and northern regions of England are particularly marked. London is seen to be a strong performer, but not nearly the stellar performer that some of the currently popular narratives suggest. However, and as with the regional case, when compared with other cities across the OECD, there is no evidence of any positive effects of London's strong performance on the rest of the UK's cities which are located outside of London's hinterland regions or Scotland. London simply appears to be quite different to other UK cities or UK regions, and the apparent lack of spillover effects between London and the rest of the UK suggests that in reality London displays very few linkages with the rest of the UK beyond its immediate hinterland regions. Yet, why this should be the case is as yet unanswered. In the following chapter we will discuss how modern globalisation has re-shaped the role of the London economy in ways which are quite different to other UK cities and regions. Then in Chapter 5 we will discuss in much greater detail the nature and extent of the various interregional linkages between London and the rest of the UK economy. In Chapter 5 we will also return to the question of the UK city-size stricture and we will examine the extent to which the UK land use planning system may artificially have distorted the UK urban distribution and hindered the realisation of agglomeration economies in many cities.

Appendix 3.1

The growth performance of UK and OECD comparator metropolitan urban areas

Table A3.1 Growth performance of OECD comparator cities for the UK's economically weaker metropolitan areas

City	GDP per Capita 2000	GDP per Capita 2010	% Change in GDP per Capita 2000–2010	Percentage Point Difference between Urban and National % Growth in GDP per Capita 2000–2010
Manchester	35,795[†]	32,395	−9.5[†]	−21.0[†]
Birmingham	31,466[†]	28,270	−10.1[†]	−21.6[†]
Leeds	37,175[†]	32,491	−12.6[†]	−24.1[†]
Liverpool	25,002	26,742	6.95	−4.55
Sheffield	22,747	25,485	12.0	+0.5
Newcastle	22,268	24,954	12.1	+0.6
Nottingham	27,511	28,513	3.64	−7.86
Leicester	28,524	29,139	2.15	−9.35
Cardiff	27,048	29,034	7.34	−4.16
Bradford	24,745	24,341	−1.63	−13.1
Average for 10 UK Cities			**1.04**	**−10.5**
Budapest	21,279	28,417	33.5	9.4
Ghent	26,433	29,377	11.1	12.7
Winnipeg (Canada)	21,867	27,287	24.78	6.64
Quebec (Canada)	29,711	33,956	14.3	−3.84
Montreal (Canada)	29,912	31,044	3.78	−4.32
Prague (Czech Republic)	29,154	41,543	42.5	6.05
Berlin (Germany)	26,536	29,971	12.9	2.43
Bochum (Germany)	27,929	29,714	6.39	−4.11
Bonn (Germany)	28,763	39,281	36.7	26.1
Saarbrucken (Germany)	27,521	32,095	16.6	6.11
Duisburg (Germany)	27,654	36,790	33.0	22.5
Essen (Germany)	26,070	33,971	30.3	19.8
Dortmund (Germany)	25,559	31,041	21.4	10.9
Münster (Germany)	28,072	31,921	13.7	3.2
Barcelona (Spain)	30,318	32,012	5.58	−1.05
Valencia (Spain)	22,980	25,135	9.37	2.74
Zaragoza (Spain)	26,666	29,522	10.7	4.07
Las Palmas (Spain)	23,689	23,930	1.01	−5.62

Bilbao (Spain)	29,351	33,541	14.3	7.67
Toulouse (France)	30,085	31,775	5.61	0.68
Strasbourg (France)	29,386	29,724	1.15	−3.78
Bordeaux (France)	28,336	29,196	3.03	−1.9
Nantes (France)	28,215	29,611	4.94	0.01
Montpellier (France)	23,430	26,078	11.3	6.37
Saint-Étienne (France)	22,424	24,896	11.0	6.07
Grenoble (France)	28,249	29,917	5.90	0.97
Toulon (France)	22,697	24,112	6.23	1.3
Marseille (France)	27,652	30,152	9.04	4.11
Nice (France)	27,779	30,195	8.69	3.76
Rouen (France)	27,122	26,408	−2.63	−7.56
Athens (Greece)	23,099	34,460	49.1	32.2
Turin (Italy)	32,482	31,207	−3.93	−1.77
Genoa (Italy)	29,382	30,872	5.07	7.23
Venice (Italy)	31,660	31,548	−0.35	1.81
Warsaw (Poland)	24,338	37,456	53.9	7.00
Lisbon (Portugal)	29,922	30,784	2.88	0.25
Gothenburg (Sweden)	28,266	32,344	14.4	−3.0
Malmo (Sweden)	26,528	30,251	14.0	−3.37
Ljublijana (Slovenia)	26,820	34,870	30.0	3.44
Bratislava (Slovakia)	26,504	45,414	71.3	12.4
Buffalo (USA)	28,220	34,556	22.5	15.1
Fresno (USA)	30,052	29,507	−1.81	−9.25
Little Rock (USA)	29,036	30,562	5.25	−1.89
Tucson (USA)	29,720	31,960	7.53	0.09
El Paso (USA)	26,653	29,891	12.1	4.66
Sapporo (Japan)	26,730	24,893	−6.87	−13.78
Sendai (Japan)	26,978	26,827	−0.56	−7.41
Niigata (Japan)	27,625	28,739	4.03	−2.88
Toyama (Japan)	31,137	32,117	3.15	−3.76
Nagano (Japan)	27,654	30,431	10.0	3.13
Kanazawa	30,147	29,116	−3.42	−10.33
Utsunomiya (Japan)	28,885	30,685	6.23	−0.68
Maebashi (Japan)	27,643	29,796	7.78	0.87
Mito (Japan)	26,792	29,789	11.2	4.27
Kofu (Japan)	26,164	28,528	9.03	2.12
Osaka (Japan)	29,339	29,952	2.09	−4.82
Yokkaichi	27,309	31,179	14.2	7.26
Himeji (Japan)	26,218	26,657	1.67	−5.24
Okayama (Japan)	22,819	23,677	3.76	−3.15
Kurashiki (Japan)	25,685	42,098	63.9	57.0
Fukuyama (Japan)	27,310	30,917	13.2	6.29
Hiroshima (Japan)	27,721	30,487	9.97	3.06
Takamatsu (Japan)	23,846	35,720	49.8	42.9
Wakayama (Japan)	25,272	27,771	9.88	2.97
Tokushima (Japan)	25,616	28,317	9.88	2.97
Kitakyushu (Japan)	26,205	30,445	16.2	9.27
Matsuyama (Japan)	25,771	26,611	3.26	−3.65
Fukuoka (Japan)	25,904	27,361	5.62	−1.29
Koichi (Japan)	22,351	22,660	1.38	−5.53
Oita (Japan)	26,754	28,076	4.94	−1.97
Kumamoto (Japan)	23,010	23,856	3.67	−3.24

(*Continued*)

Table A3.1 Continued

City	GDP per Capita 2000	GDP per Capita 2010	% Change in GDP per Capita 2000–2010	Percentage Point Difference between Urban and National % Growth in GDP per Capita 2000–2010
Nagasaki (Japan)	22,167	24,807	11.9	4.99
Average for 72 OECD Cities			**12.96**	**3.82**
Average for 45 European and North American Cities			**15.28**	**4.35**
Average for 11 French Cities			**5.84**	**1.36**
Average for 3 Italian Cities			**0.26**	**2.42**
Average for 27 Japanese Cities			**9.87**	**2.96**

Source: OECD Metropolitan Database. All figures in US$ 2005 PPP prices.
Note: There is incomplete data for Dresden, Aachen and Bari.

Table A3.2 Growth performance of OECD comparator cities for the UK's economically stronger metropolitan areas

City	GDP per Capita 2000	GDP per Capita 2010	% Growth in GDP per Capita 2000–2010	Percentage Point Difference between Urban and National % Growth in GDP per Capita 2000–2010
Bristol	33,814.50	38,242.91	13.09	1.59
Portsmouth	27,615.27	33,891.56	22.72	11.22
Glasgow	32,000.14	37,572.01	17.41	5.91
Edinburgh	36,846.84	45,166.39	22.57	11.07
Average for 4 UK Cities			**18.94**	**7.45**
Athens (Greece)	23,099	34,460	49.1	32.2
Amsterdam (Netherlands)	36,753	39,596	7.73	−1.6
Anjo (Japan)	33,673 (2001)	33,768	2.84	−4.06
Antwerp (Belgium)	35,191	37,327	6.06	−5.04
Augsburg (Germany)	32,267	33,294	3.18	−7.42
Bilbao (Spain)	29,351	33,541	14.3	7.67
Bonn (Germany)	28,763	39,281	36.7	26.1
Bratislava (Slovakia)	26,503	45,414	71.35	12.5
Bremen (Germany)	33,745	36,431	7.95	−2.65
Brussels (Belgium)	42,738	45,749	7.05	−4.05
Changwon (Korea)	19,626	34,262	74.57	31.81
Copenhagen (Denmark)	35,808	37,432	4.53	2.38

Duisburg (Germany)	27,654	36,790	33.0	22.5
Dusseldorf (Germany)	38,057	39,505	3.80	−6.7
Eindhoven (Netherlands)	34,162	36,739	7.54	−1.79
Essen (Germany)	26,071	33,972	30.3	19.8
Florence (Italy)	35,504	34,417	−3.06	−0.9
Graz (Austria)	32,284	34,298	6.23	−4.61
Hamburg (Germany)	40,669	44,934	10.48	−0.02
Hamamatsu (Japan)	30,576 (2001)	34,018	11.25	4.35
Hanover (Germany)	32,355	36,327	12.27	1.77
Helsinki (Finland)	37,033	43,082	16.33	−2.11
Karlsruhe (Germany)	36,321	40,299	10.95	0.55
Kurashiki (Japan)	25,685 (2001)	42,098	63.9	57.0
Linz (Austria)	33,890	37,994	12.11	1.27
Ljublijana (Slovenia)	26,820	34,870	30.0	3.44
Lyon (France)	34,376	36,475	6.10	1.17
Madrid (Spain)	33,214	34,735	4.58	−5.92
Mannheim (Germany)	32,475	36,501	12.39	1.89
Münster (Germany)	28,072	31,921	13.7	3.2
Nagoya (Japan)	31,881 (2001)	33,577	5.32	−0.77
Numazu (Japan)	30,691 (2001)	34,669	12.96	6.06
Nuremburg (Germany)	37,091	38,548	3.93	−6.57
Ottawa-Gatineau (Canada)	34,913	34,446	−1.34	−19.5
Prague (Czech Republic)	29,154	41,543	42.5	6.05
Quebec (Canada)	29,711	33,956	14.3	−3.84
Rome (Italy)	35,322	35,442	0.33	−1.83
Rotterdam (Netherlands)	34,258	37,043	8.12	−1.21
Shizuoka (Japan)	30,960 (2001)	35,319	14.07	7.17
Stuttgart (Germany)	38,756	42,895	10.68	0.18
Takamatsu (Japan)	23,846 (2001)	35,720	49.8	42.9
The Hague (Netherlands)	34,456	35,170	2.07	−7.26
Toronto (Canada)	37,634	35,553	−5.53	−23.7
Vancouver (Canada)	32,711	35,293	7.89	−10.25
Vienna (Austria)	31,801	40,107	26.12	15.28
Warsaw (Poland)	24,338	37,456	53.9	7.00
Winnipeg (Canada)	21,867	27,287	24.78	6.64
Akron (USA)	35,145	35,021	−0.352	−7.79
Albany (USA)	34,167	38,216	11.85	4.41
Alberquerque (USA)	35,151	35,860	2.02	−5.42
Austin (USA)	46,070	45,405	−1.44	−8.88
Atlanta (USA)	43,486	39,867	−8.32	−15.76
Birmingham (USA)	32,028	35,748	11.61	4.17
Buffalo (USA)	28,220	34,556	22.5	15.1
Charleston (USA)	40,473	37,581	−7.14	−14.58
Charlotte (USA)	42,250	37,478	−11.29	−18.73
Cincinatti (USA)	41,714	39.974	−4.17	−11.61
Clearwater/St Petersburg	35,404	40,167	13.45	6.01

(*Continued*)

Table A3.2 Continued

City	GDP per Capita 2000	GDP per Capita 2010	% Growth in GDP per Capita 2000–2010	Percentage Point Difference between Urban and National % Growth in GDP per Capita 2000–2010
Cleveland (USA)	35,145	37,526	6.77	−0.67
Colorado Springs (USA)	39,017	38,665	−0.9	−8.34
Columbus (USA)	41,406	36,174	−12.63	−20.1
Dayton (USA)	33,889	34,107	0.64	−6.8
Des Moines (USA)	39,221	40,818	4.07	−3.37
Detroit (USA)	39,699	36,693	−7.57	−15.01
Fort Worth (USA)	42,230	45,559	7.88	0.44
Harrisburg (USA)	33,725	35,717	5.91	−1.53
Indianapolis (USA)	39,394	37,075	−5.89	−13.33
Jacksonville (USA)	37,016	39,062	5.52	−1.92
Kansas City (USA)	39,730	40,388	1.65	−5.79
Las Vegas (USA)	40,399	38,310	−5.17	−12.6
Los Angeles (USA)	40,364	42,590	5.51	−1.93
Louisville (USA)	36,773	37,593	2.22	−5.22
Miami (USA)	35,128	39,121	11.36	3.92
Memphis (USA)	32,975	35,329	7.14	−0.30
Milwaukee (USA)	39,741	42,970	8.12	0.68
Minneapolis (USA)	43,246	45,343	4.84	−2.6
Nashville (USA)	38,824	38,236	−1.51	−8.95
Norfolk (USA)	35,152	42,853	21.9	14.46
Oklahoma City (USA)	31,248	35,618	13.98	6.54
Omaha (USA)	40,706	45,618	12.06	4.62
Phoenix (USA)	37,807	38,013	0.55	−6.89
Pittsburgh (USA)	34,228	40,903	19.49	12.05
Portland (USA)	39,775	45,127	13.45	6.01
Raleigh (USA)	42,717	36,744	−13.98	−21.42
Richmond (USA)	36,650	42,763	16.67	9.23
Sacramento (USA)	40,668	39,131	−3.78	−11.22
Saint Louis (USA)	36,943	38,715	4.79	−2.65
Salt Lake City (USA)	35,441	42,390	19.6	12.16
San Antonio (USA)	33,568	36,661	9.21	1.77
Tampa (USA)	35,404	35,606	0.57	−6.87
Toledo (USA)	34,817	35,569	2.15	−5.29
Tulsa (USA)	31,016	37,243	20.1	12.7
Wichita (USA)	32,067	35,032	9.25	1.81
Average for 89 OECD Cities			**11.80**	**0.782**
Average for 47 Non-USA OECD Comparator Cities			**17.81**	**4.235**
Average for 42 USA Comparator Cities			**5.064**	**−3.083**

Source: OECD Metropolitan Database. All figures in US$ 2005 PPP prices.
Note: There are incomplete data for Cologne and Milan.

Appendix 3.2

The output and productivity performance of UK metropolitan urban regions

Table A3.3 UK metropolitan region GVA at basic prices (Millions Euros Current Prices)

	2001	2007	2010	2011
London	406,238	531,502	450,869	506,924
West Midlands urban area	52,498	60,495	49,009	52,162
Leeds	27,905	33,315	26,843	29,960
Glasgow	40,214	50,535	41,543	42,811
Bradford	9535	11,130	9488	9788
Liverpool	26,946	32,452	26,194	30,131
Edinburgh	23,584	31,761	26,224	26,918
Manchester	56,441	67,487	55,591	60,182
Cardiff	20,223	24,625	20,393	21,156
Sheffield	11,245	13,701	11,583	12,211
Bristol	27,400	34,758	29,951	32,190
Belfast	15,468	19,246	16,089	16,943
Newcastle upon Tyne	21,643	26,823	22,248	23,677
Leicester	21,165	27,500	22,099	22,791
Aberdeen	14,056	17,636	16,495	18,831
Cambridge	14,603	19,745	16,124	17,583
Exeter	13,646	17,975	15,107	15,225
Portsmouth	4938	5930	5444	5147
Coventry	19,967	23,336	19,480	20,929
Kingston upon Hull	10,505	12,741	10,371	11,185
Stoke-on-Trent	18,824	23,424	18,815	20,628
Nottingham	23,539	28,486	23,026	20,040
Kirklees	11,226	12,875	10,972	11,803
Doncaster	11,745	15,929	12,281	12,690
Sunderland	5641	6992	5517	5628
Brighton and Hove	6107	7822	6133	6740
Swansea	8466	10,717	9136	9415
Derby	6915	8139	6821	7122
Southampton	5657	7089	5254	5601
Bournemouth	14,233	17,826	15,009	16,089
Reading	30,780	39,473	32,084	36,577
Blackburn – Blackpool – Preston	27,335	32,645	26,601	28,449
Middlesbrough	10,189	12,362	10,099	10,473
Norwich	15,659	19,771	16,409	17,447
Cheshire West and Chester	14,310	16,962	13,948	15,429

Source: Eurostat.

Table A3.4 UK metropolitan region GDP per capita (Euros Current Prices)

	2001	2007	2010	2011
London	36,996.2	46,444.8	35,745.4	38,195.1
West Midlands urban area	26,098.4	29,522.2	21,384.4	23,471.9
Leeds	30,525.5	34,143.5	24,747.6	26,682.8
Glasgow	25,472.2	31,865.4	24,334.5	25,986.3
Bradford	22,812.0	25,160.4	19,552.8	20,736.8
Liverpool	20,470.1	24,781.9	18,851.5	19,948.8
Edinburgh	34,088.2	43,991.3	33,692.3	35,111.8
Manchester	25,262.9	29,508.5	21,896.0	23,687.3
Cardiff	21,733.4	25,808.4	19,016.8	20,999.7
Sheffield	24,675.0	28,715.4	21,635.5	23,361.9
Bristol	31,042.5	36,789.2	27,925.8	30,565.0
Belfast	26,917.8	33,364.7	24,843.9	27,426.4
Newcastle upon Tyne	21,964.7	26,839.0	20,300.6	21,711.9
Leicester	25,695.0	31,629.8	23,615.6	24,912.1
Aberdeen	36,068.5	44,115.1	35,955.9	39,924.4
Cambridge	29,647.7	37,370.7	26,936.8	29,317.1
Exeter	21,778.1	27,113.5	20,827.6	22,569.2
Portsmouth	29,573.6	33,816.8	25,623.6	29,447.5
Coventry	27,794.4	31,318.0	23,875.2	25,624.9
Kingston upon Hull	20,945.5	24,086.3	17,974.7	19,285.2
Stoke-on-Trent	20,241.9	24,730.8	18,300.1	19,677.0
Nottingham	24,978.4	28,883.1	21,115.8	22,744.6
Kirklees	21,688.7	24,123.7	18,458.4	20,158.7
Doncaster	17.552,9	23.348,5	16.470,5	17.805,3
Sunderland	22,319.9	27,909.3	19,805.0	21,803.2
Brighton and Hove	27,517.7	35,066.4	24,948.9	26,553.8
Swansea	19,599.3	24,071.1	18,332.1	20,291.0
Derby	33,750.1	37,762.7	26,956.8	30,957.3
Southampton	29,017.9	34,439.9	24,265.8	24,553.7
Bournemouth	23,112.8	28,190.5	22,454.2	23,516.3
Reading	43,149.4	53,423.6	38,024.4	41,546.9
Blackburn – Blackpool – Preston	21,725.2	25,291.5	19,085.2	20,563.8
Middlesbrough	20,705.0	24,892.9	18,714.5	20,080.4
Norwich	22,082.5	26,463.2	19,768.4	21,321.3
Cheshire West and Chester	27,126.0	31,477.2	23,558.1	25,698.9

Table A3.5 UK metropolitan region GDP per worker (PPS)

City	2011 GVA per Worker (Euros PPS)	2011 GDP per Worker Relative to UK	2011 GDP per Worker Relative to EU-28
London	78,821	138	138
West Midlands urban area	55,515	97	97
Leeds	56,179	99	99
Glasgow	53,407	94	94
Bradford	45,420	80	80
Liverpool	48,086	84	84
Edinburgh	62,615	110	110
Manchester	51,110	90	90
Cardiff	45,762	80	80
Sheffield	47,849	84	84
Bristol	57,906	102	102
Belfast	58,024	102	102
Newcastle upon Tyne	46,063	81	81
Leicester	48,793	86	86
Aberdeen	74,756	131	131
Cambridge	56,392	99	99
Exeter	42,972	75	75
Portsmouth	48,465	85	85
Coventry	51,972	91	91
Kingston upon Hull	41,782	73	73
Stoke-on-Trent	42,150	74	74
Nottingham	44,486	78	78
Kirklees	42,827	75	75
Doncaster	38,005	67	67
Sunderland	44,667	78	78
Brighton and Hove	51,255	90	90
Swansea	44,223	78	78
Derby	62,201	109	109
Southampton	46,870	82	82
Bournemouth	48,873	86	86
Reading	80,690	142	142
Blackburn – Blackpool – Preston	44,128	77	77
Middlesbrough	45,298	79	79
Norwich	41,920	74	74
Cheshire West and Chester	54,655	96	96
UK Metro Region Average	59,953	105	105
UK Non-Metro Area Average	50,407	88	88
UK	57,011.99	100	100

Notes

1 http://ec.europa.eu/regional_policy/activity/urban/index_en.cfm.
2 In new economic geography terminology this would reflect the 'black hole' condition.
3 See for example the Evan Davis BBC television programme *Mind the Gap: London vs the Rest: Part 1* which was broadcast on Monday 3 March 2014 on BBC2 at 21.00–22.00 and Part 2 which was broadcast on Monday 10 March 2014 on BBC2 at 21.00–22.00.
4 Seoul-Inchon has twice the population of the next largest nine Korean cities. By comparison, the population of Japan's (and the world's) largest city Tokyo is only equivalent to the total populations of the next six largest Japanese cities.
5 The 2012 population densities per square kilometre for comparator cities are: Paris 981.23; Porto 1373.33; Warsaw 349.4; Stockholm 280.2; Vienna 301.08; Brussels 776.59; Zurich 1042.66; Prague 475.59; Essen 2173.45; Dortmund 1485.42; Hamburg 520.25; Barcelona 2760.03; Madrid 587.60; Helsinki 232.52; Antwerp 913.13; Copenhagen 491.55; Valencia 1097.02; Lyon 528.46; Milan 1557.80; Naples 2285.54; Rome 717.0; Toulouse 240.73; Athens 2142.19; Amsterdam 853.26; Rotterdam 1011.23; Toronto 462.86; Boston 758.12; New York 1682.47; Los Angeles 207.68; Philadelphia 934.93; Sapporo 1013.43; Hiroshima 1182.37; Nagoya 1636.27; Maebashi 829.56; Shizuoka 627.34; Cheongjiu 1323.56; Ulsan 1443.61. The highest population density cities in the OECD are: Seoul-Incheon 5027.98; Busan 4737.23; Changwon 4446.49; Tokyo 4124.86; Mexico City 3881.50.
6 From the OECD metropolitan urban area database we see that the European city whose overall spatial morphology is the closest comparator for London is Paris which has an aggregate 2012 population density of 981.23 persons per sq km, which is markedly lower than the value of 1746.93 for London. However, the total area of London is 6921 sq km comprised of a core urban area of 2654 sq km and a hinterland area of 4267 sq km. Meanwhile the total area of Paris is 12,089 sq km which is comprised of a core area of 2031 sq km and a hinterland of 10,058 sq km. The total population of London in 2012 was 12,090,254 while that of Paris is 11,862,466. However, the 2012 population in the core urban area of London is 9,674,819 while that of Paris is 9,403,955. As such, the 2012 population density of the core area of London is 3645.4 persons per sq km and the population density of the core urban area of Paris is 4630.3 persons per sq km. In other words, the core urban area of Paris is more densely populated than London (European Union 2014). The reason that Paris as a whole displays a much lower population density than London is because its commuting hinterland is more than twice the area of London. Similarly, for New York the core area is 9882 sq km and the core city population is 16,208,862, giving a core city population density of 1640.2 person per sq km. Meanwhile, the hinterland population is 417,451 across an area of 8728 sq km, giving a hinterland population density of 47.8 persons per sq km. On a range of alternative methods of calculation (Wilson *et al.* 2010) it is clear that New York city densities are by far the highest amongst North America's very large cities.
7 Neither Bradford nor Leicester have experienced significant productivity or wage rises during this period so the relatively rapid population and population density growth experienced by these cities is likely to be a result of immigration primarily from South Asia, although without detailed local migration data broken down by origin such a conclusion must necessarily remain somewhat speculative.
8 http://epp.eurostat.ec.europa.eu/portal/page/portal/region_cities/metropolitan_regions/data_metro/database_sub3.
9 In the Eurostat definition metropolitan areas are calculated as with the OECD methodology, while the 'metropolitan regions' are defined as the NUTS-3 regional proxies of the metropolitan areas with populations of 250,000 or above.

10   London, Edinburgh, Reading, Aberdeen, Derby, Belfast, Bristol.
11   London, Edinburgh, Reading, Aberdeen, Derby.
12   As the definitions of the OECD metropolitan urban areas and EU metropolitan regions definitions differ slightly according to both geography and size there are a few cases where the results are somewhat sensitive to the definitions employed. In particular, there are new metropolitan regions whose productivity levels are greater than the UK and EU average, namely Aberdeen, Reading, Belfast and Derby, while Glasgow and Portsmouth are now slightly below the UK and EU average.
13   No comparable data are available for Australia or New Zealand.
14   For comparison purposes (OECD 2013) the equivalent figures for the contribution of metropolitan areas to national economic growth in Japan, Korea, USA and Canada are 75 per cent, 66, per cent, 63 per cent and 54 per cent respectively.
15   Yet, while this aggregate growth contribution of London during 2000–2010 may sound a high figure, on the other hand the relative growth contribution of ten of the capital cities in Europe to the growth of their national economies was actually higher than London (OECD 2013). In part this may be due to the fact that while nine of these cities were smaller than London they were also located in much smaller countries than the UK. However, the same result also holds for Paris (OECD 2013) whose relative contribution to France's national growth was also greater than London's contribution to the UK's aggregate growth.

References

Ahrend, R., Farchy, E., Kaplanis, I. and Lembcke, A., 2014, "What Makes Cities More Productive? Evidence on the Role of Urban Governance from Five OECD Countries", *OECD Regional Development Working Papers 2014/05*, Organisation for Economic Cooperation and Development, Paris.

Ball, L.M., 2014, "Long-Term Damage from the Great Recession in OECD Countries", *NBER Working Paper 20185*, Cambridge, MA.

Bank of England, 2014, "The UK Productivity Puzzle", *Bank of England Quarterly Bulletin Q2*, 114–128, June.

Beaudry, C., and Schiffauerova, A., 2009, "Who's Right, Marshall or Jacobs? The Localization versus Urbanization Debate", *Research Policy*, 38, 318–337.

Berry, C., and Glaeser, E.L., 2007, "The Divergence of Human Capital Levels Across Cities", *Papers in Regional Science*, 84.3, 407–444.

Bettencourt, L.M.A., 2013, "The Origins of Scaling in Cities", *Science*, 340.6139, 1438–1441.

Bettencourt, L.M.A., and West, G.B., 2011, "Bigger Cities do More with Less", *Scientific American*, 305, 52–53

Bettencourt, L.M.A., and West, G.B., 2014, "Bigger Cities do More with Less", *Scientific American MIND; Special Edition Creativity*, 23.1, 106–107, Winter.

Brakman, S., and van Marrewijk, C., 2013, "Reflections on Cluster Policies", *Cambridge Journal of Regions Economy and Society*, 6.2, 217–231.

Brakman, S., Garretsen, H. and Van Marrewijk, C., 2009, "Economic Geography Within and Between European Nations: The Role of Market Potential and Density Across Space and Time", *Journal of Regional Science*, 49, 777–800.

Ciccone, A. and Hall, R.E., 1996, "Productivity and the Density of Economic Activity", *American Economic Review*, 86, 54–70.

Combes, P-P, Duranton, G. and Gobillon, L., 2008, "Spatial Wage Disparities: Sorting Matters!", *Journal of Urban Economics*, 63.2, 723–742.

De Groot, H.L.F., Poot, J. and Smit, M., 2009, "Agglomeration Externalities, Innovation and Regional Growth: Theoretical Perspectives and Meta-Analysis", in Cappello, R., and Nijkamp, P., (eds.), *Handbook of Regional Growth and Development Theories*, Edward Elgar, Cheltenham.

De Melo, P., Graham, D. and Noland, R., 2009, "A Meta-Analysis of Estimates of Urban Agglomeration Economies", *Regional Science and Urban Economics*, 39.3, 332–342.

Dijkstra, L., Garcilazo, E. and McCann, P., 2013, "The Economic Performance of European Cities and City-Regions: Myths and Realities", *European Planning Studies*, 21.3, 334–354.

Duranton, G., 2006, "Some Foundations for Zipf's Law: Product Proliferation and Local Spillovers", *Regional Science and Urban Economics*, 36.4, 542–563.

Duranton, G., 2007, "Urban Evolutions: The Fast, the Slow, and the Still", *American Economic Review*, 97.1, 197–221.

Duranton, G., 2011, "California Dreamin': The Feeble Case for Cluster Policies", *Review of Economic Analysis*, 3.1, 3–45.

Duranton, G., and Puga, D., 2001, "Nursery Cities: Urban Diversity, Process Innovation, and the Life Cycle of Products", *American Economic Review* 91.5, 1454–1477.

ESPON, 2013, *New Evidence on Smart, Sustainable and Inclusive: First ESPON 2013 Synthesis Report*, Luxembourg, www.espon.eu.

European Commission, 2007, *State of European Cities Report: Adding Value to the European Audit*, Directorate-General for Regional Policy, Brussels.

European Union, 2011, *The Urban and Regional Dimension of Europe 2020: Seventh Progress Report on Economic, Social and Territorial Cohesion*, Publications Office, Brussels.

European Union, 2013a, *The Urban and Regional Dimension of the Crisis: Eighth Report on Economic, Social and territorial Cohesion*, Publications Office, Brussels.

European Union, 2013b, *Quality of Life in Cities: Perception Survey in 79 European Cities*, Publications Office, Brussels.

European Union, 2014, *Investment for Jobs and Growth – Promoting Development and Good Governance in EU Regions and Cities: Sixth Report on Economic, Social and Territorial Cohesion*, Publications Office, Brussels.

Eurostat, 2013, "Regional GDP Per Capita in the EU in 2010: Eight Capital Regions in the First Ten Places", *Eurostat News Release*, 46/2013, 21 March 2013.

Faggian, A., and McCann, P., 2009, "Human Capital and Regional Development", in Capello, R., and Nijkamp, P., (eds.), *Regional Dynamics and Growth: Advances in Regional Economics*, Edward Elgar, Cheltenham.

Fingleton, B., Garretsen, H. and Martin, R., 2012, "Recessionary Shocks and Regional Employment: Evidence of Recessionary Resilience", *Journal of Regional Science*, 52.1, 109–133.

Gabaix, X., 1999a, "Zipf's Law and the Growth of Cities", *American Economic Review: Papers and Proceedings*, 89.2, 129–132.

Gabaix, X., 1999b, "Zipf's Law for Cities: An Explanation", *Quarterly Journal of Economics*, 114.3, 739–767.

Glaeser, E.L., 2011, *Triumph of the City: How Our Greatest Invention Makes Us Richer, Smarter, Greener, Healthier, and Happier*, Penguin Press, New York.

Glaeser, E.L., 2014, "Engines of Innovation", *Scientific American MIND; Special Edition Creativity*, 23.1, 102–105, Winter.

Glaeser, E.L., Kallal, H.D., Scheinkman, J.A. and Shleifer, A., 1992, "Growth in Cities", *Journal of Political Economy*, 100, 1126–1152.

Krugman, P., 1991a, "Increasing Returns and Economic Geography", *Journal of Political Economy*, 99, 483–499.

Krugman, P., 1991b, *Geography and Trade*, MIT Press, Cambridge, MA.

Lee, N., 2014, "Grim Down South? The Determinants of Unemployment Increases in British Cities in the 2008–2009 Recession", *Regional Studies*, 48.11, 1761–1778.

McCann, P., 2013, *Modern Urban and Regional Economics*, Oxford University Press, Oxford.

McCann, P., and Acs, Z.J., 2011, "Globalisation: Countries, Cities and Multinationals", *Regional Studies*, 45.1, 17–32.

Maddison, A., 2006, *The World Economy. Volume 1: A Millennial Perspective; Volume 2: Historical Statistics*, Organisation for Economic Growth and Development, Paris.

Mameli, F., Faggian, A. and McCann, P., 2014, "The Estimation of Local Employment Growth: Do Sectoral Aggregation and Industry Definition Matter?", *Regional Studies*, 48.11, 1813–1828.

MGI, 2011, *Urban World: Mapping the Economic Power of Cities*, McKinsey Global Institute.

MGI, 2012a, *Urban World: Cities and the Rise of the Consuming Class*, McKinsey Global Institute.

MGI, 2012b, *Urban America: US Cities in the Global Economy*, McKinsey Global Institute.

MGI, 2013, *Urban World: The Shifting Global Business Landscape*, McKinsey Global Institute.

OECD, 2006, *Competitive Cities in the Global Economy*, Organisation for Economic Cooperation and Development, Paris.

OECD, 2009a, *How Regions Grow*, Paris: Organisation for Economic Growth and Development, Paris.

OECD, 2009b, *Regions Matter: Economic Recovery, Innovation and Sustainable Growth*, Organisation for Economic Growth and Development, Paris.

OECD 2011, *OECD Regional Outlook 2011: Building Resilient Regions for Stronger Economies*, Organisation for Economic Cooperation and Development, Paris.

OECD, 2012, *Redefining "Urban": A New Way to Measure Metropolitan Regions*, Organisation for Economic Cooperation and Development, Paris.

OECD, 2013, *OECD Regions at a Glance 2013*, Organisation for Economic Cooperation and Development, Paris.

OECD, 2014, *OECD Regional Outlook 2014 – Regions and Cities: Where Policies and People Meet*, Organisation for Economic Cooperation and Development, Paris.

OECD, 2015, *The Metropolitan Century: Understanding Urbanisation and Its Consequences*, Organisation for Economic Development and Cooperation, Paris.

Porter, M.E., 1990, *The Competitive Advantage of Nations*, Free Press, New York.

PWC, 2012, *Cities of Opportunity*, Price Waterhouse Coopers.

Rosenthal, S.S., and Strange, W.C., 2004, "Evidence on the Nature and Sources of Agglomeration Economics", in Henderson, V., and Thisse, J-F., (eds.), *Handbook of Urban and Regional Economics Vol 4*, North-Holland, Amsterdam.

Scott, A.J., 1988, *New Industrial Spaces*, Pion, London.

The Economist, 2014a, "Free Exchange: Wasted Potential", 14 June.

UNFPA, 2007, *State of the World Population 2007, Unleashing the Potential of Urban Growth*, United Nations Population Fund, New York.

UN-Habitat, 2012, *State of the World's Cities 2012/2013. Prosperity of Cities*, United Nations Human Settlements Programme, Nairobi.

United Nations, 2012, *World Urbanization Prospects 2011: The 2011 Revision*, Department of Economic and Social Affairs: Population Division, ST/ESA/SER.A/322, New York.

Wilson, S.G., Plane, D.A., Mackun, P.J., Fischetti, T.R., Goworowska, J., Cohen, D., Perry, M.J. and Hatchard, G.W., 2010, *Patterns of Metropolitan and Micropolitan Population Change: 2000 to 2010: 2010 Census Special Reports*, United States Census Bureau, Washington DC.

World Bank, 2009, *World Development Report 2009: Reshaping Economic Geography*, Washington DC.

4 The UK's international economic engagement and the London 'global city' argument

4.1 Introduction to the UK's international positioning in the global economy

The two previous chapters have demonstrated that the UK regional and urban patterns of development display a very strong core-periphery geographical structure with London and its hinterland regions representing the core and the rest of the UK, except possibly Scotland, broadly reflecting a periphery. The UK's economic inequalities between the core and the periphery are very high by OECD and EU standards and moreover, they are increasing on various dimensions. However, the regional problems are not simply urban questions. Indeed, discussing UK urban issues without setting them squarely within the specifics of the UK regional setting makes little or no sense. Similarly, discussing UK regional issues without discussing the performance of the local cities also makes little or no sense. Rather, a region-urban setting is the most appropriate way to analyse the economic geography of the UK and also to understand the major challenges that the UK faces. Yet, why the UK's core-periphery structure is today so pronounced and why UK interregional inequalities are nowadays so marked in part is heavily related to the effects of globalisation on the UK. In particular, as we will see in this chapter, the effects of modern globalisation since the early 1990s appear to have transformed the economy of London and its hinterland in ways for which there is simply no parallel in other UK regions and cities. These transformations also have impacted on other UK regions but in rather different ways.

The chapter begins by examining the nature of modern globalisation and then sets the international experience of the UK economy over six decades in the light of these more recent developments. We discuss the sectoral, geographical and multinational features of UK trade and investment and then examine the scale of the impacts of internationalisation on the UK economy.[1] What becomes clear from the World Input-Output Database (WIOD) model is that the economic importance of the EU Single Market to the UK economy is far larger than many observers understand and moreover, this is relatively even more important to the non-core regions of the UK than it is to the core regions. The analysis then proceeds to examine the global city nature of the London economy and its role within the wider UK economy. The chapter focuses on the UK's trade, investment and global value-chain aspects of international engagement, while the issues relating to immigration and international labour mobility are discussed in Chapter 5 alongside the issues of interregional migration.

4.2   The global environment for trade, foreign investment and global value-chains

Much of the twentieth century, and in particular the period spanning the second to the seventh decade of the twentieth century, was characterised by a period of anti-globalisation in which countries were increasingly isolated from each other. This isolation was due to the catastrophes of the two world wars, the intervening depression years, and the architecture of the subsequent Bretton-Woods reconstruction era (Iammarino and McCann 2013). During this period, many trade and international engagement structures were largely 'frozen' in the sense that the pre-existing structures inherited from the late nineteenth century and the first decade of the twentieth century, were largely reinforced. The international engagement of a country such as the UK was heavily oriented towards far-distant countries located in Australasia and the Pacific arena, southern and eastern Africa, the Caribbean, South Asia and North America. Similarly, the international engagement of The Netherlands was heavily oriented towards far-distant countries in the East Indies and Caribbean, while that of France was heavily oriented towards far-distant countries in North and West Africa, South Asia, the Pacific and the Caribbean. In other words, the logic of international trade and international investment patterns for many advanced economies was heavily shaped by the earlier empire-era experiences of these countries. It was only from the post-war decades of the twentieth century onwards that this logic started to change as the previous empire systems largely disintegrated and were re-shaped by multiple emerging forces. As a result, these former colonial powers re-oriented their emerging international trade and investment relationships away from far-distant countries and increasingly towards other advanced economies away from developing countries and towards other advanced economies, many of which were geographical neighbours.

Yet, as these processes progressed, it was only really during the 1960s and 1970s that the western economies increasingly started to reintegrate at a global scale but these processes of reintegration accelerated dramatically from the 1990s onwards following the onset of 'modern globalisation'. In the period spanning 1988–1994 a coincidence in timing regarding: the establishment of the EU Single Market; the creation of NAFTA; the establishment of the WTO; the rapid opening up of China, South Africa, India and Indonesia; the fall of the Berlin Wall; and the creation of the internet all conspired to completely reconfigure the global economy within a matter of just a few years. A third of the world's potential labour market suddenly appeared

open for business (Venables 2006), and the resulting enormous reconfiguration in trade (Reyes *et al.* 2009) and investment relationships involved: the
enormous growth of out-sourcing an off-shoring of economic activities; huge
increases in exports and imports; the development of new forms of what are
known as 'global value-chains'; the increasingly dominant positions of what
have become known as 'global cities' (Taylor 2004; Sassen 2006); and often
also greater inequalities between skills and income groups as well as between
regions (Autor *et al.* 1998; Goos *et al.* 2009). The interactions between the
major features of modern globalisation, the role of global cities, and the
nature and patterns of foreign investment are discussed in detail in Iammarino
and McCann (2013). However, for our purposes here it is important to outline
a few key features of these relationships.

The single most important feature of modern globalisation is not trade, but
multinationalism (McCann and Acs 2011; Iammarino and McCann 2013),
and in particular the relationship between foreign direct investment and
the global coordination of flows of knowledge, goods, services and finance.
Contrary to many popular perceptions, globalisation is primarily a story
of the interactions between rich countries rather than interactions between
advanced and developing countries. Today, some 85 per cent of FDI emerges
from advanced economies while two-thirds of inward FDI enters advanced
economies, with Europe being the largest arena of cross-border FDI. The
number of multinationals grew by more than ten-fold between the 1970s and
the millennium with the majority emerging in the last years of the twentieth
century as global markets opened up and surged in ways which were hith-
erto entirely unexpected (Iammarino and McCann 2013). The top 700 multinational firms account for almost half of all global R&D and two-thirds of
private sector R&D (Iammarino and McCann 2013) while the top 500 multinational firms account for 90 per cent of FDI and half of global trade. Indeed,
just 100 multinationals account for 10 per cent of globally held foreign assets.
The overwhelming importance of multinationals in the modern economy is
underscored by the fact that today the sales of foreign-owned multinational
affiliates are now some 2.5 times larger than total global exports (Iammarino
and McCann 2013), and the greatly increased sales of multinational affiliates
are facilitated by enormous increases in intra-organisational trade which have
driven the trade boom since the 1990s (Iammarino and McCann 2013). These
companies tend to make most of their key investments in global cities, and in
particular they are very heavily represented in cities such as London in terms
of their headquarter functions, high-level decision-making facilities and global coordination roles. The global cities, of which London is a prime example,
have become the key nerve centres and nodes in the modern international
networks and flows of money, people, knowledge, services and goods (Taylor
2004; Sassen 2006; McCann and Acs 2011; Iammarino and McCann 2013).

No one in the 1980s could have foreseen these 1990s changes. Yet, the surge
in modern globalisation was, in some sense, a return to long-run globalising
trends which had been evident from the late sixteenth century through to the

early twentieth century. Yet the scale and pace of the recent changes is simply many orders of magnitude greater and more profound than in any previous era (Iammarino and McCann 2013). These trends were to some extent stalled, in the wake of the 2008 global economic crisis, and since then at a global scale, the recovery from the 2008 global financial crisis remains very uneven (IMF 2014). However, even allowing for this stalling, almost all of the technological and organisational changes taking place in today's companies and organisations point to the continuation of these trends over the coming decades (UNCTAD 2012; Ghemawat and Altmann 2012). Yet, even in spite of the enormous changes in the international engagement that we have experienced since the late 1980s, in reality it remains the case that the world today is still much less globally connected than most people would imagine from reading the popular press. For very large economies such as the USA or the EU, or even for large national economies such as Japan, Germany or UK, typically some 80 per cent or above of the value-added in an economy is accounted for by domestic demand (European Commission 2012). As such, the international and external sector typically accounts for something of the order of 20 per cent of the economic activity of the large economies, with smaller and highly open economies exhibiting higher shares. However, international activities are rather different in nature and patterns to domestic activities.

In terms of trade activities, services currently account for two-thirds of global GDP but only 20 per cent of global trade, with goods trade accounting for some 80 per cent of international trade but only one-third of domestic activity (Ghemawat and Altmann 2012). Moreover, these shares have remained fairly stable over long periods. BIS (2010a) estimates that global trade in services currently accounts for 21 per cent of global trade, which is markedly up from 15 per cent in 1980 and slightly up from the 19–20 per cent which has been typical since 1992, with goods exports now accounting for 79 per cent of global trade. This is a result of the fact that global trade in both goods and services increased markedly in all parts of both the developed and developing world since the 1980s and the years immediately prior to the global financial crisis of 2008 (BIS 2010a). Indeed, increasing global liberalisation in merchandise trade over recent years has fostered international growth of some 2–3 per cent of global GDP (Ghemawat and Altmann 2012). The developing countries, and in particular the BRICs countries (McCann 2009a), have increased their share of all forms of international trade, but their growth has been concentrated primarily in goods trade.

Evidence suggests that around two-thirds of the global growth in trade is due to more firms entering into exporting, which is known as the 'extensive margin of trade', rather than existing exporters increasing their export volumes, which is known as the 'intensive margin of trade' (BIS 2010a). Growth via the extensive margin has been more prominent in Russia, China and India, but much less prominent in Brazil or Mexico (BIS 2010a). The result of these shifting trade patterns is that the share of goods trade accounted for by developed economies has fallen more markedly in goods trade than in services, although advanced economies have still retained their competitive advantage in the exporting of high-end goods and in services (BIS 2010a). The growth in trade in goods between 1980 and 2008 has been four times the growth of global output, and the majority of this trade is between advanced economies, although emerging economies are also growing rapidly in this regard (BIS/DFID 2011a). Yet, while global trade patterns have shifted, primarily because of the rise of the BRIICS countries and in particular China (Reyes *et al.* 2009), much of the pattern of world trade has remained largely intact over several decades (BIS/DFID 2011a). Indeed, prior to the global financial crisis in the era of modern globalisation up to 2005 the UK had only lost 4.6 per cent of its jobs due to off-shoring, a level which is only slightly above France at 3.4 per cent but markedly below that of Germany at 7.2 per cent (Hamilton and Quinlan 2008).

In recent decades, global engagement via cross-border investment and FDI has increased even more dramatically than trade (BIS/DFID 2011a). All dimensions of multinational engagement have increased enormously since the onset of the modern era of globalisation in the late 1980s, and there are now just under 80,000 multinational companies with some 800,000 foreign affiliates (Iammarino and McCann 2013). The number of firms which have become multinationals has increased enormously along with the number of bilateral investment treaties and double taxation treaties, and the sales of multinational affiliates located outside of their parent countries is now some 2.25 times the scale of global exports (Iammarino and McCann 2013). In other words, in the modern era of globalisation, international economic engagement is at least as much about increasing cross-border investment as it is about changes in trade.

This greater cross-border investment and global engagement is increasingly associated with the exploitation of multinational firms' internal knowledge assets and their attempts to build on and source new knowledge from emerging economies (McCann 2011; Iammarino and McCann 2013). The unbundling (Baldwin 2011) of multinational establishments into different types of activities and the resulting increased geographical specialisation according to activities and functions rather than sectors has been widespread in recent decades. As such, the enormously increasing scale of cross-border investment flows has been both driven by, and also the result of, the fact that since the early 1990s, multinational investment activities have out-performed domestic activities on almost every indicator and in almost every arena of the global economy (McCann 2011). Indeed, much of the success of the London financial markets is related to the surge in international mergers and acquisitions (M&As) associated with these changes. Yet whereas much of the popular press characterises globalisation primarily in terms of rich countries investing in poor and developing countries, for most of the era of modern globalisation until just after the 2008 global financial crisis it is actually the case that advanced economies overwhelmingly accounted for the majority of both inward FDI (Iammarino and McCann 2013) and outward FDI.[2] In the wake of the crisis the share of inward and outward FDI accounted for by emerging economies increased markedly.[3] Although emerging economies are growing in terms of FDI, their growth in this arena is not nearly as much as in terms of export growth. Moreover, advanced economies still account for the vast majority of both inward and outward FDI stocks and assets (Iammarino and McCann 2013). Some two-thirds of global investment flows are within service industries, with infrastructure services being one of the largest sub-components of these flows (Iammarino and McCann 2013). These patterns, in which advanced economies are still by far the major beneficiaries of global investment as well as the major source of these investments, along with the service sector bias of FDI, present a very different picture from many popular perceptions.

The rise of global regionalisation, rather than globalisation per se, is a key feature of the modern international economy (Rugman 2000; Geyer 2006). Internal cross-border engagement within the super-regions of EU+EFTA, NAFTA, South and East Asia, and MERCOSUR accounts for an increasing share of all forms of international economic activities, including trade in goods and services, foreign direct investment, mergers and acquisitions, bilaterial investment treaties and double taxation treaties, and the sales of multinational affiliates (Iammarino and McCann 2013). Indeed, on all dimensions of globalisation, it is actually increasing localisation and regionalisation at the international scale of adjacent and neighbouring countries which is the key defining characteristic of today's global economy. This movement toward proximity in trade and investment relationships and away from primarily far-distant trading relationships reflects the fact that even though transportation technology has improved dramatically in recent decades, many aspects of distance costs have actually risen in recent decades (Hummels 2007; Hummels and Schaur 2013; Boulhol *et al.* 2008; McCann 2008; Iammarino and McCann 2013). In part this is due to the increased need for speed and timeliness in all aspects of logistics. It is also related to the fact that greater levels of knowledge embodied in innovative products and services require much greater frequency and levels of face-to-face interaction (McCann 2007). The result of this is that certain key hubs have become increasingly important, at least in the earlier years of 'modern globalisation' as locations for activities focused on developing customised and non-routine activities or services (McCann 2008; Iammarino and McCann 2013). At the centre of each of these global 'super-regions' are certain key 'global city' regions (Sassen 2006; Scott 2001; Taylor 2004) which act as the key conduits for the flows of knowledge, people, money, goods and services, and whose influence spreads far beyond their own immediate urban or regional hinterlands. At the same time, activities which can be routinised and broken down into a template or blueprint of routine steps are those which can be most easily be out-sourced and off-shored (Iammarino and McCann 2013; Spitz 2004; Baldwin 2006; Robert-Nicoud 2008; Crinò 2009; Kemeny and Rigby 2012). This is because the principal-agent problems associated with managing arm's-length supply-chain relationships of these types of activities are very much lower than for non-routinised activities. The results of the different types of spatial transactions costs inherent in managing these different types of activities within global value-chains means that the world is not becoming 'flat' (Friedman 2005) in the sense of being more equal and similar and nor is it becoming more 'global' in the sense of simply spreading out (Leamer 2007). It is becoming more differentiated around very large local groupings of specific countries and cities (Iammarino and McCann 2013, 2015a, 2015b) and these processes continued and accelerated unabated from 1990 through to 2008 (McCann 2009).

Another aspect of these changes is that classical and traditional notions of comparative advantage whereby countries specialise and then trade are also becoming increasingly out-dated and of limited use in understanding much of today's global engagement. As new international trade theory and new economic geography already make clear, most trade takes place between countries, sectors, regions and cities which are the most similar to each other, and this is also true for FDI. Flows of goods and services move largely forwards and backwards across geographical borders within the same sector, and between countries that are the most alike. In addition, and to a greater extent than at any stage in the past, the borders across which these goods and services flow are between neighbouring countries (Iammarino and McCann 2013, 2015a, 2015b; Ascani *et al.* 2015; Crescenzi *et al.* 2015a), and one key part of these processes is the rise of global value-chains (GVCs).

Much of the recent increase in global trade over the last two and a half decades is related to the increasing geographical fragmentation of the value-chains which largely comprise the internal production activities of multinationals from advanced economies (McCann 2008; McCann and Acs 2011). A large proportion of international trade, and particularly relating to the BRICs countries, is in reality internal flows of goods and services within foreign-owned multinational firms (Iammarino and McCann 2013). The geographical fragmentation and spatial reconfiguration of global value-chains is reflected in the increasing scales of cross-border investments, in which multinational firms from advanced economies restructure their activities both by direct investments in new host markets, along with much greater out-sourcing and off-shoring of their previously domestic activities (Iammarino and McCann 2013). This greater fragmentation and recombination of global value-chains tends to be heavily oriented towards the same global regions in which multinational firms originate, such that both trade flows (Kohl and Brouwer 2014) and cross-border investment flows become more heavily concentrated across the borders of neighbouring or adjacent countries, rather than across the borders of distant countries (Iammarino and McCann 2013).

The global financial crisis of 2008 led to an immediate fall in global exports of one-third, which by late 2009, one year after the crisis, was still some 23 per cent lower than a year before (BIS/DFID 2011a). The OECD suggests that the effect was particularly significant where imports were re-exported, although this only accounts for part of the fall. Similarly, global FDI inflows fell by 16 per cent in 2008 and a further 37 per cent in 2009, much of which was accounted for by the decrease in mergers and acquisitions, but these had stabilised by 2010, albeit at a lower level than in 2007/2008 (BIS/DFID 2011a). The effects of contractions in the global financial markets were particularly evident in the UK which was specialised in these particular sectors, leading to a national output contraction of 4.1 per cent in 2009 alone. It was only in 2014 that the UK reached again its 2007 nominal output levels.

As we have seen, the enormous disruption caused by the global financial crisis means that by 2011 the world was actually less globally interconnected than it was in 2007 prior to the crisis. Many firms began to reverse some of their earlier out-sourcing and off-shoring processes and to re-concentrate some of their activities in their home countries (*The Economist* 2013a, 2013b). However, this did not represent a reversal of globalisation but a partial reconfiguration. Although from 2011 onwards there was clear evidence of a return to the trend towards increasing global trade (BIS 2012a) and global connectedness (Ghemawat and Altmann 2011; UNCTAD 2012), there were only slow gains between 2009 and 2011 as the global economy gradually emerged from the effects of the 2008 crisis. Much of the very slow recovery was in goods trade and not services (Ghemawat and Altmann 2012) and re-globalisation processes stalled temporarily in 2012 before re-emerging in 2013 (Ghemawat and Altmann 2014). Indeed, by 2013 the global economy had regained its overall pre-crisis levels of interconnectedness in terms of depth but not breadth. In other words, the total number of cross-border connections had recovered to its pre-crisis levels but the diversity of these connections with different countries was still lower than it was in 2008 (Ghemawat and Altmann 2014; *The Economist* 2014a). Re-globalisation involves concentrating on deeper but fewer global linkages, and although there are concerns in some quarters that international trade has peaked as a percentage of global GDP, most commentators assume that it will still grow, albeit at a slower rate than in the previous two decades (*The Economist* 2014b).

The challenges and opportunities faced by the advanced economies associated with the emerging economies have been made especially more complex by the effects of the global financial crisis of 2008, partly because the adverse effects of the crisis have been overwhelmingly borne by wealthier countries, and also because many emerging and evolving trade and FDI relationships had to be curtailed due to the prevailing conditions. The result is that current re-globalisation trends are being led by growth amongst the developing economies in Asia, Latin America, the Caribbean and sub-Saharan Africa, although the actual levels of connectedness of these economies are still far below the advanced economies (Ghemawat and Altmann 2014). This also has led to a partial reversal of the global regionalisation trends described above.

As already mentioned, the general consensus is that long-run growth patterns will continue along the earlier trajectory (UNCTAD 2012) associated with rising global incomes, an increasing middle class in emerging markets and greater regional cooperation (BIS/DFID 2011a). However, such trends are not automatic, and must also be encouraged and fostered by appropriate institutional arrangements. Ghemawat and Altmann (2012) estimate that greater liberalisation of trade in services, which tends to be much less internationalised than goods trade, offers the possibility of increasing global GDP by a further 1.5 per cent in the medium term, which in total implies a 4 per cent increase in global GDP due to enhancing trade liberalisation measures and processes (Ghemawat and Altmann 2012). If the effects of the additional multinational flows of people and capital associated with trade liberalisation are also included, the combined effects could be as great as 8 per cent of global GDP (Ghemawat and Altmann 2012).

The economic implications resulting from the enormous disruption due to the global financial crisis combined with the much lower actual levels of global connectedness than is widely perceived, mean that the potential economic gains from globalisation for all countries are very much greater than are generally reflected in domestic debates (Ghemawat and Altmann 2012). In the light of this, concerns regarding the future pace of global trade liberalisation processes (BIS 2011a) are not unfounded given the ongoing domestic political pressure in many parts of the world for increased protectionism, and this also highlights what any fragmentation of the EU might put at risk (Ghemawat and Altmann 2012). Since the global financial crisis of 2008, there is evidence of increasing protectionism in the global economy amounting to close to 400 restrictive trade measures implemented amongst the G20 counties (BIS/DFID 2011b). Most estimates suggest that the adverse effects have so far only been small scale – amounting to 0.25 per cent of world trade, and affecting 1.8 per cent of G20 imports and 1.7 per cent of EU merchandise exports – although some estimates put the effect as being much higher (BIS/DFID 2011a). Many of these measures amongst trading partners of the EU are 'behind the border', making it very much harder to overcome these restrictions. The growth in the number of such measures has declined of late, although the withdrawal of these measures has also been very slow (BIS/DFID 2011a). Therefore, maintaining and even increasing the momentum towards greater global interconnectedness and international liberalisation is especially important at this moment.

These are all issues for ongoing and future discussions amongst policy-makers and political economy analysts. However, in terms of understanding the current realities of the UK economy this broad picture is an essential backdrop to beginning to make sense of what the UK has been, is currently and will be experiencing, in terms of globalisation. As we will see below, globalisation has heavily influenced the re-shaping of the internal economic geography of the UK economy over the last two and half decades, and therefore a good understanding of the nature and patterns of these processes at a global scale helps us to interpret what we observe at the scale of the UK's regions and cities. The UK has experienced both greater openness regarding imports and exports, but more strikingly, an even greater degree of opening in terms of inward and outward FDI. In particular, as we will see below, the pattern whereby a country moves away from international trade and invest-ment relationships primarily with far-distant and former colonial economies and instead is re-oriented primarily towards trade and FDI with neighbour-ing countries is very much the story of the UK. Moreover, as we will also see, this re-orientation also involves the widening and deepening of both global value-chains and global city relationships, which heavily influence different parts of the UK economy in different ways.

4.3   Trends in the UK's patterns of global engagement

In spite of its loss of empire as a whole the UK is today more globally connected in absolute terms than at any time in the past. In terms of goods and services in 1970 both UK exports and UK imports were approximately £11 billion per annum in current prices, whereas by 2011 UK exports had reached £493 billion and UK imports had reached £517 billion per annum (Allen 2012). Today the UK's values for gross exports and gross imports represent approximately one-third of the UK's total nominal GDP. Between 1970 and 2011 these increasing export and import values in current prices represent a 45-fold increase in exports and a 47-fold increase in imports over four decades. During this same period the nominal output of the UK economy increased by 27 times, so the ratio of both exports to national output and also imports to national output increased by two-fold during the period 1970–2011.[4] However, relative to the 1970 values, in 1980 the ratio of the current value of gross exports to nominal GDP had only increased to a value of 1.2 while the ratio of the current value of gross imports to GDP had only increased to 1.15. Similarly, even by 1990, the ratio of the current nominal value of gross exports to current nominal GDP was still 1.1 while the ratio of gross imports to current nominal GDP was only 1.25 (Allen 2012). In other words, the relative openness of the UK economy in terms of gross exports had only increased by 10 per cent in two decades to 1990 and by 25 per cent for imports. It was only subsequently during the 1990s that the ratios of gross exports and gross imports to national output began to increase rapidly.

As well as enormous increases in the value of trade there have also been some shifts in the composition of UK trade during this period. In 1960 the sectoral composition of both UK imports and UK exports was identical, with three-quarters of both exports and imports being in the form of goods trade, with the remaining one-quarter of each being in the form of services (Allen 2012). By 1970 the pattern of imports remained almost identical, with some 75 per cent of total imports being goods imports with the remaining 25 per cent being imports of services (Allen 2012). Indeed, these shares have remained almost constant right up to the present day, with 77 per cent of UK imports in 2011 being goods imports and 23 per cent of UK imports being services imports (Allen 2012). The sectoral pattern of UK exports remained instead very constant from the 1960s through to the end of the 1980s and the beginning of the 1990s. In 1990 UK goods exports still accounted for

74 per cent of total UK exports and services for 26 per cent of UK exports (Allen 2012). It was only during the 1990s that the sectoral composition of UK exports began to change markedly, with goods exports declining to 70 per cent of total UK exports in 1998, and falling below 60 per cent for the first time in 2007 and reaching a low point of 56 per cent in 2009 (Allen 2012). In the aftermath of the 2008 economic crisis the share of UK goods exports has since risen very slightly as a share of total UK exports accounting for some 61 per cent of UK exports in 2011 (Allen 2012). The changing UK export shares of goods exports are obviously also mirrored by changes in the UK export share of services exports. In 1990 services still accounted for 24 per cent of total UK exports and this share had remained almost entirely constant since 1960 (Allen 2012). By 1998 the share of UK exports accounted for by services had risen to 30 per cent and this share rose more or less continually between 1998 and 2009 reaching a peak of 44 per cent in 2009, before falling back slightly to 39 per cent in 2011 (Allen 2012). In other words, what we see is that the increasing importance of services in UK exports, a topic which is much vaunted in the popular media and press, is actually a very recent phenomenon dating back only to the mid-1990s.

Both the relative openness of the UK economy and also the sectoral composition of imports and exports remained largely unchanged between 1970 and 1990, with just small increases in the UK's level of openness regarding imports. Much of the rapid increase in the UK's trade openness and also the changing composition of UK exports towards a greater relative contribution of service exports are phenomena which began in the 1990s.

Meanwhile, in terms of inward and outward foreign direct investment, the UK is today more open in relative terms than any other large economy in the world with inward and outward FDI/GDP ratios of the order of 55 per cent and 75 per cent, respectively (OECD 2014a). These figures are comparable to those observed in the Nordic economies, although they are still significantly below those observed in Ireland, Switzerland and the Benelux countries (OECD 2014a). In terms of FDI annual outflows from the UK the value of FDI outflows in current prices increased from just under £1.7 billion in 1970 to well over £107 billion in 2011, although again these are markedly down from the peak values of over £230 billion per annum in the early years after the turn of the millennium (Allen and Dar 2013). In current prices this represents a 63-fold increase in outward FDI flows over four decades. Meanwhile, FDI inflows increased from just under £1.5 billion in 1970 to well over £54 billion in 2011, although again these are markedly down from the peak values of over £120 billion per annum in the early years after the turn of the millennium (Allen and Dar 2013). This represents a 36-fold increase over four decades.

Given that in current nominal prices UK output grew 27-fold[5] between 1970 and 2012, these figures suggest that the ratio of outward FDI to UK GDP in current nominal prices increased by 2.33 times while the ratio of inward FDI to GDP in current nominal values increased by 1.33 times, respectively, over these four decades. These figures also imply that between 1970 and 2011 the ratio of UK annual outward FDI flows to UK gross exports increased from 0.15 to 0.22 while the ratio of the UK's annual FDI inflows to gross imports actually fell from 0.14 to 0.10.

There are, however, various important issues to consider when interpreting these figures. Yet, the growth in inward FDI relative to GDP had begun much earlier during the 1970s and then continued in the 1980s. Between 1970 and 1980 nominal UK GDP increased by 4.5 times in current prices, while outward FDI flows increased by a factor of 6.8 and inward FDI flows by a factor of 4.7 times (Allen and Dar 2013). Between 1970 and 1990, a period in which nominal UK GDP increased 11-fold, UK outward FDI increased in current prices by a factor of 10.6 times while that of inward FDI increased by 20.5 times (Allen and Dar 2013). In other words, between 1970 and 1990 there was no change in the UK's level of outward FDI openness but a doubling of the UK's level of inward openness to FDI. In contrast, the value of UK outward FDI in comparison to UK GDP only began to surge during the 1990s. Indeed, after 1990 we see rapid growth in both UK inward and outward FDI and this continued through into the early years after the turn of the millennium. Between 2000 and 2007 the UK's FDI inflows and outflows fluctuated significantly but typical levels far exceeded today's levels (ONS 2011). In 2000 the ratio of UK FDI outflows to exports had reached some 86 per cent while the ratio of UK FDI inflows to imports had reached 41 per cent (Allen 2012). However, the sharp contractions in FDI globally in the aftermath of the 2008 global economic crisis have also been reflected in the UK. In the aftermath of the 2008 global economic crisis, these investment flows contracted sharply. The current UK figures for both inward and outward FDI flows are markedly down from the highs during the early years of the twenty-first century. Similarly, the current UK FDI/trade ratios largely reflect these sharp contractions in global FDI flows in the aftermath of the 2008 global economic crisis.

In the 1960s and 1970s foreign direct investment was almost entirely accounted for by the primary and secondary extraction and manufacturing sectors, with only relatively very limited cross-border investments taking place in service industries. Except for inward investment associated with the establishment of the Eurodollar markets in London during the 1960s and UK outward investment in Commonwealth countries (Casson and McCann 1999), this also remained the case for the UK. Market regulations, trade restrictions, numerous state monopolies and also lack of overseas awareness all contributed to service industries being largely domestically oriented activities during this period (Iammarino and McCann 2013). In marked contrast, today some two-thirds of global FDI is accounted for by service industries (Iammarino and McCann 2013). Modern globalisation is most notably characterised not only by surges in multinational investing and ownership as well as rapid growth in trade, but in particular it is multinational surges in investing and ownership in the services industries which is the key feature (Iammarino and McCann 2013), and these are areas in which the UK has tended to display advantages. As such, in spite of the recent sharp contractions in global engagement in the aftermath of the 2008 crisis, it is the case that on every relevant indicator, the UK today is significantly more globally engaged today than at any stage in the twentieth century. Yet, as a global exporter or importer the UK has actually slipped down the international league tables (Allen 2012). Prior to the 1970s the UK ran on average a balance of trade deficit for goods of some £0.2 billion per annum, but from 1970 to 2011 the balance of trade deficit for goods averaged £27 billion per annum. Between 1980 and 2000 the UK was ranked either the fourth or fifth largest exporter of goods in the world, with a ranking position behind Germany and France and ahead of Italy and The Netherlands. Between 1980 and 2000 the UK's share of global goods exports fell from 6 per cent to 4 per cent. By 2010, however, the UK had fallen to 12th position in the world rankings, behind much smaller countries including The Netherlands and Belgium, and its share of global goods exports had fallen to 2 per cent (Allen 2012). In contrast, for the exports of services the pattern is almost a mirror image for that of goods exports. Prior to 1970 the UK trade in services was typically in surplus with an average value of £0.1 billion per annum, whereas since 1970 the average has risen to £17.5 billion per annum (Allen 2012). Taken together, from 1946 to 1970 the UK balance of overall trade was on average £0.1 billion. From 1977 to 1985 the UK trade balance was in surplus but every year from 1985 onwards except for 1994–1997, the UK trade balance has been in deficit (Allen 2012).

Today the UK is the 25th most open economy in the OECD in terms of the value of exports and imports relative to GDP and the 19th most open in Europe, ranked equal with Spain and just slightly above France, Greece and Italy (OECD 2014a). Total exports and imports along with FDI outflows and inflows, however, only tell part of the story of how internationalised a country is. In addition, we need to consider the positioning of a country in global value-chains (GVCs) and also its contributions and exposure to foreign direct investment. The reason why we also need to consider these additional issues is that during the last two decades the relationships between trade and output have been dramatically restructured due to international fragmentation and re-constitution of GVCs. Johnson (2014) highlights several key features of the current worldwide patterns of international economic engagement associated with GVCs, and in particular how they affect the relationships between domestic value-added and exports. Because of the widespread emergence of GVCs which involve re-importing and re-exporting, the relationship between gross exports and the domestic value-added in exports has changed with gross exports typically over-stating value-added by as much as 25 per cent (Johnson 2014). Furthermore, these gaps are still increasing and they tend to make manufacturing trade appear relatively larger than services than their value-added content implies. At the same time, however, there is enormous heterogeneity in these patterns between countries, between trade partners and also over time with fast-growing emerging economies and countries' bilateral trade agreements witnessing greater falls in value-added relative to gross exports (Johnson 2014). These GVC changes have also been heavily shaped by the enormous increases in foreign direct investment because complex value-chains are almost entirely coordinated within multinational firm networks, rather simply by 'stay-at-home' exporters.

In terms of its overall participation in GVCs, the UK is ranked 26th out of the 34 OECD countries (OECD 2013a). This participation ranking is comprised of two sub-components. First, at 17 per cent the share of foreign inputs used in UK exports (backward participation) is the fifth lowest in the OECD after USA, Australia, Japan and Norway (OECD 2013a). Moreover, along with Belgium, Italy, Canada, Estonia and Norway, the UK is one of only six OECD countries for whom this backward participation share has fallen since 1995 (OECD 2013a). Conversely, since 1995 the share of domestic value-added in UK exports has risen slowly but steadily from 79 per cent to 81 per cent in 2005 and to 83 per cent in 2009 (OECD 2013a). On the other hand, although the share of foreign-produced inputs in UK exports is shrinking, for those intermediate inputs originating overseas, in the UK over 60 per cent of the foreign value-added embodied in the UK's exports originates from within Europe. This 60 per cent is not too dissimilar from most EU economies' respective scores which typically range between approximately 50 per cent in Ireland to over 70 per cent in Austria. The equivalent scores for France, Germany, The Netherlands and Italy are almost identical to that of the UK (OECD 2013a).

Meanwhile, in terms of forward participation in GVCs, the share of UK domestically produced goods and services embodied in third-country exports is the sixth highest in the OECD after the USA, Norway, Japan, Chile and Australia (OECD 2013a). In contrast, the UK share of re-exported intermediates as a percentage of intermediate imports is only 30 per cent and this is the fifth lowest in the OECD after the USA, Australia, Japan and Greece (OECD 2013a). As such, rather than relying on high shares of intermediate imports, the UK appears to add a great deal of value domestically to its exports, a high proportion of which are then embodied as intermediate inputs into third-country exports. Moreover, this share of domestic value-added embodied in third-country exports is increasing (OECD 2013a). However, clues as to why these patterns are evident arise from the fact that not only does the UK exhibit the sixth highest share of total service inputs in its exports out of all OECD countries (OECD 2013a), but also the UK's share of total exports accounted for by domestic rather than foreign service inputs is the second[6] highest in the OECD (OECD 2013a).

Taken together what we see is that the value-added contribution of the UK in GVCs is very similar to what we observe in other major European economies, and Europe accounts for approaching two-thirds of the value-added in the UK's intermediate imports which are then embodied in UK exports. This highlights the fact that the UK is already heavily integrated into European GVCs. However, the key difference is in terms of the positioning of the UK within these GVCs, in that the UK is situated further upstream than many other European economies, and in this respect is more similar to Australia,

Japan, Norway, Canada and the USA. Whereas in the cases of Canada, Norway and Australia this upstream positioning is due to the dominant role of raw material extraction activities in their export profiles, in the case of the UK it appears to be largely related to the increasing share of service inputs embodied into UK exports and the declining share of manufacturing exports.

4.4   UK trade patterns: a sectoral perspective

In terms of trading activities, the share of services and manufacturing exports varies significantly between different countries. In the UK, services accounted for an average value of 40.5 per cent of exports during 2007–2011 (European Commission 2012). In total, the UK service sector exports accounted for 6.2 per cent of the global service exports (BIS 2012a) and the UK's exports of services are second only to those of the USA (BIS 2010a). The UK is one of the few advanced economies to have actually increased its share of global services exports since 1990. Over the last decade UK exports in services grew by 7.5 per cent per annum (BIS 2012a). The UK trade in services has been in surplus every year since 1966, and this surplus has increased since 1990, whereas the UK trade in goods has been in deficit since 1983 (BIS 2010a).

Data from McKinsey Global Institute show that manufacturing is growing in most parts of the world in terms of GDP, at around 2.4 per cent in advanced economies and at around 7.4 per cent in developing economies during 2000–2007 (MGI 2012). Manufacturing contributes disproportionately to innovation and exports, and also to tackling societal challenges such as reducing energy and resource consumption and limiting greenhouse gas emissions (MGI 2012).

In terms of manufacturing and goods trades, over the last decade UK exports in manufactured goods grew by 2.8 per cent (BIS 2012a). The UK is currently the world's ninth largest manufacturing economy by value-added, down from the fifth ranked nation in 1990 (MGI 2012). These structural changes are also reflected in terms of goods exports in that with a share of total global economic output of 2.4 per cent (OECD 2013a), the UK currently accounts for 2.7 per cent of global goods exports, a figure which along with all advanced economies has declined, due to the economic surge in China and many of the other emerging countries (BIS 2012a). However, there are large variations between sub-sectors and between trading partners and the UK's highest sectoral deficits are in electrical equipment, vehicles, mineral oils and fuels (BIS 2012a). Yet, the picture is becoming rather more complex, because many manufacturing jobs are also service activities. In advanced economies manufacturers have increasingly aimed at combining goods with services, so-called 'servitisation' (BIS 2010b), such that these simple sectoral distinctions are increasingly blurred. Service-type activities make up to half of manufacturing jobs, and their share is correlated with the overall skills levels (MGI 2012). In 2005 UK manufacturers accounted for around 14 per cent of UK service exports (BIS 2010b). In the USA 34 per cent of manufacturing employment is in service-type activities such as marketing, R&D and sales, and the range of 30–55 per cent is typical for advanced economies, while services typically account for some 20–25 per cent of manufacturing inputs (MGI 2012).

In 2011 the UK had a trade deficit of −3.6 per cent of GDP, similar to the levels which were typical across the previous decade (BIS 2012a). Part of the reason for this was that UK exports in total grew slower than competitor nations such as France or Germany, except in exports of services, where UK export growth was faster (BIS 2012a). The result is that the share of services in UK exports is now the highest in the world for any large economy, surpassed in Europe only by Luxembourg, Ireland, Greece, Cyprus and Malta, while western European EU-15 countries on average exhibit export shares for services of 25.56 per cent (European Commission 2012).

One of the areas where the UK has made significant exporting strides is in the arena of the Low Carbon and Environmental Goods and Services (LCEGS) sector, which includes traditional environmental activities as well as activities in the renewable energy and emerging low carbon market. Globally this sector accounted for an estimated £3 trillion in 2007/2008 and this sector grew globally by 4 per cent in 2007/2008 and was expected to grow at a similar pace over the coming decade (BIS 2009). Importantly, almost half of this market value stems from activities in the wider supply and value-chain (BIS 2009). The UK accounted for £106 billion of this global market implying its share was 3.5 per cent, and in terms of employment this amounted to some 881,000 jobs, almost half of which were in the emerging low carbon sector. The UK was a net exporter of LCEGS in 2007/2008, primarily in environmental consultancy, wind energy and construction technologies, with China being the largest market (BIS 2009), and this is a sector which appears to offer UK businesses enormous long-term opportunities throughout the supply and value-chain.

4.5   UK trade and international investment patterns: a geographical perspective

In terms of the geography of UK exports, the top five markets for UK exports for both goods and services are the USA, Germany, The Netherlands, France and Ireland (BIS 2010a). This reflects the fact that Europe and other advanced OECD economies still dominate the trade and multinational investment relationships of the UK economy. Indeed, across all countries gravity models show that, as expected, UK exports are positively related to both the GDP and GDP per capita of a country, and negatively related to the geographical, cultural and linguistic distance of the market (BIS 2012a). As is repeatedly found empirically for countries such as the UK, most trade and also most cross-border inward and outward foreign direct investment is with neighbouring and nearby countries and also countries which are the most similar in terms of institutional and cultural issues (Gagliardi *et al.*

2015). This is why although the rise of China and other BRICs countries offer important new markets for UK firms, the future of UK trade and international engagement remains largely contingent on the performance of European and other advanced economies.

4.5.1   UK Trade with Europe and the Rest of the World

In terms of international trade what becomes immediately clear from these figures is the enormous extent to which the UK is interconnected with other European economies, followed by the USA, and to a much lesser extent the UK's former dominions and colonies. Even though the economy of the USA is slightly larger than that of the EU the UK currently exports almost three times[7] the value of goods to the EU than it does to the USA. In 2011 the value of UK exports to the EU accounts for 47.5 per cent of all UK exports with the Eurozone economies accounting for 42 per cent of total UK exports, and this figures rises to 51.8 per cent if we include the full European Single Market including the EFTA economies. Currently, our largest individual export country is the USA (16.2%) followed by Germany (8.9%), The Netherlands (6.9%), France (6.5%), Ireland (5.6%), Belgium (3.9%), Italy (3.2%), Spain (3.1%), China (2.5%), Sweden (1.9%), India (1.7%), Russia (1.5%), Denmark (1.2%) and Poland (1.2%) and all other countries individually account for less than 1% of our exports (Allen 2012). As we see the UK's exports to the USA are more or less equivalent to the UK's exports to Germany and The Netherlands combined (Allen 2012). Moreover, after allowing for the EU+EFTA, the USA and the BRICs countries, the more than 160 countries making up the rest of the world together account for only 25.5 per cent of the UK's exports (Allen 2012).

In terms of imports some 50.6 per cent of the UK's imports come from the EU which includes the 43 per cent of the UK's imports coming from Eurozone economies and this rises to 57.8 per cent if we also include the EFTA countries within the Single Market (Allen 2012). Our largest individual source of imports is Germany (11.5%) followed by the USA (9.4%), France (6.4%), and then China (6.3%) and The Netherlands (6.3%) in joint fourth position. These are followed by Belgium (4.2%), Spain (4.1%), Italy (3.6%), Republic of Ireland (3.3%), Sweden (1.9%), Poland (1.7%), India (1.7%), Russia (1.6%) and Denmark (1.4%). All other countries individually account for less than 1 per cent of our imports. Again, after allowing for the EU+EFTA, the USA and the BRICs countries, the more than 160 countries making up the rest of the world together account for only 22 per cent of the UK's imports (Allen 2012).

Regarding the large emerging economies, while China is the major emerging economic superpower, as with all BRICs countries, the importance of the UK's current trading links with emerging economies is largely in terms of imports, while the UK's export share in these markets is still very small indeed. Indeed, the UK's exports to the Republic of Ireland are greater than to the combined sum of all of the UK's exports to China[8], Brazil and India and only marginally smaller than our exports to all of the BRICs countries together (Allen 2012). The overall share of exports from the UK to the BRICs countries is currently the lowest of any EU country and the second lowest amongst the advanced OECD economies. Moreover, this apparently very limited engagement of the UK with BRICs economies is not because of the different positioning of the UK within global value-chains in comparison to many other OECD countries. Indeed, in terms of the overall domestic value-added component of the UK's exports to the BRICs countries, this share again is the second lowest amongst both the EU and also the advanced OECD economies. In both cases these UK shares amount to approximately one-half of the OECD average values and little more than half of the equivalent shares exhibited by countries such as Germany or Sweden (OECD 2014a).

In 1960 the UK's top ten goods export markets were the USA followed by the five major Commonwealth economies of Australia, Canada, India, South Africa and New Zealand along with Germany, The Netherlands and Sweden. Together the five Commonwealth economies accounted for a quarter of the UK's goods exports while amongst the UK' top 15 goods export destinations the European economies accounted for only 15 per cent of UK goods exports (Allen 2012). By 1970 Belgium, Luxembourg and France had entered the top 10 export destination economies and European economies in the top 15 UK goods export destinations accounted for 29 per cent of UK exports. By 1980 all of the Commonwealth economies had slipped out of the UK's top 10 ranking of goods export destination countries, being replaced by Italy, Sweden and the Republic of Ireland and European economies in the top 15 goods export destinations now accounted for 49 per cent of UK exports (Allen 2012). By the 1990s Spain had also entered the rankings, which have remained largely stable since then with UK goods exports to European economies in the top 15 export destinations accounting for some 53 per cent of UK goods exports. Overall the share of UK goods exports accounted for by the European economies has remained remarkably constant since 1980 (Allen 2012), although its composition has changed along with the enlargement of the EU. UK exports of goods and services to the EU-12 new member states were worth over £11.6 billion in 2009, which were almost three times as much as the £4.5 billion worth of exports in 1999 (BIS/DFID 2011b). The UK's constant share of its total goods exports which are accounted for today by the EU is almost exactly the same as the respective share of both Norway's and Switzerland's goods exports (Allen 2012), and again, these have all remained remarkably constant since 1980 (Allen 2012). Similarly, the share of UK goods exports accounted for by both the USA and Germany has also remained remarkably constant since 1960s (Allen 2012). In contrast, by 2011 the highest ranked Commonwealth UK goods export destination was India at 13th position, accounting for less than 2 per cent of UK exports (Allen 2012). The only other noticeable change was the temporary appearance of

Japan in the UK's top ten goods export destinations in the 1980s and 1990s, but since the millennium Japan has fallen out of the rankings.

In terms of goods imports the geographical patterns looked similar to those for exports, with 1960s goods imports arriving from the USA, Germany, The Netherlands plus the five major Commonwealth economies (Allen 2012). European economies amongst the UK's top 15 goods import origins accounted for only 15 per cent of total UK goods imports. During the 1970s and 1980s other European economies such as France, Sweden, Belgium, Republic of Ireland, Italy and Denmark first appeared in the rankings, followed later in the 1990s by Switzerland and then Spain. This pattern remains today. Amongst the top 15 UK goods import origins, in 1970 some 26 per cent of UK goods imports were from European economies and this number rises to 52 per cent by 1980 (Allen 2012). Again, and as with goods exports, the importance of the EU and also Germany as sources of the UK's goods imports have remained remarkably constant since 1980.[9] The share of the UK's goods imports accounted for by the USA remained remarkably constant between 1960 and 2000 and it is only since then that the share has fallen from some 13 per cent to 7 per cent, being replaced largely by China (Allen 2012). Again, the only other noticeable change was the temporary appearance of both Japan and Hong Kong in the rankings in the 1990s (Allen 2012).

The reason for these particular trade patterns is because of geographical proximity. Trade relationships are generally far more intensive between countries which are geographically close to each other and, as we have seen, one of the ironies of modern globalisation is that the importance of proximity in driving economic relationships has actually been increasing over recent decades, and not decreasing as many people would have presumed (Cairncross 1997; Friedman 2005). In the case of the UK our trade relationships in the era of modern globalisation are dominated by Europe, and this is to be expected given the logic of modern multinational investment and global value-chain behaviour. Yet, the geographical shifts and re-orienting of the UK economy away from former Empire colonies and Commonwealth countries towards Europe began in the late 1960s and accelerated after UK entry into the EEC or Common Market in 1973. As well as altering the UK's trade composition, these international shifts also heavily re-oriented the internal UK geography of port-trade towards ports on the south and east coast of Britain which were close to EEC countries and away from the more northern and western ports which were further away from the rest of Europe (Overman and Winters 2005, 2011), an outcome which is consistent with the worldwide evidence (Brülhart 2011). The era of modern globalisation beginning in the late 1980s and early 1990s simply deepened and accelerated these already-existing trends towards the EU through to 2007. In the aftermath of the 2008 global financial crisis the UK's trade deficit with the rest of Europe reached its highest levels yet recorded (HM Revenue and Customs 2013).

In advanced economies such as the EU Single Market arena, for the UK the importance of the nearby EU markets lies in fostering both the extensive margin of trade as well as the intensive margin (BIS/DFID 2011b, 2011c). For new firms aiming to export for the first time, entering markets which are geographically close is easier than distant markets. Early-stage exporting is an iterative process of trial and error and proximity allows for the frequent face-to-face interaction with distributors, agents and customers necessary to adapt to overseas markets. The EU market provides an important test-bed for fostering fledgling exporters. Accessing more distant markets is easier for experienced exporters, so fostering early-stage exporting in more local EU markets is also critical for providing the experience required to access other more distant markets including the BRICs countries. The EU market also drives improvements in the intensive margin of trade, whereby firms aim to increase their competitiveness by developing innovations to ensure success in a tough market environment.

Economic downturns are periods when market competition is greater than ever, and the need for innovation is absolutely paramount in order to compete successfully. At the same time, achieving competiveness in difficult periods also ensures that firms are best-placed to reap significant benefits when the economy again expands.

The EU Single Market is vital to the UK's prosperity, giving business access to the world's largest market of 500 million people and it has been a key driver of UK and EU growth (BIS/DFID 2011b) via greater trade and cross-border investment. The Single Market is reflected in terms of improved and cheaper network connectedness, easier business travel, mutual agreement on stand-ards, easier access to cheap and competitive inputs, easier and wider options for leisure travel; the realisation of economies of scale (BIS/DFID 2011b); and most importantly the innovation opportunities associated with greater competition, diversification and specialisation opportunities. The reduction in mark-ups associated with the Single Market, which are estimated to be around 3.9 per cent in the 1990s, clearly illustrates the competitive pressures for survival, and OECD estimates suggest that an increase in trade exposure of 10 per cent increases output per worker of some 4 per cent, with lower productivity firms exiting the fiercer competition (BIS/DFID 2011c).

4.5.2   *UK Foreign Investment with Europe and the Rest of the World*

As well as imports and exports, a key feature, and in many ways an even more important feature of modern globalisation than pure trade (Iammarino and McCann 2013), is that of multinationalism and flows of foreign direct investment (FDI). As of 2012, some 4.6 per cent of total world inward FDI was into the UK while 5.8 per cent of total world outward FDI originated from the UK (ONS 2014). As such, today the UK is still the third largest source of outward FDI in the world and the third largest recipient of FDI in the world.[10] Typically, therefore, the Gross National product of the UK is higher than the Gross Domestic product of the UK and this reflects the fact that the UK has a surplus of outward over inward FDI. As well as with trade effects, other EU nations are also both the main source and also the main location of UK FDI. Europe is by far the most globally connected region containing nine out of the ten most globally connected countries (Ghemawat and Altmann 2014). European countries display the highest global connectedness scores for flows of trade and people, while North America displays the highest scores for capital and information flows (Ghemawat and Altmann 2014).

In terms of outward FDI, in 2000 UK outward FDI in the rest of the EU accounted for 55.1 per cent of total UK outward FDI stocks (Allen and Dar 2013). Meanwhile, in 2008, some 44 per cent of UK outward FDI went to other EU-27 nations, generating 48 per cent of total UK foreign investment earnings (BIS/DFID 2011b). The value of the UK's inward and outward FDI flows fell in the aftermath of the global financial crisis, but still over recent years the outward flows of FDI from the UK to the rest of Europe have been greater than the inflows of FDI from Europe to the UK (ONS 2013). By 2011 UK outward FDI stocks to the rest of the EU amounted to £531.5 billion which accounted for 48.4 per cent of the total worldwide UK outward FDI stocks of some £1098 billion (Allen and Dar 2013). For comparison purposes, the US and EU economies are largely equivalent in size. Yet, as of 2011 the stocks of UK outward FDI in the USA account for just 19.1 per cent of total UK outward FDI stocks and only 39.6 per cent of the UK outward FDI stocks within the EU (Allen and Dar 2013).

In terms of inward FDI in 2000 there was some £151 billion worth of inward FDI from the EU-15 in the UK (Allen and Dar 2013; BIS/DFID 2011b) which represented 43.3 per cent of total inward FDI stocks within the UK (Allen and Dar 2013). These figures increased during the period prior to the 2008 crisis such that by 2008, inward FDI stocks from the rest of the EU amounted to £465 billion, representing some 49 per cent of total UK inward FDI stocks. By 2011 total inward FDI stocks from Europe had fallen slightly to £365 billion but these still accounted for 47.7 per cent of all of the £766 billion worth of worldwide inward FDI stocks within the UK (Allen and Dar 2013). Again, for comparison purposes, the US and EU economies are largely equivalent in size. Yet, as of 2011 the stocks of US inward FDI into the UK accounted for 26.6 per cent of all inward FDI stocks within the UK and some 55 per cent of the value of the inward FDI stocks from the EU (Allen and Dar 2013).

In terms of the balance of inward and outward FDI stocks between the UK and the rest of the EU as of 2011 the UK exhibited a net outward FDI surplus with the EU amounting to £166.2 billion.[11] Meanwhile, the UK's net outward FDI surplus with the rest of the world in 2011 was £332.0 billion.[12] In other words, in 2011 the rest of Europe accounted for exactly 33 per cent of the total net surplus balance between UK outward FDI stocks and UK inward FDI stocks to and from the rest of the world (Allen and Dar 2013). That this is the case is even though the EU as a whole accounts for less than 23 per cent of global GDP and only some 7.3 per cent of the global population. In comparison, in 2011 the UK's net outward FDI balance of stocks with the USA, whose economy is largely equivalent in size to that of the EU, is only £6528 million or just 1.9 per cent of the UK's net global FDI surplus.[13] This is half of the UK's net FDI surplus with Hong Kong and more or less equivalent to the UK's net FDI surplus with its own UK Offshore Islands (Allen and Dar 2013). In other words, the UK's outward FDI net balance with the EU is 26 times larger than the UK's outward FDI net balance with the USA.

The scale of the UK's net FDI surplus with the rest of the EU is extremely important in terms of the UK's overall global FDI position. As already mentioned, the UK's Gross National Product (GNP) or Gross National Income (GNI) is currently larger than the UK's Gross Domestic Product (GDP).[14] The difference amounts to some 1.5 per cent of GDP (OECD 2014b) and this reflects the net flows of property and investment asset incomes between the UK and the rest of the world. At present the UK stock of overseas-based property and investment assets of all forms is larger than the total stock of foreign-owned property and investment assets of all forms located within the UK (Allen and Dar 2013). In other words, the UK-owned outward FDI stocks are larger than the UK's foreign-owned inward FDI stocks and the difference between the UK's outward FDI stocks in the EU and its inward FDI stocks from the EU is exactly half of the total net outward FDI stocks of the UK at a global scale. Assuming that the UK's portfolio of outward FDI stocks within the EU displays a broadly similar risk-return profile to the UK's portfolio of outward FDI stocks in the rest of the world, and also assuming that that the risk-return profile of the UK's portfolio of inward investments from the EU is not different to those from the rest of the world, we can therefore also conclude that one-half of the total difference between the UK's GNP or GNI and its GDP is accounted for by economic activity within the rest of the EU. In other words, 0.75 per cent of UK GDP is associated with net profit inflows from the EU associated with UK FDI in the EU.

The slowdown in the global economy has meant that net income flows from UK overseas investments have diminished sharply since the 2008 crisis (*The Economist* 2015a) and these flows will only recover as the global economy recovers. Yet, since the 2008 economic crisis there has been something of a resurgence, albeit a patchy one, of FDI flows at both the global and the EU scales (*Financial Times* 2014; Ernst and Young 2013). Some 55 per cent of FDI inflows into EU economies originates in other EU economies, with 27.5 per cent originating from the USA (Ernst and Young 2013). In contrast, the combined BRICs economies account for only 6.5 per cent of FDI inflows into European economies (Ernst and Young 2013). Amongst European countries, the UK is the largest recipient of FDI inflows with Germany ranked a very close second (Ernst and Young 2012, 2013). Indeed, the UK has been the largest recipient of inward FDI in Europe for much of the last three decades, although its position of relative dominance is continually shrinking. Over the last few decades inward FDI has provided the UK with a diverse and positive range of economic and innovation impacts (Crescenzi *et al.* 2015b).

In terms of the UK, as a base for inward FDI recent evidence in terms of the job-creation effects of inward FDI has been generally positive (Breeze Strategy 2010, 2012), as have the general levels of demand and supply for UK inward FDI (UKTI 2012). Even in the immediate aftermath of the 2008 global financial crisis, in 2009 UKTI projects of new inward FDI investments created 53,358 jobs in the UK, inward investors accounted for some 40 per cent of UK business R&D, and in 2008 foreign residents filed some 40 per cent of UK domestic patents (BIS/DFID 2011c). By 2011 inward FDI projects still numbered 1406 and accounting for 112,000 new or safeguarded jobs (UKTI 2012). Of these, some 42 per cent of projects and some 37 per cent of associated jobs were from inward investment projects originating from other European countries (UKTI 2012), and these levels were lower than in previous years, largely because the severe impacts of the crisis on Europe. As well as shifting patterns regarding both the nature and origins of inward FDI there are also changes in the likely areas of priority. International expectations are that high-technology services and infrastructure services will increasingly dominate FDI projects over the coming years along with sectors such pharmaceuticals and 'cleantech' activities (Ernst and Young 2013).

4.5.3 UK Trade and Investment with the Emerging Economies

As we have already seen, the UK's share of exports and also domestic value-added content in exports to the BRICs countries is currently the second lowest in both the EU and the advanced OECD economies (OECD 2014a). This suggests that many of the currently popular UK political narratives about moving away from European markets to Asian and emerging markets are heavily overplayed. However, although the UK's exports to emerging economies countries are currently very small Ernst & Young ITEM Club have forecasted that UK export growth will average at 8.5 per cent per annum over the next decade (BIS 2012a), with UK exports to the BRICs countries likely to grow at 11.7 per cent per annum. This forecast export growth is argued to be driven primarily in response to rising middle-class consumer demands in these countries (BIS 2012a). At the same time, however, the exports by BRICs countries to the UK and other advanced economies are also likely to continue to increase. This means that an improvement in the UK's trade balance with the BRICs countries depends on both China's success in the five-year plan to rebalance its growth towards domestic consumption and also a successful rebalancing of UK growth away from consumption and imported final goods to exporting and investment (BIS 2012a). Yet, some of these earlier trade growth forecasts are now seriously in doubt, given the economic difficulties faced by China and other BRICs countries, most notably Russia and Brazil.[15] As such, the tiny share of UK economic and trade activity which is associated with the BRICs countries, or even the broader groups of BRIICS countries (McCann 2009a), including Indonesia and South Africa, along with their faltering growth prospects, implies that the potential for UK exporting firms to switch away from EU customers in favour of emerging countries is extremely limited.

At present the UK's exports to BRICs countries are concentrated in machinery, vehicles and consumer goods and services. As such, UK exports tend to be competing more against other advanced economies in emerging BRICs markets than against other emerging economies (BIS 2012a). Although over time this will change as developing countries move up the value-chain, this focuses attention on the need to consider the UK's current and future performance in the high-value-added manufacturing and services sectors in comparison to other advanced economies in competition for these emerging export markets. Europe is increasingly shifting towards medium- and high-value manufacturing activities and is actually increasing its relative global dominance in these fields, and Germany and The Netherlands have increased their share of activity in all levels of the manufacturing global value-chains (Jaegers *et al.* 2013). At the same time, however, the UK, along with Greece, Portugal and Italy, has experienced falling shares in all levels of the manufacturing value-chain (Jaegers *et al.* 2013). The UK is the only northern European economy to exhibit falling trends in all stages of the manufacturing value-adding chains, and this poses real challenges to maintaining and enhancing the UK's present and future role in the global economy.

In terms of the long-run opportunities for UK firms to export to BRICs countries, the demand for imported differentiated goods on the part of emerging countries is very high. However, countries such as the UK, which already trade with most countries across most products, have less scope for gains from the extensive margin of trade than from the intensive margin of trade (BIS 2010a) and must increasingly focus on product differentiation and increased value-added in order to capture greater market share in the emerging markets. This is particularly difficult in the case of Latin America where UK export performance is particularly low. This is partly due to trans-shipment issues in that UK firms often export from US locations, and partly due to the fact that where UK firms do export directly to Latin America our goods and services are then perceived as being directly in competition with US firms (BIS 2012a). Yet, research suggests that although the number of markets and product categories targeted by UK exporters is similar to the UK's competitor countries, for some reason UK firms sell less and at a higher price than their competitor country firms (BIS 2010a). It is unlikely to be a result of currency issues because exchange rate effects on trade often tend to be rather small, with currency depreciation tending to favour trade at the extensive margin rather than at the intensive margin, which is where UK firms tend to operate (BIS 2010a). More likely these patterns are due to the fact that UK firms use outward FDI to sell lower quality goods and exporting to sell higher quality goods (BIS 2010a). Whatever the reasons, however, it is clear that the UK's challenges associated with developing new overseas markets are very real indeed.

This poses an additional challenge for UK firms seeking overseas markets and investment opportunities in the BRICs because the impact on the extensive margin of trade of various types of market entry costs – such as search, adaptation and regulatory costs – tends to be higher for differentiated goods, whereas variable costs – including transport costs – affect the extensive margin more for homogeneous goods because of price effects (BIS 2010a). Social networks often influence trade patterns from differentiated goods and services and new or unconventional products, but the barriers associated with these features are particularly high for innovative firms (BIS 2010a, 2011b), and are also magnified in the case of the BRICs countries due to their cultural, geographical and linguistic distance from the UK.

Outside of certain extraction industries UK foreign investment to developing and emerging economies is very small indeed (Allen and Dar 2013), although it is rapidly increasing (Gagliardi *et al.* 2015). UK outward FDI investments in India represent 1.2 per cent of total UK global outward FDI stocks, while UK FDI in China represents less than 0.6 per cent of total UK outward FDI stocks (Allen and Dar 2013). As of 2010, total outward investment in Asia and Africa (including Japan, Korea, Hong Kong and Taiwan as well as India and China) accounted for just 12.4 per cent of UK overseas outward FDI assets (ONS 2011). Meanwhile, total inward investments in the UK from Asia and Africa accounted for only 7.6 per cent of total inward FDI stocks (ONS 2011). For comparison, both outward and inward UK FDI stocks in and from Australasia and Oceania account for approximately one-fifth of the total combined equivalent values from Asia and Africa, even though the population of Australasia and Oceania is only 0.5 per cent of the total population of Asia plus Africa. These patterns reflect the differing historical economic ties between these different parts of the world.

4.6   The demand impacts of international trade and global value-chains on the UK economy

Taken together all of the issues discussed here relating to international trade, foreign investment and financial transactions contribute to the overall impacts on the UK economy of modern globalisation. However, one issue which we have not yet discussed is the question of how the emerging global value-chains (GVCs) (Gereffi 1999) are changing the international economic relationships between countries. In the modern era of globalisation the increasing fragmentation and changing spatial configurations of GVCs span both services and manufacturing industries. These increasingly myriad GVCs also cut across national borders in far more complicated arrangements than simple textbook-type Ricardian discussions of specialisation and trade imply. As such, simple observations of either gross or net exports or imports hide many of the underlying features of modern international economic engagement.

In order to capture these complex effects alongside the more orthodox trade-related effects we can employ the World Input-Output Database (WIOD),[16] developed at the University of Groningen in The Netherlands in conjunction with a range of international partner institutions. This database integrates the input and output structural and trade relationships across 35 industries and 40 countries, including 27 EU nations plus Canada, USA, Mexico, Brazil, Turkey, Russia, India, China, South Korea, Taiwan, Japan, Indonesia and Australia, which together account for 85 per cent of global GDP and more than 90 per cent of UK trade.[17] The WIOD database provides estimates of all value-added, trade and employment activities for each country decomposed according to the domestic and international sources of demand and supply, and explicitly allowing for the GVC systems we have already discussed. The estimates are generated from a full international input-output system which captures all of the domestic demand interactions between manufacturing, services and other industries (mainly land-based sectors including agriculture and extraction) as well as all of the external interactions between final demand and intermediate demand between countries, while also allowing for the evolving structures of GVCs. As well as the countries in the database, estimates for an aggregate 'Rest of the World' 'country' containing all remaining countries are also included. The data cover the period since 1995 to 2011. The WIOD database allows for the calculation of all of the output and employment effects on each economy of all the currently evolving value-chains, multipliers and feedback effects in the global economy, broken down according to socio-economic categories along with the environmental effects (European Commission 2012).[18]

The data from the WIOD system allow us to disentangle and calculate the value-added and employment effects on the UK economy which are derived from domestic versus international effects, and also broken down by sector. Table 4.1 sets out the various components of UK demand levels all of which are calculated in terms of current US$ prices for the years 1995, 2008 and 2011. These specific years coincide with the regional and urban data provided in the previous two chapters and allow us to observe both the effects on the UK economy of the modern era of globalisation which commenced in the late 1980s onwards, plus the economic downturn effects since the 2008 global financial crisis.

The rows in Table 4.1 each allow us to identify one particular feature of the sources of UK value-added. Row 1 indicates the UK value-added (VA) which is due to UK domestic final demand, while Row 2 indicates the UK value-added which is due to foreign final demand from all overseas markets. Rows 1 and 2 sum up to the total final UK demand given in Row 7. Row 3 indicates the UK value-added which is due to final demand in other EU countries, while Row 4 indicates the UK value-added which is due to final demand in non-EU countries. Rows 3 and 4 sum up to give Row 2. The UK value-added which is derived from demand from non-EU countries is broken down in Rows 5 and 6 into two separate components. Row 5 indicates the UK value-added which is due to intermediate demand associated with final products from EU countries which are actually serving final demand in

Table 4.1 Sources of value-added in the UK economy 1995, 2008, 2011 (in Millions of Current US$)

	UK Value-Added (VA)	1995	2008	2011
1	VA from UK Domestic Final Demand	823,202	1,909,687	1,702,122
2	VA from Foreign Final Demand	224,314	541,999	503,150
3	– of which from EU Final Demand	101,517	231,416	193,703
4	– of which from non-EU Final Demand	122,797	310,583	309,447
5	– of which is served via EU GVCs	5925	21,537	21,632
6	– the rest of non-EU Final Demand	116,872	289,046	287,815
7	Total UK Value-Added (GDP)[a]	1,047,516	2,451,686	2,205,272

Source: WIOD World Input-Output Database, University of Groningen.

[a] The WIOD database suggests that between 2008 and 2011 the UK economy contracted by some 10 per cent, a value which is much greater than UK and OECD official statistics (OECD 2014b). This is because all WIOD data for all countries are calculated at current exchange rates and are neither adjusted for purchasing power parities nor inflation adjusted using the GDP deflator. The important point, however, is that the WIOD data are base-invariant so this does not affect the relative shares of the individual sources of demand in each country. For details see Timmer *et al.* (2013).

non-EU countries. Row 6 indicates the value-added which is due to non-EU final demand on UK markets, including from NAFTA and the BRICs countries. Row 7 provides the total UK value-added (GDP in basic prices).

The figures in Row 5 capture the role of the UK and EU in global value-chains (GVCs) which are serving final demand in other non-EU countries (Timmer *et al.* 2013). An example of the UK role in these types of GVCs would be the case of a UK-based firm providing computer-systems services to a manufacturing firm in The Netherlands which then sells its products to final consumers in Brazil or China. Alternatively, another example could be a UK firm providing financial services to a plastics company in Germany which then sells its products to the USA, or finally a UK high-technology manufacturer producing components for an automobile firm in France which sells its cars in Russia and Japan.

In Table 4.2 the figures in Table 4.1 are converted into shares calculated with respect to either UK Final Domestic Demand; with respect to All Foreign Final Demand; with respect to All Non-EU Final Demand; or with respect to All UK Domestic and Foreign Demand. In Table 4.2, as we see from Row A, the share of UK domestic value-added which is due to overseas demand is 29.56 per cent. In other words the UK economy is a very open economy. At the same time, this share has only increased very slowly between 1995 and 2011, by some 2.3 percentage points, so the increasing influence of modern globalisation in terms of economic openness has only been very gradual. In other words, for all of the popular discussions regarding the transformative impacts of globalisation, over two decades the UK has only shifted very slowly and slightly in terms of its global engagement and the value-added share of its global activities relative to its domestic activities.

Table 4.2 Shares of value-added in the UK economy 1995, 2008, 2011

	UK Value-Added (VA)	1995	2008	2011
A	VA from Foreign Final Demand Relative to VA from UK Domestic Final Demand [2/1]	0.2725	0.2838	0.2956
B	VA from EU Final Demand Relative to VA from All Foreign Final Demand [3/2]	0.4525	0.4269	0.3849
C	VA which is created for EU GVCs serving Non-EU Final Demand relative to VA from All Non-EU Final Demand [5/4]	0.0482	0.0693	0.0699
D	VA from All EU-final Demand + VA which is created for EU GVCs serving Non-EU Final Demand relative to VA from All Foreign Final Demand [(3+5)/2]	0.4789	0.4667	0.4279
E	VA from All EU-final Demand + VA which is created for EU GVCs serving Non-EU Final Demand relative to VA from UK Domestic Final Demand [(3+5)/1]	0.1305	0.1324	0.1265
F	VA from Foreign Final Demand Relative to VA from Total UK Domestic and Foreign Final Demand (GDP) [2/7]	0.2141	0.2211	0.2281
G	VA from All EU-final Demand + VA which is created for EU GVCs serving Non-EU Final Demand, relative to all UK VA from UK Domestic and Foreign Final Demand (GDP) [(3+5)/7]	0.1025	0.1031	0.0976

Source: WIOD World Input-Output Database, University of Groningen.
Note: The figures in square brackets indicate the respective rows in Table 4.1 from which the data are derived.

From Row B we see that UK value-added due to EU final demand had fallen slowly between 1995 and 2008 by some 2.5 percentage points, but then fell by an extra 4.2 percentage points as a result of the European demand contraction in the wake of the global financial crisis (European Union 2014).

These UK's value-adding shares associated with both domestic and foreign activities have shifted slightly over the last two decades. From Row C we see that the share of UK value-added which is due to EU-based GVCs that are serving final demand in non-EU markets has increased steadily since 1995 by some 2.2 percentage points from 4.8 per cent to 7 per cent. These GVCs are a result of the multinational fragmentation and spatial reconfiguration processes outlined above. Deepening intra-EU integration and the cross-border investment processes associated with this, mean that the EU has been a central hub in these processes of value-chain fragmentation and global reconfiguration. These processes of value-chain fragmentation and recombination are very important because indices of 'final' demand alone do not capture these evolving value-chains. As such, the correct indicator of the EU-related demand on the UK economy is given by the effects of EU final demand plus the effects of the EU GVCs serving non-EU markets. In Table 4.2 these effects are given in Rows D, E and G, calculated with respect to total Foreign Demand, total UK Domestic Demand, and with respect to total UK output, respectively[19].

If we consider the total impact of the EU on the UK economy we see from Row E that EU demand plus the demand from EU GVCs serving non-EU final demand is 12.65 per cent of total UK domestic demand and from Row G that it represents 9.76 per cent of total UK domestic plus foreign demand. In other words, the overall share of UK domestic plus foreign demand which is accounted for by EU demand including EU value-chains serving foreign demand, is 9.76 per cent. These figures capture the total demand effect of the EU on the UK economy including those effects which are generally impossible to identify from simple trade statistics, and these figures imply that the total demand effect of the EU on the UK is currently £157.33 billion per annum. In addition, as we have already seen some 0.75 per cent of UK GDP relates to repatriated profit incomes generated by UK assets located within the EU. In other words, the total economic effect of the EU on the UK economy must be at least 10.51 per cent of total UK GDP, or some £168.84 billion per annum. Moreover, if Norway, which accounts for 5 per cent of UK imports, and Switzerland, which accounts for 7 per cent of UK exports (Allen 2012), are also included as part of the European Single Market, then this EU-related demand effect of £168.84 billion per annum clearly represents a lower-bound estimate of the total economic effect of the EU Single Market on the UK's economy, and will shift this value upwards to over £170 billion.

To give a sense of the relative scale of these EU demand impacts on the UK economy, calculations using the WIOD indicate that 10.49 per cent of the total domestic plus foreign demand driving the Canadian economy is accounted for by the USA, while the equivalent figure for Mexico is 9.58 per cent. In other words, EU-related demand accounts for a share of UK GDP which is almost exactly the same as the effects of the US economy on either Canada or Mexico. Moreover, this is the case even though the economy of the rest of EU is 5.15 times larger than the UK economy, while the USA economy is some 11 times and 14 times larger than the Canadian and Mexican economies, respectively (OECD 2014b). The UK economy is a little under twice the size of the Canadian economy and well over twice the size of the Mexican economy, while the EU and US economies are of similar orders of magnitude. On the basis of these pure scale comparisons, however, we might have expected demand in Canadian and Mexican economies to be far more dependent on the USA than the effects of EU demand on the UK. However, in reality, the UK economy is more deeply integrated with the rest of the EU than would be suggested purely on the basis of the relative size and location of the neighbouring economies, and this also underscores the fact that the EU is the world's most deeply interconnected global trade block. Similarly, from WIOD we see that the demand effects of China on the Australian economy associated with Chinese raw materials imports from the Australian extraction industries, and which are widely credited with driving Australia's success over the last two decades, still only account for 5.4 per cent of total Australian domestic and foreign demand. In other words the demand effects of the EU on the UK are twice the relative size of the effects of China's demand on the Australian economy. Moreover, even if we add India to the Australian export story the total combined demand share of China plus India is still only 5.9 per cent of total Australian domestic plus foreign demand. As such, the example of Australia, along with examples of Canada and Mexico, underscore the scale and the depth of economic integration between the UK and the rest of the EU.

In Table 4.3 we see that in comparison to all UK foreign demand effects, between 1995 and 2008 the share of value-added due to EU-related final and intermediate demand remained constant at 47 per cent, while between 2008 and 2011 this share fell to 43 per cent. This fall was due to the demand contraction in Europe which accounted for 96.7 per cent of UK demand contractions which were due to adverse international trade-transmission effects. However, this is not in any way to argue that Europe is the major source of the UK's domestic demand contractions because the scale of this fall should be put into perspective. As we see in Table 4.1, since 2008 the fall in UK value-added due to the demand contraction associated with European activities is only 15.2 per cent, or just under one-seventh of the fall in UK value-added due to the contraction of UK domestic demand. More than 84 per cent of the total demand contraction within the UK is simply due to domestic demand contractions, and not due to international issues.

As we also see from Tables 4.3 and 4.4, the value-added and employment relationships between UK and Europe differ very little between services and manufacturing. The coefficients differ only slightly between manufacturing

Table 4.3 Shares of value-added by UK sector due to EU final demand + EU GVCs serving non-EU final demand 1995, 2008, 2011

UK Value-Added (VA) from All EU-final Demand + VA which is created for EU GVCs serving Non-EU Final Demand relative to VA from All Foreign Final Demand [(3+5)/2]	*1995*	*2008*	*2011*
– in Other Sectors (Agriculture, Extraction, Utilities)	0.420	0.574	0.486
– in Manufacturing	0.513	0.476	0.462
– in Services	0.455	0.443	0.401
– in All Sectors	0.479	0.467	0.428

Source: WIOD World Input-Output Database, University of Groningen.

Table 4.4 Shares of UK employment by sector due to EU final demand + EU GVCs serving non-EU final demand 1995, 2008, 2011

UK Employment due to All EU Final Demand + UK Employment for EU GVCs serving Non-EU Final Demand relative to employment due to All Foreign Final Demand [(3+5)/2]	1995	2008	2011
– in Other Sectors (Agriculture, Extraction, Utilities)	0.508	0.567	0.520
– in Manufacturing	0.512	0.474	0.459
– in Services	0.458	0.436	0.389
– in Total UK Employment	0.484	0.453	0.417

Source: WIOD World Input-Output Database, University of Groningen.

and services, with the value-added interconnectedness between the UK and Europe in manufacturing being only 15.2 per cent higher than for services while for employment it is only 8.7 per cent higher.

In terms of employment, as we see in Table 4.4 the total effect on UK employment of the EU-related activities, including the effect of European GVCs, is that in 2011 just under 42 per cent of all overseas-related employ-ment was dependent on EU-related activities, a figure which had fallen slightly from 48 per cent in 1995 and 45 per cent in 2008 due to the aftermath of the 2008 crisis. Interestingly, by comparing Table 4.4 with Table 4.3 we also see that the UK overseas-related employment shares which are associ-ated with EU final demand plus the non-EU final demand which is served via EU global values, closely exactly reflect the equivalent value-added shares accounted for by the same combined sources of EU demand. EU demand most significantly affects demand and employment in sectors such as utilities, agriculture and extraction industries, followed very closely by manufacturing industries. In each of these cases EU demand accounts for more or less half of total overseas-related demand and employment. Somewhat differently, the reliance of the UK service industries on EU-related demand is noticeably less, at around some 40 per cent of demand and employment.

Often, observations of international data suggest that international and multinational activities tend to exhibit higher value-added shares than employment shares. Here, however, the WIOD data suggest that within the UK the employment and value-adding shares of all foreign-related demand which are due to EU demand are very consistent with each other.

The WIOD data imply that some 2.5 million jobs in the UK are directly linked to EU-related demand. If in addition to the UK jobs based on EU demand we also include the workers from other EU countries working in the UK – of which the largest groups are from Poland, Ireland and Germany (ONS 2012) – this figure is then larger than the 3.5 million UK-based jobs assumed to be directly related to the EU (BIS/DFID 2011b).[20]

Other evidence also provides support for the magnitude of these WIOD-based numbers regarding the number of UK-based jobs due to the

EU economy. Some 3.706 million people in the UK work in foreign-owned establishments, accounting for 13.32 per cent of total UK employment. Of these, 2.374 million (64.1 per cent of those in foreign-owned units) work in EU immediately owned units and 1.332 million (35.9 per cent) work in non-EU immediately owned units, while 1.882 million (50.8 per cent) work in EU ultimately owned units and 1.823 million (49.2 per cent) work in non-EU ultimately owned units.[21] In terms of relative shares, 2.374 million employees in EU immediately owned establishments represent 8.54 per cent of total UK employment, while 1.882 million in EU ultimately owned represents 6.77 per cent of total UK employment.[22]

To put these UK-based EU-related employment figures into context, the total number of jobs directly linked to EU-related demand is the equivalent to total employment associated with UK manufacturing, and ten times the number of workers in the City of London Financial Services industry (CEBR 2012a, 2012b). Moreover, just over twice as many UK-based jobs directly due to EU-related demand are in the service industries than in the manufacturing industries. In other words, more than two-thirds of EU-related employment demand within the UK is in services, and these figures have been increasing (BIS 2012a).

Finally, we turn to the trade and economic potential of the UK which is associated with the rise of BRICs countries). In 1995 the share of UK demand which is driven by demand from the BRICs countries was just 0.91 per cent of total domestic and foreign UK demand., just 4.24 per cent of total UK foreign demand, and just 1.1 per cent of domestic UK demand. In other words, the overall economic interactions between the UK and the BRICs countries in 1995 were tiny and had only very marginal effects on the UK economy. As the BRICs countries started to grow rapidly from the 1990s onwards, between 1995 and 2008 the UK value-added related to the demand increases in the BRICs countries increased by 0.71 percentage points to 1.62 per cent. Relative to total UK foreign demand the share had increased by 3.1 percentage points to 7.33 per cent and relative to UK domestic demand by 0.98 percentage points to 2.08 per cent. During the post-crisis period, as the

Table 4.5 Shares of UK value-added arising from final demand in the BRICs countries 1995, 2008, 2011

UK Value-Added (VA)	1995	2008	2011
VA from BRICs Final Demand	0.011	0.0208	0.0291
– in comparison to UK Final Demand			
– in comparison Total Foreign Final Demand	0.0424	0.0733	0.0984
VA from BRICs Final Demand	0.0091	0.0162	0.0225
– in comparison to Total UK Domestic and Foreign Final Demand			

Source: WIOD World Input-Output Database, University of Groningen.

Table 4.6 Shares of UK value-added by sector due to BRICs final demand 1995, 2008, 2011

UK VA due to BRICs Final Demand in comparison to Total UK Domestic and Foreign Final Demand	1995	2008	2011
– in Other Sectors (Agriculture, Extraction, Utilities)	0.0072	0.0115	0.0162
– in Manufacturing	0.0223	0.0508	0.0712
– in Services	0.0053	0.0118	0.0160

Source: WIOD World Input-Output Database, University of Groningen.

BRICs economies continued to grow while most OECD economies generally contracted, the respective percentage point increases between 2008 and 2011 following the global financial crisis are 0.62 with respect to total UK domestic plus foreign demand, 2.51 points with respect to total foreign demand, and 0.83 with respect to total domestic demand only. In 2011 the combined demand effects from BRICs economies still only accounted for 9.84 per cent of total foreign demand effects on the UK economy, only 2.91 per cent of UK domestic demand, and in total only 2.24 per cent of all of the domestic and foreign demand effects on the UK economy.

The share of value-added across all UK sectors associated with BRICs final demand has increased more or less threefold since 1995. At just over 7 per cent the relative importance of BRICs demand is 4.5 times larger in manufacturing than in services and in all other industries in which it is only 1.6 per cent. Yet, even for manufacturing industries BRICs demand is still only a tiny component. Moreover, the fact that the coefficients are of this magnitude underscores the important point that in spite of all of the talk regarding the potential UK growth effects of the BRICs economies, it still remains the case that the combined effect of the BRICs countries on the UK economy is tiny.

To put these figures into perspective, the total European demand-related value-added and employment figures are some 4.35 times the total demand associated with all of the BRICs countries combined. In other words, the total value-added and employment impacts of China, India, Russia and Brazil combined on the UK economy are less than 23 per cent of the economic impacts of the EU on the UK economy. This is not surprising when we consider that, as we have already seen, UK exports to the Republic of Ireland are larger than the UK's combined exports to all of the BRICs countries,[23] and the UK's imports from The Netherlands and the Republic of Ireland together far outweigh the UK's imports from all of the BRICs economies. The result of the UK trade patterns being heavily weighted towards neighbouring countries, as is also the case for all economies across the globe, is that the UK-BRICs growth in trade is increasing from a tiny original baseline. As such, the combined contribution of the geographically distant BRICs economies to UK demand remains very small even though the BRICs countries have been growing rapidly. This means that the overall effect of export-led demand from the Rest of the World, and in particular from the BRICs countries, on the UK economy, still remains very small.[24]

There is a final group of economies that we need to consider, and these are the 'western offshoots' (Maddison 2006) comprising the USA and the large westernised Commonwealth economies of Canada and Australia. Up to the 1960s and prior to joining the EEC European Common Market in 1973, these North American and Commonwealth economies had traditionally been key components of the UK trading and overseas investment relationship. However, as we have seen the global engagement of the UK has changed dramatically since then, so an understanding of these relationships today also helps to underscore the scale of these changes.

In Table 4.7 we see that the demand impacts of final demand in the USA on the UK economy are very small indeed, and are only of the order of just over 3 per cent. However, this has been the case for the last two decades. Most of the impacts on the UK economy associated with US final demand are in manufacturing industries, accounting for some 8 per cent of manufacturing demand, a value which we see from Table 4.6 is higher than the combined value of all BRICs demand on UK manufacturing. The effects of US demand on both the UK service industries and all other UK industries accounts for just below or just above 3 per cent of total demand on these sectors.

Similarly, if we also add to the US demand effects on the UK the impacts of the final demand from the other 'Western Offshoots' of Canada and Australia, the picture remains largely unaltered. As we see by comparing Table 4.8 with Table 4.7, the combined effects on UK output, which is associated with final demand from the three 'Western Offshoots', are marginally larger than the effects of the USA alone, increasing by one-third to 4.5 per cent. The demand effects on UK manufacturing are three times greater than for services or all other industries.

As a whole what is clear is that the combined demand effects on the UK economy associated with both the three 'Western Offshoots' of USA, Canada and Australia plus the BRICs countries are only two-thirds of the EU demand

Table 4.7 Shares of UK value-added arising from final demand in the USA 1995, 2008, 2011

UK Value-Added (VA)	1995	2008	2011
VA from USA Final Demand – in comparison to Total UK Domestic and Foreign Final Demand	0.0373	0.0342	0.0341
– in Other Sectors (Agriculture, Extraction, Utilities)	0.0245	0.0300	0.0304
– in Manufacturing	0.0734	0.0865	0.0811
– in Services	0.0282	0.0271	0.0275

Source: WIOD World Input-Output Database, University of Groningen.

Table 4.8 Shares of UK value-added Arising from final demand in the 'western offshoots' of the USA, Canada and Australia 1995, 2008, 2011

UK Value-Added (VA)	1995	2008	2011
VA from 'Western Offshoots' Final Demand	0.0471	0.0442	0.0455
– in comparison to Total UK Domestic and Foreign Final Demand			
– in Other Sectors (Agriculture, Extraction, Utilities)	0.0291	0.0357	0.0383
– in Manufacturing	0.0903	0.1103	0.1097
– in Services	0.0368	0.0357	0.0368

Source: WIOD World Input-Output Database, University of Groningen.

effect on the UK. Most noticeably, the impacts of both 'Western offshoot' and BRICs demand on UK service industries remains remarkably small, even as Europe has struggled in the aftermath of the global financial crisis. While the 'servitisation' of UK exports is widely discussed, in reality the contribution to UK service industries due to demand from the USA, Canada and Australia is not only tiny, but also has not grown since 1995. Meanwhile, the contribution of demand from Brazil, Russia, India and China to the UK's service industries remains tiny, and as we see from Table 4.6 has only changed by just over 1 per cent since 1995. The much-vaunted role of services in UK exports to far-distant and emerging economies is not to be found in the data in the case of these seven countries. Instead the UK's international engagement with both the 'Western Offshoots' and the BRICs is dominated by manufacturing industries. In reality, the service sector exports including the 'servitisation' of UK manufacturing exports is dominated by demand from the EU. This global regionalisation of service exports makes perfect sense given that services generally require much more face-to-face interaction between customers and suppliers than many types of manufacturing activities. As we see from Tables 4.3 and 4.4 Europe nowadays accounts for some 40 per cent of foreign-related demand and employment in UK services.

This underscores the immense importance of the EU for UK demand and also underpins the need to understand our ongoing levels of international economic engagement with our EU partners. The EU today still accounts for something of the order of half of the UK's overall foreign trade and also half of its total foreign inward and outward investments and one-third of its total net profit inflows. Eight out of the top ten of the UK's export markets are in the EU, and EU countries currently trade with each other twice as much as they would without the Single Market. As a result, it has been estimated that around 3.5 million jobs in the UK are estimated to be directly linked to the exports of goods and services to the EU (BIS/DFID 2011b), a figure which accounts for just under 12 per cent of the UK workforce. These various trade, FDI and global value-chain interactions which we have discussed above together produce the combined EU demand effects on UK GDP that we observe here. To re-cap, the WIOD figures imply that the some 77 per cent of total UK GDP is due to domestic demand while 23 per cent of UK GDP is due to foreign-related demand. Moreover, some 44.4 per cent of this total foreign-related demand is accounted for by the EU economies, including the UK–EU global value-chains. Taken together, what we see is that the EU Single Market in 2011 accounted for £168 billion per annum, or 10.50 per cent of total UK economic demand, and this figure comprises 9.76 per cent associated with direct and indirect demand effects plus 0.75 per cent associated with profit inflows from the EU. Given that in 2011 there were currently some 25.7 million UK households, and using current output levels[25] this implied that the EU economy was then 'worth' (CBI 2014) at least £6537 per household per annum, irrespective of whether or not household members work directly in EU-related or export-related activities.

This figure of close to £170 billion per annum for 2011 is a very large figure, and is associated with all of the static and dynamic effects associated with EU economic integration, including trade, global value-chain and foreign investment activities. However, it also represents a lower-bound estimate as it does not include any of the beneficial economic effects associated with immigration (Dustmann and Frattini 2014), and nor does it include the induced competition, innovation and efficiency-enhancing effects within the UK domestic economy due to greater external economic integration. This figure of £168 billion per annum – or 10.5 per cent of GDP – is more than twice as high as the figure of £62–78 billion – or 4–5 per cent of GDP – which the CBI (2014) reported that the Single Market is 'worth' net to the UK, or the 6 per cent of GDP reported by the BIS 2010 estimates submitted to the House of Lords EU Select Committee on Re-launching the Single Market.[26] The major difference, however, between the CBI and BIS reported figures and the WIOD estimates is due to the fact that the WIOD model is far more sophisticated than the literature review research of the CBI (2014) or the counter-factual approach of Boltho and Eichengreen (2008). The WIOD data allow for formal demand calculations based on the systems of national accounts integrated across 40 countries and 35 sectors.[27]

If we translate this 2011 EU Single Market year-on-year figure of £6537 per UK household per annum into a present value, or total mortgage value equivalent, then the total value per UK household of the EU Single Market in 2011 prices is between £81,713 for a time preference discount rate of 8 per cent and £130,740 for a time preference discount rate of 5 per cent. If we net out the EU budget contribution of the UK the present value of the EU Single Market per UK household still was worth more than £77,000 for a time preference discount rate of 8 per cent and £124,000 for a time preference discount rate of 5 per cent.[28]

In order to put these numbers into perspective, the importance of the EU Single Market to the UK economy is underlined by the fact that today it is worth almost half of what the whole economy of London is currently worth to the UK, or almost three-quarters of what the economy of the South East of England is worth to the UK, and more than what any of the UK's other ten regions are worth to the UK. In other words, whichever way we choose to characterise these issues, the important point is that the demand effects of the EU Single Market on the UK economy are enormous.

If we now consider the additionality effects of the EU Single Market, or rather the long-run growth effects due to EU integration which would otherwise not have been possible, previous estimates suggest that the Single Market is likely to be responsible for income *gains* of the order of 5–6 per cent for long-standing EU member states (Boltho and Eichengreen 2008). In the case of the UK this implies an income increase of some £3300 per annum per household for all UK households over what would have been the case without the EU Single Market (BIS/DFID 2011b), again irrespective of whether the household employment is directly related to the EU Single Market or not. In order to arrive at this figure Boltho and Eichengreen (2008) used a counter-factual approach similar in methodology to Fogel (1964) rather than employing a formal econometric or modelling approach. However, these figures can now be re-assessed in the light of the results presented here based on the WIOD estimates and foreign investment data.

We know that since the 1960s and early 1970s the UK trade and foreign investment patterns have gradually shifted away from the far-distant Commonwealth countries and towards the neighbouring European economies. In the case of the UK, since the 1960s, the UK's goods export trade with the EU as a share of total UK goods export trade has increased by just under 30 percentage points while that of import trade has increased by more than 30 percentage points (Allen 2012). These figures imply that approximately 60 per cent of today's UK–EU trade represents the increased share of UK trade accounted for by this shift towards the European economies and away from the Commonwealth economies. A rapidly increasing share of today's international trade in reality is comprised of intra-firm trade within multinational companies. The increasing 'global regionalisation' of trade (McCann 2009a) is closely tied to the emergence of global value-chains and reflects a pattern which is seen all across the world (Iammarino and McCann 2013) whereby today some 60–70 per cent of all multinational investments, sales and employment are contained within the same 'global region' of neighbouring countries as the headquarter locations of the parent companies (Rugman 2000, 2005; MGI 2010). If we apply the 60 per cent figure to the WIOD demand estimates, then given that current EU-related total demand accounts for 10.25 per cent of UK economic activity and along with a similar figure for employment, these shifting trade-pattern figures suggest that the additional UK income associated with the EU is $0.6 \times 10.25 = 6.15$ per cent of total UK GDP, or equivalent to over £100 billion per annum. In other words, even if we also allow for the more than £10 billion annual net contribution of the UK to the EU (Robinson 2015),[29] in terms of absolute orders of magnitude the 5 per cent estimate of Boltho and Eichengreen (2008) as regards the GDP per capita gains associated with EU integration was likely to have been an under-estimate of the order of one-quarter. The WIOD 2011 data demonstrate that the UK's net annual benefit of EU Single Market membership allowing for the UK's net payments into the EU and not including the EEA countries, was of the order of £160 billion per year in 2011. Moreover, the increase in UK household incomes associated with EU Single Market membership by 2011 was of the order of £1666 per person per annum and £4000 per household per annum.

As before, if we translate the likely UK household net income gains associated with EU membership of £4000 per UK household per annum year-on-year into a present value, or total mortgage value equivalent, then the total value per UK household of the EU Single Market in 2011 prices is between £34,000 for a time preference discount rate of 8 per cent and £80,000 for a time preference discount rate of 5 per cent.

If we now assume that the shares of the different WIOD components of demand have remained almost constant between 2011 and 2014, then in current UK output[30] terms the EU economy is 'worth' some £188 billion per annum to the UK in current prices. If we subtract the UK's current net annual EU contribution of £11.7 billion per annum this gives a net economic surplus of £176 billion per annum. Given that there are currently 26.4 million UK households this implies that the EU Single Market is currently 'worth' some £2750 per person per annum and £6650 per UK household per annum.

Again, if we translate this EU Single Market year-on-year figure of £6650 per UK household per annum into a present value or total mortgage equivalent value, then the total present value per UK household of the EU Single Market is currently between £83,125 for a time preference discount rate of 8 per cent and £133,000 for a time preference discount rate of 5 per cent.[31]

There are two ways of judging the likely veracity of these figures which are generated by linking the WIOD calculations to long-run geographical changes in international trade and investment patterns. First, the importance today and also the positive long-run gains from EU membership are more or less a mirror image of the likely negative effects of an exit of the UK from the EU, in that WIOD-based estimated effects of integration and separation are of similar orders of magnitude to each other, although of course in opposite directions (Ottaviano *et al.* 2014; Dhingra *et al.* 2015). Second, and as discussed in detail in Appendix 4.3, an additional check on the likely veracity of these estimates can also be provided by considering the experience of New Zealand, a country which is very similar to the UK in terms of institutions, governance and culture, but which for reasons of economic geography was simply unable to engage in the extensive forms of global regionalisation of the types enjoyed by the UK with the EU. Again, the adverse experience of New Zealand was almost a mirror image of the UK's positive experience of global regionalism.

To give a sense of the scale of the WIOD-based and FDI-based impacts reported here regarding the effects of the EU Single Market on the UK economy's current income and also on its long-run growth, there are two key reference points. First these positive estimates are of a similar order of magnitude to the losses the UK experienced since the 2008 global economic crisis (Ottaviano *et al.* 2014). In other words they are enormous. Second, if we recall the regional and city-based counter-factual exercises in Chapter 2 and Chapter 3, we see that the estimates are of the same order of magnitude as the additionality effects of the growth of the London and South East economies on the wider UK economy during the same time period. The key difference, however, is that the EU Single Market is likely to have benefited all UK regions, whereas the growth of London and the South East appears not to have had any beneficial effects on seven of the other UK regions or the major cities contained in these same regions.

4.7   The international trade and FDI patterns of UK regions

Until now we have focused on UK national trade patterns and impacts. However, it is also possible to examine the interregional trade patterns of UK regions both at the domestic interregional or intra-national level, and also at the international interregional level across Europe, along with key trading beyond countries. In order to do this we can employ the new intra-EU interregional and international trade data sets (Thissen *et al.* 2013a, 2013b, 2013c)[32] developed by PBL in The Netherlands. These are calibrated in millions of Euros and provide detailed interregional trade data for 256 EU NUTS2 regions plus other non-EU countries disaggregated for 10 sectors and for the years 2000, 2005 and 2010 as well as trade data with macro-areas including the USA, Asia, China, Africa, the Rest of Asia, Australasia and Singapore. The Thissen *et al.* (2013a, 2013b, 2013c) estimates can be considered to be robust as they are consistent with the available regional input-output data.[33]

In terms of international trade if we consider the OECD-TL1/EU-NUTS1 large statistical regions, we see from Table 4.9 that Greater London generates the highest value of exports per capita, followed by Northern Ireland, the South East and Scotland. Meanwhile the highest international balance of payments surplus per capita is displayed by Scotland, followed in descending order by Greater London, the North East and the North West. Conversely, the regions with the largest per capita international balance of payments deficits are Northern Ireland, followed by the West Midlands, the East and the East Midlands. There is also a group of regions, namely Wales, the South West, Yorkshire and Humberside and the South East, all of which display something close to balance of payments equilibrium values whereby international imports and exports are largely equivalent to each other.

Instead of considering international imports and exports per capita we consider international trade values relative to regional GDP then a rather different picture appears. In particular, although Greater London generates the highest exports per capita of the OECD-TL2/EU-NUTS1 regions, relative to the size of its own economy Greater London is actually very closed. Indeed, relative to the

Table 4.9 UK regional-international trade patterns 2010

OECD-TL2/EU-NUTS1 Large Statistical Regions and the Nested EU-NUTS2 Regions	2010 Pop[a]	Foreign Exports as a % of Regional GDP	Foreign Imports as a % of Regional GDP	Foreign Exports per Capita €	Foreign Imports Per Capita €
North East	2,587,000	25.66	23.23	5310	4808
North West	6,939,000	26.97	25.96	6173	5942
Yorkshire and Humberside	5,247,000	25.68	25.46	5715	5667
East Midlands	4,489,000	24.99	26.29	5810	6112
West Midlands	5,479,000	26.45	31.28	5923	7003
East	5,771,000	22.50	23.73	5648	5959
Greater London[b]	7,950,000	16.29	14.84	7416	6757
South East	8,498,000	21.85	21.90	6275	6290
South West[c]	5,252,000	20.81	20.97	5419	5460
Scotland	5,262,200	22.91	20.30	6031	5346
Wales[d]	3,050,000	27.31	27.16	5151	5123
Northern Ireland[e]	1,804,800	30.43	38.20	6421	8059

Note: In the EU-NUTS2 components of the OECD-TL2/EU-NUTS1 regions there are no GDP figures for Kent or the Welsh NUTS1 regions in the EU interregional trade data set so the GDP figures are imputed here from Eurostat. All figures are in Euros at current prices. See: http://appsso.eurostat.ec.europa.eu/nui/show.do?dataset=nama_r_e2gdp&lang=en.

[a] The 2010 regional populations for England are taken from: www.ons.gov.uk/ons/rel/snpp/sub-national-population-projections/2010-based-projections/stb-2010-based-snpp.html. For Scotland, Wales and Northern Ireland see: www.ons.gov.uk/ons/dcp171778_345500.pdf.

[b] The London Development Plan website suggests that London exports £37 billion worth of goods and services while London's GDP is £565 billion. However, this implies that London's export share accounts for only 6.5 per cent of the city-region's output. This figure is incredibly small and likely to be a mistake, based on the fact that the figure quoted for London's GDP is far too high. If we employ the figures from the OECD regional database which are reported in US$ and then convert these using the current OECD £/$ deflator the correct value for the GDP of the 2012 London NUTS1 regional economy is £341 billion while for the OECD 'Metropolitan Urban Area' definition of London the total city GDP is £381.5 billion. Using the former NUTS1 large statistical area Greater London definition of the London economy so as to be consistent here with the Thissen data, the London Development Plan's export estimate implies that London's share of exports is 10.8 per cent of its GDP, while the share falls to only 9.7 per cent if we employ the 'Metropolitan Urban Area' definition. See: www.uncsbrp.org.

At the other end of the spectrum, the *Experian* efforts to build a London Input-Output Tables using the LQ, CILQ and FLQ formulas (McCann 2013) generate London exports in 2003 of £54.3 billion and imports of £48.7 billion all in 2000 constant prices. Again, by using the OECD regional database and setting in 2000 constant prices via the OECD £/$ deflator for that year we arrive at a 2003 Greater London output of £242 billion. This suggests that London's exports and imports amount to 22.3 per cent and 20.12 per cent, respectively of London's GDP. See: www.london.gov.uk/mayor/economic_unit/docs/CapImpact_andrew_burrell.pdf.

The Thissen *et al.* data reported in Table 4.9 are almost exactly halfway between the London Development Plan and the *Experian* figures.

[c] The South West Input-Output regional tables estimate that exports account for 21.5 per cent of regional GVA and imports 25.9 per cent of regional GVA. See: www.economicsystems.co.uk/south-west/help.php.

[d] The 2007 Welsh Input-Output Tables estimate the Welsh export share as 24.8 per cent of GVA and the Welsh import share as 27.8 per cent of GVA. See: http://business.cardiff.ac.uk/sites/default/files/IO_2007_Final_30_6.pdf.

[e] The prototype 2008 Northern Ireland Input-Output tables estimate that the Northern Ireland export share is 28.2 per cent of total final demand in Northern Ireland and the import share as 34.0 per cent. See Iparraguire D'Elia (2008).

size of their own economies, the more prosperous regions of the UK, namely, London, the South East, the East, the South West and Scotland are all relatively more closed internationally than the economically weaker regions of the West Midlands, the East Midlands, the North West, Yorkshire and Humberside, the North East, Wales and Northern Ireland. Moreover, this relationship appears not to be particularly size-related. The international export and import values relative to the respective regional GDP levels are all below 0.25 for the more prosperous regions, whereas for the less prosperous regions all of these values are 0.25 or above. As such, the less prosperous regions are also the most open regions for international trade, relative to the total size of their economies.

This inverse relationship between trade openness and regional prosperity is most marked in the case of London, whose international trade values are relatively small in comparison to the scale of its economy. The fact that London is relatively closed internationally and relatively more domestically oriented has already been observed before (CLC 2004a, 2005a, 2008, 2009) although previous data were subject to severe limitation (CLC 2009), but what is meant here by 'closed' is only in relative terms to GDP. Greater London is a region displaying very high absolute levels of international trade activities and high levels per capita. At the same time, however, London also has such large and locally oriented service industries that relative to the overall size of the regional economy, these international trade values are actually very small. In contrast, a region such as the North West has a similar population to Greater London also slightly lower levels of international trade per capita as Greater London. However, these trade values for the North West are much greater relative to its overall regional size. Part of the explanation is likely to be that the North West region has a smaller scale of locally oriented and service industry activities than is the case with the London economy.

For those regionally based activities that do result in international exports, we see from Table 4.10 that there are noticeable regional variations in terms of the geographical patterns of regional exports orientation. The exports of all UK regions are clearly dominated by trade with the EU which typically accounts for between 57 per cent and 63 per cent of regional-international export trade for 10 of the 12 UK large statistical OECD-TL2/EU-NUTS1 regions. The share tends to be higher in the more geography-peripheral regions although the pattern only varies very slightly. However, the two noticeable exceptions here are Greater London and Scotland. London exports slightly less than half of its internationally traded output to the EU and slightly more than half to countries beyond the EU. London is relatively more oriented to other parts of the world (CLC 2014a) than other UK regions, and in particular BRIICS countries. Yes, as we have already seen, total UK trade with the BRIICS countries is relatively tiny and so are the demand effects on the UK economy. Scotland is the other region which slightly differs from the typical pattern in that while the majority of Scotland's international exports go to the EU, the share is much more evenly spread with only slightly more than half of Scottish exports going to the EU.

Table 4.10 Shares of regional-international export trade with EU and the rest of the world 2006

OECD-TL2/EU-NUTS1 Regions	% Exports to the EU	% Exports to Rest of the World	% Imports from the EU	% Imports from Rest of the World
North East	62.0	38.0	53.5	46.5
North West	58.5	41.5	50.6	49.4
Yorkshire and Humberside	60.8	39.2	50.6	49.4
East Midlands	60.1	39.9	47.1	52.9
West Midlands	62.6	37.4	58.6	41.4
East	60.9	39.1	61.3	38.7
Greater London	48.6	51.4	39.8	60.2
South East	57.0	43.0	57.4	42.6
South West	61.7	38.3	41.6	58.4
Scotland	51.7	48.3	35.5	64.5
Wales	60.2	39.8	40.5	59.5
Northern Ireland	63.3	36.8	68.7	31.3

Source: ONS (2008: Table 13.7).

In terms of imports, regions in the north, the midlands and the east of England typically bring in between 50 per cent and 60 per cent of their imports from the EU, with the share for Northern Ireland being noticeably higher. In contrast, the shares for London, Scotland and Wales are much lower. For Scotland and Wales, the lower shares are likely to be related to the significant presence of large American and Asian multinational firms in their local economies. On the other hand, for London the reason for the lower EU import share is again likely to be related to the wider global orientation of the London economy, as also reflected in the relatively much lower EU export share for London. The different regional consequences of a possible Brexit become all too obvious, with the UK's weaker regions being the most adversely affected by such a decision if it were to happen.

On the basis of the relative openness and trade-orientation arguments discussed here, one interpretation of the regional and urban patterns of relative economic weakness described in Chapters 2 and 3 might be that this is related to the relative openness of the weaker regions. In particular, it might be in some way due to their greater relative exposure to the adverse international shocks associated with the 2008 global economic slowdown, and in particular the sluggishness of the EU economies. In contrast, the regions which are relatively the most closed or oriented to the rest of the world may be somewhat more insulated from these adverse external shocks. However, there are three reasons why this explanation may not be appropriate. First, as we saw in Table 2.1, Table 2.2 and Table 3.6 in Chapters 2 and 3, respectively, the regions which have been struggling and also the major cities contained within them, were all experiencing decline relative to the UK average during the strong national and global growth period between the millennium and the 2008 financial crisis. If the arguments regarding the role of international exposure to global economic shifts had any substance, then we would also have expected these weaker regions and cities to thrive during the period of strong global economic growth. This is not what we observe. Second, apart from Greater London the differences in relative trade openness between the rest of the UK regions are typically only a very few percentage point differences, and much less than the relative differences in either GDP per capita or GDP per capita growth over the last decade. This is also the case with EU trade. Moreover, the weakness of the European economies cannot be an explanation because as we have already seen in Chapter 1, since 2008 both the EU-28 and the Eurozone have out-performed the UK economy. Moreover, the WIOD data confirm that 82 per cent of the UK demand contraction post-2008 was due to internal, and not external issues. Third, if such simple relative trade-openness explanations were indeed correct, then this would also imply that all of the economic arguments regarding the importance of openness and global orientation would be largely incorrect, and that prosperity would be gained by autarky. These arguments are clearly not sensible.

Instead, we need to search for alternative and more nuanced explanations, and two main arguments appear to be most pertinent here. The first argument relates to the importance of agglomeration and spillover effects, and the evidence in Chapters 2 and 3 suggests that these are far more limited outside of the southern regions of England plus Scotland. We will also discuss these issues in further detail in Chapter 5. Second, another potentially fruitful line of enquiry relates to the nature and quality of trade-related investments. As we have already seen, the UK still remains the preferred European location for inward FDI, although its relative lead has been declining for many years and it is nowadays only very marginally ahead of Germany. However, the various types of UK FDI inflows appear to continually offer strong opportunities for a wide range of UK regions to upgrade their technologies and to help them take greater advantage of the possibilities associated with global markets. In particular, building up knowledge-related capabilities via inward FDI in manufacturing is a priority for many UK regions because of their historical strengths (NESTA 2013) and this also offers an opportunity for upgrading the regional production system. Part of the reason for this is that knowledge spillovers in manufacturing are typically distributed more widely across the country than other sectors, and are not confined primarily to particular core regions or to cities in general (Harris and Moffat 2012). However, these inward investment flows are also likely to have major regional and local impacts. Today, London is the top-ranked European city for inward FDI projects, followed by Paris in second place (Ernst and Young 2013) and these figures highlight the role played by cities as host for inward FDI. Indeed, the top ten European cities in terms of FDI inflows accounted for 30.1 per cent of all Europe's total inward FDI projects. However, there also appear to be increasingly marked differences between London, in particular, and the rest of the UK when it comes to inward FDI, and there are two aspects to these differences. First, since the 1990s London has increasingly captured the lion's share of new projects along with to a much lesser extent the South East, Scotland or Northern Ireland (Dimitropoulou *et al.* 2013; Ernst and Young 2012). In contrast, during the 1980s and 1990s non-core UK regions had received large inflows of FDI in manufacturing (Hill and Munday 1994; Hill and Morgan 1998) and during the 1990s and 2000s FDI inflows into non-core UK regions had increasingly involved the upgrading or expansion of existing assets. Second, relatively few of the inward FDI projects outside of London and the South East during the 1990s and 2000s represented head-quarter functions (Dimitropoulou *et al.* 2013). These qualitative differences have also been reflected in terms of quantitative differences. Since the 1990s, there has also been something of a North-to-South shift in inward manufac-turing FDI in favour of southern regions (Jones and Wren 2006; Wren and Jones 2012; BIS 2012b). Between 2004 and 2011 London and the South East of England accounted for more inward FDI projects than the rest of England put together (Ernst and Young 2012). While there is also some evidence of a countervailing spread effect regarding inward FDI in services, this effect is not strong enough to compensate for the overall southward drift in manu-facturing in inward FDI. As such, as a whole, these two trends are leading to something of a convergence of the geography of inward FDI patterns across both manufacturing and services, a geography which appears to be related primarily to the agglomeration advantages of certain regions over others (Wren and Jones 2012), although identifying these effects remains very dif-ficult (Jones and Wren 2006). While regional policy can partially alter these patterns, it can only do so as long as it is being implemented, and once it is withdrawn, in some cases FDI reverts to its earlier trends and pattern (Wren and Jones 2012).

These diverging patterns appeared to have accentuated in various dimen-sions following the global financial crisis. By 2011 the only regions experi-encing an increase in the number of inward FDI projects were London and the South East while the Eastern region experienced only a very marginal decline in projects (Ernst and Young 2012). All other UK regions faced not only declining numbers of projects, but double-digit percentage declines. In 2011 London for the first time alone accounted for more than 50 per cent of the UK's inward FDI projects, while London and the second ranked region of the South East together accounted for more than 60 per cent of the UK's inward investment projects (Ernst and Young 2012).

On the other hand, in terms of employment generation or safeguarding, the picture is still rather different. In 2011 Scotland remained by quite some margin the largest recipient of employment related to inward FDI, with almost twice as many jobs as regions in the midlands and north of England of similar sizes and with similar structural profiles (Ernst and Young 2012). The success of Scotland in attracting inward FDI appears to be related to the continuing efforts of Scottish Development International (Ernst and Young 2012). However, these successes need to be set against a context whereby the

English Regional Development Agencies (RDAs) were disbanded from 2010[34] onwards and the Welsh Development Agency was abolished in 2006 (Ernst and Young 2012). Although the final formal abolition of the English RDAs was not until March 2012, as we will see in Chapter 7, their institutional capacity began to crumble almost as soon as the abolition announcements were made in 2010 due to the undermining of their FDI negotiation and inter-mediation capabilities and the associated haemorrhaging of key personnel.

These data and narratives suggest that qualitative shifts in the nature of FDI and trade-related activities coming into UK regions have increasingly favoured London, the South East and Scotland over other regions. As such, within global value-chains the relative position of these more prosperous regions may well be improving. If so, the increasingly favourable positioning of these regions in international markets may be largely due to geography (Overman and Winters 2005). Yet, while this might be relevant for southern English regions it is rather difficult to justify in the case of Scotland. Alternatively, the combination of geographical shifts plus qualitative shifts in trade-related activities may be favouring certain regions over others. Again, however, the case of Scotland suggests that additional institutional explanations might also need to be sought. Indeed, this suggestion that qualitative and institutional issues as well as scale-related quantitative issues may also be relevant in explaining performance of the UK's weaker regions is also likely to be just as pertinent in terms of understanding the global performance of the successful London economy.

4.8   The performance of London as a 'global city'

Most of the popular and also academic narratives surrounding the London economy talk of a globally connected and highly diversified city, an environment which is ideal for fostering knowledge spillovers and innovation. London is seen as quintessentially a model of a modern 'global city' (Sassen 2006; Taylor 2004) with a wide array of world-leading cultural and heritage assets (Smith 2014) including the first 9 out of the UK's top 10 tourist attractions and 17 out of the UK's top 20 tourist attractions,[35] a diverse multicultural population with almost 40 per cent of its residents being borne outside of the UK,[36] world-class centres of research (CfL 2011; *Times Higher Education* 2014) many of which rival Oxbridge and appear to be gaining primarily at the expense of universities located in UK regions outside of London and the South East,[37] and numerous overseas investors scrambling to buy up London real estate assets. In terms of global real estate investment flows into office markets during the period 2007–2014 London was ranked as the world's number 1 city with US$107 billion worth of deals. The second and third most highly positioned UK cities in the global rankings were Birmingham, ranked at 56th with US$2.3 billion worth of deals and Manchester at 60th with US$2.1 billion worth of deals, followed by Reading and Glasgow which are ranked as 74th and 76th with flows of US$1.2

billion, and Edinburgh at 90th with flows of US\$0.78 billion. The rest of the UK's cities are all ranked outside of the top 100 cities in the global real estate ranking.[38] As such London displays an overwhelming dominance as a location for inward real estate capital flows which is some 50 times larger than any other UK city. Meanwhile, these financial flows are also mirrored by flows of people. With a throughput of some 70 million passengers per annum, while being the third busiest airport in the world after Atlanta and Beijing,[39] Heathrow Airport is still the world's second most globalised airport in terms of the number of international passengers it handles.[40] Indeed, on a range of empirical indicators (Taylor 2004) relating to the location of headquarter functions and decision-making power, along with the movements of people, money (Hoyler *et al.* 2014) and goods, in many years London is found to be the most globalised city in the world both in terms of the global connectivity of its city-functions (Clark 2015) and also specifically in terms of its role in international finance (McCann and Acs 2011; Iammarino and McCann 2013).

Yet, many of today's global city characteristics of the London economy are largely a product of recent global transformations. Of course, as the nerve centre of the British Empire and later as the 1960 and 1970s location of the emerging Eurodollar markets London has for many years played something of a global city role in trade and international finance (Casson and McCann 1999). However, an enormous transformation within the London economy took place in the 1990s, building on various fortuitous developments which had taken place in earlier years. The 1980s deregulations of the London capital markets and the enormous influx of US, European and Japanese investment banks, as well as smaller numbers of trading houses from Hong Kong, Singapore and Australia, were also accompanied by major infrastructure investments including the Channel Tunnel rail link, the Docklands Development and the Heathrow Terminal 5 expansion. In addition, the 1980s shift to electronic trading within the London markets meant that as the communication revolution driven by the world wide web began earnest in the early 1990s the London markets were already at the forefront of the innovation possibilities offered by such technologies in international finance. As such, when the modern era of globalisation emerged at the dawn of the 1990s, London found itself uniquely placed to capitalise on these globalisation processes. The reason is that modern globalisation and multinationalisation depends crucially on the provision of international investment finance for cross-border mergers and acquisitions, and the London markets were perfectly situated to capture the lion's share of the surge in demand for these services (McCann 2009a; Iammarino and McCann 2013). Yet, none of this could have been predicted or expected beforehand. The 1980s influx of American and Japanese investment banks was primarily aimed at capturing the investment opportunities associated with the ongoing market integration of the European markets. However, as the whole global economy underwent such rapid and unexpected transformations, spurred on also by the communications revolution in the wake of the invention of the world wide web, the London capital markets burgeoned as did all of the associated business service industries supplying these markets, including legal services, IT services, marketing services, human resource services, architectural services and various allied consultancy activities. The influx of high-value activities into the London economy, not surprisingly, was also accompanied by a range of numerous household and consumer services as well as cultural and entertainment services, all of which were aimed primarily at the growing cohort of very high-income customers and clients. In addition, large inflows of high human capital, the origins of which initially largely matched the nationalities of the incoming investment banks, spurred the skills base of the London economy. As the London economy diversified, so did the nationalities of these inflows. Nowadays more than 15 per cent of the London labour force are highly skilled immigrants, a share which is almost twice that of Paris, and along with Vancouver and Toronto, this represents the highest share of highly skilled immigrants of any city in the world (OECD 2011). These international inflows of human capital were also accompanied by graduate inflows from other parts of the UK which also displayed higher human capital levels than the average levels for UK university graduates. These issues of interregional and international human capital mobility into the London economy are discussed in much more detail in Chapter 5.

The London economy was already being totally transformed by the mid-1990s from the city which had existed in the early 1980s, and the productivity and income surges from the early 1990s onwards outlined in the previous chapters are testament to this. Some recent books (Rosewell 2013; Clark 2015) have discussed these transformations in detail and the most notable feature is not only just how recent these transformations have been, but also how largely unexpected, fortuitous and unplanned many of these transformations were.

Of course, as we have already seen in Chapter 3, not all Londoners benefited from these changes. London's income inequality increased markedly since the 1980s, primarily as a result of income surges amongst the highly paid cohorts of London's economy, working primarily in the financial services and allied industries. London's GDP per capita is now either the second or the eighth[41] highest in Europe depending on the definition of London used, while at the same time London's income inequality is also now the highest in Europe.[42]

Somewhat surprisingly to some observers, however, is the fact that in terms of industrial structure the London economy is actually rather more specialised than most parts of the UK. Indeed, the London region is the one of the least diversified regions of the UK (Dewhurst and McCann 2002). The reason for this is that in London there is a relatively larger share of employment in tertiary industries and services-sector activities than other regions and a smaller share associated with manufacturing and other industries (ONS 2008). In particular, within the broad generic grouping of service activities, the largest range of London-based activities are actually in financial business services (CLC 2009). While the UK average employment share for financial and business services is some 20 per cent (ONS 2008) the Greater London share is of the order of 32 per cent, and the only other region with a share higher than the national average is the South East at 23 per cent (ONS 2008). Business services themselves represent a diverse group of activities and employment roles and some commentators argue that the observation that London is sectorally very specialised rather than diversified is simply due to the fact that the Standard Industrial Classification (SIC) schemes we currently employ do not fully reflect the diversity of service activities. While there may be some credence in these arguments, it also remains the case that the design and organisation of SIC schemes are benchmarked and standardised internationally. As such, the observation that London displays a high degree of sectoral specialisation is still likely to hold even irrespective of any future potential re-classification efforts, none of which are immediately on the horizon. Moreover, to the extent that some City-type activities have been out-sourced or off-shored these specialisation patterns may actually be reinforced over time (CLC 2005b).

Amongst London's service industries the international financial markets are by far the most high-profile, and in many ways also the most iconic, of all of London's economic activities. Today, many of these banking-related activities take place in the London Docklands–Canary Wharf area, a purpose-built development undertaken in the late 1980s and early 1990s (Clark 2015). However, it is still the case that the majority of London's international financial intermediation activities take place within an area known as The City of London. This is a very small neighbourhood within the overall London metropolitan context which has a certain degree of self-governing autonomy going back to the late Middle Ages. In the world of business and commerce it is colloquially referred to as either 'The City' or the 'Square Mile'. Although it only houses a small number of residents, due primarily to the extremely high land prices, it is very densely populated in terms of businesses and employment. In 2012 The City accounted for 17,750 businesses employing over 365,500 people contributing £39 billion to the UK economy (CLC 2014b).[43] Output per employee in The City in 2012 was £105,000 in comparison to £57,000 across Greater London and £38,000 across the UK as a whole (CLC 2014b). While The City accounts for just 4 per cent of Greater London's stock of businesses it generates some 16 per cent of Greater London's economic output and therefore something less than 4 per cent of all of the UK's economic output (CLC 2014b).[44]

The City contains five major and quite distinct clusters of activity. The largest is: the financial services cluster which represents 2230 firms and 87,000 employees and generates a 2012 output of £9.7 billion (CLC 2014b); the second cluster is the insurance and re-insurance cluster which accounts for 1200 firms and 50,500 firms generating £10.4 billion; the third cluster is the professional services cluster with 3780 and 79,800 firms producing an output of £8.1 billion (CLC 2014b); the fourth cluster is that of technology, media and telecommunications activities accounting for 1300 firms, 25,550 employees and an output of £2.3 billion;[45] and the fifth cluster is the retail and hospitality cluster accounting for 1930 businesses employing 22,700 people and generating an output of £0.8 billion, representing 2 per cent of The City's output (CLC 2014b).

The City is still the hub of the London financial markets but in many ways is also the hub of the overall London economy in that it is widely regarded as the bellwether of the buoyancy of the overall London economy, even though it accounts for only 16 per cent of Greater London's output. Indeed, in certain political circles and in much of the popular press the performance of The City is widely interpreted as a bellwether for the whole UK economy, even though it only accounts for 4 per cent of UK output. In the immediate aftermath of the 2008 global financial crisis The City experienced sharp contractions of output and employment as a result of being specialised precisely in those financial intermediation activities which were central to the shock. Between 2008 and 2012 employment in The City fell by just over 5000 and the number of firms fell by 2300 (CLC 2014b). However, during this period the output of The City actually increased by £2.7 billion (CLC 2014b). The increase in The City output and the relatively small declines in employment and firm numbers were to a great extent driven by the in-migration of more than 200 new firms into The City since 2008, which generated some 13,500 new jobs and £3.5 billion in output (CLC 2014b). As already explained, although financial services jobs are spread across London as a whole, the vast majority are primarily contained within The City and in the secondary centre of the London Docklands–Canary Wharf Development. Across London, the number of 'city-type' jobs has been forecast to fall from a 2007 high of 354,000 in 2007 to 236,000 in 2014[46] and the pressure on the London financial services industry is also reflected by the fact that the financial bonuses paid in these types of jobs have also fallen markedly.[47] During 2008 and 2009, while the contraction in overall UK exports was the sixth largest amongst the advanced OECD economies, the contraction in business and financial services was by far the highest in the OECD.[48] Yet, in terms of employment the various activities within The City itself have proved remarkably resilient, and as we have seen in the preceding chapters, this resilience in the aftermath of the 2008 crisis also reflects the fortunes of the wider London economy. Indeed, London is also forecast to out-perform the UK economy in the coming years in terms of output growth.[49]

Yet, there is also some evidence to suggest that London may be changing somewhat in the wake of the crisis. As we have already seen, during the 1990s and the early 2000s London occupied the very top spot in both the global city rankings and also the global financial centre rankings (McCann and Acs 2011; Iammarino and McCann 2013), in the aftermath of the 2008 global economic crisis, London's position as the premier financial centre was increasingly under threat (CLC 2014b). These threats to London's pre-eminence arise primarily from Hong Kong and Singapore which have benefited from the strong and continuing growth in Asia. Meanwhile, the New York financial services displayed higher levels of resilience in response to the stronger recovery in the US economy in comparison to the UK and Europe. As of 2014, London had fallen one place and is now second to New York in both the global city rankings (AT Kearney 2014) and also the global financial centre (Long Finance 2014). The potentially greater vulnerability of London's financial services industries in the coming decades in comparison to earlier decades suggests that the pattern of many of London's dynamic growth activities may somewhat shift away from financial intermediation and increasingly towards technology, computer, media and business services. As a result of these predictions, the centre of gravity of much of London's growth is also forecast to shift eastward towards east London boroughs.[50] Indeed, evidence suggests that some of these employment shifts have already been under way since the 1990s (CfL 2012). Along with the financial markets, the London 'Tech City' cluster (CfL 2012) which spans both The City of London and also neighbouring boroughs of Tower Hamlets, Hackney and Islington is nowadays also often in the popular press and media.[51] As a whole in 2012 this 'Tech City' cluster contained 21,130 firms employing 243,000 people and generating an output of some £17.3 billion (CfL 2012), and as such it accounted for 4.7 per cent of Greater London's total number of firms and 5.7 per cent of Greater London's total employment (CfL 2012). Yet, its perceived importance as a *national* asset is highlighted not only by the fact that the UK Prime Minister has an 'Ambassador' to Tech City (CfL 2012).[52]

Although there is some evidence of the changing global roles of the wider London economy, and in particular its possible relative decline as an international financial intermediation centre and its diversification into wider technology-related services, it still remains the case that London will be a key centre for global commerce during the coming decades and a key focus for many aspects of UK economic activities. As we have already seen, the wider London economy has proved to be very resilient in the aftermath of the 2008 crisis and both employment and real estate demand has continued to remain very buoyant. Indeed, central London's employment growth to date since the crisis has been even stronger than in the pre-crisis years, driven almost entirely by the central London City-type jobs (Gordon 2015). However, whether London's economic performance is actually as stellar and as critical for the whole UK economy as many narratives in the popular press and in influential London-centred policy-circles suggest can be questioned (Kay 2015).

As has already been mentioned in previous chapters there have been several attempts to outline the effects of the London economy on the wider UK economy (CLC 2004b, 2009, CEBR 2012). These reports tend to focus on the shares of UK output and employment activities which are accounted for by the London regional economy and they also provide estimates of the employment-associated effects in other regions due to interregional linkages. As we have already seen in Chapter 1, the general picture painted by these reports is that London provides important assets and market conditions which potentially can benefit the wider UK economy. However, as our counter-factual analyses in Chapters 2 and 3 have also demonstrated, there is simply no evidence of this. Indeed, the evidence from numerous comparator OECD regions and cities is that London has provided no beneficial effects on the majority of UK regions. It is true that London generates a trade international surplus with the rest of the world. However, using 2003 data at 2000 prices the scale of this London trade surplus was £5.6 billion, while the UK as a whole experienced an international trade deficit of £41.7 billion. Yet, in order to put these figures into context, London's trade surplus amounts to only 2.3 per cent of London's GDP and just 0.46 per cent of overall UK GDP.[53] In other words, many of the narratives which position London as a crucial 'national' asset on the basis of its ability to realise trade surpluses are often over-stating the case. Similarly, The City itself, or London's 'City-type jobs', which are argued to account for over 40 per cent of London exports[54] account for something between 3 per cent and 4 per cent of UK output,[55] less than 1 per cent of UK employment,[56] and a trade surplus of less than 0.2 per cent of UK GDP. Again, the contribution of these activities to the overall UK economy appears to be far smaller than most of the popular narratives[57] regarding the importance of the City would suggest (Kay 2015).

These tiny figures, combined with the evidence in the previous two chapters, present us with something of a paradox given the numerous narratives about London as a 'motor' or 'engine' of the UK national economy. Again, the most direct way to assess the extent to which London's performance is as stellar and as critical for the whole UK economy is to compare it with appropriate OECD comparison cities.

As we see in Table 4.11, both the absolute growth of GDP per capita in London 2000–2010 and also the growth relative to the national growth compare favourably when benchmarked against either four or seven other rich OECD mega-cities of some 10 million people or over. However, the difference between London and the average performance of these comparators is very marginal. It also compares favourably to the seven comparator but much smaller European cities whose GDP per capita was very similar to that of London in 2000. If the sample is then extended to include the other 15 or 18 smaller European cities whose 2010 GDP per capita is also similar to London (see Table A4.1) then London under-performs relative to this wider sample.

Again, if we extend our sample to include those 19 US cities whose GDP per capita in 2000 was similar to that of London in 2000, or if we also include in the sample those additional 10 US cities whose 2010 GDP per capita is similar to London in 2010, then in both cases we see that London's absolute growth in GDP per capita is very similar to these comparison groups but under-performs relative to national performance. The latter effect is due to the fact that the UK was one of the strongest growing economies during this period.

These figures suggest that while the GDP per capita growth performance of London has been strong since the millennium, it is not nearly as stellar as many narratives in the UK popular press suggest. In absolute terms the

Table 4.11 The economic performance of London assessed against comparator cities

OECD Metropolitan Urban Area	Population 2012	GDP per Capita 2000 (2000 constant prices)	GDP per Capita 2010 (2000 constant prices)	Urban Area % Change in GDP per Capita 2000–2010	National % Change in GDP per Capita 2000–2010	Difference between Regional and National % Change
London	11,650,153	41,557.05	46,532.13	**11.97**	11.5	**+0.47**
Paris	11,862,466	44,606.76	49,497.90	10.96	4.93	+6.03
New York	16,626,313	51,091.88	57,534.33	12.60	7.44	+5.16
Chicago	9,406,812	45,546.49	48,296.18	6.03	7.44	–1.41
Los Angeles	17,378,937	40,363.95	42,589.72	5.51	7.44	–1.93
Average for 4 OECD Mega-Cities				**8.78**		**+1.96**
Tokyo	35,441,287	35,495.71	37,021.50	4.29	6.91*	–2.62
Osaka	17,294,189	29,339.17	29,952.46	2.09	6.91*	–4.82
Seoul	23,496,373	19,630.55	26,243.01	33.68	42.76	–9.08
Average for 7 OECD Mega-Cities				**10.74**		**–1.24**
Average for 7 European Comparator Metropolitan Urban Areas				**8.28**		**–0.93**
Average for 15 European Comparator Metropolitan Urban Areas				**16.91**		**+1.22**
Average for 18 European Comparator Metropolitan Urban Areas				**14.11**		**+1.23**
Average for 19 North American Comparator Metropolitan Urban Areas				**10.19**		**2.02**
Average for 29 North American Comparator Metropolitan Urban Areas				**11.75**		**+3.83**

* The base year for the Japanese estimates in the database is 2001 and not 2000 but the GDP per capita values in the macroeconomic data are almost identical between these two years (OECD 2006).

productivity growth of London since the millennium is largely consistent with those other OECD cities whose GDP per capita scores were very similar to those of London in 2000. On the other hand, relative to national performance it appears that London's productivity growth has been somewhat less impressive when benchmarked against these comparator cities, although this was largely because the UK as a whole was growing strongly on average during the decade prior to the 2008 global economic crisis.

The data presented in Table 4.11 suggest that London is somewhat still less productive than Paris and that London's productivity growth since the millennium has only been very marginally ahead of that of Paris. In 2010 Paris still had a GDP per capita level which is some 6.37 per cent higher than London and a population which is just 1.8 per cent larger than London. Paris had a larger share of French national output growth 2000–2010 than the London share of the UK national growth 2000–2010 (OECD 2013b, 2014a) but this was because much more of the UK's growth during this period was accounted for by many non-metropolitan areas. This is rather different from many of the narratives in the UK popular press which often describe London as being the 'capital of the world' and the world's most dynamic city and other such comparisons. Part of the reason why these data tell a rather different story to these popular narratives is that as we see in Appendix 4.2 the data which are typically discussed in the press regarding the performance of cities relate to city administrative data rather than to data which are standardised according to functional urban area logic, as is done in the OECD Metropolitan Urban Area data set.

A second issue here is the degree of openness of London ascribed to its 'global city' status and role. We have already seen that it is the most closed region within the UK, relative to its GDP. However, again we can consider its limited openness in comparison to comparator regions. As we see in Table 4.12, when benchmarked against other large and prosperous comparator European city-regions, London again emerges as being relatively less open and relatively more closed than other similar types of regions. Much of the economic activity in London is in locally oriented business and household services and although some sub-sectors of the London economy including international finance and tourism are globally oriented (CLC 2004b), as a whole London is actually a rather closed economy (CLC 2009).

One final observation is that in the immediate post-crisis years the Bank of England and the UK Government initiated quantitative easing and facilitated enormous financial support worth more than £1 trillion in the form of guarantees, £120 billion in actual cash commitments (Gordon 2015) and implicit subsidies of over £100 billion in order to maintain the stability of the banking system (Gordon 2015), particularly where banks were deemed too big to fail, while direct quantitative easing asset purchases amounted to some £375 billion (Gordon 2015; Kaletsky 2015). Yet, within the UK the only observable effect of these measures in the aftermath of the crisis was increased employment in City-type jobs in London (Gordon 2015). This raises the question of why were the beneficial effects not UK-wide, apart from possibly Edinburgh?[58] One

Table 4.12 The trade openness of London in comparison with other European 'global city-regions'

OECD-TL2/ EU-NUTS1 Large Statistical Regions and the Included EU-NUTS2 Regions	2012 Pop	GDP per Capita 2010	Foreign Exports as a % of Regional GDP	Foreign Imports as a % of Regional GDP
Greater London NUTS1	8,136,285	47,200	**16.28**	**14.83**
– Inner London	3,210,633	83,300	12.40	11.23
– Outer London	4,925,652	23,700	24.96	22.90
Paris/Ile de France	11,914,812	49,700	15.95	18.69
North Holland including Amsterdam	2,709,822	40,400	33.42	38.12
Munich	4,430,706	41,500	24.77	23.30
Comunidad de Madrid	6,387,824	29,500	19.08	19.60
Lombardy including Milan	9,992,548	33,600	26.52	22.24
Stockholm	2,091,473	50,700	29.11	28.30
Brussels	1,159,448	61,200	30.91	28.61
Hovedstaden including Copenhagen	1,714,589	52,700	40.54	41.47
Hamburg	1,798,836	51,700	19.27	18.18
Catalonia including Barcelona	7,318,513	26,500	27.75	22.56
Average for 10 Comparator European NUTS2 regions	6,143,338	43,750	**26.73**	**26.12**

suggestion is that the credit easing resulted in enormous capital injections and flows within London which resulted in the observed local growth of jobs, and which in turn spurred a nation-wide credit expansion. However, as we will see in the following chapter there is no evidence of this in the national credit conditions. Rather, the UK credit contraction was one of the most severe in the OECD. A more realistic suggestion is that the implicit subsidies were passed on in greater international financial activities with emerging markets, rather than with the rest of the UK (Gordon 2015), exactly as would be expected from the globalisation argument in which London's engagements are primarily with respect to other countries and places, rather than with the rest of the UK.

4.9   Conclusions

In this chapter we have examined the various trade, investment and global value-chain impacts associated with internationalisation and modern globalisation on the UK economy, its regions and in particular on the London economy. Between the 1960s and the 1980s the UK economy gradually re-oriented itself towards the European economies as the logic of the former British Empire-based trading system collapsed in the post-war era while the processes of European integration weighed more heavily on UK trading patterns. By far the biggest changes, however, were heralded by the advent of modern globalisation, at the transition between the late 1980s and early 1990s. Modern globalisation is characterised primarily by multinationalism rather than by free trade-based internationalism, by foreign investment rather than by trade exports and imports, and most importantly by knowledge and technology flows within corporate structures, rather than by market-based knowledge transactions. Against this backdrop, and as much by chance and accident as by planning and foresight, London emerged in these transitions as a key player in the new global economy. Indeed, on many indicators London now represents the quintessential 'global city', operating at a key junction or node in global investment relationships. In particular, at more than £170 billion per annum, the EU Single Market is today worth (CBI 2014) far more to the UK economy than most commentators understand, amounting to more than 10 per cent of UK GDP. To put this into perspective, the impact of the EU Single Market on the UK economy is equivalent to almost half of the London economy, two-thirds of the economy of the South East, and larger than any other UK region. Although as with all other UK regions, the EU still provides the largest sphere of international influence for the London economy and in turn the EU arena exerts the largest international influence on the London economy, today, the non-core regions of the UK are relatively even more dependent on the rest of the EU for trade and investment than are the core regions of London and the South East. As such, an EU exit would hurt the UK's non-core regions relatively more than London and the South East, although the scale of integration means that the overall effect of a so-called Brexit would be disastrous on the UK economy.

In recent years since the millennium, and in particular since the 2008 global economic crisis, we have witnessed a southward shift in investment patterns towards primarily London, and to a lesser extent the London hinterland regions, and in particular this southward drift is reflected in terms of higher quality investments and newer investments. This suggests that the global city role of London, induced as it was primarily by external effects, has subsequently led to further induced effects with internal and domestic consequences on the economic geography of the UK. At the same time, the London economy is relatively more closed as an international and interregional economic centre than is often realised. The contribution of the London economy and in particular of The City-type financial markets to the wider UK economy, either in terms of output or taxes, is also much smaller than is generally perceived in popular narratives (Kay 2015). Indeed, and following on from the empirical insights of Chapters 2 and 3, as we will see in the next chapter, the lack of linkages between London and the wider UK economy appears to have limited the ability of the London economy to act as an economic driver stimulating other parts of the UK economy, beyond its immediate hinterland regions. Having said all of this, the future role of the London economy in the wider UK system, and in particular the role of international finance as London's economic driver, is now in doubt (Rosewell 2013; Clark 2015), as the global economic centre of gravity shifts eastward (Reyes *et al.* 2009), as the rate of global transformation slows (*The Economist* 2015b), and as regulatory changes are being implemented in response to the fact that the role played by international finance in the 2008 global financial crisis becomes more widely understood.

The one major issue regarding the UK's international and global engagement and the impacts on its regions and cities which we have not yet examined is that of immigration and international migration. This issue will be discussed in detail alongside the issue of interregional migration. Importantly for our purposes, as we will see shortly, the conclusions of this chapter are further substantiated and bolstered when immigration is also considered.

Appendix 4.1

OECD metropolitan urban area international comparators for London

Table A4.1 provides details of all of the OECD metropolitan urban areas whose GDP per capita scores in either 2000 or 2010 are within plus or minus 10 per cent of the London values.

Table A4.1 OECD comparator cities for London

OECD Metropolitan Urban Area	GDP per Capita 2000 (2000 constant prices)	GDP per Capita 2010 (2000 constant prices)	Urban Area % Change in GDP per Capita 2000–2010	National % Change in GDP per Capita 2000–2010	Difference between Regional and National % Change
London	41,557.05	46,532.13	**11.97**	11.5	**+0.47**
Paris	44,606.76	49,497.90	10.96	4.93	+6.03
Hamburg	40,668.69	44,934.66	10.49	10.49	0.0
Munich	51,269.39	51,349.67	0.15	10.49	−10.34
Frankfurt	43,691.00	48,801.78	11.69	10.49	+1.20
Dublin	41,682.35	48,181.79	15.6	7.67	+7.93
Brussels	42,738.15	45,749.58	7.04	11.1	−4.06
Utrecht	41,209.12	42,060.37	2.06	9.33	−7.27
Average for 7 European Comparator Metropolitan Urban Areas			**8.28**		**−0.93**
Edinburgh	36,846.84	43,380.18	17.7	11.5	+6.2
Stockholm	39,900.79	48,364.37	21.2	17.4	+3.8
Helsinki	37,033.09	43,081.99	16.33	14.73	+1.6
Stuttgart	38,755.95	42,894.94	10.67	10.49	+0.18

Vienna	38,170.78	40,106.71	5.07	10.84	−5.77
Karlsruhe	36,321.03	40,299.70	10.95	10.49	+0.46
Prague	29,153.93	41,543.09	42.5	36.45	+6.05
Bratislava	26,503.89	45,414.05	71.3	58.9	+12.4
Average for 15 European Comparator Metropolitan Urban Areas			**16.91**		**+1.22**
Zurich	49,369.65 (2008)	48,128.28	−2.51	−5.1	+2.59
Geneva	40,792.62 (2008)	40,039.17	−1.85	−5+	+3.25
Oslo	46,010.78 (2008)	48,180.08	4.71	6.74	−2.03
Average for 18 European Comparator Metropolitan Urban Areas			**14.11**		**+1.23**
New York	51,091.88	57,534.33	12.60	7.44	+5.16
Chicago	45,546.49	48,296.18	6.03	7.44	−1.41
Los Angeles	40,363.95	42,589.72	5.51	7.44	−1.93
Washington	50,144.26	57,167.33	14.0	7.44	+6.56
Seattle	48,518.44	51,909.82	6.98	7.44	−0.46
Boston	46,873.79	51,225.46	9.28	7.44	+1.84
Philadelphia	43,870.53	49,286.39	12.34	7.44	+4.9
Austin	46,070.48	45,405.28	−1.44	7.44	−8.88
Fort Worth	42,229.60	45,559.35	7.88	7.44	+0.44
San Diego	48,105.66	50,349.29	4.66	7.44	−2.78
Dallas	42,229.60	46,450.86	9.99	7.44	+2.55
Omaha	40,705.67	45,617.58	12.1	7.44	+4.66
Baltimore	50,144.26	63,126.03	25.88	7.44	+18.4
Houston	47,442.34	50,680.57	6.82	7.44	−0.62
San Francisco (Bay Area)	52,282.50	57,228.03	9.45	7.44	+2.01
Minneapolis	43,245.55	45,342.78	4.84	7.44	−2.6
Providence	46,873.79	52,614.69	12.24	7.44	+4.8
Edmonton	47,162.72	56,603.93	20.0	14.3	+5.71
Calgary	48,718.45	55,803.40	14.5	14.3	+0.2
Average for 19 North American Comparator Metropolitan Urban Areas			**10.19**		**2.02**

(*Continued*)

Table A4.1 Continued

OECD Metropolitan Urban Area	GDP per Capita 2000 (2000 constant prices)	GDP per Capita 2010 (2000 constant prices)	Urban Area % Change in GDP per Capita 2000–2010	National % Change in GDP per Capita 2000–2010	Difference between Regional and National % Change
Portland	39,775.46	45,127.02	13.45	7.44	+6.01
Norfolk	35,152.34	42,852.75	21.9	7.44	+14.46
Richmond	36,650.14	42,763.12	16.67	7.44	+9.23
Kansas City	39,730.49	40,388.16	1.65	7.44	−5.79
Salt Lake City	35,441.27	42,389.87	19.6	7.44	+12.16
Des Moines	39,220.55	40,818.12	4.07	7.44	−3.37
Milwaukee	39,740.77	42,969.78	8.12	7.44	+0.68
Pittsburgh	34,228.27	40,902.62	19.49	7.44	+12.05
St Petersburg	35,404.19	40,166.82	13.45	7.44	+6.01
Baton Rouge	38,152.58	49,125.47	28.76	7.44	+21.32
Average for 29 North American Comparator Metropolitan Urban Areas			**11.75**		**+3.83**

These estimates do not include New Orleans, whose GDP per capita increased from US$33,776.69 in 2000 to US$54,395.07. However, the city population declined from 1,289,753 in 2000 to 1,144,722 in 2010 in the aftermath of Hurricane Katrina in 2005 and this period also saw enormous inflows of state and federal funds. If New Orleans is also included in the estimates then the average productivity growth of US comparator cities for London 2000–2010 is 13.39 per cent and 5.48 percentage points above the US national growth performance during this period.

Appendix 4.2

OECD-TL2/EU-NUTS1 Greater London and Paris/Ile de France regional comparisons

In terms of the OECD Regional Database, at the OECD-TL2/EU-NUTS1 level the only really appropriate European comparator region for the Greater London region is that of the Paris/Ile de France region. As we see in Table A4.2 in 1995 these two city-regions exhibited largely similar GDP per capita performance with the Paris score being just over 4 per cent higher than that of London. By 2011, however, the London GDP per capita score was now some 16 per cent higher than that of Paris. These data suggest that London has out-performed Paris during this period in terms of absolute growth but under-performed in terms of growth relative to the national economy. This latter result is partly due to the fact that the overall national growth of France during this decade was much lower than the UK. However, the former effect is partly due to differences in administrative area classification systems. The problem with making such comparisons at the city level is that the OECD regional definitions of cities are not standardised according to the geographical and functional structure of the city but instead are based on the administrative boundaries, which differ across countries. In contrast, the OECD metropolitan urban area definitions are standardised exactly according to these principles. With the standardised metropolitan urban measures we see that the absolute growth in GDP per capita in both Paris and London has been very similar whereas Paris has out-performed London when benchmarked against national performance.

Table A4.2 London and Paris metropolitan urban area comparisons

OECD Metro Urban Area	Population 2012	Pop Density	Pop Annual Ave Growth Rate % 2000–2010	Pop of the Core Area	Pop of the Hinter-land	Sprawl Index	Metro Urban Area sq km	% Metro Area Urban
London	12,090,254	1,746.93	1.189	9,674,819	2,415,435	-6.776	6921	34.99
Paris	11,862,466	981.0	0.689	9,403,955	2,458,511	-2.366	12,090	19.99

From the OECD metropolitan urban area database and as noted in Chapter 3, the European city whose overall spatial morphology is the closest comparator for London is Paris which has an aggregate 2012 population density of 981.23 persons per sq km, which is much lower than the value of 1746.93 for London. However, the total area of London is 6921 sq km comprised of a core urban area of 2654 sq km and a hinterland area of 4267 sq km. Meanwhile the total area of Paris is 12,089 sq km which is comprised of a core area of 2031 and a hinterland of 10,058. The total population of London in 2012 was 12,090,254 while that of Paris is 11,862,466. However, the 2012 population in the core urban area of London is 9,674,819 while that of Paris is 9,403,955. As such, the 2012 population density of the core area of London is 3645.4 persons per sq km and the population density of the core urban area of Paris is 4630.3 4 persons per sq km. In other words, the core urban area of Paris is more densely populated than London (European Union 2014). The reason that Paris as whole displays a much lower population density than London is because its commuting hinterland is more than twice the area of London.

Table A4.3 London and Paris comparisons Using OECD-TL2/EU-NUTS1 regional definitions

OECD-TL2 Region	GDP per Capita 1995 (2000 constant prices)	GDP per Capita 2000 (2000 constant prices)	GDP per Capita 2010 (2000 constant prices)	Regional % Change in GDP per Capita 1995–2010	Difference between Regional and National % Change 1995–2010	Regional % Change in GDP per Capita 2000–2010	Difference between Regional and National % Change 2000–2010
London	37,022	49,438	58,344	57.6	+23.8	18.0	+6.5
Paris	38,463	44,447	50,256	30.6	+13.06	13.0	+8.23

Within the OECD-TL2/EU-NUTS1 Greater London region there are also enormous productivity variations at the OECD-TL3/EU-NUTS3 levels. While the overall average for the OECD-TL2/EU-NUTS1 region of Greater London in 2010 is US$58,344 (2000 prices) the figures for the OECD-TL3/EU-NUTS3 regions of Inner London West are US$182,522, for Inner London East US$58,121, for Outer London East and North East US$21,510, for Outer London South US$25,011 and for Outer London West and North West US$38,094.

Table A4.4 London and Paris inequality comparisons using OECD-TL2/EU-
NUTS1 regional definitions

	Gini Index of Inequality After Taxes and Transfers	Gini Index of Inequality Before Taxes and Transfers	Poverty Rate After Taxes and Transfers 60% Line	Poverty Rate After Taxes and Transfers 50% Line
Greater London	0.405	0.555	0.163	0.100
Paris/Ile de France	0.344	0.504	0.124	0.069

Appendix 4.3

The counter-factual New Zealand experience of globalisation and the adverse demand impacts due to a lack of global regionalism

In order to assess the role of economic geography and EU economic integration in the long-run performance of the UK economy it is very difficult to develop a counter-factual analysis. However, given their numerous institutional and cultural similarities, it is very instructive to compare the UK's long-run trade and globalisation experience with the case of New Zealand. New Zealand probably shares more institutional, governance and cultural features with the UK than any other country, and in terms of these various dimensions is the country which is most alike the UK. In economic geography terms, however, New Zealand is one of the most different countries to the UK being both small and extremely isolated. For more than a century up to the late 1960s New Zealand and the UK engaged in a sophisticated and managed set of bilateral trading and investment relationships based on relatively simple textbook-type comparative advantage principles. During this period the New Zealand and UK GDP per capita levels closely followed each other although in the majority of years New Zealand typically exhibited slightly higher levels than the UK and markedly higher levels in the 1960s (Maddison 2006). It was only in the late 1980s, however, that the UK started to overtake New Zealand in terms of GDP per capita (McCann 2009b). A major part of this was because although both countries undertook radical economic liberalisation reforms in the 1980s and both also engaged in deep economic integration with neighbouring countries (McCann 2009b), with the onset of modern globalisation New Zealand had very limited options to engage in the types of global regionalism undertaken by the UK. Due to its integration within the EU the UK was able to exploit much greater cross-border trading, investment and global value-chain (GVC) opportunities with neighbouring countries than was possible for New Zealand, which really only had Australia to integrate with as part of the CER (Closer Economic Relations) market integration programme (McCann 2009b). Due to its geographical location New Zealand had very few options to engage in the global regionalisation of its international economic engagement activities except with Australia, an economy which is more or less equivalent to just those of The Netherlands and Belgium combined. Yet even Australia is not close by. The Tasman Sea which separates Australia from New Zealand can accommodate almost all of the EU within its boundaries and the types of enormous market integration opportunities available to the UK simply did not exist for New Zealand. In this particular case Australia gained almost all of the benefits of the trans-Tasman integration, as would be expected from New Economic Geography models (Krugman and Venables 1995; McCann 2009b), because New Zealand had neither the scale, nor the home market, nor the accessibility advantages associated with economic integration which were enjoyed by the UK.

In the case of the UK, as we have seen, towards 60 per cent of the increased openness of the UK's trade activities was with the rest of the EU, rather than the whole world. As such, at least 6.15 per cent of the UK's productivity-enhancing effects associated with the UK's experience of modern globalisation is actually one of global regionalisation with the EU. An additional check on the estimate of 6.15 per cent of UK GDP per capita being the additional UK growth effects attributable to EU membership, as is implied by the fact that a figure approaching 60 per cent of the increasing trade openness exhibited by the UK in the last four decades is associated with increased UK–EU trade, can be derived from consideration of another comparator country case. Here the experience of New Zealand in globalisation and global regionalism is very instructive. Prior to the early 1970s the trade relationships of New Zealand were dominated by largely managed bilateral trade linkages with the UK (McCann 2009b), and prior to the early 1970s New Zealand had for almost a century been one of the world's very richest countries and consistently richer than the UK, particularly in the post-war era. However, as global trade relationships evolved from the mid-1970s onwards, and with the UK re-orienting itself away from Commonwealth countries and towards much more geographically concentrated trade-linkages with Europe, New Zealand was forced to seek new markets primarily in Asia and Australasia. However, as the global economy transformed with the onset of modern globalisation in the early 1990s, New Zealand has found its peripheral geographical location to be a major disadvantage. Trade and development is now driven far more by the advantages of proximity than in previous eras and New Zealand's productivity has fallen continuously over the last five decades relative to the OECD average, even though its governance reforms have meant that its institutional set-up is one of the very best in the world. Immediately prior to the 2008 global financial crisis, on purely institutional and governance criteria the productivity of New Zealand should be some 27 per cent higher than the OECD average, whereas in reality its productivity is below the OECD average, and 55 per cent of this gap is due to the problem of economic geography (de Serres *et al.* 2014). This 55 per cent share of the long-run relative decline in the GDP per capita of New Zealand relative to the OECD average productivity levels, is almost a mirror image of the estimated UK growth in goods trade (Springford *et al.* 2014) and economic output (Boltho and Eichengreen 2008; CBI 2014) due to four decades of EU integration processes. Over more than four decades the UK has enjoyed the benefits of having an enormous and rapidly integrating global market on its doorstep, and this has helped to slow down or partly reverse some of the long-run downward productivity trends the UK had been experiencing in the post-war era. On the eve of the 2008 global economic crisis the GDP per capita of the UK was 25 per cent higher than New Zealand and some 9 per cent above the OECD average (OECD 2014b) and, as we have already seen, towards 60 per cent of the increased openness of the UK's trade activities was with the rest of the EU. This reflects the general global pattern that today some 60–70 per cent of all multinational activities (trade, investment, sales) typically take place within the same global region in which a firm is located (Rugman 2000, 2005; McCann 2009a; Iammarino and McCann 2013; MGI 2010). It is this global regionalism which has driven the lion's share of the international aspects of growth during the modern era of globalisation, and from which the UK has benefited primarily due to its integration with the EU. In contrast, because of its problematic geography, New Zealand has very limited possibilities for exploiting the potential advantages of globalisation, given that by way of comparison, almost the whole of the EU can be inserted into the Tasman Sea separating Australia from New Zealand. Indeed, for reasons of contrasting geography this has meant that over more than four decades the economy of New Zealand has been deprived of many of the benefits of modern trade and globalisation to almost an identical extent that the UK has benefited from them.

Notes

1 Some of the material in this chapter is based on McCann (2013), but the chapter draws on numerous different sources of material.

2 Outward FDI from advanced economies accounted for 84 per cent of total global outward FDI in 2009 down from 89 per cent in 1980.

3 Emerging and transition economies accounted for 52 per cent of FDI inflows and 35 per cent of FDI outflows by 2012 (UNCTAD 2012).

4 See: www.bankofengland.co.uk/publications/.../threecenturiesofdata.xls. This nominal growth between 1970 and 2011 is equivalent to a growth of 250 per cent in real terms. See: www.ons.gov.uk/ons/rel/elmr/explaining-economic-statistics/long-term-profile-of-gdp-in-the-uk/sty-long-term-profile-of-gdp.html.

5 Ibid.

6 After Greece whose overall low export propensity is dominated by tourism and shipping.

7 And comfortably more than three times if we include EFTA (EEA + Switzerland).

8 "We Can Pivot Too", *The Economist*, 24 October 2015.

9 The EU provides a slightly smaller share of the UK's total imports than is the case for Norway, while Switzerland is even more dependent on the EU for imports than Norway (Allen 2012).

10 Assuming that Hong King and China are combined. See: OECD, 2013, *OECD Science, Technology and Industry Scoreboard: Innovation for Growth*, Organisation for Economic Cooperation and Development, Paris and *The FDI Report*, www.fdiintelligence.com.

11 £531,479–£365,268 million (Allen and Dar 2013).

12 £1,098,177–£766.166 million (Allen and Dar 2013).
13 £210,356–£203,828 = £6528 million. This has changed little from the value of £6392 in 2000 (Allen and Dar 2013).
14 In 2010 net earnings from UK foreign investment abroad were £79.1 billion while overseas companies' investment in the UK earned £37.5 billion, giving a 2010 net surplus of £41.6 billion (ONS 2011).
15 "He Warned of Trouble for China", *New York Times*, 26 August 2015; "Taking a Tumble. Briefing: China and the World Economy", *The Economist*, 29 August 2015; "The Great Fall of China", *The Economist*, 29 August 2015.
16 www.wiod.org/database/index.htm.
17 http://atlas.media.mit.edu/profile/country/gbr/.
18 Similar models have also been developed by the OECD (2013a) and by the OECD in conjunction with the World Trade Organisation (WTO) using trade data as the starting point rather than input-output production and use tables. This system allows for value-decompositions of the global value-chains but does not allow for calculation of the derived demand effects. Other trade input-output type models have also been developed by JETRO Japan and the OECD (Johnson 2014). However, while their various starting points of these models and databases differ, these various systems largely provide very similar global value-chain decomposition estimates, as do those based on GTAP models (Johnson 2014).
19 As such, the WIOD model estimates incorporate the so-called 'Rotterdam Effect' trans-shipment effect plus UK-mediated trans-shipments effects along with all other broader GVC related effects. See: Docx, E., 2015, "Nigel Farage's Dream", *Prospect*, December.
20 Some 1.8 million people from other EU countries are currently working in the UK. Including their dependents this implies that some 2.7 million people from the rest of the EU are currently resident in the UK. At the same time, some 1.3 million UK citizens are currently living in other EU countries of which some 900,000 are in employment. See: www.migrationwatchuk.org/briefing-paper/4.30.
21 'Immediately' owned refers to the nationality of the company officially listed as owning the establishment, while 'ultimately' owned refers to any higher level parent companies which own the 'immediately' owning company.
22 See:www.ons.gov.uk/ons/rel/regional-analysis/foreign-ownership-of-businesses-in-the-uk/foreign-ownership-of-businesses-in-the-uk/index.html.
23 As of the first half of 2014 both Lufthansa and Air France each carried more than three times as many passengers to China as did British Airways, which actually carried fewer passengers to China than even Finnair. See: the BBC television programme *A Very British Airline* broadcast on BBC4 at 23.00 on 14 April 2015.
24 The direct multiplier effect is calculated from the value-added/gross output ratios plus the intermediate demand coefficients and the final demand levels, and as such represents the first round multiplier effects, while the indirect multiplier effects represent all subsequent rounds plus those demand effects mediated the alternative demand pathways provided by GVCs. If we consider the ratio of the indirect/direct value-added multipliers associated with UK demand for each of the years 1995, 2001 and 2011 from the EU-27 countries, the BRICs countries, the 'Western Offshoots' and the Rest of the World, the ratios for 1995, 2001 and 2011 for the EU-27 are 2.6, 2.5 and 2.4, respectively; for BRICs countries are 3.1, 3.4 and 3.3; for the 'Western Offshoots' are 2.4, 2.6 and 2.4; and for the Rest of the World are 2.7, 2.7 and 2.7. For the indirect/direct employment multiplier ratios, the ratios for 1995, 2001 and 2011 for the EU-27 are 2.6, 2.5 and 2.5, respectively; for BRICs countries are 3.0, 3.2 and 3.0; for the 'Western Offshoots' are 2.5, 2.6 and 2.5; and for the Rest of the World are 2.8, 2.7 and 2.7. As such, in the case of both the value-added multipliers and the employment multipliers the ratios of the indirect/

direct multipliers is more or less the same for UK demand emanating from both the EU-27 and also the 'Western Offshoots' whereas the ratios of indirect/direct multipliers associated with demand emanating from the Rest of the Word and the BRICs countries are typically more than 12 per cent and 30 per cent higher, respectively. Yet, the reason for these differences is primarily associated with the GVCs mediated via the EU-27, which serve demand emanating in the BRICs and the Rest of the World and indirectly channel demand to the UK via the EU-27.

25 http://stats.oecd.org/Index.aspx?DatasetCode=SNA_TABLE1.
26 "Leaving the EU", *Research Paper 13/42*, House of Commons Library, 1 July, page 7.
27 Involving the inversion of matrices of dimension $40 \times 40 \times 35 \times 35 = 1.96$ million cells.
28 In 2012 the £10 billion UK annual net contribution to the EU represented some 0.7 per cent of UK GDP and 1.5 per cent of UK public expenditure. See: "Leaving the EU", *Research Paper 13/42*, House of Commons Library, 1 July 2013. If we adjust the WIOD figures for the £10 billion net UK annual EU contribution as of 2011–2012 then the net economic demand effect of the EU Single Market on UK households in 2001 was £6214 per UK household per annum. Using a range of discount rates with an upper bound of 8 per cent and a lower bound of 5 per cent this implies that the net household contribution of the EU Single Market was between £77,675 and £124,280 in 2011.
29 In 2014 the net contribution of the UK was £11.7 billion. These payments currently represent an average annual cost of some £440 per UK household and £180 per person. To put these figures into perspective, this figure is marginally higher than the current annual BBC TV licence fee of £145 (Robinson 2015).
30 http://stats.oecd.org/Index.aspx?DatasetCode=SNA_TABLE1.
31 This Input-Output analysis also demonstrates the absurd logic underpinning Andrew Marr's comments to Sir Richard Branson that the annual 'cost' of the UK's EU membership is the UK's net annual EU budget contribution plus the value of the UK's trade deficit with the EU. See *The Andrew Marr Show*, broadcast on BBC1 at 09.00 on Sunday 28 June 2015. This type of logic represents either a total misunderstanding or a complete lack of understanding of how trade, global value-chains and demand are interrelated.
32 http://themasites.pbl.nl/eu-trade/. Additional background and related material to the data sets and their applications can be found at: www.pbl.nl/en/publications/european-regional-competitiveness-scoreboard; http://s3platform.jrc.ec.europa.eu/s3-tools.
33 The Scottish Input-Output tables estimate the Scottish export share as 20.7 per cent of regional GVA and the Scottish import share as 18 per cent of regional GVA. See: www.gov.scot/Topics/Statistics/Browse/Economy/Input-Output/Downloads.
34 The announcement regarding the closure of English RDAs was made in 2010 and they were largely disbanded in 2011, albeit with formal closure in March 2012 (Ernst and Young 2012).
35 "British Museum Tops UK Visitor Attractions", BBC News, 16 March 2015, see: www.bbc.com/news/entertainment-arts-31877819.
36 See: www.migrationobservatory.ox.ac.uk/number-foreign-born-local-area-district.
37 www.bbc.com/news/education-30521423.
38 The calculations were kindly undertaken by Colin Lizieri of Cambridge University on the basis of the Real Capital Analytics Top 1000 Office Transactions. See also: Lizieri and Pain (2014, 2015) and Lizieri and Mekic (2015).
39 "The Freight Debate", *The Economist*, 18 October 2014.
40 In terms of international passengers as of 2014 Heathrow was the busiest international airport closely followed by Dubai, Hong Kong, Paris Charles de Gaulle,

Singapore and Amsterdam Schiphol. See: "Dubai Looks to Cement Mega-Hub Status", *Financial Times*, 10 September 2014. However, by 2015 it was overtaken by Dubai, and all of the other competitor airports except Singapore were all growing more quickly than Heathrow. See: "London's Airports: Decision Time" and "Airports in London: Now Get on With It", *The Economist*, 4 July 2015. There is also some recent evidence that UK regional airports outside of London are making progress towards increasing their global long-haul connectivity in response to regional industry demands, but the global connectivity gap between the London airports and the rest of the UK in this regard is still enormous. See: Hackett (2014) and "UK Provincial Airports Go Over Head of London", *Financial Times*, 7 December 2014. In terms of the issues raised in this book this connectivity gap is important because for European cities it is inter-continental airport connectivity rather than intra-continental connectivity which is the most critical influence on the location of corporate headquarter and high-level decision-making functions (Bel and Fageda 2008) rather than anything related to urban specialisation, size or diversity.

41 At 2005 US dollar PPP prices the highest OECD-TL2/EU-NUTS1 regions GDP per capita values for 2011 in descending order are: Brussels $60,637; Greater London $58,344; Hamburg $57,136; Ile de France (Paris) $50,256; Oslo $48,160; Zurich $49,536. See: http://stats.oecd.org/Index.aspx?datasetcode=REG_DEMO_TL2. With a total output of $549 billion, London is the sixth largest city in the world after Tokyo $1295 billion, New York $944 billion, Los Angeles $750 billion, Seoul-Incheon $589 billion and Paris $579 billion, followed by Osaka with $517 billion in seventh position and Chicago with $450 billion in eighth position, all calculated in 2005 US dollar PPP. However, in terms of GDP per capita London is the 23rd richest city in the OECD. For the OECD Metropolitan Urban Areas the highest European GDP per capita scores in 2005 US dollar PPP values in descending order are: Munich $51,349; Paris $49,498; Frankfurt $48,802; Stockholm $48,364; Dublin $48,181; Oslo $48,180; Zurich $48,128; London $46,532; Brussels $45,749; Hamburg $44,934; Milan $44,453; Edinburgh $43,380; Helsinki $43,082; Stuttgart $42,895; Utrecht $42,060; Prague $41,543. As such London is the eighth richest city in Europe. For North American cities the 15 cities which are richer than London in descending order are Baltimore $61,839, San Francisco $56,703, Edmonton $56,604, Washington DC $56,590, New York $56,021, Calgary $55,804, Seattle $51,910, Providence $52,615, Boston $51,225, San Diego $50,112, Houston $48,539, Chicago $48,296, Denver $48,343, Philadelphia $48,122 and New Orleans $47,520. See: http://stats.oecd.org/Index.aspx?datasetcode=CITIES.

42 For Greater London the 2010 Gini Indices of Inequality Before Taxes and After Taxes and Transfers are 0.565 and 0.405, respectively. For other OECD global cities and global city-regions the equivalent values in descending order of the before-taxes Gini index are: Washington DC 0.585 and 0.478; New York State (New York) 0.534 and 0.403; California (Los Angeles and San Francisco Bay Area) 0.534 and 0.408; Illinois (Chicago) 0.522 and 0.401; New Jersey (New York) 0.508 and 0.389; Brussels 0.518 and 0.347; Ile de France (Paris) 0.504 and 0.344; Massachusetts (Boston) 0.498 and 0.377; Kansai (Osaka) 0.497 and 0.337; Berlin 0.491 and 0.281; New South Wales (Sydney) 0.477 and 0.344; Hamburg 0.475 and 0.330; Southern Kanto (Tokyo) 0.473 and 0.335; Catalonia (Barcelona) 0.462 and 0.303; Denmark Capital Region (Copenhagen) 0.445 and 0.282; West Netherlands (Randstad) 0.439 and 0.303; Madrid 0.439 and 0.317; Stockholm 0.438 and 0.302; Ontario (Toronto) 0.436 and 0.314; Zurich 0.430 and 0.320; Lazio (Rome) 0.341 and 0.325; Lombardy (Milan) 0.308 and 0.297. See: http://stats.oecd.org/Index.aspx?datasetcode=REG_DEMO_TL2.

43 The BRES Business Register Employment Survey estimated that The City employment in 2011 was 382,700 while the UK 2011 Census estimates gave a figure of 357,000. See *City of London Workforce CENSUS 2011 Introduction*, Corporation for the City of London, May 2015.

44 This CLC (2014b) reported figure of 4 per cent of UK economic output is a result of rounding-up. From Chapter 2 we see that Greater London accounts for 22.3 per cent of 2011 UK output, so 16 per cent of this suggests The City generates 3.568 per cent of total UK economic output.

45 The media and technology activities which are actually located within the boundaries of The City are located primarily in the neighbourhoods of Farringdon and Coleman Street (CLC 2014b).

46 "City Job Numbers to Fall by 13,000 in 2013 and to Fall Further in 2014 to Lowest Level since 1993", News Release, Centre for Economics and Business Research, 6 November 2012.

47 "City Bonuses Join the Real World – Down from £33,000 a Head to £6,400 a Head", News Release, Centre for Economics and Business Research, 12 November 2012.

48 OECD, 2013, *OECD Science, Technology and Industry Scoreboard: Innovation for Growth*, Organisation for Economic Cooperation and Development, Paris.

49 "Life Beyond the City: London's Shifting Centre of Gravity", "London Loses Top Spot as World Financial Centre", News Releases, Centre for Economics and Business Research, 12 November 2012.

50 "Life Beyond the City: London's Shifting Centre of Gravity", News Release, Centre for Economics and Business Research, 12 November 2012.

51 See for example the Evan Davis BBC television programme *Mind the Gap: London vs the Rest: Part 1* which was broadcast on Monday 3 March 2014 on BBC2 at 21.00–22.00.

52 Moreover, the 'ambassador' argues that nowhere except diverse and globalised mega-cities such as London can succeed in these twenty-first century media technologies, and that public policy support to nurture these clusters in London is therefore justified (CfL 2012). This assertion and these policy-related conclusions are stated in spite of widespread evidence to the contrary including the fact that almost all of the computer animation and filming of both *The Lord of Rings* and *The Hobbit* trilogies, along with other blockbusters such as the *Chronicles of Narnia* and *The Last Samurai*, took place in one of the OECD's least globalised, least populated economies, and least accessible locations, namely New Zealand.

53 www.london.gov.uk/mayor/economic_unit/docs/CapImpact_andrew_burrell.pdf. These estimated figures are very close to the PBL estimates.

54 www.uncsbrp.org.

55 The London Development Plan (LDP) states that The City produces 10 per cent of UK national income. However, this figure is three times larger than the figure reported by CLC (2014b) which itself is based on employment estimates which are also largely consistent with those provided by CEBR (2012a). Indeed, in order for the LDP figures to be accurate it would require that The City alone generates 45 per cent of Greater London's output. Yet combining LDP with CEBR (2012a) and CLC (2014b) data it is clear that 'City-type' employment is less than 10 per cent of the total London employment level, such that City-type jobs would have to generate productivity levels on average some five times higher than all other London jobs. These figures are unrealistic. As such, the LDP reported figures only become meaningful if they are taken to refer to all of London's financial and business service jobs combined, including those which are not located in either The City or Docklands, and including all of those business service jobs which are part of financial services.

56 www.ons.gov.uk/ons/rel/lms/labour-market-statistics/june-2013/sty-uk-employment.html.
57 "London Centric", BBC News, 30 September 2015, www.bbc.co.uk/news/resources/idt-248d9ac7-9784-4769-936a-8d3b435857a8.
58 Edinburgh is the UK's second financial services city and the dominant employment centre for Scotland's 85,000 financial services workers (Kay 2015).

References

Allen, G., 2012, "UK Trade Statistics", *Standard Note SNEP 6211*, House of Commons Library, 8 October.

Allen, G., and Dar, A., 2013, "Foreign Direct Investment", *SN/EP/1828, Economic Policy and Statistics, House of Commons Library*, 14 March.

Ascani, A., Crescenzi, R. and Iammarino, S., 2015, "Economic Institutions and the Location Strategies of European Multinationals in their Geographical Neighbourhood", Discussion Paper Henley Business School, JHD-2015-07.

AT Kearney, 2014, *2014 Global Cities Index and Emerging Markets Cities Outlook*, Korea.

Autor, D.H., Katz, L.F. and Kreuger, A.B., 1998, "Computing Inequality: Have Computers Changed the Labor Market?", *Quarterly Journal of Economics*, 113.4, 1169–1213.

Baldwin, R., 2006, *The Great Unbundling(s)*, Prime Minister's Office, Economic Council of Finland, Helsinki, 20 September.

Baldwin, R., 2011, "Trade and Industrialisation after Globalisation's 2nd Unbundling: How Building and Joining Supply Chains are Different and Why it Matters", *NBER Working Paper 17716*, Cambridge, MA. www.nber.org/papers/w17716.

Baldwin, R., and Evenett, S., 2012, "Value Creation and Trade in 21st Century Manufacturing; What Policies for UK Manufacturing?", in Greenaway, D., (ed.), *The UK in a Globalised World: How Can the UK Focus on Steps in Global Value-Chains that Really Add Value?*, CEPR, Centre for Economic Policy Research, London.

Bel, G., and Fageda, X., 2008, "Getting there Fast: Globalization, Intercontinental Flights and Location of Headquarters", *Journal of Economic Geography*, 8, 471–495.

BIS, 2009, *Towards a Low Carbon Economy – Economic Analysis and Evidence for a Low Carbon Industrial Strategy*, BIS Economics Paper No. 1, Department for Business Innovation and Skills, July.

BIS, 2010a, *UK Trade Performance: Patterns in UK and Global Trade Growth*, BIS Economics Paper No. 8, Department for Business Innovation and Skills, November.

BIS, 2010b, *Manufacturing in the UK: An Economic Analysis of the Sector*, BIS Economics Paper No. 10a, Department for Business Innovation and Skills, December.

BIS, 2011a, *World Trade and the Doha Round: Final Report of the High-Level Trade Experts Group*, Department for Business, Innovation and Skills, London.

BIS, 2011b, *Internationalisation of Innovative and High Growth SMEs*, BIS Economics Paper No. 5, Department for Business Innovation and Skills, March.

BIS, 2012a, *UK Trade Performance Across Markets and Sectors*, BIS Economics Paper No. 17, Department for Business Innovation and Skills, February.

BIS, 2012b, *Commentary on Regional Economic Performance Indicators*, Department for Business, Innovation and Skills, London, September.

BIS/DFID, 2011a, *Global Context – How Has World Trade and Investment Developed, What's Next?*, Trade and Investment Analytical Papers Topic 1 of 18, Department for Business, Innovation and Skills Department for International Development Joint BIS/DFID Trade Policy Unit.

BIS/DFID, 2011b, *The UK and the Single Market*, Trade and Investment Analytical Papers Topic 4 of 18, Department for Business, Innovation and Skills Department for International Development Joint BIS/DFID Trade Policy Unit.

BIS/DFID, 2011c, *Economic Openness and Economic Prosperity*, Trade and Investment Analytical Papers Topic 2 of 18, Department for Business, Innovation and Skills Department for International Development Joint BIS/DFID Trade Policy Unit.

Boltho, A., and Eichengreen, B., 2008, *The Economic Impact of European Integration*, CEPR Discussion Paper 6820, Centre for Economic Policy Research, London.

Boulhol, H., de Serres, A. and Molnar, M., 2008, "The Contribution of Economic Geography to GDP per Capita", *OECD Economic Journal*, Organisation for Economic Growth and Development, December.

Breeze Strategy, 2010, *Inward Investment Begins at Home: A Localist Approach to Attracting Jobs and Investment*, see: http://breeze-strategy.blogs.com/files/inward-investment-begins-at-home-3.pdf.

Breeze Strategy, 2012, *UK Projects Database: Job Creating Investments by UK and foreign Companies 2011/12*, see: http://breeze-strategy.blogs.com/files/uk-projects-database.pdf.

Brülhart, M., 2011, "The Spatial Effects of Trade Openness: A Survey", *Review of World Economics*, 147.1, 59–83.

Cairncross, F., 1997, *The Death of Distance: How The Communications Revolution will Change our Lives*, Orion Business Books, London.

Casson, M.C., and McCann, P., 1999, "Globalisation, Competition, and the Corporation: The UK Experience", in Whitman M., (ed.), *The Evolving Corporation: Global Imperatives and National Responses*, Group of Thirty, Washington DC.

CBI, 2014, *Our Global Future: The Business Vision for a Reformed EU*, Confederation of British Industry, London.

CEBR, 2012a, "City Job Numbers to Fall by 13,000 in 2013 and to Fall Further in 2014 to Lowest Level since 1993", News Release, 6 November, Centre for Economics and Business Research, London, www.cebr.org.

CEBR, 2012b, "London Loses Top Spot as World Financial Centre", News Release, 12 November, Centre for Economics and Business Research, London, www.cebr.org.

CEBR, 2012c, "One Pound in Five Earned in London Subsidises the Rest of the UK – Northern Ireland, Wales and North East Receive More Than a Fifth of Their Income as Subsidies from Outside of the Region", News Release, 13 February, Centre for Economics and Business Research, London, www.cebr.org.

CfL, 2011, *London's Calling: Young Londoners, Social Mobility and Access to Higher Education*, Centre for London, London.

CfL, 2012, *A Tale of Tech City: The Future of Inner East London's Digital Economy*, Centre for London, London.

Clark, G., 2015, *The Making of a World City: London 1991 to 2021*, Wiley Blackwell, Oxford.

CLC, 2004a, *London's Place in the UK Economy 2004*, City of London Corporation, London.

CLC, 2004b, *London's Linkages with the Rest of the UK*, City of London Corporation, London.

CLC, 2005a, *London's Place in the UK Economy, 2005–06*, City of London Corporation, London.

CLC, 2005b, *Offshoring and the City of London*, City of London Corporation, London.

CLC, 2008, *London's Place in the UK Economy 2008–09*, City of London Corporation, London.

CLC, 2009, *London's Place in the UK Economy, 2009–10*, City of London Corporation, London.

CLC, 2014a, *London's Finances and Revenues*, City of London Corporation, London.

CLC, 2014b, *The Impact of Firm Migration on the City of London*, City of London Corporation, London.

Crescenzi, R., Datu, K. and Iammarino, S. (2015a), "European Cities and Foreign Investment Networks", Department of Geography & Environment, LSE, mimeo.

Crescenzi, R., Gagliardi, L. and Iammarino, S. (2015b), "Foreign Multinationals and Domestic Innovation: Intra-industry Effects and Firm Heterogeneity", *Research Policy*, 44:3, 596–609.

Crinò, R., 2009, "Offshoring, Multinationals and Labour Markets: A Review of the Empirical Literature", *Journal of Economic Surveys*, 23.2, 197–249.

de Serres, A., Yashiro, N. and Boulhol, H., 2014, "An International Perspective on the New Zealand Productivity Paradox", *New Zealand Productivity Commission Working Paper 2014/01*, Organisation for Economic Cooperation and Development, Paris.

Dewhurst, J.H.Ll., and McCann, P., 2002, "A Comparison of Measures of Industrial Specialisation for Travel-To-Work Areas in Great Britain 1981–97", *Regional Studies*, 36.5, 541–551.

Dhingra, S. Ottaviano, G. and Sampson, T., 2015, *Should We Stay or Should We Go? The Economic Consequences of Leaving the EU*, Centre for Economic Performance, London.

Dimitropoulou, D., McCann, P. and Burke, S.P., 2013, "The Determinants of the Location of Foreign Direct Investment in UK Regions", *Applied Economics*, 45.27, 3853–3862.

Dustmann, C., and Frattini, T., 2014, "The Fiscal Effects of Immigration to the UK", *Economic Journal*, 124.580, F593–F643.

Ernst and Young, 2012, *Staying Ahead of the Game: Ernst and Young's Attractiveness Survey UK*, see: www.ey.com/attractiveness.

Ernst and Young, 2013, *Coping with the Crisis, the European Way*, see: www.ey.com/attractiveness.

European Commission, 2012, *European Competitiveness Report 2012: Reaping the Benefits of Globalisation*, European Commission Directorate-General for Enterprise and Industry, Brussels.

European Union, 2014, *Investment for Jobs and Growth – Promoting Development and Good Governance in EU Regions and Cities: Sixth Report on Economic, Social and Territorial Cohesion*, Publications Office, Brussels.

Fogel, R.W., 1964, *Railroads and American Economic Growth: Essays in Econometric History*, Johns Hopkins Press, Baltimore.

Financial Times, 2014, *The FDI Report 2014: Global Greenfield Investment Trends*, FT Intelligence, London.

Friedman, T.L., 2007, *The World is Flat: A Brief History of the Twenty-First Century*, 3rd edition, Picador, New York.

Gagliardi, L., Iammarino, S. and Rodriguez-Pose, A., 2015, "Outward FDI and the Geography of Jobs: Evidence from the UK", Department of Geography & Environment, LSE mimeo.

Gereffi, G., 1999, "International Trade and Industrial Upgrading in the Apparel Commodity Chain", *Journal of International Economics*, 48, 37–70.

Geyer, H.S., 2006, (ed.), *Global Regionalization: Core Peripheral Trends*, Edward Elgar, Cheltenham.

Ghemawat, P., and Altmann, S.A., 2011, *DHL Global Connectedness Index 2011: Analysing Global Flows and their Power to Increase Prosperity*, IESE Business School, Barcelona.

Ghemawat, P., and Altmann, S.A., 2012, *DHL Global Connectedness Index 2012: Analysing Global Flows and their Power to Increase Prosperity*, IESE Business School, Barcelona.

Ghemawat, P., and Altmann, S.A., 2014, *DHL Global Connectedness Index 2014: Analysing Global Flows and their Power to Increase Prosperity*, NYU Stern School of Business and IESE Business School, Barcelona.

Goos, M., Manning, A. and Salomons, A., 2009, "Job Polarization in Europe", *American Economic Review*, 99.2, 58–63.

Gordon, I.R., 2015, "The Quantitative Easing of a Finance Capital: How London Came So Well Out of the Post-2007 Crisis", Working Paper, Department of Geography and Environment, London School of Economics, and *Paper Presented at the Divergent Cities Conference*, St Catharine's College, Cambridge, 16–17 July.

Hackett, P., 2014, (ed.), *Making Global Connections: The Potential of the UK's Regional Airports*, Smith Institute, London.

Hamilton, D.S., and Quinlan, J.P., 2008, *Globalization and Europe: Prospering in the New Whirled Order – Germany and Globalization*, Centre for Transatlantic Relations, Paul H. Nitze School of Advanced International Studies, Johns Hopkins University. See: http://transatlantic.sais-jhu.edu/publications/books/GermanyandGlobalization-eng.pdf.

Harris, R., and Moffat, J., 2012, "Is Productivity Higher in British Cities", *Journal of Regional Science*, 52.5, 762–786.

Hill, S., and Morgan, B., 1998, (eds.), *Inward Investment, Business Finance and Regional Development*, Macmillan, Basingstoke.

Hill, S., and Munday, M., 1994, *The Regional Distribution of Foreign Direct Investment in the UK*, Macmillan, Basingstoke.

HM Revenue and Customs, 2013, "EU Overseas Trade Statistics October 2013", London.

Hoyler, M., Lizieri, C., Pain, K., Taylor, P., Vinciguerra, S., Derudder, B. and Pelckmans, D., 2014, "European Cities in Advanced Producer Services and Real Estate Capital Flows: A Dynamic Perspective", in Pain, K., and van Hamme, G., (eds.), *Changing Urban and Regional Relations in a Globalizing World*, Edward Elgar, Cheltenham.

Hummels, D., 2007, "Transportation Costs and International Trade in the Second Era of Globalization", *Journal of Economic Perspectives*, 21.3, 131–154.

Hummels, D., and Schaur, G., 2013, "Time as a Trade Barrier", *American Economic Review*, 103.7, 2935–2959.

Iammarino, S., and McCann, P., 2013, *Multinationals and Economic Geography: Location, Technology, and Innovation*, Edward Elgar, Cheltenham.

Iammarino, S. and McCann, P., 2015a, "MNE Innovation Networks and the Role of Cities", in Archibugi, D., and Filippetti, A., (eds.), *The Handbook of Global Science, Technology and Innovation*, Wiley-Blackwell, Oxford.

Iammarino, S. and McCann, P., 2015b, "Network Geographies and Geographical Networks. Co-Dependence and Co-Evolution of Multinational Enterprises and Space", in Clark, G.L., Feldman, M.P., Gertler, M.S. and Wójcik, D. (eds.), *The New Oxford Handbook of Economic Geography*, Oxford University Press, Oxford, Forthcoming.

IMF (International Monetary Fund), 2014, *World Economic Outlook: Recovery Strengthens, Remains Uneven*, Washington DC.

Iparraguire D'Elia, J.L., 2008, "Northern Ireland's Input-Output Table: An Application of the Kronenberg's Derivative Approach", Northern Ireland Economic Research Institute, Belfast.

Jaegers, T., Lipp-Lingua, C. and Amil, D., 2013, "High-Technology and Medium-High Technology Industries Main Drivers of EU-27's Industrial Growth", *Eurostat Statistics in Focus 1/2013*, European Commission.

Johnson, R.C., 2014, "Five Facts about Global Value Added Exports and Implications for Macroeconomics and Trade Research", *Journal of Economic Perspectives*, 28.2, 119–142.

Jones, J., and Wren, C., 2006, *Foreign Direct Investment and the Regional Economy*, Ashgate, Aldershot.

Kaletsky, A., 2015, "Corbynomics – Almost Right", *Prospect*, October.

Kay, J., 2015, *Other People's Money: Masters of the Universe or Servants of the People?*, Profile Books, London.

Kemeny, T. and Rigby, D., 2012, "Trading Away What Kind of Jobs? Globalization, Trade and Tasks in the US Economy", *Review of World Economics*, 148, 1–16.

Kohl, T., and Brouwer, A., 2014, "The Development of Trade Blocs in an Era of Globalisation", *Environment and Planning A*, 46, 1535–1553.

Krugman, P., and Venables, A.J., 1995, "Globalization and the Inequality of Nations", *Quarterly Journal of Economics*, 110.4, 857–880.

Leamer, E.E., 2007. "A Flat World, a Level Playing Field, a Small World After All, or None of the Above? A Review of Thomas L Friedman's *The World is Flat*", *Journal of Economic Literature*, 45.1, 83–126.

Lizieri, C., and Mekic, D., 2015, "Real Estate and Global Capital Networks: Drilling into the City of London", Paper Presented at the 2015 European Real Estate Society Conference, Istanbul.

Lizieri, C., and Pain, K., 2014, "International Office Investment in Global Cities: The Production of Financial Space and Systemic Risk", *Regional Studies*, 48.3, 439–455.

Lizieri, C., and Pain, K., 2015, "International Office Investment Networks and Capital Flows in the Financialization of City Space", Paper Presented at the 2015 Association of American Geographers Conference, Chicago.

Long Finance, 2014, *The Global Financial Centres Index 16*, Qatar Financial Centre, Corporation of the City of London and Z/Yen Group, Qatar.

McCann, P., 2007, "Sketching out a Model of Innovation, Face-to-Face Interaction and Economic Geography", *Spatial Economic Analysis*, 2.2, 117–134.

McCann, P., 2008, "Globalization and Economic Geography: The World is Curved, Not Flat", *Cambridge Journal of Regions, Economy and Society*, 1.3, 351–370.

McCann, P., 2009a, "Globalisation, Multinationals and the BRIICS Countries", in Lattimore, R., and Safadi, R., (eds.), *Globalisation and Emerging Economies*, Organisation for Economic Growth and Development, Paris.

McCann, P., 2009b, "Economic Geography, Globalisation and New Zealand's Productivity Paradox", *New Zealand Economic Papers*, 43.3, 279–314.

McCann, P., 2011, "International Business and Economic Geography: Knowledge, Time and Transactions", *Journal of Economic Geography*, 11.2, 309–317.

McCann, P., 2013, "The North East (NELEP) Area in the Context of the Global Economy", Paper Commissioned as an Independent Expert 'Thinkpiece' for the *North of England Independent Economic Review*. Available at: www.nelep.co.uk/ne-economic-review/evidence/.

McCann, P., and Acs, Z.J., 2011, "Globalisation: Countries, Cities and Multinationals", *Regional Studies*, 45.1, 17–32.

Maddison, A., 2006, *The World Economy. Volume 1: A Millennial Perspective; Volume 2: Historical Statistics*, Organisation for Economic Growth and Development, Paris.

MGI, 2010, *Growth and Competitiveness in the United States: The Role of its Multinationals*, McKinsey Global Institute.

MGI, 2012, *Manufacturing the Future: The Next Era of Global Growth and Innovation*, McKinsey Global Institute.

NESTA, 2013, *Foreign Direct Investment and UK Suppliers: The Impacts on Innovation Capabilities*, London.

OECD, 2006, *OECD Factbook 2006: Economic, Environmental and Social Statistics*, Organisation for Economic Cooperation and Development, Paris.

OECD, 2011, *OECD Regions at a Glance 2011*, Organisation for Economic Cooperation and Development, Paris.

OECD, 2012c, *International Migration Outlook 2012*, Organisation for Economic Cooperation and Development, Paris.

OECD, 2013a, *Interconnected Economies: Benefiting from Global Value-Chains*, Organisation for Economic Growth and Development, Paris.

OECD, 2013b, *OECD Regions at a Glance 2013*, Organisation for Economic Growth and Development, Paris.

OECD, 2014a, *Netherlands: OECD Reviews of Innovation Policy*, Organisation for Economic Growth and Development, Paris.

OECD, 2014b, *OECD Factbook 2014: Economic, Environmental and Social Statistics*, Organisation for Economic Growth and Development, Paris.

ONS, 2008, *Regional Trends 40*, Stationery Office, London.

ONS, 2011, "Foreign Direct Investment Involving UK Companies", 2010 Release, *Statistical Bulletin*, 8 December, Office for National Statistics, London.

ONS, 2012, "2011 Census Key Statistics for England and Wales, March 2011", *Statistical Bulletin*, 11 December, Office for National Statistics, www.ons.gov.uk/ons/dcp171778_290685.pdf,

ONS, 2013, "Foreign Direct Investment Involving UK Companies, 2013 (MA4), *Statistical Bulletin*, 7 February 2012, Office for National Statistics, London.

ONS, 2014, "Foreign Direct Investment Involving UK Companies, 2012 (MA4), *Statistical Bulletin*, 6 February 2014, Office for National Statistics, London.

Ottaviano, G.I.P, Pessoa, J.P., Sampson, T. and van Reenen, J., 2014, "The Costs and Benefits of Leaving the EU", *Centre for Economic Policy*, London School of Economics, London.

Overman, H.G., and Winters, L.A., 2005, The Port Geography of UK International Trade", *Environment and Planning A*, 37.10, 1751–1768.

Overman, H.G., and Winters, L.A., 2011, "Trade and Economic Geography: The Impact of EEC Accession on the UK", *The Manchester School*, 79.5, 994–1017.

Reyes, J., Garcia, M. and Lattimore, R., 2009, "The International Economic Order and Trade Architecture", *Spatial Economic Analysis*, 4.1, 73–102.

Robert-Nicoud, F., 2008, "Offshoring of Routine Tasks and (de) Industrialisation: Threat or Opportunity – and for Whom?", *Journal of Urban Economics*, 63.2, 517–535.

Robinson, W., (Bill), 2015, "The Brexit and Investments", *The New Statesman: Spring Investment Special supplement*, 10–16 April.

Rosewell, B., 2013, *Reinventing London*, London Publishing Partnership, London.

Rugman, A., 2000, *The End of Globalization: Why Global Strategy is a Myth & How to Prosper from the Realities of Regional Markets*, Amacom, New York.

Rugman, A., 2005, *The Regional Multinationals*, Cambridge University Press, Cambridge.

Sassen, S., 2006, *Cities in a World Economy*, Pine Forge Press, Thousand Oaks, CA.

Scott, A.J., 2001, *Global City-Regions: Trends, Theory, Policy*, Oxford University Press, Oxford.

Smith, A., 2014, *London Theatre Report*, The Society of London Theatre and the National Theatre, London.

Spitz, A., 2004, "Are Skill Requirements in the Workplace Rising? Stylized Facts and Evidence on Skill-Biased Technological Change", *ZEW Discussion Paper 04-33*, ZEW Centre for European Economic Research, Mannheim.

Springford, J., Tilford, S., and Whyte, P., 2014, *The Economic Consequences of Leaving the EU: The Final Report of the CER Commission on the UK and the EU Single Market*, Centre for European Reform, London, June.

Taylor, P.J., 2004, *World City Network: A Global Urban Analysis*, Routledge, London.

The Economist, 2013a, "Here, There and Everywhere, Special Report: Outsourcing and Offshoring", 19 January.

The Economist, 2013b, "Reshoring Manufacturing: Coming Home", 19 January.

The Economist, 2014a, "Free Exchange: Signs of Life", 15 November.

The Economist, 2014b, "International Trade: A Troubling Trajectory", 13 December.

The Economist, 2015a, "The Current Account. Britain's Biggest Export: Wealth", 10 January.

The Economist, 2015b, "The Global Economy: Diminished Hopes", 11 April.

Thissen, M., Diodato, D. and Van Oort, F.G., 2013a, *Integration and Convergence in Regional Europe: European Regional Trade Flows from 2000 to 2010*, PBL Netherlands Environmental Assessment Agency, The Hague, www.pbl.nl/sites/default/files/cms/publicaties/PBL_2013_European%20Regional%20Trade%20Flows%20from%202000-2010_1036.pdf.

Thissen, M., Diodato, D. and Van Oort, F.G., 2013b, *Integrated Regional Europe: European Regional Trade Flows in 2000*, PBL Netherlands Environmental Assessment Agency, The Hague, www.pbl.nl/sites/default/files/cms/publicaties/PBL_2013_European%20Regional%20Trade%20Flows%20in%202000_1035.pdf.

Thissen, M., van Oort, F.G., Diodato, D. and Ruijs, A., 2013c, *Regional Competitiveness and Smart Specialization in Europe: Place-Based Development in International Economic Networks*, Edward Elgar, Cheltenham.

Times Higher Education, 2014, "Capital Gains: London Universities Have Advantages Not Found Elsewhere in the UK But Also Face Unique Challenges", 29 May.

Timmer, M.P., Erumban, A.A., Los, B., Stehrer, R. and de Vries, G.J., 2012, "New Measures of European Competitiveness: A Global Value Chain Perspective", WIOD Working Paper, www.wiod.org/index.htm.

Timmer, M.P., Los, B., Stehrer, R. and de Vries, G.J., 2013, "Fragmentation, Incomes and Jobs: An Analysis of European Competitiveness", *Economic Policy*, 613–661.

UKTI, 2012, *Great Britain and Northern Ireland: Inward Investment Report 2011/12 UK Trade and Investment*, London.

UNCTAD, 2012, *World Investment Report 2012: Towards a New Generation of Investment Policies*, United Nations Conference on Trade and Development, New York.

Venables, A.J., 2006, "Shifts in Economic Geography and their Causes", *Federal Reserve Bank of Kansas City Economic Review*, 91.4, 61–85.

Wren, C., and Jones, J., 2012, "FDI Location Across British Regions and Agglomerative Forces: A Markov Analysis", *Spatial Economic Analysis*, 7.2, 265–286.

5 The UK interregional economic system

Structures, linkages and spillovers

5.1 Introduction

As we saw in Chapter 1, the geographical core-periphery structure of the UK's economic performance is extremely marked by OECD and EU standards, and also almost entirely out of step with the UK's governance system. The subsequent three chapters have then outlined the key regional, urban and globalisation-related characteristics of the UK economy, all of which confirm these broad core-periphery relationships. It is clear that the economy of London and its hinterland regions have prospered from the experience of modern globalisation in ways which have no parallels in the rest of the UK, and this has further cemented and exacerbated the pre-existing core-periphery structure of the UK economy to levels which are unparalleled since the nineteenth century. Yet, these observations still leave unanswered the questions as to why these core-periphery relationships are so marked in the case of the UK. There is no automatic or inevitable relationship between increasing globalisation and interregional inequality (Brülhart 2011). Whether increasing international openness and engagement results in intra-national and interregional convergence or divergence depends on the specific features of the country. These features refer variously to the internal economic geography of the country, as well as the country's specific industries, its labour markets, its financial and monetary systems, and its governance and institutional system. In this chapter we examine the role played by each of the issues, except for the question of the governance and institutional system, issues which will be addressed in Chapters 6 and 7.

In order to better understand the role played by various economic mechanisms and linkages across space in mediating interregional adjustments Overman *et al.* (2010) describe a two-region 'North–South' framework as a parsimonious construct of the UK interregional economic system. This framework helps us to consider how the interregional allocation of workers is related to, and also adjusts in response to changes in, productivity, wages and housing costs. A more detailed discussion of many of the specific features evident in these types of interactions is provided by Combes *et al.* (2005a), although for our purposes here the parsimonious schema of Overman *et al.* (2010) is perfectly illustrative.

Assuming that workers migrate interregionally in response to real wage variation between regions, various outcomes in terms of interregional wage and productivity inequalities are possible depending on the local returns to scale and the local housing cost functions. In the schema they set out the national population is assumed to be fixed and the analysis therefore focuses on the shares of the national population in each region both prior to and following a positive exogenous productivity shock in the 'South'. Any changes in the interregional shares are effected by internal interregional migration. Yet, it is also possible that the endowment shares of specific factors can give rise to different partly-endogenous responses to exogenous shocks. The existing skills sets or industrial structures may bring about different regional responses to external shocks, and this implies that the causality may partly run from the factor shares to the productivity shocks as well as the other way around.

Moreover, if we re-label housing costs as land costs and insert profits for wages, a similar set of potential interregional outcomes can be generated in the Overman *et al.* (2010) framework if we focus only on the shares of national investment capital entering each region. In this case all interregional adjustments can be effected by interregional capital flows, with no labour migration required. Indeed, the observation that interregional adjustments can be mediated either just by labour reallocations, or just by capital reallocations, or by combinations of both forms of factor reallocation, has been understood for more than half a century (Borts and Stein 1964; McCann 2013). Yet, considering the realities of the UK over the last three decades there is no particular reason why the national population needs to be assumed to be fixed. Indeed the Overman *et al.* (2010) framework can easily be adjusted instead to the case of an immigration-induced rapidly growing population by aiming the analysis purely on the interregional shares of immigrant workers, leaving the national native population levels fixed. Under these conditions exactly the same sets of potential outcomes described by Overman *et al.* (2010) can also be generated with zero internal migration on the part of native population and all interregional labour adjustments taking place via the distribution of immigrants. Moreover, a similar set of outcomes can even be generated if we focus solely on the shares of foreign investment capital entering into UK regions in the case of either a stable or a growing immigrant population.

Of course inflows of external labour or capital may be associated with additional complications not addressed in the Overman *et al.* (2010) framework. For example, it is possible that inflows of immigrants or foreign capital into a region will raise local land prices and therefore to some extent may crowd out native residents or domestic investments. These competition and substitution effects associated with inflows of immigrants into a region may encourage the out-migration of existing residents from the region (Rowthorn 2008, 2009), thereby rendering the labour market displacement effects relatively benign (Hatton and Taini 2005). In the UK there is some evidence for such immigration-induced outflows from southern regions, and this implies that purely observing the effects of local immigration on local wages and unemployment understate the real effects on the overall economy (Hatton and Taini 2005). In fact, any exogenous population shock, including a higher local birth rate, generates similar results to the effects of migration (Rowthorn 2008, 2009), unless immigration is also associated with qualitative differences in skills and human capital. Similar types of impacts can be envisaged for firms as well as households. The local costs increases associated with large inflows of foreign investment capital in real estate and land markets, or in industrial and commercial investments, in particular may bring about adverse displacement effects or greater failure for existing local businesses, many of which will be unable to relocate to other regions given their local business relationships. In either the labour market or the capital market cases, the regional displacement of native labour and domestic capital will always be locally evident unless there are productive complementarity effects between the external factor inflows and the domestic factors which more than compensate for the induced local cost increases.

Yet, even allowing for these additional complications, for our purposes there are two key insights here. First, in each of these alternative scenarios sketched out here on the basis of the Overman *et al.* (2010) framework, no internal migration on the part of the native population is required in order to generate interregional adjustments. In other words interregional factor allocation adjustments can take place without any labour-related economic linkages actually operating across space. Second, the nature and role of economic linkages across space is also partly endogenous to the allocated factor shares. If the relationship between wages, productivity and factor shares is depicted by a strongly upward-sloping slope[1] this implies that the interregional linkages of knowledge, trade and technology are very weak whereas the local intra-regional linkages of knowledge, trade and technology are very strong. Conversely, if knowledge, technology and trade flow easily between regions then this upward-sloping relationship will tend to be very flat. In general, the steeper is this relationship the more responsive will be the factor reallocations to exogenous shocks to these relationships, although there is no reason why internal migration amongst natives ought to be the major adjustment mechanism. This depends on which of the potential interregional factor reallocation mechanisms – via native-born workers, via domestic investment capital, via foreign-born workers, via foreign investment capital – exhibits the least interregional adjustment frictions. Cultural and attachment-value arguments would suggest that native-born worker flows may exhibit greater interregional adjustment frictions than the other mechanisms (Evans 1985; McCann 2013). Yet, this also implies that interregional adjustments can take place even where there is a lack of economic linkages operating across space and where factor reallocations do not involve domestic factors.

Many other EU and OECD advanced economies do not experience interregional inequalities which are as large or as persistent as those which are evident in the UK. Therefore, understanding the underlying causes of the interregional inequalities is critical (Rice and Venables 2003). Inequalities may not necessarily be the result of market failures. Indeed, there are cases of equilibrium disparities where utilities are equalised across space and where there are no welfare gains associated with removing the inequalities (Rice and Venables 2003). On the other hand, there are cases where even when markets are working and utilities are equalised across space, aggregate welfare will be increased by removing the underlying causes of the interregional disparities (Rice and Venables 2003). It depends on the causes of the interregional inequalities and the mix of exogenous and endogenous mechanisms and linkages which bring about these inequalities. In terms of linkage mechanisms, various different arguments have been put forward for the underlying causes of UK inequalities, including: interregional differences in human capital distributions and spatial sorting; the nature and scale of interregional trade linkages; the nature and scale of interregional financial and fiscal linkages; and the nature and scale of interregional knowledge linkages in the light of prevailing industrial and structural changes. There are also arguments which suggest that UK interregional differences may be related to land use constraints either via the effects of land supply restrictions in limiting of the interregional flows of human capital to non-core regions (Duranton and Monastiriotis 2002) or via the inhibiting of potential agglomeration effects in non-core regions. Whatever are the underlying reasons, it is clear from all of the foregoing that combinations of exogenous effects, endogenous effects, interregional linkages across space and land use constraints within locations are all likely to play a part in mediating interregional adjustments and in determining UK inequalities. However, in order to assess the likely contribution of each of these individual linkages or constraints to the shaping of UK interregional disparities it is necessary in the following sections to consider all of the available evidence pertaining to each of these potential explanations for UK interregional inequalities.

5.2   Human capital, labour mobility and 'sorting' arguments

One of the key arguments regarding the widening regional disparities has been the role played by human capital, and also the interactions between human capital and interregional migration, in which migration from low to higher demand regions is also potentially accompanied by human capital gains to the destination regions. However, in order to assess the importance of the mechanisms we begin by examining the human capital indicators at the regional level and also the changes in these, and we then move on to discussing interregional mobility.

In terms of human capital, the share of the UK population whose highest level of education is only below the upper secondary-level education is one percentage point below the OECD average and exactly equals the EU average (OECD 2012b). Meanwhile, the share of the UK population whose highest level of educational attainment is the upper secondary-level education falls short of the OECD and EU averages by 7 percentage points and

11 percentage points, respectively (OECD 2012b). In contrast, at the tertiary level of education the UK out-performs the OECD and EU averages by 7 and 10 percentage points, respectively (OECD 2012b). The result of these patterns is that when we consider the whole population aged 25–64 the UK share of the population which has at least upper secondary education is exactly the same as the EU average and one percentage point above the OECD average (OECD 2012b). These patterns largely reflect the changes in educational opportunities and access. The younger age groups 25–34 exhibit upper secondary and tertiary education rates which are some 18 and 16 percentage points higher than the older age groups 55–64, respectively (OECD 2012b), and these figures imply, respectively, that some 27 per cent and 53 per cent more of the younger age cohorts achieve upper secondary and tertiary education levels than the older age groups (OECD 2012b). These figures reflect both a significant widening and upgrading of the UK educational offerings and opportunities over the last six decades, along with changes in the relationships between different educational and skills-training and the alternative pathways into employment. For at least upper secondary education levels, the UK education scores relative to the OECD and EU averages very closely correspond to the UK's productivity ranking relative to both the OECD and EU. However, these cannot be treated simply as accounting for the UK's current productivity position given that the variation in these shares across richer EU economies is very small and many richer countries than the UK such as The Netherlands, Belgium, Austria, Germany, Denmark and Sweden, all have much lower tertiary attainment levels than the UK (OECD 2012c). The relationships between national education performance and national productivity performance are clearly very complex.

These changes in UK educational provision and opportunities are a result both of policy changes and also industrial restructuring, but there are still significant differences in terms of individual educational attainment. UK educational scorings and the perceived inequality of educational opportunities and attainments are frequently discussed topics in the national media and political arenas. Such differences are in part related to family behaviour and aspirations (Sutton Trust 2014) and access to social and financial networks (Jerrim 2014) as well as differences in the subjects studied and institutions attended (De Vries 2014), and this of course is also true in other countries (*The Economist* 2015a). Yet, even after controlling for the subject studied and the performance of the students, there still appear to be deep social reasons for UK differences in individual educational opportunities[2] and outcomes including income-related limits on downward social mobility (McKnight 2015). However, as part of these discussions recent years have also seen increasingly frequent references in the popular and national media regarding differences in educational performance across the UK regions but also increasing differences in higher level educational opportunities and outcomes across regions (*The Times* 2015). As such, another potentially fruitful line of enquiry into the reasons why UK interregional inequalities are so high and also increasing concerns human capital explanations. In particular, if there are significant UK interregional differences in the local human capital stock, or if migration behaviour alters these stocks to a sufficiently great extent, then an examination of the interaction between the levels of human capital and labour mobility processes may provide some clues as to the nature and scale of UK interregional inequalities.

If we consider regional stocks of human capital, observations from the 1980s reveal only very limited differences between regions in terms of their levels of educational participation, skills training and educational attainment. In 1981/1982 participation in education for 16 year olds was typically 57–58 per cent with most UK regions varying only by one or two percentage points from these figures, except for the North, Yorkshire and Humberside, East Midlands and East Anglia, all of which displayed figures some 3–5 percentage points below the national average (CSO 1990, 1992). By the late 1980s and the start of the 1990s the gap between these regions and the national average had been almost entirely closed with educational participation rates for 16 year olds in many of these regions now surpassing the national averages (CSO 1990, 1992). Presumably this was in part related to declining employment opportunities associated with the dramatic industrial restructuring evident at the time in some of these regions, as well as to changes in educational provision. By far the highest educational participation rates were in Scotland (CSO 1990, 1992). In terms of students leaving school the variation in examination performance across UK regions is also very limited. Assessing regions in terms of the proportion of school leavers with certain numbers of A-levels/Scottish Highers or GCSEs, again the variation across regions is typically just one to two percentage points and there is no particular north–south pattern to these variations, other than the fact that the scores for both Scotland and Northern Ireland are systematically higher than for all other regions (CSO 1990, 1992). In terms of the destinations of students, the proportions entering higher and further education during the 1980s rose from just over 28 per cent to some 37 per cent by the end of the decade (CSO 1990). In other words, at this point higher and further education was still much more of a niche arena than today with approximately only 9 per cent of school-leavers England and Wales entering degree courses in 1988 (CSO 1990) rising to 12 per cent by 1990 (CSO 1992). However, interregionally the shares entering higher and further education barely vary again by just one or two percentage points, with the exception of the North and Yorkshire and Humberside, where the shares remained at 4–6 percentage points below the national average throughout the 1980s (CSO 1990, 1992). In terms of educational expenditure and investment again there are only small variations across UK regions during the 1980s, with the only observable difference being that the share of local authority expenditure in the South East on higher and further education is just over one percentage point higher than the national average while the share of secondary education was just over one percentage point below the national average (CSO 1990). Total local government plus central government expenditure per capita on education rose by some 5 per cent between 1981/1982 and 1987/1988 across England and Wales but interregionally the levels hardly varied at all across UK regions during the 1980s, except for the fact that it was some 22 per cent higher in Scotland and 28 per cent higher in Northern Ireland and some 10 per cent lower in East Anglia and the South West (CSO 1990).

By the mid-1990s some interregional differences in educational attainment start to become more apparent. Although there were no differences in terms of exam scores, except for the fact that Wales slightly lagged the rest of the country, by 1994/1995 the relative numbers of students achieving two or more A-levels or Scottish Higher equivalents was some 7–9 percentage points higher in the South East, East and South West than in other parts of the UK, including London (ONS 1997). These differences were maintained through until after the turn of the millennium (ONS 2001). From the mid-1990s through to the millennium, at the GCSE level, the share of students achieving five or more GCSEs at grades A* to C was again some 7–9 percentage points higher in the South East, East and South West than in other UK regions, including London (ONS 1997, 2001). On the other hand, between 1994/1995 and 2000/2001 in terms of further education in 1994/1995 there were few if any systematic differences in terms of regional participation rates, and the same was also true for those on foundation courses or in job-related training or on government-supported training schemes (ONS 1997, 2001). Meanwhile, an area of emerging difference between regions concerns the local labour force in employment. In 1996 the share of people in employment qualified to at least NVQ level 3 or equivalent was some 6–9 percentage points higher in London and Scotland than the rest of the UK while for those qualified to NVQ level 4 or equivalent the difference between London and the rest of the UK was some 10 percentage points, while for Scotland it was 3–4 percentage points (ONS 1997). For A-level or equivalent qualifications or for GCSEs or equivalent qualifications, by 2001 the differences between all UK regions had become very small indeed, except again for the cases of Scotland and London (ONS 2001). In Scotland there was still a relatively higher share of the workforce qualified to A-level/Scottish Higher equivalent levels than in other UK regions, although this gap had fallen to typically some 4–7 percentage points (ONS 1997). The convergence across regions in educational attainment during the 1980s and early 1990s was observed by Duranton and Monastiriotis (2002).

In 1996 the share of males employed in the Northern Ireland workforce with NVQ level 4 or equivalent was the lowest in the UK while that for women was only one percentage point below that of Scotland and above the rest of England and Wales (ONS 1997). By 2001 the skills profile of the Northern Ireland workforce was similar to many other UK regions, except for the fact that the region still exhibited a large share of workers with no formal qualifications. Again, Wales also lagged other UK regions in terms of exhibiting a relatively larger share of workers with either no formal qualifications or only with lower level qualifications (ONS 2001).

In the years immediately preceding the 2008 global financial crisis when the UK economy was growing strongly, many aspects of the basic situation which pertained at the turn of the millennium largely continued to hold, except for a few noticeable changes. Most notably, in terms of both A-level scores and GCSE scorings, the gaps between regional attainments levels had fallen, to typically less than 4–5 percentage points across the whole country (ONS 2008). Similar scale interregional narrowing trends are also reflected in terms of the share of 19 year olds with National Qualifications Framework (NQF) Level 2 and Level 3 skills, whereas Levels 4 and 5 skills which correspond to higher education skills, show some trends towards interregional divergence in favour of London and the South East (BIS 2012a). A marked narrowing of interregional gaps is also evident in terms of participation in training schemes, job-related training programmes, and also the attainment of various primary and secondary learning milestones (ONS 2001). Meanwhile, there was no difference at all in high school attainment scores between rural areas and urban areas (DEFRA 2015). Across the whole UK workforce aged between 19 and 64 the share of people with each particular NQF level of skills, ranging from NQF Level 2 to NQF Level 5, has increased (BIS 2012a) and the share of people with no skills has consistently fallen over time (BIS 2012a).

Duranton and Monastiriotis (2002) find that between the early 1980s and the mid-1990s differences in educational outcomes and rewards to education played a major role in the worsening UK interregional inequalities, and this role took place in various subtle ways. First, London gained because its workforce became more educated over the period while second the returns to education increased at a national scale, thereby favouring regions with higher educational levels (Duranton and Monastiriotis 2002). Although the returns to education had initially been lower in London,[3] London partially caught up with the rest of the UK because there was also a rapid convergence across regions in terms of the determinant of individual wages (Duranton and Monastiriotis 2002). Social class effects on educational attainment favouring the south are substantially offset by crowding-out effects on teacher supply in economically successful areas (Gordon and Monastiriotis 2007), thereby attenuating differences in interregional educational attainment.

At this stage, however, the extent to which we can attribute any of the observed UK interregional inequalities to the geography of UK schooling performance is still not yet clear. This is because the observed mobility of UK university graduates must also be considered in the light of differences in educational attainment and the consequences for spatial 'sorting'. There are two reasons for this. First, higher education skills are increasingly understood as being critical for economic development in today's economy and it is differences in the distribution of graduates that is widely believed to differentiate regions rather than simply the number of people who have completed high school, which is almost universal in today's economy. Second, young people between the ages of 18 and 34 dominate interregional migration flows

(Fielding 2012), and these include students entering higher education and those leaving higher education and entering employment. We have already seen that the interregional variations in educational attainment are very small, but the interregional mobility of university graduates has the potential to markedly alter the human capital composition of regions if interregional flows are large and if there are also significant differences in the educational qualities of those moving to different regions. To assess both the quantitative and qualitative aspects of interregional graduate flows it is also necessary to consider these flows within the context of the overall system of interregional and international labour mobility displayed by the UK, a system which itself has changed dramatically over the last three or four decades.

Given the greatly increased importance of university education in the UK economy, especially since the 1990s expansion of higher education, the role of graduate human capital would be expected to be particularly important in shaping the fortunes of different regions. At an estimated 14–15 per cent, the social rates of return on UK higher education are high by OECD standards due to the short duration of courses and high completion rates and regions such as London are argued to benefit significantly from such educational investments.[4] Between 2000 and 2007 the proportion of the overall UK workforce with university degrees had risen from 15.2 per cent to 19.6 per cent and during this period the share of university graduates in UK regional workforces had also increased by 4–5 percentage points in all of the UK regions (ONS 2008). Meanwhile, by the millennium the typical gap between Scotland and other UK regions in terms of the share of its workforce with university degrees or equivalent qualifications had not only fallen to less than 1.5 percentage points, but by now all of the southern and eastern regions of England had overtaken Scotland in terms of the proportion of their employed workforce with degree or degree-equivalent qualifications (ONS 2001). In marked contrast, in the case of London by 2001 the typical gap between the share of the local workforce with university degrees or degree-equivalent qualifications over other UK regions had increased slightly to between 10 and 13 percentage points, such that the graduate share of the London workforce was by now 40–60 per cent higher than what was typically observed in the other southern and eastern regions of England and between 80 and 100 per cent of what was typical in the rest of the other UK regions (ONS 2001). The proportion of the London workforce with university degrees or equivalent qualifications had by now risen to more than 30 per cent and between the millennium and the 2008 crisis the London economy continued to display a 1–13 percentage point gap between the share of its own workforce share with university degrees or degree-equivalent qualifications and the share which was typically evident in other UK regions (ONS 2008). Indeed, by 2007, on the eve of the 2008 global financial crisis, the graduate share of the London workforce had continued to be approximately 40–60 per cent higher than what was typical in other southern and eastern regions of England, and some 80–100 per cent higher than what was typically evident in the rest of the UK regions (ONS 2001).

In other words, the much greater relative share of university graduates in the London workforce which had become evident by the turn of the millennium had remained in place up to the eve of the crisis, even though the graduate share of all regional workforces had been increasing during this period. The situation today remains largely as it was prior to the crisis.[5] Some 60 per cent of the non-student working age population over the age of 21 living in Inner London are graduates and 45 per cent of those living in Outer London.[6] The figures for Scotland and the South East are 41 per cent and 40 per cent, followed by South West and East on 37 per cent and 36 per cent, respectively. The figures for Wales and the North West are 33 per cent, with 32 per cent in Yorkshire and Humberside, 31 per cent in East Midlands, followed by West Midlands and North East on 30 per cent and 29 per cent, respectively.[7] In other words, every UK region has a higher share of its workforce with tertiary education than either Germany, Austria or France and more or less equivalent to The Netherlands, all of which are richer countries than the UK.[8]

Over the last three decades, the greater and also more differentiated presence of university graduates in the local workforce has emerged as being one of the key features of the evolution of the UK regional labour market system. Yet, these differences are not simply a result of the geographical structure of the UK higher education system, but also different propensities to move both for education and for employment. In the mid-1990s typically between 61 per cent and 68 per cent of university students domiciled in the regions of North East, North West, Yorkshire and Humberside, London and Wales, attended university studies in their home domicile region (ONS 1997). In the cases of the East Midlands, West Midlands, the East, the South East and the South West, typically between 43 per cent and 56 per cent of students studied in their home region, while in Northern Ireland and Scotland the figures were 73 per cent and almost 95 per cent, respectively (ONS 1997). Scotland has such a different educational and university system to the rest of the UK that the Scottish case is unsurprising (Faggian *et al.* 2007a). Yet, by 2001 it is possible to detect a slight increase in the tendency of students to study in their home regions with the figures for the North East, Yorkshire and Humberside, London and Wales, typically now being between 66 per cent and 72 per cent of students studying in their domicile regions (ONS 2001). In the cases of the North West, the East Midlands, West Midlands, the East, the South East and the South West, typically between 43 per cent and 58 per cent of students studied in their home region, while again in Northern Ireland and Scotland the figures were much higher at almost 78 per cent and 95 per cent, respectively (ONS 2001).

The shift towards more home-based learning in the majority of regions may reflect the withdrawal of university grants and the introduction of student loans and increasing tuition fees in the years either side of the turn of the millennium. This shift becomes even clearer by 2005/2006 with between 68 per cent and 77 per cent of students in the North East, North West, Yorkshire and Humberside, London and Wales all studying in their home regions (ONS

2008), while for East Midland, West Midlands, the East and the South West the proportion of locally domiciled students studying locally ranged between 41 per cent and 61 per cent. Again, the respective figures for Northern Ireland and Scotland in 2005/2006 are higher at 78.8 per cent and 94.1 per cent (ONS 2008). Overall, what we observe is that between 1995/1996 and 2005/2006 in eight UK regions – namely the North East, North West, Yorkshire and Humberside, East Midlands, West Midlands, South West, Wales and Northern Ireland – the proportion of university students educated locally increased by more than 5 percentage points and in two cases, the North East and North West, the increase was more than 10 percentage points (ONS 1997, 2008). The four regions in which this share remained constant over the decade were Scotland, London, the South East and the East (ONS 1997, 2008).

In other words, in terms of education provision some regions appear to have benefited particularly well from the major restructuring within the UK higher education system which was taking place during these years. In 1995/1996 the national share of university students being educated in each region varied by less than 1.5 percentage points from the share of national population in each region, except for the cases of the South West, where some 1.7 percentage points fewer students were educated at home than the region's national population share, and the cases of London and Scotland, where the positive differences between the national share of students who were locally educated and the local regional population share were 3.3 percentage points and 3.1 percentage points, respectively (ONS 1997). By 2005/2006, however, there had been something of a shift in these patterns. The number of regions which were educating a share of the national student cohort, which differed by more than 1.5 percentage points from the population share of the region, had increased. Now the regions which were educating a markedly smaller share of the national student cohort than might be expected on the basis of their population shares were the East and the South East, while the regions of London and Scotland all educated shares of the national student cohort which were more than 3 percentage points above their respective population shares (ONS 2001). Overall, however, rural areas exhibited slightly higher rates of participation in higher education than urban areas (DEFRA 2015).

When we consider the employment destinations of UK university graduates according to the type of jobs, employment, training or educational roles they enter into, there are remarkably few differences across UK regions according to the types of occupations and employment roles accessed (ONS 2001, 2008), except for the fact that graduates from the East display a higher tendency to pursue postgraduate qualifications while West Midlands graduates display a greater propensity to combine employment and further study (ONS 2008). However, apart from these minor differences, it is clear that the distribution of graduate employment and educational roles is largely consistent across all UK regions (ONS 2001, 2008). In other words, there are no major structural or sectoral differences across regions in terms of the opportunities taken up by locally educated graduates. Rather, any differences appear to relate to where these opportunities are taken up.

In terms of the geography of employment of UK graduates the increasing localisation tendency which is evident in terms of accessing higher education is also evident in terms of employment locations. In 1994/1995 and 1995/1996 the shares of graduates and also postgraduates entering employment in their home domicile regions was very low for all English regions, and typically between 15 per cent and 37 per cent, whereas for the devolved regions it was typically between 50 per cent for Wales through to over 70 per cent for both Northern Ireland and Scotland.[9] In general, at this stage there were still relatively very few university graduates and postgraduates in the UK labour market and this cohort displayed high levels of interregional mobility. By 2000/2001 there was a marked shift towards more local employment with typically between 50 per cent and 67 per cent of English- and Welsh-domiciled graduates and postgraduates entering employment in their home domicile region, while in Northern Ireland and Scotland the equivalent figures were between 74 per cent and 85 per cent.[10]

This localisation tendency has increased further over recent years. The UK Higher Education Statistics Agency (HESA)[11] shows that in 2005/2006 some 90 per cent, 81 per cent and 79 per cent, respectively, of Scotland-domiciled, Northern Ireland-domiciled and London-domiciled graduates entered employment in their own region. These were the highest shares of locally domiciled graduates entering employment in their local region. The equivalent shares in all other UK regions were between 64 per cent and 76 per cent, except for the East Midlands, South East and East where the shares were 60 per cent, 59 per cent and 52 per cent, respectively. For postgraduate qualifications the respective shares entering employment in the domicile region are higher and typically between 69 per cent and 79 per cent, except for the South East and East in which the shares were 64 per cent and 60 per cent, respectively, and Scotland, London and Northern Ireland for which the shares were 90 per cent, 82 per cent and 81 per cent, respectively. Some 20 per cent of graduates domiciled in the South East move to London for employment, demonstrating the role of the region as a dormitory region for the London labour market. These patterns have remained largely stable in the aftermath of the 2008 global economic crisis. In 2012/2013 the highest local employment rates for locally domiciled graduates were again in Scotland (89 per cent), Northern Ireland (79 per cent) and London (81 per cent). The figures for most other regions varied between 64 per cent and 77 per cent, except for the South East (60 per cent), the East (56 per cent) and 61 per cent for the East Midlands (HECSU 2015).

If we consider the employment location relative to the region of higher education rather than the region of domicile, we observe much more mobility amongst graduates than when the domicile region is the reference point. In 2005/2006 some 95 per cent and 86 per cent of the Northern Ireland-educated and Scotland-educated graduates entered employment in the same region as their university. The share in London was 69 per cent and in the North West was 66 per cent. The equivalent shares in all other UK regions were between 50 per cent and 59 per cent, except for the East Midlands in which the share was 38 per cent. For postgraduate qualifications again the respective shares are generally higher and typically between 61 per cent and 71 per cent, except for the East Midlands and East in which the shares were 47 per cent and 55 per cent, respectively, and Scotland and Northern Ireland for which the shares were 90 per cent and 91 per cent, respectively. Some 20 per cent of graduates and 33 per cent of postgraduates educated in the East move to London for employment, demonstrating the role of the East region in supplying London-employed graduates. Again, these figures have remained largely stable in the aftermath of the 2008 global financial crisis with 2012/2013 local retention rates for graduates who were locally educated being the highest in Northern Ireland (92 per cent), Scotland (83 per cent), London (70 per cent) and the North West (66 per cent). The proportions evident in most other regions are typically between 48 per cent and 59 per cent, except for the South East (43 per cent) and the 39 per cent in the East Midlands (HECSU 2015).

If we now consider the subsequent employment-migration behaviour of graduates three years after graduating, the longitudinal surveys of the UK Higher Education Statistics Agency (HESA) show that typically between 80 per cent and 90 per cent of graduates initially employed in London and in the northern English regions and also in the three devolved regions after graduation remained in employment in the same region over three years later. The respective shares are markedly lower, and typically between 70 per cent and 78 per cent, in the regions of the midlands and the south of England outside of London.

The overall localisation pattern is also evident in the northern English regions plus the three devolved regions tend to generate university graduates and also local graduate employment opportunities which are largely in line with the national population shares. On the other hand, it is the regions in the midlands, east and south of England which tend to attract relatively fewer undergraduates or to subsequently retain graduates in local employment, to the same levels as other UK regions. This suggests that these regions have rather more fluid labour markets acting as springboards or conduits to subsequent employment elsewhere, and primarily in London.[12] The total share of UK graduates in employment in London was 19 per cent of the national graduate cohort, and some 22 per cent of the national postgraduate cohort. In other words, in 2006 London accounted for 42 per cent more graduates and 65 per cent more postgraduates in local employment than its national population share would predict. In total London now accounts for 19.4 per cent of the total national employed graduate plus postgraduate cohort, and therefore some 46.5 per cent more university graduates in local employment than its national population share would predict. Yet, the majority of these graduate inflows into the London economy come from London's own hinterland regions. The total number of graduates domiciled in the South East,

East and South West entering employment in London is twice that of the rest of the UK regions combined. Indeed, the South East alone accounts for more London-employed graduates than the regions of the north and midlands of England plus the three devolved regions combined.[13] These mobility patterns are largely unchanged since the 2008 global economic crisis (HECSU 2015).

Overall, what we observe from the rapid expansion of UK higher education from the early 1990s onwards is that the overall interregional mobility of the UK labour market is likely to have increased because the total number of young people moving into higher education has increased by more than three-fold since then, and many of these students also move away to study. However, at the same time, the average mobility of university graduates and postgraduates has fallen sharply over the last two decades as more and more young people choose either to enter higher education or to enter employment or both, in the same region as their domicile location. A greater localisation tendency for both education and employment is clearly evident amongst university graduates across the whole of the UK. Between 1995 and 2005 the proportion of graduates entering employment in their home region has more than doubled in English regions, and also increased in the devolved regions, such that the overall mobility of the UK graduate labour force is likely to have increased by a factor of approximately 1.5 during the last two decades.[14] Yet, as regards London the increased mobility relates primarily to London's own hinterland regions rather than the UK as a whole. Indeed, typically only between 3 per cent and 6 per cent of the locally domiciled graduates in the regions outside of the southern and eastern part of England enter into employment in London, and even after three and half years in the workforce the additional share moving to London for subsequent employment is typically only between 1.3 per cent and 3.6 per cent. In contrast, for the southern and eastern regions of England the subsequent London mobility share for the South West is 4.7 per cent, for the South East is 12.9 per cent and for the East is 16.1 per cent.

The data from the HESA first-destinations and longitudinal surveys demonstrates that while the combined population of the southern regions of England including London accounts for 44.3 per cent of the UK population, these regions only account for 39.5 per cent of university graduates in their first employment. This figure rises to 47.3 per cent of employed graduates after their subsequent employment moves. The relatively low initial figure is a result of the fact that these regions account for a relatively low number of university places while the relatively higher second figure is a result of subsequent migration behaviour. One might expect that the differences in the regional distribution of higher education opportunities along with the interregional differences in the share of graduates within the regional workforces and their employment-mobility behaviour would provide much of the explanation of the currently observed UK interregional productivity differences. Yet, taken together, the interregional differences in graduate and postgraduate human capital are not large. The distribution of UK-educated graduate and postgraduate employment across the UK differs only slightly from the regional population shares. Moreover, the quality of education provision also differs relatively very little in the UK, due to the constant monitoring from the education funding councils and also the external examiner system. As such, the spatial distribution of UK-educated graduates and postgraduates does not appear to be sufficiently large to explain interregional productivity differences.

On the other hand, however, it may be that there are sufficiently significant differences in the quality of graduates working in different regions, as a result of human capital-migration interactions (Faggian and McCann 2006, 2009a, 2009b; Abreu *et al.* 2015) which give rise to the interregional spatial sorting of graduates on the basis of skills (D'Costa and Overman 2014; Gibbons *et al.* 2014b). In order to consider these issues it necessary to understand that if for example we take the case of London which is widely presumed to offer and generate a graduate quality premium, the university graduates employed in London comprise different groups according to their employment-migration behaviour. There are those who were already domiciled in London prior to entering university, those domiciled in other regions and who migrated to London for employment soon after graduation, and also those who originally entered employment in other UK regions and who then subsequently moved to London for later employment. Each of these groups displays quite different features. Similarly, those university graduates who work in other UK regions also display quite different features according to their employment-migration behaviour. There are those who remained in their home region for employment after graduating, those who were domiciled outside of London and who took up jobs in other UK regions outside of London, those who were originally domiciled in London but who entered employment positions in other UK regions, and those who subsequently moved into other UK regions for employment after a few years of working. In order to cast further light on the extent to which London enjoys a graduate quality premium it is essential to consider each of these different types of graduate employment-mobility groups.

Tables 5.1a, 5.1b and 5.2 are constructed from data derived from the Higher Education Statistics Agency (HESA) First Destinations Survey (FDS) which connects the original domicile location of the university student to their first employment destination six months after graduation and also from the 2010 Longitudinal Destination of Leavers from Higher Education (LDLHE) survey undertaken in November 2010 for the 2006/2007 graduate cohort which also identifies their employment location 3.5 years after graduation. Table 5.2 also uses data from the UK University and Colleges Admissions Service (UCAS) which coordinates all university applications from secondary school students and the data here are linked to individuals contained in the FDS and LDLHE surveys. The FDS contains between 128,000 and 140,000 observations each year, the linked LDLHE survey contains some 25,000 observations, and the linked UCAS data contain between 65,000 and 104,000 for the FDS and 18,000 for the LDLHE survey.

Table 5.1a Percentage of graduates moving more than 15 Miles from domicile to employment (six months after graduation)[a]

	2002/2003	*2003/2004*	*2004/2005*	*2005/2006*	*2006/2007*
Class 1 or 2:1 Degree	55.95	55.97	56.12	56.69	57.45
Class 2:2 or 3 Degree	47.07	46.90	46.96	47.28	47.26
All Graduates	52.46	52.42	52.59	53.15	53.75

[a] The calculations for this table were kindly undertaken by Dr Maria Abreu from Pembroke College, Cambridge and the Department of Land Economy at the University of Cambridge.

Table 5.1b Percentage of graduates moving between counties or unitary authorities from domicile to employment (six months after graduation)

	2002/2003	*2003/2004*	*2004/2005*	*2005/2006*	*2006/2007*	*2010/2011*
Class 1 or 2:1 Degree	52.54	52.07	52.30	52.40	52.73	54.21
Class 2:2 or 3 Degree	43.92	43.95	43.93	43.56	43.60	48.92
All Graduates	49.15	48.89	49.06	49.06	49.40	52.41

Note: These data include only undergraduate honours degrees and exclude Northern Ireland.

We are able to use the HESA data to consider whether geographical mobility and spatial sporting has increased over recent years by considering how the actual geographical distance of the migration movements of graduates is related to educational attainment. In order to do this Table 5.1a provides details of the percentage of graduates of different degree classes who move more than 15 miles from domicile to employment, and Table 5.1b details the percentage of graduates of different degree classes who move between counties or unitary authorities. As we see the figures are very similar between the two different area and distance definitions.

As expected, higher human capital graduates are more mobile. However, what we also see is that the levels of interregional graduate migration mobility have remained remarkably stable over time. While the average distance of migration-employment movements has generally increased over time, these increases are almost imperceptibly small. For each of the different skills cohorts and mobility definitions the changes in graduate mobility typically amount to no more than 2–3 percentage points over the whole decade. These observations suggest that there has been no surge in the interregional spatial sorting of graduate human capital even remotely sufficient to explain the UK's burgeoning interregional inequalities. This conclusion can also be further bolstered by a decomposition of these graduate mobility flows by region, as is done in Table 5.2.

Table 5.2 Graduate quality, interregional employment movers and non-movers[a]

	1 2002/2003 FDS	2 2003/2004 FDS	3 2004/2005 FDS	4 2005/2006 FDS	5 2006/2007 FDS	6 2010* LDLHE Relative to Original Domicile Location	7 2010* LDLHE Relative to First Employment Location
Non-London Domiciled	**69.15**	**68.44**	**70.05**	**70.88**	**71.9**	**73.69**	**63.19**
Moved to London for Employment	8.4	8.6	8.6	9.0	9.8	6.8	14.1
	1.04	1.06	1.13	1.14	1.14	1.06	1.13
Non-London Domiciled	**57.06**	**57.33**	**57.95**	**58.16**	**62.4**	**63.25**	**58.75**
Moved to Other UK Regions for Employment	18.0	17.6	17.2	16.7	20.3	13.6	21.9
	1.16	1.16	1.08	1.07	1.08	1.03	1.06
London Domiciled	**53.80**	**54.67**	**54.77**	**53.81**	**52.71**	**54.64**	**63.29**
Remained in London for Employment	10.4	10.6	10.7	11.0	10.5	16.3	10.33
	0.88	0.86	0.93	0.92	0.90	1.03	0.91
London Domiciled	**51.93**	**49.64**	**50.71**	**50.12**	**54.66**	**58.56**	**60.26**
Moved Away from London for Employment	2.3	2.3	2.4	2.5	2.8	3.4	2.7
	0.99	1.02	0.99	0.97	0.98	1.04	0.99
Non-London Domiciled	**53.00**	**53.35**	**53.09**	**54.17**	**53.95**	**53.60**	**54.07**
Remained in Home Region for Employment	60.9	60.9	61.2	60.9	56.7	59.9	51.5
	0.97	0.97	0.96	0.97	0.95	0.97	0.94

* The figures for the 2010 longitudinal LDLHE survey and also the 2006/2007 graduate leavers FDS (First Destinations Survey) contain sampling weights to correct for the oversampling. The figures reported here are those adjusted for oversampling.

[a] The calculations for this table were kindly undertaken by Dr Sarah Jewell from the Department of Economics at the University of Reading.

Each cell of Table 5.2 reports three numbers. The top number is the share of graduates with class 1 and class 2:1 degrees for each type of interregional employment mobility displayed by UK-domiciled university graduates, calculated for the movements across and within the 12 UK large statistical regions. The second number is the relative size of each flow in comparison to all graduates entering into employment in that particular cohort. The third number is the average UCAS grade on entry to university, relative to the UK average. In columns 1–6 of Table 5.2 the geographical reference point is the domicile region of the student prior to entering higher education and the region of first employment, while in column 7 the geographical reference point is the region of employment six months after graduation. In order to assess the extent to which there is a quality premium associated with the graduates entering employment in London we explicitly calculate all London-related movements, while all other UK regions are grouped together.

As we see from the top number in columns 1–6 of Table 5.2, in terms of the relationship between the mobility of graduates and the quality of university of graduates in each type of movement or non-movement category, the overall picture again is one of remarkable stability over time. In columns 1–6 of Table 5.2 there has been almost no change during the decade since the millennium in terms of the quality of each of these flows. Although qualitative differences do exist there has been no surge or increase in qualitative differences between these different types of employment-migration flows. The flows of graduates into London do have the highest shares of class 1 and 2:1 degrees, followed by those from outside of London moving to other UK regions for work, some 10–12 percentage points below. The flows away from London as well as those who remain in their same domicile region for employment all exhibit more or less the same characteristics with lower shares again of graduates with class 1 and 2:1 degrees. Importantly, the London-domiciled cohort who remain in London after graduation for work are really no different to the non-movers in other UK regions or those who move away from London.[15] In other words, any graduate quality premium associated with gaining a first employment in the London economy is entirely due to inflows from outside of London. Moreover, these broad conclusions also hold when we consider the UCAS points scores.

The only slight differences to this broad picture concern the subsequent migration behaviour. The onward flows relative to the original domicile location reported in column 6 are entirely consistent with those reported in columns 1–5. However, when we use the first employment region as the reference point we see from column 7 that the graduate quality of subsequent onward movements to employment in London and also other UK regions is lower, suggesting that something of a first-mover advantage effect may be operating. The only exception is the case of those who were originally domiciled in London and had taken up jobs in other UK regions and who then subsequently moved back to London. These are a higher quality cohort than those Londoners who always remained in London for employment after graduation, and who in fact are no different whatsoever from those from other UK regions and who also remained in their home region for employment. While graduate inflows into London are of a higher quality than other graduate employment-migration flows, the differences are not sufficient to account for the UK interregional inequalities. Each year approximately half a million UK-domiciled Bachelor students graduate from UK universities accounting for more than three-quarters of all university students (UUK 2013). Employment-migration flows to London from other UK regions, which are the key quality premium enjoyed by the London economy, in reality only amount to less than 10 per cent of all interregional graduate migration flows and are less than half of the interregional migration flows of graduates into employment in other UK regions. To put these figures into perspective, given that total annual inflows of people into London from the rest of the UK are of the order of 200,000 per annum or rather less than 2 per cent of the Greater London population (GLA 2013; Dickey 2014), the annual inflows of fewer than 50,000 UK university graduates into London represent an inflow of rather less than 0.5 per cent of the population of London. In contrast, and as already explained, between two-thirds and three-quarters of all UK graduates enter into employment in their home region. While many aspects of the observed interregional flows of the native-born population do tend to conform to the theoretical predictions of human capital-migration models (Hughes and McCormick 1985; Faggian and McCann 2006, 2009a, 2009b, 2009c; Faggian *et al.* 2007a, 2007b; Abreu *et al.* 2015), these flows have been stable for decades and are also too small to account for either the exogenous productivity shocks in the 'South' or any interregional differences in skills. Even in the case of new university graduates, the very group which theory would suggest are the most mobile group and for whom interregional differences in wages and house prices are of little relevance (Overman *et al.* 2010), interregional mobility is both small and non-increasing. As such, on the basis of the relative scale of the graduate quality composition of each of the interregional employment-migration flows and also on the relative scale of these interregional employment-migration flows, it would appear that as the UK higher education sector expanded in the 1990s and early 2000s, the qualitative differences in the regional distribution of graduates is simply nowhere near large enough to account for the observed UK interregional inequalities that grew at that time.[16]

In reality, what we observe today is that the UK graduate labour market displays something of the fragmented pattern dependent on the domicile residence, as is evident in the overall UK regional and urban system discussed in Chapters 2 and 3. Broadly, what we see is one graduate labour market comprising London and its hinterland regions plus to some extent also the regions of the midlands of England, plus a second graduate labour market comprising the northern regions of England plus the three devolved regions and which displays a much more localised and fragmented structure. Duranton and Monastiriotis (2002) argued that higher existing formally educated human capital stocks gave London and the South East a relative advantage in the 1980s and early 1990s as the economy shifted towards activities which favoured such kinds of skills, and these advantages in turn gave rise to further endogenous adjustments of factor stocks, themes which are also frequently picked up by the literature on 'sorting' (Combes *et al.* 2005b; D'Costa and Overman 2014; Gibbons *et al.* 2014b). However, Rice and Venables (2003) suggest that while regional differences in skills endowments can lead to inter-regional differences in the composition of production, it still seems unlikely that skills differences alone can account for the UK's observed interregional inequalities. The reason is that if there are endogenous regional effects oper-ating mediated via market size, prices, transport costs and migration, then small exogenous productivity differences associated with skills differences, for example, may give rise to much larger differences in incomes, house prices and populations (Rice and Venables 2003). Indeed, the observed regional human capital stocks and their productivity returns are just as endogenous as the regional industrial composition (Duranton and Monastiriotis 2002).

As we have already seen, Duranton and Monastiriotis (2002) find that prior to the mid-1990s shifting educational returns favoured London and the South East over other UK regions. Yet, it is rather difficult to link some of their insights and conclusions to much of the more recent evidence presented here, for three reasons. First, because their index of education was simply in terms of the number of years of schooling and the cohorts which they were examin-ing, which spanned those born between 1917 and 1982, contained very large numbers of people who had left school well before the age of 16 to work in industry and only tiny numbers who had entered higher education. Since the late 1990s, however, the educational picture in the UK has been totally different. Second, the end of the cohorts that Duranton and Monastiriotis (2002) were examining were by 1997 all in full-time employment and this was before the UK's widespread higher educational reforms of the 1990s. It is also immediately before the cohort whose detailed UCAS and HESA results along with their migration behaviour was reported in Table 5.1. Indeed, the detailed quality of educational outcomes for these more recent cohorts display such little variation across regions, except for interregional migrants, that it calls into question the usefulness of educational scorings based solely on years of education, and particularly in today's context. Third, the migration variable they employed did not distinguish between local intra-regional moves and long-distance interregional moves, while both theoretical arguments and also the empirical evidence suggest that these are quite distinct mechanisms reflect-ing responses to different employment and amenity-related incentives (Biagi *et al.* 2011). Moreover, while as we have already seen there is indeed something of a small graduate quality premium in the London economy as sorting argu-ments would suggest, this is associated almost entirely with inflows from other regions and appears not to be associated in any way with existing London human capital. Furthermore, the scale of these marginally higher quality inflows, and also the changes in these inflows over three decades, appear to be too small to make any significance difference to regional productivity levels. Other interregional transmission or non-transmission mechanisms must also be operating beyond simply the spatial sorting of human capital.

Overall, when we consider all of the evidence regarding interregional differences in secondary school attainment, interregional differences in the numbers and quality of the university graduates, and also the interregional migration flows and greater overall localisation tendencies of UK university graduates, it is very difficult to argue that these pieces of evidence are sufficient for accounting for the growing interregional productivity differences between UK regions (Webber *et al.* 2009). Over the last 30 years, the regional differences in human capital and the changes in the types of migration behaviour that would give rise to spatial sorting are just so small that sorting explanations become difficult to justify. That is the case, at least, when we consider in detail the level of formal education qualifications acquired by UK domiciled secondary school and university students. Of course, it may be the case that these detailed formal education data are still wholly insufficient for capturing skills because other largely non-observable individual characteristics such as ambition (Gordon 2015a) are part of the requisite successful skill-set over and above formal educational qualifications. If this is indeed the case then data on formal qualifications alone may not accurately reflect the role of skills in processes of spatial sorting (Overman *et al.* 2010). Yet, why there should be such enormous differences in these unobservable characteristics across UK regions in order to make such sorting arguments tenable is theoretically unclear as well as being inconsistent with the available evidence (European Commission 2013). Rather, it is more realistic to argue that the detailed evidence on the formal secondary and tertiary education performance of UK secondary and tertiary educated human capital displays only tiny interregional variations, and these variations are far smaller than would be required in order for spatial sorting to be a major explanation for the UK's observed interregional inequalities.

As a whole, the UK appears to display broadly two separate labour markets for UK domiciled graduates and postgraduates which largely co-exist with each other and which display very few interactions between. This co-existence pattern is one which has already been observed regarding the apparent lack of interregional growth interactions between the London economy and the more geographically peripheral regions of the UK. From a development perspective these observations should lead to concerns regarding the long-term national and local impacts of the UK university system whose funding is increasingly oriented towards institutions in London and its hinterland regions (*The Times* 2015),[17] especially at a time when governments are increasingly keen for universities to help foster local growth.[18]

5.2.1   *UK Interregional Migration*

Observation of spatial features of the UK's university graduate cohorts is important for understanding both UK regional differences in human capital and also the UK's interregional labour market adjustment processes. As well as displaying high human capital and relatively low reservation wages, new university graduates are largely unaffected by regional house price variations and are also society's most geographically mobile grouping (Overman *et al.* 2010). However, while we find little evidence of large interregional variations in graduate human capital or mobility, the UK labour market is much broader than simply new graduates. As such, the interregional movements of UK university graduates also need to be understood in the light of the overall UK interregional migration patterns.

If we consider overall labour mobility arguments, then we see that today the UK is now one of the most mobile societies in the world. Interregional mobility at the OECD-TL3 level is higher in the UK than in almost any other country (OECD 2013a). Some 4 per cent of the UK population, or 2.5 million people, move between UK-TL3 areas annually,[19] a proportion which is more than double the OECD average for OECD-TL3 regions (OECD 2013a), more than triple the EU-wide average for the larger NUTS2 regions (ESPON 2013), and one which is also much higher than the equivalent OECD-TL3 figure for the USA (OECD 2013a).[20] Along with The Netherlands the UK today exhibits the highest share of population moving interregionally per annum at the level of OECD-TL3 regions. Meanwhile, at the level of OECD-TL2/EU-NUTS1 regions in 1995 some 1.196 million people moved interregionally while in 2007 some 1.364 million people moved interregionally.[21] As a share of the UK national population these 1995 and 2007 figures represent interregional annual migration rates of 2.06 per cent and 2.22 per cent, respectively.[22]

In order also to help put these interregional labour mobility figures into perspective, the total population change of the cities and towns in the southern and eastern regions of England 2003–2013 was 1.671 million of which 1.130 million was the expansion of London alone,[23] while the population increase in the towns and cities of the rest of the UK was 979,300.[24] Moreover, during the first decade following the turn of the millennium the UK population expanded by some 4.5 million of whom some 2.6 million were new in-migrants from overseas countries. Given that a large proportion of immigrants moved to London in particular as well as other more prosperous southern and eastern regions, this suggests that the scale of north–south internal flows was actually relatively very limited. Indeed, taking the Severn–Wash line as the demarcation between 'north' and 'south' there was only a very small population gain in the south due to migration from the north (Fielding 2012). Furthermore, during this same period there were something of the order of 25 million interregional movements of people between the UK OECD-TL3 regions and some 12 million interregional movements at the level of OECD-TL2/EU-NUTS1 regions. In other words, the vast majority of UK interregional movements do not involve migration from northern, midland or the devolved regions towards southern and eastern English regions. Indeed, as a whole such 'north–south' type movements are actually only a tiny minority of the migration flows which are evident between UK regions.

That this is the case can be seen by considering gross and net flows of people between broad regions. The London economy currently receives labour inflows from the rest of the UK of the order of 200,000 while it generates labour outflows to the rest of the UK of some 250,000 per annum (GLA 2013; Dickey 2014). In other words, in terms of net interregional migration London currently loses 50,000 people per annum to the rest of the UK (GLA 2013). Out-migration from London to the rest of the UK is the single largest gross migration flow within the UK (Fielding 2012) and net outflows of people from London to the rest of the UK are a long-standing feature of the London economy (Dickey 2014; GLA Economics 2005). Over the last two decades prior to the 2008 crisis between 1991 and 2007 the annual gross inflows and outflows from the London economy were typically of the order of 2–3 per cent of the population, while net outflows from Greater London had typically been 50,000–80,000 people, or rather less than 1 per cent of the London population. These gross annual inflows and outflows to and from the rest of the southern regions of England combined were approximately twice the scale of those associated with London, again accounting for just over 2 per cent of the combined regional population, while the annual net inflows into the rest of the southern regions of England typically amounted to just 0.35 per cent of their combined population (Dickey 2014). Indeed, gross inflows and outflows in southern and eastern regions of England are far larger than in other parts of the UK with net inflows to the South West the largest migration flows in the UK, driven primarily by amenity-related issues (Fielding 2012). Annual gross inflows and outflows to and from the combined regions in the midlands of England were typically some 2 per cent of the population, but the net outflows and inflows were typically close to zero. Meanwhile, the annual gross inflows and outflows to and from the three northern regions of England combined were never more than 1.5 per cent of the population, and the negative net balance of inflows and outflows was typically just between 0.02 per cent and 0.2 per cent of the population (Fielding 2012; Dickey 2014). Annual gross inflows and outflows to and from Wales were typically 2 per cent of the population while the annual net balance fluctuated around zero. Finally, gross inflows and outflows to and from Scotland were typically 1 per cent of the population while the net balance was typically between 0.07 per cent and 0.25 per cent (Dickey 2014) with Scotland being slightly positive and Northern Ireland slightly negative.

As we see in Table 5.3, the relative scale of UK interregional inflows and outflows has barely changed between 1995 and 2007, the economically buoyant years associated with the beneficial impacts of modern globalisation on the UK economy. More specifically, interregional inflows and outflows as a share of the regional population have typically only increased by no more than 0.6 percentage points for any UK region and in most regions the increases have only been of the order of 0.1–0.4 percentage points. In other words, changes in the scale of interregional flows are imperceptible. Similarly, if we consider net flows, the change in net flows has only been of the order

Table 5.3 Annual interregional inflows and outflows 1995 and 2007[a]

	1995 Pop Inflows as a % of Reg Pop	1995 Pop Outflows as a % of Reg Pop	1995 Net Pop Flows as a % of Reg Pop	2007 Pop Inflows as a % of Reg Pop	2007 Pop Outflows as a % of Reg Pop	2007 Net Pop Flows as a % of Reg Pop
North East	1.45	1.75	−0.30	1.75	1.77	−0.02
North West	1.50	1.68	−0.18	1.63	1.72	−0.09
Yorks & Humber	1.81	1.94	−0.14	2.02	2.08	−0.06
East Midlands	2.46	2.22	+0.23	2.75	2.56	+0.18
West Midlands	1.70	1.85	−0.15	1.94	2.09	−0.16
East	2.56	2.26	+0.03	2.78	2.49	+0.31
Greater London	2.44	2.96	−0.53	2.54	3.56	−1.02
South East	2.79	2.50	+0.29	2.98	2.70	+0.28
South West	2.73	2.24	+0.49	2.88	2.32	+0.56
Wales	1.88	1.82	+0.05	2.11	1.88	+0.23
Scotland	0.94	1.01	−0.07	1.08	0.81	+0.28
Northern Ireland	0.86	0.75	+0.11	0.68	0.64	+0.05

[a] The data for this table were constructed by combining interregional migration calculations kindly undertaken by Dr Heather Dickey from the University of Aberdeen using the data sets in Dickey (2014) with regional population data (ONS 1997, 2009). International in-migration and out-migration flows are not included in these data.

of 0.01–0.5 percentage points between 1995 and 2007, and as such again is barely perceptible.

These percentage figures in Table 5.3 also translate into changing inter-regional in-migration and out-migration flows for the individual UK regions. Total interregional migration inflows and outflows have increased by less than 10,000–15,000 per annum between the years 1995 and 2007 for the regions of Yorkshire and Humberside, West Midlands, South West, while for the East Midlands and the East the increases are more than 20,000. Meanwhile, for the North West, Scotland, Wales and Northern Ireland the changes in in-migration and out-migration flows between 1995 and 2007 have been less than 10,000 per annum in each case. For the South East the changes in annual inflows and outflows between 1995 and 2007 have been of the order of 30,000 while for London annual inflows have increased by more than 20,000 while annual outflows have increased by some 60,000 between 1995 and 2007.

In the years immediately preceding and following the 2008 global financial crisis, at the level of the UK's 12 OECD-TL2/EU-NUTS1 large statistical regions annual gross UK interregional migration had reached some 1.6 per cent of the UK population while annual net interregional migration flows var-ied between more or less zero in the northern English regions and Northern Ireland, to approximately 0.2–0.3 per cent in the Midlands and Scotland, 0.3–0.5 per cent in southern English regions, to around 1 per cent in London (Fielding 2012; Dickey 2014). The types of interregional gross migration fig-ures we observe today are therefore roughly just 1.5–2 times the interregional mobility flows that were typical between the 1960s and 1980s (Gordon and Molho 1998; Hughes and McCormick 1987, 1994; McCormick 1991,[25] 1997), while the net interregional flows are almost entirely unchanged during three to four decades. Overall, these figures suggest that the UK has experienced only a very slight increase in interregional mobility in more than three dec-ades of deregulation, and interregional migration is still tiny in overall rela-tive terms. Moreover, this almost glacial rate of change in UK interregional mobility has been evident during a long period which has involved a whole-sale deregulation of the UK economy. In particular, the fundamental changes to the UK housing markets and the deregulation of whole swathes of the UK council housing system have not resulted in the greatly increased mobility outcomes previously expected in some quarters (Minford and Stoney 1991). Interestingly, the lack of responsiveness of migration to varying regional demand and supply conditions may not necessarily be UK-specific phenom-enon, with similar observations also evident within the USA where interre-gional migration rates have continually dwindled since at least 2000 (Partridge *et al.* 2012, 2015).

Within the UK the most notable interregional mobility changes which are observable relate primarily to flows in and out of London. Indeed, between 1991 and 2007 London experienced increasing gross annual inflows and out-flows of 40,000 and 66,000, or rather increases of 28 per cent and 32 per cent (Dickey 2014). At larger spatial scales; the rest of southern England combined including the East experienced increased gross inflows and outflows of 110,000 and 90,000, representing 25 per cent and 22 per cent increases; the combined regions in the midlands of England experienced increased gross inflows and outflows of some 50,000, 30 per cent and 33 per cent; while the three combined northern regions of England and Wales all experienced increased gross inflows and outflows of the order of 40,000, or some 18 per cent and 19 per cent (Dickey 2014). Wales also experienced increased gross inflows and outflows of 19–21 per cent, but in this case the larger flow numbers are only of the order of 10,000 per annum, while Scotland has experienced no change in gross interregional inflows or outflows between 1991 and 2007 (Dickey 2014).

If we consider smaller spatial units such as counties, annual gross interregional migration flows for the UK currently amount to 3.22 per cent of the population (Fielding 2012) and these rates vary between 5 per cent in south-eastern counties such as Berkshire, to 3 per cent in London and 2 per cent in many of England's other large urban metropolitan counties (Fielding 2012). The vast majority of movements between UK local authority areas are movements between urban areas, with intra-London movements accounting for half of the total of these types of movements in England (DEFRA 2015). Movements between local authorities within England and Wales have remained largely unchanged between 2002 and 2014, with just marginal rises in 2007 and 2014 (ONS 2015). In other words, as a whole interregional mobility within the UK has hardly changed over several decades and where it has changed, the UK's increasing interregional mobility since the early 1990s has been primarily associated with interregional mobility between London and the other southern and eastern regions of England. Meanwhile, the increases in gross interregional migration associated with all other regions of England and also the devolved regions are all smaller than those observed in southern English regions, as are the related net migration flows.

However, to put these various increases into perspective, between 1991 and 2007 which spans the buoyant years when migration grew due to its pro-cyclical nature, the increase in annual gross interregional inflows and outflows to and from the Greater London economy was actually less than 0.5 per cent of the current London population and smaller in absolute terms than the number of people currently employed at Heathrow airport.[26] Similarly, the increases in annual interregional gross inflows and outflows to and from other three regions in southern and eastern England are of the order of 0.5 per cent of their combined population and are equivalent to the total number of people currently employed at Heathrow and Gatwick airports.[27] For the two regions in the midlands of England the increase in gross interregional migration between 1991 and 2007 is 0.5 per cent and for the three northern regions the growth in gross interregional mobility is equivalent to 0.25 per cent of their combined population. For Wales the figure is 0.33 per cent and for Scotland it is zero. In other words, what these figures underscore at the level of large combined regions is that even though the UK is one of the most mobile societies in the world, the annual gross population inflows and outflows as well as the annual net balance of these flows are still just a tiny fraction of the overall regional populations, and that the much-vaunted growth in UK interregional mobility that we have witnessed over the last two and half decades still in reality only related to a tiny fraction of the UK population.

One possible manifestation of all of these changes in interregional mobility and also the structure of the housing market since the 1980s is that overall unemployment differentials between UK regions are now in the lowest third of the OECD rankings for the whole population and for the youth population and in the lowest half for long-term unemployed (OECD 2013a). Traditionally, the UK interregional unemployment gap would increase in economic downturns and fall in upturns (Gordon 1985). However, it may well be the case that interregional mobility has played only a very limited role in lowering the UK's regional employment differentials, with changes to employment rights and reductions in secure job-tenures being far more important. As such, although it still largely remains the case that regional unemployment differentials are counter-cyclical it is nowadays much harder to interpret these changes partly because they are now much smaller than before and also because they are now manifested primarily in differential wage and income effects (Hemmings 1991). The previously high interregional unemployment differentials have been reduced as national unemployment levels have fallen, and been replaced instead by much higher interregional productivity, income (OECD 2013a) and wealth differentials. The nature of the UK interregional problem has fundamentally changed since the early 1990s.

The currently somewhat higher levels of geographical and interregional mobility evident nowadays within the UK relative to both other countries and also the UK in earlier decades reflects something of a slightly different picture to the 1970s and 1980s. A series of papers at that time argued that the marked and persistent UK interregional unemployment differences were largely a result of the fact that UK interregional migration was far too low, constrained primarily by the workings of the housing market. One the one hand, for lower income workers the prevalence of social housing with secured tenure was argued to inhibit incentives to migrate from weaker to stronger employment demand regions (Hughes and McCormick 1981, 1987; Minford *et al.* 1988). On the other hand, interregional differences in house prices meant that many owner-occupiers, and particularly those who were lower down on the income scales, systematically faced mortgage credit constraints due to their inability to sell their houses at prices which were high enough to provide sufficient collateral for a subsequent house purchase following migration from a weaker to a more prosperous region (Bover *et al.* 1989). Given that housing was the only major form of saving for many lower income groups, these interregional house price differentials therefore created a set of incentives which act as a barrier to mobility (Henley 1998). This was particularly marked in the case of lower income groups, many of whom at this time were also new home owners following the widespread 1980s housing market deregulations and the 'right to buy' public housing schemes. Far from promoting mobility, home ownership created another form of interregional mobility restrictions amongst lower income groups, and in particular those who might have benefited in employment terms by moving from the north to the south. As interregional inequalities have increased the greater differences in mortgage thresholds required to be reached on moving from the north to the south militate against migration for those in the non-core regions who are home owners. The marked differences between the institutional situation today and that which existed in the 1970s and 1980s means that not all of the issues pertinent then are quite so relevant today. Given the current burgeoning house price disparities between UK regions the adverse effect of home ownership on migration is probably even more relevant today than it was in the 1980s, whereas the council house explanation is now of relatively much more limited merit. Large swathes of former council housing are now either owner-occupied or in the private rented sector.[28] What we see is that at different times the operation of both the publicly owned rented housing sector and the private owned housing sector have in different ways limited migration from the northern non-core northern to the core regions of the south. At the same time, however, migration from the south to the north has also rather surprisingly been hindered by home-ownership. In order to see this we need to reconsider the insight derived from spatial price equilibrium models (McCann 2013), as is discussed in Appendix 5.1.

There is much evidence which points to these types of effects. In terms of labour mobility, although today the UK is relatively a highly mobile society, there are still marked differences in UK interregional migration patterns according to age cohorts. The most geographically mobile groups are those between the ages of 18 and 34 (Fielding 2012) and almost all young people who move within the UK move into predominantly urban areas (OECD 2011b, 2013a). On the other hand, across all age groups the majority of interregional migration moves within the UK are actually away from predominantly urban areas and towards intermediate areas and predominantly rural areas (OECD 2013a). Indeed, some 60 per cent of the UK's predominantly urban areas experience population outflows (OECD 2011a). These patterns suggests that interregional migration in the UK exhibits life-cycle features, and in particular, what is known as an 'escalator' process (Fielding 1992a, 1992b, 2012). Younger workers, and particularly those in their twenties with high qualifications and skills tend to move towards higher productivity and more dynamic regions (Faggian and McCann 2006, 2007b, 2009a, 2009b; Abreu *et al.* 2015) in search of employment opportunities (Faggian *et al.* 2006, 2007b; Abreu *et al.* 2015), and in the UK these movements are almost entirely to urban centres (OECD 2011b). These highly skilled workers typically work in these urban locations in order to build their careers for a period of 10–20 years, after which they seek to move away to smaller towns and rural areas, largely for family and lifestyle reasons. As they move away these older and more experienced workers are in turn replaced by other younger, highly skilled and lower wage workers who themselves are moving into the cities. In other words, UK interregional migration is dominated by flows of particular cohorts or people, at particular stages in their life-cycles, and into and out from particular types of places (Fielding 1992a, 1992b, 2012), rather than by general interregional movements of people randomly distributed across age groups and places. Moreover, given its size and its global city nature, the role of the London economy and its hinterland regions appears to be particularly crucial in the UK version of this 'escalator' phenomenon (GLA Economics 2005). The London economy appears to dominate these escalator flows, with certain other UK cities also mirroring these patterns, but to a much lesser extent (Champion 2012; Champion *et al.* 2014). The regional escalator argument was set primarily as a core-hinterland process within a city-region setting, such as London and its environs. However, these escalator-type effects are also complemented by 'elevator' effects (Gordon *et al.* 2013) involving relocations between city-regions rather than escalator processes within an individual city-region setting. Yet, these escalator and elevator arguments also emphasise that employment progression is not purely a combination of city-size agglomeration and human capital arguments, but also is very much a social argument (Fielding 1989) where ambition (Gordon 2015a) coupled with access to particular types of jobs and their associated social and professional networks and communities of practice may be just as important as urban scale and personal skills. Yet, overall migration into UK cities and regions, and most notably London in particular, is also heavily shaped by international immigration flows, and in order to understand the dynamics of UK regional population change we also need to consider the nature and scale of these international flows relative to interregional migration flows.

5.2.2   *International and Interregional Migration*

Within the escalator pattern described above, the population relationship between the London economy and the rest of the UK has a particular structure to it, which is also heavily shaped by international labour flows. Immigration and international migration into the UK have increased markedly over the last two decades, with migrants arriving from a diverse range of countries, including those which are members of the European Union. The 2011 UK census revealed that 12 per cent of the UK population were foreign-born, up from 9 per cent in 2001, with a figure of 13 per cent for England and Wales, 6 per cent for Scotland[29] and 4.5 per cent for Northern Ireland[30] (ONS 2012b). The 2014 estimate is that this value is now 13 per cent.[31] As of 2013 some 16 per cent of the UK working age population were born outside of the UK, a proportion which has doubled from 8 per cent since 1995 (Wadsworth 2014). The EU Single Market also allows 1.5 million UK citizens to live and work freely elsewhere in the EU without requiring a work permit, and reciprocal rights for EU citizens bring valuable skills, experience and money into UK universities and businesses (BIS/DFID 2011a). EU nationals today work primarily in the sectors of retail, restaurants and bars, education, food manufacturing, commercial cleaning and gardening, health care, construction and hotels.[32] Between mid-2001 and mid-2010 38 per cent of the UK population growth was accounted for by a greater number of births than deaths while 56 per cent was accounted for by net immigration.[33] However, the 2011 UK census revealed that immigration into the UK from within the EU only accounted for 27 per cent of the foreign-born population of the UK, although by 2013 this figure was 28 per cent (Wadsworth 2014) and was forecast to have risen to 29.7 per cent by the end of 2014.[34] Current inflows from the EU are now 1.85 times larger than those from outside of the EU.[35] Yet, even with the recent increases in immigration from the UK, the important point here is that more than 70 per cent of the foreign-born population of the UK have not originated from within the EU. The reasons for this are twofold. First, as well as earlier migration from Commonwealth countries, in the last two and half decades political conflicts and natural disasters have also led to a surge in international migration at both a global and European level from migrants originating outside of the developed world (OECD 2013b). All advanced OECD countries have experienced increased inflows of immigrants for these reasons in recent years and while many of these patterns are related to previous colonial ties, proximity is also a major factor, with richer EU countries in particular which are geographically close to many of the most troubled regions receiving heavy inflows of illegal immigrants. Second, global and international flows of students have also increased dramatically in recent decades and the UK higher education system has been at the forefront of these internationalisation processes. The surge in student inflows to the UK university system has been heralded in many quarters as evidence of the status and quality of the system, and a huge boost to UK exports. The largest numbers of foreign-born in the UK by country of origin come from India, Poland, Pakistan, Ireland, Germany, Bangladesh, Nigeria, South Africa, United States and Jamaica, in descending order, respectively (ONS 2012b). The Republic of Ireland and the UK have always maintained a free movement single labour market ever since the creation of the Irish Free State, so if we remove Ireland from the list, the ordering is India, Poland, Pakistan, Germany, Bangladesh, Nigeria, South Africa, United States and Jamaica.

As well as political and security considerations, migration and immigration also tend to be very pro-cyclical, with migration flows strongly correlated with employment demand. The highest year for immigration into the UK was 2007 immediately prior to the 2008 crisis and the highest outflows were in 2009 immediately following the crisis.[36] As of late 2014 net immigration flows into the UK had largely recovered to their pre-crisis levels driven primarily by inflows from the rest of the EU as growth in the UK economy had strengthened relative to many other EU countries,[37] the result of which is that the population of England grew by just over half a million between 2011 and 2014.[38] Yet, a major difference here between the EU and non-EU immigrants cohorts is that that whereas EU immigrants enter primarily for work reasons, non-EU immigrants are much more likely to enter the UK for study reasons (Wadsworth 2014). However, even allowing for these increases in international migration, at 12 per cent[39] (ONS 2012b) the proportion of the UK population which are foreign-born is more or less the same as in most other large advanced OECD countries and markedly lower than in many small advanced OECD economies (OECD 2014a; ONS 2012b). Moreover, although there is much political emphasis on migration flows from central and eastern Europe, in reality apart from inflows from Poland, which the second largest source of immigrants after India and slightly above the inflows from both Pakistan and Ireland, the total aggregated influx of migrants from the eastern European countries over many years is generally very small (ONS 2012b). After Poland, whose secondary school students out-perform UK secondary school students by PISA scores of 24, 19 and 12 in mathematics, reading and science, respectively,[40] the next largest source of immigrants from eastern Europe is Lithuania, and this is ranked as only the 21st largest source of immigrants into England and Wales, followed by Romania which is ranked as just the 26th largest source of immigrants into England and Wales (ONS 2012b). Indeed, along with Poland (ONS 2012b) the largest increases in UK immigration since the millennium are from the South Asian sub-continent countries plus China (OECD 2012c). This is rather different to the period prior to the millennium in which large shares of immigration were primarily associated with the 'Western Offshoots' (Maddison 2006) of Australia, New Zealand, South Africa and USA along with France and Germany (OECD 2008). Asian immigration was at much lower levels during these years (OECD 2008). Between 2001 and 2011 the number of foreign-born who arrived in the UK was just under 4 million (ONS 2012b) and these inflows accounted for almost 90 per cent of the net UK population increase during this decade.

Across almost every indicator of migration the UK is close to the OECD average, except for in terms of three key criteria. First, in terms of the in-migration of foreign students into tertiary education, the UK ranks as second only to the USA (OECD 2012c); second, in terms of the average education gap between UK immigrants and UK natives the UK ranks as one of the very highest amongst all OECD countries (OECD 2014b); and third, the average education levels of all classes of immigrants into the UK according to the length of time that they are resident is higher than in any other OECD country except Canada (OECD 2014b). Importantly, on all of these criteria the UK out-performs Australia, New Zealand the USA, all of which are countries with points-based immigration systems (OECD 2014b). In other words, in spite of much political rhetoric the UK is not particularly different from most other advanced economies in terms of the intensity and scale of immigration (Portes 2013), but it is markedly different to most countries in terms of the higher educational quality of immigrants to the UK (OECD 2014b).

Within these international and interregional labour flows London plays a critical role. Although London experiences net outflows of interregional migrants to the tune of 50,000 per annum (GLA 2013; Dickey 2014), on the other hand, London also currently receives inflows of some 200,000 international immigrants per annum while generating international outflows of some 125,000 people per annum. In other words, in terms of net international migration London currently gains some 68,000–75,000 per annum (Fielding 2012; GLA 2013). As a whole, the contribution of labour mobility and migration to the population growth of London is currently some 25,000 per annum, and this is driven almost entirely by net gains in international immigration (GLA 2013). The main periods of in-migration into London coincided with the expansion of the EU and the opening of the UK to international inflows from the eight new EU accession countries in 2004/2005 and also more recently, the impact of the crisis has reduced interregional outflows from London to the rest of the UK, as the adverse impacts of the crisis on other UK regions have been more severe than on London. Meanwhile, international immigration into London has not been affected by the aftermath of the 2008 global economic crisis (GLA 2013). Current projections suggest that the net outflows from London to the rest of the UK will increase to some 100,000 per annum over the coming decades while net inflows from international immigration will remain fairly stable at around 75,000 per annum (GLA 2013). In other words, in the coming decades the overall impact of interregional migration and international immigration on London's population is expected to become negative to the tune of minus 25,000 per annum.

This does not mean, however, that London will contract. This is because, even more important than in-migration, is the role of natural population change which today is the major driver of London's population change. Natural population growth is a function of previous immigration plus increased ageing of the population (GLA 2013), and in particular inflows of younger people increase the number of new births. The replacement ratio of the UK without immigration is too low to sustain current population levels so immigration plus births due to immigrants account for the vast majority of UK population growth.[41] Indeed, fertility rather than migration is also the major explanation for the population growth of many of the major cities across Europe whereby young people move into cities (European Union 2014). In the case of London, at present natural population growth is of the order of 70,000–80,000 per annum, and current projections suggest that these rates of natural population growth will be maintained for the coming two to three decades. As such, although London is expected to lose some 25,000 people annually due to net out-migration to the rest of the UK, the overall London population is expected to increase by 55,000 per annum over the coming decades, due to the higher natural population growth (GLA 2013).

The foreign-born share of the population of London currently stands at 39 per cent[42] which is slightly over three times the UK average of between 12 per cent and 13 per cent (ONS 2012b). At present, London alone accounts for some 38 per cent of all international immigrants and just under 40 per cent of all international emigrants (ONS 2013b). In other words, London has three times as many immigrants and emigrants as would be expected purely on the basis of London's population,[43] while the rest of the UK has one-third fewer immigrants on average than might have been expected purely on the basis of population levels. Outside of the three core regions of London, the South East and the East the share of foreign-born in the rest of the UK is currently just 8 per cent,[44] levels which are lower than in all but two of the EU-15 economies and also lower than in half of the EU-13 countries (ONS 2012b). Indeed, many parts of northern England and the three devolved regions have immigrant shares of between 1 per cent and 3 per cent of the population (ONS 2012b; Wadsworth 2014).[45] Meanwhile, in marked contrast, in some London boroughs immigrants account for some 60 per cent of the local working age population (Wadsworth 2014). Primarily as a result of immigration, overall population densities in London have risen during the last decade from 2.3 persons per household to 2.5 persons per household.[46] Moreover, London appears to have benefited especially from immigration. Along with Brussels, London is one of the two cities with the largest share of recent immigrants in the OECD while the rest of the UK is actually below the OECD average (OECD 2011b). At the same time, more than 15 per cent of the labour force of London are highly skilled immigrants, and along with Ontario (Toronto) and British Columbia (Vancouver) this is the highest share of any OECD region and almost twice that of Paris (OECD 2011b). In terms of human capital inflows, both in terms of scale and the quality premium, London is unique within the UK. These observations underscore the importance of considering the labour market roles of the London economy as reflecting a quite different phenomenon from other parts of the UK driven primarily by international immigration and not interregional migration. The skills and human capital experience of London needs to be set against the backdrop of the international economy and the recent era of modern globalisation, rather than discussions regarding the spatial sorting of the domestic population.[47]

Between 1997 and 2000 the UK moved to rather more of an open-door policy on immigration (Coleman and Rowthorn 2004a) with the perceived economic and possibly also social[48] benefits of immigration underpinning the shift in policy. These purported benefits include increased productivity, greater labour supply, an improved demographic age structure, and the associated fiscal advantages of these expected effects (Coleman and Rowthorn 2004a). However, there are also important social and environmental arguments for restrictions on immigration, which centre on the potential displacement effects on vulnerable sections of the labour market, greater congestion and access costs for housing and public services, along with complex social cohesion impacts (Coleman and Rowthorn 2004a). Yet, although there are many UK political debates regarding the case for restricting immigration, there is often something of a mismatch between public perceptions and actual impacts (Rolfe *et al.* 2013; Gallup 2013). For example, immigrants do not account for the majority of new jobs, but rather their share of new jobs reflects their share of the population (Wadsworth 2014). In terms of the economic characteristics of UK immigration, immigrants tend to be over-represented in very high-skill and very low-skill occupations (Wadsworth 2014). Indeed, the overall wide-ranging international and UK evidence suggests that on average immigrant workers tend to be more highly skilled or willing to work under more challenging conditions than the native-borne population (*The Guardian* 2008; Rolfe *et al.* 2013; *The Economist* 2013; OECD 2013b, 2014b; Wadsworth 2014). This is particularly the case for immigrants to the UK from the EU-15 countries which were members of the EU prior to 2004 (Wadsworth 2014). Furthermore, the evidence for the UK also suggests that immigrants do not reduce the wages of natives (Manacordia *et al.* 2012). The reason is that immigrants and natives are not close substitutes for each other, as they tend to work in different occupations (Manacordia *et al.* 2012) both at the top and bottom of the labour market (Wadsworth 2014). Yet, although the dispersion patterns of skills and employment for immigrants differ from those of natives which tend to be much more concentrated in middle-skills and middle-incomes jobs, the overall result is that on the basis of OECD-PISA scores in aggregate even UK immigrants from outside of the EU display almost identical educational levels on average to UK natives, which as we also saw in Chapter 1 are also almost identical to the overall OECD average.[49]

As a whole, the Bank of England considers that immigration has kept UK wage inflation and interest rates at lower levels than otherwise would have been the case.[50] Moreover, in spite of enormous public misperceptions and beliefs regarding the 'welfare tourism' activities of immigrants (Kellner 2015)[51] and the numbers of asylum seekers,[52] in reality immigrants are also found to be less of a strain on the UK public purse than natives (Dustmann and Frattini 2014), contributing far more in taxes than they receive in terms of benefits. However, the overall effects of immigration on both GDP and GDP per capita are likely to be small, with the major effect being on the overall scale of the population, reduced pressure on government debt, and the growth of the economy (Vargas-Silva 2015; Rowthorn 2014).

These observations are largely consistent with the international evidence. Overall, the evidence from across the world generally points to the fact that in the long run immigration tends to be beneficial for the national economy (Borjas 1995, 1999; Peri 2011; Sanderson 2013; Nijkamp and Poot 2012; Orrenius *et al.* 2012), although the economic effects are often found to be small (Coleman and Rowthorn 2004a). In the specific case of the UK there are a series of reports which also largely point to this same conclusion holding for the economy as a whole (House of Lords 2008; MAC 2014; Wadsworth 2014; Rowthorn 2014) and in particular on urban areas (Nathan 2011a, 2011b, 2011c). Obviously, immigration may lead to displacement and wage-reduction effects on lower skills native-borne groups, and these short- and medium-term adjustments to openness may be difficult to ascertain because the distributional effects of openness are complex (Wadsworth 2010; BIS/DFID 2011b MAC 2012, 2014; Devlin *et al.* 2014). However, such displacement effects are often found to be more severe on other recent immigrants rather than on native-born (Longhi *et al.* 2010) and across all international studies the adverse wage effects on native-born workers tend to cluster around zero (Longhi *et al.* 2005). In other words, as already mentioned the international evidence from many countries suggests that in the long run immigration tends to be generally beneficial for the overall economy (Peri 2011; Nijkamp and Poot 2012). This thinking dominated UK immigration policy in the years around the millennium (Balch 2009), and particularly in the light of the rejuvenated global role of London. Indeed, in reality UK immigration has partly mitigated the long-term demographic problems exacerbating secular stagnation faced by many other economies (*The Economist* 2014a) and also kept the costs of the provision of public and social services lower than it would otherwise have been (House of Lords 2008; *The Spectator* 2008). Consequently, if successfully implemented, the efforts to cut UK immigration inflows in response to domestic political pressures are likely to lead to adverse long-term economic and fiscal consequences for the UK, although the scale of these is disputed with some commentators arguing the adverse effects will be relatively minor (Collier 2014a, 2014b) while others argue that it will be very severe (Lisenkova *et al.* 2013).[53]

Part of the problem in terms of motivating a serious discussion about these matters, and particularly in the context of UK regional and urban issues, is the fact that in economic terms immigration has broadly similar impacts to inward foreign direct investment (FDI) in domestic industry. Indeed, in the case of highly educated immigrants FDI and immigration often display complementarity effects. The social cohesion impacts may differ but while there is much material on the social cohesion effects of immigration there is very little written about the social cohesion impacts of FDI, so it is not possible to pursue this argument any further here. However, given the economic parallels, many of the political arguments advocating cuts in labour immigration on economic grounds ought to be matched with widespread pressure to cut inward FDI inflows into UK cities. Yet, the fact that this is not the case suggests that debates in the public media display a serious lack of appreciation of the long-run economic impacts of immigration, and this also greatly hampers discussions about UK regional and urban issues. Therefore, outlining the parallels between immigration and inward FDI is instructive in order to better appreciate the induced economic mechanisms.

Immigrant FDI increases competition in domestic markets and in many cases there are displacement effects on various domestically owned firms. At the same time, the new inward FDI also provides new possibilities for local suppliers to generate new local and overseas markets. Overall, the diverse competition effects associated with inward FDI tends to lead to a re-ordering of domestic industrial structures and to a re-shaping of the relative primacy of certain key firms and industrial networks. In general, however, the overall welfare effects on the economy are largely positive because of the increased competition induced in the domestic economy, and also because of the fact that inward FDI also often provides for inward technology transfer and knowledge spillovers as best-practice and state-of-the-art technologies from international markets are introduced into the domestic UK economy. A certain share of the realised profits are repatriated to the parent country, but some of these profits will also be re-invested in the domestic host economy. On average, greater FDI and firm investment competition is welfare enhancing.

In the case of inward labour immigration there may also be displacement effects on the local population (MAC 2012, 2014) and increased labour market competition. At the same time, diversity and also the inflow of ideas from external markets tend to drive labour productivity gains and increased overall economic welfare (Nathan 2013a, 2013b), and this appears to be particularly relevant in the case of London (Nathan 2011b) and to a lesser extent other UK cities (Nathan 2011c). Again, some immigrant earnings will be re-patriated to the origin country while some of these earnings will also be re-invested in the domestic host economy. These labour immigration-related productivity and distributional mechanisms are largely equivalent to those associated with inward FDI and on average the competition effects are welfare enhancing.

The only real difference between the two mechanisms relates to the factor proportions. In a traditional neo-classical model inward FDI is likely to be associated with higher capital-labour ratios and increasing wages whereas labour immigration is associated with lower capital-labour ratios and lower wages (McCann 2013). However, allowing for the endogenous factor-complementarity effects associated with human capital, technology transfer, learning effects and knowledge spillovers, this simple dichotomy disappears. Indeed, these conclusions are bolstered by a further twist to these arguments. Immigration of higher educated workers tends to spur inward FDI (Nijkamp *et al.* 2011) because immigration also helps to establish greater international economic networks and linkages with the origin countries. In the case of the UK both the in-migration of labour and also the location of FDI investments tend to be heavily focused on UK cities such that complementarities between immigration and FDI are likely to be most evident in urban settings. Indeed, the evidence in Chapter 4 for London points to exactly these conclusions. In other words, in economic terms immigration and FDI not only tend to mirror each other, but they also tend to complement each other. They are only substitutes in the case where immigrants are of very low education levels (Nijkamp *et al.* 2011). In the UK immigrants on average are more highly educated than natives (Wadsworth 2014) such that immigration and FDI ought to display largely complementarity properties which are beneficial to the economy.

Unsurprisingly, in the case of immigrant FDI any displacement effects often impact particularly heavily on those firms which previously enjoyed advantageous or largely monopoly-type positions, and these firms will therefore also tend to be the most vocal in calling for state protection. However, while these types of mercantilist narratives still do exist, they are generally very much at the margins of public debate. As such, in the UK there is almost no political pressure to cut inward foreign investment, and nor is there any pressure to reduce UK investments overseas. On the other hand, there is mounting political pressure to cut immigration. Yet, the fact that so many of the competition and distributional mechanisms are almost identical between inward FDI and labour immigration suggests that most anti-immigration arguments are based largely on cultural narratives rather than on economic arguments.

As with inward FDI, even allowing for any labour market displacement effects the majority of the UK research suggests that the net effects of immigration on the UK economy have been positive. Indeed OECD research suggests that only about 20 per cent of the rising income inequality of the last decades is associated with openness, with the remaining 80 per cent being related to technology and skills (BIS/DFID 2011b). Immigrants into the UK are better educated on average than the native population and more recent immigrants are the most highly educated group (Wadsworth 2014). Moreover, even allowing for these possible displacement effects, it still remains the case almost all of the worldwide evidence on this topic suggests that the long-run immigration tends to be beneficial for the national economy as a whole (Borjas 1995, 1999; Peri 2011; Sanderson 2013; Nijkamp and Poot 2012; Orrenius *et al.* 2012).

The UK is indeed typical of such patterns (Dustman and Frattini 2014). In terms of the fiscal effects of immigration between 2001 and 2011, the estimated net tax contributions (£24 billion) plus education-related efficiency savings (£18 billion) associated with immigrants are found to amount to £42 billion in total, or equivalently some £4.2 billion per annum (Dustmann and Frattini 2014). This is largely a result of the fact that consistent with the wider evidence not only are immigrants into the UK more educated and work longer hours than their native-born counterparts (Wadsworth 2010; OECD 2014b) but also the UK does not have to pay for their education (Dustmann and Frattini 2014),[54] and this positive net fiscal effect is most marked for EU immigrants[55]. However, these skills-enhancement effects are not only important at the lower wage segments of the labour market but also at the higher wage segments, as manifested by the fact that the inflows of scientists into the UK are also of higher quality than the outflows of scientists from the UK, although the UK exhibits net outflows of scientists as a whole.[56] Indeed, the gap between the higher skill immigrants and those of the native-born in the case of the UK is one of the highest in the OECD (OECD 2012c). As such, in economic terms at least, the successful integration of foreign workers takes place in the UK in a manner which is generally more effective than in almost all other countries, as witnessed by the fact that in the UK immigrants account for a lower share of long-term unemployed than in most other OECD countries (*The Economist* 2013; MAC 2012; OECD 2012c).

As Collier (2014a, 2014b) points out, the estimated figures suggest that the broadly positive economic and fiscal effects of immigration are likely to be very small in comparison to the overall UK economy. Yet, when we consider these issues at the regional or local level then the picture is rather more complex. The effects on London of immigration are not small. Indeed, as we have already seen, London benefits from the human capital-enhancing effects of immigration more than almost any other city in the world. While London's property prices spiral partly in response to these inflows, the social impacts of these cost increases depend on complex distributional effects, depending primarily on one's tenure within London's property markets. In contrast, many parts of the UK, and in particular non-core regions, exhibit only very small levels of immigration, and in many of these cases immigration has recently reversed decades of local population decline. At the local level population decline can be even more pernicious than population growth, undermining local real estate markets, weakening local government fiscal positions and thereby the ability of local government to provide long-term public services. Yet, many of these economic arguments are often overlooked in public debates regarding immigration.

When discussing immigration issues, some commentators argue that England is one of[57] if not the most crowded country in Europe (Collier 2014a) and that purely economic arguments in favour of immigration (Dustmann and Frattini 2014) miss many of the crucial cultural and political perspectives[58] out of which concerns arise regarding the effects of immigration on social integration, on the demands on public services (Drinkwater 2010) and on the cost and availability of housing (Collier 2013, 2014b). In particular Collier (2013, 2014b) argues that it is not whether or not immigration is beneficial to the UK which is the central question, but rather what scale of immigration is desirable and advisable. In other words perceptions rather than economic issues are fundamental. Not surprisingly, much of the recent UK anti-immigration sentiment has increased in the aftermath of the 2008 global economic crisis, reflecting a pattern which is more widely observed following downturns in the business cycle (Johnston and Lordan 2014). In parallel, while anti-immigrant sentiment tends to harden during economic downturns popular misperceptions regarding the numbers and scale of benefits received by welfare claimants also tend to be exacerbated during these periods (Kellner 2015). Yet, although there is pressure on public service resources associated with population growth (CWI 2012), as we have already seen, on the whole immigration has benefited the UK economy over recent years. However, while the cultural and political perspectives on issues such as immigration (Collier 2014b; Goodhart 2013), cultural diversity (West 2013) and national identity (Wellings 2012; Riddoch 2014, 2015; Colley 2014; Macwhirter 2014) are clearly deep-seated and profoundly held on the part of many people, they are also often very confusing and contradictory,[59] and therefore in terms of serious discussions regarding the effects of population change on UK cities and regions in the context of modern globalisation (Geddes 2013), it is important to be both careful and accurate regarding the data and evidence we refer to.

Many political views are driven by ideological or cultural perspectives and as such are both held and maintained quite independently of available evidence or 'facts' or changes in the evidence (Krugman 2015a, 2015b). In this context, discussions about data or evidence may appear to be largely meaningless because so many people simply refuse to allow their views to be influenced by the evidence (Krugman 2015a, 2015b). However, in the case of issues related to population, migration and 'crowding', the mismatches between public perceptions and the available evidence are so great that it is imperative to make some headway in this regard in order to have any realistic discussion about UK urban and regional issues.

Similarly, in terms of the issue of population scale and population 'crowding' it is important to be consistent when making international comparisons. For example, as long as Scotland remains part of the UK[60] the relevant 'country' which is the correct benchmark for international comparisons on population and all other social, economic and environmental issues is the United Kingdom of Great Britain and Ireland, and not England as Collier (2014a) refers to. Otherwise, we may as well arbitrarily compare England with the Dutch province of North Holland, Flanders in Belgium, Massachusetts in the USA, Sydney in Australia, Shikoku Island in Japan or just the North Island in New Zealand. Indeed, on this arbitrary approach there are numerous sub-national units across both the EU and the OECD with far higher population densities than England as a whole or even the most densely populated regions of England (Niemietz 2012). Moreover, as we will see shortly, more than 7 million people in England, a figure almost equal to the total combined population of the eight English core cities, live in extremely low density environments and in rural settlements of less than 2500 people (OECD 2011a), a figure which rather undermines many of the population 'crowding' arguments.

For consistency reasons and to ensure proper comparisons, therefore, either we compare national data or we adopt comparisons based on standardised cross-country sub-national regional comparisons using for examples the EU-NUTS system or the OECD-TL2 and TL3 systems, as employed in Chapters 2 and 3. In the end it doesn't really matter which approach we adopt, because either using national data or standardised EU or OECD data the results do not particularly change. As we will see below when we discuss the UK's land use constraints, the UK is not even nearly the most 'crowded' country in Europe and nor is it in any way 'crowded' due to population and immigration issues. To the extent that the UK is in any way 'crowded' this is almost entirely because of the artificial restrictions imposed by the UK's land use planning system. Well over 90 per cent of the UK's land area is almost empty and another 7 million UK residents, almost the same as the population of London or of the combined population of the core cities, live in extremely low density environments. As such, whatever may be the emotional or cultural foundations of certain political perceptions, the argument that the UK or England are 'crowded' is simply to ignore all of the available data and evidence, and what 'crowding' does exists is almost entirely an outcome of the land use planning system. On almost all population-related or migration-related issues many public perceptions on these matters are not even nearly accurate, however deeply felt are the emotional concerns.

The available evidence therefore points to a series of key insights. First, as we will see below, the UK is neither Europe's most crowded country in terms of population densities, with a population density which is far below those of both The Netherlands[61] and Belgium and also one which is only 7 per cent higher than Germany (Evans and Hartwich 2005b; Dorling 2011). Second, using either EU or OECD data we see that even the UK's most densely populated regions are not particularly densely populated in comparison to many other EU and OECD regions (Evans and Hartwich 2005b; Niemietz 2012). Third, the southern and eastern regions of England are not even particularly densely populated in comparison to other parts of the UK such as the North West or West Yorkshire.[62] Fourth, immigration places only limited demands on housing supply (Whitehead *et al.* 2011) and relatively lower demands on public services than does the native population (Dustmann and Frattini 2014). Fifth, there is no evidence whatsoever of European migration flows being related to national social security expenditure (Giulietti *et al.* 2011; ICF-GHK 2013; Gallup 2013), although these concerns are particularly commonplace in the UK media. Sixth, there is no evidence that immigration from the EU and in particular from eastern Europe has been in any way associated with increased crime (Bell and Machin 2011). Seventh, the UK is not the country in Europe with the most immigrants per capita (Portes 2013), and eighth, overall immigration into the UK from the EU is less significant than immigration from outside of the EU (Barrell *et al.* 2010).

Immigration does, however, appear to have played an important and beneficial role in UK regions and cities in two different arenas. First, it appears to have helped to rejuvenate many regions and cities which had previously been facing population decline. The restructuring of public services in the face of slow population ageing or population decline may be largely manageable as the population moves to a new stable equilibrium growth trajectory (Coleman and Rowthorn 2004b). However, at a local and regional level population decline, and in particular declines associated with outflows of young and highly educated people may be a far more serious and pernicious economic and fiscal problem than population growth, and in severe cases can lead to a lack of viability of many aspects of public service provision, depressed local housing markets and the fiscal insolvency of local governments. Indeed, many regions in Europe are already facing these challenges. Yet, current UK political narratives have barely raised these issues, choosing instead to focus on the perceived adverse relationships between immigration and population growth. In reality, however, renewed population growth, and in particular the growth in the working age population, can offer a major boost to cities and regions, helping to improve the long-term fiscal positions of local government as well as buoyancy in housing and employment markets.

Second, in particular immigration appears to have significantly helped to spur the economic growth of London over the last two decades in terms of both population and productivity. London's large immigrant cohort is especially highly skilled on average and the inflows of workers from outside of the

UK over the last two decades have been heavily associated with productivity improvements. However, whether the purported beneficial UK effects associated with so-called 'Tier 1' high-value immigrant investors are as large as is often claimed is doubtful (MAC 2014). Instead the London productivity boosts associated with immigration are more likely to be related to the widespread immigration of highly skilled workers from many countries (OECD 2011b) and in particular the EU (Wadsworth 2014).

However, a broad picture which emerges for the last three decades is that the UK is not, and has not been, experiencing a widespread internal north–south drift of people. There has been some southward movement but in comparison to the overall population it is only marginal, and this is also true for university graduates. The scale of the internal north–south flows is simply far too small to account for the observed interregional disparities. On the other hand, the effects of international migration into the UK, and in particular into primarily the London economy but also into the South East and the East, and the embodied human capital increases that these inflows offer, have provided London and the South East with a major skills-enhancing injection over other UK regions. These human capital inflows have also been accompanied by enormous international investment injections, which as we saw in Chapter 4, appear to be continually upgrading the capital stock of first the London economy, and second the economies of the South East and the East. What appears from observation of simple population data to suggest that there is an internal north–south drift of productive resources within the UK reflects in reality a major international injection of human and financial capital into London and the southern and eastern regions of England. Yet, even here the picture is still more nuanced. If we examine all of the components of population change including replacement ratios, fertility and mortality rates, as well as both interregional and international migration, we see that natural population growth in London in 2008–2009 was more than ten times more important than all forms of migration combined, in explaining London's population growth, whereas in in 2000/2001 it was migration which was 40 per cent more important than natural population growth (Fielding 2012). As a result of demographics including both interregional and international migration, the more youthful population of London has higher fertility rates which drive the majority of population growth, an experience which is also typical of many other prosperous European cities (European Union 2014). However, the evidence suggests that these favourable demographic shifts in London pre-dated the 2004 eastward expansion of the EU.

Today, natural population growth accounts for 55 per cent of UK population growth with immigration accounting for 45 per cent, whereas in 2000/2001 it accounted for only one-third of UK population growth, two-thirds of which was accounted for by immigration (Fielding 2012). In 2008/2009 natural population growth was more important for population change than in-migration in the five regions of the North West, West Midlands, East Midlands, Northern Ireland (Fielding 2012) and London, whereas in 2000/2001 natural population growth was only higher than migration in the West Midlands (Fielding 2012). Today, the regions with the very low or declining natural population growth such as Scotland, Wales and the North East are those in which immigration plays a relatively more important role in population changes (Fielding 2012). As we saw in Chapter 2 these are regions which have experienced the adverse demographics during many years of economic difficulties, and which only since the turn of the millennium (Fielding 2012) have started to turn a corner due to immigration. In contrast, in the prosperous regions in the south and east of England outside of London, interregional and international in-migration together play a relatively more important role than natural population changes as people are attracted to these regions (Fielding 2012). In other words, the role played by migration in driving population change is different in different UK regions.

The wide range of evidence provided here regarding the UK regional distribution of human capital, the nature and scale of UK interregional migration patterns, and the regional patterns of international immigration, all point to two major conclusions. First, UK interregional migration proves not to be a significant contributor or explanation of the observed growth in UK regional disparities. The nature and scale of human capital-migration interactions are simply not large enough nor sufficiently different in terms of quality to make any significant contribution to the observed inequalities. Spatial 'sorting' according to skills has been argued to be a major (Rice *et al.* 2006), if not the most important (Gibbons *et al.* 2014b; D'Costa and Overman 2014) driving force behind the UK's growing interregional inequalities. Yet, as the national levels of formally educated human capital have soared in recent decades relative to previous decades, the scale of UK interregional migration flows of human capital have remained relatively tiny, they have also hardly changed over the last three decades and, if anything, have actually favoured the non-core regions. Where mobility has increased this largely concerns the interactions between London and its hinterland regions in the south and east of England. Interregional human capital mobility involving non-core regions is largely unrelated to the London economy.

In contrast, international immigration into the UK has heavily favoured London, both in terms of absolute scale and also in terms of the quality of human capital inflows. These processes do not reflect the spatial sorting of an existing national human capital stock of labour but rather certain forms of global spatial sorting driven by international migration behaviour. Much of this is largely independent of the internal and interregional labour dynamics of other UK regions. Of course, international inflows into the London economy allied with the local land use constraints may well have inflated London housing prices more rapidly than otherwise would have been the case, thereby artificially inhibiting interregional inflows into London from non-core regions (Overman *et al.* 2010). Yet, such interregional flows have barely changed over more than two to three decades and migration flows have not markedly changed even for new university graduates, which weakens the possible explanatory power of such a hypothesis. The interregional linkages of human capital appear to be of relatively very limited importance in the UK economy. This observation, allied with the fact that according to the most detailed data available the differences in regional human capital endowments are also negligible, suggests that the role of 'sorting' in accounting for the UK's observed interregional inequalities is likely to be less than is often assumed.

Since the 1980s the labour markets in all UK regions have become more flexible and the north–south differences in labour market flexibility evident in the 1970s and 1980s have narrowed markedly (Monastiriotis 2005). However, this narrowing in regional labour market flexibility is pro-cyclical, with the narrowing being most rapid in economically buoyant periods (Monastiriotis 2007a). Moreover, the observed UK regional labour market flexibility is now also highly heterogeneous (Monastiriotis 2005, 2007a), with southern regions displaying greater flexibility in terms of wages and labour mobility while regions outside of the south display greater levels of production flexibility (Monastiriotis 2005, 2007a), such that institutional issues including the forms of unionisation (Monastiriotis 2007b) appear to play important roles (Monastiriotis 2007a). Local wages in the UK are negatively related to unemployment as would be expected from the 'wage curve' arguments (Longhi 2012) with higher unemployment reflecting greater supply-side competition for labour and a stronger monopsony position for employers. In contrast, in more buoyant regions wages are higher as workers face less severe supply-side competition and employers have less monopsony power. Women also appear to be more sensitive to these local competition effects providing reasons for the observed gender pay gaps (Longhi 2012). In general, while the spatial or sectoral concentration of human capital in the UK does tend to lead to increasing returns, human capital measured by experience appears to be far more important in explaining wages than human capital measured by years of schooling (Monastiriotis 2002). Given the empirical evidence here regarding the tiny interregional variations in secondary and tertiary educated human capital as well as the interregional flows in human capital, these observations all suggest that the regional industrial composition is still critical in determining wages because it is experience in particular sectors which allows individuals to build on their formal education skills. Again, given the fact that the UK interregional inequalities are large while human capital stocks are largely identical, this still suggests that different sectors located in different regions only interact interregionally to a very small extent. These are the issues to which we now turn.

5.3   Interregional linkages and transmission mechanisms

The connections and linkages between regions are of various different types and each of these play somewhat different roles in mediating the relationships between different types of regions. As well as human capital migration flows, interregional linkages can also be considered in terms of trade and demand linkages, fiscal and financial linkages and knowledge-spillover linkages. It may be the case that the increasing UK interregional inequalities are in part also a result of the nature and patterns of these different types of linkages, and also potentially changes in these linkages.

5.3.1 Trade Linkages

As we have already seen in Chapter 4, the London region runs a small international trade surplus. At the same time, one of the arguments for the importance of London to the national economy is that it provides a major market for goods and services produced in other UK regions, containing highly specialised expertise and services, and also acts as a conduit for all UK regions to global networks of knowledge (CLC 2004; Coyle and Rosewell 2014). London is a net exporter of services to the rest of the UK and a net importer of manufactures and other sectors. Estimates of the size of London's exports to the rest of the UK suggest that they are between 35.5 per cent[63] and 51.2 per cent of London's GDP (CLC 2004) while London's imports are between 40 per cent and 44.6 per cent of London's GDP. Indeed, various models suggest that the interregional demand effects of London lead to a trade deficit with other UK regions. Estimates of the size of London's interregional trade deficit with the rest of the UK derived from adjusting national input-output tables suggest that it is of the order of 4.2 per cent of UK GDP and 9.2 per cent of UK GDP if we include all of London's commuting population.[64] In other words, well over 90 per cent of the markets engaged with by the rest of the UK's regions do not involve London. However, the scale of this interregional demand effect should not be over-stated.[65]

For comparison purposes the Scottish Input-Output tables suggest that Scotland's exports to the rest of the UK account for 41.5 per cent of Scotland's regional gross value-added (GVA) and Scotland's imports from the rest of the UK for 51.3 per cent of Scotland's regional GVA.[66] The Welsh Input-Output tables suggest that Wales' exports to the rest of the UK amount to 64.9 per cent of regional GVA and imports from the rest of the UK account for 75.9 per cent of Wales' GVA.[67] The South West Input-Output tables suggest that the South West region's exports to the rest of the UK amount to 59.1 per cent of regional GVA and the region's imports from the rest of the UK amount to 60.5 per cent of regional GVA.[68] As such, by UK regional standards the London economy is relatively closed to the demand and supply markets in other UK regions. Linked to this is the fact that London exhibits the third lowest output multipliers of any UK regions (Iparraguire D'Elia 2008), above only the North East and Northern Ireland. This is unusual given that in general, multipliers increase both as the total regional GVA increases and also as the GVA per capita increases (Iparraguire D'Elia 2008). Yet, as we have already suggested in previous chapters, this might be a result of the widespread international linkages of the London economy which in many ways appear to be more important than its domestic linkages. Indeed, even after accounting for local and regional UK markets, sales to London by the rest of the UK regions still only account for 40 per cent of their sales to international export markets, while their imports from London only account for one-third of the international imports into the rest of the UK's regions.[69] On this approach, although the rest of the UK regions run an international trade deficit while their trade with London runs a trade surplus, in terms of their total scale of trade engagement, the rest of the world is far more important to the rest of the UK's regions than is London. Moreover, this argument holds even stronger if London runs a trade surplus with the rest of the UK's regions (CLC 2004).

Curiously, if we follow the type of logic which posits that one of the national benefits associated with London is that the London economy provides an important market for the rest of the UK, then conversely, and rather surprisingly to many observers, the rest of the UK plays a more important role for the London economy than overseas markets. London's exports to the rest of the UK are approximately 60 per cent higher than its international exports while its imports from the rest of the UK are double its international imports.[70] This would appear to go counter to many popular narratives which perceive London as primarily a global city, whereas these data suggest that it is still primarily a domestically oriented city. Yet, the problem with all of these types of narratives regarding the importance of domestic versus global markets is that they are primarily a matter of relative scale, as well as distance. It is well known that international trade is much lower than domestic interregional trade when we consider only the effects of geographical distance. Other institutional and cultural aspects of distance play a much bigger role in inhibiting trade across countries than simply geographical distance, and these distance deterrence effects mean that domestic interregional trade tends to be far greater than international trade, even for global cities (McCann 2013). This is part of the explanation as to why London trades far more with the rest of the UK than it does with other countries, even though it does so with relatively less intensity than other UK regions. At the same time, as well as these distance deterrence effects, relative scale also matters. London can never be the main market for the regional exports of the rest of the UK's regions, simply due to the fact that its economy is only one-quarter of the combined size of the economy of the rest of the UK's regions. Similarly, the rest of the UK is four times the size of the London economy, and without the barriers associated with international borders the much weaker distance deterrence effects between regions rather than nations account for the fact that UK domestic markets still account for the majority of London's trade. However we look at these issues, it is clear that the net demand contribution of the London market to the rest of the UK is actually very small, if it exists at all, and that the reverse demand relationship from the rest of the UK to London may actually be far more important on many levels, in spite of the global city arguments. This may in part explain why the dynamic growth links between London and the rest of the UK appear to be so weak, as we have already discussed in detail in Chapters 2 and 3.

5.3.2 Financial and Fiscal Linkages

As well as trade linkages, another set of interregional linkages which may shape regional fortunes are financial linkages, both in terms of private sector financial linkages and also public sector financial linkages. These different types of financial linkages may affect the ability of both entrepreneurs and existing enterprises to create new businesses or business models, to access and develop new technologies, and foster local innovation. However, in the wake of the 2008 global financial crisis one of the issues which has recently been highlighted is the ability of SMEs to access credit finance. In the years prior to the 2008 global financial crisis loans to SMEs had been steadily declining but the rate of decline accelerated markedly after 2008 (OECD 2015a). Over recent years since the crisis the UK has faced a general collapse in credit availability, such that the overall levels of business finance contracted sharply and across all types of business lending to both large and small firms, in comparison to the years prior to the crisis. In reality, the financial retrenchment in the UK has actually been more severe than across the Eurozone (Monteiro 2013). The result of this is that SMEs in particular, appear to have faced especially severe and adverse credit availability conditions by both EU and OECD standards (OECD 2015a). UK business loan rejections increased from just 4–6 per cent in 2007 prior to the crisis to some 20–30 per cent in the years following the crisis (Monteiro 2013). Indeed, the UK ranked sixth highest in Europe terms of overall business loan rejection levels and second highest for business loan rejections to the service sector. The proportion of SMEs using external finance fell to something of the order of 40 per cent. On the other hand, the UK fared relatively well in terms of equity finance and other non-loan sources of finance such as leasing, overdrafts and credit lines (Monteiro 2013). Yet, UK SMEs still tend to be largely reluctant about external equity participation and instead rely heavily on debt finance in the form of fixed term loans or overdraft finance and similar credit lines (Ennew and Binks 1995). Overall, therefore, the pessimism of UK businesses regarding credit conditions was more marked than in many other EU countries (Monteiro 2013), although the actual number of UK bankruptcies was of an average value relative to the OECD and below that of ten other European countries (OECD 2013c). Aggregate lending to UK businesses continued to contract for six years until the middle of 2014 (BoE 2014), after which it began to increase again as the UK economy grew from 2014 onwards (OECD 2015a). Yet, lending to the smallest (OECD 2015a) SMEs has continued to fall[71] even as aggregate lending has increased. Given that the UK's 4.8 million (NAO 2013) SMEs make up 99.9 per cent of UK companies and account for 14 million workers (NAO 2013) or 60 per cent of UK private sector employment[72] and more than half of total UK private sector turnover,[73] any such variations in credit conditions will heavily affect the prospects for local and regional economies.

Given that business performance in the UK largely mirrored EU averages the relatively severe UK credit contractions suggest that supply side factors may be at play, and possible market failures provide a rationale for government intervention in this arena (BIS 2012b). There are currently various national and local policy initiatives to try to improve SME credit access (BIS 2013; NAO 2013; ACCA 2014) and access to investment finance (BIS 2013). These policy initiatives also include efforts to improve the sharing of SME credit data[74] between banks and financial institutions (HM Treasury 2014a), movements towards a Business Bank (BIS 2013; BBB 2014) type of scheme, and the creation of local SME-related credit institutions (Appleyard 2013), and all such policies are intended to improve the supply of business credit in all regions.

The overall deteriorating credit conditions may have exacerbated already-existing financial or fiscal biases in UK regions. It has long been argued that business in different regions will face differential access to credit, according to the local demand conditions and that these differences will also have implications for the functioning of regional economies (Dow 1987; Dow and Rodriguez-Fuentes 1997; Dow and Montagnoli 2007). Within a single currency interregional context one national base rate operates across all regions. Therefore, rather than credit-finance being prices by interest rate variations, it is argued that finance is primarily apportioned out on the basis of structured credit constraints determined in part by the hierarchical structure of the banking system.[75] In these circumstances, credit availability for firms will be dependent both on the deposit base of the local bank branch and also linked to issues such as the level of collateral provided by the firms (Dow 1987; Dow and Rodriguez-Fuentes 1997; Dow and Montagnoli 2007). In other words, the levels of financial gearing and leveraging may differ across regions, and these differences are often argued to affect primarily SMEs.

While these theoretical arguments are persuasive, in reality it is very difficult to provide evidence for these types of effects, so indirect approaches are required. There is some evidence that UK regional investment yields reflect heuristic mark-ups on London prices which are primarily related to familiarity rather than economic fundamentals and as such may result in systematic mispricing (Henneberry and Mouzakis 2014). For example, if such SME financial constraints operate differentially across regions, then one would expect there to be significant differences in SME start-up rates between regions. Yet, at the scale of the 12 UK OECD-TL2/EU-NUTS1 large statistical regions the rate of business start-ups as a percentage of the active enterprises varies across seven of the English regions plus Scotland by less than 1 percentage point, with the range varying between 10.3 per cent in East Midlands to 11.2 per cent in the North East. The only outliers here are London where the rate is 14.6 per cent and the South West where the rate is 9.6 per cent, along with Wales at 9.3 per cent and Northern Ireland with 6.5 per cent. In terms of business death rates the range across the whole of the UK is much smaller, varying between 8.6 per cent in Northern Ireland and 10.7 per cent in the North West. Indeed, the death rates in nine regions vary just between 9.1 per cent in Scotland and 10 per cent in the West Midlands and Yorkshire and

Humberside, with the most heavily urbanised regions of the North West (10.7 per cent) and London (10.4 per cent) exhibiting the highest death rates.[76] Yet, at the scale of the large regions entrepreneurship rates appear to explain little about UK interregional disparities, except at the very top of the productivity scale in London and at the very bottom in Northern Ireland and Wales. These findings today largely reflect the findings from two decades earlier (Barkham *et al.* 1996).

Entrepreneurship performance, however, is about far more than simply the number of firm start-ups and deaths. While SME turnover is a partial index of the creative and destructive dynamism of the economy the quality and outcomes of entrepreneurial actions are key to economic development. The differences in UK regional entrepreneurial dynamism reflect a range of different economic, social, institutional and attitudinal factors (European Commission 2013) all of which come together to shape the potential for local start-ups. When considering all of these factors together, as a whole, the entrepreneurship performance of the UK scores well in terms of the overall quality of its entrepreneurial environment relative to other EU countries, and all UK regions actually perform well in this regard, although there is still significant variation between the individual UK regions. The Regional and Entrepreneurship and Development Index (REDI) (European Commission 2013) ranks the Greater London region as having the second highest entre-preneurship score in Europe out of 125 EU-NUTS1 regions behind only the Copenhagen region and just very marginally ahead of the Ile de France region. The South East regions ranks as 9th in Europe followed by the East and South West, both of which are ranked between the 22nd and the 25th EU regions. The rest of the UK's regions rank as: North West (28) and Scotland (29), West Midlands (33), Northern Ireland (35), Yorkshire and Humberside (40), East Midlands (42), Wales (45–46) and the North East (59). The picture which emerges from the combination of both the aggregate firm turnover data plus the REDI indices is that while entrepreneurial issues are clearly import-ant, at the level of the OECD-TL2/EU-NUTS1 large statistical regions, the variations are not sufficiently large to account for the major productivity vari-ations within the UK, and within England in particular. However, at the level of smaller regions the picture is rather different.

One of the best candidates for explaining interregional differences in the links between entrepreneurship and regional access to finance (Dow 1987; Dow and Rodriguez-Fuentes 1997) relates to the operation of the UK hous-ing market. There is also a literature going back to the late 1980s and early 1990s which suggests that capital market constraints prevent low wealth indi-viduals from setting up businesses (de Meza and Webb 1999), and the level of collateral provided by entrepreneurs appears to be an important determinant of the credit availability for entrepreneurial start-ups. In particular, housing equity appears to play an important role in the provision of UK entrepreneur-ial credit (Henley 2005). Movements in housing markets are closely related to the flows of entrepreneurial capital (Reuschke and Maclennan 2014) and the

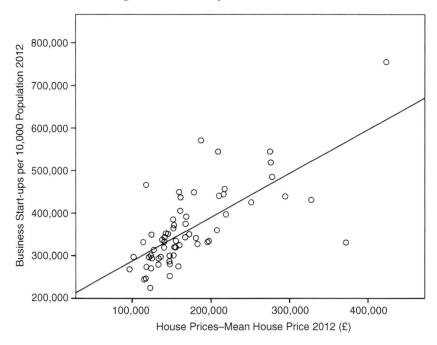

Figure 5.1 House prices and business start-ups
Source: www.citiesoutlook.org/.

links between local housing markets and the flows of start-up and SME credit appear to work both by influencing the levels of collateral which borrowers can provide and also via the increased incentives for greater efforts associated with committing one's own resources (Black *et al.* 1996). During the growth period between the millennium and the global financial crisis the number of insolvencies in London was both relatively lower and also shrinking faster relative to other parts of the UK (Bishop 2013). As we will see below the operation of the UK housing market greatly distorts the interregional variation in UK prices and housing equity growth, and it may be the case that these house price distortions have also interregionally distorted the ability of individual entrepreneurs to access start-up or seed finance.

As we see in Figure 5.1 the relationship between UK house prices and levels of entrepreneurship is indeed closely correlated, although the relationship is likely to be complex. On the one hand, house prices will be higher the more buoyant is the local economy. On the other hand, if entrepreneurial conditions are shaped by local economic conditions then entrepreneurship and house prices will be correlated. However, this relationship is not necessarily automatic. House prices also reflect housing demand due to amenity-driven in-migration, irrespective of any demand associated with local economic buoyancy (Graves 1980, 1983), although this amenity-related aspect has been argued to be of relatively limited importance in the UK, with house prices regarded as primarily reflecting economic demand conditions (Evans 1990, 1993), particularly in London and parts of the South East of England. Yet, if house prices do reflect local and regional economic buoyancy it is difficult to argue that this economic buoyancy is primarily related to levels of entrepreneurship and new firm foundation, unless housing collateral also plays an important role in the availability of SME start-up credit in which case entrepreneurship will also be related in a causal manner to both house prices and the overall economic conditions. The evidence of Black *et al.* (1996) suggests that this is indeed the case, although entrepreneurship is heavily shaped by many other issues as well (European Commission 2013).

Rather than entrepreneurship and new firm start-ups, in the case of firms which are already in operation the most recent evidence available suggests that while there are arguments that business finance within the UK may be generally too short-term in nature and with a preference for dividend payments over reinvestment (Cox 2015)[77] to foster many types of activities (Hutton 1995), and in particular manufacturing activities (Christopherson 2015) and R&D-intensive activities, there are actually very few systematic regional differences in SME access to finance between UK regions (Armstrong *et al.* 2013; Lee and Drever 2014). Previous evidence (Deakins *et al.* 2008) suggests that newer, smaller and more geographically isolated SMEs tended to face more significant financial barriers than established and larger SMEs. However, although businesses in non-core regions do perceive local credit conditions to be particularly adverse, in reality there are few if any substantial differences in SME credit availability for businesses already in operation. This would suggest that many aspects of the UK financial supply systems are broadly efficient and effective in accessing firms in different locations, notwithstanding the overall capital withdrawal shocks associated with the 2008 crisis. Markets for equity finance are the main area where London is far ahead of other UK regions (CLC 2010; SQW 2013), and on various criteria SMEs in London still appear more able or ready to access these types of finance than SMEs in other UK regions (SQW 2013; Armstrong *et al.* 2013), although some of these differences are also likely in part to be due to self-selection characteristics (SQW 2013; Lee and Drever 2014). As such, beyond the housing equity-collateral and external equity-finance arguments, the workings of the financial system would appear to be an unlikely candidate for explaining the long-term UK interregional productivity differences, except in one particular respect. In the years since the 2008 crisis the employment performance of London has outpaced all other parts of the UK, and this has been driven by the City-type jobs in central London. Much of the stimulus appears to be associated with the combination of quantitative easing and also guarantees and implicit subsidies to the banking systems provided by the Bank of England and the UK Government, which amounted to over £100 billion (Gordon 2015b). Yet, such enormous capital injections were not mirrored in UK-wide improvements in credit conditions, although the policies were ostensibly undertaken in the national interest. This raises the question as to where the money went. The most plausible suggestion is that these guarantees and implicit subsidies were carried over into London-based international financial activities with emerging markets, rather than the rest of the UK (Gordon 2015b). This outcome is perfectly consistent with the globalisation argument that London's most important and primary economic linkages and modes of operation are with the rest of the world, rather than the rest of the UK.

Another possible way in which money and financial issues may shape regional fortunes comes via the interregional transfers of public funds. It is perfectly possible to envisage situations in which local public sector employment crowds out local private sector employment (Faggio and Overman 2013), and these substitution-type effects would be all the more likely in times of tight labour markets, and rather less likely in times of slack labour markets, as many parts of the UK are currently experiencing. This crowding-out type of argument would reflect a rather orthodox interpretation of the relationship between public and private sector activities, while a rather more unorthodox argument is something of a regional analogy of Baumol's Law or 'Baumol's Cost Disease' (Baumol 1967, 2012). Baumol's Law or 'Baumol's Cost Disease' argues that if high-productivity sectors exist side by side with low-productivity sectors, and in particular low-productivity service industries, then observation suggests that the costs in the low-productivity sectors tend to increase much faster than the average thereby further reducing their relative productivity growth. The Moynihan Corollary (Moynihan 1996) to Baumol's Law is that in order to continue to exist an ever greater number of these service-related sectors will tend to end up in the public sector or will rely heavily on public sector support (Summers 2013). The regional analogy is that if high-productivity regions co-exist with low-productivity regions, then over time a larger share of the activities in the low-productivity regions will end up being underpinned by the public sector. Crowding out is one possible response, but so is co-option. However, a third option arises from observations of the workings of many capital cities, of many university and college towns, and of areas hosting publicly funded national research institutes. These observations also suggest that there can be a range of powerful complementarities between public and private sector employment relationships. As such, rather than public employment per se, what appears to be more important regarding substitution effects versus complementarity effects is exactly what types of public sector roles are undertaken in a particular place and how these dovetail with local private sector roles.

These relationships will in part be reflected in the national fiscal system and in particular interregional fiscal transfers, so it is instructive to consider interregional fiscal flows. It is widely understood that in general the London economy generates more tax revenue than it receives in public expenditure. The relative scales of UK interregional fiscal transfers have been estimated by the LSE (CLC 2009), Oxford Economics (CLC 2011a, 2012) and CEBR (2012a) and the broad picture is that between the millennium and the global financial crisis of 2008 the annual net contribution of the Greater London economy to the UK fiscal balances was typically of the order of £10–20 billion (CLC 2009, 2012), or between 4 per cent and 9 per cent of Greater London's GVA. In the years immediately following 2008 these figures shrank to between zero and £10 billion (CLC 2012) or between and zero and 3 per cent of Greater London's GVA. Typically the other net contributor regions are the South East and the East (CLC 2012),[78] both of which typically display a larger net fiscal surplus relative to their regional GVA than London (CLC 2012).[79] The rest of the UK regions typically run fiscal deficits although around the time of the millennium some years the South West and the regions in the English midlands also ran overall fiscal surpluses (CLC 2012). All other UK regions effectively receive net fiscal subsidies of between 13 per cent and 20 per cent of regional GDP,[80] with the highest net subsidies being in Northern Ireland, followed by Wales and the North East (CEBR 2012a; CLC 2012), all of which received net fiscal subsidies of between 32 per cent and 40 per cent of regional GDP.[81] The most recent estimates (CLC 2014a) show that the net fiscal deficits in the North East, Wales and Northern Ireland have fallen by around 7 percentage points in 2013 relative to their peak in 2011, and by 3–4 percentage points in the regions of the midlands and north of England (CLC 2014a).

Overall, there tends to be a very clear core-periphery structure to the relative size of these regional fiscal deficits with more peripheral regions exhibiting higher relative deficits, except for the case of Scotland. In the years around the turn of the millennium Scotland displayed a fiscal deficit relative to GVA which was similar to or even worse than those of most other English regions outside of southern England. Yet, while the deficit positions of these English regions deteriorated by 6–8 percentage points in the years prior to the 2008 global financial crisis the fiscal deficit of Scotland increased by only 3 percentage points (CLC 2012). CEBR (2012a) estimated that the net transfers to Scotland in 2010/2011 were exactly zero after factoring in Scotland's share of oil and gas revenues (CEBR 2012a).[82] However, as of 2013 the Scottish deficit position had deteriorated by 2 percentage points (CLC 2014a) and the issues regarding the compensatory role of Scottish oil and gas revenues to the UK Exchequer have been thrown into sharp relief by the recent and dramatic oil price falls.[83]

These very clear core-periphery patterns across the UK which are observed in the region-wide patterns are also broadly reflected if the local fiscal surplus and deficits are constructed at the sub-regional scale (McGough and Swinney 2015). Yet, the regional picture is also rather more complex than these simple fiscal surplus and deficit descriptions suggest for various reasons.

First, as we have indicated above, the current fiscal positions of all UK regions are not typical of earlier years (CLC 2011b). Prior to the crisis London, the South East and the East ran fiscal surpluses of between 6 per cent and 12 per cent of regional GVA whereas most English regions outside of southern England along with Scotland typically displayed fiscal deficits of between 3 per cent and 11 per cent of GVA. At the same time, the deficits in the North East and Wales were of the order of 14–22 per cent of GVA while that in Northern Ireland was typically 20–27 per cent of GVA (CLC 2012). However, in the immediate aftermath of the 2008 crisis the fiscal surpluses of London declined by 4–6 percentage points of GVA while the declines for the South East and the East were of the order of 9–13 percentage points of GVA, with the East actually becoming a net recipient region (CLC 2012). The fiscal deficits of all other net recipient regions relative to their GVA have typically increased by more than 15–18 percentage points since the 2008 global financial crisis (CLC 2012), except for Wales and Northern Ireland where the increases were of the order of 20 percentage points (CLC 2012).[84] In contrast, between the millennium and the 2008 crisis the deficits in the net recipient English regions had only increased by 6–7 percentage points while those in Wales and Northern Ireland had increased by 7–8 percentage points (CLC 2012). As such, regional fiscal deficits increased by a factor of 2.5 in the immediate wake of the crisis relative to their growth prior to the crisis, and there is clearly something of a UK core-periphery geographical structure to these increasing deficit positions. The only slight exception to this UK core-periphery pattern is the case of Scotland, where in the years prior to the crisis the Scottish fiscal deficit had only increased by 3 percentage points, and in the aftermath of the crisis it had increased threefold by 9 percentage points (CLC 2012), but from a much lower level at the time of the crisis relative to the English regions outside of southern England. Since then, as already mentioned, the fiscal deficits in the regions of the midlands and north of England have fallen by 3–4 percentage points between 2011 and 2013 (CLC 2014a). At the same time, the East has returned from a net deficit position to being fiscally neutral while both London and the South East are net fiscal contributors of the order of 10 per cent of their respective regional GVA (CLC 2014a). These various figures reflect the fact that the post-crisis recovery has been far stronger in London and the South East and then followed by the East, than anywhere else in the UK, while there has been little or no growth in the more peripheral regions, accompanied by severe contractions in public expenditure.[85] The spatial distribution of taxes raised and spent is therefore heavily shaped by the geography of the economic recovery, and this is also clear at the sub-regional scale (McGough and Swinney 2015).

Second, the net fiscal subsidies received by all regions outside of the south of England are almost entirely the result of welfare payments. When these transfer payments are factored out, each of these regions actually provides a fiscal surplus to the Treasury in most years, if not all years (CLC 2012). Indeed, the only UK region which continually displays a fiscal deficit when welfare payments are excluded is Northern Ireland, and this deficit was typically between 2 per cent and 6 per cent of Northern Ireland's GVA (CLC 2012). Prior to the 2008 crisis the fiscal surpluses of Greater London excluding welfare payments were typically 13–17 per cent of London's GVA, while those of the South East and East were 14–23 per cent (CLC 2012). For English regions outside of the south of England prior to the crisis the fiscal surpluses excluding welfare payments were of the order of 7–14 per cent while in the North East and Wales they were between zero and 5 per cent of regional GVA (CLC 2012). Again, these fiscal surpluses all declined in the wake of the crisis, and typically these declines were all around 8 percentage points for the regions in the midlands and north of England. The surplus of Wales decreased by 11 percentage points while that of Scotland remained largely unchanged at 10–12 per cent of regional GVA. Meanwhile, the fiscal deficit of Northern Ireland excluding welfare payments increased by 12 percentage points (CLC 2012). Again, the effects of welfare spending on shaping the geographical patterns of fiscal deficits and surpluses is very evident at the sub-regional scale (McGough and Swinney 2015).

Third, if we consider the total public expenditure across all classes of public transfers and investments, we see that London receives a relatively high level of public expenditure (CLC 2009; HM Treasury 2013, 2014b) and a share of national public purse which is typically 1.5 percentage points above its UK population share (CLC 2012) but below its GDP share. London typically receives more public expenditure per head than any other UK region except Scotland and Northern Ireland, and above the public expenditure levels in other English regions (CLC 2014a). On the other hand London receives less public expenditure relative to either GDP or GVA than any other UK region. Indeed, even today in the wake of the 2008 crisis where its economy had largely recovered while those of the northern English and the devolved regions are still struggling, London's per capita public expenditure levels are still only marginally below those of the North East of England and not very different even to those evident in the three devolved regions (CLC 2014a). More particularly, if we consider only 'productive' public investments such as those in education, health, transport, crime prevention and economic development (CLC 2009) rather than welfare-related transfer payments, we see that London receives more public expenditure per capita than the rest of the UK in all of these investment areas (CLC 2012). In particular, public expenditure on transport is far higher in London than in any other region, and public expenditure on housing and economic development in London is the second highest of any UK region (CLC 2009). This is also evident at the sub-regional scale. London receives the highest levels of per capita 'productive' public expenditure than anywhere in England and Wales, and only Edinburgh and Glasgow receive more than London (McGough and Swinney 2015).

These observations are very important because they highlight the fact that the way we interpret public expenditure shares relative to GDP requires a great deal of nuance. From microeconomic theory we know that the mutual relationships between different production factors and difference sources of investment may exhibit either complementarity properties or anti-complementarity priorities. If public investments and private investments exhibit complementarity properties then higher levels of public investment per capita will increase the marginal productivity of private investments, resulting in relatively lower public expenditure/GDP ratios. In contrast, if public and private investment exhibit anti-complementarity properties then higher public invest-ments per capita will reduce public expenditure/GDP ratios. As such, while understanding public expenditure per capita is straightforward, interpreting the links between per capita public expenditure and output is more complex. Given that UK interest rates and credit conditions are largely invariant across all regions,[86] the 'concerns'[87] raised by some economists that higher public expenditure in more peripheral UK regions will crowd out local private invest-ments makes little or no sense. Of course 8 out of the UK's 12 OECD-TL2/EU-NUTS1 regions have no budget responsibility or fiscal roles and as such these fiscal deficit or surplus calculations are simply using large statistical regions for data purposes. If instead we therefore consider the OECD-TL3/EU-NUTS3 regions with explicit budgetary and fiscal responsibilities then two of the three UK areas running the highest fiscal deficits and receiving relatively the highest fiscal transfers related to employment and infrastruc-ture will be the highly prosperous areas of Oxford and Cambridge.[88] A sim-ple reading of the local fiscal position might view these figures with extreme 'concern'. However, as with the London case, in these two areas high levels of per capita public expenditure appear to exhibit primarily complementarity effects rather than anti-complementarity effects, thereby allaying such 'con-cerns'. As we have already seen in Chapter 2, London receives far more public funding per capita in heritage and cultural issues, but again, little concern is raised regarding the possible local crowding-out effects of these investments. The reason, as almost everyone recognises, is that these public investments invariably act as complements to private investments ad very rarely, if ever, as anti-complements. In reality, therefore, the issues involved in interpreting public expenditure/GDP ratios are not about crowding effects but about the existence of complementarity or anti-complementarity effects, and discussing these issues requires careful consideration of the nature of the public expen-ditures and the extent to which the public expenditures are productive invest-ments or in largely non-productive transfer payments. Moreover, if the funds are primarily in the form of transfer payments, then the major issues are not about crowding out, but rather about weak local demand and limited resili-ence in the face of adverse shocks.

Indeed, while London benefits from very high per capita levels of produc-tive investments, the only public expenditure arena where London appears to falls short of the rest of the UK is in terms of welfare payments.[89] London receives more welfare payments than the South East and East due to higher local unemployment (CLC 2012). However, housing costs are far higher in London than in other regions and given that the London unemployment is similar to many other UK regions outside of southern and eastern England, the additional housing-related benefit payments to London residents relative to regional GVA are likely to be far higher than elsewhere, although these have not been factored in to existing calculations of regional fiscal positions (CLC 2012). Recent evidence suggests that housing benefits grew by more than £3.25 billion between 2009/2010 and 2014/2015 with half a million more people claiming housing benefit, which is expected to reach £25 billion by 2017, and that the vast majority of these housing benefit increases are in London and the South East of England.[90]

In terms of the sources of taxation (McGough and Swinney 2015), although the national per capita tax contribution of London is higher than in any other UK region due to the role played by progressive taxes on higher incomes and also higher total corporate taxes, some parts of the total tax contribution of London, and in particular, National Insurance Contributions (NICs) and VAT payments, are highly regressive and relatively low in comparison to London's incomes (CLC 2012). As such, since the millennium London's share of the UK tax base has typically been between 3.5 and 4.5 percentage points below (CLC 2012) its relative output share of UK GDP (ONS 2013c; Harari 2014). However, recent estimates forecast that the net fiscal contribution of Greater London to the UK's public finances will recover beyond its typical pre-crisis values of over £20 billion per annum to more than £30 billion per annum (CLC 2014a) as London grows and gains in productivity relative to other UK regions. The forecast growth of London means that its share of total UK taxes will become very close to its relative share of UK output in the coming years (CLC 2014a). However, all of these estimates are likely to some extent to over-state the actual London tax contribution relative to other regions because most corporate headquarters for multiplant and multinational companies are located in London. In particular, although tax receipts are apportioned across the four constituent nations of the UK wherever possible, these are not disaggregated within England.[91] As such, tax receipts generated by economic activities taking place in other English regions or overseas will typically be reported as being based in London, the address of the corporate financial headquarters.

Within the London economy, the financial services are a major contributor of London's overall tax base. Nationally, the financial services sector is estimated to account for 11.5 per cent of the overall UK tax base (CLC 2014b), a value which is very similar to that generated by each of manufacturing, distribution and also North Sea industries. Indeed, each of these four broad sectors now account for around 10–12 per cent of UK taxes, with the remaining half of UK taxes being accounted for by all other industries combined (CLC 2014b). Today's situation is rather different to earlier years. Prior to the 2008 global financial crisis the UK tax revenues generated by financial services were larger than those generated by the UK manufacturing and distribution sectors combined and almost double those generated by North Sea oil and gas companies (CLC 2011b). Between 2008 and 2011, however, corporate tax receipts from the UK financial services sector fell to around two-thirds of those generated by manufacturing and distribution and were largely similar to those generated from North Sea oil and gas companies (CLC 2011b). By 2014, tax receipts from manufacturing and distribution were double those from financial services (CLC 2014b). Indeed, by then the tax receipts from the three sectors of manufacturing, distribution and financial services, were all almost equal to each other (CLC 2014b). In contrast, corporate tax receipts from North Sea oil and gas firms fell sharply in 2013 and 2014 in response to global oil price falls (CLC 2014b). Given that the financial services sector is estimated to comprise 1.1 million people nationally, or 3.7 per cent of the total UK workforce, this implies that the sector pays much higher contributions per capita than other sectors (CLC 2014b) due to relatively high wages and profits. In particular, the contribution of banks is important as a source of UK taxes. Banks account for 71.9 per cent of the taxes borne and 59.5 per cent of the taxes collected within financial services, while employing just 29.5 per cent of the people employed in the financial services sector (CLC 2014b). City-type financial service jobs in London account for between one-quarter and one-third of UK national financial services jobs. At the same time, many of the financial services activities in London are qualitatively very different to financial services in most other parts of the UK, except possibly Edinburgh. A large component of London City and Docklands-based financial services are in wholesale financial services, providing finance to investors, corporate organisations, other financial institutions and public sector bodies including governments in many different countries as well as in the UK (CLC 2014c), rather than providing financial services to individuals and households. These types of international financial services play a relatively large role in the UK economy. Indeed, the UK, and London in particular, accounts for more than one-third of all of wholesale financial services within the EU (CLC 2014c), and more than three times larger than France, and in particular Paris, the next largest EU centre of such services (CLC 2014c). Wholesale financial services now account for 5.5 per cent of GVA in both the UK and The Netherlands, only relatively behind Ireland with 6.1 per cent and Luxembourg with 21.1 per cent (CLC 2014c), both of which are much smaller economies than the UK. In the rest of the EU-15 countries the range varies between 0.5 per cent in Finland and 0.8 per cent in Germany, through to 3.2 per cent and 3.8 per cent in Belgium and Denmark, respectively, with the EU-28 average being 1.5 per cent (CLC 2014c). As we have already seen, these 'City-type' jobs in London (CEBR 2012b), most of which are in wholesale financial services, account for 16 per cent of Greater London's economic output and less than 4 per cent of UK output (CLC 2014c), while the City of London area, not including Canary Wharf–Docklands,[92] alone accounts for some 10 per cent of Greater London tax receipts (CLC 2014a). London currently accounts for 18.5 per cent of the total UK tax base (CLC 2012, 2014a) and 12.9 per cent of the UK population; this means that London's total tax rate is 29 per cent higher than the UK average.[93] These various figures imply that all of the City-type financial activities in the London markets are at the most likely to account for no more than 3–4 per cent of the total UK tax base, and at the most towards one-third of the total taxation revenues of UK financial services sectors.

Meanwhile, the estimated 2013 net surplus of both the Greater London region and also the South East regions is 10 per cent of the GVA of each region while the latest estimate for the East is that it will be fiscally neutral

(CLC 2014a). Given that combined size of the Greater London and South East regions in 2012 was 37.7 per cent of UK GVA this implies that the net fiscal surplus generated by these two regions combined, currently amounts to 3.8 per cent of UK GVA, or is equivalent approximately to some 10 per cent of the total UK tax base. If we assume that all of the fiscal surplus generated by London and the South East is transferred to other regions in the form of welfare payments,[94] then the total value of interregional welfare transfers amounts to less than 4 per cent of UK GVA.

In terms of orders of magnitude, the total tax generated by the City-type jobs in London is more or less equivalent to the total fiscal surpluses generated by London and the South East, and which themselves account for 80–90 per cent of welfare payments in other UK regions. In other words, in aggregate accounting terms there are some grounds to argue that the taxes generated by the UK-wide financial services industries fund the net welfare payment deficits incurred by UK regions outside of southern England. However, this claim is based on the equivalence of accounting flows whereas the economic reality is far more complex. To put these numbers into perspective, some 80 per cent of the UK taxation base does not involve London and more than 96 per cent of the UK taxation base does not involve London City-type financial industries. Similarly, more than 96 per cent of the activity of the UK economy does not involve transfer payments between UK regions. It is simply the interregional 4 per cent deficit margin of GVA, or some 10 per cent of the UK tax base, between local public expenditure payments and local tax receipts in other UK regions, which is funded by net outflows of public funds generated by economic activities in southern English regions.[95] This margin happens to be similar to the tax base generated by the UK-wide financial service industries, or three times the tax that is generated London City-type jobs, but it is also similar to the taxes generated by each of the UK manufacturing industries, or similar to the taxes generated by the UK distribution industries. Given that the majority of the UK's manufacturing and distribution activities are not in London so using the same aggregate accounting numbers it is just as accurate following this logic to say that welfare payments in other UK regions are funded by the UK manufacturing industries or the distribution industries outside of the south of England. The economic logic underpinning these arguments starts to look weak, to say the least, and is simply based on accounting equivalent numbers. What is clear is that even following this logic, the taxes generated by London City-type jobs are only equivalent to 4 per cent of UK GVA, less than 4 per cent of UK taxes, and only one-third of the interregional fiscal transfers. As such, popular narratives about the role played by City financial industries in generating UK tax revenues are largely overblown. The scale of their contribution is relatively tiny when considered at a national scale, and even the scale of Greater London's overall contribution to the UK fiscal position is little different from its overall share of national output, and also likely to be over-stated due to the fact that the tax generated by multiplant operations will typically be reported with respect to the London headquarter address. Moreover, since the 2008 global financial crisis any fiscal surplus generated by London for interregional transfers appears to have been largely cancelled out by expenditure on the 2012 Olympics plus the bank bail-outs (Clark 2015).

As with the private sector financial matters discussed above, the various figures reported here also suggest that these public financial matters are unlikely to provide a major explanation for the observed scale of UK interregional disparities. In any country, the scale of interregional fiscal transfers depends on three major issues. First, the level of fiscal transfers depends in part on the overall structure of the national tax system and in particular on the extent to which it is progressive. Second, it also depends on the levels of income inequality between regions, and third it depends on the levels of fiscal federalism operating in the national system. The higher are each of these three features, the higher will be the levels of interregional fiscal transfers. In the case of the UK, until now the levels of fiscal federalism have been tiny, although it appears that this is likely to change as the new constitutional arrangements regarding Scotland are implemented. In terms of its progressiveness the UK tax system is close to the average OECD levels on a range of criteria (OECD 2014b) but most importantly, the interregional inequalities in the UK are very significant. In other words, in the UK the scale of interregional fiscal transfers is driven primarily by the scale of the UK interregional inequalities rather than issues related to tax structures. At the same time, the observed scale of these fiscal transfers within the UK is tiny relative to the scale of the interregional inequalities. As such, although it is possible to consider crowding-out types of arguments in reality the observed fiscal transfers within the UK are primarily an outcome of, and not a cause of, the interregional inequalities.

5.4   Structural transformation and knowledge spillovers arguments

One of the most commonly heard arguments regarding the poorer performance of the UK's non-core regions is that they have suffered historically from being too specialised in either manufacturing activities or public sector activities at the very time when the global economy was shifting in favour of service sector activities. The effects of structural change, and in particular the effects of deindustrialisation on the balance of payments situation on national (Rowthorn and Ramaswamy 1999) and regional (Thirlwall 1980; Dow 1986) economies, has been long discussed. In the absence of a separate currency and differential prices for finance, interregional capital flows are argued to accommodate for regional balance of payments problems (Thirlwall 1980), and as such hide the balance of payments problem. However, if these flows are not accommodating then the adverse effects on deficit regions may be far more serious than on countries with separate currencies because they require income rather than currency adjustment (Dow 1986). Yet, this is not simply a matter of the adverse effects of globalisation, in that de-industrialisation has been found to be primarily associated with internal structural shifts within advanced economies including changing patterns of demand, more rapid productivity growth in manufacturing and relative price changes. In reality, growing trade with emerging economies only accounts for less than one-fifth of deindustrialisation processes (Rowthorn and Ramaswamy 1999). In the case of the UK, improvements in the non-manufacturing arenas such as knowledge-intensive services have partly compensated for the poor trade performance of UK manufacturing (Rowthorn and Coutts 2004) and these activities have tended to be heavily concentrated in London and the southern regions of England. The structural argument therefore concludes that these southern regions have naturally therefore proved to be relatively buoyant in the face of these structural shifts while non-core regions have not.

Yet, if this structural argument is indeed to be considered as being broadly correct then three other questions would need to be addressed. First, why have other countries which have faced much less deindustrialisation than the UK, such as Germany, Korea, Sweden, Finland, Denmark, Belgium, Switzerland, The Netherlands and Israel, all proved to be at least as productive (OECD 2014a) and resilient (Jaegers *et al.* 2013) as the UK economy over the last three decades? Second, why are so many of Europe and North America's richest cities such strong manufacturing and engineering centres, including Europe's richest city Munich? Third, given that the UK uses more or less similar technologies and skills to these other countries why have UK interregional knowledge transfers and spillovers been so apparently ineffective in helping UK regions to adjust to the emerging realities relative to these other countries? In order to begin to answer these questions we need a more considered view of deindustrialisation experience of the UK's regions.

The most striking feature of UK deindustrialisation is the fact that it was common to all UK regions since the early 1970s, with large long-run falls in employment in manufacturing and increases in service sector employment (Rowthorn 2010). The growth in these tertiary service-related sectors was relatively more rapid in southern regions, and in particular the financial, business and market-related sector grew much more rapidly in the south between 1970 and 2010. In terms of employment, in spite of more rapid deindustrialisation in the northern and non-core regions than in the southern and eastern regions of England, the overall regional unemployment rates differ markedly less than the decline in secondary sectors, partly because more highly qualified individuals were better able to move between jobs across regions and sectors and partly because of increased public sector activity (Rowthorn 2010). Not surprisingly, higher unemployment rates have always tended to be focused on low-skills individuals with the lowest levels of mobility, including those even in the prosperous London economy. Indeed, those who have really benefited from the prosperity of London are the highly skilled groups, many of whom live outside of London (Rowthorn 2010) or who have originated from outside of the UK.

Yet, if we split the southern regions of England from the rest of the UK into a simple 'North–South' framework we see that the picture is rather more nuanced than this rather blunt characterisation suggests, for two reasons (Rowthorn 2010). First, the relative population decline in the North has been slower than its industrial decline in part because increasing public sector employment in these regions partly offset the declines in manufacturing. Although total public sector employment grew between 1999 and 2005 after which it remained constant until the public sector cuts began in 2010 (IFS 2012), the growth in public sector employment nationally was actually much slower than the growth in private sector employment between 1999 and 2008 (IFS 2012). It was only in the immediate aftermath of the 2008 global economic crisis during which private sector employment contracted sharply while public sector employment levels remained unchanged, that the ratio of public to private sector employment increased (IFS 2012). Yet, even allowing for these private sector contractions, in 2011 before the public sector cutbacks began in earnest the UK's ratio of public sector to private sector employment was still less than it had been in 1999, because the increase in the number of private sector jobs between 1999 and 2011 was still twice that of the increase in public sector jobs during the same period (IFS 2012).[96] Meanwhile, in terms of wages, growth in private sector pay either out-performed or at least matched the growth in public sector pay every year between 1999 and 2011 except for the period spanning the middle of 2008 to the end of 2009 (IFS 2012). Many of the new public sector jobs were located outside of London and the South East and the more peripheral regions tended to benefit from these jobs both in terms of the numbers of jobs and also in terms of the relative wages they paid. Due to national public sector bargaining agreements, public sector wages tend to vary little across regions, and certainly much less so than interregional productivity variations. Public sector pay levels tend to out-perform private sector pay levels in the lower two-thirds of the income distribution and as such lower income regions have generally benefited markedly from public sector employment over recent years. The gaps between local public sector wages and local private sector wages tend to be much larger in economically weaker regions (IFS 2012). Given that skilled people will be attracted away from the private sector by higher wages, a cursory look at these data suggests that the relatively greater role of the public sector in the UK's weaker regions may have hampered their long-run economic dynamism and partly accounts for their economic weaknesses. However, the picture is more complex than this.

Until recently the North was not more dependent on public sector employment than the South (Rowthorn 2010). London and the southern regions of England were the parts of the UK which traditionally had enjoyed relatively higher public sector employment for many decades and it was only after a 30-year process of catching up via intentional government policies (Marshall *et al.* 2005; Gay 2006) that the North finally caught up (Rowthorn 2010). The relative shares in public sector employment in the North related to health, education and public administration were only for the first time equal to those in the South in 1990, 1997 and 1998 (Rowthorn 2010). In other words, the relatively higher role of public sector employment in the non-core regions outside of London and the southern regions of England is only a very recent phenomenon and post-dates the widespread 1980s deregulations of the UK economy and the initial effects of modern globalisation on the UK economy. Moreover, the period following this catching up between the late 1990s and the 2008 global economic crisis was a period in which private sector employment grew faster than public sector employment and private sector wage growth more than matched public sector wage growth (IFS 2012).

As such, arguments which suggest that one of the major contributory factors to the relative weakness of the UK's peripheral regions has been a historical over-reliance on public sector employment which has for many years crowded out private investment simply cannot be true. While as already mentioned some local crowding out of private investment is likely and particularly so in times of relatively tight labour markets susceptible to wage inflation (Faggio and Overman 2013), as a general explanation of national and regional structural weakness this argument is wholly insufficient, and in some cases is counter-intuitive, for two reasons. First, although there was indeed growth in the public sector in the decade prior to the 2008 crisis, in 2007 the UK government debt to GDP ratio was still close to its lowest level in a century while both the budget deficit and the levels of inflation were also small in comparison to previous decades (Krugman 2015c, 2015d).[97] Second, the relationships between public and private capital injections may exhibit either substitution features or alternatively complementarity features. For example, in terms of their relative local share of employment, two of the outstanding stellar performing parts of the UK over the last three decades, namely Oxford and Cambridge, represent two out of the three most public sector dependent areas of the UK.[98] Moreover, if we were to consider overall public sector investment and expenditure shares, and not just employment shares, then the dependence of these areas on public sector injections is likely to be relatively even greater. The success of these areas cannot be explained purely by recourse to private sector incentives, because clearly public sector and private sector investments in these cases have been highly complementary for decades, and continue to be so. Therefore, policy recommendations which argue that in the national interests reductions in land supply restrictions to allow the expansion of places like Oxford and Cambridge (Leunig *et al.* 2007; Leunig and Overman 2008; Crafts 2013) implicitly come very close to arguing in favour of public sector-led regional development processes. As such, these arguments appear to be somewhat more in tune with other arguments regarding the potential interactions between the public and private spheres (Mazzucato 2014) and curiously out of step with arguments which had previously criticised the public sector-led supply-side attempts at shaping the regional economic system (Crafts 2012). Similarly, the counter-cyclical characteristics of increasing public sector employment in the late 1980s and early

1990s may have helped regions in the 'North' to adjust to new structural challenges, and thereby partly limited the rate of increase of interregional inequalities, by providing ongoing income injections into the regions and some complementarities between public and private sector investments. During this period productivity growth in the public sector was approximately zero while the sector as a whole expanded nationally although since 2010 productivity has started to show an upward trend (IFS 2013). The national falls in productivity since 2008 are not primarily a result of structural changes bur rather declines within industries (IFS 2013). Again, the relatively greater role of public sector employment in many non-core regions of the 'North' is only a very recent phenomenon. As a whole, therefore, using public sector arguments as a basis for understanding the UK's interregional inequalities only makes sense on the basis of observations since the 2008 crisis, many years after the inequalities were already emerging, and only in terms of understanding how regions may adapt to the post-crisis realities, given that the crisis was not caused by public sector employment but by private sector activities and neither was it caused by peripheral regions (Roubini and Mihm 2011; Krugman 2004).

Another difficulty with the structural arguments as a basis for understanding the UK's interregional inequalities is that from economic theory it is not quite clear what the expected regional deindustrialisation responses ought to have been and how large they would have been expected to have been. Regions need an export base (Rowthorn 2010; Thirlwall 1980; McCann 2013) in order to generate the tradeables that can be exported to other regions and countries in order to drive local growth, and if services are to grow in the face of declining productive sectors, these service industries must also provide the tradeable-based export potential. However, given that so many service industries are part of the non-basic and non-tradeable sectors while manufacturing still accounts for some 80 per cent of global exports and more than 60 per cent of UK exports, in terms of the export base composition of UK regions, growing services cannot always be expected or relied on to fully compensate for any weaknesses in UK manufacturing (Rowthorn and Coutts 2004). Part of the problem is that there are only a small number of service industries with international and interregional export potential, namely, higher education, tourism, media and communications, and financial services. In the UK context, given that London and the South East had already long heavily dominated all four of these sectors, it becomes rather difficult to identify exactly what role in these other regions services were expected to play. Regions cannot diversify and grow in the long run on the basis of household and local consumer services, and in most cases services link into other export base sectors including manufacturing, energy and other forms of industry. The limited resilience of the UK's non-core regions in the aftermath of the 2008 crisis has meant that today there are again growing concerns that UK deindustrialisation processes may have led to excessive hollowing out (Bailey *et al.* 2015) in many UK regions while the role of financial services may have become too large in other regions (Crafts 2012). In response to these particular concerns, ways to reignite the UK's manufacturing technologies (GOFS 2013) and to better link knowledge actors and institutions such as universities to industry are being widely considered (House of Commons 2013; Witty 2013), and these lines of thinking suggest that the flows of knowledge and technology throughout the economy are much weaker than might have been envisaged.

Urban economists have tended to emphasise the role played by agglomeration effects and local knowledge spillovers in driving regional economic growth and transformation. In the UK there do appear to be positive externalities associated with urban density and particularly for service industries (Graham 2007a) which tend to be more clustered than other sectors (Bennett *et al.* 1999). The types of services industries typically oriented towards central business districts tend to benefit the most from agglomeration effects (Maré and Graham 2013), and as a result, although for some other sectors the agglomeration benefits of urban density are heavily attenuated in the face of urban transport congestion (Graham 2007b), for these type of CBD-oriented firms agglomeration-density effects appear to continue.

Such agglomeration benefits may arise through, for example, the better employer-employee matching afforded by larger markets (Melo and Graham 2014), depending on the spatial structure (Simpson 1992; Melo *et al.* 2012), and indeed in the case of the UK there is an urban wage premium which increases with city size, although controlling for sorting there is no evidence for any urban wage growth premium (D'Costa and Overman 2014). Workers do receive wage increases also from moving to cities but this affect attenuates after one year. However, experience in cities does seem to contribute to long-run wage growth in comparison to those who have never worked in cities (D'Costa and Overman 2014).

As well as matching and sorting, the literature suggests that there are also likely to be knowledge spillover and learning advantages from being in cities (Athey *et al.* 2008) especially related to intangible assets, and these may help to foster entrepreneurship and the creation of a new generation of high-growth firms (NESTA 2009, 2011). However, in the UK there is surprisingly little real evidence on the nature and spatial extent of UK knowledge spillovers, and especially in the light of the prominence these issues are being given by the city-based narratives underpinning many aspects of UK government policy. For example, Mason *et al.* (2013) find strong local spillovers for production industries from innovative inputs and external knowledge sources associated with UK city-regions. However, no similar effects are found for knowledge intensive services or other sectors. Similarly, positive relationships between the innovative performance of production firms and city-region skills levels are evident but again they are not evident for knowledge intensive services. Mason *et al.* (2013) speculate that the reason for these observations might be that knowledge intensive services may not be constrained by their local city-region. Meanwhile, the evidence for creative industries is also similarly equivocal. While creative industries do tend to introduce more new products and services than other industries, Lee and Rodriguez-Pose (2013a, 2013b, 2014) find no evidence that SMEs in creative industries are more productive in UK cities than in other types of localities. However, they do find that creative occupations are used by SMEs in cities to introduce innovations learned elsewhere.

Along similar lines, Harris and Moffat (2012) find that manufacturing and business service plants located in UK cities perform better than plants in the same region but outside of the city. They also find that multiplant or multinational (Harris and Moffat 2013) establishments exhibit higher productivity than single plant and domestic firms (Harris and Moffat 2012) and that agglomeration externalities in these types of cases extend well beyond an individual city-region arena. However, with the exception of Bristol, no UK city has significantly higher total factor productivity levels than the overall South East regions (Harris and Moffat 2012).

While cities enhance productivity relative to their hinterlands, in terms of the characteristics of the city, although spatial effects are found to benefit business service sectors the effects of urbanisation economies and diversity on high-technology firms were not found to be significant, such that there are few grounds for arguing that diverse cities are the ideal locations for fostering growth, particularly in high-technology industries (Harris and Moffat 2012). Neither do intangible assets appear to play a critical role (Konstantinos and Spence 2014; Artis *et al.* 2012). Other local factors may also play a positive role. For example, rather than any large city-effect it is the effects of Oxbridge which mean that regional R&D as a share of regional GVA is highest in the East and South East (BIS 2012a). Local university-industry collaborations are generally found to have positive effects on innovation and total factor productivity (Harris *et al.* 2013a, 2013b), but overall being located in the South East was found to be more important than being located in a city (Harris and Moffat 2012; Breheny 1999) and similar results are also found for the effects on labour inflows (Champion *et al.* 2014).

These findings are also largely mirrored by Athey *et al.* (2008) who find that in terms of innovation performance measured either by patenting or by the Oslo-manual (OECD 2005) Community Innovation Survey-type indicators, most of the top UK towns and cities are located in the southern or eastern regions of the UK, while the weakest performers are located in the midlands and northern regions of England (Athey *et al.* 2008). The geography of high-growth firms (Anyadike-Danes *et al.* 2013) and high net worth individuals (Dorling 2014a) is dominated by London and its hinterland, with much smaller positive effects in cities outside of the South East, and similar observations also hold for both the UK's creative industries (NESTA 2010; Ball *et al.* 2010), its high-technology sectors (NESTA 2015) and its fastest growing companies (Coutu 2014). The result is that today none of the FTSE 100 businesses which were based north of Birmingham when the FTSE index began in 1984 are still in the index.[99] In 1984 there were 10 such companies but now there are just 6, in comparison to 66 in London and the South East, a number which itself has fallen from 79 in 1984. Of course many FTSE 100 companies have major operations in northern regions as well as northern companies in private hands or which are part of larger corporate groups. However, many of these are in back-office type functions,[100] such that even with rapidly rising land and labour costs in London and the South East, there has been no northward drift at all in corporate activities in the last 30 years. Moreover, this southward drift has also been mirrored in the case of foreign investments into the UK (Wren and Jones 2012; Dimitropoulou *et al.* 2013), a process which is also associated with higher local and regional wage inequality (Driffield and Taylor 2000).

As such, the evidence on the productive role of cities and the relationship between cities, knowledge spillovers, intangible assets (Artis *et al.* 2012; Konstantinos and Spence 2014), entrepreneurship and SMEs (CfC 2014) is at best very mixed, whereas the difference in the performance of London and its hinterland regions and the rest of the UK is very clear. Yet, why the knowledge spillover and knowledge linkage features of the UK should be either so weak or so localised is not clear. Part of the difficulty in unpicking these different agglomeration-type mechanisms is that causality may run in different directions, both from agglomeration to productivity and also from productivity to agglomeration (Graham *et al.* 2010). The standard urban economic arguments (Mills 1972; Brueckner 2011) tend to adopt the former causal mechanism as an analytical departure point whereas the orthodox regional or interregional economic models tend to give more weight to the latter causal mechanism (McCann 2013). While there is no strict demarcation between these analytical approaches which are not mutually exclusive and as such exhibit a great deal of overlaps, the potential for two way causality suggests that there is no naturally preferred starting point for thinking about the interactions between geography and economic performance. As such, whether we adopt more of an urban or a regional perspective as our analytical departure point heavily depends on the context, the available data, and also the intended objectives that the research questions are aiming to address or respond to. The approach employed in this book obviously uses both urban and regional approaches but generally leans towards the latter, given the questions being addressed and the range of evidence emerging.

From this broader regional type of perspective, across the UK's regions the different local regimes of prosperity and areas of low incomes in the UK may be partly a result either of differences in occupational composition or in productivity differences. Patacchini and Rice (2007) find that the 'winner's circle' areas in the south and east of England benefit from both the occupational mix and relatively high-productivity performance whereas weaker areas in the north of England are hampered particularly by a poor occupational mix. In addition, while human capital is important, the evidence presented here and elsewhere (Webber *et al.* 2009) suggests that it is less important than official publications tend to imply. These productivity differences are also found to be related to proximity to economic mass (Rice *et al.* 2006; Graham 2007b; Webber *et al.* 2009), an issue central to many new economic geography (NEG) insights. If proximity is measured in terms of travel time, a doubling of working age population proximate to an area increases productivity by 3.5 per cent, although these effects decline steeply with time and disappear beyond approximately 80 minutes (Rice *et al.* 2006). Indeed, with various assumptions NEG models can indeed be operationalised to estimate UK local and regional wages on the basis of market potential (Fingleton 2005a). Yet, while NEG models are seen to perform better in accounting for UK regional wage variations than traditional neo-classical growth models (Fingleton 2005b), they are less powerful than urban economic models (Fingleton 2006) in explaining UK regional wage data.[101] This is particularly so at the level of small areas (Fingleton 2006, 2011) because they do not capture the producer service effects (Fingleton 2003) associated with employment density (Fingleton 2006). However, as we have also already seen in the previous chapters, urban economic models also fail to capture many of the key features of the UK's local and regional labour markets. Why neither NEG nor orthodox urban economic models are able to capture so many aspects of the UK interregional system is somewhat puzzling, and may be related to other constraints or issues which are typically not considered in such models. Two candidates which have already been proposed relate to the role of the UK's land use planning systems and also the role of the UK's city-size distribution.

5.5   The possible effects of land use constraints on UK interregional inequalities

As mentioned above, one of the arguments regarding the scale of the UK's observed interregional inequalities is that the UK's land supply restrictions may have contributed to these inequalities, and there are two ways of arguing this. First, it may be the case that land supply restrictions may have limited the ability of high-quality human capital to disperse more evenly including to non-core regions (Duranton and Monastiriotis 2002) and thereby limited the ability of these non-core regions to shift away from a manufacturing-dominated economy to one dominated by service industries. As we have already seen the UK interregional variations in all forms of secondary and tertiary human capital are now tiny, but also so are interregional migration flows, and these limited interregional migration flows may be an unintended by-product of the restrictive land use planning system. Second, the UK land use constraints may have artificially limited the ability of cities in non-core UK regions to achieve their full potential agglomeration effects, and this has given rise to an unfortunately skewed urban size distribution which is inefficient in terms of national productive capacity. In this next section we deal with the land supply argument and in the following section we will address the city-size distribution argument.

5.5.1   *Land Supply and Land Use Planning Constraints*

On the basis of the 2011 census, the Town and Country Planning Association projects that every year from 2011 to 2031 England needs 245,000 new homes, while in reality annual completions are less than half of this number and already the UK is more than half a million homes behind this target, pushing the requirements even higher.[102] How this situation could arise, and what the broader implications for all aspects of the UK economy are from this housing shortage, are key issues for understanding the regional, urban and the interregional features of the UK economy. Indeed, one of the major points of debate concerning UK urban and regional issues over recent years is the role played by the UK land use planning system in potentially distorting the location and performance of economic activities (Cheshire *et al.* 2014a, 2014b; Leunig and Overman 2008). This debate has nowadays received such a high profile both academically and politically that it is important for us to consider the extent to which the UK interregional inequalities may be in some ways related to these potential distortionary effects. In order to consider these issues it is necessary to discuss both the current debates and also to set these debates in a historical context.

The first three decades of the twentieth century saw four Westminster government acts between 1909 and 1932 which heralded the first movements towards a comprehensive urban and rural planning framework in the UK. The 1947 introduction of the current UK land use planning system was a result of these initial acts plus the experience of widespread urban squalor of the nineteenth century and the early twentieth century, along with observations of the largely uncoordinated ribbon development of the 1920s and 1930s. In an era when less than a quarter of households (ONS 2013a) were land and real estate property owners[103] the vast majority of the population were subject to the vagaries of the free market, with little or no official protection regarding the quality of their living conditions or environment (Hall 1998). These market-led challenges created enormous problems for local and municipal government not only in terms of basic infrastructure provision but also the upgrading and maintenance of public health standards (Mumford 1961; Hall 1998). The early experiences of modern types of urban planning interventions alongside the ideas promoted by the Garden Cities movement (Fishman 1982) suggested that in order to upgrade the quality of the built environment a more comprehensive public governance system intentionally structured to encourage coordinated land use actions was required. These demands were subsequently bolstered by the findings of both the Barlow Commission (1937) on the distribution of the UK's industrial population, the Scott Committee (1942) inquiry into rural land use (Macgregor 1943), the Uthwatt Report (1942) into the challenges and issues associated with compensation and betterment and finally the Reith Report (1947) into the case for new towns.

The inter-war years of the twentieth century had seen a boom in middle-class housing and a spreading of property ownership, but these improvements still largely evaded the much larger populations of lower income groups who tended to be densely concentrated in the major urban areas. The 1947 introduction of the Land Use Planning Act can therefore be seen in many ways as a progressive post-war policy response intended to improve the living conditions not only of society as a whole but in particular of the lower and primarily urban classes, in a similar vein to the introduction of the National Health Service and of compulsory secondary schooling. One aspect of this improved quality of life was much greater accessibility to the countryside in the vicinity of the major cities with local rural areas adapted to offer leisure and education possibilities for the urban population. Indeed, as a measure of success, today greenbelt land in England has a higher concentration of woodlands, walkways, country parks, nature reserves, and historic parks and gardens, than non-greenbelt land (CPRE 2010a). Yet, greenbelts were also developed in an era when the vast majority of the urban population spent their one-week-long summer holidays at their nearby seaside resort, and when mass car ownership, widespread motorway systems and low cost air travel could not be conceived of. The possibility that the majority of the population might be able to routinely access leisure pursuits in other parts of the UK or Europe had not then been considered. Nor, given the fact that this era was immediately prior to the onset of the post-war 'baby boom', could post-war greenbelt planners envisage the enormous demographic changes about to take place including population increases of the order of 15 million or more[104] alongside enormous increases in the numbers of households allied with falling annual house building numbers.[105] As such, in hindsight some of the social and aesthetic aspirations and aims which inspired early post-war greenbelt policies (Mumford 1961; Hall 1975, 1988, 1998; Lynch 1981; Fishman 1982; Cullingworth 1985; Greed 1993; Rydin 1993; Cullingworth and Nadin 1994) may nowadays appear in some sense to be rather paternalistic, romantic[106] and middle class in motivation, yet at the time of their introduction they contained very strong and socially progressive elements, given the social contexts at the time.

In the three or four decades following the introduction of the 1947 Land Use Planning System the positive social and environmental impacts of the policy were viewed by economists largely in a positive and constructive light and economists were largely sanguine regarding their ability to adjust and adapt the system and plan resources and needs according to market imperatives without undermining the system (Barlowe 1958; Lean and Goodall 1966; Netzer 1970; Stone 1970; Goodall 1972; Evans 1973; Bish and Nourse 1975; Newell 1977; Parry Lewis 1979; Willis 1980; Harvey 1981; Walker 1981; Whitehead 1983; Mathur 1986). Indeed, the UK land use planning system has succeeded in many regards over the last 60 decades, especially in terms of the upgrading of housing quality, infrastructure provision and environmental quality, and these benefits were particularly noticeable in the first three decades of the policy. More recently, however, during the late 1980s and early

1990s many economists (Evans 1988; 1991a, 1991b, 1996; Whitehead 1991; Balchin *et al.* 1995) started to raise deep concerns regarding long-run impacts of the policy as a result of both observation and also economic analysis of the workings of the current policy frameworks, which have given rise to severe unintended and adverse pricing effects. These severe and adverse pricing effects operate both in the short run and the long run and from a social inclusion perspective are particularly pernicious on lower income groups. While local greenbelts were initially aimed at providing rural engagement possibilities for the local urban population, it was never intended that such policies would also increasingly reduce the long-run property-owning and wealth accumulation opportunities of these lower income groups while enhancing the wealth accumulation possibilities for higher income groups. These adverse and unintended pricing effects were never foreseen by the architects of the system and were not even particularly apparent during the first four decades of the operation of the system. It was only in the early 1990s that government started to become more systematically aware of these issues (Evans and Hartwich 2005a).

The contemporary economic critique of the current UK land use planning system is largely a product of the last three decades and is not fundamentally an ideological argument in terms of the left or right of the political spectrum, but rather it is a normative social welfare and social inclusion argument based on a positivist analysis of the unintended and adverse effects of the system (Vigar *et al.* 2000). The area and quantity constraint challenges facing the land use planning system as the UK population increased and the economy restructured had already been raised specifically in relation to London and the South East (Hall 1966; Hall *et al.* 1973). Moreover, subsequently warnings regarding the wealth distortion effects of the growth of home ownership and the links between housing wealth-transfers and social and interregional inequality were also raised (Hamnett *et al.* 1991), although no explicit link was made here with the operation of the land use planning system. The approach which pulls each of these elements together in a systematic framework follows the work of Evans (1988, 1991a, 1991b, 1996; 2004a, 2004b), Whitehead (1991), Meen (1996), Barker (2004, 2008, 2014), Evans and Hartwich (2005a, 2005b, 2006, 2007), Meen and Andrew (2008), Cheshire (2008), Cheshire *et al.* (2014a, 2014b), and the basic argument is that over many years UK land prices have become too high due to the restrictive land use planning system. This effectively imposes an implicit 'tax' on UK land use (Cheshire and Hilber 2008)[107] such that the UK now has some of the highest land prices in the world (Hilber and Vermeulen 2012).[108] A result of this is that the UK now builds the smallest new homes in the western world[109] and the land use restrictions also increase the volatility of both housing markets and macroeconomic conditions (Hilber and Vermeulen 2012), the cost and price distortion effects of which reduce the productive efficiency of UK firms and also the affordability of home ownership for numerous people. In particular the effects of the urban green belt are particularly pernicious in this regard because

they increasingly tend to price out lower income groups from home ownership and to bolster poverty traps (Stephens *et al.* 2014) while increasing the
housing-based and land-based wealth of property owners.[110] Some of these
issues, whereby land price cost and price distortions limit access to housing
markets to the extent that they subsequently also generate wealth distortion
effects favouring higher income and older groups, are also highly relevant in
many rural regions as well as in more heavily urbanised regions (NHF 2014),
and relate very closely to some of the increasing wealth inequality arguments
of Piketty (2014),[111] Dorling (2014b) and Atkinson (2015a, 2015b).[112]

In economic and welfare terms both an obvious and an essential structural
reform is therefore to remove many of these land use planning restrictions so
as to increase the supply of greenfield land and housing and thereby to reduce
the price of accessing home ownership. Urban brownfield redevelopment is
often extremely expensive and typically requires major public subsidies to
become viable while the long-run social and fiscal outcomes are very uncertain. As such, these commentators argue that reducing greenbelt land is the
optimal strategy, on the grounds that greenbelt development can be relatively
cheap and rapid and is more likely to be attractive to market investors and
less of a financial burden on the state. Moreover, as pointed out by Cheshire
et al. (2014a), Clarke *et al.* (2014) and Evans and Hartwich (2007), rather
small areas of UK greenbelt land immediately surrounding our existing cities
or existing infrastructure would be perfectly sufficient to make a significant
difference to overall UK house prices and to greatly increase home-ownership
especially amongst lower income groups. Indeed, the London greenbelt
alone could sustain the building of 1.6 million homes at average densities.[113]
Moreover, encroachment on the greenbelt does not imply either ribbon or
haphazard development, with garden city-type designs being an obvious
option (DCLG 2014a). Moreover, the reduction of planning restrictions also
needs to be accompanied by various other legal and taxation reforms which
following the Henry George theorem would include some sort of land taxation system,[114] and many different options have been proposed (Pennington
2002; Corkindale 2004; Evans and Hartwich 2006) on the basis of observations which have been shown to be workable in other countries (Evans and
Hartwich 2005b, 2007).

In marked contrast to these arguments, however, there are other views, which
argue that increased housing should be concentrated in existing urban areas
rather than on greenbelt land. Proponents of these views include high-profile
bodies analysing urban issues (Urban Task Force 1999) as well as institutions
marshalling public support against development encroaching on the greenbelts (CPRE 2009, 2010a, 2010b, 2011, 2014) and instead campaign for future
development to be almost entirely focused on current urban 'brownfield' sites
and in town centres. These latter brownfield-development arguments tend to
be dominated by architectural, cultural-aesthetic and more traditional planning approaches to development, rather than on the basis of economic and
welfare arguments which tend to dominate the former greenbelt-development

arguments.[115] These approaches tend to see urban housing and development problems as being largely a matter of good city design and good city form (Lynch 1981), largely eschewing any real role for markets.[116] At the same time, however, there is compelling evidence that the aesthetic arguments on which many brownfield approaches are based, and which tend to centre on the building of flats and apartments, are not in line with the housing preferences of the vast majority of UK residents (Evans and Hartwich 2005a), and as such reflect the design preferences of architectural elites rather than the preferences of UK residents and households.[117]

These brownfield arguments also enter into wider debates about the relationship between the location of different types of activities including residential housing, commercial activities (Barkham *et al.* 2014), and changing retail markets (Grosvenor 2002) which threaten the viability of the 'high street' (Portas 2011; DCLG 2012a; Wrigley and Lambiri 2014, 2015; Wrigley and Brookes 2014; Cheshire *et al.* 2014b). Indeed, the brownfield-development proponents raise many important issues regarding the day-to-day social, cultural and heritage functioning of cities, neighbourhoods and communities and how such compact city types of ideas (OECD 2012a) can help to shape and improve citizens' quality of life.[118] In the case of town centres many high street retail markets are becoming increasingly vulnerable,[119] although the evidence also shows that there is a strong north–south dimension to these discussions with southern towns generally faring much better than northern towns (Wrigley and Lambiri 2014). In particular, town centres and high streets in smaller northern and midlands towns are especially vulnerable, displaying a poor quality mix of services (RSPH 2015)[120] and losing shops at a relatively more rapid and increasing rate due to weak local demand conditions[121] whereas high streets in small towns in southern England tend to be relatively more buoyant, prosperous and offering higher quality services (Wrigley and Lambiri 2014). Obviously, there are also variations within regions reflecting the fact that towns and cities differ greatly, but it is the interregional differences rather than intra-regional differences which are generally the most marked.

The counter-argument against the brownfield types of approaches begins from the fact that if a piece of land is listed as 'brownfield' it often means either the market sees no value in it at the current price (including a price of zero) or in the conditions and that there is an intra-urban or interregional spatial mismatch between demand and supply for land. As such, unless local real estate demand is very strong and the brownfield land can be rehabilitated into the market simply by means of an existing use re-designation,[122] almost invariably public subsidies will be required in order to make the brownfield land attractive for investors and developers. Moreover, given the spatial demand mismatches as well as the reclamation and rehabilitation issues, it is argued that only a small share of the required housing can be provided by building on brownfield land (Evans and Hartwich 2005a). As Cheshire *et al.* (2012) point out this is because a hectare of available brownfield land in Bradford is not a substitute for a hectare of development land required in Cambridge, and the reason is that many firms looking for locations do not treat these as possible substitutes and therefore neither do real estate investors. As such, this implies that some of the arguments used by proponents of brownfield development which are based on calculating the total UK-wide area of brownfield sites relative to the total UK-wide demand for housing (CPRE 2014) are of limited value as they ignore the inherent spatial demand and supply mismatches.[123] Either way, there will be real financial and social costs and also significant wealth distributional effects involved in rehabilitating or upgrading the brownfield land as part of these compact city types of approaches (Barkham *et al.* 2014; Cheshire *et al.* 2014b) which can only provide a very partial solution to the overall problem of wealth-related social costs. This raises the question of the extent to which society will or should tolerate such costs and wealth effects.

In terms of systematically and continually prioritising urban brownfield development over greenfield development so as to preserve the 'natural' environment, it is very difficult to argue today that significant tracts of greenbelt land in the immediate vicinity of the urban fringe are generally of such high cultural and heritage value as to be of national and international importance and therefore to be protected at all costs. Today, even though some two-thirds of greenbelt land is agricultural land, not surprisingly, greenbelt land has a lower concentration of Areas of Outstanding National Beauty, agricultural land, open access land and nature reserves of national importance, than land which is outside of the greenbelts. While tourists may flock to the Lake District, the Cotswolds or the Peak District, few national or international tourists take their holidays visiting the greenbelt land in the immediate vicinity of Croydon, Hillingdon, Wolverhampton or Oldham. Indeed, almost nowhere in the UK is 'natural' with almost all rural environments as well as urban environments being the product of millennia of human intention and design (Pryor 2010).

Even allowing for many cultural, aesthetic and heritage arguments, in economic and welfare terms, the arguments of Evans (1991a, 1991b, 1996, 2004a, 2004b), Whitehead (1991), Meen (1996), Barker (2004, 2008, 2014), Evans and Hartwich (2005a, 2005b, 2006, 2007), Meen and Andrew (2008), Cheshire (2008), Cheshire *et al.* (2014a, 2014b), the unintended price and costs impacts of planning are fundamentally correct both theoretically and empirically. Moreover, the scale of the current UK housing problem now means that the originally enlightened and socially progressive greenbelt policy has become a deeply anti-progressive phenomenon.[124] Young people in particular are increasingly locked out of the home-ownership possibilities (Willets 2010). The proportion of 25–34 year olds renting has more than doubled since 2003 and the proportion owning their own homes is now only just over 60 per cent of what it was in 2013.[125] Unless ways can be found to make urban brownfield development systematically attractive to investors, and no such way has been found without significant public subsidies, then these changing realities over six decades would suggest that it ought to be in the UK national economic and welfare interest to find ways to reduce the greenbelt planning constraints so as to allow for the lowering of land use costs and housing prices on the urban fringes. Notwithstanding the current supply constraints in the construction industry,[126] the current scale and urgency of these issues and the need to spread opportunities for accessing the wealth accumulation amongst younger and lower income groups (Willets 2010) ought to trump many of the local greenbelt heritage-amenity interests.[127]

Yet while the arguments of Evans (1991a, 1991b, 1996, 2004a, 2004b), Whitehead (1991), Meen (1996), Barker (2004, 2008, 2014), Evans and Hartwich (2005a, 2005b, 2006, 2007), Meen and Andrew (2008), Cheshire (2008), Cheshire *et al.* (2014a, 2014b) regarding the house price and wealth distortion effects of the overly restrictive UK land supply constraints are basically correct, a more difficult problem is how to bring about such a change. Urban, regional and real estate economic models of a theoretical nature are very good at handling comparative statics or small dynamic changes but they are largely incapable of handling large and rapid structural changes such as the intra- and interregional effects of the 2008 financial crisis, or of fundamental and underlying changes, such as widespread changes to the UK land use planning system. The problem here is that such changes are not comparatively static or even dynamic in nature, but rather are inherently institutional problems related to perceptions, unaligned incentives and conflicting wealth interests. These types of institutional and incentive problems exist in many areas of the economy such as in health care and education. However, they are notoriously complex in the case of real estate markets. Following what are known as 'user costs of capital' arguments (Meen 2001), the reason for this is that land and housing not only display the characteristics of consumption goods or services but they also simultaneously display a unique array of asset characteristics. Many areas with strong demand which are primarily in southern and eastern England plus parts of eastern Scotland also display high amenity-related quality of life characteristics even when controlling for these user costs of capital type arguments (Gibbons *et al.* 2011), and if these amenities in part are protected and internalised by the land use planning system then the local resistance to institutional change will be significant. These problems are very difficult to respond to by policy changes because the interaction of land markets and the land use planning system generates a whole series of wealth-related and amenity-consumption-related incentive problems which are primarily local in nature but also display both interregional and national manifestations. These wealth-related problems are typically of an 'insider–outsider' form (Lindbeck and Snower 2001) and the key distinction here relates to household housing tenures. 'Insiders' are home-owners and 'outsiders' are renters and in this context the wealth-related incentives and interests associated with home ownership lead to conflicting interests between both individuals and also groups and these typically lead to deep and conflicting political and political economy implications (Castro Coelho *et al.* 2014).

In the UK today, housing is the most direct means of wealth accumulation and not surprisingly housing currently accounts for the vast majority of UK household wealth (*The Economist* 2015b; Kumar *et al.* 2014). Interests and incentives imply that individuals and local communities will act so as to preserve their wealth and wealth accumulation possibilities and this is more relevant and widespread in the case of housing than almost any other area of the economy. Therefore any reforms or changes to the current land use planning system which change the balance of wealth accumulation possibilities related to housing will face enormous resistance at many different levels, irrespective of the merits of the wider economic and welfare arguments for reform. Such resistance will take the form of individual or community-related actions and will tend to use a mixture of both legal and political measures. If development control is decided locally, then the outcomes of local politics will tend to be heavily influenced by the nature, form and strength of any such opposition.

Any reform to the UK land use planning system which is aimed at increasing land supply and reducing land prices in specific areas will immediately be at odds with the interests of recent house buyers in the same local area. In particular, the potential for lower local house prices will most directly and severely threaten the interests of recent first-time buyers who will immediately be in jeopardy of their recent housing-asset purchase entering into negative equity. Long-standing local housing owners with substantial equity who have also recently remortgaged for consumption or commercial reasons will also be the group which is the second most threatened by any rise in the local housing supply and associated falls in local home-ownership costs. Only long-standing local home owners with substantial housing equity or recent in-migrants to the local area who bring substantial wealth with them, will be largely insured against the adverse effects of local house price falls. Indeed, increasing local housing supply may actually provide new buy-to-let house purchase opportunities for these latter groups, so rather than being a threat, increased local housing supply may provide further wealth generating opportunities.

As well as these differing opposition incentives to increasing local land supply which are driven by housing wealth-related issues there are also differing amenity-consumption effects on incentives. Many home-owners who already have very significant housing equity may be relatively less concerned about their long-term equity positions but rather may be more concerned about their immediate amenity consumption possibilities. In these cases high-wealth individuals often display preferences in which their preference ordering ranks amenity-consumption issues more highly than wealth-related issues. If such home owners perceive that the quality of their immediate environment is likely to be adversely affected by increased local land supply, increased local housing and further local development, then of course they have an incentive to oppose it. These issues tend to be particularly apparent on the urban fringes of the greenbelt, where following a textbook urban economic model (McCann 2013), the housing will tend to be dominated by higher income groups trading off improved environmental consumption over increased journey times.

These high-income groups will also tend to be particularly well-positioned to use political power in order to influence local political decisions in their favour. Land law has 70 years of intense interaction and engagement with the land use planning system and over time has built up numerous precedents which limit the ability of government authorities to alter the land use trajectory. In contrast, if development is perceived by local residents to potentially upgrade the quality of a local area's environment, then local property owners will tend to support it both for reasons of both amenity-consumption and also equity-generation if local housing prices are expected to rise. This is one of the reasons why urban 'brownfield' redevelopment schemes in low-income urban neigbourhoods often receive relatively strong local backing, or at least much lighter resistance than development schemes on greenbelt land. Where opposition in such cases does exist, it tends to be on the part of residents who are long-term local renters who fear either an appreciation in their rental costs of living or the disappearance of their homes in the redevelopment schemes. Yet, as a general rule these groups tend to be lower income groups with generally rather limited political or institutional influence. These patterns are also exacerbated by national political considerations. Political parties on the centre-right have little incentive to campaign for development in greenbelt and higher income areas in that such activities tend to risk upsetting their own natural constituents. Meanwhile centre-left parties tend to favour brownfield development as it offers the possibility of upgrading the local environment of weaker inner city neighbourhoods, many of which reflect their own constituencies. As such across the political spectrum there are incentives to favour brownfield development.

The point about these observations is that both the wealth-related and amenity-related incentives against increased local land supply and greater local housing provision as well as the political incentives tend to give rise to very large implicit coalitions of both higher and lower income people whose incentives are largely aligned with each other favouring brownfield development and against greenfield development. Diverse groupings of individuals and implicit coalitions acting in their own interests collectively act against the national interest. The key distinction here is between those who are already home-owners – the 'insiders' – and those who are not – the 'outsiders' and insider–outsider arguments (Lindbeck and Snower 2001) are central to understanding many of the most important aspects of UK regional and urban phenomena. In the case of housing, the people who are the home-owner insiders will tend to be those on higher incomes and those who are older, while outsiders who rent will generally be those on lower incomes and younger people. In addition, there is also a group of outsiders who for temporary rather than long-term reasons wish to enjoy the locational flexibility afforded by renting. Often these are young and highly skilled people or those embarking on a career move which may involve job switching or employment-related migration. In the short term renting suits these people but in line with their aspirations in the long term many of this group eventually become insiders. What insider–outsider models predict is that those who are home owners and whose wealth-acquisition possibilities are related primarily to housing will use all political and legal means in order to act against the (supply increase and price reduction) interests of those who are not home owners, irrespective of their individual incomes or political perceptions. This rather perverse alignment of incentives even encourages local authorities in supply-constricted localities to sell off the existing green spaces for profit (Nathan and Overman 2011a).

What this demonstrates is that the ability or willingness of policy-makers to reduce local housing constraints and house prices via extensions of the land which is made available for development is limited because such policies often lead to complex and confrontational processes. Local housing demand is related to both national demographic changes, migration and also local economic conditions. However, housing supply is largely seen as a local, rather than a national issue, and although there appears to have been some softening in attitudes towards increased local house-building with those favouring it in England having risen from 28 per cent in 2010 to 56 per cent in 2015, the ability of national government to fundamentally alter the UK housing trajectory is open to question because of local political economy considerations[128] as well parliamentary opposition.[129] In this polarised political economy environment characterised by a lack of alignment of institutional views and people's interests and ambiguities regarding what 'sustainable development' means (Nathan and Overman 2011b), local politicians therefore have little incentive to oppose the preferences of the majority of local residents.[130] Moreover, the fact that the incentives against greenbelt development also often involve groupings of households which span a wide range of income groups and political preferences, means that the local political centre ground tends to be dominated by such groupings. Moreover, if we consider the possibilities for regional rather than local institutional changes to overcome supply restrictions, then from insider–outsider arguments it is also clear that there are no real options for achieving this. Politicians and numerous interested parties in the non-core more northern regions of the UK have little or no incentives to argue for greatly reduced land supply restrictions in the south of England, as long as there are concerns that the reductions of such southern land supply restrictions would encourage greater out-migration and lead to something of a 'hollowing out' of these more northern regions.[131]

Even though home-ownership in the UK has recently fallen by some five percentage points from its peak of close to 70 per cent at the turn of the millennium (ONS 2013a),[132] as long as the majority of society are home owners, as they currently are, then this situation whereby little or no major changes are made to greenbelt planning constraints, will continue for the foreseeable future. The insider–outsider problem is an example of what is known in methodological literature as a 'wicked problem', namely a problem which cannot be analysed, nor fully understood, nor solved, by means of one specific model or analytical framework, and policy attempts to alleviate or respond to such problems can only ever be partial or gradual at best (Edwards 2015).[133] Many social issues involving property rights, individual rights and group rights related to institutional settings represent classic 'wicked problems', including climate change mitigation, gun control in the USA, land rights and inequality in Latin America, and the political economy of the capital city versus the rest of the country in Thailand. The UK land market interactions with the planning system are also a clear example of a 'wicked problem'. As such, in reality, the ability of UK national government to reduce the restrictiveness of the land use planning system by partially dismantling the greenbelt is in reality extremely limited, even though the underlying economic argument is almost entirely correct. The insider–outside nature problems mean that the combined legal and political costs involved in attempts at deregulating land use in buoyant areas of the South East of England are extremely high, and any arguments which suggest that the costs of doing this are relatively small in reality ignore most of the most significant costs. This is not just an economic argument, but rather it is a broader political economy argument, as is the case with most institutional and governance issues. These opposition and confrontation realities also mean that UK house prices are likely to remain far higher than they ought to be and fewer young and lower income people will be able to afford to buy houses than should be the case, given the fact that more than 92 per cent of UK land is rural land (Evans and Hartwich 2005b), the majority of which is relatively of low productivity in comparison to urban land. The UK is becoming an environment in which housing-related wealth is increasingly favouring older-age groups at the expense of younger-age groups,[134] and without fundamental and sweeping reforms for land use policies, this situation will continue.

This is not to say that planning policy settings have not been altered. There have been some recent planning policy reforms (DCLG 2012b, 2012c; TCPA 2010a) which aim to overhaul the planning systems in England and Wales so as to provide a more strategic national approach (TCPA 2010b, 2010c) and to speed up development process (DGLG 2012d, 2012e) as well as delivering more socially and environmentally sustainable development (TCPA 2010c). These reforms in essence aim both to shift the local planning policy default position from being anti-development centre to pro-development (Heywood 2014) and also to foster greater levels of engagement of local actors and communities in these development decisions. Yet, although the years following the 2008 economic crisis saw a sharp fall in both house building (DCLG 2014b) as well as real estate development in general, it is unlikely that these reforms will have any long-lasting effects even as the UK economy emerges from the post-crisis years, in the sense of sufficiently altering the overall UK land use planning context so as to bring about significantly lower house prices. There are two major reasons for this contention.

First, the local incentive and institutional issues discussed above still remain in place (CPRE 2010b) and the policy reforms do little to address these issues. Moreover, to the extent that prime UK agricultural land achieves high investment returns (Savills 2012; *The Economist* 2015c) the financial-institutional pressures to encroach on the greenbelt will remain limited.

Second, national monetary authorities are likely to be very cautious regarding major deregulations to development control. The experience of the 2008 global economic crisis, which originated in real estate and housing markets and then spread into the 'real' economy, underscored our lack of understanding of the transmission mechanisms between the real estate and financial markets and the wider economy. Furthermore, the post-2008 experience of countries with limited land use restrictions and wide-ranging local discretion in terms of land supply, such as Ireland, Spain, Greece and Mexico, is that they now have enormous real estate debt overhangs and widespread negative equity-related housing loans. In these countries a relaxed approach to land use planning policies may have been beneficial in times of boom but has clearly been problematic in times of bust. As such, national monetary authorities in countries such as the UK are now well aware of their current lack of understanding regarding the nature of the interrelationships between real estate markets, finance and the macro economy (Miles 2004; Haldane 2013; Benford and Burrows 2013; Bank of England 2014; Ellis and Naughtin 2010; IPF 2014) and in this context are also likely to be very reticent or reluctant about policy changes favouring rapid or widespread land use deregulation. This reluctance is also likely to be bolstered if the changes in expectations brought by any such widespread deregulations could potentially be associated with surges in development finance along with complex, little-understood and nationwide price, wealth and incomes effects (Duranton and Monastiriotis 2002).

Taken together these two insights suggest that we are unlikely to witness major changes in the physical land coverage or urban areas area or the spatial morphology of UK cities in the coming years and that greenbelt and restrictive land use planning regimes are likely to remain largely in place for the foreseeable future, irrespective of the intellectual quality and rigour of the economic and welfare arguments of Evans, Whitehead, Meen, Cheshire, Barker and the like. However, in terms of the wider issues discussed in this book regarding the UK regional economic problem there are therefore three key insights which are particularly pertinent here.

First, it is really only since the early 1990s as the UK was rapidly becoming more interregionally unequal that the unintended and adverse cost impacts of the land use planning system started to become increasingly apparent. In particular, the academic and public awareness of these housing issues only really emerged as the economies of London and the South East surged and housing costs in London became increasingly unaffordable for many local residents. That this is the case is also demonstrated by the fact that as we have already seen, not only did UK academics start to comment on these problems only from the early 1990s onwards, but also that this greater awareness only started to filter into wider public debates around the time of the millennium as interregional inequalities (Urban Task Force 1999; Barker 2004).

Second, these debates (Urban Task Force 1999; Barker 2004, 2014) are dominated by the experience of London and the South East, with much less recourse to the issues and challenges faced by other UK cities and regions which tend to centre much more on weak rather than strong local real estate demand. This is also the case with discussions about housing affordability in rural areas (Best and Shucksmith 2006; DEFRA 2006; Satsangi *et al.* 2010; RHPR 2015) where the vast majority of the 62 areas[135] where house prices are less affordable when compared with local wages than London are in the South East and South West regions (NHF 2014). By mid-2015 average house prices in London had reached £370,000,[136] current sales were averaging over £600,000 per deal and average monthly rents had exceeded £900,[137] and during recent years London house prices have been increasing annually by more than the UK average wage, such that London houses typically 'earn' more than their owners.[138] However, these housing wealth acquisition effects also give credence to wider public perceptions that a London-based elite are benefiting inordinately from market trends while others struggle with rising costs of living.[139] Indeed, these housing cost issues are now very much in the public domain, but people's perceptions, incentives and actions regarding these issues are heavily shaped by their specific tenure status and location within the housing market. As such, although the general awareness of these land price-planning issues has emerged as a result of the increasing interregional UK inequalities driven by the surging London and South East economies, it is still the case that our knowledge of exactly how these land use and planning issues actually relate to the wider long-run UK interregional inequalities is as yet rather limited.

Third, we know that UK interregional price and costs transmission mechanisms in real estate markets tend to display a strong core-periphery patterns House price cycles tend to originate first in London and the South East and then spread to more geographically peripheral regions with a time lag (Meen 1996; 2001; CLC 2004; Deutsche Bank 2014), although both the correlation and responsiveness of regional house price movements with London fall with distance (Deutsche Bank 2014). Although house prices in London and the South East along with many other parts of southern and eastern England are high, it is not possible to conclude that house prices in other UK regions are too high due to a London effect (CLC 2004). However, the generally weaker economic demand in the more peripheral regions means that outside of southern England the levels of housing equity (Smith Institute 2013) tend to be much less than in London and the South East, as are the affordability constraints for new first-time buyers (Deutsche Bank 2014). Indeed, the house price transmission mechanisms between London, the South East and the rest of the UK are little understood and it is not possible to say whether London house prices are 'too high' or not, given the supply and demand conditions (CLC 2004). On the other hand short-term house price volatility tends to be higher in London and the South East (Hilber and Vermeulen 2012) due to supply constraints although in the long run house prices also appear to be less volatile and more resilient in London and the South East (Deutsche Bank 2014) than in other UK regions. Indeed, London and the southern and eastern English regions display such different housing market features from the rest of the UK that it becomes difficult in the UK case actually to talk about aspects of the 'national' housing market (Deutsche Bank 2014). In reality there are two (Smith Institute 2013) or possibly even three broadly different housing markets in the UK (Deutsche Bank 2014). Housing demand in London and the South East is today being driven primarily by the effects of globalisation, and in particular both by overseas investors and population immigration (Deutsche Bank 2014) as well as internal UK migration. The London housing market alone is becoming increasingly isolated from the rest of the UK (Deutsche Bank 2014) while at the same time having a disproportionate effect on the valuations of the UK housing market. In terms of scale the Greater London housing market accounts for 15 per cent of the UK housing stock, but on the basis of value it accounts for almost 30 per cent of the UK market, even though the population and output shares are only 12.8 per cent and 22.3 per cent, respectively.[140] As such, the overall 'national' housing picture and the interactions between monetary policy and housing asset markets (Deutsche Bank 2014) are heavily shaped by the behaviour of the London market plus to a lesser extent the housing market of the South East, even though in reality they are regional rather than national markets.[141]

This core-periphery structure is also reflected in real estate investment markets. Returns in UK commercial real estate investments are robust (*The Economist* 2015d) and if we adopt London as the benchmark reference point, it is clear that UK regional inequalities cannot be due to inefficient financial and investment markets. We see that the pattern and variations in UK real estate rents for offices, retail and industrial spaces (CBRE 2014a, 2014b) are not inconsistent with the pattern and variations in UK interregional and inter-urban productivity performance, as described in Chapters 2 and 3, except for the additional risk premia associated with investments. UK real estate financial allocations as displayed by the yields in the UK office, retail and industrial sectors across UK cities and regions (CBRE 2014c), tend to rise as the distance from London increases although in general they only differ slightly across most of the UK cities and regions (CBRE 2014c), except for the cases of London and the South East and also to a lesser extent the East, which systematically all display lower yields across all classes of real estate. As such, real estate financial investors tend to view the UK as comprising two broadly separate investment markets, with London and the South East plus to a lesser extent the East as comprising one broadly safer market, and the rest of the UK comprising a second broadly more risky market. Moreover, these general points regarding the overall efficiency of UK commercial property markets are not contradicted by the observation that the interregional range of UK house prices,[142] is rather greater than the UK interregional productivity variations, because over and above the expected price ranges (Evans 1995), in UK-wide terms housing in London and its immediate environs represents largely risk-free prime core investments with extremely low yields.[143] Obviously, these yields may rise or prices may fall somewhat if planning policy changes allowed for widespread housing development on greenbelt land surrounding London and in other South East urban areas. However, as argued here, such changes are very unlikely to be sufficiently widespread to fundamentally alter the high UK housing and land prices, and especially those pertaining in the southern regions of England (Leunig and Overman 2008). Moreover, prime real estate in global cities is regarded as being the least overvalued asset class in the long run, so there is no reason to expect central London real estate prices to fall or for yields on these properties to increase.[144]

On the other hand, meanwhile, the various arguments outlined here suggest that land supply restrictions in reality explain little about the observed productivity fortunes of the UK's more geographically peripheral cities or the reasons why UK interregional inequalities are now so high. Indeed, the weaker performance of many of the UK's non-core cities and regions does not appear to be primarily or even particularly related to supply restrictions. Moreover, not only do such land supply explanations offer fewer insights into inequalities than other demand-related and structural explanations, but that more biting planning restrictions in southern cities may actually limit these interregional inequalities, especially if migration-growth effects exhibit cumulative features (Fingleton 2008; Overman *et al.* 2010), as discussed below. At the same time, the strength and resurgence and resilience of the London and South East economy also casts some doubt on the arguments that land use planning heavily limits local productivity growth (Roger Tym and Partners 2002a, 2002b, 2003), particularly if agglomeration effects are in some way related to density. Moreover, the role played by planning in terms of both correcting for negative externalities and enhancing positive externalities (Ahlfeldt *et al.* 2012; Gibbons *et al.* 2014a) tends to be overshadowed by the debates regarding the adverse effects of planning (Roger Tym and Partners 2002a, 2002b, 2003).

Further evidence casting doubt on any land supply-related explanations of UK interregional inequalities also emerges from international comparisons. For example, many other countries such as The Netherlands, Switzerland, Austria, Germany, Sweden, Denmark, Japan, Korea and Belgium all operate tight land use planning systems and therefore many of the arguments in favour of reducing UK planning restrictions should be largely just as applicable in these countries as in the UK. Yet, in none of these other countries do the interregional inequality questions arise to nearly the same extent as in the UK, except for possibly Korea and Belgium. This observation therefore casts doubt on the possible link between interregional inequalities and the operation of restrictive planning systems.

The lack of any systematic relationship between restrictive planning systems and interregional inequalities can also be examined by comparing the UK with The Netherlands. The proportion of UK land which is 'urban' – including roads and urban development in rural areas, is 6.8 per cent with 93.2 per cent of the UK being rural land, comprising agriculture, woodland and recreational and natural environment land (UKNEA 2011).[145] Some 71 per cent of the total UK land area is arable land (DEFRA *et al.* 2014; UKNEA 2011). Meanwhile, at 12.7 per cent of the total UK area woodland (ONS 2012a) alone accounts for almost double the total space occupied by towns and cities although it accounts for almost zero per cent of the UK population, while the 6.8 per cent of land which is urban accounts for some 80 per cent of the total UK population.[146] Moreover, not all 'urban' land is actually built on, in the sense that it is 'concreted over' to provide housing, industrial spaces, offices, car parks, public facilities and buildings, roads and transportation facilities. In England only 21.4 per cent of urban land is actually built on, with 54 per cent of urban land being in the form of gardens, parks, allotments and sports pitches,[147] 6.6 per cent in the form of canals, lakes and reservoirs, and 18 per cent in the form of domestic gardens.[148] In other words, the total area of UK land which is actually built on, in the sense of actually being 'concreted over', is only a tiny 2.2 per cent.[149]

The vast majority of the UK population are squashed into relatively tiny but densely populated large urban areas. This high and dense urban concentration of population is also manifested in the fact that those who are not squashed into urban areas enjoy extremely low density rural living. Today, as we have also seen in Chapter 2, in 2011 some 20 per cent of the English population (UKNEA 2011), or 10.6 million people, live in rural areas of whom 6.7 per cent, or over 3.5 million, lived in hamlets of fewer than 500 people, and another 3.5 million lived in villages of between 500 and 2500 people (OECD 2011a). In other words, just in England, over 7 million people live in villages of fewer than 2500 people (OECD 2011a). The final third of the rural population live in settlements of between 2500 and 30,000 people (OECD 2011a). The 7 million people in England living in hamlets and villages of no more than 2500 people is equivalent to 85 per cent of the total combined population of the eight English core cities[150] or three-quarters of the total combined population of these cities and their commuting[151] hinterlands.[152] Moreover, only a fraction of these residences are related to agriculture. Some 464,000 people are employed in UK agriculture including farmers, spouses and employed farm managers and workers (DEFRA *et al.* 2014). Given the Type-II employment multipliers for agriculture are of the order of 1.7 (Scottish Government 2014) this implies that the number of people resident in English hamlets and small villages is almost ten times what would be expected on a rural employment basis, and if we include all small towns across rural England this figures rises to something of the order of 16 times larger than what would be expected on the basis of required rural employment demand. In other words, the motives for rural dwelling for 90 per cent and 95 per cent of English rural dwellers in England are primarily related to amenities and environment and largely unrelated to local employment demands, and there are likely to be significant amenity-related house price effects (Gibbons *et al.* 2014a). These 20 per cent of the English population live in extremely low density environments, while some 80 per cent of the English population live in just 11 per cent of England's land area in squashed and densely populated surroundings. These types of figures also largely hold for the three devolved regions.[153] The observed price and wealth distortion effects on UK land use and housing which are engendered by these largely policy-induced spatial population distributions imply that the current UK population patterns are highly inefficient both economically and socially.[154] Indeed, just how restrictive and inefficient are these residency patterns can be understood by comparing the UK with other similar countries.

The Dutch and German land use planning systems are also restrictive in many ways and in some cases even more so than the UK land use planning system. For comparison purposes with these countries we will use the broad definition of 'urban', which in the UK accounts for 6.8 per cent of land. In The Netherlands, the proportion of Dutch land which is urban is 17 per cent,[155] leaving 83 per cent left as natural and rural spaces (Daams *et al.* 2014) while the equivalent proportion of urban land in Germany is 13.6 per cent, leaving 86.4 per cent as rural land.[156]

Comparing the UK with The Netherlands we see that the proportion of land which is urban in The Netherlands is almost 2.5 times the UK equivalent value, and twice as much in Germany. In the case of The Netherlands, the Dutch national population density on land[157] is 1.88 times that of the UK, so the urban land area per capita in The Netherlands is 1.33 times larger than that in the UK. In other words, the operation of the UK land use planning system means that UK residents inhabit parcels of urban land which on average are only 75 per cent of the size of those available for people living in The Netherlands. Moreover, given the fact also that at 74 per cent the shares of both the UK and the Dutch populations are living in functional urban areas of over 50,000 people are identical to each other (OECD 2013a), this means that these differences are not related either to urbanisation rates. As such, the more intensive use of urban land associated with the UK greenbelt policies also partly explains why urban land in the UK is more expensive than in The Netherlands, even though the Netherlands is a much more densely populated country and richer country than the UK.[158]

In the case of Germany, the proportion of land which is urban is exactly twice that of the UK. Given that the population density of the UK is 16.4 per cent higher than that of Germany this implies that the urban land area per resident of Germany is 2.32 times that of each UK resident. Although at 64 per cent the total share of the population living in functional urban areas in Germany is ten percentage points below the UK (OECD 2013a), again these differences cannot account for the differences in the urban land area per capita. These differences must be due to differences in the land use planning systems between the UK on the one hand and The Netherlands and Germany on the other hand. When comparing the UK with these two other cases we see that the UK urban land allocations per capita bear no relationship to the national population densities.

These urban land relationships also allow us to understand the levels of UK rural land prices in comparison to these other countries. In contrast to urban land prices, Dutch agricultural land is much more expensive than UK land, which in turn is slightly more expensive than German agricultural land (Savills 2014). Specifically, UK agricultural land prices are one-third of those prevailing in The Netherlands, the world's most productive agricultural land, and also are even one-third higher than those in Germany (Savills 2014), even though UK agriculture is less productive than German agriculture. Yet, these land price patterns make sense if we understand that the share of UK land which is used for agriculture is amongst the highest in the western and northern European countries (Evans and Hartwich 2005a). If we consider all non-urban land, the area of all rural land per capita in the UK is 1.66 times that in The Netherlands while in Germany the rural land area per capita is 1.25 times that of the UK. The observed land prices plus these urban and rural land ratios per capita therefore suggest that in the UK insufficient land is allocated to urban activities while too much land is preserved for rural activities.

In spatial terms the UK, along with The Netherlands, can be considered as being broadly monocentric, with London being the UK centre and also therefore the origin of the national (envelope) bid-rent curve (McCann 2013), while in The Netherlands Amsterdam would play this role. Given that London is now on some criteria[159] the most expensive city in the world (CBRE 2014a) the UK national bid-rent curve displays a very high origin but only declines relatively slowly for urban land, with very much lower prices for the intervening rural land. The overall result of the various UK urban and rural land allocations in comparison to these other countries means that UK urban land prices are too high and insufficient urban land is made available while rural land prices are too low as too much rural land is protected.

If we now consider the questions of interregional inequalities, we see that The Netherlands, which has identical levels of urbanisation to the UK, much higher population densities and not very dissimilar levels of urban land coverage per capita, still exhibits extremely low interregional productivity variations relative to the UK. Meanwhile, Germany has higher interregional inequalities than The Netherlands but ones which are still much lower than the UK, even though it has much lower aggregate urban population densities and indices of urbanisation than the UK. Both countries are richer in terms of GDP per capita than the UK. While the planning system may induce land price distortions, these various observations therefore suggest that the UK interregional productivity variations, which are amongst the highest in the group of rich EU and OECD countries, cannot therefore be primarily related to land supply restrictions. Instead, the high land and housing prices which are evident in the southern regions of England along with much of Edinburgh and parts of Cheshire, are largely a result of the UK interregional inequalities in demand, rather than land supply constraints per se. It is the former rather than the latter which is the dominant underlying mechanism. Of course, it may be the case that land supply restrictions have limited the ability of high human capital to move away from London and the South East to other areas, as was originally speculated by Duranton and Monastiriotis (2002). For example, if during the late 1980s and early 1990s highly skilled home owners working in the southern regions of England were increasingly reluctant to leave for employment elsewhere as they expected relatively greater capital gains from their local housing due to supply restrictions, then this may have inhibited high human capital labour outflows to other regions. Yet, there is simply no evidence of these effects operating, as reflected by the fact that interregional migration flows have changed so little between the 1990s and today. We could just as easily argue that in the 1980s and early 1990s the emerging house price differentials may have encouraged highly skilled individuals to remain in employment in their domicile regions rather than relocating to London, and this discouragement effect was beneficial for other regions. If these two effects were indeed operating, then the fact that interregional migration flows have changed so little over three decades suggests that they cancelled each other out. However, the available data provide us with no clues as to either the existence of, or the likely scale of, these mechanisms, other than pointing to the general fact that land supply restrictions and the ensuing land price distortions were primarily outcomes, and not causes of, the UK's growing interregional inequalities. The only other candidate for arguing that land supply restrictions have contributed to and exacerbated the UK's interregional inequalities relates to the interactions between house prices and firms start-up rates. There may well be some important effects here where house price distortions also engender further interregional distortions in the ability of entrepreneurs to access seed-funding. Again, however, these distortions are likely to be very much an outcome, rather than a cause of, the UK's interregional inequalities. As a whole, even allowing for these possible specific contributory mechanisms, all of the available evidence points to the conclusion that the high interregional differences in UK housing prices and their associated wealth distortion effects which are evident in certain regions, are primarily a symptom rather than a cause of UK interregional disparities.

If this is indeed the case, then a reform of the planning system of itself is likely to do little to reduce or solve the UK interregional inequalities, unless there are other mechanisms at play related to land use issues. For land supply restrictions to be part of the explanation for the UK's interregional inequalities, other reasons need to be sought. One possibility, as we will see shortly, is that in the long run the effects of land-based wealth distortions on access to credit and seed-funding capital will induce further regional distortions in entrepreneurship opportunities, thereby exacerbating existing inequalities. Another possibility, as we discuss now, is that the land use planning system has adversely impacted on the structure of the UK urban system in a manner which inhibits agglomeration economies, and that this problem is particularly acute outside of the southern regions of England. This is the issue to which we now turn our attention.

5.5.2   *The UK City-Size Distribution Constraint Argument*

Given that there is little evidence so far that restrictive planning policies per se are systematically linked to interregional inequalities, in terms of the issues which this book is primarily concerned with, there is another remaining set of potential arguments which may link high UK land prices and land use planning restrictions to the observed UK interregional inequalities, and as we will see below these are related to the Zipf's Law (Zipf 1949) type of arguments regarding city sizes. In the case of the UK a possible argument is that almost seven decades of restrictive land use planning policies have artificially constrained the growth of UK's large cities (Cheshire *et al.* 2014a) and as such many of our cities have failed to achieve their potential in terms of realising productivity-enhancing agglomeration effects (Crafts 2012). If this argument is correct, then this failure to grow would also be reflected in terms of lower productivity than would have been expected if the land use restrictions had not been in place.

In this line of enquiry one of the arguments which has been put forward is that the UK's second order cities are 'too small' and that land use planning constraints may have limited the growth of these cities and may have had a pernicious effect on their long-term productivity performance. In particular, these cities are viewed as being 'too small' relative to London. At the same time, others view London as being 'too large' relative to the rest of the UK's cities and regions and that London's size dominance is in some way problematic for the whole country.[160] Yet any discussion such as this suffers from the obvious problem that London's size relative to the other UK cities is simply the inverse of their size relative to London, so in some sense the question is not entirely answerable in objective terms. It depends on what our analytical benchmark or reference point is. As we will see immediately below Zipf's Law provides some sort of reference framework for discussing these issues. However, any analysis based on this framework, and in particular questions regarding the role played by the planning system in shaping UK city sizes, are only precursors to much deeper analytical questions, such as 'too small for what?' and 'too large for what?'. Are the UK's second tier cities too small to achieve sufficient agglomeration economies? Are the UK's second tier cities too small to achieve economies of scale in service provision? Are the UK's second tier cities too small to achieve sufficient political representation in central government? Are the UK's second tier cities too small to allow for the provision of environmentally efficient infrastructure and services? Conversely, is London too large to ensure a sufficiently diverse range and level of political representation in central government from across the UK? Is London too large to allow for the political concerns of other regions to be sufficiently well-represented in London-based public and media debates? Is

London so large that the social and economic issues facing London receive over-representation in the media and political debates? Is London too large to allow for the provision of environmentally efficient infrastructure and services? Is London relatively too large and are the UK's second tier cities relatively too small to allow the UK's urban system to best allow for national network externalities? Or even is London actually too small to fully realise the global city benefits afforded by globalisation (Coyle and Rosewell 2014), even though it is consistently ranked at the top or very close to the top of all global city connectivity rankings (Clark 2015). These issues are discussed in detail in the following chapter, so for the moment we will leave these questions aside and return to them in due course.

In terms of the city-size productivity arguments, as we have already seen above and also in Chapter 3, many of the textbook-type city-agglomeration-productivity arguments do not appear to hold in the UK, unless we also set these urban observations in the broader regional context. Moreover, cross-country comparisons throw some further doubts on mechanistic interpretations of these arguments without more discussion of the national and regional context. For example, the OECD metropolitan data discussed in Chapter 3 show us that there are seven cities in Europe which are richer than London and all of them are smaller than London. Similarly, if we take the case of Manchester, which is often hailed as something of a success story,[161] there are 30 urban areas across the rest of Europe plus 5 other urban areas within the UK all with populations in excess of 500,000, and which are smaller than Manchester but which also are richer than Manchester. If we also include the numerous small and medium-sized towns and cities across the Europe and the UK which are richer than Manchester (Ahrend *et al*. 2014; Overman and Gibbons 2011) then the numbers increase even further. These observations plus many of the observations outlined in Chapters 2, 3 and 4 suggest that city size is only one possible part of a much more complex story of the relationships between cities, scale and productivity. Regional and national issues relating to connectivity, networks, governance and institutional arrangements are also likely to play a critical role in shaping individual city productivity levels (McCann and Acs 2011; Iammarino and McCann 2013). However, notwithstanding these caveats we will proceed with discussing the question of the UK features of the city-size distributions using a Zipf's Law type of approach and this will also allow us to consider whether land use planning restrictions have historically acted as a break on the urban productivity of UK second tier cities by artificially distorting the size-related patterns of UK city growth.

The data generated by research using Zipf's Law types of approaches applied to many countries show that when we regress the natural logarithm of the rank order of the city against the natural logarithm of the population size of the city, the slope of the estimated function is typically quite close to a value of -1 (Rozenfeld *et al*. 2011), and that over many decades the city-size distributions of many countries tend to converge to these values as economic development progresses (Matlaba *et al.* 2014). As such, over many centuries of industrialisation and development we might expect the same to be true in the case of the UK. Yet, while these types of expected results do largely hold across all of the UK's smaller towns and settlements with populations of over 5000 people (Rozenfeld *et al.* 2011), rather strangely, the current data suggest that this Zipf's Law regularity does not apply in the case of most of the UK's large cities below the level of London. This may be due in part to land use planning policies. However, before we apply the Zipf's Law type of logic to the UK to assess the possible effects of land use policy on UK city sizes it is important to note that the Zipf's Law approach displays various well-known limitations (Overman and Rice 2008). First, Zipf's Law types of observations reflect a particular class of statistical power-law relationships which are commonly found in a wide range of natural and social phenomena (Robson 1973; Ball 2004). As such, in the case of cities as with any other phenomena conforming in some way to these types of patterns, the interpretation of such statistical regularities needs to be undertaken with care and allied with other evidence and complementary data. Indeed, even in the case of city sizes the observations of these statistical regularities had been analysed by at least five authors before George Zipf (1949) and the first of these preceded Zipf's analysis by some three and a half decades (Robson 1973). Their observations and subsequent analyses by many different authors also demonstrate that there is no correct way of interpreting these relationships (Cliff *et al.* 1975) in a geographical or behavioural setting (Haggett 1965; Robson 1973). As such, the approach we adopt to interpret these pattern regularities will be heavily shaped by our chosen theoretical framework. Our rank size rule arguments derive from central place theory (Batty 2005; McCann 2013) while our Zipf's Law arguments derive from empirical observations (Zipf 1949), yet the rank size 'rule' is not strictly a rule and Zipf's 'Law' is not strictly a law (Batty 2005; McCann 2013). The fact that these empirical regularities do not hold strictly, combined with the fact that there are only a relatively small number of economic papers which aim to provide a theoretical underpinnings of Zipf's Law (Duranton 2006, 2007; Fujita *et al.* 1999; Gabaix 1999a, 1999b; Rozenfeld *et al.* 2011),[162] means that using Zipf's Law and rank-size rule type arguments as a basis for thinking about UK city and regional policies is not at all straightforward. This is because, as just mentioned, they are neither rules nor laws, and second because our understanding of what rank-size and Zipf's Law type distributions imply for the real world and policy is still very limited. While Zipf's Law patterns often capture well the size distribution of numerous small towns and cities these types of explanations tend to be much weaker in explaining the size of large cities, and especially the cases where the primal city is also the capital city (Krugman 1996; Gabaix 1999b). Zipf's Law cannot shed any real light on why the two largest cities in each of Australia, USA and Italy are almost the same size as each other, nor why the three largest cities in The Netherlands are almost the same size as each other, nor why the primal cities in Korea, Thailand, Ireland, Uruguay, are so large relative to the second tier cities in their own countries. Nor can Zipf's Law tell us whether the size of the city size relative to its national economy is possibly more relevant than the absolute city size. The fact that Zipf's Law is weak in explaining large cities (Cristelli *et al.* 2012; Batty 2015) means that an overly mechanistic recourse to such arguments tends to miss much of what determines a country's urban history and structure. Having acknowledged all of these important caveats, we are now able to return to the basic question as to whether UK second tier city sizes are 'too small' or whether London is 'too large' and whether the city-size patterns we observe are due to UK land use planning restrictions.

Following the logic employed by Overman and Rice (2008) and Cheshire *et al.* (2014a) the initial evidence for his possible line of argument arises from observations of the current UK city-size distribution. As we have already seen in Figure 3.2 and Figure 3.9 of Chapter 3, many of the UK's second tier cities below London do not follow the type of a city-size distribution that might have been expected on the basis of Zipf's Law. In particular, they are generally 'too small' relative to Zipf's Law patterns and for this reason are likely to fail to achieve their agglomeration potential (Crafts 2012). Indeed, on face value, the evidence from Figure 3.2 and Figure 3.9 suggests these arguments might be especially relevant to the dozen or so UK second tier cities, and in particular those which are geographically close to each other, such as those large cities located in the northern regions of England. According to Cheshire *et al.* (2014a) this possible failure to reach higher city population levels and also to achieve maximum agglomeration economies, is likely to be in part due to the UK's land use planning and greenbelt restrictions.

For ease of exposition we exactly reproduce Figure 3.2 and Figure 3.9 here as Figure 5.2 and Figure 5.3, respectively, and for comparability purposes we also include Figure 5.4 which plots the 2011 city-size distribution using the data reported by Champion (2014) which is based on the 2001 definition of primary urban areas (PUAs). As we already know from Chapter 3, Figures 5.2, 5.3 and 5.4 are constructed by plotting the natural logarithm of the rank of the city against the natural logarithm of the city population size. On the basis of Zipf's Law we would expect that the slope would have a value of -1. As we see in Figures 5.2–5.4, on the basis of Zipf's Law, the second tier cities of the UK appear to be 'too small' relative to the size of London (Cheshire *et al.* 2014a), or conversely that London is 'too large' relative to these second tier cities. Moreover, as we see here this conclusion holds irrespective of whether we employ the OECD Metropolitan Urban Area data set as in Figure 5.2, the Eurostat Metropolitan Urban Region data set as in Figure 5.3, or the Champion (2014) data set in Figure 5.4.

While these figures (Figure 5.2, 5.3 and 5.4), depicting the twenty-first-century UK city-size distributions do suggest that UK cities currently deviate significantly from what might be expected from Zipf's Law, these figures of themselves cannot explain why this is the case. Yet, if the greenbelt land use restrictions are indeed the root of the problem, then this would imply that such deviations from the expected distributions must fundamentally be

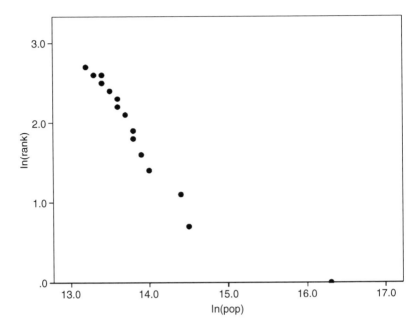

Figure 5.2 Zipf's Law for UK metropolitan urban areas in 2010
Source: OECD Metropolitan Urban Area Database.

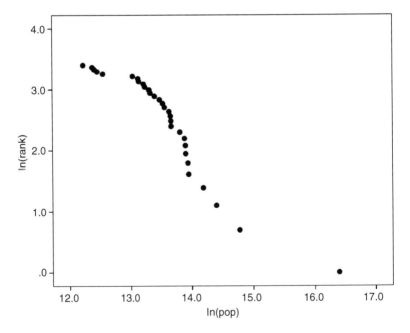

Figure 5.3 Zipf's Law and the UK metropolitan urban regions in 2010
Source: Eurostat Metropolitan Urban Region Database.

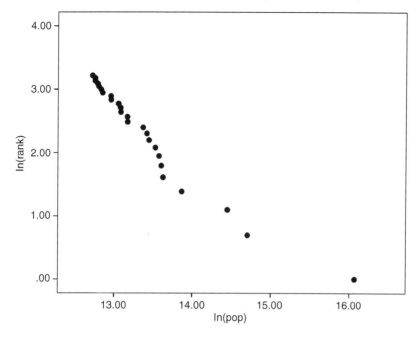

Figure 5.4 Zipf's Law and the UK urban areas in 2011
Source: Champion (2014).

post-war phenomena, given that the current planning system was initiated in 1947. In order to shed additional light on these issues we can plot similar city-size distributions for earlier time periods. Figures 5.5, Figure 5.6, Figure 5.7, Figure 5.8, Figure 5.9 and Figure 5.10 plot the UK[163] city-size distributions for the years 1851, 1900, 1925, 1950, 1981 and 2000, respectively.

One of the issues which becomes immediately apparent from observation of Figures 5.5–5.10 is that the UK city-size distributions have always been characterised by second tier cities which are 'too small' relative to London or where London is 'too big' relative to all of the second tier cities. The shape of this UK's city-size distribution which differed markedly from a Zipf's Law type of distribution remained remarkably constant between the middle of the nineteenth century and the late 1920s, and this pattern occurred during a period with almost no land use restrictions going back more than a century prior to the 1947 implementation of the UK land use planning system. At the same time, today's distribution also closely resembles the distribution which was evident in those days, and differs markedly from the distributions evident between 1950 and 1981 which more closely follow a Zipf's Law type of pattern. As such, the fact that the current UK city-size distribution today differ markedly from what might be expected on the basis of Zipf's Law is unlikely to be specifically related to the greenbelt and land use planning policies introduced in the post-war era, because for much of this planning era

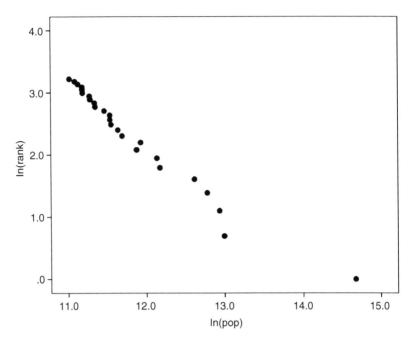

Figure 5.5 Zipf's Law and the UK city-size distribution in 1851
Source: Chandler (1987).

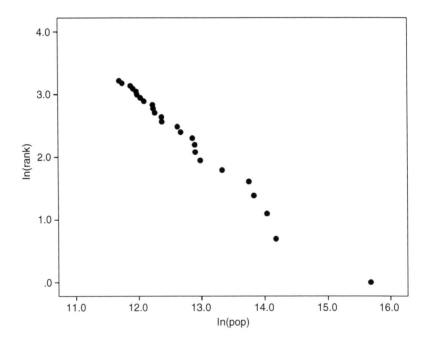

Figure 5.6 Zipf's Law and the UK city-size distribution in 1900
Source: Chandler (1987).

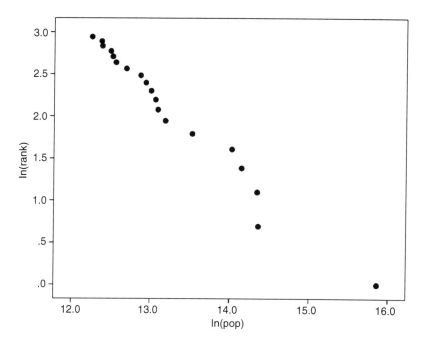

Figure 5.7 Zipf's Law and the UK city-size distribution in 1925
Source: Chandler (1987).

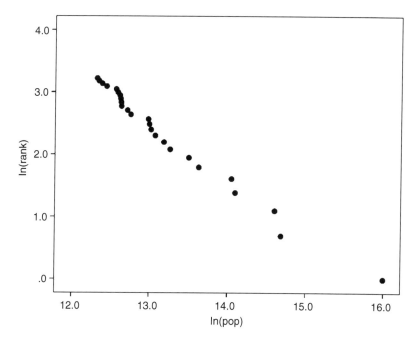

Figure 5.8 Zipf's Law and the UK city-size distribution in 1950
Source: Chandler (1987).

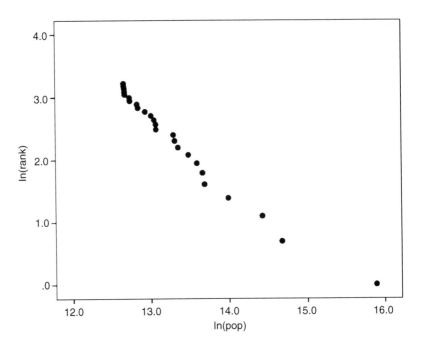

Figure 5.9 Zipf's Law and the UK city-size distribution in 1981
Source: Champion (2014).

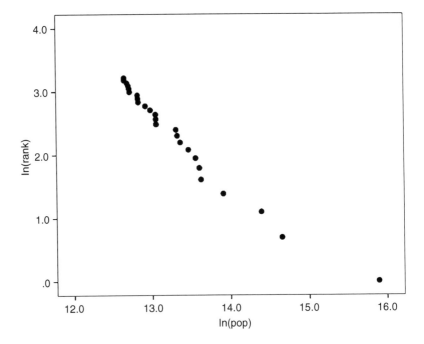

Figure 5.10 Zipf's Law and the UK city-size distribution in 1991
Source: Champion (2014).

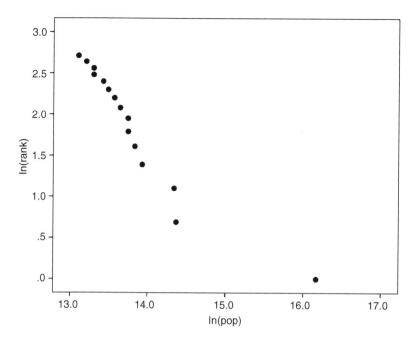

Figure 5.11 Zipf's Law and the UK city-size distribution in 2000
Source: OECD Metropolitan Urban Area database.

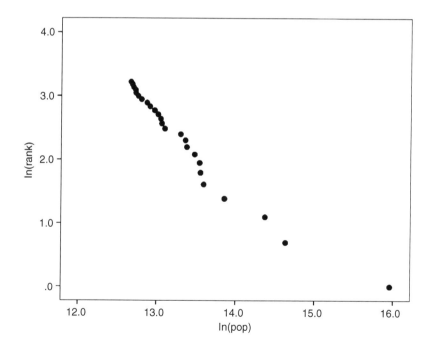

Figure 5.12 Zipf's Law and the UK city-size distribution in 2001
Source: Champion (2014).

it closely resembled Zipf's Law and only recently has reverted to its previous pattern. Nor by comparing Figure 5.11 with Figure 5.3 and Figure 5.12 with Figure 5.4 are the current patterns purely a post-millennium phenomenon. As such, the current UK city-size distribution cannot just be primarily the result of the recent immigration from eastern Europe following the 2004 removal of immigration restrictions to migrants from the new EU member states. Instead, the current UK city-size patterns appear to have much deeper and more long-standing historical roots.

London's primacy within Great Britain and the broad economic distinction between those areas settled by the Anglo-Saxon and those regions inhabited primarily by Celtic and Nordic peoples are long-standing (Pryor 2010). If we consider the geographical area which exactly defines the UK today across a span of seven centuries,[164] we see that in 1300 London was 1.8 times larger than the next largest city, Norwich. Between 1400 and 1500 this ratio remained between 2.25 and 2.5 with Edinburgh emerging as the second largest city above Norwich (Chandler 1987). During the sixteenth century this ratio started to increase markedly, reaching more than 5.3 by 1600. However, the enormous increase in the relative primacy of London commenced in the seventeenth century. By 1700 the population of London was almost 16 times the population of the next largest city, Edinburgh and some 19 times the size of the third largest city, Norwich. The relative sizes of London in each century are almost certainly a result of the fact that since the late Middle Ages England was one of the western world's two oldest and most highly centralised states, in which political factors were at least as significant as internal trade costs in determining the level of urban primacy (Ades and Glaeser 1995). A similar argument can be applied to France.

The relative primacy of London then slowly began to fall with the onset of the industrial revolution. In 1750 the population of London was 12.3 times the second largest city and by 1800 this ratio had fallen to 10.25, at which point Glasgow emerged as the UK's second largest city (Chandler 1987). By 1850 the ratio had fallen to 5.45 with Liverpool emerging as the UK's second largest city followed by Manchester, Glasgow and Birmingham and other newly industrialising cities (Chandler 1987). Between 1900 and 1925 the ratio of the size of the population of London over the next largest city was 4.5 times larger than the next largest city, with Manchester now being the UK's second city followed in size ordering by Birmingham, Glasgow, Liverpool, Newcastle, Leeds and Sheffield. By 1950 this ratio had fallen to 3.72, its lowest level since the late Middle Ages (Chandler 1987).

This slow downward shift in the ratio of the population of London relative to other UK cities continued for two centuries between the onset of the industrial revolution and the Second World War. Two centuries of UK industrialisation and globalisation led to the rise of many other large second tier cities which gradually reduced the relative primacy of London. The result was that between the early 1930s and the late 1970s the UK city-size distribution increasingly shifted towards what might be expected from Zipf's Law and this shift coincided with the five-decade-long narrowing of the interregional inequalities (Geary and Stark 2015). This five-decade period of interregional convergence processes from the early 1930s through to the late 1970s also very closely mirrored the narrowing of UK-wide income inequalities, with national income inequalities being at their historic lows in the late 1970s.[165] In the United States this phenomenon was known as the 'Great Compression' (Goldrin and Margo 1992) and was a result primarily of a combination of unionisation, minimum wage legislation and increased government intervention in various arenas of the economy which together re-shaped social norms (Krugman 2015e). In the UK this long-run process of income convergence and interregional convergence went into reverse during the last two decades of the twentieth century. There is some initial evidence of this in terms of slight changes in the 1991 UK city-size distribution, as depicted in Figure 5.10, but this becomes much clearer during the following decade. By 2000 at the turn of the millennium, as we see in Figure 5.11 and Figure 5.12, the ratio of the population of London relative to the UK's two second largest cities of Birmingham and Manchester whose populations are almost identical to each other, had again grown to some 6.1, and by 2010 after the increasing immigration into the UK in the years following the millennium as we see in Figure 5.2 this ratio had grown further to 6.3 (Chandler 1987), its highest level since the early 1800s. As of 2015 London had reached its highest population level ever, overtaking its peak population levels at the outbreak of the Second World War.[166]

These historical observations over seven centuries plus the detailed city-size distributions depicted in Figures 5.2–5.10 suggest that the growth of the UK's second tier cities over long historical periods has been driven by the enormous changes associated by industrialisation and globalisation, as the UK emerged during the eighteenth and nineteenth centuries as the leading global economy (Findlay and O'Rourke 2007; McCann and Acs 2011; Iammarino and McCann 2013). Industrialisation and the expansion of the UK canal and railway systems from the mid-eighteenth and mid-nineteenth centuries onwards, respectively, created the network conditions by which other towns and cities started to grow rapidly (Musson 1978; Lawless and Brown 1986). In geographical terms there was little or no real interregional convergence during the second half of the nineteenth century or the first two decades of the twentieth century, whereas between the early 1930s and the late 1970s interregional convergence was the dominant feature (Geary and Stark 2015). As such, the five-decade-long period of twentieth-century UK interregional convergence processes was also associated with a convergence more towards what might have been expected on the basis of Zipf's Law. It was only during the 1980s that widespread structural and labour market reform was introduced in the UK, although there was no discernible effect on either the UK city-size distribution or on UK interregional inequalities during this period. In part, this is likely to be due to the fact that very few large cities were growing during this period (Champion 2014). Subsequently, however, from the

1980s and 1990s onwards these long-running regional convergence processes all went into reverse, and at the upper end of the city-size distribution the UK city-size scatterplots also all moved away from a Zipf's Law type pattern. Moreover, the similarity evident in the patterns displayed in both Figure 5.2 with Figure 5.11 indicates that it was during the 1980s and 1990s that these city-size patterns really started to shift, rather than today's distribution being primarily the result of the post-2004 EU immigration from eastern Europe.

In reality, all of the UK city-size distributions evident at various points during the nineteenth, twentieth and early twenty-first centuries are successively superimposed on an inherited spatial structure of UK cities which for many centuries had been highly unequal and far from what might be expected on the basis of Zipf's Law. The city-size distributions prevailing in 2000, 2010 and 2011 are still remarkably similar to those prevailing in the period spanning 1851, 1990 and 1925, when Britain was at the height of its global imperial power and when there were little or no land planning restrictions. Meanwhile the distributions between 1950 and 1991 are so different from both the more recent and also earlier patterns. These observations all suggest that the particular structure and pattern of today's UK city-size distribution is related not only to the cumulative long-term hysteresis effects resulting from a range of possible historical influences, but also from the effects of modern globalisation. We can speculate that the influences shaping the historical UK city-size distributions are likely to be related to issues such as infrastructure, skills, technologies, trade-patterns, governance features, and also numerous decisions made by both private sector and public policy government makers. However, the particular impacts of modern globalisation and governance also appear to have played a major role. London was the financial and commercial centre of the world in the second half of the nineteenth century, and again, at the beginning of the twenty-first century in the era of modern globalisation, London has again become one of, if not the, pre-eminent 'global cities'.

Historically over the last four and a half centuries London has always been far 'too large' relative to the UK's second tier cities according to a simple interpretation of Zipf's Law. However, industrialisation slowly but steadily reduced the relative primacy of London, but still, throughout this period, the UK's second tier cities were always 'too small' relative to London. In particular, over the last 165 years since Britain's other major industrial cities emerged, the UK's 15 or so second tier cities have always been 'too small' relative to London according to the logic of Zipf's Law. These historical insights prior to 1950 all point away from planning-related explanations of the current UK city-size distributions. Moreover, even if we ignore the evidence from the century spanning 1851–1950 prior to the widespread implementation of greenbelt-type planning policies and consider only the last half century or more, for the argument to hold that greenbelts have subsequently and severely limited the growth of these cities it would also require that greenbelt land use planning policies were more restrictive and biting in the rest of the UK's large cities than in London. Yet, there is simply no evidence of this. Indeed, the current house price data suggest entirely the opposite, namely that the restrictions have been relatively more biting in London and the southern cities than in cities in other regions of the UK, and that without greenbelt policies southern cities may have grown even larger.

Alternatively, therefore, it could be argued that these greenbelt policies have restricted the growth of southern cities (Leunig and Overman 2008) such as Bristol, Portsmouth, Oxford and Cambridge and that over the last six decades market-led north–south migration would have allowed these southern cities to grow and move up the urban hierarchies above cities such as Manchester, Birmingham, Newcastle and Leeds, so as to 'correct' the 'incorrect' Zipf's Law slope. Yet, as Champion (2014) demonstrates, most urban areas including the majority of urban areas in the south were either stable in terms of population or were actually losing population in the 1980s. Very few experienced noticeable population growth. Indeed, only 20 out of the top 64 UK cities and towns experienced a population growth of more than 2 per cent for the whole decade, and even London only grew by 0.3 per cent during this period (Champion 2014). Moreover, the handful of towns which did grow by more than 5 per cent during the 1980s were largely small towns in southern England including Cambridge, Peterborough, Gloucester, Milton Keynes, Northampton, Reading, Swindon and Bournemouth, with only one town outside of the southern English regions growing by more than 5 per cent across the ten-year period. Meanwhile 26 out of the top 64 UK cities exhibited declines in population, including many of the largest urban areas (Champion 2014). Between 1981 and 1991, amongst the 25 largest UK urban areas, all of which had populations of over 315,000 people, 15 experienced population decline including 13 out of the top 20 cities, while only 4 of the 10 growing cities in this group were outside of the southern regions of England (Champion 2014). As such, for the UK city-size distribution to be fundamentally altered during the post-war era cities such as Bristol and Portsmouth would need to have grown fourfold or fivefold from their current size since the late 1980s or early 1990s in order for the slope parameter to be 'corrected'.[167] Yet, whether this hypothetical growth pattern would indeed have taken place if greenbelt policies had not been in place since the post-war era is highly debatable, especially given the fact that the rank order position of these cities in the historical city-size rankings has changed very little over 160 years. Yet, even if this argument were to be correct, such that the growth of these southern cities was indeed to be fuelled by migration from cities outside of southern England, then this argument would actually imply that many of the UK's current second tier cities, and particularly those outside of the south of England, are actually be 'too big' rather than 'too small' and that in reality it is the UK's third tier cities which are 'too small'.

While in general we can largely rule out planning-related explanations of the current UK city-size distributions, we can still return to the discussion regarding whether London is today 'too big' relative to other UK cities or whether the UK second tier cities are 'too small' according to Zipf's Law types of arguments. Yet, resolving or just making progress on these discussions becomes very difficult because in reality it depends on how we classify second tier cities and third tier cities and also what statistical reference points we choose in order to benchmark our observations, and there are no generally agreed methods for doing this. In particular, the responses to this question hinge on what our statistical benchmark is and how we interpret the behavioural underpinnings of the city-size distributions.

If we adopt international comparisons as a benchmark we see from the OECD data sets that the UK's second tier cities are not particularly small in comparison to the second tier cities in most other advanced OECD economies, and in particular in comparison to the other large OECD economies of Germany, France, Canada, Italy, Spain, Australia. In fact, of all of the advanced economies, the UK's second tier cities are only small in comparison to those in the USA, Japan and Korea. Moreover, the UK's second tier cities are relatively large in comparison to the primal cities in many of the world's most prosperous countries. International comparisons therefore do not suggest that the UK's second tier cities are too small. On the other hand, what international comparisons do show is that in unitary states the ratio of the size of the primal city relative to the second city is on average double what is observed in federal states (OECD 2015b), and in the UK case this ratio is more than 1.5 times the average for unitary states (OECD 2015b).

If we adopt as a benchmark deviations from a Zipf's Law type of distribution, the question is whether we assess these deviations by using the intercept term or the slope parameter as our reference point for deciding how far the observed patterns deviate from what would be expected. One approach is to assume that the estimated slope is 'correct' in the sense that it is the outcome of numerous economic shocks and influences across the urban system, and then to consider the extent to which the largest city deviates from what would be expected on the basis of the experience of the rest of the urban system. Alternatively, we could assume that the intercept generated by largest city size is 'correct' and then consider the extent to which the rest of the city-size distribution as reflected by the estimated slope parameter deviated from what would be expected.

If at first we adopt the former approach and we use the estimated slope parameter as our benchmark, we see that for the largest urban areas in the UK for each of the years 1851, 1900, 1925, 1950, 2000 and 2010 the slope parameter for the urban size distribution has changed relatively little over more than one and a half centuries. For all of the years between 1851 and 2010 London is larger than would be predicted based on the slope parameter generated by population distributions of the rest of the large UK cities. Indeed, in (natural) logarithmic terms for all of these years London is larger by a factor of between 0.25 and 1.0 than would be expected on the basis of the other large UK cities.

The 'gap' between the size of London and what would be expected on the basis of the slope parameter based on the other large UK cities was initially highest in the middle of the nineteenth century at approximately 0.5 falling to around 0.25 for the period between 1900 and 1950. Importantly, this 'gap' existed, in other words London was 'too large' according to the slope parameter based on the urban population distributions, during a century in which there were no widespread land use restrictions, little or no explicit urban planning policies except at a very small scale, and in particular, no general greenbelt type of policy was in operation. A free market environment in land markets gave rise to London being 'too large' relative to the rest of the urban population distribution. However, by the millennium the 'gap' between the size of London and what would be expected on the basis of the other large UK cities had now risen to something of the order of 1.0. This is the largest gap in the last one and a half centuries, and has arisen during more than six decades during which explicit urban greenbelt policies have dominated UK land markets and land use planning systems. Following this logic, the 2010 population of London ought to be approximately 4.4 million and not 11.79 million.

An alternative approach to interpreting Zipf's Law is to use the intercept of London as the benchmark reference point and to consider the extent to which the slope derived from the UK urban population distribution deviates from what would be expected if the intercept – i.e. the size of London was 'correct' and the slope was somehow 'incorrect'. Following this logic, we see that all of the UK's large cities between 1851 and 2010 were 'too small' relative to what they should have been assuming that London was 'correctly' sized and the Zipf's Law slope parameter should have been −0.5. While it may be possible to argue as Cheshire *et al.* (2014a) do that the 'incorrect' slope in part has been due to greenbelt policies, this potential argument could only be applicable when observing the changes between 1950 and 2010 when the greenbelt policy was in operation across the UK. Yet, such an argument cannot account for the fact that if London was 'correctly' sized the slope parameter derived from the rest of the UK's large cities was systematically 'incorrect' during the whole of the preceding century in which there were no generally restrictive land use planning policies in operation. The historical data suggest that the argument that London is 'correctly' sized while the 14 or so second tier UK cities are 'too small' according to Zipf's Law starts to become difficult to justify. The idea that one city should be 'correctly' sized and the next 14 or 15 large cities should be 'incorrectly' and under-sized over one and a half centuries becomes unrealistic, unless of course we avoid an overly mechanistic interpretation of Zipf's Law. A more realistic interpretation is simply that the combined hysteresis effects related to transport infrastructure, industrial structures, industrial relations, skills-profiles and institutional settings, as well as land use planning policies, are together both real and long-lasting, and that London has always been very large relative to the rest of the UK's other large cities and this still remains the case. While it may be useful for expositional purposes, from an analytical perspective at least, any recourse to Zipf's Law explanations is largely unnecessary and unhelpful.

A third approach, which is something of a halfway house between the first two approaches, is to consider the extent to which London's size deviates from what would be expected according to a Zipf's Law slope parameter of -1 with the regression line being centred on the existing distribution of the rest of the UK cities excluding London. Following this approach, the data suggest that between 1851 and 1925 London was 'too big' in (natural) logarithmic terms by a value of approximately 0.5 while between 1950 and the present day London is 'too big' in (natural) logarithmic terms by a value of approximately 0.25. Given the actual populations observed for the rest of the UK large cities at each time period, this implies that the 1851 population of London should have been approximately 1.45 million rather than 2.36 million, the 1900 population of London should have been some 3.9 million rather than 6.48 million, and the 1925 population of London should have been approximately 4.85 million rather than 7.74 million. For 1950 this approach suggests that the population of London should have been some 6.9 million rather than 8.86 million, for 2000 the population of London should have been approximately 8.2 million rather than 10.49 million, and for 2010 the population of London should have been approximately 9.2 million rather than 11.79 million. Following this argument, during the twentieth century London has always been 'too big' by somewhere between 2 million and 2.9 million, with London's 'excess' population being just over 900,000 in 1851, 2.58 million in 1900, 2.89 million in 1925, 1.96 million in 1950, 2.29 million in 2000 and 2.58 million in 2010.

Interestingly, the 'excess' population of London calculated on this basis was minimised in 1950. The year 1950 is also the distribution which most closely corresponds to the textbook case. However, the major difference between the 1925 and 1950 distributions is the growth of London, Manchester and Birmingham. London grew to its greatest size in the twentieth century during the 1920s and 1930s. However, while the South East was relatively buoyant during this period (Scott 2007) the effects of the 1930s Depression on the London financial markets narrowed the gap between London and other UK cities (Geary and Stark 2015). Meanwhile, both Manchester and Birmingham expanded significantly during the inter-war and war years, and a major part of this growth was also associated with the war effort, in which many civilian engineering activities in both cities were transformed into military engineering activities. In the latter decades of the twentieth century, the transformation of the London economy in response to the impacts of modern globalisation has again reversed these trends, and on the basis of this specific approach, the 'excess' population of London is now exactly the same as it was in 1990. As we have already seen in Chapter 2, UK interregional inequalities are now at similar levels to what they were at the beginning of the twentieth century, and this is also the case for the 'excess' population of London, at least as understood from the historical structure of the UK city-size distribution.

On the question of whether these second tier cities are actually 'too small' or whether London is 'too large', almost all of the evidence presented from seven centuries of observations plus the changing patterns evident during the twentieth century, all suggests that London is indeed relatively 'too large' in comparison to all of the other large UK cities, on the basis of what might be expected from international comparisons (Rozenfeld *et al.* 2011; Soo 2005). Indeed, the only case where the Zipf's Law evidence suggests that the UK's second cities are 'too small' is where we a priori assume that London is 'correctly' sized and then observe the city-size distribution from this particular standpoint. All of the other approaches suggest that London is too large.[168]

An alternative approach is to focus only on the relationship between London and the UK's small and medium-sized towns (Overman and Rice 2008) below say the top 25 UK cities (Overman 2013), and on this basis then indeed the UK's large second tier cities are 'too small' and London is appropriately scaled (Overman 2013). However, this approach ignores the vast majority of UK industrial and urban history, and we simply have no theoretical justification or analytical basis for such an approach. Indeed, this is part of the problem with Zipf's Law, in that it gives us no real guidance as to how to interpret many of these issues nor what to do about them, if anything. As such, a third approach to the question of the sizes of UK cities is simply to ignore the rank size and Zipf's Law types of explanations as providing little or no real basis for policy or for thinking about policy issues (Haggett 1965; Cliff *et al.* 1975; Robson 1973), because as we have seen from the previous sections it becomes very difficult and somewhat arbitrary to decide precisely how to interpret these rank-order and city-size patterns (Batty 2005). Moreover, our historical data do not support such a mechanistic application of Zipf's Law to the specifics of the UK case, but call for a more nuanced historical approach in tandem with other data on interregional inequality.

Taken together, these various cumulative historical influences plus the specific experience of UK cities and regions at different stages of the nineteenth, twentieth and twenty-first centuries, have led to a pattern whereby today London is relatively very large in comparison to the dozen or so second tier UK cities. A range of different factors and influences together appear to have shaped the specific character of the UK city-size distributions historically in the long run and right up to today, rather than specifically post-war land use planning policies. In other words, the argument offered on the basis of Zipf's Law that the second tier cities of the UK cities are 'too small' relative to London, rather than London being 'too big', and that this is in some significant part due to a restrictive land use planning environment (Cheshire *et al.* 2014a) cannot be supported or substantiated on the basis of the available historical data.

Instead a much simpler and more direct approach is to argue that today's city-size patterns reflect diverse and changing long-term demand trends for different activities in different regions, and the population and employment demand in particular cities also depends on where they are located in the overall UK core-periphery structure. As we have already seen in Chapters 2 and 3, cities located in the southern regions of England have generally experienced consistently stronger demand during the last four decades than cities in other regions. As such, the fact that many of the UK's second tier cities are smaller than might be expected given the size of London cities may simply be a reflection of these long-run differences in demand. The majority of the UK's large second tier cities are located in regions which have experienced relatively weak long-term demand, and not surprisingly their population growth over many decades has been limited. Indeed, as a whole the UK is one of the few European countries where population growth prior to the 2008 economic crisis in rural, small town and non-metropolitan urban regions was consistently higher than in metropolitan urban regions of over 250,000 inhabitants (Dijkstra *et al.* 2013; OECD 2011b, 2013a) and as we saw in Chapter 2 these trends have continued since the crisis. Yet, although in the UK demand for rural living is stronger than demand for urban living, in the last two decades demand for urban living has re-emerged primarily in London as well as other southern cities, bolstered in particular by international immigration. Although there has been some limited resurgence in UK cities (Overman and Rice 2008), these effects are still relatively much weaker in cities located outside of the southern regions of England or Scotland. As such, a regional core-periphery type of explanation is still far more useful than a Zipf's Law type of explanation of UK city sizes or alternatively any explanations based on the effects of greenbelt land use planning policies.

However, even though this specific land use planning argument for the possible under-sizing of second tier UK cities has been ruled out here on the basis of historical data, the city scale-related issues raised by this discussion are still very important indeed. Some commentators have argued that in order to correct the possible under-sizing of UK second tier cities it would be appropriate for these cities to find ways to merge in some way.[169] This is also a very important issue which is discussed in more detail in the following chapters. However, as we will see in these chapters it will be argued that institutional and governance approaches (OECD 2015b) provide a much stronger grounding for these types of city-size arguments than analyses based on Zipf's Law or restrictive land use planning approaches. Scaling laws such as Zipf's Law explain very little about the structure of the UK urban system because of the overwhelming presence of London on almost every economic and social indicator (Arcaute *et al.* 2015) and in particular because of the role of London in attracting immigrants. Instead, London's size and performance is likely to be far more related to its role in global city networks rather than its relationships with other second tier UK cities, a group which represent quite a different cohort of urban centres playing quite different roles within the UK economy (Arcaute *et al.* 2015). On this basis, institutional and governance arguments also provide a potentially far more powerful set of policy solutions to the current UK interregional problem than do land use planning arguments.

5.6   Discussion and conclusions

All of the evidence presented so far in this book suggests that the drivers of prosperity in London and the southern and eastern regions of England do not transfer to the rest of the UK and that regional growth remains highly localised even after three and a half decades of massive structural change in UK regions. This points to the conclusion that in the UK the 'South–North' interregional linkages of human capital, knowledge, trade and technology are all very limited. The UK's interregional trade, financial and fiscal linkages as well as human capital and knowledge linkages are all too small to account for the observed interregional productivity differences, and so are their associated adjustment mechanisms. Moreover, the observed land use and city-size-related constraints, which are very real, are also not fundamental reasons for the inequalities, but rather are largely outcomes. Again, this requires to reflect on, and reconsider, the potential reasons for what we observe.

We know from previous chapters that the UK's city-scale-productivity relationships are both very weak and also are overwhelmingly dominated by the case of London. There are no generally applicable UK-wide agglomeration types of relationships, but rather different relationships in different regions, and for many UK urban areas there are few or no such relationships which are at all evident. Where agglomeration-productivity relationships do exist, the productivity benefits of being in cities tend to be far less important than being located in the southern regions of England (Breheny 1999). In other words, on many levels the geography-productivity geography-inequality story of the UK is really much more of a regional core-periphery issue rather than it is an urban issue.

The core-periphery aspects of the UK interregional inequalities have become increasingly serious over recent years, and part of the problem appears to be the fact that while the economy of London is broadly successful the various linkages between London and the rest of the UK economy are both very weak and largely limited to the southern regions of England. These potential interregional linkages include human capital linkages, trade linkages, financial and fiscal linkages, and knowledge and technological linkages. Yet, the most recent and detailed evidence along with evidence going back over the recent decades all points to the general conclusion that these linkages are weak.

One of the areas which has frequently been discussed concerns the differing regional distributions of human capital as possible contributors to interregional inequalities. Indeed, we know that human capital is important in driving productivity and human capital-migration interactions are important for shaping regional development. Yet, the productivity differences between UK regions cannot simply be ascribed to sorting and self-selection amongst the UK native population on the basis of skills in the face of technological progress. The secondary and tertiary education levels of London domiciled graduates are not particularly different to other regions so the only potential human capital advantage that London has relates to inflows from other regions. However, these inflows are unlikely to provide much of an explanation for the UK inequalities because the skills differences are very small, and second because the interregional migration flows have hardly changed at all over the last two decades. While London does play an important role in the migration patterns which are evident in the UK system of cities, it does not play an overwhelmingly dominant role in these patterns. London is obviously crucial in shaping the labour flows to and within the southern and eastern regions of England. Outside of these regions, however, the London labour market appears to largely co-exist with the labour markets of the rest of the UK, with very limited domestic interregional labour market connections between London and the northern English and the devolved regions. Apart from with its hinterland regions, most of the important labour market linkages in the London economy are either internal and local linkages or international global linkages. As with the regional and urban evidence, again it appears to be the case that in terms of labour markets the London and southern English economy is simply decoupling and drifting away from most of the rest of the UK. As such, the reasons for the UK's interregional inequalities do not appear to be primarily related to internal matters, and better explanations need to be sought elsewhere, and particularly related to external and global matters.

In terms of the shocks associated with modern globalisation since the late 1980s, London has benefited from these worldwide transformations and on many levels it is clearly a very successful hub within the global networks of trade, knowledge and communications. In contrast, many of the UK's more peripheral regions have struggled in the face of the global headwinds with economic restructuring. Yet, the regional decoupling and disconnection we observe in the UK between the 'South' and the 'North' is primarily as a result of a decoupling between London and the rest of the UK. The regions of the South East, East and South West represent the hinterland of the London economy and their performance is inextricably related to that of London. However, the reasons for this decoupling and disconnection are not fundamentally internal to the London economy. They have been driven by the profound changes associated with the modern era of globalisation. The key characteristics of modern globalisation are related to multinationalism and foreign investment rather than simply trade, and the core of multinationalism is foreign ownership. At the heart of these transformations are cross-border mergers and acquisitions, alongside new international investments. The structural changes within the 1980s financial markets of London including the inflows of foreign investment banks, allied with the UK's membership of the EU which emerged as being the largest arena of cross-border ownership and financial flows, along with the pipeline of other London infrastructure investments – such as the Channel Tunnel link, the Docklands development and Heathrow Terminal 5 – all combined fortuitously to position London in a pivotal role in the ensuing global transformations. No-one in the 1980s, and least of all UK policy-makers, could have foreseen the scale of the global transformations from the early 1990s onwards nor the dramatically increased international role to be played by the London capital markets in modern globalisation. It is these external shocks that triggered the economic transformation processes widely evident within the London economy today. Importantly for our purposes, the UK-owned presence in the London capital markets in the late 1980s and early 1990s was relatively small (Casson and McCann 1999) and of almost no importance whatsoever in terms of triggering the overall growth of the London markets from 1990 onwards (Iammarino and McCann 2013). At the same time, the advent of the EU Single Market allowed large numbers of highly qualified and primarily young European citizens, to enter the burgeoning London capital markets. The inflows of Europeans into the London capital markets were primarily from the other EU countries with large banking sectors including Germany, France and The Netherlands, plus Switzerland. These EU inflows were also accompanied by inflows of large numbers of young people from Australia, New Zealand, Canada and South Africa who took advantage of the Commonwealth-related labour-mobility agreements. These EU and Commonwealth inflows of human capital were also mirrored by large inflows of financial market workers from the USA and Japan and to a much smaller extent also Hong Kong and Singapore, all of which were the same origin countries of the inflows into London of many new banks and financial market actors. In other words, the external global shocks which triggered the demand for the types of international financial services which London was able to provide then also themselves triggered inflows of high-quality human capital from many countries into the London economy, the majority of whom were university educated. In other words, from the 1990s onwards London enjoyed a human capital surge which was largely independent of the ongoing structure of UK internal migration flows. It was also largely independent of any of the 1990s internal changes within the UK education system, except for the extent to which foreign students within the UK university system, and especially those from the EU and some Commonwealth countries, were increasingly able to enter employment positions within the London economy after graduation.

These particular ways in which these types of adjustment processes have taken place in London are not necessarily evident in exactly the same ways in other global cities. Indeed, and contrary to popular perceptions,[170] there is no automatic reason why these types of large global hub cities such as London should necessarily grow faster than other kinds of areas or why they should play an increasingly important role in their national economies in the medium to long term. Indeed, the empirical evidence from across the world suggests that this is not at all the case (OECD 2011c, 2012d, 2014c). As such, while the increasing role played by a global hub city is evidently the case in the UK there is nothing automatic or natural about this process. Rather, the experience of London's role within the UK is something which is specific to the UK, and this itself raises a particular conundrum in that while the UK uses broadly similar technologies and displays similar levels of education to other advanced OECD economies we observe that the interregional inequalities in many other countries are much smaller than the UK and their interregional linkages and spillovers appear to be much stronger. In particular, why is it the case that having such a world-trading centre for knowledge, finance and communications as London also appears to be associated with such limited interregional flows of knowledge, finance and communications, the very issues which London deals in? This conundrum still remains unanswered. However, in order to avoid potentially problematic inferences, Coyle and Rosewell (2014) argue that those who perceive that London's success might be at the expense of other UK regions are wrong because this is not an interregional 'zero-sum game'. In other words, while the puzzle still remains, it is important that potential solutions to the puzzle are not sought in line of argumentation which may be at the expense of London's economic interests. Yet curiously Coyle and Rosewell are also partly incorrect. The wide-ranging evidence so far presented in this book suggests that the UK interregional 'game' is one which rather than being a zero-sum game is one which is separable and additive, to use mathematical jargon, in which the core regions of the 'South' – i.e. London and the southern regions of England (plus in some sense also Scotland) – are to a large extent simply decoupled and disconnected from the 'North'- i.e. the rest of the UK's regions. Rather than a zero-sum interregional game, in the UK what we experience is there is actually no 'game' as such, because a game requires interactions and competition whereas the UK interregional reality is one of decoupling, disconnection and an almost total absence of interconnections. As such, the 'national' performance of the UK economy may well improve as the economy of London and the 'South' grows but this southern growth does not translate into the growth of the 'North', as reflected in the growing interregional inequalities. In national growth accounting terms what may appear to be 'good' for the UK economy on the basis of London's performance may not be particularly good for almost half of the UK's citizens.

As Krugman (2015e) points out income inequality in many countries has risen far faster than the wages of the vast majority of highly educated individuals which have remained flat since the late 1990s, just as aggregate productivity growth has remained largely stagnant since then. As a result, increasing doubts are raised as to the relative value of tertiary education skills gained over recent decades and also the long-term viability of the recently expanded tertiary education sectors.[171] Moreover, allied with the stability of UK interregional migration flows these also raise doubts about the role of human capital as drivers of regional productivity. This is particularly the case in the UK and the USA where during this same period, corporate profits and profit-related remuneration have soared as a share of national income even though the rates of return on capital have remained flat (Krugman 2015e). In part, this is due to the fact that increasing numbers of workers are employed in service industries, and in particular in financial and business services, in which technological progress is very limited (Jorgensen and Timmer 2011), and this appears to have been particularly so in the case of the UK (Coutts and Gudgin 2015). Aggregate inequality is driven by the surging incomes of a tiny minority of the population in senior corporate positions or in finance[172] and this suggests that monopoly power is central to the modern inequality story rather than skills (Krugman 2015e; Stiglitz 2015).[173] In terms of income inequality the UK is now more unequal than almost every other advanced economy except the USA and far more unequal than the rich Commonwealth countries which are seen as culturally more similar to us.[174] Meanwhile, in terms of the growing UK interregional inequalities which we have observed since the early 1990s, although human capital is very important, the labour skills, labour sorting and labour self-selection arguments are unlikely candidates for explaining the UK's rising interregional inequalities. Rather, the increasing decoupling and dislocation of London from the rest of the UK all point to these same monopoly-type explanations offered by Krugman and Stiglitz amongst others. These monopoly positions were generated by fortuitous demand surges for the services of London's international capital markets and these in turn triggered further inflows of human capital and investment capital. A range of London's allied non-basic business service activities and occupations were also spurred by these changes within the capital markets, and nowadays they account for a larger part of London's output and employment than the financial services sectors. However, in terms of causality it was the international financial service industries, which represent a major part of London's export-base (Rowthorn 2010; McCann 2013), which triggered the demand increases for London's larger non-basic sectors, and not the other way around. In other words, what we see overall is that across three critical dimensions, namely: in terms of structural changes, in terms of changes in firm and investment capital injections, and in terms of changes in human capital injections, the exogenous shocks which spurred the growth of the London economy during the last two and a half decades were almost entirely external to the UK economy, and they commenced around 1990/1991 as the whole global economy began to reorganise (Iammarino and McCann 2013), as we have already discussed in detail in Chapter 4. These were not primarily a result of internal adjustment processes driven by changing factor reallocations or by human capital spatial sorting, but rather these features were partial responses to fundamental exogenous and externally driven changes.

The detailed observations provided in this chapter, along with the detailed material examined in the previous four chapters, also allows us to consider and comment on the veracity of some of the popular narratives currently circulating in the UK's academic and policy literatures.

First, the idea that the UK's interregional inequalities are not very 'real' is incorrect. Even allowing for processes of skills selection and spatial sorting which reduce the usefulness of headline indicators of average income differences as indicators of inequalities, they are indeed still very real indeed, and amongst the most marked of any advanced OECD country.

Second, and as we have already seen in Chapters 2 and 3, the idea that it is more or less inevitable that London as a 'big hub' will increasingly benefit from productivity gains associated with increasing global knowledge flows and investments is simply not corroborated by the available international evidence. London is a strong performer but there is nothing automatic or inevitable about this network phenomenon. Rather, the performance and role of London within the UK economy is something which is specific to the UK.

Third, the idea that London is the key driver or motor of the UK economy is also not supported by the evidence. As we have already seen in Chapters 2 and 3 there is no evidence of any general UK-wide beneficial spread effects or 'trickle down' effects emanating from London's growth, except those operating in the southern and eastern regions of England which represent London's hinterland. This also implies that the 'jam and Ryvita' analogy of Boris Johnson referred to in Chapter 2 is also implausible.[175]

Fourth, the description of London as a 'dark star'[176] which is inexorably pulling in resources and people from the rest of the UK is also not supported by the evidence. London pulls in resources from its hinterland regions (*The Economist* 2014b) but beyond this hinterland of the southern and eastern regions of England the effect appears to be very limited indeed. If the UK had a highly deregulated land market which allowed for rapid house-building at little cost then it is indeed possible that London would have acted as a 'dark star' and may therefore have sucked resources out of everywhere else. Yet, this is not the case and the highly restrictive UK land use planning system may have resulted in rapidly increasing land use and housing prices which in turn may have limited interregional migration into London. However, this can only be speculated as we have no alternative counter-factual evidence.

Fifth, while on the one hand the view that London is the driver or motor of the UK economy is largely incorrect, on the other hand the view that London grows at the expense of the rest of the UK economy is also not necessarily correct (GLA Economics 2005). Indeed, the evidence in this book strongly suggests while it is incorrect to argue that growth in London is complementary to aggregate UK growth it is also not correct to argue that interregional growth is a zero-sum game and that limits on London's growth will hurt the rest of the UK (GLA Economics 2005; Coyle and Rosewell 2014). Both of these descriptions are incorrect because in reality the economy of London increasingly just appears to co-exist with the rest of the UK in a decoupled and largely disconnected manner. On many different levels, the global city nature of the London economy means that London's most important linkages are primarily with its other global city regions in other countries, and especially those which are financial centres, and then secondarily with its own hinterland regions, rather than within the rest of the UK.

Sixth, while they have led to complex and in some cases pernicious wealth-related and inter-generational effects, the house price distortions due to the land supply restrictions imposed by the UK land use planning system are primarily a result of the interregional inequalities, and not a cause of them. It may well be the case, however, that the supply restrictions have exacerbated and will continue to exacerbate the inequalities via long-term wealth-related effects, housing-collateral-based effects on access to credit and limits on downward social mobility.

Seventh, the historical evolution of the structure of the UK city size-distribution patterns suggest that these patterns are primarily a result of the specific industrial and urbanisation history of the UK over many centuries, and not a result of the 1947 planning system. Moreover, the weight of evidence in the context of the changing industrial experience of the UK points, if anything, to London being too large relative to the other UK cities, rather than the UK's second tier cities being too small. The relative size of London is most likely to be related to the fact historically England and then Great Britain were amongst the world's first highly centralised modern nation-states, a situation which has continued through to today, in which London acted as the capital of a global empire. London continues today as something of a global capital, of finance.

These seven observations suggest that overall, the linkages between London and the 'South' and the 'North' or the rest of the UK – defined in terms of human capital linkages, trade and demand linkages, financial and fiscal linkages, and knowledge linkages – are in reality very limited and much weaker than many popular political narratives suggest. Moreover, in the aftermath of the 2008 global economic crisis which initially emerged in the financial markets, doubts are now being raised (Rosewell 2013; Clark 2015) as to the ability of international finance to continue to drive the London economy in the long run, particularly as the centre of gravity of the global economy shifts eastwards (Reyes *et al.* 2009). These various concerns, allied with the lack of any real evidence of widespread spillovers and linkages between London and the wider UK economy, raise further doubts as to the ability of London to be relied on drive the UK economy as a whole. Notwithstanding the 2012 London Olympics, this in turn has progressively weakened the wider public perceptions regarding the potentially beneficial role played by the London economy in the wider life of the UK (Clark 2015).

Given all of the available evidence, the best description of the current relationship between London and the rest of the UK economy is that since the very late 1980s the London economy has been slowly and increasingly decoupling, disconnecting and 'floating away' from the rest of the UK. London and its hinterland is increasingly becoming its own 'island' economy. As the *Financial Times* puts it, today we have a "Disunited Kingdom [with] London in a World of Its Own".[177] Indeed, in many arenas of government, public policy, the media and academia, the suspicion that this gradual process of disconnection and decoupling is today's UK reality is also what best accounts for some of the curious public debates currently being aired and some of the rather strange public policy decisions now being made in central government policy regarding regional and urban issues. There has been a recent political rush towards major investments in high-speed rail and also towards city-region governance decentralisation. Some aspects of these agendas are very welcome and have been based on good thinking and careful analysis set against the backdrop of increasing international evidence on these matters. Meanwhile, there are also other aspects of these agendas which appear to be rather less strongly grounded, either in terms of analytical or empirics and based rather more heavily on shorter-term political priorities. Indeed, in some cases there appears to be little or any real economic justification for such debates and decisions if we are to base these arguments on purely conventional urban economic arguments and conventional efficiency frameworks. Yet, part of the fundamental problem that the UK faces is that it is these very orthodox analytical frameworks which are now so much in doubt, given the prevailing UK evidence, and therefore extremely important decisions for the whole country are being made regarding local and regional governance re-organisations, infrastructure investments and responses to globalisation, on a variety of rather ad hoc criteria influenced primarily by other political narratives. Unpicking the various different arguments underlying these decisions and political choices is therefore absolutely essential if we are to put some sort of economic framework on the current political economy of the UK, and to impose some sort of analytical logic as to how current and future policy decisions ought to be framed. These issues are the subjects to be addressed in the following two chapters.

Appendix 5.1

The spatial pricect equilibrium model with housing assets

Spatial price equilibrium frameworks are extremely important for understanding the likely geographical economic adjustments associated with changes in individual factor or market prices. However, the interpretation of these frameworks is not so straightforward when we consider different employment probabilities and also the role of housing and home ownership in the context of real options and user costs of capital types of framework.

Given interregional differences in employment spatial price equilibrium models based on real wage equalisation frameworks need to incorporate unemployment probabilities in the wage structure in order to construct an expected wage (Harris and Todaro 1970). Real wages therefore need to be adjusted for breaks in employment. Today in the UK this is important, because although headline unemployment rates vary very little by region, 'involuntary non-standard employment' (INSE) (Green and Livanos 2015), which includes all involuntary part-time working and involuntary temporary working, varies markedly by region, with the level of INSE in London being significantly below the levels observed in all other UK regions. Lower levels of INSE increase the expected nominal and real wages in London relative to the rest of the UK above the values that would be derived simply by observing nominal wages and local living costs and headline regional unemployment rates.

In addition, traditional urban economics models assume that all land users are renters with all land owned by absentee landlords. Under these conditions the spatial price equilibrium arguments are very simple. For example, if we consider two hypothetical regions 'the north' N and 'the south' S in which amenities are equal between both regions, while nominal wage incomes in the south are twice as high as those in the north, then according to the disequilibrium model of migration (McCann 2013) labour will move from the lower nominal wage region to the higher nominal wage region until the nominal costs of living – housing rents plus consumption – are exactly twice as high in the south as those in the north. At this point, migration will cease because the real wages are now equalised. However, if home ownership is introduced, then the model changes fundamentally.

If, instead of renting, we assume that all workers take out 25-year housing mortgages, and if incomes in the south are twice as high as those in the north, this also means that north–south migration will continue until the equilibrium is reached whereby the living costs (both inclusive and exclusive of housing) in the south are twice those in the north. At this point the nominal house prices in the south will be twice as high as in the north and the size of the required mortgage for purchasing the equivalent house in the south as could be purchased in the north will also be twice as high in the south. Monthly interest payments in the south will therefore also be double those in the north. As with the model in which all labour are assumed to be renters, one understanding of the spatial price equilibrium is characterised by southern nominal incomes and the nominal costs of living including housing mortgage costs in the south being exactly twice those which prevail in the north. Yet, how we interpret these mortgage costs is important. If there is no house price appreciation then the equity gain depends on the form of mortgage repayment. If the mortgages are interest-only payments, then this is no different to the renting case, and indeed there is no real incentive to take out such a mortgage rather than renting. Alternatively, if the mortgages are full repayment mortgages then for spatial equilibrium models if we calculate the housing costs as the total monthly (interest plus capital) repayment and assume no long-term capital gains,[178] after 25 years the residents located in the south will have generated twice as much housing equity as those in the north. After a given period they are twice as wealthy The reason is that even though the price or cost of money – the interest rate – is the same between the two regions, the higher nominal mortgage repayments imply higher rates of capital accumulation. Most UK housing mortgages are repayment mortgages so this would appear to be the most reasonable deflator for real wages.[179]

The fact that in nominal terms the residents in the south are twice as wealthy as those in the north even though in day-to-day real wage terms calculated on a full repayment mortgage basis they were equivalent to each other also means that the long-term residents of the south can eventually exercise their wealth by moving to another less expensive region such as the north, and enjoy a standard of living which is twice as high as the long-term residents of the north. If, however, at the end of mortgage the residents in the south choose to stay in the south then they will be no better off in real terms than the residents in the north who have also repaid their mortgage.[180] This is the equivalent of the model in which all are renters. Alternatively, following an equilibrium model of migration (McCann 2013) the long-term residents of the south could also choose to move to a third region, the south west *SW*, which is less expensive than the south *S* but more expensive than the north *N*, due to higher natural amenities. In contrast, the residents of the north are unable to move in later life to either the south or the south west without severely reducing their standard of living. This is because they are budget constrained by their lower housing wealth. These housing-assets effects mean that there will be little or no long-term movements of older cohorts from the north to either the south or the south west but there will be large numbers of older cohort movements from the south to the south west.

Following a real options and user cost of capital argument, irrespective of which region the residents of the south do or do not move to, the fact that they have much greater ability to move at the termination of the mortgage period is a long-term housing asset-related consumption effect (Mishkin 2001, 2007), and one which demonstrates that a spatial price equilibrium based only on the interest costs plus the day-to-day living costs, does not reflect a spatial price equilibrium when asset-based wealth is incorporated into the framework. A spatial price equilibrium derived purely from daily living plus housing costs generates an interregional housing-asset disequilibrium which favours the higher nominal wage region, while one which is also asset-based implies markedly lower real wages in the south. The difference between the two is due to the fact that prices for finance do not vary according to the region and also nominal mortgage values are real values which cannot be normalised downwards according to living costs. These differences imply long-term life-cycle-related differences in consumption mediated via regionally differentiated housing asset effects, and the more that we shift consumption towards asset-related goods and services (Summers 2013) the more important these issues become. Moreover, these pressures are increased even further given the fact that pension payments are based on nominal incomes, which vary by region, and not on real incomes.

This argument provides a powerful reason why so many workers employed in the south are reluctant to move to the north during the majority of their careers, because residence and employment in the south provide greater opportunities for long-term wealth acquisition, even allowing for relatively higher living costs. Relocation to other regions only makes sense for most southern residents at much later stages in life where the wealth can be realised via equity-withdrawal. These hysteresis arguments therefore provide a rationale for some of the escalator arguments in the southern regions of England. They also provide a rationale for the relatively lower real wage observations in south eastern locations (Gibbons *et al.* 2011) without the recourse to amenity-based explanations which are rather doubtful in the case of towns such as Slough, Reading and Luton. Moreover, while this regional labour hysteresis and escalator-type of effect holds even with either zero or equal house price growth in all regions, it is obviously greatly entrenched by house price growth in the south east outpacing that of other UK regions, as has been evident in the UK over recent decades. The higher house price growth in London and the South East, allied with the land use restrictions, is likely to both transmit and distort national monetary policy by converting asset price appreciation into increased long-term consumption (Mishkin 2001, 2007). In particular, if consumers believe both that London will continue to be favoured as a national economic champion while at the same time land use restrictions will not be fundamentally altered, underpinned as they are by the prevalent insider–outsider features of the UK land markets discussed above, then the South East-dominated transmission mechanisms between UK monetary policy, housing assets and consumption will continue. Given that the UK is now less of an optimal currency area than either the Eurozone or the EU-28, the housing asset-related consumption effects in many cases are likely to undermine much of national UK monetary policy by generating long-term unintended outcomes. Indeed, the evidence in this book regarding the decoupling of London from the rest of the UK (Deutsche Bank 2013, 2014) suggests that this has to a large extent already happened.

Notes

1 The upper left hand quadrant in the Overman *et al.* (2010) figures.
2 "Pupils in Some Areas are Not Offered 'Vital' GCSEs". See: www.bbc.com/news/education-30983083?print=true.
3 If returns to education were relatively lower in London, a relatively prosperous region, and relatively higher in less prosperous regions, then we would expect from human capital investment theory that educational self-investments should have fallen in London rather than increased during this period and risen in less prosperous regions. However, the apparently counter-intuitive results observed by Duranton and Monastiriotis (2002) which suggest that educational returns had been higher in less prosperous regions are primarily due to the fact that the index of education they employ is simply the number of years in formal schooling, rather than the total number of years in formal plus in situ on-the-job training. For most of the twentieth century the average number of years in formal education was lower in many of the less prosperous regions which were dominated by manufacturing and heavy industry where many years of on-the-job, placement and part-time educational training in skilled trades was a normal part of the employment trajectory for those entering employment as young teenagers, or even earlier. Indeed, in the earlier decades of the twentieth century it was the most able students who left school earlier as they achieved the 'leaving standard' more rapidly. It was only as the mandatory school leaving age of 14 which was originally implemented in 1918 was raised to 15 in 1947 and then to 16 in 1972, that the years of formal education increased and many of those in the cohorts observed by Duranton and Monastiriotis (2002) fell into these groupings. The apparently relatively higher returns to formal education in these less prosperous regions which Duranton and Monastiriotis (2002) observed are likely to be largely a result of the lower number of years in the formal education system, so it is also likely that a large portion of these apparent differences in returns to education would disappear if the number of years involved in on-the-job training for trades was also included in the education index. Evidence in support of this interpretation emerges from sectoral educational profiles over time. In 1978 only 5.5 per cent of the UK labour force has university or university-equivalent qualifications while for manufacturing and all non-manufacturing sectors the figures were 3.3 per cent and 6.5 per cent, respectively. For secondary school or equivalent qualifications the national, manufacturing and all non-manufacturing shares were 30 per cent, 28.7 per cent and 30.75 per cent, while the national, manufacturing and all non-manufacturing figures for those with no formal qualifications were 64.4 per cent, 68 per cent and 62.8 per cent (Prais 1981; Alford 1996). As such, sectoral differences in skills profiles were negligible, and given that tertiary educational skills were also relatively so small at the onset of the 1980s, it casts doubt on the primarily supply-side argument that, allowing for regional structural differences, London benefited so markedly in the 1980s and early

1990s from having higher shares of a higher skills workforce. In 1996 the proportion of the UK 18 year olds participating in full-time education was still only the second lowest in the EU, behind Portugal and ahead of Greece (Dorling 2013). By 1992 the total national graduate share of the UK population had risen to 17 per cent and 25 per cent by the end of 2000. By 2013 the national figure had risen to 38 per cent. See: www.ons.gov.uk/ons/dcp171776_337841.pdf; www.historyextra.com/feature/school-leaving-age-what-can-we-learn-history.

4 See: www.london.gov.uk/mayor/economic_unit/docs/world_city_world_knowledge.rtf. However, these long-run social rates of return may be reduced by the aftermath of the 2008 global financial crisis if short- and medium-term graduate employment and employment-progression opportunities have been adversely affected.

5 www.ons.gov.uk/ons/rel/regional-trends/regional-economic-indicators/july-2014/rep-regional-economic-indicators.html#tab-Skills.

6 www.ons.gov.uk/ons/dcp171776_337841.pdf.

7 Ibid.

8 At 40 per cent, the UK has the seventh highest share of its worksforce with tertiary education. See: OECD, 2013, *Education at a Glance 2013*, Organisation for Economic Cooperation and Development, Paris.

9 https://www.hesa.ac.uk/index.php?option=com_content&view=article&id=832; https://www.hesa.ac.uk/index.php?option=com_content&view=article&id=828.

10 https://www.hesa.ac.uk/index.php?option=com_content&view=article&id=808.

11 https://www.hesa.ac.uk/index.php?option=com_pubs&Itemid=&task=show_year&pubId=1714&versionId=54&yearId=260.

12 https://www.hesa.ac.uk/index.php?option=com_pubs&Itemid=&task=show_year&pubId=1714&versionId=54&yearId=292.

13 https://www.hesa.ac.uk/index.php?option=com_pubs&Itemid=&task=show_year&pubId=1714&versionId=54&yearId=260.

14 On the other hand, it can be argued that because of the enormous expansion of UK higher education since the 1990s, the appropriate comparison group for analysing changes in graduate mobility patterns relative to the previous decades would also include those young people in earlier decades with high school qualifications but who had not entered university. It is realistic to assume that the vast majority of this group would have largely entered employment in their own region, given that in the 1980s UK interregional migration was typically of the order of just 1 per cent per annum for employed workers and 2 per cent for unemployed workers seeking work (Hughes and McCormick 1981). On this basis, again, it is clear that overall UK interregional labour market mobility has increased since the 1980s.

15 In fact a very detailed examination of the data according to individual degree classification suggests that they are very slightly worse, but these differences are tiny.

16 In very recent years London and Scotland appear to have relatively better schooling and results than other areas, along with university admission rates, as to a smaller extent also do cities such as Birmingham and Manchester. This 'London effect' appears to be related in part to ethnic composition and/or early improvements in London's primary schooling, and relates in particular to children not from disadvantaged backgrounds. However, these effects post-date the emerging interregional inequalities described throughout this book, although they may well exacerbate them in the future. See: "Regional Developers: Participation Rates", *Times Higher Education*, 11 October 2012 and also: www.suttontrust.com/researcharchive/mobility-map-background/; www.suttontrust.com/wp-content/uploads/2016/04/Social-Mobility-Index-further-information.pdf; www.bristol.ac.uk/cmpo/publications/papers/2014/wp333.pdf; www.gov.uk/government/uploads/attachment_data/file/321969/London_Schools_-_FINAL.pdf; www.bbc.com/news/education-34778514; www.bbc.com/news/education-34964522. See also: http://www.smf.co.uk/publications/educational-inequalities-in-england-and-wales/.

17 "South Secures Research Cash", *Times Higher Education*, 16 February 2007; "Capital Gains", *Times Higher Education*, 29 May 2014; "Crick Institute Remark Betrays Southern Bias, Fears VC", *Times Higher Education*, 3 July 2014; "South Secures Research Cash", *Times Higher Education*, 16 February 2007; "High Notes Need to Be Balanced", *Times Higher Education*, 3 October 2013; "REF 2014: Is London Now Dominant?", *Times Higher Education*, 18 December 2014; "N8 Remains Bullish Despite Fall in Rankings and Research Income", *Times Higher Education*, 9 April 2015; "QR Funding: 10 Campuses in the South to Get More than £2K per Student", *Times Higher Education*, 7 May 2015.

18 "Turning Cold Spots Hot", *Times Higher Education*, 2 October 2014; "All in This Together", *Times Higher Education*, 24 July 2014; "Government Sees That Growth is Already in the University Mission", *Times Higher Education*, 24 July 2014; "Centre Sparks", *Times Higher Education*, 27 November 2014; "The Engines of Regional Prosperity?", *Times Higher Education*, 27 November 2014; "Concerns Over New Universities and Science Minister's Dual Role", *Times Higher Education*, 17 July 2014.

19 Gibbons *et al.* (2011) calculate that 3.5–4 per cent of the population, or some 680,000 households, move annually between the 157 UK labour market areas that they construct, figures which are very consistent with orders of magnitude reported by the OECD (2013a).

20 The 179 OECD-TL3 areas in the USA on average are just under three times the area of the 274 EU-NUTS2 regions, ignoring Alaska, but only 96 per cent of the average NUTS2 area population. However, in the densely populated north-eastern and coastal states many of the US TL3 areas are of similar sizes to many of the OECD-TL3 regions in Europe. The 1.3 per cent per annum interregional migration rate of the USA is therefore very similar to the 1.39 per cent interregional migration rates across EU-NUTS2 regions in Europe.

21 The figures were kindly provided by Dr Heather Dickey from the University of Aberdeen.

22 Interestingly, when calculated on a population basis the scale of interregional mobility within the UK is little different to that which is observed in USA. Annually some 1.3 per cent of the US population move between the 179 OECD-TL3 regions of the USA (OECD 2013a), whose average population is 1.76 million people per TL3 region. Meanwhile, some 4 per cent of the UK population move annually between the 139 OECD-TL3/EU-NUTS3 regions (OECD 2013a), whose average population is 460,000. The ratio of the UK migration rate divided by the US migration rate (4/1.3 = 3.08) is very close to the ratio of the average population of the US OECD-TL3 regions divided by that of the UK OECD-TL3 regions (1.76/0.46 = 3.82). Similarly, if we compare the US OECD-TL3 regions with the UK's 12 OECD-TL2/EU-NUTS1 regions whose average population is 5.33 million people, we see that the ratio of the population of the UK OECD-TL2 regions divided by the average population of the US OECD-TL3 regions is 4.1 Yet, rather than being smaller as might be expected, the UK interregional migration rates are still 1.7 times larger than the equivalent US figures. On the other hand, if we consider these issues according to geographical areas the US OECD-TL3 areas are on average 2.71 times larger than the OECD-TL2 regions of the UK, so the ratio of the areas and the migration rates comes much closer.

23 www.centreforcities.org/data-tool/#graph=table&indicator=population\\ actual\\2003--2013&city=aldershot&city=bournemouth&city=brighton&city= bristol&city=cambridge&city=chatham&city=crawley&city=gloucester&city=hast ings&city=ipswich&city=london&city=luton&city=milton-keynes&city=northam pton&city=norwich&city=oxford&city=peterborough&city=plymouth&city=por tsmouth&city=reading&city=southampton&city=southend&city=swindon&city= worthing.

24 www.centreforcities.org/data-tool/#graph=table&indicator=population\\
actual\\2003--2013&city=aberdeen&city=barnsley&city=belfast&city=birkenh
ead&city=birmingham&city=blackburn&city=blackpool&city=bolton&city=
bradford&city=burnley&city=cardiff&city=coventry&city=derby&city=donc
aster&city=edinburgh&city=glasgow&city=grimsby&city=huddersfield&city=
hull&city=leeds&city=leicester&city=liverpool&city=manchester&city=mansfi
eld&city=middlesbrough&city=newcastle&city=newport&city=preston&city=
rochdale&city=sheffield&city=stoke&city=sunderland&city=swansea&city=
telford&city=wakefield&city=warrington&city=wigan&city=york.

25 McCormick (1991) reports that in the 1970s UK interregional migration rates for
non-manual workers were of the order of 1 per cent per annum while for manual
workers it was just 0.5 per cent per annum. In the 1980s the unemployment rates
of the former group only rose slightly while those of the latter group rose markedly
(Minford and Stoney 1991).

26 www.heathrowairport.com/static/Heathrow/Downloads/PDF/Heathrow-Related-
Employment-Report.pdf.

27 www.gatwickairport.com/business-community/about-gatwick/at-a-glance/
facts-stats/.

28 Some 1.9 million former council houses were transferred into the private sector
since the 1980 Housing Act which ushered in the 'Right to Buy' scheme and later
on also the 'Right to Acquire' houses scheme from housing associations, with only
345,000 social houses built subsequently. See "Housing and the Election: The
Right to Buy ... Votes", *The Economist*, 18 April 2015. The result is that more
former council houses are now in the private sector than still remain in the public
sector. See: *Panorama* "What Britain Wants: Somewhere to Live", broadcast on
BBC1 at 22.40 on Monday 9 March 2015.

29 www.migrationobservatory.ox.ac.uk/sites/files/migobs/Briefing%20-%20
Migrant%20stock%20in%20Scotland%20intl%20comparison.pdf.

30 www.migrationobservatory.ox.ac.uk/sites/files/migobs/Briefing%20-%20
Northern%20Ireland%20census%20profile_0.pdf.

31 See: www.migrationobservatory.ox.ac.uk/number-foreign-born-local-area-district.

32 *The Economist*, "European Immigrants: What Will Become of Them?", 30 May
2015.

33 *Revised Annual Mid-Year Population Estimates, 2001 to 2010*, Office for National
Statistics, 17 December 2013.

34 www.migrationobservatory.ox.ac.uk/number-foreign-born-local-area-district.

35 www.migrationobservatory.ox.ac.uk/number-foreign-born-local-area-district.

36 *Revised Annual Mid-Year Population Estimates, 2001 to 2010*, Office for National
Statistics, 17 December 2013.

37 "Net Migration up to 298,000 as Conservative Target Missed", www.bbc.com/
news/uk-politics-31638174.

38 www.migrationobservatory.ox.ac.uk/number-foreign-born-local-area-district-
www.bbc.com/news/uk-31748422.

39 These figures come from the 2011 census. The 2014 estimate is that this value is 13
per cent. See: www.migrationobservatory.ox.ac.uk/number-foreign-born-local-area-
district.

40 OECD, 2014, *PISA 2012 Results: What Students Know and Can Do (Volume I,
Revised Edition, February 2014): Student Performance in Mathematics, Reading
and Science*, Organisation for Economic Cooperation and Development, Paris.

41 www.migrationwatchuk.org/pdfs/BP15_5.pdf; www.migrationwatchuk.org/briefing-
paper/7.18.

42 See: www.migrationobservatory.ox.ac.uk/number-foreign-born-local-area-district.

43 There are also intra-urban differences in foreign-born within London. See "The
London Effect", *The Economist*, 15 December 2012.

44   See: www.migrationobservatory.ox.ac.uk/number-foreign-born-local-area-district.

45   Various small municipalities and localities in the East Midlands have some of the highest immigrant shares in the UK which are associated primarily with agricultural industries, and this is argued to strain local service provision. However, from an economic perspective immigration has been broadly beneficial to the region (EMC 2014) which as a whole still reflects the generally much lower immigrant shares evident outside of London and the South East.

46   "Two Birds with One Stone", *The Economist*, 18 July 2015.

47   https://lselondonmigration.files.wordpress.com/2014/12/full-book_migrationand-londonsgrowth.pdf; www.london.gov.uk/olc/2015/part2/docs/Fitting%20a%20 Quart%20into%20Pint%20Pot%20-Ian%20Gordon.pdf.

48   www.migrationwatchuk.org/briefing-paper/11.36.

49   "Looking for a Home", *The Economist*, 29 August 2015.

50   "Interest Rates Would Be Higher Without Immigrants", BBC News, 14 May 2015. See: www.bbc.com/news/business-32739852.

51   Which at the most are between just 2 and 3 per cent of the total £205 billion UK welfare bill in 2013/2014, whereas the perceived levels calculated from surveys of the general public are 23 per cent (Kellner 2015). In other words, public perceptions over-inflate the issue by a factor of between 8 and 10. Similarly, in terms of the number of immigrants claiming a job-seeker's allowance, public attitudes and perceptions point to a figure of between 300,000 and 500,000 while the actual number is around 60,000 (Kellner 2015).

52   "Immigration Worries", *The Economist*, 22 August 2015.

53   "Britain's Immigration Policy: How to Kneecap the Recovery", *The Economist*, 20 June 2015.

54   Some commentators question the empirical measures employed in this analysis but not the econometric methodology. www.migrationwatchuk.org/pdfs/BP1_37. pdf.

55   "The Snarling Dud of May", *The Economist*, 10 October 2015.

56   See: www.bruegel.org/nc/blog/detail/article/1483-brain-drain-gain-or-circulation/.

57   www.migrationwatchuk.org/pdfs/BP15_4.pdf.

58   www.migrationwatchuk.org/pdfs/BP12_4.pdf.

59   www.economist.com/news/britain/21627666-britons-views-immigration-are-perple xing-blend-myth-and-reality-melting-pot.

60   "Scotland Tipped to Leave the Union, Survey Shows", *Financial Times*, 16 March 2015.

61   The overall population densities in both The Netherlands and Belgium is much higher than in the UK. The UK population density as a whole is 263 people per sq km or 265 per sq km if we remove lakes and waterways. The population density of Belgium is 366 people per sq km while the population density of The Netherlands as a whole is 401 people per sq km, or 495 people per sq km if we remove lakes and waterways. The Netherlands contains 4.5 times as much surface area covered by water – comprising lakes and waterways – as the whole of the UK and the vast majority of this is accounted for by the large artificial inland brackish sea of 1100 sq km known as the Ijsselmeer, which alone is almost four times the size of Lough Neagh and is the largest lake in western Europe, plus the very low lying Waddensee between the northern Dutch coast and the Friesian island. The Ijsselmeer alone is equivalent to two-thirds of the surface area of all of the UK's lakes and waterways.

62   Indeed, outside of London, most of the southern and eastern regions of England actually exhibit low levels of urbanisation (Evans and Hartwich 2005a).

63   www.london.gov.uk/mayor/economic_unit/docs/CapImpact_andrew_burrell.pdf.

64   Ibid.

65 Oxford Economic Forecasting estimated that London ran a small interregional trade surplus of the order of less than 7 per cent of UK GDP (CLC 2004).
66 www.gov.scot/Resource/0045/00457487.pdf.
67 http://business.cardiff.ac.uk/sites/default/files/IO_2007_Final_30_6.pdf.
68 www.economicsystems.co.uk/south-west/help.php.
69 www.london.gov.uk/mayor/economic_unit/docs/CapImpact_andrew_burrell.pdf.
70 The Experian estimates for London's imports from the rest of the UK are 90 per cent of those estimated previously by Oxford Economic Forecasting (CLC 2004) and therefore are close to each other. Where they differ substantially, however, is in terms of London's exports to the rest of the UK. The Experian estimates are only 70 per cent of those provided by Oxford Economic Forecasting (CLC 2004) which suggest that London runs a trade surplus with the rest of the UK and conversely that the rest of the UK runs a trade deficit with London. Moreover, if it were the case that London runs a trade surplus with the rest of the UK (CLC 2004) then many of the positive arguments regarding London's role as a market for UK regions would largely disappear. See: www.london.gov.uk/mayor/economic_unit/docs/CapImpact_andrew_burrell.pdf.
71 "Credit Where It's Due: The SME Lending Puzzle". See: www.smf.co.uk/credit-where-its-due-the-sme-lending-puzzle/.
72 www.cbi.org.uk/business-issues/smes/.
73 https://www.gov.uk/government/uploads/system/uploads/attachment_data/file/32263/12-539-sme-access-external-finance.pdf.
74 https://www.gov.uk/government/consultations/competition-in-banking-improving-access-to-sme-credit-data/competition-in-banking-improving-access-to-sme-credit-data.
75 Bank lending plays a relatively much more important role in business finance than in the US. See: "Financing Europe's Small Firms: Treasure Hunt", *The Economist*, 27 June 2015.
76 www.ons.gov.uk/ons/regional-statistics/index.html.
77 A point examined in the radio programme *The City* presented by Will Hutton and broadcast on BBC Radio 4 on 5, 12 and 19 January 1995, and also reiterated by the UK's Most Successful Investor Neil Woodford on *Hardtalk*, broadcast on BBC World at 08.30, 6 April 2015.
78 The latest CEBR (Centre for Economics and Business Research) figures suggest that in 2014 the net contribution of London to the public revenues was £34 billion. See *BBC London News*, broadcast at 18.30–19.00 on 16 April 2015. Moreover, the fiscal relationships between London and the rest of the UK are expected to be one of the major campaign issues in the forthcoming London Mayoral Election campaign. See *BBC London News*, broadcast at 18.30–19.00 on 15 June 2015.
79 "The 'Beverly Hills' of Surrey Pays More Income Tax Than Big Cities of the North", *The Independent*, 22 May 2013.
80 The Oxford Economics estimates for the net fiscal contributions of London inclusive of welfare payments and relative to GVA (CLC 2012) are far lower than the CEBR (2012a) estimate of these net contributions relative to GDP. In part this is because their 2010/2011 estimate is 8 percentage points lower than the CEBR estimate and also in part because CEBR benchmark the regional fiscal position relative to the national fiscal position at the time.
81 www.bbc.co.uk/blogs/thereporters/markeaston/2008/06/map_of_the_week_public_spendin.html.
82 Other analyses paint a rather less optimistic picture into the future situation (McLaren *et al.* 2013, 2014). However, the figures reported here are also affected by the fact that issues such as defence spending, foreign and diplomatic services, and many other government services and activities including debt servicing are

not broken down by region and instead are classed as 'national' expenditure with everyone contributing and benefiting equally (CLC 2014a). These activities tend to heavily favour London and the southern regions of England. See also: Maxwell, J., 2011, "Enough of the Scottish Subsidy Myth: Scotland Pays its Way in the Union – It's Time the London Commentariat Acknowledged That", *Prospect*, 6 November.

83 www.oilandgasuk.co.uk/2014-economic-report.cfm.

84 The current ratio of public expenditure to tax receipts is 1.14 for the UK, 1.13 for England, 1.88 for Wales, 1.95 for Northern Ireland and 1.30 for Scotland – excluding North Sea Oil and Gas-related tax receipts. The figures were kindly calculated by Professor Stephen Gibbons of SERC and LSE on the basis of HMRC regional tax receipts reports and HM Treasury public expenditure data.

85 Of course 8 out of the UK's 12 OECD-TL2/EU-NUTS1 regions have no budget responsibility or fiscal roles and as such are simply large statistical regions for data purposes. If we therefore consider OECD-TL3/EU-NUTS3 regions with explicit budgetary and fiscal responsibilities then two of the three UK areas running the highest fiscal deficits and receiving relatively the highest fiscal transfers related to employment and infrastructure will be Oxford and Cambridge. See: www.centreforcities.org/data-tool/.

86 Except for housing-related issues.

87 www.bbc.co.uk/blogs/thereporters/markeaston/2008/06/map_of_the_week_public_spendin.html.

88 See: www.centreforcities.org/data-tool/.

89 Britain's total welfare bill in 2013/2014 was £205 billion, of which by far the largest component is state pension and pension-related credits, amounting to some £90 billion. Benefits for families with children total £37 billion, those for sick and disabled people amount to £36 billion. A further £34 billion helps people on low incomes, of which two-thirds is accounted for by housing benefits. Unemployment benefits amount to just £4.5 billion, or rather just 2 per cent of total welfare spending (Kellner 2015).

90 "Half a Million More People Claiming Housing Benefit Under Coalition", *The Observer*, 15 March 2015.

91 See: *A Disaggregation of HMRC Tax Receipts between England, Wales, Scotland & Northern Ireland: Methodology Note*, HM Revenue & Customs, October 2014.

92 Which with a workforce of at 100,500 the Canary Wharf–Docklands area is just over a quarter as large as The City whose total employment is approximately 365,000, although estimates vary between 357,000 and 382,700. See: ONS, 2013, *Big Developments Provide Work for London*, Office for National Statistics, London, 8 August; *City of London Workforce CENSUS 2011 Introduction*, Corporation for the City of London, May 2015.

93 In 2010/2011 total taxes accounted for 45.2 per cent of Greater London's GDP (CEBR 2012a) whereas the UK average tax share is 35 per cent of GDP (OECD 2014a). London's per capita tax contribution is therefore 29 per cent higher than the UK average. At the other end of the spectrum Northern Ireland's tax contribution is only 27.7 per cent of GDP (CEBR 2012a).

94 This assumption is realistic, given that in the years between the turn of the millennium and the 2008 crisis the total fiscal surpluses generated by UK regions excluding welfare payments typically accounted for some 80 per cent of the total fiscal deficits incurred by UK regions including welfare payments, and after the crisis this figure rose to 90 per cent (CLC 2012). In other words, typically 10–20 per cent of these welfare transfer payments were paid for as part of overall UK government borrowing. See: www.ons.gov.uk/ons/guide-method/compendiums/compendium-of-uk-statistics/economy/index.html.

95 The relative size of these interregional fiscal transfers is much lower than the equivalent shares which are evident in Canada, USA or Germany. See: Sandbu, M., 2015, "The Case Against 'Cash for Reform'", *Financial Times*, 19 August.

96 These IFS calculations treat the banks which had been taken into public ownership in the aftermath of the 2008 crisis as still being part of the private sector. See IFS 2012, p. 110.

97 Moreover, budget deficits are the relatively very small differences between two enormous numbers, namely public spending and government revenues, and the ability of the government to predict or control these with any accuracy over the medium or long term is very limited (Kaletsky 2015).

98 www.centreforcities.org/data-tool/.

99 "Lure of the South Too Strong for Northern Businesses", *Financial Times*, 15 March 2015.

100 Ibid.

101 While urban economic models are seen to perform better than NEG models, these results only hold for females and not for males (Fingleton and Longhi 2013). The reasons may be related to gender differences in commuting patterns associated with joint household and employment choices (Fingleton and Longhi 2013). These gender differences also appear in terms of local job competition effects.

102 "Westminster: Where Houses Earn More than People", BBC News, 17 March 2015. See: www.bbc.com/news/uk-31919109.

103 See also: "The Super Rich and Us: Part 1" broadcast on BBC2 on 8 January 2014 at 21.00.

104 The UK population has increased by 15 million since 1947, by more than 10 million since 1964, and by more than 5 million since 2001. See: www.ons.gov.uk/ons/rel/pop-estimate/population-estimates-for-uk--england-and-wales--scotland-and-northern-ireland/2013/index.html.

105 www.lloydsbankinggroup.com/globalassets/documents/media/press-releases/halifax/2010/50_years_of_housing_uk.pdf.

106 Many of these rather romantic aesthetic notions are related to the cultural underpinnings of Englishness (Paxman 2002) and in many ways appear to be just as pertinent today as they were some 60 years ago. See: www.cpre.org.uk/magazine/features/item/3665-the-countryside-and-englishness.However, apart from a minority of genuine ecological concerns, many of the values today underpinning campaigns to protect the greenbelt range from being conservative (Scruton 2012, 2014) to reactionary (Robin 2011) in nature, while also spanning across the political spectrum. Scruton, R., 2012, *How to Think Seriously About the Planet: The Case for An Environmental Conservatism*, Oxford University Press, Oxford; Scruton, R., 2014, *How to Be a Conservative*, Bloomsbury, London; Robin, C., 2011, *The Reactionary Mind: Conservatism from Edmund Burke to Sarah Palin*, Oxford University Press, Oxford.

107 Reductions or removal of most planning restrictions would reduce UK house prices by 25–35 per cent (Hilber and Vermeulen 2012; Overman 2013). The equivalent figures for houses in New Zealand are 10–15 per cent, but in the NZ case these implicit taxes are found to be relatively more significant on affordable housing, and are of the order of 35 per cent (Grimes and Mitchell 2015), and this is also likely to be the case in the UK. Meanwhile London's office construction costs are amongst the highest in the world, but this is also due to history and the physical morphology of the city as well as planning-related issues. See: "London's Costly Construction: Bodies, Bombs and Bureaucracy", *The Economist*, 9 August 2014.

108 "Through the Roof", *The Economist*, 26 September 2015; "Global Housing Markets: Upwardly Mobile", *The Economist*, 3 October 2015.
109 McDermott, J., "The London Syndrome: The World's Money and People are Pouring into the Capital. Don't Knock it.", *Prospect*, 14 November 2013.
110 England currently has 14 greenbelts covering 1.6 million square hectares, or some 13 per cent of the total land area of England (CPRE 2010a).
111 Although Piketty does not directly address there housing and land-supply related issues on intergenerational wealth inequalities. See Willets, D., 2015, "Mind the Gap", *Prospect*, September. See also: "http://www.ft.com/intl/cms/s/0/1ad5c43a-a593-11e5-a91e-162b86790c58.html" \l "axzz3uqwpyYSW" \t "_blank" http://www.ft.com/intl/cms/s/0/1ad5c43a-a593-11e5-a91e-162b86790c58.html#axzz3uqwpyYSW http://www.theguardian.com/money/2015/dec/18/britain-private-wealth-owned-by-top-10-of-households.
112 "The Paradox of Soil", *The Economist*, 4 April 2015; Krugman, P., 2015, "Inequality and the City", *New York Times*, 1 December.
113 "Two Birds with One Stone", *The Economist*, 18 July 2015.
114 "Space and the City: Poor Land Use in the World's Greatest Cities Carries a Huge Cost", *The Economist*, 4 April 2015.
115 As Evans and Hartwich (2005a) point out, the Urban Task Force consisted entirely of architects and planners with no urban, land or regional economists on the panel. As such there was little or no consideration of the price and wealth-related impacts of the UK housing and real estate markets associated with the impacts of the brownfield proposals. This lack of market perspective also resulted in some incorrect interpretations being made regarding international cross-country comparisons of house sizes (Evans and Hartwich 2005b).
116 Except for the argument that at present there are some 330,000 planning permissions which have been granted for dwellings to be built and which have not yet been acted upon. The Chair of the Urban Task Force Richard Rogers interprets this as implying that insufficient finance rather than land supply is the major problem. See; "Finance is the Best Path to Development", *Financial Times*, 10 September 2012. However, the fact that major "UK builders hold back enough land for 600,000 new homes" (*The Guardian*, 31 December 2015) suggests that there are major supply inefficiencies and dysfunctionalities within the UK land markets, which builders blame on the planning system.
117 Martin Wolf describes the greenbelt as being the "holiest" of all "sacred cows". See: Wolf, M., 2015, "A More Radical Solution for England's Housing Crisis", *Financial Times*, 11 December.
118 https://www.atcm.org/policy_practice/future_high_streets_forum/future_high_streets_forum2014.
119 "Shops Desert High Street at Faster Rate in 2014". See: www.bbc.com/business-31899346.
120 "Preston Tops Table of UK's 'Unhealthiest High Street' ". See: www.bbc.com/news/uk-32058929.
121 "Local Data Company: Empty Shops Show North-South Divide". See: www.bbc.com/news/business-311245506.
122 Today this is often associated with re-designating existing urban open space and land designated for sport and leisure activities – and which have a high social value due to their immediate accessibility for local residents – into land which can be made available for housing or commercial development (Cheshire *et al.* 2012).
123 Evans and Hartwich (2005a) contend that only some 14 per cent of UK housing needs can be accommodated by brownfield developments. However, the fact that this spatial mismatch argument is also based on the degree of substitutability also implies that the observation that office rents in the pre-2008 crisis boom in Birmingham and San Francisco were very similar (Overman 2013) is also of

limited value for understanding the workings of land markets within the UK interregional economy, because for the vast majority of service sector firms and investors these cities are not substitutes. Similarly, today's office rents in Leeds are exactly the same as those in Ho Chi Minh City Vietnam (CBRE 2014a), but again this tells us little about the workings of land markets in the UK interregional economy. As such, the Birmingham–San Francisco comparability argument does not relate primarily to spatial market demand and supply price mismatches but rather to the excess levels of gross capital flows into UK real estate markets. Since the post-2008 crisis correction, office rents today in Birmingham are 62 per cent of those in San Francisco (CBRE 2014a).

124 Including the higher environmental costs associated with average commuting distances which are greater than would otherwise be the case. See: "Commuting; Metroland Spreads Out", *The Economist*, 5 April 2014.

125 www.bbc.com/news/business-31690194.

126 "Can We Fix It? No We Can't", *The Economist*, 15 August 2015.

127 Following many of the original Garden City ideas there is no reason why housing development on greenbelt land cannot be both environmentally sensitive and also sensitive to the quality of life considerations of different age and income groups (Evans and Hartwich 2006). However, there is a key distinction between the housing-related and the retail-related arguments. The social welfare conclusions of the housing-related arguments do not relate directly to retail location questions, because retail does not directly involve distortions in wealth accumulation opportunities. As such, pro-greenbelt housing development conclusions do not necessarily or automatically imply that edge-of-city and out-of-town superstore shopping mall-type retail development should automatically also be encouraged over town centre approaches. Access to a combination of retail, cultural and heritage services in a safe social and public context is an important aspect of quality of life and livability for citizens (Grimsey 2013) and this differs markedly according to location and also age and income groups. For reasons of both residential location patterns and also transportation access and possibilities, out-of-town retail facilities often favour higher income groups. As such, the trade-offs between the costs and benefits of providing such services in central or out-of-town locations are very different to their housing questions and need to be considered from the perspective of the preferences of local residents, as well as from the profitability perspective of businesses (Wrigley and Lambiri 2014).

128 "Westminster: Where Houses Earn More than People", BBC News, 17 March 2015. See: www.bbc.com/news/uk-31919109.

129 www.publications.parliament.uk/pa/bills/cbill/2014-2015/0139/15139.pdf; Cash, W., 2011, "A Very English Revolution", *New Statesman*, 12 September.

130 The only possible exceptions here are where local development is championed by central government on the basis of the perceived 'national' interest, such as in the cases of Heathrow Terminal 5 or the HS2 project.

131 Overman *et al.* (2010) show that under increasing returns to scale in the south that this is indeed a possibility with southern house prices eventually again reaching existing or even greater levels (Fingleton 2008). This scenario is something like the land use equivalent of the transport problem (Duranton and Turner 2011).

132 See also: www.lloydsbankinggroup.com/globalassets/documents/media/press-releases/halifax/2010/50_years_of_housing_uk.pdf.

133 www.prospectmagazine.co.uk/features/how-to-fix-the-housing-crisis.

134 The UK is demographically one of the most unequal countries in the world. The wealth of the average 55–64 year old is over five times that of the average 16–34 year old, whereas in Italy it is only three times as high. Similarly, the household debt of British twentysomethings is fives higher than those in their fifties and sixties. See: "The Only Way is Up", *The Economist*, 8 August 2015. See also: "No

Country for Young Men – UK Generation Gap Widens", *Financial Times*, 23 February 2015; "Britain's Twentysomethings and the Broken Promises of a Future", *Financial Times*, 23 February 2015; www.theguardian.com/money/2015/jul/22/pwc-report-generation-rent-to-grow-over-next-decade; "Old Displace Young on Income Ladder", *Financial Times* interactive age-income distribution calculator, see: www.ft.com/ig/features/old-displace-young-on-income-ladder/.

135 www.bbc.com/news/business-28648704.

136 "Two Birds with One Stone", *The Economist*, 18 July 2015.

137 BBC London News, broadcast on BBC1 at 18.30–19.00 on 15 June 2015.

138 "Westminster: Where Houses Earn More than People", BBC News, 17 March 2015, see: www.bbc.com/news/uk-31919109.

139 Ibid.

140 OECD Regional Database. Note also that in 2011 only 49.6 per cent of London households were property owners with 50.4 per cent being renters (ONS 2011). This suggests that not only is the overall value of the London housing market overvalued relative to the share of the Greater London population and its output contribution, but also that these excessive property values accrue to a minority of the London population.

141 Across the UK and across all housing tenures some 54 per cent of people do *not* perceive there to be a housing 'crisis' in their local area whereas 76 per cent of London residents *do* perceive there to be such a crisis situation. The 54 per cent of UK people who do not perceive any housing crisis in their local area also very closely relates to the 55.6 per cent of the UK population who as we have seen in Chapter 2 are not resident in the southern and eastern regions of England. For renters, the national picture is that 60 per cent perceive there to be a housing crisis in their local area. See: www.cih.org/news-article/display/vpathDCR/template-data/cih/news-article/data/Three_quarters_of_public_and_two_thirds_of_MPs_think_there_is_a_housing_crisis_in_Britain.

142 www.bbc.com/news/business-30630655.

143 London experiences significant capital inflows from all over the world into its real estate markets, some of which is primarily for property development purposes and some of which is primarily for investment purposes, with the London real estate markets acting somewhat as a reserve currency. See: "Capital Returns", *Investors Chronicle*, 17–25 July 2015; Goldfarb, M., "London's Great Exodus", *New York Times*, 12 October 2013; McDermott, J., "The London Syndrome: The World's Money and People are Pouring into the Capital. Don't Knock it.", *Prospect*, 14 November 2013.

144 "What is in Demand in 2015 in Real Estate", *Financial Times* FDI Intelligence, 12 February, 2015, www.fdiintelligence.com.

145 The Wibberley (1959) estimate for the share of UK land which was urban in 1950 was 9.7 per cent rising from 5.4 per cent in 1900. Stone (1970) estimated the 1970 share at 7 per cent and Best calculated the 1981 share of UK land which was urban as being 8 per cent (Evans and Hartwich 2005a), Today the Centre for Cities provide a 2015 figure of 9 per cent (CfC 2015) on the basis of local authority areas, while the 6.8 per cent figure calculated by UKNEA (2011) based on remote sensing and geographic information systems is by far the most detailed and accurate estimate currently available.

146 The aggregate value of 6.8 per cent is comprised of 10.6 per cent for England, 1.9 per cent for Scotland, 3.6 per cent for Northern Ireland and 4.1 per cent for Wales (UKNEA 2011). See: "The Great Myth of Urban Britain", BBC News, 28 June 2012, www.bbc.com/news/uk-18623096.

147 Even allowing for the rapid decline of urban green spaces including allotments and playing fields over the last three and a half decades due to land sales and land conversion (UKNEA 2011).

148 Which also explains why central London urban population densities are relatively low in comparison to many other EU cities.

149 See: "The Great Myth of Urban Britain", BBC News, 28 June 2012, www.bbc. com/news/uk-18623096.

150 According to the city population definitions employed by the Centre for Cities. See: www.centreforcities.org/data-tool/.

151 Commuting across the greenbelt is estimated to cost the UK £12 billion per annum, or 0.75 of UK GDP. "Two Birds with One Stone", *The Economist*, 18 July 2015.

152 As calculated according to OECD (2012b) metropolitan urban areas definition.

153 In Scotland only 2 per cent of the land area is urban while 80 per cent of the population are urban dwellers. In Northern Ireland 65 per cent of the population are urban dwellers covering 3 per cent of the land area. In Wales 6 per cent of the land area is urban (UKNEA 2011).

154 In addition, UK house prices are overvalued on the basis of both housing rents and housing incomes relative to all other European countries except Belgium. See: "Property Puzzles", The Economist, 18 April 2015. Today almost two thirds of UK households wish they could live in a larger home. See: http://corporate. postoffice.co.uk/our-media-centre#/pressreleases/close-knit-families-the-uk-s-space-starved-children-struggle-for-room-1062730.

155 The 1981 estimate by Best for The Netherlands was 15 per cent (Evans and Hartwich 2005a) whereas the actual value today is 17 per cent (Daams *et al.* 2014). Given the respective population densities (263 and 495) and the urban land shares (6.8 per cent and 17 per cent) for the UK and The Netherlands, respectively, these figures imply that the urban area per resident in The Netherlands is currently 12.9 per cent higher than the equivalent figure for the UK.

156 See: www.destatis.de/EN/FactsFigures/EconomicSectors/AgricultureForestry Fisheries/LandUse/Tables/Areas.html. Given that the population density in Germany is 226 per sq km, this implies that the urban land area per German resident is almost exactly double that of UK residents. See also chapter 4 of Cheshire *et al.* (2014a) for more details on these international comparisons.

157 The UK population density of 263 persons per sq km is far below the overall population densities in both The Netherlands and Belgium and only 16 per cent more densely populated than Germany. The UK population density as a whole is 263 people per sq km or 265 per sq km if we remove lakes and waterways. The population density of Belgium is 366 people per sq km while the population density of The Netherlands as a whole is 401 people per sq km, or 495 people per sq km if we remove the artificial inland sea-lakes and waterways. The Netherlands contains 4.5 times as much surface area covered by water – comprising lakes and waterways – as the whole of the UK and the vast majority of this is accounted for by the large artificial inland brackish sea of 1100 sq km known as the Ijsselmeer, which alone is almost four times the size of Lough Neagh and is the largest lake in western Europe, plus the very low lying Waddensee between the northern Dutch coast and the Friesian island. The Ijsselmeer alone is equivalent to two-thirds of the surface area of all of the UK's lakes and waterways.

158 UK land rents for various types of urban uses are typically some 20–25 per cent above those evident in other European countries (CBRE 2014b). While higher UK urban land prices might be expected, given that the UK is much more densely populated than countries such as Spain, Sweden and Finland, and rather more densely populated than France or Poland, these population distribution arguments alone cannot explain why there is such a UK urban land price premium over The Netherlands given that both countries have identical levels of urbanisation, or an urban land price premium over Germany which has similar population density levels and is more productive. However, if we acknowledge the different

urban land allocations per capita due to the different planning systems then the figures start to make sense.

159 In contrast, Deutsche Bank (2014) find that in terms of skyscraper costs and prices that Hong Kong, Tokyo, New York and Singapore are all more expensive than London, with London being only marginally more expensive than Sydney, Beijing, Shanghai. Moreover, in relation to its role as a global financial centre, London appears to be relatively inexpensive, and not significantly more expensive than cities whose global financial role is much more limited than London's. Similarly, the EIU (Economist Intelligence Unit) finds Singapore to be the most expensive city in the world with several other European cities also being more expensive than London, and most notably Paris. See: www.worldwidecostofliving.com/asp/wcol_WCOLHome.asp.

160 "Cities Unshackled from Whitehall's Dead Hand", *Financial Times*, 14 May 2015.

161 "Manchester: The UK's New Order?", *Financial Times*, 20 February 2015; "Greater Manchester: The Start of Something Big?", BBC News, 25 February 2015. See: www.bbc.com/news/health-31590885.

162 Rozenfeld *et al.* (2011) provide a detailed list of contributions over more than six decades. However, apart from two major contributions in the early 1950s, almost all economic comments on these Zipf's Law types of issues have only emerged since the mid-1990s.

163 For reasons of consistency and comparability we remove observations from what is now the Republic of Ireland from the 1851 and 1900 data sets.

164 Rather than the different and shifting geopolitical entities which had London as its official capital city, and which prior to 1557 would include various different parts of today's France, which prior to 1707 would rule out Scotland, which prior to 1776 would include parts of today's USA, which between 1801 and 1922 would also include all of the island of Ireland, and which in the early nineteenth century would also include Australia and New Zealand.

165 See: "The Super Rich and Us: Part 2", broadcast on BBC2 on 15 January 2014 at 21.00.

166 www.bbc.com/news/uk-england-london-31056626; www.bbc.com/news/uk-england-london-31082941.

167 In the cases of Oxford and Cambridge the required growth would have to be more than fifteen-fold. Yet, Oxford and Cambridge are not especially useful examples for an analysis of wider potential market-led structural changes, given that they are very particular cases of towns dominated by world-famous universities and with Oxford displaying the highest public employment shares of any UK city and with Cambridge displaying the third highest share. Moreover, Oxford lost population during the 1980s (Champion 2014). The argument would therefore appear to be more credible if examples such as Reading, Slough, Basingstoke, Peterborough or Bournemouth were to be used. However, again, in the absence of greenbelt policies, whether or not these small southern towns would have grown by some fifteen-fold since the early 1990s, as would be required in order to really alter the national city-size distributions, can only be a matter of speculation and is certainly open to serious doubt. See: www.citiesoutlook.org/ratio/table#all.

168 Coyle and Rosewell (2014) also contend on the basis of a Zipf's Law type argument that the UK's second cities are too small but they also argue that on the basis of a 'world cities' or 'global cities' argument that London is too small in comparison to other world cities. In reality, however, London is rather large in comparison to most other world cities (Iammarino and McCann 2013; McCann and Acs 2011). Moreover, the UK's second tier cities are not small in comparison to the second tier cities of most OECD countries of similar levels of development to the UK. The only advanced OECD countries with markedly larger primal and second tier cities are the USA, Japan and Korea, and those in Korea and Japan

were largely a result of intentional industrialisation-urbanisation policies over many decades in a context of severe limited space constraints due to mountainous terrain. As such it is difficult to draw lessons for the UK from comparisons with Japan and Korea. In the case of the USA, relative to the national population, US cities are actually much smaller than UK cities, so again drawing inferences for the UK becomes problematic.

169 Less seriously, it has been suggested that in the case of Manchester and Leeds the newly merged city might centre on the village of Hebden Bridge, located in a narrow valley approximately halfway between the two centres. See Part 2 of the Evan Davis BBC television programme *Mind the Gap: London vs the Rest* broadcast on Monday 10 March 2014 on BBC2 at 21.00–22.00.

170 In Part 1 of the Evan Davis BBC television programme *Mind the Gap: London vs the Rest* which was broadcast on Monday 3 March 2014 on BBC2 at 21.00–22.00.

171 "Excellence Versus Equity: Special Report on Universities", *The Economist*, 28 March 2015.

172 UK income inequality defined in terms of the 90:10 ratio of the top and bottom deciles has narrowed since 1990 while the income share of the top 1 per cent (or 300,000 workers) has doubled since the 1980s. Many of the top 1 per cent are employed in London's 'City-type' jobs, of which, as we saw in the previous chapter, there are approximately 300,000 such jobs. See: "The Inequality Puzzle", *The Economist*, 18 July 2015.

173 See also "Stiglitz on Inequality", 21 May 2015, BBC Podcast www.bbc.co.uk/podcasts/series/bizdaily.

174 "Inequality is Bad for Growth, Says OECD", BBC News, 21 May 2015, www.bbc.com/business-32826643.

175 Overman (2013) refers to the problem whereby political logic encourages a 'jam spreading' approach to the distribution of policy funds which then leads to fragmentation and a lack of resource concentration. This is an important point and one which is examined in the next two chapters. In contrast, Boris Johnson uses the same metaphor but it is unclear as to whether Johnson intends the 'jam' to refer to market-related economic benefits or to public and fiscal resources. Clarification on this issue is essential because the purported 'spreading' mechanism may differ significantly depending on what is being referred to. Yet, even without any such clarity, in either case Johnson implies that concentration of economic benefits and resources in London will automatically lead to some sort of 'trickle down' type of spread effect emanating from London to the rest of the UK economy. However, extending this analogy it is obvious that this argument is clearly not only analytically incorrect – in that any purported spread effects also depend on the jam's viscosity, the Ryvita's surface porosity and roughness, and the specifics of the 'spoon' mechanisms employed for delivering the jam – but also that the empirical evidence simply doesn't support this contention.

176 See the Tony Travers reference in Chapter 1.

177 "Disunited Kingdom: London in a World of Its Own", *Financial Times*, 2 March 2015.

178 Which Gibbons *et al.* (2011) refer to as the 'myopic' case.

179 For a mortgage which is 2.5–3.0 times annual gross income, and assuming that direct taxes are of the order of one-third of gross incomes, then for a 25-year mortgage the average annual wealth accumulation due to the capital repayments even without nominal house price growth is of the order of 15–18 per cent of the nominal after-tax income. In a housing-based spatial equilibrium model this savings-income premium needs to be added to the income side or numerator of the model, and not the denominator which contains the cost components relating to interest payments in the gross mortgage payments.

180 Except for the fact that long-term consumption costs of services such as health and social care are unlikely to be twice as high in the high housing price region.

References

Abreu, M.A., Faggian, A. and McCann, P., 2015, "Migration and Inter-Industry Mobility of UK Graduates", *Journal of Economic Geography*, 15.2, 353–385.

ACCA, 2014, *Innovations in Access to Finance for SMEs*, Association of Chartered Certified Accountants, London.

Ades, A.F., and Glaeser, E.L., 1995, "Trade and Circuses: Explaining Urban Giants", *Quarterly Journal of Economics*, 110, 195–227.

Ahlfeldt, G., Holman, N. and Wendland, N., 2012, *An Assessment of the Effects of Conservation Areas on Value*, Report Submitted to English Heritage, Department of Geography and SERC Spatial Economics Research Centre, London School of Economics and Political Science, London.

Ahrend, R., Farchy, E., Kaplanis, I. and Lembcke, A., 2014, "What Makes Cities More Productive? Evidence on the Role of Urban Governance from Five OECD Countries", *OECD Regional Development Working Papers 2014/05*, Organisation for Economic Cooperation and Development, Paris.

Alford, B.W.E., 1996, *Britain in the World Economy Since 1880: A Social and Economic History of Britain*, Longman, London.

Anyadike-Danes, M., Bonner, K. and Hart, M., 2013, "Exploring the Incidence and Spatial Distribution of High Growth Firms in the UK and their Contribution to Job Creation, *NESTA Working Paper No. 13/05*, London.

Appleyard, L., 2013, "The Geographies of Access to Enterprise Finance: The Case of the West Midlands, UK", *Regional Studies*, DOI: 10.1080.00343404.2012.748979.

Arcaute, E., Hatna, E., Ferguson, P., Youn, H., Johansson, A. and Batty, M., 2015, "Constructing Cities, Deconstructing Scaling Laws", *Journal of the Royal Statistical Society: Interface*, 12, DOI: dx.doi.org/10.1098/rsif.2014.0745.

Armstrong, A., Davis, E.P., Liadze, I. and Rienzo, C., 2013, "Evaluating Changes in Bank Lending to UK SMEs Over 2001–12: Ongoing Tight Credit?", *NIESR Discussion Paper No. 408*, National Institute of Economic and Social Research, London.

Artis, M., Miguelez, E. and Moreno, R., 2012, "Agglomeration Economies and Regional Intangible Assets", *Journal of Economic Geography*, 12, 1167–1189.

Athey, G., Nathan, M., Webber, C. and Mahroum, S., 2008, "Innovation and The City", *Innovation: Management, Policy & Practice*, 10, 156–169.

Atkinson, A.B., 2015a, *Inequality: What Can be Done?*, Harvard University Press, Cambridge, MA.

Atkinson, A.B., 2015b, "What Can Be Done About Inequality?", *Juncture*, 22.1, 32–41.

Bailey, D., Hildreth, P. and de Propris, L., 2015, "Mind the Gap! What Might a Place Based Industrial and Regional Policy Look Like?", in Bailey, D., Cowling, K. and Tomlinson, P., (eds.), *New Perspectives on Industrial Policy for a Modern Britain*, Oxford University Press, Oxford.

Balch, A., 2009, "Labour and Epistemic Communities: The Case of 'Managed Migration' in the UK", *The British Journal of Politics and International Relations*, 11, 613–633.

Balchin, P.N., Bull, G.H. and Kieve, J.L., 1995, *Urban Land Economics and Public Policy*, 5th edition, Palgrave, Basingstoke.

Ball. L., Pollard, E. and Stanley, N., 2010, *Creative Graduates Creative Futures*, Institute for Employment Studies, Brighton, www.creativegraduates.com.

Ball, P., 2004, *Critical Mass: How One Thing Leads to Another*, Heinemann, Random House, London.

Bank of England, 2014, *Financial Stability Report: Section 2*, June, London.

Barker, K., 2004, *Review of Housing Supply: Delivering Stability, Securing our Future Housing Needs, Final Report – Recommendations*, HM Treasury and HMSO, London.

Barker, K., 2008, "Planning Policy, Planning Practice, and Housing Supply", *Oxford Review of Economic Policy*, 24.1, 34–49.

Barker, K., 2014, *Housing: Where's the Plan?*, London Publishing Partnership, London.

Barkham, R., Gudgin, G., Hart, M. and Hanvey, E., 1996, *The Determinants of Small Firm Growth: An Inter-Regional Study in the United Kingdom, 1986–90*, Jessica Kingsley, London.

Barkham, R., Grilli, M. and Parpa, C., 2014, "Financial Markets in London Metropolitan Commercial Real Estate", in Nozeman, E.F., and van der Vlist, A., (eds.), *European Metropolitan Commercial Real Estate Markets*, Springer, Heidelberg.

Barlow, M., 1937, Royal Commission on the Distribution of the Industrial Population (Barlow Commission): Minutes and Papers. HLG27. See: www.discovery.nationalarchives.gov.uk/details/r/C8722.

Barlowe, R., 1958, *Land Resource Economics: The Political Economy of Rural and Urban Land Resource Use*, Prentice-Hall, Englewood-Cliffs, NJ.

Barrell, R., Fitzgerald, J. and Riley, R., 2010, "EU Enlargement and Migration: Assessing the Macroeconomic Effects", *Journal of Common Market Studies*, 48.2, 373–395.

Batty, M., 2005, *Cities and Complexity: Understanding Cities with Cellular Automata, Agent-Based Models, and Fractals*, MIT Press, Cambridge, MA.

Batty, M., 2015, "Competition in the Built Environment: Scaling Laws for Cities, Neighbourhoods and Buildings", Working Paper, University College London, 18.07.2015, *NEXUS*, Forthcoming.

Baumol, W.J., 1967, "Macroeconomics of Unbalanced Growth: The Anatomy of Urban Crisis", *American Economic Review*, 57.3, 415–426.

Baumol, W.J., 2012, *The Cost Disease: Why Computers Get Cheaper and Health Care Doesn't*, Yale University Press, New Haven.

BBB, 2014, *Small Business Finance Markets*, British Business Bank, London, www.british-business-bank.co.uk.

Bell, B., and Machin, S., 2011, *The Impact of Migration on Crime and Victimisation*, A Report for the Migration Advisory Committee, LSE Consulting, London.

Benford, J., and Burrows, O., 2013, "Commercial Property and Financial Stability", *Bank of England Quarterly Bulletin Q1,* London.

Bennett, R.J., Graham, D.J. and Bratton, W., 1999, "The Location and Concentration of Businesses in Britain: Business Clusters, Business Services, Market Coverage and Local Economic Development", *Transactions of the Institute of British Geographers*, 24, 393–420.

Best, R., and Shucksmith, R., 2006, *Homes for Rural Communities*, Joseph Rowntree Foundation, York.

Biagi, B., Faggian, A. and McCann, P., 2011, "Long and Short Distance Migration in Italy: The Role of Economic, Social and Environmental Characteristics", *Spatial Economic Analysis*, 6.1, 111–131.

BIS, 2012a, *Commentary on Regional Economic Performance Indicators*, Department for Business, Innovation and Skills, London, September.

BIS, 2012b, *SMEs Access to External Finance*, BIS Economics Paper No. 16, Department for Business, Innovation and Skills, London.

BIS, 2013, *SMEs Access to Finance Schemes: Measures to Support SME Growth*, Department for Business, Innovation and Skills, London, April.

BIS/DFID, 2011a, *The UK and the Single Market*, Trade and Investment Analytical Papers Topic 4 of 18, Department for Business, Innovation and Skills Department for International Development Joint BIS/DFID Trade Policy Unit, London.

BIS/DFID, 2011b, *Economic Openness and Economic Prosperity*, Trade and Investment Analytical Papers Topic 2 of 18, Department for Business, Innovation and Skills Department for International Development Joint BIS/DFID Trade Policy Unit, London.

Bish, R.L., and Nourse, H.O., 1975, *Urban Economics and Policy Analysis*, McGraw-Hill, New York.

Bishop, P., 2013, "The Spatial Distribution of Personal Insolvencies in England and Wales, 2000–2007", *Regional Studies*, 47.3, 419–432.

Black, J., de Meza, D. and Jeffreys, D., 1996, "House Prices, the Supply of Collateral and the Enterprise Economy", *Economic Journal*, 106, 60–75.

BoE, 2014, *Trends in Lending*, Bank of England, London, July.

Borjas, G.J., 1995, "The Economic Benefits from Immigration", *Journal of Economic Perspectives*, 9.2, 3–22.

Borjas, G.J., 1999, "Does Immigration Grease the Wheels of the Labor Market?", *Brookings Papers on Economic Activity*, 2001.1, 69–119.

Borts, J.H., and Stein, J.L., 1964, *Economic Growth in a Free Market*, Columbia University Press, New York.

Bover, O., Muellbauer, J. and Murphy, A., 1989, "Housing, Wages and UK Labour Markets", *Oxford Bulletin of Economics and Statistics*, 51.2, 97–136.

Breheny, M., 1999, (ed.), *The People: Where Will They Work?*, Report of the TCPA Research into the Changing Geography of Employment, Town and Country Planning Association, London.

Brueckner, J.K., 2011, *Lectures on Urban Economics*, MIT Press, Cambridge, MA.

Brülhart, M., 2011, "The Spatial Effects of Trade Openness: A Survey", *Review of World Economics*, 147.1, 59–83.

Casson, M.C., and McCann, P., 1999, "Globalisation, Competition, and the Corporation: The UK Experience", in Whitman M., (ed.), *The Evolving Corporation: Global Imperatives and National Responses*, Group of Thirty, Washington DC.

Castro Coelho, M., Ratnoo, V. and Dellepiane, S., 2014, *Housing that Works for All: The Political Economy of Housing in England*, ESRC and Institute for Government. See: www.instituteforgovernment.org.uk.

CBRE, 2014a, *Cost Increases Signal Economic Momentum: Global Prime Office Occupancy Costs*, CBRE Global Research and Consulting, London, December.

CBRE, 2014b, *EMEA Rents and Yields: Market View Q3 2014*, CBRE Global Research and Consulting, London.

CBRE, 2014c, *UK Prime Rent and Yield Monitor: Market View*, CBRE Global Research and Consulting, London.

CEBR, 2012a, "One Pound in Five Earned in London Subsidises the Rest of the UK – Northern Ireland, Wales and North East Receive More Than a Fifth of Their Income as Subsidies from Outside of the Region", *News Release*, 13 February, Centre for Economics and Business Research, London, www.cebr.org.

CEBR, 2012b, "City Job Numbers to Fall by 13,000 in 2013 and to Fall Further in 2014 to Lowest Level since 1993", *News Release*, 6 November, Centre for Economics and Business Research, London, www.cebr.org.

CfC, 2014, *Small Business Outlook 2014*, Centre for Cities, London, www.centreforcities.org.

CfC, 2015, *Cities Outlook 2015*, Centre for Cities, London, www.centreforcities.org.

Champion, A.G., 2012, "Testing the Return Migration Element of the 'Escalator Region' Model: An Analysis of Migration Into and Out of South-East England", *Cambridge Journal of Regions, Economy and Society*, 5, 255–270.

Champion, A.G., 2014, *People in Cities: The Numbers*, Future of Cities Working Paper, Foresight – Government Office for Science, London.

Champion, A.G., Coombes, M. and Gordon, I.R., 2014, "How Far do England's Second-Order Cities Emulate London as Human Capital 'Escalators'?", *Population, Place and Space*, 20.5, 421–433.

Chandler, T., 1987, *Four Thousand Years of Urban Growth: An Historical Census*, 2nd edition, The Edwin Mellen Press, Lewiston, NY.

Cheshire, P., 2008, "Reflections on the Nature and Policy Implications of Planning Restrictions on Housing Restrictions. Discussion of 'Planning Policy, Planning Practice and Housing Supply' by Kate Barker", *Oxford Review of Economic Policy*, 24.1, 50–58.

Cheshire, P.C., and Hilber, C.A.L., 2008, "Office Space Supply Restrictions in Britain: The Political Economy of Market Revenge", *Economic Journal*, 118. 529, F185–F221.

Cheshire, P.C., Leunig, T., Nathan, M. and Overman, H.G., 2012, "Links Between Planning and Economic Performance: Evidence Note for LSE Growth Commission", Evidence Note Submitted as Part of the LSE Growth Commission.

Cheshire, P.C., Nathan, M. and Overman, H.G., 2014a, *Urban Economics and Urban Policy: Challenging Conventional Wisdom*, Edward Elgar, Cheltenham.

Cheshire, P.C., Hilber, C.A.L. and Kaplanis, I., 2014b, "Land Use Regulation and Productivity – Land Matters: Evidence from a UK Supermarket Chain", *Journal of Economic Geography*, Forthcoming.

Christopherson, S., 2015, "How Does Financialization Affect Manufacturing Investment? Preliminary Evidence from the US and UK", in Bryson, J.R., Clark, J. and Vanchan, V., (eds.), *Handbook of Manufacturing Industries in the World Economy*, Edward Elgar, Cheltenham.

Clark, G., 2015, *The Making of a World City: London 1991 to 2021*, Wiley Blackwell, Oxford.

Clarke, E., Nohrová, N. and Thomas, E., 2014, *Delivering Change: Building Homes Where We Need Them*, Centre for Cities, London.

CLC, 2004, *London's Linkages with the Rest of the UK*, Oxford Economic Forecasting and the City of London Corporation, London.

CLC, 2009, *London's Place in the UK Economy, 2009–10*, City of London Corporation, London.

CLC, 2010, *The City's Role in Providing for the Public Equity Needs of UK SMEs*, City of London Corporation, London.

CLC, 2011a, *London's Competitive Place in the UK and Global Economies*, City of London Corporation, London.

CLC, 2011b, *Total Tax Contribution of UK Financial Services: Fourth Edition*, City of London Corporation, London.

CLC, 2012, *London's Finances and Revenues*, City of London Corporation, London.

CLC, 2014a, *London's Finances and Revenues*, City of London Corporation, London.

CLC, 2014b, *Total Tax Contribution of UK Financial Services: Seventh Edition*, City of London Corporation, London.

CLC, 2014c, *The Impact of Firm Migration on the City of London*, City of London Corporation, London.

Cliff, A., Haggett, P., Ord, J.K., Bassett, K. and Davies, R., 1975, *Elements of Spatial Structure: A Quantitative Approach*, Cambridge University Press, Cambridge.

Coleman, D., and Rowthorn, R., 2004a, "The Economic Effects of Immigration into the United Kingdom", *Population and Development Review*, 30.4, 579–624.

Coleman, D., and Rowthorn, R., 2004b, "Who's Afraid of Population Decline? A Critical Examination of Its Consequences", *Population and Development Review*, 37, Issue Supplement 1, 217–248.

Colley, L., 2014, *Acts of Union and Disunion: What Has Held the UK Together – and What's Dividing It?*, Profile Books, London.

Collier, P., 2013, "How Much is Enough?", *Prospect*, 18 September.

Collier, P., 2014a, "A New Deal on Immigration: The Crisis is Real and We Can Solve it Without Leaving Europe", *The Spectator*, December.

Collier, P., 2014b, *Exodus: Immigration and Multiculturalism in the 21st Century*, Penguin Books, London.

Combes, P-P., Duranton, G. and Overman, H.G., 2005a, "Agglomeration and the Adjustment of the Spatial Economy", *Papers in Regional Science*, 84.3, 311–349.

Combes, P-P., Duranton, G. and Gobillon, L., 2005b, "Spatial Wage Disparities: Sorting Matters!", *Journal of Urban Economics*, 63, 723–742.

Corkindale, J., 2004, *The Land Use Planning System: Evaluating Options for Reform*, IEA Hobart Paper 148, Institute of Economic Affairs, London.

Coutts, K., and Gudgin, G., 2015, *The Macroeconomic Impact of Liberal Economic Policies in the UK*, Centre for Business Research, Judge Business School, University of Cambridge, Cambridge.

Coutu, S., 2014, *The Scale-Up Report on UK Economic Growth*, An Independent Report to the Government, www.scaleupreport.org.

Cox, G., 2015, *Overcoming Short-Termism within British Business: The Key to Sustained Economic Growth: An Independent Review by Sir George Cox Commissioned by the Labour Party*, www.yourbritain.org.uk/agenda-2015/policy-review/cox-report.

Coyle, D., and Rosewell, B., 2014, "Investing in City Regions: How Does London Interact with the UK System of Cities and What Are the Implications of this Relationship", *Future of Cities Essay*, Foresight: Government Office for Science, London.

CPRE, 2009, *2026 A Vision for the Countryside*, Campaign to Protect Rural England, London.

CPRE, 2010a, *Green Belts: A Greener Future*, Campaign to Protect Rural England, London.

CPRE, 2010b, *Neighbourhood Plans: How They are Working Towards CPRE's Vision for the Countryside*, CPRE Briefing, Campaign to Protect Rural England, London, December.

CPRE, 2011, *Building in a Small Island? Why We Still Need the Brownfield First Approach*, Campaign to Protect Rural England, London.

CPRE, 2014, *From Wasted Space to Living Spaces: The Availability of Brownfield Land for Housing Development in England*, Campaign to Protect Rural England, London.

Crafts, N., 2012, "Creating Competitive Advantage: Policy Lessons from History", in Greenaway, D., (ed.), *The UK in a Global World: How Can the UK Focus on Steps in Global Value Chains That Really Add Value?*, CEPR Centre for Economic Policy Research and BIS Department for Business Innovation and Skills, London.

Crafts, N., 2013, Comments by Professor Nickolas Crafts in the BBC Radio 4 Current Affairs Documentary Programme *Analysis: Regions*, presented by Alison Wolf at 20.30–21.00 on 3 June 2013.

Cristelli, M., Batty, M. and Pietronero, L., 2012, "There is More Than a Power Law in Zipf", *Scientific Reports*, 2.812, 1–7, DOI: 10.1038.srep00812.

CSO, 1990, *Regional Trends 25*, Central Statistical Office, ISSN 0261-1783, London.

CSO, 1992, *Regional Trends 27*, Central Statistical Office, ISSN 0261-1783, London.

Cullingworth, J.B., 1985, *Town and Country Planning in Britain*, 9th edition, George Allen and Unwin, London.

Cullingworth, J.B., and Nadin, V., 1994, *Town and Country Planning in Britain*, 14th edition, Routledge, London.

CWI, 2012, *Shortage Occupation List (SOL) Update*, Report Prepared by the Centre for Workforce Intelligence for the Migration Advisory Committee, London.

Daams, M.N., van der Vlist, A.J. and Sijtsma, F.J., 2014, "The Spatial Extent of Natural Spaces Effects on Property Prices: A Perceived Value Adjusted Hedonic Model", Working Paper, Faculty of Spatial Sciences, University of Groningen.

DCLG, 2012a, *Re-Imagining Urban Spaces to Help Revitalise our High Streets*, Department of Communities and Local Government, London, July.

DCLG, 2012b, *National Planning Policy Framework*, Department of Communities and Local Government, London, March.

DCLG, 2012c, *Technical Guidance to the National Planning Policy Framework*, Department of Communities and Local Government, London, March.

DCLG, 2012d, *Streamlining Information Requirements for Planning Applications*, Department of Communities and Local Government, London, March.

DCLG, 2012e, *External Review of Government Planning Practice Guidance*, Report Submitted by Lord Matthew Taylor of Goss Moor, Department of Communities and Local Government, December, London.

DCLG, 2014a, *Locally-Led Garden Cities*, Department of Communities and Local Government, London, April.

DCLG, 2014b, "Net Supply of Housing, 2013–2014", Department of Communities and Local Government, *Housing Statistical Release*, 13 November, London.

D'Costa, S., and Overman, H.G., 2014, "The Urban Wage Growth Premium: Sorting or Learning?", *Regional Science and Urban Economics*, 48, 168–179.

Deakins, D., North, D., Baldock, R. and Whittam, G., 2008, "SMEs' Access to Credit: Is There Still a Debt Finance Gap?", Institute for Small Business and Entrepreneurship, Belfast, 5–7 November.

DEFRA, 2006, *Affordable Rural Housing Commission. Final Report. Goodman Report*, Department for Environment, Food and Rural Affairs, London.

DEFRA, 2015, *Statistical Digest of Rural England*, Department for Environment, Food and Rural Affairs, London, April.

DEFRA, DARD (NI), DRAH (WA) and RERAD (Scottish Government), 2014, *Agriculture in the United Kingdom 2013*, Department for Environment, Food and Rural Affairs, Department of Agriculture and Rural Development (Northern Ireland), Welsh Assembly Department for Rural Affairs and Heritage, Scottish Government Rural and Environment Research and Analysis Directorate, London.

De Meza, D., and Webb, D., 1999, "Wealth, Enterprise and Credit Policy", *Economic Journal*, 109, 153–163.

Deutsche Bank, 2013, *London and the UK: In for a Penny, in for the Pound*, Deutsche Bank Markets Research Special Report, London, 27 November.

Deutsche Bank, 2014, *UK Housing: London vs The Rest*, Deutsche Bank Research, London, 18 July.

Devlin, C., Bold, O., Patel, D., Harding, D. and Hussain, I., 2014, *Impacts of Migration on UK Native Employment: An Analytical Review of the Evidence*, Home Office and Department for Business, Innovation and Skills, London.

De Vries, R., 2014, *Earnings by Degree: Differences in the Career Outcomes of UK University Graduates*, Sutton Trust, London.

Dickey, H., 2014, "The Impact of Migration on Regional Wage Inequality: A Semiparametric Approach", *Journal of Regional Science*, 54.5, 893–915.

Dijkstra, L., Garcilazo, E. and McCann, P., 2013, "The Economic Performance of European Cities and City-Regions: Myths and Realities", *European Planning Studies*, 21.3, 334–354.

Dimitropoulou, D., McCann, P. and Burke, S.P., 2013, "The Determinants of the Location of Foreign Direct Investment in UK Regions", *Applied Economics*, 45.27, 3853–3862.

Dorling, D., 2011, *So You Think You Know About Britain?*, Constable, London.

Dorling, D., 2013, *The Population of the UK*, 2nd edition, Sage, London.

Dorling, D., 2014a, *Inequality and The 1%*, Verso, London.

Dorling, D., 2014b, *All That is Solid: How the Great Housing Disaster Defines Our Times, and What We Can Do About It*, Penguin Books, London.

Dow, S.C., 1982, "The Regional Composition of the Money Multiplier Process", *Scottish Journal of Political Economy*, 29.1, 22–44.

Dow, S.C., 1986, "The Capital Account and Regional Balance of Payments Problems", *Urban Studies*, 23.3, 173–184.

Dow, S.C., 1987, "The Treatment of Money in Regional Economics", *Journal of Regional Science*, 27.1, 13–24.

Dow, S.C., and Montagnoli, A., 2007, "The Regional Transmission of UK Monetary Policy", *Regional Studies*, 41.6, 797–808.

Dow, S.C., and Rodriguez-Fuentes. C.J., 1997, "Regional Finance: A Survey", *Regional Studies*, 31.9, 903–920.

Driffield, N., and Taylor, K., 2000, "FDI and the Labour Market: A Review of the Evidence and Policy Implications", *Oxford Review of Economic Policy*, 16.3, 90–103.

Drinkwater, S., 2010, "Immigration and the Economy", *National Institute Economic Review*, 213: R1, NIESR National Institute of Economic and Social Research, London.

Duranton, G., 2006, "Some Foundations for Zipf's Law: Product Proliferation and Local Spillovers", *Regional Science and Urban Economics*, 36.4, 542–563.

Duranton, G., 2007, "Urban Evolutions: The Fast, the Slow, and the Still", *American Economic Review*, 97.1, 197–221.

Duranton, G., and Monastiriotis, V., 2002, "Mind the Gaps: The Evolution of Regional Earnings Inequalities in the UK, 1982–1997", *Journal of Regional Science*, 42.2, 219–256.

Duranton, G., and Turner, M.A, 2011, "The Fundamental Law of Road Congestion: Evidence from US Cities", *American Economic Review*, 101.6, 2616–2652.

Dustman, C., and Frattini, T., 2014, "The Fiscal Effects of Immigration to the UK", *Economic Journal*, 124.580, F593–F643.

Edwards, M., 2015, *Prospects for Land, Rent and Housing in UK Cities*, Future of Cities Working Paper, Foresight, Government Office for Science, June.

Ellis. L., and Naughtin, C., 2010, "Commercial Property and Financial Stability: An International Perspective", *Reserve Bank of Australia Quarterly Bulletin*, June, Canberra.

EMC, 2014, *The Impact of International Migration on the East Midlands*, East Midlands Councils, July. See: www.emcouncils.gov.uk/write/ImpactOfMigration-6-A4-AW.pdf.

Ennew, C.T., and Binks, M.R., 1995, "The Provision of Finance to Small Businesses: Does the Banking Relationship Constrain Performance?", *Journal of Small Business Finance*, 4.1, 57–73.

ESPON, 2013, *New Evidence on Smart, Sustainable, and Inclusive: First ESPON 2013 Synthesis Report*, Luxembourg, www.espon.eu.

European Commission, 2013, *REDI: The Regional Entrepreneurship and Development Index – Measuring Regional Entrepreneurship Final Report*, Directorate-General for Regional and Urban Policy, Brussels, November.

European Union, 2014, *Investment for Jobs and Growth – Promoting Development and Good Governance in EU Regions and Cities: Sixth Report on Economic, Social and Territorial Cohesion*, Publications Office, Brussels.

Evans, A.W., 1973, *The Economics of Residential Location*, Macmillan, Basingstoke.

Evans, A.W., 1985, *Urban Economics: An Introduction*, Blackwell, Oxford.

Evans, A.W., 1988, *No Room! No Room! The Costs of the British Town and Country Planning System*, IEA Institute for Economic Affairs, London.

Evans, A.W., 1990, "The Assumption of Equilibrium in the Analysis of Migration and Interregional Differences", *Journal of Regional Science*, 30.4, 515–531.

Evans, A.W., 1991a, "Rapid Hutches on Postage Stamps: Planning, Development and Political Economy", *Urban Studies*, 28.6, 853–870.

Evans, A.W., 1991b, "Investment Diversion and Equity Release: The Macroeconomic Consequences of Equity Release", *Urban Studies*, 28.2, 173–182.

Evans, A.W., 1993, "Interregional Equilibrium: A Transatlantic View", *Journal of Regional Science*, 33.1, 89–97.

Evans, A.W., 1995, "The Property Market: Ninety Percent Efficient?", *Urban Studies*, 32.1, 5–29.

Evans, A.W., 1996, "The Impact of Land Use Planning and Tax Subsidies on the Supply and Price of Housing in Britain: A Comment", *Urban Studies*, 33.3, 581–585.

Evans, A.W., 2004a, *Economics, Land Use and Planning*, Blackwell Publishing, Oxford.

Evans, A.W., 2004b, *Economics, Real Estate & the Supply of Land*, Blackwell Publishing, Oxford.

Evans, A.W., and Hartwich, O., 2005a, *Unaffordable Housing: Fables and Myths*, Localis and Policy Exchange, London.

Evans, A.W., and Hartwich, O., 2005b, *Bigger Better Faster More*, Localis and Policy Exchange, London.

Evans, A.W., and Hartwich, O., 2006, *Better Homes, Greener Cities*, Localis and Policy Exchange, London.

Evans, A.W., and Hartwich, O., 2007, *The Best Laid Plans: How Planning Prevents Economic Growth*, Localis and Policy Exchange, London.

Faggian, A., and McCann, P., 2006, "Human Capital Flows and Regional Knowledge Assets: A Simultaneous Equation Approach", *Oxford Economic Papers*, 58.3, 475–500.

Faggian, A., and McCann, P., 2009a, "Universities, Agglomerations and Graduate Human Capital Mobility", *TESG Journal of Economic and Social Geography*, 100.2, 210–223.

Faggian, A., and McCann, P., 2009b, "Human Capital, Graduate Migration and Innovation in British Regions", *Cambridge Journal of Economics*, 33.2, 317–333.

Faggian, A., and McCann, P., 2009c, "Universities, Agglomerations and Graduate Human Capital Mobility", *TESG Journal of Economic and Social Geography*, 100.2, 210–223.

Faggian, A., McCann., P. and Sheppard, S.C., 2006, "An Analysis of Ethnic Differences in UK Graduate Migration", *Annals of Regional Science*, 40.2, 461–471.

Faggian, A., McCann., P. and Sheppard, S.C., 2007a, "Human Capital, Higher Education and Graduate Migration: An Analysis of Scottish and Welsh Students", *Urban Studies*, 44.13, 2511–2528.

Faggian, A., McCann, P. and Sheppard, S.C., 2007b, "Some Evidence that Women are More Mobile than Men: Gender Differences in UK Graduate Migration Behaviour", *Journal of Regional Science*, 47.3, 517–539.

Faggio, G., and Overman, H.G., 2013, "The Effect of Public Sector Employment on Local Labour Markets", *Journal of Urban Economics*, 79, 91–107.

Fielding, A.J., 1989, "Inter-Regional Migration and Social Change: A Study of South East England Based Upon Data from the Longitudinal Study", *Transactions of the Institute of British Geographers*, 14, 24–36.

Fielding, A.J., 1992a, "Migration and the Metropolis: Recent Research on the Causes and Consequences Migration to the Southeast of England", *Progress in Human Geography*, 17.2, 195–212.

Fielding, A.J., 1992b, "Migration and Social Mobility: South East England as an Escalator Region", *Regional Studies*, 26, 1–15.

Fielding, A.J. (Tony Fielding), 2012, *Migration in Britain: Paradoxes of the Present Prospects for the Future*, Edward Elgar, Cheltenham.

Findlay, R., and O'Rourke, K.H., 2007, *Power and Plenty: Trade, War, and the World Economy in the Second Millennium*, Princeton University Press, Princeton.

Fingleton, B., 2003, "Increasing Returns: Evidence from Local Wage Rates in Britain", *Oxford Economic Papers*, 55, 716–739.

Fingleton, B., 2005a, "Towards Applied Geographical Economics: Modelling Relative Wage Rates, Incomes and Prices for the Regions of Great Britain", *Applied Economics*, 37, 2417–2428.

Fingleton, B., 2005b, "Beyond Neoclassical Orthodoxy: A View Based on the New Economic Geography and UK Regional Wage Data", *Papers in Regional Science*, 351–375.

Fingleton, B., 2006, "The New Economic Geography Versus Urban Economics: An Evaluation Using Local Wage Rates in Great Britain", *Oxford Economic Papers*, 58, 501–530.

Fingleton, B., 2008, "Housing Supply, Housing Demand, and Affordability", *Urban Studies*, 45.8, 1545–1563.

Fingleton, B., 2011, "The Empirical Performance of NEG with Reference to Small Areas", *Journal of Economic Geography*, 11, 267–279.

Fingleton, B., and Longhi, S., 2013, "The Effects of Agglomeration on Wages: Evidence from the Micro Level", *Journal of Regional Science*, 53.3, 443–463.

Fishman, R., 1982, *Urban Utopias in the Twentieth Century*, MIT Press, Cambridge, MA.

Fujita, M., Krugman, P. and Mori, T., 1999, "On the Evolution of Hierarchical Urban Systems", *European Economic Review*, 43, 209–251.

Gabaix, X., 1999a, "Zipf's Law and the Growth of Cities", *American Economic Review: Papers and Proceedings*, 89.2, 129–132.

Gabaix, X., 1999b, "Zipf's Law for Cities: An Explanation", *Quarterly Journal of Economics*, 114.3, 739–767.

Gallup, 2013, *Poll of Romanians*, Report Prepared from the BBC, March–April.

Gay, O., 2006, *The Lyons and Gershon Reviews and Variations in Civil Service Conditions*, Standard Note SN/PC/2588, House of Commons Library, 26 January, London.

Geary, F., and Stark, T., 2015, "What Happened to Regional Inequality in Britain in the Twentieth Century?", *Economic History Review*, Forthcoming, DOI: 10.1111/her.12114.

Geddes, A., 2013, *Britain and the European Union*, Palgrave, Basingstoke.

Gibbons, S., Overman, H.G. and Resende, G., 2011, *Real Earnings Disparities in Britain*, SERC Discussion Paper 65, Spatial Economics Research Centre, London.

Gibbons, S., Mourato, S. and Resende, G.M., 2014a, "The Amenity Value of English Nature: A Hedonic Price Approach", *Environmental and Resource Economics*, 57, 175–196.

Gibbons, S., Overman, H.G. and Pelkonen, P., 2014b, "Area Disparities in Britain: Understanding the Contribution of People vs. Place Through Variance Decompositions", *Oxford Bulletin of Economics and Statistics*, 76.5, 745–763.

Giulietti, C., Guzi, M., Kahanec, M. and Zimmerman, K.F., 2011, "Unemployment Benefits and Immigration: Evidence from the EU", *IZA Discussion Paper No. 6075*, Bonn.

GLA, 2013, *GLA 2012 Round Population Projections: Intelligence Update 05-2013*, GLA Intelligence, London, February.

GLA Economics, 2005, *Growing Together: London and the UK Economy*, London.

GOFS, 2013, *The Future of Manufacturing: A New Era of Opportunity and Challenge for the UK*, Foresight, Government Office for Science, London.

Goldrin, C., and Margo, R., 1992, "The Great Compression: The U.S. Wage Structure at Mid-Century", *Quarterly Journal of Economics*, 107, 1–34.

Goodall, B., 1972, *The Economics of Urban Areas*, Pergamon, London.

Goodhart, D., 2013, *The British Dream: Successes and Failures of Postwar Immigration*, Atlantic Books, London.

Gordon, I.R., 1985, "The Cyclical Sensitivity of Regional Employment and Unemployment Differentials", *Regional Studies*, 19.2, 95–110.

Gordon, I.R., 2015a, "Ambition, Human Capital Acquisition and the Metropolitan Escalator", *Regional Studies*, 49.6, 1042–1055.

Gordon, I.R., 2015b, "The Quantitative Easing of a Finance Capital: How London Came So Well Out of the Post-2007 Crisis", Working Paper, Department of Geography and Environment, London School of Economics, *Paper Presented at the Divergent Cities Conference*, St Catharine's College, Cambridge, 16–17 July.

Gordon, I.R., and Molho, I., 1998, "A Multi-Stream Analysis of the Changing Pattern of Interregional Migration in Great Britain, 1960–1991", *Regional Studies*, 32.4, 309–323.

Gordon, I.R., and Monastiriotis, V., 2007, "Education, Location, Education: A Spatial Analysis of English Secondary School Public Examination Results", *Urban Studies*, 44.7, 1203–1228.

Gordon, I.R., Champion, A.G. and Coombes, M., 2013, "Urban Escalators and Inter-Regional Elevators: The Difference that Location, Mobility and Sectoral Specialisation Make to Occupational Progression", *SERC Discussion Paper 139*, Spatial Economics Research Centre, London.

Graham, D.J., 2007a, "Agglomeration, Productivity and Transport Investment", *Journal of Transport Economics and Policy*, 41.3, 317–343.

Graham, D.J., 2007b, "Variable Returns to Agglomeration and Effect of Road Traffic Congestion", *Journal of Urban Economics*, 62, 103–120.

Graham, D.J., Melo, P.S., Jiwattanakulpaisarn, P. and Noland, R.B., 2010, "Testing for Causality Between Productivity and Agglomeration Economies", *Journal of Regional Science*, 50.5, 935–951.

Graves, P.E., 1980, "Migration and Climate", *Journal of Regional Science*, 20.2, 227–237.

Graves, P.E., 1983, "Migration with a Composite Amenity: The Role of Rents", *Journal of Regional Science*, 23.4, 541–546.

Greed, C., 1993, *Introduction to Town Planning*, 2nd edition, Longman, London.

Green, A.E., and Livanos, I., 2015, "Involuntary Non-Standard Employment and the Economic Crisis: Regional Insights from the UK", *Regional Studies*, 49.7, 1223–1235.

Grimes, A., and Mitchell, I., 2015, "Impacts of Planning Rules, Regulations, Uncertainty and Delay on Residential Property Development", *Motu Working Paper 15-02*, Motu Economic and Public Policy Research, Wellington, New Zealand, January.

Grimsey, W., 2013, *The Grimsey Review: An Alternative Future for the High Street*, Independent Report, see: www.vanishinghighstreet.com/wp-content/uploads/2013/09/GrimsetReview04.092.pdf.

Grosvenor, 2002, *Shopping Centre Futures*, Report by the Future Foundation for BCSC and Grosvenor, London.

Haggett, P., 1965, *Locational Analysis in Human Geography*, Edward Arnold, London.

Haldane, A., 2013, "The Commercial Property Forum Twenty Years On", Lecture Presented to the Commercial Property Forum, London.

Hall, P., 1966, *The World Cities, World University Library*, Weidenfeld and Nicolson, London.

Hall, P., 1975, *Urban and Regional Planning*, Pelican Books, London.

Hall, P., 1988, *Cities of Tomorrow: An Intellectual History of Urban Planning and Design in the Twentieth Century*, Blackwell, Oxford.

Hall, P., 1998, *Cities in Civilization*, Weidenfeld & Nicolson, London.

Hall, P., Gracey, H., Drewett, R. and Thomas, R., 1973, *The Containment of Urban England. The Planning System: Objectives, Operations, Impacts*, George Allen & Unwin, London.

Hamnett, C., Harmer, M. and Williams, P., 1991, *Safe as Houses: Housing Inheritance in Britain*, Paul Chapman Publishing, London.

Harari, D., 2014, "Regional Economic Output Statistics", *Standard Note SN/EP/5795, Economic Policy and Statistics*, House of Commons Library, London.

Harris, J.R., and Todaro, M.P., 1970, "Migration, Unemployment and Development: A Two-Sector Analysis", *American Economic Review*, 60.1, 126–142.

Harris, R., and Moffat, J., 2012, "Is Productivity Higher in British Cities", *Journal of Regional Science*, 52.5, 762–786.

Harris, R., and Moffat, J., 2013, "The Direct Contribution of FDI to Productivity Growth in Britain, 1997–2008", *The World Economy*, 36.6, 713–735.

Harris, R., Li, Q.C. and Moffat, J., 2013a, "The Impact of Higher Education Institution-Firm Knowledge Links on Firm-Productivity in Britain", *Applied Economics Letters*, 18.13, 1243–1246.

Harris, R., Li, Q.C. and Moffat, J., 2013b, "The Impact of Higher Education Institution-Firm Knowledge Links on Establishment-Level Productivity in British Regions", *The Manchester School*, 81.2, 143–162.

Harvey, J., 1981, *Urban Land Economics*, Macmillan, Basingstoke.

Hatton, T.J., and Taini, M., 2005, "Immigration and Inter-Regional Mobility in the UK, 1982–2000", *Economic Journal*, 115, F342–358.

HECSU, 2015, *Loyals, Stayers, Returners and Incomers: Graduate Migration Patterns*, Ball, C., February, Higher Education Careers Services Unit, London.

Hemmings, P.J., 1991, "Regional Earnings Differences in Great Britain: Evidence from the New Earnings Survey", *Regional Studies*, 25.2, 123–133.

Henley, A., 1998, "Residential Mobility, Housing Equity and the Labour Market", *Economic Journal*, 108.447, 414–427.

Henley, A., 2005, "Job Creation by the Self-Employed: The Roles of Entrepreneurial and Financial Capital", *Small Business Economics*, 25.2, 175–196.

Henneberry, J., and Mouzakis, F., 2014, "Familiarity and Determination of Yields for Regional Office Property Investments in the UK", *Regional Studies*, 48.3, 530–546.

Heywood, A., 2014, *Housing and Planning: What Makes the Difference? A Smith Institute Survey and Discussion Paper on the Relationship between Councils and House Builders*, Smith Institute, London, December.

Hilber, C.A.L., and Vermeulen, W., 2012, "The Impact of Supply Constraints on House Prices in England", *CPB Discussion Paper 219*, CPB Netherlands Bureau for Economic Policy Analysis, The Hague.

HM Treasury, 2013, *Public Expenditure Statistical Analysis 2013, Cmd 8663*, London, July.

HM Treasury, 2014a, *Improving Access to SME Credit Data: Summary of Responses*, London, June.

HM Treasury, 2014b, *Public Expenditure Statistical Analysis 2014, Cmd 8902*, London, July.

House of Commons, 2013, *Bridging the Valley of Death: Improving the Commercialisation of Research*, Science and Technology Committee, 8th Report of Session 2012–13, HC348, The Stationery Office, London, 13 March.

House of Lords, 2008, *The Economic Impact of Migration Volume I: Report*, Select Committee on Economic Affairs, 1st Report of Session 2007–08, The Stationery Office, London.

Hughes, G., and McCormick, B., 1981, "Do Council House Policies Reduce Migration Between Regions", *Economic Journal*, 91, 919–938.

Hughes, G., and McCormick, B., 1985, "Migration Intentions in the UK Which Households Want to Migrate and Which Succeed?", *Economic Journal*, 95, 113–123.

Hughes, G., and McCormick, B., 1987, "Housing Markets, Unemployment and Labour Market Flexibility in the UK", *European Economic Review*, 31, 615–645.

Hughes, G., and McCormick, B., 1994, "Did Migration in the 1980s Narrow the North-South Divide?", *Economica*, 61, 509–527.

Hutton, W., 1995, *The State We're In*, Random House, London.

Iammarino, S., and McCann, P., 2013, *Multinationals and Economic Geography: Location, Technology and Innovation*, Edward Elgar, Cheltenham.

ICF-GHK, 2013, *A Fact-Finding Analysis on the Impact on the Member States' Social Security Systems of the Entitlements of Non-Native Intra-EU Migrants to Special Non-Contributory Cash Benefits and Healthcare Granted on the Basis of Residence*, Final Report Submitted by ICF GHK in Association with Mileu Ltd to DG Employment, Social Affairs and Inclusion via DG Justice Framework Contract, Brussels.

IFS, 2012, *The IFS Green Budget*, Institute for Fiscal Studies, February.

IFS, 2013, *The IFS Green Budget*, Institute for Fiscal Studies, February.

IPF, 2014, *A Vision for Real Estate Finance: Recommendations for Reducing the Risks of Damage to the Financial System from the Next Commercial Real Estate Market Crash*, Investment Property Forum, London.

Iparraguire D'Elia, J.L., 2008, "Northern Ireland's Input-Output Table: An Application of the Kronenberg's Derivative Approach", Northern Ireland Economic Research Institute, Belfast.

Jaegers, T., Lipp-Lingua, C. and Amil, D., 2013, "High-Technology and Medium-High Technology Industries Main Drivers of EU-27's Industrial Growth", *Eurostat Statistics in Focus 1/2013*, European Commission.

Jerrim, J., 2014, Family Background and Access to 'High Status' Universities, Sutton Trust, London.

Johnston, D.W., and Lordan, G., 2014, "When Work Disappears: Racial Prejudice and Recession Labour Market Penalties", *CEP Discussion Paper No. 1257*, Centre for Economic Performance, London.

Jorgensen, D.W., and Timmer, M.P., 2011, "Structural Change in Advanced Nations: A New Set of Stylised Facts", *Scandinavian Journal of Economics*, 113.1, 1–29.

Kaletsky, A., 2015, "Getting Credit for Everything: The Chancellor's Cunning Plan", *Prospect*, April.

Kellner, P., 2015, "The Truth About Welfare", *Prospect*, April.

Konstantinos, M.A., and Spence, N., 2014, "The Impact of Intangible Assets on Regional Productivity Disparities in Great Britain", *Environment and Planning A*, 46, 629–648.

Krugman, P., 1996, *The Self Organizing Economy*, Blackwell, Oxford.

Krugman, P., 2004, *The Great Unraveling: Losing Our Way in the Twenty-First Century*, Norton, New York.

Krugman, P., 2015a, "Fighting the Derp", *New York Times*, 8 June.

Krugman, P., 2015b, "Walmart's Visible Hand", *New York Times*, 4 March.

Krugman, P., 2015c, "This Snookered Isle", *New York Times*, 24 April.

Krugman, P., 2015d, "Seriously Bad Ideas", *New York Times*, 13–14 June.

Krugman, P., 2015e, "Knowledge Isn't Power", *New York Times*, 24 February.

Kumar, A., Ussher, K. and Hunter, P., 2014, *Wealth of Our Nation: Rethinking Policies for Wealth Distribution*, Smith Institute, London.

Lawless, P., and Brown, F., 1986, *Urban Growth and Change in Britain: An Introduction*, Harper and Row, London.

Lean, W., and Goodall, B., 1966, *Aspects of Land Economics*, The Estates Gazette Limited, London.

Lee., N., and Drever, E., 2014, "Do SMEs in Deprived Areas Find it Harder to Access Finance? Evidence from the UK Small Business Survey", *Entrepreneurship and Regional Development*, 26.3–4, 337–356.

Lee, N., and Rodriguez-Pose, A., 2013a, "Creativity, Cities and Innovation: Evidence from UK SMEs", *NESTA Working Paper 13/10*, www.nesta.org.uk.

Lee, N., and Rodriguez-Pose, A., 2013b, "Original Innovation, Learnt Innovation and Cities: Evidence from UK SMEs", *Urban Studies*, 50.9, 1742–1759.

Lee, N., and Rodriguez-Pose, A., 2014, "Creativity, Cities and Innovation", *Environment and Planning A*, 46.5, 1139–1159.

Leunig, T., and Overman, H., 2008, "Spatial Patterns of Development and the British Housing Market", *Oxford Review of Economic Policy*, 24.1, 59–78.

Leunig, T., Swaffield, J. and Hartwich, O., 2007, *Cities Unlimited: Making Urban Regeneration Work*, Policy Exchange, London.

Lindbeck, A., and Snower, D., 2001, "Insiders versus Outsiders", *Journal of Economic Perspectives*, 15.1, 165–188.

Lisenkova, K., Sanchez-Martinez, M. and Mérette, M., 2013, "The Long-Term Economic Impacts of Reducing Migration: The Case of the UK Migration Policy", *NIESR Discussion Paper No. 420*, National Institute of Economic and Social Research, London.

Longhi, S., 2012, "Job Competition and the Wage Curve", *Regional Studies*, 46.5, 611–620.

Longhi, S., Nijkamp, P. and Poot, J., 2005, "A Meta-Analytic Assessment of the Effect of Immigration on Wages", *Journal of Economic Surveys*, 19.3, 451–477.

Longhi, S., Nijkamp, P. and Poot, J., 2010, "Meta-Analysis of Labour-Market Impacts of Immigration: Key Conclusions and Policy Implications", *Environment and Planning C: Government and Policy*, 28.5, 819–833.

Lynch, K., 1981, *Good City Form*, MIT Press, Cambridge, MA.

MAC, 2012, *Analysis of the Impacts of Migration*, The Migration Advisory Committee, London, January.

MAC, 2014, *The Growth of EU and Non-EU Labour in Low-Skilled Jobs and Its Impact on the UK*, The Migration Advisory Committee, London, July.

McCann, P., 2013, *Modern Urban and Regional Economics*, Oxford University Press, Oxford.

McCann, P., and Acs, Z.J., 2011, "Globalisation: Countries, Cities and Multinationals", *Regional Studies*, 45.1, 17–32.

McCormick, B., 1991, "Migration and Regional Policy", in Bowen, A., and Mayhew, K., (eds.), *Reducing Regional Inequalities*, Kogan Page, London.

McCormick, B., 1997, "Regional Unemployment and Labour Mobility in the UK", *European Economic Review*, 41, 581–589.

McGough, L., and Swinney, J., 2015, *Mapping Britain's Public Finances: Where is Tax Raised and Where is It Spent?*, Centre for Cities, London.

Macgregor, D.H., 1943, "The Scott Committee Report", *Economica*, New Series, 10.37, 1–11.

McKnight, A., 2015, *Downward Mobility, Opportunity Hoarding and the 'Glass Floor'*, Social Mobility and Child Poverty Commission, Research Report, June.

McLaren, J., Armstrong, J. and Gibb, K., 2013, *Measuring an Independent Scotland's Performance*, Centre for Public Policy Research Briefing Paper, University of Glasgow, 23 April.

McLaren, J., Armstrong, J. and Gibb, K., 2014, *Analysis of Scotland's Past and Future Fiscal Position: Incorporating GERS 2014 and the 2014 UK Budget*, CPPR Briefing Note, Centre for Public Policy Research, University of Glasgow, March.

Macwhirter, I., 2014, *Disunited Kingdom: How Westminster Won a Referendum but Lost Scotland*, Cargo Publishing, Glasgow.

Maddison, A., 2006, *The World Economy. Volume 1: A Millennial Perspective; Volume 2: A Historical Perspective*, Organisation for Economic Cooperation and Development, Paris.

Manacordia, M., Manning, A. and Wadsworth, J., 2012, "The Impact of Immigration on the Structure of Wages: Theory and Evidence from Britain", *Journal of the European Economic Association*, 10.1, 120–151.

Maré, D., and Graham, D.J., 2013, "Agglomeration Elasticities and Firm Heterogeneity", *Journal of Urban Economics*, 75, 44–56.

Marshall, J.N., Hodgson, C. and Bradley, D., 2005, "Public Sector Relocation and Regional Disparities in Britain", *Environment and Planning C: Government and Policy*, 23.6, 883–906.

Mason, G., Robinson, C. and Bondibene, C.R., 2013, "Firm Growth and Innovation in UK City-Regions", *NESTA Working Paper 13/11*, www.nesta.org.uk.

Mathur, A.S., 1986, *Land Use*, Longman, London.

Matlaba, V., Holmes, M.J., McCann, P. and Poot, J., 2014, "A Century of the Evolution of the Urban System in Brazil", *Review of Urban and Regional Development Studies*, 25.3, 129–151.

Mazzucato, M., 2014, *The Entrepreneurial State: Debunking Public vs. Private Sector Myths*, Anthem Press, London.

Meen, G.P., 1996, "Ten Propositions in UK Housing Macroeconomics: An Overview of the 1980s and Early 1990s", *Urban Studies*, 33.3, 425–444.

Meen. G.P., 2001, *Modelling Spatial Housing Markets: Theory, Analysis and Policy*, Kluwer Academic, London.

Meen, G., and Andrew, M., 2008, "Planning for Housing in the Post-Barker Era: Affordability, Household Formation and Tenure Choice", *Oxford Review of Economic Policy*, 24.1, 79–98.

Melo, P.S., and Graham, D.J., 2014, "Testing for Labour Pooling as a Source of Agglomeration Economies: Evidence for Labour Markets in England and Wales", *Papers in Regional Science*, 93.1, 31–53.

Melo, P.S., Graham, D.J. and Noland, R.B., 2012, "The Effect of Labour Market Spatial Structure on Commuting in England and Wales", *Journal of Economic Geography*, 12, 717–737.

Miles, D., 2004, *The UK Mortgage Market: Taking a Longer-Term View: Final Report and Recommendations*, HM Treasury, London.

Mills, E.S., 1972, *Urban Economics*, Scott Foresman and Company, Glenview, IL.

Minford, P., and Stoney, P., 1991, "Regional Policy and Market Forces: An Assessment", in Bowen, A., and Mayhew, K., (eds.), *Reducing Regional Inequalities*, Kogan Page, London.

Minford, P., Ashton, P. and Peel, D., 1988, "The Effects of Housing Distortions on Unemployment", *Oxford Economic Papers*, 40, 322–345.

Mishkin, F.S., 2001, "The Transmission Mechanism and the Role of Asset Prices in Monetary Policy", *NBER Working Paper 8617*, National Bureau of Economic Research, Cambridge, MA.

Mishkin, F.S., 2007, "Housing and the Monetary Transmission Mechanism", *NBER Working Paper w13518*, National Bureau of Economic Research, Cambridge, MA.

Monastiriotis, V., 2002, "Human Capital and Wages: Evidence for External Effects from the UK Regions", *Applied Economics Letters*, 9.13, 843–846.

Monastiriotis, V., 2005, "Labour Market Flexibility in the UK: Regional Variations and the Role of Global/Local Forces", *Economic and Industrial Democracy*, 26.3, 443–477.

Monastiriotis, V., 2007a, "Labour Market Flexibility in UK Regions, 1979–1998", *Area*, 39.3, 310–322.

Monastiriotis, V., 2007b, "Union Retreat and Regional Economic Performance: The UK Experience", *Regional Studies*, 41.2, 143–156.

Monteiro, D., 2013, *The Flow of Credit in the UK Economy and the Availability of Financing to the Corporate Sector*, European Commission, Brussels.

Moynihan, D.P., 1996, *Miles to Go: A Personal History of Social Policy*, Harvard University Press, Cambridge, MA.

Mumford, L., 1961, *The City in History: Its Origins, Its Transformations, and Its Prospects*, Harcourt Brace Jovanovich, New York.

Musson, A.E., 1978, *The Growth of British Industry*, Batsford Academic and Educational Publishers Ltd, London.

NAO, 2013, *Improving Access to Finance for Small and Medium Sized Enterprises*, Report to the Department for Business, Innovation and Skills and HM Treasury, HC-734, Session 2013–2014, 1 November, National Audit Office, London.

Nathan, M., 2011a, "Does Cultural Diversity Help Innovation in Cities? Evidence from London Firms", *SERC Discussion Paper 69*, Spatial Economics Research Centre, London.

Nathan, M., 2011b, "The Economics of Super-Diversity: Findings from British Cities, 2001–2006", *SERC Discussion Paper 68*, Spatial Economics Research Centre, London.

Nathan, M., 2011c, "The Long-Term Impacts of Migration in British Cities: Diversity, Wages Employment and Prices", *SERC Discussion Paper 67*, Spatial Economics Research Centre, London.

Nathan, M., 2013a, "The Wider Economic Impacts of High-Skilled Migrants: A Survey of the Literature", *NIESR Discussion Paper No. 413*, National Institute of Economic and Social Research, London.

Nathan, M., 2013b, "Top Team Demographics, Innovation and Business Performance: Findings from English Firms and Cities 2008–9", *SERC Discussion Paper 129*, Spatial Economics Research Centre, London.

Nathan, M., and Overman, H.G., 2011a, "What We Know (and Don't Know) About the Links Between Planning and Economic Performance", *SERC Discussion Paper 10*, Spatial Economics Research Centre, London, November.

Nathan, M., and Overman, H.G., 2011b, "Assessing the Government's Proposals to Reform the UK Planning System", *SERC Policy Paper 11*, Spatial Economics Research Centre, London, November.

NESTA, 2009, *The Vital 6 Per Cent: How High Growth Innovative Businesses Generate Prosperity and Jobs*, London.

NESTA, 2010, *Creative Clusters; Putting Creativity in the Map*, Chapain, C., Cooke, P., De Propris, L., MacNeill, S. and Mateos-Garcia, J., London.

NESTA, 2011, *Vital Growth: The Importance of High-Growth Businesses to the Recovery*, London.

NESTA, 2015, *The Geography of the UK's Creative and High-Tech Economies*, Bakhshi, H., Davies, J., Freeman, A. and Higgs, P., London.

Netzer, D., 1970, *Economics and Urban Problems: Diagnosis and Prescriptions*, Basic Books, New York.

Newell, M., 1977, *An Introduction to the Economics of Urban Land Use*, The Estates Gazzette Limited, London.

NHF, 2014, *Rural Housing: Countryside in Crisis*, National Housing Federation, London.

Niemietz, K., 2012, "Abundance of Land; Shortage of Housing", *IEA Discussion Paper No. 38*, Institute of Economic Affairs, London.

Nijkamp, P., and Poot, J., 2012, "Migration Impact Assessment: A State of the Art", in Nijkamp, P., Poot, J. and Sahin, M., (eds.), *Migration Impact Assessment: New Horizons*, Edward Elgar, Cheltenham.

Nijkamp. P., Gheasi, M. and Rietveld, P., 2011, "Migrants and International Economic Linkages: A Meta-Overview", *Spatial Economic Analysis*, 6.4, 359–376.

OECD, 2005, *Oslo Manual: Guidelines for Collecting and Interpreting Innovation Data*, Organisation for Economic Cooperation and Development, Paris.

OECD, 2008, *International Migration Outlook*, Organisation for Economic Cooperation and Development, Paris.

OECD, 2011a, *OECD Rural Policy Reviews: England, United Kingdom*, Organisation for Economic Cooperation and Development, Paris.

OECD, 2011b, *OECD Regions at a Glance 2011*, Organisation for Economic Cooperation and Development, Paris.

OECD, 2011c, *OECD Regional Outlook 2011: Building Resilient Regions for Stronger Economies*, Organisation for Economic Development and Cooperation, Paris.

OECD, 2012a, *Compact City Policies: A Comparative Assessment*, Organisation for Economic Cooperation and Development, Paris.

OECD, 2012b, *Education at a Glance 2012 OECD Indicators*, Organisation for Economic Cooperation and Development, Paris.

OECD, 2012c, *International Migration Outlook 2012*, Organisation for Economic Cooperation and Development, Paris.

OECD 2012d, *Promoting Growth in All Regions*, Organisation for Economic Cooperation and Development, Paris.

OECD, 2013a, *OECD Regions at a Glance 2013*, Organisation for Economic Cooperation and Development, Paris.

OECD, 2013b, *International Migration Outlook 2013*, Organisation for Economic Cooperation and Development, Paris.

OECD, 2013c, *OECD Science, Technology and Industry Scoreboard: Innovation for Growth*, Organisation for Economic Cooperation and Development, Paris.

OECD, 2014a, *OECD Factbook 2014: Economic, Environmental and Social Statistics*, Organisation for Economic Cooperation and Development, Paris.

OECD, 2014b, *Matching Economic Migration with Labour Market Needs*, Organisation for Economic Cooperation and Development, Paris.

OECD, 2014c, *OECD Regional Outlook – Regions and Cities: Where Policies and People Meet*, Organisation for Economic Development and Cooperation, Paris.

OECD, 2014d, *PISA 2012 Results: What Students Know and Can Do (Volume I, Revised Edition, February 2014): Student Performance in Mathematics, Reading and Science*, Organisation for Economic Cooperation and Development, Paris.

OECD, 2015a, *Financing SMEs and Entrepreneurs: An OECD Scoreboard*, Organisation for Economic Development and Cooperation, Paris.

OECD, 2015b, *The Metropolitan Century: Understanding Urbanisation and Its Consequences*, Organisation for Economic Development and Cooperation, Paris.

ONS, 1997, *Regional Trends 32*, Office for National Statistics, The Stationery Office, ISSN 0261-1783, London.

ONS, 2001, *Regional Trends 36*, Office for National Statistics, The Stationery Office, ISSN 0261-1783, London.

ONS, 2008, *Regional Trends 40*, Office for National Statistics, ISSN 0261-1783, Palgrave Macmillan, Basingstoke.

ONS, 2009, *Regional Trends 41*, Office for National Statistics, ISSN 0261-1783, Palgrave Macmillan, Basingstoke.

ONS, 2011, "Foreign Direct Investment Involving UK Companies", 2010 Release, Statistical Bulletin, Office for National Statistics, London, 8 December.

ONS, 2012a, *UK Environmental Accounts*, Office for National Statistics, London.

ONS, 2012b, *International Migrants in England and Wales*, Office for National Statistics, London, 11 December.

ONS, 2013a, *A Century of Home Ownership and Renting in England and Wales (full story)*, Office for National Statistics, London, 19 April.

ONS, 2013b, *Migration Statistics Quarterly Report*, Office for National Statistics, London, 28 November.

ONS, 2013c, "Regional Economic Indicators, March 2013", Office for National Statistics, London, 4 June.

ONS, 2015, *Internal Migration, England and Wales, Year Ending June 2014*, Office for National Statistics, London, 25 June.

Orrenius, P.M., Zavodny, M. and LoPalo, M., 2012, *Gone to Texas: Immigration and the Transformation of the Texas Economy*, Federal Reserve Bank of Dallas, Dallas.

Overman, H.G., 2013, "The Economic Future of British Cities", *Centrepiece*, 2–5, Summer.

Overman, H.G., and Gibbons, S., 2011, "Unequal Britain: How Real Are Regional Disparities?", *Centrepiece*, Autumn.

Overman. H.G., and Rice, P., 2008, "Resurgent Cities and Regional Economic Performance", *SERC Policy Paper 1*, Spatial Economics Research Centre, London.

Overman. H.G., Rice, P. and Venables, A.J., 2010, "Economic Linkages Across Space", *Regional Studies*, 44.1, 17–33.

Parry Lewis, J., 1979, *Urban Economics: A Set Approach*, Edward Arnold, London.

Partridge, M., Rickman, D.S., Olfert, M.R. and Ali, K., 2012, "Dwindling Internal U.S. Migration: Evidence of Spatial Equilibrium or Structural Shifts in Local labor Markets?", *Regional Science and Urban Economics*, 42, 375–388.

Partridge, M., Rickman, D.S., Tan, Y. and Olfert, M.R., 2015, "U.S. Regional Poverty Post 2000: The Lost Decade", *Economic Development Quarterly*, 29.1, 38–48.

Patacchini, E., and Rice, P., 2007, "Geography and Economic Performance: Exploratory Spatial Data Analysis for Great Britain", *Regional Studies*, 41.4, 489–508.

Paxman, J., 2002, *The English: A Portrait of a People*, Penguin, London.

Pennington, M., 2002, *Liberating the Land: The Case for Private Land-Use Planning*, IEA Hobart Paper 143, Institute of Economic Affairs, London.

Peri, G., 2011, "The Labor Market Effects of Immigration: A Unified View of Recent Developments", in Maloney, T.N., and Korinek, K., (eds.), *Migration in the 21st Century: Rights, Outcomes and Policy*, Routledge, London.

Piketty, T., 2014, *Capital in the Twenty-First Century*, Translated from French by Arthur Goldhammer, Harvard University Press, Cambridge, MA.

Portas, M., 2011, *The Portas Review: An Independent Review into the Future of Our High Street*, Department for Business, Innovation and Skills, London.

Portes, J., 2013, "David Goodhart's British Fantasy" 27 March, http://notthetreasuryview.blogspot.nl/2013/03/david-goodharts-fantasy.html.

Prais, S., 1981, "Vocational Qualifications of the Labour Force in Britain and Germany", *National Institute Economic Review*, 98, 47–59.

Pryor, F., 2010, *The Making of the British Landscape: How We Have Transformed the Land, from Prehistory to Today*, Penguin Books, London.

Reith Report, 1947, New Towns Committee (Reith Committee): Minutes, Papers and Report, HLG84. See: http://discovery.nationalarchives.gov.uk/details/r/C8779.

Reuschke, D., and Maclennan, D., 2014, "Housing Assets and Small Business Investment: Exploring Links for Theory and Policy", *Regional Studies*, 48.4, 744–757.

Reyes, J., Garcia, M. and Lattimore, R., 2009, "The International Economic Order and Trade Architecture", *Spatial Economic Analysis*, 4.1, 73–102.

RHPR, 2015, *Affordable Housing: A Fair Deal for Rural Communities*, Report of the Rural Housing Policy Review. See: www.hastoe.com/page/772/Affordable-Housing-A-Fair-Deal-for-Rural-Communities.aspx.

Rice, P. and Venables, A.J., 2003, "Equilibrium Regional Disparities: Theory and British Evidence", *Regional Studies*, 37.6, 675–686.

Rice, P., Venables, A.J. and Patacchini, E., 2006, "Spatial Determinants of Productivity: Analysis for the Regions of Great Britain", *Regional Science and Urban Economics*, 36, 727–752.

Riddoch, L., 2014, *Blossom: What Scotland Needs to Flourish*, Luath Press, Edinburgh.

Riddoch, L., 2015, *Wee White Blossom: What Post-Referendum Scotland Needs to Flourish*, Luath Press, Edinburgh.

Robson, B.T., 1973, *Urban Growth: An Approach*, Methuen, London.

Roger Tym and Partners, 2002a, *Planning, Competitiveness and Productivity: Memoranda Submitted to the Committee*, House of Commons, ODPM: Housing, Planning, Local Government and the Regions Committee, HC 114-II of Session 2002–03, 2 December, London.

Roger Tym and Partners, 2002b, *Planning, Competitiveness and Productivity: Research Commissioned from Roger Tym and Partners*, House of Commons, ODPM: Housing, Planning, Local Government and the Regions Committee, HC 114-III of Session 2002–03, 12 December, London.

Roger Tym and Partners, 2003, *Planning, Competitiveness and Productivity: Fourth Report of Session 2002–03: Volume 1*, House of Commons, ODPM: Housing,

Planning, Local Government and the Regions Committee, HC 114-I of Session 2002–03, 27 January, London.

Rolfe, H., Rienzo, C., Lalani, M. and Portes, J., 2013, "Migration and Productivity: Employers' Practices, Public Attitudes and Statistical Evidence", National Institute of Economic and Social Research, London, November.

Rosewell, B., 2013, *Reinventing London*, London Publishing Partnership, London.

Roubini, N., and Mihm, S., 2011, *Crisis Economics: A Crash Course in the Future of Finance*, Penguin, New York.

Rowthorn, R., 2008, "Returns to Scale and the Economic Effects of Migration", *Spatial Economic Analysis*, 3.2, 151–158.

Rowthorn, R., 2009, "Returns to Scale and the Economic Effects of Migration: Some New Considerations", *Spatial Economic Analysis*, 3.2, 151–158.

Rowthorn, R., 2010, "Combined and Uneven Development: Reflections on the North-South Divide", *Spatial Economic Analysis*, 5.4, 363–388.

Rowthorn, R., 2014, *Large Scale Immigration: Its Economic and Demographic Consequences for the UK*, Civitas: Institute for the Study of Civil Society, London.

Rowthorn, R., and Coutts, K., 2004, "De-Industrialisation and the Balance of Payments in Advanced Economies", *Cambridge Journal of Economics*, 28, 767–790.

Rowthorn, R., and Ramaswamy, R., 1999, "Growth, Trade and Deindustrialization", *IMF Staff Papers*, 46.1, 18–41.

Rozenfeld, H.D., Rybski, H.D., Gabaix, X. and Makse, H.A., 2011, "The Area and Population of Cities: New Insights from a New Perspective on Cities", *American Economic Review*, 101, 2205–2225.

RSPH, 2015, *Health on the High Street*, Royal Society for Public Health. See: www.rsph.org.

Rydin, Y., 1993, *The British Planning System: An Introduction*, Macmillan, Basingstoke.

Sanderson, M.R., 2013, "Does Immigration Promote Long-Term Economic Development? A Global and Regional Cross-National Analysis, 1965–2005", *Journal of Ethnic and Migration Studies*, 39.1, 1–30.

Satsangi, M., Gallent, N. and Bevan, N., 2010, *The Rural Housing Question*, Policy Press, Bristol.

Savills, 2012, *International Farmland Focus 2012, Savills Research*, London.

Savills, 2014, *Market Survey UK Agricultural Land, Savills World Research*, London.

Scott, P., 2007, *Triumph of the South: A Regional Economic History of Early Twentieth Century Britain*, Ashgate, Aldershot.

Scott Committee, 1942, *Report of the Committee on Land Utilisation in Rural Areas (Scott Report)*, Ministry of Works and Planning, Cmd 6378, HMSO.

Scottish Government, 2014, *Scottish Input–Output Tables and Multipliers: Type II Leontief Multipliers and Effects Table*, August, Edinburgh. www.scotland.gov.uk/Topics/Statistics/Browse/Economy/Input-Output/Downloads/IO1998-2011L2.

Simpson, W., 1992, *Urban Structure and the Labour Market: Worker Mobility, Commuting, and Underemployment in Cities*, Clarendon Press, Oxford.

Smith Institute, 2013, *The Great House Price Divide*, Briefing Paper, Smith Institute, London, December.

Soo, K.T., 2005, "Zipf's Law for Cities: A Cross-Country Comparison", *Regional Science and Urban Economics*, 35.3, 239–263.

SQW, 2013, SME Finance in London: Final Report to the Greater London Authority, Segal Quince Wicksteed and CEEDR Centre for Enterprise and Economic Development Research, Middlesex University, November, www.sqw.co.uk.

Stephens, M., Leishman, C., Bramley. G., Ferrari, E. and Rae A., 2014, *What Will the Housing Market Look Like in 2040?*, Joseph Rowntree Foundation, York.

Stiglitz, J.E., 2015, *The Great Divide*, Penguin, London.

Stone, P.A., 1970, *Urban Development in Britain: Standards, Costs, and Resources 1964–2004. Volume 1: Population Trends and Housing*, NIESR National Institute of Economic and Social Research, Cambridge University Press, Cambridge.

Summers, L.H., 2013, "Economic Possibilities for Our Children: The 2013 Martin Feldstein Lecture", *NBER Reporter*, 4, www.nber.org/reporter.

Sutton Trust, 2014, *Research Brief: Extra-Curricula Inequality*, 1 September.

TCPA, 2010a, *Making Planning Work. National Planning Framework*, Briefing Paper 2, Town and Country Planning Association, London.

TCPA, 2010b, *Making Planning Work. The Bigger Picture and the Longer View: Really Useful Strategic Planning*, Briefing Paper 3, Town and Country Planning Association, London.

TCPA, 2010c, *A Framework for National Infrastructure Development: Revised Energy and Waste Water NPSs*, TCPA Briefing, Town and Country Planning Association, London.

The Economist, 2013, "Immigration and the Public Finances: Boon or Burden?" 15 June.

The Economist, 2014a, "Free Exchange: No Country for Young People", 22 November.

The Economist, 2014b, "Glass Half Empty: London's Great Suction Machine Affects the South Too", 26 July.

The Economist, 2015a, "An Hereditary Meritocracy", 24 January.

The Economist, 2015b, "The Balance Sheet Boom", 3 January.

The Economist, 2015c, "Barbarians at the Farm Gate", 3 January.

The Economist, 2015d, "The Sky's the Limit: Commercial Property Has Been Delivering Excellent Returns", 14 February.

The Guardian, 2008, "British Workers Lack Skills and Drive of East Europe's Migrants, Says Study", 12 June.

The Spectator, 2008, "The Real Immigration Lie", 5 April.

The Times, 2015, "Top Universities Ordered to End the North-South Split", 17 January.

Thirlwall, A.P., 1980, "Regional Problems are 'Balance of Payments' Problems", *Regional Studies*, 14, 419–425.

UKNEA, 2011, *UK National Ecosystem Assessment: Understanding Nature's Value to Society: Synthesis of Key Findings*, Cambridge.

Urban Task Force, 1999, *Towards an Urban Renaissance: The Final Report of the Urban Task Force*, E&FN Spon, London.

Uthwatt Report, 1942, *Expert Committee on Compensation and Betterment* (Uthwatt Committee): Minutes and Papers, HLG81. See: http://discovery.nationalarchives.gov.uk/details/r/C8776.

UUK, 2013, *Patterns and Trends in UK Higher Education 2013. Higher Education: A Diverse and Changing Sector*, Universities UK in Collaboration with HESA, London.

Vargas-Silva, C., 2015, *Briefing: The Fiscal Impact of Immigration in the UK*, The Migration Research Observatory, 27 March.

Vigar, G., Healey, P., Hull, A. and Davoudi, S., 2000, *Planning, Governance and Spatial Strategy in Britain; An Institutionalist Analysis*, Macmillan, Basingstoke.

Wadsworth, J., 2010, "The UK Labour Market and Immigration", *National Institute Economic Review*, 213: R35, NIESR National Institute of Economic and Social Research, London.

Wadsworth, J., 2014, "Immigration, the European Union and the UK Labour Market", *CEP Policy Analysis Paper*, Centre for Economic Performance, London.

Walker, B., 1981, *Welfare Economics and Urban Problems*, Hutchinson, London.

Webber, D.J., Hudson, J., Boddy, M. and Plumridge, A., 2009, "Regional Productivity Differentials in England: Explaining the Gap", *Papers in Regional Science*, 88.3, 609–622.

Wellings, B., 2012, *English Nationalism and Euroscepticism*, Peter Lang AG, Bern.

West, E., 2013, *The Diversity Illusion: What went Wrong About Immigration and How to Solve It*, Gibson Square, London.

Whitehead, C.M.E., 1983, "The Rationale for Government Intervention", in Dunkerley, H., (ed.), *Urban Land Policy: Issues and Opportunities*, World Bank Publications, World Bank, Washington DC.

Whitehead, C.M.E., 1991, "From Need to Affordability: An Analysis of UK Housing Objectives", *Urban Studies*, 28.6, 871–887.

Whitehead, C.M.E., Edge, A., Gordon, I.R., Scanlon, K. and Travers, T., 2011, *The Impact of Migration on Access to Housing and the Housing Market*, A Project for the Migration Advisory Committee, 16 December, LSE Consulting, London.

Wibberley, G.P., 1959, *Agricultural & Urban Growth: A Study of the Competition for Rural Land*, Michael Joseph, London.

Willets, D., 2010, *The Pinch: How the Baby-Boomers Took Their Children's Future – and Why They Should Give it Back*, Atlantic Books, London.

Willis, K.G., 1980, *The Economics of Town and Country Planning*, Granada Publishing, St Albans.

Witty, A., 2013, *Encouraging a British Revolution: Sir Andrew Witty's Review of Universities and Growth*, Department for Business, Innovation and Skills, London.

Wren, C., and Jones, J., 2012, "FDI Location Across British Regions and Agglomerative Forces: A Markov Analysis", *Spatial Economic Analysis*, 7.2, 265–286.

Wrigley, N., and Brookes, E., 2014, Evolving High Streets: Resilience & Reinvention, Perspectives from Social Science, University of Southampton and ESRC.

Wrigley, N., and Lambiri, D., 2014, *High Street Performance and Evolution: A Brief Guide to the Evidence*, University of Southampton and ESRC.

Wrigley, N., and Lambiri, D., 2015, *British High Streets: From Crisis to Recovery? A Comprehensive Review of the Evidence*, University of Southampton and ESRC. See: http://thegreatbritishhighstreet.co.uk/research-reports.

Zipf, G., 1949, *Human Behavior and the Principle of Least Effort*, Addison-Wesley, New York.

6 The sub-national economic policy agenda

Governance devolution and interregional connectivity

6.1 Introduction

The previous five chapters have all argued that the UK exhibits long-standing and serious interregional inequalities and imbalances in productivity, incomes, quality of life and wellbeing, and that these imbalances have been very heavily shaped by the impacts of globalisation on the UK economy. In addition, the governance and institutional structure of the UK has so far been largely unable to respond to these growing core-periphery imbalances. Indeed, Rodrik (2011) has argued that against the backdrop of modern globalisation nation-states and democracy cannot continue to exist and function in the manner that was possible prior to the advent of modern globalisation, and that fundamental changes must arise. Indeed, in the UK we do now appear to be entering a new era in which major changes in the UK's governance system and also major changes in the UK's infrastructure delivery system are afoot. However, many of the current debates tend to be framed in legal and constitutional terms, and of course, these are essential features of devolution and decentralisation discussions (Renwick 2014; Bogdanor 2015; Hazell 2015). Yet, the arguments in this book are that such changes are fundamentally driven by economic trends. The suggestion that the UK's highly centralised and London-centric governance system artificially skews UK macroeconomic, structural, housing-related and infrastructure policies in favour of London-related issues rather than one which relates to the realities of the wider UK economy has recently started to enter mainstream public policy debates (NESTA 2014; CfC 2014).[1] This chapter aims to document the arguments underpinning these changes in thinking and will highlight the likely areas of consensus and uncertainty regarding the role which governance and infrastructure-related changes may play in the UK's future governance and economic performance.

The background to these issues is that in the wake of the 2008 global economic crisis many of the issues examined in this book have re-emerged in mainstream public and political debates, whereas for several decades previously they had been largely sidelined in public discourses. However, the ways in which these issues have re-surfaced in public debates is sometimes markedly still out of step with the economic realities. In particular, many of the recent 'national' discussions about productivity-related issues in the wake of the 2008 global financial crisis still fail to fully take into consideration the explicit core-periphery regional structure of productivity performance.

As we have seen, there is a very clear and long-standing core-periphery structure to UK productivity performance which long pre-dates the 2008 financial crisis by more than three decades. However, in the aftermath of the 2008 crisis the UK's poor productivity performance is in many ways now regarded as the most important economic challenge facing the UK economy (Kaletsky 2015), and the international comparison figures reported in Chapter 1 underpin the scale of the challenge. Yet, there is no unanimous agreement as to the causes of the UK's poor productivity performance, which is why as we saw in Chapter 1 it is described as a mystery or a puzzle. Most academic economists plus the Bank of England regard it to be primarily a result of a severe demand contraction in the aftermath of the 2008 global financial crisis which was exacerbated by a fiscal contraction from 2010 onwards (Krugman 2015a, 2015b; Kaletsky 2015). Alternatively, The Treasury regard it to be primarily a result of supply side factors, to be rectified by the upgrading of skills and infrastructure, while others suggest it may be a statistical problem whereby conventional growth accounting frameworks somehow underplay the productivity role of services (Kaletsky 2015) which figure so heavily in the UK economy. Yet for our purposes the possible responses to these different explanations each raise important issues. First, regarding the purported statistical problems, the work of Jorgensen and Timmer (2011) which directly addresses these types of issues using the most comprehensive data available would point in precisely the opposite direction; namely, that most services do indeed generate very poor productivity growth. As such, the argument that London prospers relative to other parts of the UK because its economy is more service-oriented than other parts of the UK becomes problematic unless we also explicitly acknowledge the specific role played by international finance in modern globalisation, because services per se do not heavily drive productivity growth. Second, the main problem with the supply side argument is that it is almost entirely unclear as to why UK skills and infrastructure would have apparently and so suddenly become so much less productive (Kaletsky 2015). In particular, for our purposes it is unclear from the supply side argument why in the wake of the 2008 crisis areas outside of London and the southern regions of England should have become relatively even less productive in comparison to London, given that the financial crisis originated in the international financial markets. Finally, in terms of the demand contraction argument, again this appears to have a marked core-periphery interregional structure, but the reasons for this are still somewhat opaque, given that again the demand contractions originated in the international financial markets. Some of the geography of the demand contractions and responses may be in part related to interactions between access to finance and geographically determined housing asset-based wealth effects, and some may be related to the geography of public sector cuts. Yet, as with all major economic issues it is likely that there may be some elements of truth in more than one of these possible explanations although which is the dominant causal mechanism is still a matter of debate. As such, questions regarding the reasons why the UK interregional inequalities are both so large and continually increasing still remain.

However, the wide-ranging evidence reviewed in this book provides us with some clear lines of thinking. As we have seen in Chapters 2 and 3, urban and local economic explanations alone do not fit the facts, so regional explanations are also essential to the story. In this regard, the most popular supply side explanation which has been circulating in recent years is that of the differential effects of the spatial sorting of human capital. However, as we have already seen in detail in previous chapters the levels of UK interregional migration are tiny relative to the overall population and in addition they have barely changed in almost four decades. Moreover, this observation, allied with the fact that UK interregional secondary and tertiary skills profiles are today almost identical, makes the spatial sorting of the native population inadmissible as a major explanation of the UK's interregional inequalities. Supply side explanations relating to spatial sorting simply don't fit the evidence, and consequent calls for 'people-based' improvements focused on education become largely impotent, given the fact that as we will see in the following chapter UK educational investments have for decades totally dwarfed 'place-based' spatial policy investments, and decades of educational policy reforms have led to largely invariant educational outcomes at the large region scale.

The only sense in which supply side human capital and spatial sorting explanations gain traction in the UK relates to the skills enhancement effects associated with international immigration, from which, as we have already seen in Chapters 4 and 5, London has benefited more than any other city in the world. UK education policy debates therefore have effectively nothing to say about the skills-sorting effects associated with immigration of human capital because the human capital of immigrants has by definition been largely developed outside of the UK. Furthermore, the burgeoning UK interregional inequalities examined in this book pre-date the surges in UK migration by more than a decade. These observations therefore suggest that the immigration of human capital is likely to be largely an induced result of London's demand shocks driven by the renewed globalisation of capital markets rather than a cause. Demand side explanations favouring London's key role in the global capital markets alongside the overwhelming primacy of the South East in UK global connectivity provide much more sensible explanations as to what we observe. As such, from this perspective, the induced effects relating to inflows of human capital and investment primarily into London and the southern regions of the UK are largely unsurprising consequences, except possibly for the scale of these inflows.

Yet, even ruling out domestic spatial sorting as a major explanation of UK interregional inequalities, however, the problem still remains as to why these inequalities are both so intractable and also why they display such a persistent core-periphery structure in which London appears to provide few if any positive spillovers beyond its southern hinterland regions. On this matter, the UK Government has for many years appeared to be almost entirely ignorant as to both the underlying causes of these inequalities and also therefore precisely what to do about the problem. Part of the reason for this is that it was largely assumed as being patently obvious in most government and policy circles from the mid-1980s through to the onset of the 2008 crisis that the prosperity of London was beneficial to the UK as a whole. However, as we have seen in the previous chapters, in terms of aggregating total UK output growth this may be true, but in terms of London generating spillovers which positively spur growth in other UK regions beyond its immediate hinterland, there is almost no evidence whatsoever that this has been the case. Yet, it is only in the years since the 2008 global financial crisis in which the performance of London and the South East has diverged so markedly from other parts of the UK that many analysts and policy-makers have begun to suspect that London may not have been the driver of the national economy as was previously imagined. Heavily influenced by growing political pressures for devolution, central government has recently started to undergo significant shifts in some of its attitudes towards these issues. From a range of international as well as national sources and influences national government has embarked on a two-pronged attack on the UK's regional and national economic problem. This two-pronged attack involves enhancing both regional decentralisation and devolution, while at the same time enhancing interregional connectivity.

As we will see in this chapter, these two policy agendas are distinct, but not separate, and while they are heavily influenced by political pressures, they are also based on responses to three fundamental economic problems which go way beyond the UK context, namely the optimal currency area problem, the optimal size of a nation problem and the place-based versus space-blind problem. The UK state is heavily centralised and now it faces severe underlying challenges to its governance efficacy associated with each of these problems. After discussing the enormous centralisation of the UK state this chapter will therefore explain each of these fundamental problems and will examine the implications of these problems for the UK's economic and political governance. This will then provide the backdrop against which the UK policy debates are currently being framed, and will also allow us to consider how the changing governance systems and public investment efforts are likely to respond to the fundamental interregional economic problems faced by the whole of the UK polity.

6.2 The problem of UK governance centralisation

The UK state has been gradually centralising over the last 70 or more years (Mulgan and Bury 2006). In the nineteenth and early twentieth centuries large shares of public finance were locally generated (Diamond and Carr-West 2015). Many spheres of civic and institution building went hand in hand with locally generated and locally raised finance and investment, and this was particularly evident in the growing industrial cities of the midlands and the north of England.[2] However, the centralisation of the UK state began in earnest with the post-war establishment of the National Health Service (Mulgan and Bury 2006), but greater centralisation also occurred for political reasons under the 1980s Thatcher government, specifically limiting the power of city authorities.[3] Today the ratio of central government employees to local government employees is at its highest level ever.[4] Yet, as we have already suggested in Chapter 1, today's high degree of governance centralisation and the low degree of sub-national government autonomy[5] appears to be strangely out of step with the UK's interregional inequalities, which are some of the most marked in the (OECD 2013a). In particular, the ability of a highly centralised governance system (Hazell 2015) to respond to the diverse challenges raised by these differences is now open to widespread debate, and indeed there are some real grounds for these concerns (Hope and Leslie 2009). Yet, the political consequences of various devolution and decentralisation shifts which were already evident prior to 2014–2015, allied with the fallout from both the 2014 Scottish independence referendum and the 2015 UK general election, means that governance issues are likely to dominate much of the 2015–2020 parliament (Riddell 2015). However, the governance and devolution issues facing the constituent nations of the UK are not independent of the EU membership question (Geddes 2013; Riddell 2015), and nor are they independent of the governance questions facing English cities and regions (Bogdanor 2012; LGA 2012).

One of the issues which is closely intertwined with this national lack of trust in public institutions and governance relates to the structure of the UK governance system. In particular, in many quarters, as we have already seen in Chapter 1, there is widespread and increasing public disquiet regarding the overly top-down and highly centralised nature of the UK and these concerns are beginning to have real and long-lasting impacts on UK politics in public discourses. The UK is generally regarded as being a country with largely strong institutional capabilities (OECD 2013b), and in particular regarding economic freedoms (Miller and Holmes 2009) and the ease of doing business the UK is consistently ranked in the top ten countries in the world (World Bank 2009a). As such, the quality of the UK governance and institutional environment might be expected to be highly conducive to the development of well-designed local and regional development strategies. Yet, as we have also seen in Chapter 2, there are noticeable variations in access to services and levels of civic engagement across UK regions which correspond largely to the levels of regional wealth. As a whole, by OECD standards many of the economically weaker regions of the UK are only middle-ranking performers in terms of institutional engagements, and relatively much weaker performers than the national aggregate ease-of-doing-business institutional rankings would suggest (World Bank 2009a). Moreover, these regional variations are set against the backdrop of current UK levels of public trust in national political institutions which are well below the OECD average (OECD 2013b). The recent gains in UK public confidence in national government since just before the 2008 crisis are well above the OECD average (OECD 2013b), but it still remains the case that public confidence in UK government institutions is relatively low in comparison to many other advanced OECD economies. As we will see below, however, these subtle differences in the perceived value and roles played by different national, regional and local institutional elements are leading to profound changes and consequences for the whole UK governance system and regional and urban concerns are very much driving these changes.

In the UK the levels of sub-national government funding and sub-national government capital expenditure are currently not only both very low by OECD standards (OECD 2011a) but indeed they are amongst the lowest of any large OECD economy (HoC 2014a). Local taxes account for just 1.7 per cent of GDP.[6] Although since the late 1990s the UK national governance structure became somewhat less centralised due to the enhanced roles of the devolved administrations in Scotland, Wales and Northern Ireland, the UK as a whole is still a heavily centralised economy and institutional changes such as the 2010 abolition of the regional government offices and the Regional Development Agencies in England mean that in terms of economic development issues England is still very highly centralised.

In this highly centralised state, the funding streams for sub-national government activities come overwhelmingly from fiscal transfers from the central national government (OECD 2013b). In terms of regional, urban and local development matters there are now widespread public concerns that this very high degree of national governance centralisation may inhibit the ability of policy-makers to design and deliver public policies and the provision of public goods and services that are well-tailored to the needs and preferences of local citizens. Moreover, these long-standing concerns have now increased markedly in the aftermath of the 2008 global economic crisis as public sector cut-backs orchestrated from central government are perceived to potentially exacerbate these problems. Yet, whether these concerns are justified depends on: first, the extent to which these centralisation perceptions reflect actual realities; second, the social and political objectives which centralised structures are intended to respond to and address; and third, the extent to which centralised governance systems are better able to achieve these objectives than more decentralised systems. In other words it depends on the degree of governance centralisation, the objectives of centralisation and the performance of governance centralisation.

On the first point, namely the degree of governance centralisation, as we have already seen the UK is indeed already one of the most highly centralised states in the OECD (RSA 2015). It is also a state where the civil service structure is strongly federal in an organisational but not geographical sense, with high degrees of autonomy between departments (IfG 2013), except for the ultimate controlling hand of the Treasury (NESTA 2014). However, in actual fact the realities of sub-national governance changes in the UK, and in particular the perceived trends towards greater centralisation, are rather more nuanced and subtle than the picture painted by many rather simple public discourses and perceptions. Technically whether or not the UK has been entirely a unitary state is a matter of debate (IfG 2014), although UK central government dominates revenue collection and funding allocations to a greater degree than almost any other advanced economy. The main roles of sub-national government within the UK relate primarily to both education and also social protection (OECD 2013a) while the level of sub-national governance activities associated with economic affairs or regional development is one of the lowest in the OECD (OECD 2013a). The level of these particular types of activities, and especially economic development, which is undertaken by sub-national government has indeed fallen markedly over recent years in England, whereas on the other hand Scotland and Wales have benefited from greater levels of devolution. These various local government reductions and reorganisations of service provision activities have led to widespread public concerns regarding the potential role played by different tiers of government, but these impacts are likely to differ according to the service provision objectives. In the UK the relative importance of education and social protection is much greater at the local level than is economic development, which is now either largely sidelined or very much centralised.

As a whole, however, the share of national investment accounted for sub-national government in the UK has actually increased slightly since 2008 and the UK experience has therefore been slightly different to many other OECD economies. Since 2008 the share of public investment undertaken by OECD sub-national governments has actually increased very slightly after the crisis (OECD 2013a, 2013c). On average the general OECD-wide (OECD 2013c) and EU-wide (Dotti and Bubbico 2014) trends are towards greater sub-national government expenditure relative to national government expenditure, and the directions of these trends since 2008 tend to coincide with the degree of governance decentralisation at the national level. For example, the share of national public investments which are undertaken by sub-national governments have tended to fall sharply in highly centralised states while in more decentralised states the share of sub-national government expenditure has tended to increase markedly. Interestingly, the UK has slightly moved against the trend associated with other highly centralised states in that there has been a slight increase in the share of national government expenditure accounted for by local and regional governments. Yet, even in spite of these shifts, it still remains the case that the share of direct investment accounted for by sub-national local and regional government is very low by OECD standards (OECD 2013a), as is the share of sub-national government revenue which is generated by taxes and also the share of the national debt which is accounted for by sub-national government (OECD 2013a, 2013c).

On the second point regarding the service provision objectives of government systems, governance centralisation is not necessary of itself a problem any more than governance decentralisation is of itself a problem. Rather it depends on the particular issues which governance systems are expected to address and the public goods which governance systems are expected to provide. This also brings us directly to the third point, namely the performance of the highly centralised governance system. At present, in current debates on the UK regional economic problem the second and third points are very closely intertwined and, as such, questions of the intended objectives as well as the performance of the UK governance system need to be considered together.

In the case of the increasing UK interregional inequalities the greater differences between regions are increasingly perceived by many citizens as requiring a different form of UK governance system which may be better able to respond to these differences. However, the results of these shifting 'bottom-up' public perceptions on UK governance systems also depend crucially on how they shape national political decision-making and in turn how this influences the 'top-down' responses of central state, and on these matters, there is already a fairly clear broad direction of travel which has emerged.

Whenever problematic issues arise in society there are a range of different possible responses within government, the media and wide public discourses, the framing of which in each case depends on a variety of external political, philosophical, cultural, practical and pragmatic influences. In the case of the UK regional economic problems and the widening interregional inequalities, there have been long-standing debates about these matters and over recent decades we have witnessed a variety of such responses. These responses to the problem have variously included: (i) there is no problem; (ii) there is a problem but there is nothing that we ought to do as the alternative will be worse, which is a kind of implicit crowding-out type of argument; (iii) there is a problem but there is nothing much we can do even if we wished to do so as it is a natural outcome of systems or processes beyond our control; (iv) there is a problem and it is important to try to effect something of a response or a solution by using new policy approaches to re-shape current trajectories, which is a kind of 'crowding in' type of argument (Zoellick 2012); (v) there is a problem and the scale of public perceptions about it means that it is imperative we implement a substantial response. As already initially outlined in Chapter 1 and as will be seen in this chapter and the following chapter, over recent years, and particularly in the wake of the 2008 global financial crisis, the debates and responses to the UK regional economic problems have shifted towards the latter sets of responses. In the 1980s and the early 1990s the public responses from national government were largely characterised by responses (i) and (ii) while the late 1990s and early 2000s were characterised rather more by responses (iii) and (iv). In the aftermath of the 2008 crisis, the responses have shifted markedly towards (iv) and (v), and especially towards response (v), as reflected in the raft of recent policy initiatives being put forward regarding regional governance changes and greater city devolution along with major high-speed rail infrastructure investments aimed at enhancing interregional connectivity.

Public discourses regarding the UK regional economic problems are indeed shifting, but precisely in which direction exactly they are moving is as yet not quite so clear, as more than one trend is already observable. As we will see below the somewhat ambiguous and occasionally conflicting narratives framing public discourses aimed at overcoming the UK regional economic problems are not entirely aligned or consistent with each other, and there are two main reasons for this. On the side of the policy-makers, part of the problem is a certain degree of confusion in central government as to precisely what is the nature of the problem, what are the causes of the problem, and in particular what is the role played by London in the problem. Meanwhile, amongst the wider public there is also a range of different perceptions. At one end of the spectrum to many observers many of the UK's current policy initiatives regarding governance devolution and infrastructure investments merely reflect some degree of panic amongst the Westminster elites, particularly around the time of the 2014 Scottish independence referendum (Platt 2015), and the resulting devolution promises and offers were simply a myopic and knee-jerk reaction by a highly centralised and top-down governance system to a potential loss of political influence and traction at various levels. As such, these initiatives are perceived to have no real substance and are merely political tools. At the other end of the spectrum these developments reflect a long wished-for and long-considered set of devolution and connectivity initiatives that the UK economy needs in order to best address twenty-first-century economic realities, and these initiatives are based on increasing international evidence of best-practice regarding governance and connectivity. On this view these types of policy initiatives do have real substance and, as such, their veracity is not contingent on the politics surrounding independence debates.

While the views of many observers are likely to sit somewhere between the two polar opposites there is also an important third perspective to consider. Both of the polarised views outlined here share common ground in that they both accept that devolved or decentralised governance has important economic and social advantages and that governance reform is an important step towards realising these advantages at the regional or urban levels. On the other hand, there are some who consider that the architecture of governance is largely unrelated to issues of economic development and that good horizontal and framework policies ensuring good institutions, well-defined property rights and the enforceability of contracts is all that is required to ensure economic development. The UK is generally regarded as scoring well on these criteria and if one adopts this type of minimalist interpretation of institutional issues then many of the current UK public discussions regarding the importance of devolution and decentralisation as well as connectivity and accessibility would be regarded as being largely meaningless. However, these arguments ignore a vast literature in regional studies, political science and development studies which suggests that there are important relationships between the nature, structure and the quality of governance and economic development. Moreover, although the evidence on the relationship between governance decentralisation and economic growth is weak (Ezcurra and Rodriguez-Pose 2013), there is much stronger evidence that regional inequalities are lower in decentralised (Ezcurra and Pasqual 2008) and higher quality (Ezcurra and Rodriguez-Pose 2014) political and governance systems. The minimalist approach has little to say about these issues, and in particular is out of step with the UK observations. In the case of the UK, the observed combination of a high-quality national governance system with high interregional inequalities means that the UK is therefore something of an outlier in comparison to other countries, and this also suggests that issues of political and governance decentralisation are likely to be key to the UK observations.

Given the issues and arguments raised in this book, we focus on three fundamental lines of argument which assume that governance and regional development are interrelated issues and therefore that UK discussions about governance devolution, decentralisation and interregional connectivity do have some real credibility and substance to them. However, these three lines of argument which in the literature are posed as analytical problems, namely the optimal currency area problem, the optimal size of nation problem and the place-based versus space-blind problem, are not specific to the UK. Rather, they have emerged from international debates in diverse literatures spanning economics, political science, geography and development studies. However, more than almost any other OECD country the current regional realities of the UK throw these issues into sharp relief and challenge many aspects of previously accepted UK political and policy-related narratives. Therefore, before we can discuss the emerging (partial) policy consensus currently arising within the UK regarding regional governance matters it is crucial that we first consider these three basic analytical problems, each of which has profound impacts for understanding the challenges facing the UK.

6.3   Governance problems relating to the size of the currency area, the size of nation and the underlying regional policy logic

In order to understand the underlying long-run governance challenges facing the UK's interregional economic system there are three different analytical problems which must be reflected upon, even before we begin to discuss the possible approaches to public policy. These analytical problems concern, first, the optimal monetary arrangements linking regions together, second, the optimal governance arrangements linking regions together within an integrated economic system, and third the place-based versus space-blind logic of governance and policy. It is essential to understand the issues raised by these three analytical problems because first the current debates about the UK's internal governance arrangements all depend on providing responses to these three problems, and second, because any changes to the UK's interregional governance arrangements will automatically face challenges associated with these problems. Once we understand these three problems then we can begin a more serious discussion of the theoretical underpinnings of the different policy approaches.

6.3.1   *The Optimal Currency Area Problem*

The first theoretical problem which is essential for understanding the long-run governance challenges facing the UK's interregional economic system is known as the 'optimal currency area' or the 'optimal currency region' problem and this problem is associated originally with the work of Mundell (1961). The argument of Mundell (1961) is that a single common currency system becomes both inefficient and ineffective in a situation where areas or regions within the single currency system differ greatly. For a multi-regional market area to be appropriate for a common currency there need to be the free mobility of both capital and labour across regions, a risk-sharing system of fiscal transfers assisting weaker regions or regions facing downturns, and also all of the regions should broadly move through business cycles together. Otherwise, if there are severe and asymmetric business cycle shocks between regions then some or all of the regions will face long-standing problems within the system (Mundell 1961). On the other hand, a common currency system may also be able to shield individual regions from severe localised and adverse shocks by spreading the risk across the whole system (Mundell 1973). At the same time, however, if overall national aggregate economic volatility is limited the adverse effects of divergences in regional business cycles are mitigated, whereas the adverse effects of a lack of interregional synchronisation are greater in times of greater economic volatility (Partridge and Rickman 2005).

Although these various features necessary for an optimal currency area may only be met to different extents in different regions, the introduction of the Euro is also argued by its proponents to have helped to spur interregional convergence across Europe (Marsh 2009) and, as such, helped to facilitate conditions more appropriate for such a common currency. Yet, while these various optimal currency area arguments have previously been used for and against the introduction of the Euro and also for and against the UK's decision not to adopt the Euro, in reality common currency systems tend to be endogenous to the institutional contexts (Frankel and Rose 1998). As such the outcomes regarding the currency area tend to be political and institutional in nature rather than purely economic and monetary in nature (Deutsche Bank 2013).

As we saw in Chapter 1, at present the UK economy is actually less of an optimal currency area than either the EU-28 or the Eurozone (Deutsche Bank 2013). The reason is that the UK regional economies (Deutsche Bank 2014a) and business cycles (Deutsche Bank 2013) have become so divergent on a range of dimensions and, in particular, the business cycle of London and the South East is increasingly decoupled from that of the rest of the UK's regions (Deutsche Bank 2013, 2014a). The fact that the Sterling area zone is diverging so far from being an optimal currency area means that national economic governance becomes increasingly difficult. Macroeconomic decisions and national public policy decisions made on aggregate 'national' criteria will increasingly have uneven interregional impacts and are likely to lead to different and often unintended impacts in different places. These interregional differences are in turn likely to weaken the effectiveness of national policy for three reasons. First, in purely economic terms, if regions become more heterogeneous and their business cycles less synchronised then a national top-down economic policy of any particular form is likely to exhibit a weaker fit and lower effectiveness with increasing numbers of regions and localities (OECD 2011b). Second, in governance terms, the effectiveness of national economic policy will become increasingly undermined due to its inability to generate similar outcomes across all parts of the UK. The reason is a question of justice. Government policies require public support in order to be implemented and to be effective and a failure to produce more equivalent outcomes in different places starts to undermine the policy in terms of the critical criteria of public credibility, legitimacy and salience (Cash *et al.* 2003). Greater interregional divergence means that fewer people perceive that they are being treated either equally to people in other regions, and also that their own specific concerns are being incorporated into the design of national policies. These optimal currency area-related concerns are now very real in the UK, and nowhere more so than in Scotland as they relate directly to questions of fiscal federalism (Hallwood and MacDonald 2005), and outlining some of the Scottish issues is very instructive for considering how these issues also relate to other parts of the UK's regions and cities. Third, the enormous aggregate volatility along with a lack of interregional synchronisation exhibited by the UK in the post 2008-crisis era implies that UK monetary policy is likely to have had only a very limited effectiveness during this period, confined primarily to just a limited number of regions.

While it remains part of the UK, Scotland in economic terms is a region of the wider UK state, even though on various cultural and legal criteria it can be considered a country. However, the differences between Scotland as a region and as a nation and also the nature of the relationships between regions and nations came under the spotlight during the 2014 Scottish independence referendum. The partial break-up of the common Sterling area defined by the UK became a real possibility with the 2014 Scottish independence referendum, and in the ensuing debates the latent links between national-regional governance and the common currency system for the first time became partially exposed. While these public debates related to the relationship between Scotland and the rest of the UK, in reality they are every bit as pertinent, if not even more so, regarding the relationships between the UK's other economically weaker regions and its stronger regions, so a review of the issues which arose in the Scottish case is extremely instructive in terms of helping us consider the monetary issues relating to the UK interregional systems as a whole, and the extent to which this is optimal, and the national and regional governance issues inextricably tied up with these questions.

Around the time of the 2014 referendum on Scottish independence the various publicly debated arguments about whether Scotland would, could or should maintain its use of Sterling in the event of a UK break-up, exposed the two different features of a common currency system and its operation within an interregional setting, namely the medium-of-exchange aspect of the currency and the wealth-holding asset aspect of a currency.

On the one hand there is the medium-of-exchange aspect of a currency, in which a currency simply acts as a denominator index allowing the relative values of all goods and services to be standardised and benchmarked against each other. Yet, as we saw in Chapter 2, Scotland is very close to the UK average values in terms of productivity and incomes. Moreover, as we also saw in Chapter 5, in terms of budget deficits Scotland also does not diverge markedly from a fiscally neutral position, particularly if North Sea Oil revenues are included in the discussion. As such, on various current indicators at least, a shared common currency between an independent Scotland and the rest of the UK would indeed closely reflect the true underlying relationship between the economic realities of Scotland vis-à-vis the rest of the UK.[7] This means that at least in terms of the medium-of-exchange feature of a currency, whereby the currency simply acts as a value denominator index, Scotland is actually one of the UK regions for which a common currency system with the rest of the UK makes the most sense (Deutsche Bank 2013), whereas the case for other economically weaker regions is in reality much less clear.

On the other hand, a currency is not purely a dominator, as the Euro crisis has made abundantly clear. A currency is also partially an asset and a stock of wealth. Yet, there are two fundamental differences between a currency as an asset class and many other classes of assets. First, while the values of all assets may move up or down relative to each other, scarcity means that in the long run the value of precious metals will never collapse, nor will the values of paintings by Van Gogh or Caravaggio, nor will the most valuable central London prime real estate next to Hyde Park or Buckingham Palace. The supply of assets whose wealth holding properties is based on long-term scarcity cannot be significantly increased, and as such, the wealth stored by these types of assets remains safe in the long term relative to all other means of holding wealth. In contrast, the supply of a currency can easily be increased by a central bank simply by adjusting the money supply through any one of a variety of different mechanisms, and this reduces the wealth holding potential of a currency. In addition, even without increases in the money supply the wealth holding features of a currency also depend on both the expected and actual long-run performance of the economy underpinning the currency issue, whereas there is no analogous or equivalent question regarding the long-run 'performance' of a Van Gogh or a Caravaggio. Finally, and crucially, a common currency system requires a lender of last resort to underpin the currency and to ensure the successful pooling and sharing of risks and this is a key role of the central bank. As a wealth holding asset a currency requires that the monetary authorities issuing the currency build and maintain long-term credibility in the international financial markets. The role of lender of last resort and the associated credibility requirements imply that the government issuing the currency must have both the ultimate responsibility and also the ultimate power to enforce currency and budgetary discipline over lower levels of government. This is in order to ensure that the money supply is not unilaterally increased by lower level tiers of government without the consent of the highest levels of monetary authority (Ahmad and Brosio 2015). In other words, a common currency system also implies a partial or total pooling of sovereignty and a partial or total surrendering of government independence to higher authorities.

In the case of Scotland following on from the disastrous financial consequences of the Darien adventure (Paterson 1994; Schama 2001), the loss of monetary sovereignty involved in the 1707 Act of Union meant that the ultimate financial and monetary authority for Scotland as well as the rest of Britain of necessity shifted to London. In other words, whatever the actual political economy interests prevailing at the time both within and between Scotland and England (Paterson 1994; Colley 2014), at least in economic and financial terms what was formerly an independent country or nation-state now became a region of Britain. Yet, although Scotland surrendered financial and monetary independence and pooled its monetary base with that of the rest of Great Britain, Scotland never fully surrendered nor pooled all of its governance sovereignty (Colley 2014; Paterson 1994).[8] It managed to maintain many of its previous national institutional features, particularly relating to legal, religious and educational matters, as distinct regional institutional arrangements within the new united and integrated British polity (Paterson 1994). The following two centuries saw Scotland experience a flowering of economic (Paterson 1994) and cultural development as Scotland became increasingly integrated into the wider British global markets and its emerging Empire system (Schama 2001). Yet, in this case the precise relationship between integration and economic development still remains open to some debate.[9] However, this raises the more wide-ranging and important point which we will discuss in more detail shortly, namely the relationship between economic integration, economic geography and economic growth.

The issues surrounding the relationships between Scotland and the rest of the UK reflect a much wider and much more complex set of arguments relating to fiscal federalism and multi-level finance, and there are many asymmetries between governance integration and monetary union. For example, monetary integration does not necessarily imply the total surrendering or pooling of governance sovereignty, as reflected in the differing institutional arrangements governing the Eurozone, the relationship between the UK and the Channel Island or the Isle of Man, or the cases of the relationships between states such as Puerto Rico or Ecuador and the

USA.[10] In contrast, the total pooling of governance sovereignty does imply monetary integration. Meanwhile, the break-up of countries, nation-states, or empires, into smaller sub-components, until now has always involved monetary separation because the logic of separation is for part of a country to claim or re-claim its sovereignty and, as such, to eschew permitting the ultimate governance authority over its financial and monetary affairs to be ceded to another country. Indeed, while the official position of the Scottish Government in the 2014 independence referendum was to share 'ownership' of Sterling (Scottish Government 2013), the stated position of the Bank of England[11] was that a UK break-up involving a reclaiming of ultimate self-governance sovereignty on the part of Scotland would also imply a break-up of the Sterling common currency system, with Scotland needing to issue a separate country or join the Euro.[12] There are very complicated monetary and fiscal issues here which also have implications for the probity of many aspects of the wider UK city-regional devolution agenda, and reflect the fact that fiscal federalism (Oates 2011) and the relationships between multi-level governance and finance even within a single country (Ahmad and Brosio 2015) is a far more complex arena than political debates tend to reflect. Moreover, when fiscal federalism also involves the creation of independent states the relationships become even more complex (Armstrong and Ebell 2014a, 2014b, 2014c, 2014d, 2014e). In the era of floating currencies[13] there is simply no precedent for the break-up of a country to still involve the sharing of a currency between the former parts of the same country because the different multi-level governance roles appear to change and conflict[14] with one another as the polity moves from a unified state to two independent states. For our purposes, however, regarding the UK regional economic problems we can put these monetary-authority and currency-related issues to one side for the remaining chapters of this book, as they will only again become relevant if Scotland again seeks independence.[15] They do, however, have implications for the emerging and differing multi-level governance arrangements evolving in the three devolved administrations and also the English city-regions. In particular, different regional–national devolution agreements and different 'city deals' across England will imply differing financial and governance relationships between HM Treasury and different parts of the UK, with no Westminster parliamentary representation formally reflecting these differences, as would be the case in a truly federal state. Finance, governance and the functioning of regional economies are always closely interrelated issues, but in a highly centralised state these issues appear to disappear, whereas in a decentralised and devolved state they surface. What is therefore important to emerge from these discussions about Scotland is that in an interregional economic system matters of governance and monetary policy are always closely interrelated, partly because of the issues regarding the ultimate monetary authority, and also partly because of the question of the value of the medium of exchange. In addition, as we have also seen from Chapter 5, both national and regional fiscal issues are also inter-twined with governance and monetary matters.

If we return just to the question of the medium-of-exchange role of a currency, as we have seen the sharing of a currency as a value denominator index between Scotland and the rest of the UK makes some sense given the fact that Scotland is close to average UK values on many economic and fiscal dimensions. In contrast, many of the other English regions along with the other two devolved regions of Wales and Northern Ireland are nowhere near being close to the UK averages on a whole host of economic criteria. As already mentioned in Chapter 1, the UK is now less of an optimal currency area than is the case either in the whole of the EU or the Eurozone (Deutsche Bank 2013) and, as such, the Sterling area zone fails the first optimal currency criterion (Mundell 1961) regarding the degree of integration and level of convergence between its various regional components. Moreover, the Sterling zone also fails the second optimal currency area criterion (Mundell 1973) regarding the extent to which integration has driven convergence (Dow and Montagnoli 2007). As we have already seen in Chapter 2, the UK experience over the last three decades is largely one of divergence.

As such, these observations raise doubts about whether a Sterling zone as it is currently constructed really is optimal for the UK.[16] The increasing UK interregional inequalities and increasingly decoupled north–south regional business cycles weaken the effectiveness of UK national policies both in economic terms (Dow and Montagnoli 2007) and also in terms of governance legitimacy. In particular, there are increasing doubts as to whether UK monetary policy as a whole is too heavily focused on the specific issues facing the economy of London and the South East. For example, a focus on restricting house price growth in London and the south may be beneficial for the UK economy and for certain sections of society in London whereas a less restrictive monetary policy and a lower value of Sterling may be relatively more beneficial for trade positions of the UK's weaker regions.[17] In particular, the extent to which London effectively trades interregionally and internationally on an undervalued currency while the weaker regions effectively trade interregionally and especially internationally on the basis of an overvalued currency becomes increasingly unclear.

Over recent years public perceptions appear to have shifted to greater concerns that London and South East economic issues are increasingly seen by central government as being synonymous with national issues, while much of the general public outside of these regions rarely perceive these issues as being synonymous. The point is that the shifting public perceptions across the UK and these perceptions appear to be increasingly unaligned. As with housing and land use issues, in terms of perceptions regarding national governance, the UK polity is increasingly characterised by insider–outsider features. While of course, no-one is publicly currently suggesting or speculating that the Sterling common currency system operating across the UK and its small neighbouring island states is going to be dissolved between all UK regions, the recent Scottish independence debates and the current UK interregional inequalities also do raise fundamental questions as to whether the UK in its current form with its common currency system is the most appropriate governance system for the 64 million or so people living within its borders (Dow and Montagnoli 2007). Any regional governance reforms and fundamental changes in the UK governance structures will need to be cognisant of these issues, in particular if these changes also involve some further devolution of fiscal and financial powers, as will definitely be the case with Scotland (Smith Commission 2014), and probably will be the case in Wales (Silk 2014; HM Government 2015) and Northern Ireland (IfG 2014), and also is likely to be the case with some of England's city-regions (ICLGF 2014, 2015).

6.3.2   *The Optimal Size of the Nation Problem*

The second theoretical problem which is essential for understanding the long-run governance challenges facing the UK's interregional economic system is known as the 'optimal size of a country' problem, and this problem is associated originally with the work of Alesina and Spolaore (2005). This problem is based on the argument that a nation's optimal size is the result of a trade-off between the costs of provision of national public goods and the heterogeneity of preferences of local electorates. The provision of national public goods includes health services, defence services, diplomatic representation, infrastructure provision, and the provision of monetary and legal authorities, and these costs per capita all fall significantly as a country increases in size. On the other hand, a larger country with a single electorate tends to dilute the preferences and needs of specific communities into a single national aggregate governance offering which reflects a broad compromise across many different groups, communities and sets of preferences. The larger is the country the less the specific needs and wishes of particular groups are responded to. If the state contains local communities with diverse and differing preferences, values or value-systems, then this dilution into a national aggregate governance offering will fail to satisfy local wishes. Moreover, the greater is the regional diversity of preference and values the greater will be the extent to which the nation-state fails to provide for the needs and wishes of its citizens.[18]

The protagonists of this approach posit that the optimal balance between these costs and preferences nowadays tends to favour a smaller size for a country (Alesina and Spolaore 2005),[19] as reflected by the fact that the number of countries has surged and the average size of countries has fallen in the second half of the twentieth century as different peoples desired greater independence, autonomy and self-determination. Alesina and Spolaore (2005) also point out that many wealthy countries are small, which they interpret as evidence that in the current context small nation-states best allow governments to respond to local preferences and these considerations increasingly outweigh the cost advantages of large-scale public service provision.

Note that this argument provides a fundamental twist on the standard income inequality arguments which assume that interpersonal inequalities are far more important than interregional inequalities. In a country in which political representation is largely determined by geographical area constituencies, the existence of high interpersonal income inequalities allied with low interregional inequalities does not challenge the optimal size of the nation-state. The reason is that under these circumstances the heterogeneity of public preferences and public values is not reflected in the geography of political representation, as is currently the case in, for example, Australia or New Zealand. The same argument also obviously holds in the case of a country with low interpersonal and low interregional inequalities, as is the case in the Nordic economies and The Netherlands. However, if there are also large interregional as well as interpersonal inequalities within a country which are also clearly reflected in different public preferences, values and needs, then these will all be manifested in a segregated geography of political preferences. It is the segregated geography of political preferences which challenges the optimal size of the nation-state. Indeed, in a country such as the UK the increasing inequalities appear to be leading to greater interregional differences in preferences, values and needs and it is the interregional inequalities rather than the inter-personal inequalities which challenge the efficacy of the optimality of the UK nation-state as it is currently incorporated.

Regions which perceive that a lack of concern by the central state to their specific needs is also associated with their economic under-performance tend to view that there are economic grounds favouring independence and a smaller nation-state. The greater are the interregional inequalities the stronger will be these perceptions, some of which have in the past been evident in the independence narratives of Scotland, Wales and Quebec (Bothwell 2006). At the same time, independence narratives aimed at shrinking the size of the nation can also arise from richer regions just as from economically weaker regions. As we have already seen in Chapter 5, in cases where interregional inequalities are large, some regions will be major net fiscal contributors to the national revenues, much of which will be manifested in fiscal transfers to other regions. The greater are the interregional inequalities, the greater will be the fiscal transfers from net donor regions to net recipient regions, for any given overall share of national public expenditure as a percentage of national GDP. The greater are the interregional fiscal transfers the greater will be the pressure from the net donor regions either to reduce the overall national levels of public expenditure and taxation, and thereby to shrink the state. Alternatively, in some cases the scale of these interregional fiscal transfers leads to regionally based political pressures arising from relatively wealthy regions to reduce the overall size of the country, as is currently the case in some regional independence narratives in parts of Italy, Spain and Belgium, as well as in some UK independence narratives from the EU.[20] Interestingly, some of the Scottish North Sea Oil-related narratives also reflect aspects of this argument. In the Alesina and Spolaore (2005) framework the reason here is that the costs of the provision of national public goods and services by the central state, including the interregional fiscal transfers, are perceived as being too high by wealthier regions.

In the case of Scotland, the gradual 30-year drift of Scottish preferences towards greater self-governance and away from the advantages of pooled sovereignty with the rest of the UK has been argued primarily and originally to be a result of a fundamental and deep-seated shift away from the Conservative Party.[21] However, the 2015 general election suggests that this shift is now also away from Labour and the Liberal Democrats. As such, the post-2014 referendum shift towards even greater demands for much greater Scottish devolution or independence does indeed suggest that there are fundamental changes in views, values and preferences (Riddoch 2014, 2015; Macwhirter 2014). In terms of the Alesina and Spolaore (2005) approach these shifts would be interpreted as preferences or values, or value-systems as having shifted over time in favour of greater local self-determination on the grounds that the specifics of the local preferences are becoming increasingly divergent and heterogeneous from those of the aggregated and pooled preferences responded to by the central state governed from London.[22] The Alesina and Spolaore (2005) argument implies that from the perspective of Scottish citizens voting for outright independence, over time the preferred optimal size of the nation-state is shrinking, even allowing for the likely adjustment costs that may be involved in reconfiguring the size of the nation-state.

Yet, as well as the Scotland case, the optimal size of a nation argument applies equally to the optimal size of any polity at the sub-national level. As such, these analytical arguments help us to understand many of the economic aspects not only of the Scottish independence movement and Welsh devolution but also the recent UK city-region devolution trends in England. In economic terms, the calls for greater devolution to UK city-regions are based largely on very similar arguments to those advocating greater devolution or even independence in Scotland and Wales. One of the key features of economic geography over the last three decades is that regions are becoming more heterogeneous within countries (OECD 2009a) and internally many countries have diverged interregionally (OECD 2011b). In particular, the different economic trends in specific city-regions are becoming more important than those operating at the national level, and this is clearly the case in the UK, as the five previous chapters have demonstrated. These observations imply that sub-national polities such as city-regions may play an increasingly important role in providing for and responding to geographically differentiated heterogeneous preferences and values (Barber 2013; Denters *et al.* 2014). Indeed, in many aspects and on many different dimensions, these sub-national polities are actually more relevant than the nation-state (Barber 2013; Denters *et al.* 2014). In other words, the Alesina and Spolaore (2005) framework can also be applied to lower level polities at the level of sub-national spatial units such as regions and cities.

Yet, while the Alesina and Spolaore (2005) argument favouring smaller polities at first appears compelling from the perspective simply of the trade-offs between preferences and service provision, a major problem with the Alesina and Spolaore (2005) framework is that it fails to incorporate one fundamental issue in their schema which is highly relevant for our discussions, namely that of economic geography. One of the most important advantages of large countries or large polities is that economic scale provides for large domestic 'home market effects' (Krugman 1991, internal agglomeration advantages, network and spillover effects (Bell and Eisner 2015), as well as the locations for major multinational and headquarter investments (McCann and Acs 2011; Iammarino and McCann 2013). In other words, the advantages associated with modern globalisation are heavily oriented towards large markets and large polities. Moreover, the greater competition possibilities associated with the scale of a polity are just as much related to the internal competition for ideas and competition between networks of domestic elites as they are to the competition between firms, products and services. A weakness of small polities, small nations and small states is that they often reduce or limit the competition for ideas and for knowledge, or limit the operation of spillovers. In social capital terminology (Putnam 1996) small states or polities face the danger of developing a political economy culture which over-emphasises the role of bonding capital at the expense of bridging capital. The danger here is that commercial, political and cultural interests become increasingly intertwined and associated with the membership of specific social networks which develop informal but very powerful monopoly positions. Such processes inhibit entrepreneurship, innovation and social experimentation and gradually limit both the internal and external connectivity of the polity to new ideas, new influences and even new technologies.

In the modern globalisation context home market effects, economic geographies of scale and global connectivity are critical for growth, and therefore the links between the size of a market and the size of a nation are central to the ability of states to succeed as independent economic entities. In the absence of large domestic home market effects (Krugman 1991) the only ways that a small nation or polity can achieve the agglomeration or network effects which are essential for realising economies of scale and for generating and marketing tradeables interregionally and internationally is via global connectivity. Such connectivity is mediated via a portfolio of key assets, of which home-based multinational firms along with hub airports are by far the two most important types of assets. Small countries such as The Netherlands, Denmark, Switzerland, Finland and Sweden are largely decentralised countries (OECD 2012a) characterised by large numbers of home-based multinational companies operating in a wide range of high-value-added and high-technology sectors (Van Den Bulcke *et al.* 2009) and based primarily in highly globalised cities (Derudder *et al.* 2012) boasting international hub airports within a wider integrated market arena.[23] These ensure the constant inflows of knowledge necessary in the global market. In contrast, as we saw in Chapter 4, New Zealand has very few such assets, and the lack of such assets means that in the modern context, even with excellent institutions, New Zealand enjoys few of the economic geography and connectivity advantages of The Netherlands or Denmark (McCann 2009; de Serres *et al.* 2014). Without such assets, a small country requires other sources of global advantage in order to prosper and these are typically related to either tourism, tax-haven status or a specific and long-standing natural resource advantage relating to extraction or marine industries. Many small countries do not have sufficient scale advantages in these types of sectors which are sufficient to counter the lack of a home market and a lack of connectivity.

As such, and rather contrary to the idea that the Alesina and Spolaore (2005) framework provides a widely generalisable hypothesis, is the observation that in reality the vast majority of the world's poorest people actually live in small countries which have become independent in the second half of the twentieth century (Collier 2006). These countries are unable to sustain home market, agglomeration or global connectivity effects and as a result have been largely left behind in modern globalisation (Collier 2006). Economic scale provides enormous advantages in terms of economic geography (Krugman and Venables 1995) and indeed, the overwhelming majority of developing countries which have experienced growth since the mid-1990s are large and contain large cities. As such, if the Alesina and Spolaore (2005) arguments favouring small polities have any veracity, in reality such arguments can only relate to a specific sub-set of possible cases where regions and countries in question are already deeply integrated and connected with each other and the wider world and where fragmentation from larger to smaller independent nations involves no significant additional adjustment costs or increasing trade barriers (McCann and Acs 2011). European regions which are already part of the UK may be possible candidates here. Not surprisingly, proponents of separatist movements in Europe typically assume and argue that these global integration conditions are already in place and that the ensuing adjustment costs of independence are therefore likely to be small. Indeed, Alesina and Spolaore (2005) also assume that these adjustment costs are likely to be relatively low in the case of those various European regions including Scotland which are seeking independence from larger national polities, and also possibly in the case of Canada. If we therefore extend the basic optimality framework of Alesina and Spolaore (2005) so as to incorporate the transactions and adjustment costs involved in reducing the size of the nation-state, the optimality results of the Alesina and Spolaore (2005) framework tell us that the greater are the transactions and adjustment costs, the larger will be the optimal size of the nation-state, for any given set of preferences and values and for any given set of economies of scale in national service provision. In contrast, if the transactions and adjustment costs associated with reconfiguring the size of the state are perceived to be small, then on balance the shifting preferences will favour a smaller nation-state. Proponents of independence tend to underplay the likely adjustment costs while opponents of independence are likely to stress the adjustment costs.

In the event of Scotland eventually becoming independent from the rest of the UK, some research has argued that the adjustments costs associated with the setting up of new national institutions in Scotland are likely to be relatively small (Dunleavy *et al.* 2014), given that many institutions already exist. However, setting up institutions is only one component of the potential adjustment and transactions costs associated with separation. Uncertainty, logjams in political bargaining, and the associated uncertainty effects on commerce are likely to be far more important, including potentially increased trade barriers with the rest of the UK.[24] Whether such adjustment costs are indeed likely to be small or large is obviously open to debate, but there are two recent precedents in OECD economies which provide some information on these matters, namely the 'Velvet Divorce'[25] of Czechoslovakia into the Czech Republic and Slovakia (Fidrmuc *et al.* 1999) and second also the experience of Canada.[26] Both of these cases suggest these uncertainty costs on business are significant and long-lasting. The experience of the Velvet Divorce was a small nation-state break-up[27] while the experience of Canada (Bothwell 2006) did not result in a country break-up. In both cases, however, the experience here suggests that the transactions and adjustment costs involved in a UK break-up are likely to be much more significant than simply setting up new institutions. Indeed, this precedent suggests that the transactions and adjustment costs associated with the separation of Scotland from the rest of the UK are likely to be very significant and long-lasting on all sides.

Many of the same types of independence and separation assumptions and arguments are typically also put forward in political narratives advocating UK independence from the European Union. In these narratives it is implicitly assumed that there will be few if any adverse impacts on the UK of such a separation and that the overall domestic and global trading position of the UK would largely benefit from this separation. Yet, as we have already seen in Chapter 4, modern globalisation is far more about multinationalism than it is about trade. From this vantage point, the available evidence presented in Chapter 4 suggests that even if the formal institutional adjustment and transactions costs involved in any disruption of the relationships between the UK and the EU in event of a separation are relatively small,[28] the absolute costs to the UK are still likely to be very large. However, the same argument is just as applicable to the case of a separation between the UK and the EU, given that as we have seen in Chapter 4, the demand impacts of the EU on the UK are relatively even greater than the demand effects of Scotland on the rest of the UK. Obviously, whether in reality these various assumptions and expectations regarding the transactions and adjustment costs in the event of separation or devolution, cannot be known in advance, but the limited evidence from Europe and Canada suggests that such costs will not always be as low as independence narratives tend to suggest.

Whatever are the actual adjustment costs involved in a UK break-up,[29] the insights provided by the Alesina and Spolaore (2005) framework, however, produce some critical insights which are also more widely applicable to many other parts of the UK. At the city-region-national scale, the wide range of different movements towards greater degrees of sub-national regional and city-region devolution and regional decentralisation also tend to assume that the associated governance transactions and adjustment costs are likely to be small. The advantages of governance centralisation are often understood by national governments in terms of more efficient provision of public goods at a national level, and advocates of a highly centralised UK state will point to the efficiency of the UK institutional set-up (OECD 2013b) as reflecting these advantages. However, the extent to which the UK interregional system now diverges from anything approaching an optimal currency area (Deutsche Bank 2013) suggests not only that these national efficiency arguments are becoming weaker but that the public is also increasingly aware of this. As a result, increasing preferences for greater devolution in Wales and Northern Ireland, as well as calls for greater devolution in the major city-regions such as Manchester, Birmingham and Leeds as well as in London, can all be understood in the context of the trade-offs between the greater need to respond to heterogeneous local preferences and also the perceived weakening in ability of the national state to provide equally effective and efficient public services across all regions. In particular, a further twist on these arguments arises from the fact that while the level of trust amongst Scottish voters in the Scottish Government in Edinburgh is higher than that of the Westminster government in London, Scottish and UK-wide preferences on a range of issues appear to be very similar (Bell and Eiser 2015). This suggests that in the case of Scotland at least, it is political accountability which appears to be an advantage of a smaller sized polity, rather than preference heterogeneity (Bell and Eiser 2015). Indeed, within England trust in local government is also higher than trust in central government.[30] In the framework of Alesina and Spolaore (2005) the desire for greater local trust and political accountability also represents a preference which reduces the optimal size of the polity.

However, the city-region cases also raise another twist on the standard Alesina and Spolaore (2005) arguments in that moving from the lowest spatial and governance level upward it raises the question of what is the effect of size on the democratic quality of municipal government (Lago-Peñas and Martinez-Vazquez 2013)? Similar to the Alesina and Spolaore (2005) approach Dahl and Tufte (1973) argue that on the one hand the smaller is the population size the greater will be the citizens' ability and effectiveness in controlling political decisions (Denters *et al.* 2014), while on the other hand small polities are less capable and display weaker problem-solving capacity for dealing with major community issues (Denters *et al.* 2014). Switzerland, Norway, Denmark and The Netherlands are examples of countries where governance reorganisations led to larger sub-national governance units via the amalgamation of very small local governance units into larger municipal and metropolitan-level governance tiers (Denters *et al.* 2014). The available evidence from municipalities in Switzerland, Norway, Denmark and The Netherlands found that increasing size is either negatively related or insignificant with respect to the level and quality of democratic participation and engagement, even after controlling for the educational levels and diversity of the local populations (Denters *et al.* 2014). However, each of these cases relates to small countries, similar in size to individual UK large statistical regions, except The Netherlands which is similar in size to London plus the South East. As such these countries each have strong governance at precisely the spatial and population scales which are largely absent in the UK case. Yet, even allowing for this, each of these countries is already much more decentralised than the UK (OECD 2013a, 2013b, 2013c) and also far more equal interregionally.

This observation links directly to another important set of insights, originally identified in the UK context by Cheshire *et al.* (1992). The two most influential policies spheres relating to UK economic and spatial development, namely local economic development and land use planning, are increasingly seen to be in conflict with the structure of UK government (Cheshire *et al.* 1992). The emerging consensus regarding the most sensible and practical approach to economic development which has gradually emerged over recent decades is a 'bottom up' approach to economic development focused on the use of supply-side instruments to work with, shape and enhance market forces (OECD 2009b). Yet in the UK, the highly centralised governance system means that on the one hand economic and development policy is largely driven from the centre while on the other hand land use planning has been largely devolved to local government. As such, the emerging worldwide consensus and emphasis on enhancing supply side instruments and the fostering of local and bottom-up approaches to economic development is largely incompatible with the current UK governance structures, except possibly in the cases of Scotland, Wales and more recently Northern Ireland, where regional[31] tiers of government operate.

The incompatibility between policy and governance arises because in the current UK governance set-up while the costs of physical development are contained at the local level the benefits of development are spread across a wider regional level (Cheshire *et al.* 1992). In other words, those who bear the costs do not fully enjoy the rewards. The automatic free-rider problem means that the incentives for encouraging development are misaligned between different spatial scales and the conflicting goals which inherently arise between different interest groups and stakeholders naturally will lead to different forms of insider–outsider behaviour, as outlined in the previous chapter. As a rule, the broad incentive structures encourage local stakeholders to systematically restrict development or to divert it to sub-optimal locations. In contrast, what is required at a broader regional and national scale is for local economic development policy and land use policy to be complementary in terms of goals and implementation, whereas the current UK governance structures ensure that this is not the case. It is therefore essential for there to be a tier of UK governance which better aligns the wider interests of both those who immediately bear the costs of economic development and the wider beneficiaries of economic development. Such a missing tier of UK governance is required in order to reconcile these conflicting incentives and interests. As such, Cheshire *et al.* (1992) argue that a regional tier of government across all of the regions of the UK, not just the already devolved administrations, would be required in order to provide an appropriate balance of functions between national, regional and local government (Cheshire *et al.* 1992).[32]

In line with the insights of Cheshire *et al.* (1992) it is fair to say that there are now widespread shifts across many parts of the UK for greater levels of regional and local autonomy and local decision-making relative to the national level, of which the Scottish case is simply the most notable and constitutionally the most important example (Bell 2015). At the same time there are also trends towards larger local governance units, of which the city-deals (O'Brien and Pike 2015) are the most notable examples.[33] In the Alesina and Spolaore (2005) framework, these various governance changes reflect changing public attitudes and preference shifts on the part of citizens for institutional and governance systems which are perceived to be better able to deliver services which are more closely tailored to local preferences. Moreover, in the Alesina and Spolaore (2005) framework, the demands for greater local autonomy which are now evident across many parts of the UK also imply that local preferences within the UK are becoming more geographically heterogeneous. The expected outcome of these shifts will therefore be either a partial break-up of the UK state or, alternatively, a reconfiguration towards a much more decentralised UK state, or indeed a combination of both of these outcomes, all of which will be further complicated by any UK exit from the EU.

Yet, irrespective of whether we consider devolution and independence at the regional–national scale, the national-international scale or at the city-region-national scale, what the economic geography issues highlight is the fact that in economic terms, the domestic and national effects of devolution and decentralisation processes can never be divorced from the effects of globalisation. In turn, much of the pressure for decentralisation, devolution and independence processes has in turn arisen in response to globalisation pressures. The critical link here is the notion of global connectivity, which we discussed in detail in Chapter 4, as high levels of national and international connectivity can often partially substitute for weaker agglomeration and home market effects. Devolution and independence can only succeed if global connectivity is also maximised, although often these considerations are ignored in UK devolution debates. Many UK domestic political narratives regarding devolution and independence tend to focus on the need for greater local autonomy at the national or regional level in order to better allow local policy-makers and domestic governance actors to bring about preferred changes in the local and regional context. However, as we have seen, many of these narratives either largely ignore the realities of globalisation or even claim to reverse some of the impacts of globalisation on the domestic context. As such, unless global connectivity issues are explicitly addressed, then exactly how the domestic devolution and independence narratives are expected to ameliorate UK interregional inequalities is still very much open to question.

6.3.3 The Place-Based Versus the Space-Blind Problem

The current debates, policy shifts and governance discussions in the UK regarding devolution and connectivity reflect fundamental and deep-seated policy debates which are taking place internationally. They are not UK specific. It is therefore important to put the UK experience into context in order to understand what is generally reflective of international experience and what is particular to the UK. The current international debates arose as a result of many years of analysis and reconsideration by analysts whose reflections were subsequently thrown into sharp relief by the 2008 global financial crisis. The debates broke onto the international arena by a series of high-level reports and publications which were published within a period of less than a year of each other, although they were motivated and organised by entirely different organisations and for different purposes. In 2009 the World Bank published the 2009 World Development Report (World Bank 2009b) which argued that given the realities of economic geography in order to best promote economic development policy should concentrate on promoting urban density, providing infrastructure to help overcome problems of distance and selectively applying spatially targeted interventions to overcome institutional and governance divisions. Fundamentally, however, the report argues that development policy should be 'space-blind', in that national economic policies should be "designed without explicit consideration to space" (World Bank 2009b: 24) and instead of having 'place-based' policies the national priority should be on 'people-based' policies which should focus, for example, on upgrading national education standards, or encouraging firm start-ups. This space-blind argument is based first on the supposition that policy-makers have no idea what the ideal spatial configuration should look like (Glaeser and Gottlieb 2008) and second that people and investments should be allowed to move freely according to market forces to where they are most productively employed. Following the original arguments of Winnick (1966), the World Bank argues that spatially targeted policies favouring weaker regions in the end simply result in limiting interregional migration and therefore limit the overall economic efficiency of the national economy (Gill 2010).

Very shortly after the publication of the World Bank (2009b) report a suite of four other independently produced reports (Barca 2009; OECD 2009a, 2009b; CAF 2010) followed by further reports (OECD 2011b, 2014a; World Bank 2010, 2011) all came to conclusions which were very similar to each other and entirely different to those posited by the World Bank (2009b).

These reports all argued for a 'place-based' approach to economic development in which policy has an explicitly geographical logic to it and the aim of policy is to overcome the under-development traps evident in specific regions. The key element of place-based policies is that many under-development traps are partly local as well as national in nature and policies aimed at local institutional transformation are required in order to allow regions to develop according to their potential. In particular, institutional reforms which either remove local monopolies or top-down central government restrictions on local initiatives and which allow coalitions of local actors and institutions to undertake development activities building on local knowledge, are key to the modern place-based approach. Overcoming the institutional bottlenecks and addressing these under-development traps is to be undertaken by the provision of locally tailored bundles of public goods (Rodrik 2007) leading to different policy 'recipes' in different places and this also requires well-working multi-level governance settings in which national government sets the overall agenda while local and regional government leads much of the local policy design and delivery. In a place-based approach such policy interventions could include, for example, education and training policies tailored to the needs of local businesses or policies designed to encourage local firm start-ups to connect with other large local enterprises.

The place-based argument is based on the assumption that national space-blind policy approaches are largely ineffective in such cases, and the reasons for this are threefold (Barca *et al.* 2012; McCann and Rodriguez-Pose 2011). First, countries are internally heterogeneous and indeed are becoming even more so (OECD 2009a), and the greater is the internal heterogeneity of a country, the less will a 'one-size-fits-all' policy logic be applicable or relevant to many of the parts of the country. Second, often what are ostensibly 'space-blind' policies in reality tend to be top-down centrally driven policies which favour the interests of the elites in the capital city or commercially dominant cities. Such policies in the long run may reduce national growth because they limit the overall portfolio of intra-national options for the inter-regional migration of people and firms (Dijkstra 2013). As such, many apparently *de jure* 'space-blind' policy settings are *de facto* inherently place-based. Third, social capital arguments imply that there is a lack of trust in top-down centrally organised policies on the part of local actors in many non-core regions who consequently typically refuse to engage with many national policies for precisely the first two reasons, and as such the widespread lack of local engagement means that there is a serious loss of national policy engagement and efficacy. Moreover, this would be particularly problematic in the case of any top-down spatially targeted interventions to overcome institutional blockages, as recommended by the World Bank (2009b). In contrast, the place-based approach advocates much more bottom-up and multi-level institutional arrangements to overcome such problems. Indeed, part of the modern place-based argument here, as with the space-blind argument (Glaeser and Gottlieb 2008), is the assumption that central government policy-makers have no idea what the ideal spatial arrangements look like. However, in contrast to the space-blind logic which advocates a top-down one-size-fits-all logic the place-based approach argues that building on local knowledge is essential and therefore argues in favour of differentiated spatially targeted approaches which in many cases, but not all cases, will include the targeting of weaker regions.

The important issues raised here by the 'space-blind' and 'place-based' nomenclature concern the nature, intentions and objectives of economic development policies and here there are four key points which need to be considered. First, the place-based argument argues that making the intentions of a policy clear is essential in order to understand both the application and the likely outcomes of the policy. So many aspects of many economic phenomena are explicitly geographical in nature, and simply ignoring these spatial aspects under the banner of a national policy which is apparently space-blind ignores the likely manifestations of the policy. This intentional ignorance underlying the space-blind logic precludes the proper evaluation of the policy at later stages, because the likely outcomes of the policy are not made explicit, and as such the intended outcomes of the policy against which any subsequent evaluation is to be undertaken are entirely unclear.

Second, the space-blind approach works on the basis that there is a well-understood dichotomy between what are 'people-based' and 'place-based' phenomena and that place-based policies are in conflict with people-based policies. This idea goes back to Winnick (1966) and has again resurfaced in recent years (Glaeser and Gottlieb 2008; World Bank 2009b; Gill 2010). However, Winnick (1966) was writing at a time when our knowledge of either technology or institutions and their complex interactions with other factors of production was almost zero in comparison to today, so apparently straightforward and simple dichotomies such as 'people-based versus place-based' appeared reasonably justifiable. Since then our understanding of how markets operate has been transformed and with this more modern understanding such simple dichotomies become much less tenable and defensible. In contrast, the modern place-based argument posits that 'people-based versus place-based' is an entirely outdated and fundamentally incorrect way of characterising most of the economy and instead a much more realistic way of describing many aspects of the economy and good economic policy settings are 'place-based in order to be people-based' (Garcilazo *et al.* 2010; Barca and McCann 2010). This does not imply that all policy-related activities necessarily have geographical elements to them. For example, it is hard to think of any explicitly geographical aspects to regulatory issues regarding internet-based advertising, such that in the Winnick (1966) terminology, there is no obvious place-based element to this. Similarly, horizontal framework policies aimed at cutting the bureaucratic and legal burdens facing firm start-ups, or policies aimed at fostering greater reliance on green energy have no obviously geographical dimensions to them. On the other hand, in the case of the reclamation of previously contaminated urban land, in the Winnick (1966) terminology there is here an entirely place-based phenomenon, as is also the construction of a new international airport. In between these extremes is a spectrum of numerous economic phenomena and mechanisms which simultaneously contain both place-based and people-based dimensions, including knowledge spillovers, worker commuting, supply-chain relationships, university-industry collaborations, energy production and consumption, industrial investment patterns, cultural and heritage issues, and institutional interaction and governance relationships. Moreover, many of these are specific to a geographical context at a sub-national level as well as at a cross-country level and cannot simply be moved from one place to another. This is the reality of economic geography. Manchester is not simply a small London and Cheltenham is not simply a small Birmingham, while Manchester and Birmingham are very different places even though they are almost identical in size. Indeed, it is the variations in each of these types of economic geography features and mechanisms which explains precisely why scale or density differences offer such little explanatory power when comparing Manchester with London, Cheltenham or Birmingham. It is also these variations which place-based policies are intended to address.

Third, the extent of migration and labour mobility is a key indicator of the likely importance of place-based and people-based aspects, to use the Winnick (1966) terminology. International labour mobility is probably the purest and strongest people-based manifestation or phenomenon, followed by long-distance interregional migration followed by short-distance intra-regional migration and last of all by non-migration. For non-migrants, who spend most of their working lives in the same locality, the various influences of local business, family, professional and cultural networks and ties are maximised and as such the relative weighting of the place-based dimensions of their lives are maximised. These place-based elements operate in addition to formal educational and skills and all contribute to human capital. In contrast, for international and long-distance migrants, who by definition break such local origin ties, these place-based influences are minimised[34] and for long periods such migrants have to rely purely on their skills and experience in order to succeed,[35] and therefore the relative weighting of place-based elements is minimised.[36] This logic also implies that place-based policy interventions are best-suited to situations where outward labour mobility is low, as most of the impacts of the policy will be felt locally, whereas if outward labour mobility is high spatially targeted interventions will be much more limited in their impact. Partridge *et al.* (2015) show that place-based policies are effective even in the USA which is one of the most geographically mobile societies, because not only is US interregional labour mobility low and falling but also because such policies tend to be targeted on the least mobile cohorts (Klein and Moretti 2013, 2014a). The same argument also holds for firm investments (Klein and Moretti 2014b). In the UK, where as we saw in the previous chapter at least 98 per cent of the population each year do not move between the UK's OECD-TL2/EU-NUTS1 large regions and 96 per cent do not move each year between the UK's OECD-TL3/EU-NUTS3 small regions, the US arguments suggest that the UK ought to be an obvious candidate for place-based policies.

For our purposes in this book, there are three additional levels of nuance which are important to add to the standard space-blind versus place-based debate, one of which is general and two of which are specific to the UK.

First, and in order to avoid any misunderstanding or misinterpretation, it is necessary at this point to explicitly state and reiterate what place-based arguments are *not* about. Place-based approaches do not advocate that all regions should exhibit equal productivity, wages and incomes, the so-called spatial equity principle. Indeed, geography itself implies that this cannot be the case. We know from economic geography, regional science and urban economics that spatial price (Glaeser 2008) and interregional equilibrium (McCann 2013) conditions require different productivity, wage, income and price levels to pertain in different regions. This is because the presence of spatial transactions costs – in other words the costs of doing business across and between places – means that for firms to successfully compete from different locations with similar levels of profitability, it is imperative that productivity, wage and land price variations exist. Although a range of countries such as The Netherlands, Australia, Sweden, Japan, Austria, Finland, New Zealand, Switzerland, Denmark, Norway, and many parts of Canada, do in reality exhibit very low levels of interregional inequality across these various indices, in a market-based economy a situation of complete interregional equality can never pertain as long as geography matters. Only communitarian-type beliefs would argue for spatial equality in wages and incomes (Barca 2011), and for the purposes of this book, this is not a realistic approach. On the other hand, however, our knowledge of what scale of interregional inequalities would be expected in order to foster growth and over what time period these would operate and whether divergence would eventually give way to convergence is still very limited and our understanding of how these issues are interrelated is still very unclear (Kanbur and Venables 2013). Indeed, what this book is examining is the issue of why the interregional inequalities in the UK are both so large and also so persistent. This is a real question and a very real issue which space-blind narratives are largely incapable of responding to.

Second, the issue of urban density enhancement raised by the World Bank (2009b) is rather ambiguous in the case of the UK. As we have seen in Chapters 2 and 3 the UK is already a relatively densely populated and highly urbanised society, which is also becoming more densely populated and urbanised due to immigration. At the same time, as we saw in Chapter 5, the question of whether UK cities should be more densely populated also touches on the questions regarding the use of greenfield or brownfield land for development, and as we have seen there are contrasting views on this matter. In general, therefore, the relevance of the space-blind density argument in the UK case is rather ambiguous.

Third, in spite of changing government narratives and in particular the recent increased interest in place-based ways of thinking in UK policy circles, it still remains the case that the UK is overwhelmingly space-blind in its governance and policy settings (Bailey and Hildreth 2013, 2014; Bailey *et al.* 2015), and it is important to put the relative weighting of these UK debates into perspective. The space-blind approach to policy-making eschews governance devolution as simply adding additional place-based layers of bureaucracy and red tape, and this in many ways still reflects the mainstream UK Treasury view. HM Treasury defends its ultimate control over all activities at the centre of the highly federalised civil service structure (IfG 2013) and allows only minimal autonomy and discretion on the part of other departments or levels of governance to make decisions (NESTA 2014, 2015). This primarily space-blind top-down logic is still the dominant central government governance orthodoxy within the Treasury and Whitehall in general. As such, the small number of analyses which argue that UK policies and expenditure should prioritise space-blind policy settings which focus on purported 'people-based' policies and not on any place-based interventions are therefore effectively arguing for the status quo and for no change of governance, institutions or policy. Indeed, this space-blind and purported 'people-based' reality is reflected by the fact that today's UK total government expenditure on education[37] currently dwarfs the various different streams of local and regional development policy expenditure[38] by a factor of 18:1.[39] If we compare education expenditure relative to just those expenditures which would be understood as reflecting regional policy type activities, then the ratio has increased from something of the order of 30:1 in the first decade following the millennium to around 45:1 today.[40] Similarly, as we have seen in previous chapters and will also see shortly, in the UK many ostensibly national and space-blind policy decisions and settings are in reality focused on enhancing the performance of London and its hinterland, exactly as the place-based argument posits, including major investments transport, education and those aimed at rescuing the banking system. As such, much of the 'people-based versus place-based' narratives in the UK are of little relevance because in reality the UK is already almost entirely space-blind and top-down in governance and policy-thinking, very highly centralised institutionally, and London-centric in terms of many aspects of policy prioritisation.

It is clear that the current place-based debates and ways of policy thinking in the UK are aiming to generate some shifts away from this centralised and top-down institutional structure, because of the increasing public awareness that while the UK is one of the most interregionally unbalanced countries in the industrialised world it has a governance and institutional system which is one of the least able to respond to these imbalances. However, the institutional issues central to the place-based approach imply that in many aspects and on many levels UK central government is really the worst actor or institution regarding deciding what to do to foster development in non-core regions. In a highly centralised state such as the UK these problems are exacerbated by the fact that civil service employment and promotion trajectories increasingly mean that few high-level civil servants remain in such a complex policy arena for long enough to develop any real specialist long-term knowledge (IfG 2013) beyond the capital and its hinterland. As such, the 'institutional memory' of central government departments tends to be very short-term as well as being sectorally rather than geographically focused. The modern place-based argument therefore advocates more locally based and bottom-up approaches to economic development, and as such would appear to be consistent with the current UK devolutionary governance trends. However, as we will see shortly, UK governance devolution is a result of a negotiation process and central government has such limited knowledge of local issues that it becomes unclear precisely what constructive role central government plays in these negotiations. Consequently, the place-based argument (Barca *et al.* 2012; McCann and Rodriguez-Pose 2011; Storper 2013) also contends that the long-standing disconnection between the UK's governance structures and the UK's spatial economic realities will itself necessarily militate against the development of local or regional economic development strategies which are appropriate for the context. Therefore the ability of UK governance systems to tailor policies to the local or regional context will be very limited unless the governance reforms are genuinely radical and sufficiently fundamental to enable much greater multi-level governance arrangements than currently exist.

What we see from the foregoing sections is therefore that in spite of much of the currently popular political rhetoric many of the UK domestic debates about cities, regions and governance are not particular to the UK but rather are set against the backdrop of these wider international debates regarding the relationships between governance, economic geography and economic development. Indeed, these wider international debates heavily shape the domestic UK debates, yet, what is particular to the UK simply relates to specific institutional and geographical features of the UK economy in which these debates are set, and the ways in which these specific features shape and frame the UK debates and policy choices. The UK is overwhelmingly space-blind, top-down and sectorally oriented in its governance and policy-making logic while its economy is overwhelmingly geographically imbalanced, and increasingly internally disconnected and decoupled. As we will see below, the current devolution trends are aimed at partially addressing one aspect of this disconnection, namely the governance aspect, while the connectivity agenda is aimed at partially correcting for the internal disconnections. The crucial importance of connectivity is highlighted both by space-blind and place-based ways of thinking, whereas the need for governance devolution and decentralisation to take place within a multi-level system of governance reflects primarily place-based lines of thinking.

Importantly for our purposes, however, taken together the insights afforded by the three analytical problems, namely the optimal currency area problem, the optimal size of the nation problem and the place-based versus space-blind problem, do help us to understand and make sense of many aspects of the rather hybrid consensus which is now emerging as to the type of policy approaches which necessarily need to be followed in the coming years in order to try to address the UK regional economic problems.

6.4   The emerging (partial) UK policy consensus

As yet, as we have seen there is no totally clear agreement or consensus concerning the underlying factors and influences driving the UK interregional inequalities, and nor therefore is there any comprehensive agreement as to the most effective, realistic and reasonable ways forward for addressing such inequalities. However, something of a broad-based consensus is slowly emerging as to what needs to be done and how this might be achieved. This emerging consensus reflects something of a hybrid and eclectic response, based both on insights from various economic geography, urban economics and regional studies research programmes (Lakatos 1970) along with shifting UK national and regional political considerations. The different research programmes differ variously in terms of their methodologies, their treatment of data and empirics, their emphases and priorities, and sometimes in terms of their policy recommendations. However, no one research programme has a monopoly of knowledge or expertise when it comes to understanding the UK regional economic problem because the problem is simply so complex and multi-dimensional. Moreover, the methodological and topical demarcation lines between these various research programmes are not always so strictly defined and although there are disagreements, many of their differing insights also overlap in different ways. This allows for such an eclectic approach to be developed and adopted when it comes to policy prescriptions.

From the rather broad and eclectic analytical base which has emerged, along with the shifting public and political debates, it is now possible to detect two rather different lines of thinking which are emerging as the two major components of the somewhat hybrid policy response to the UK regional economic problem. In particular, current UK political and policy debates regarding regions and cities are nowadays framed around two major themes, namely on the one hand governance decentralisation and devolution, and on the other hand connectivity and accessibility. These two key themes were first aired together approximately a decade ago (ODPM 2006a, 2006b, 2006c). Now, following the May 2015 UK general election, the ministerial appointment of Jim O'Neill, who had previously headed the RSA City Growth Commission, as Commercial Secretary to the Treasury with responsibility for advancing both city-region devolution and infrastructure development, underpins the fact that these two themes are seen as being heavily intertwined rather than being separate.[41]

6.4.1   *Governance Decentralisation and Devolution*

Governance decentralisation and devolution is one of the few policy areas with genuine cross-party support both prior to (Heseltine 2012; IPPR 2012;

LGALG 2014; RSA 2015), and subsequent to, the 2015 general election (Cox and Giovannini 2015). Even back in 2009 concerns were being raised from within parliament itself regarding the prevailing balance of power between central and local government and the over-centralisation of the UK state (HoC 2009; CLG 2009). The winds of change heralded during the last two or three years appear to point to genuine devolution and decentralisation changes being made within the UK governance system. However, what we do not know as yet is the exact nature of UK governance devolution and the resulting composition of the UK polity in the future, although some of the changes are already beginning to be put in place. The shifting public, cultural and political perceptions regarding the governance and constitutional challenges facing the UK today do genuinely appear to reflect something of a paradigm shift in terms of how we perceive and justify the nature of the state (Kuhn 1970a, 1970b). Perceptions regarding the nature of a broadly unified British identity (IPPR 2012; Wellings 2012; Riddoch 2014, 2015) and also the existence of a centralised constitutional and governance arrangement underpinning the unified British polity (Bogdanor 2015; Renwick 2014; HM Government 2015a, b; Silk 2012, 2014; ICLGF 2014, 2015; Smith Commission 2014) are changing rapidly and in ways which appear to be irreversible. In terms of the insights offered both by the optimal currency area problem (Mundell 1961, 1973), the optimal size of a nation or polity problem (Alesina and Spolaore 2005) and the place-based versus space-blind problem, while as yet there is no move to adjust the Sterling currency area, there are irreversible trends towards smaller and more devolved polities, even if the size of the UK nation-state for the moment is unchanging. Moreover, even if the size of the UK nation-state at some point in the future does shrink due to a Scottish secession, there is no reason to assume that this would also be associated with a re-centralisation of the state. Governance devolution and decentralisation trends nowadays are dominating OECD countries, and generally in states which are already far more devolved than the UK. Now that the governance devolution trend has commenced in the UK there is no reason to assume that it will be reversed in the foreseeable future.

In terms of Scotland and Wales the various Westminster parties and subsequent governments were independently developing clearly pro-devolution arguments[42] which while they are different in content and specifics, broadly followed a similar sets of themes. On the other hand, in terms of English cities and city-regions, the major momentum for devolution came primarily not from the political parties but from various independent reports and commissions involving numerous analysts and stakeholders, and these reports not only spanned the private sector, the public sector and civil society actors, but they also spanned the political spectrum. In many of these reports and commissions the thinking which has evolved in the UK has generally started at the city and metropolitan levels (LGA 2015; ResPublica 2014, 2015; MIER 2009; PWC and Demos 2012; HoC 2014a; ICLGF 2014, 2015) and is based primarily on arguments regarding urban scale and agglomeration, but increasingly this thinking has broadened to also consider issues related to connectivity and network effects between cities and regions (Heseltine 2012, IPPR 2012; CBI 2012; Adonis 2014; RSA 2015) and even in rural and non-metropolitan areas (NMC 2014, 2015; LGA 2015). This shift from a mono-centric to a polycentric frame of analysis clearly reflects the fact that in terms of economic geography, issues of decentralisation and devolution are often also intricately tied up with issues of connectivity. Indeed, the current narratives regarding the promotion of a 'northern powerhouse'[43] via improved infrastructure provision and local connectivity reflect many of the issues previously discussed in the 'northern way' initiative[44] (Northern Way 2009a, 2009b, 2011; SQW 2009, 2011). Indeed, notwithstanding genuine concerns over the feasibility of actually building the necessary infrastructure,[45] the profile being offered to the current 'northern powerhouse' agenda (HM Government and Transport for the North 2015) appears to be far more richer, purposeful and bolder than any of the previous initiatives (HM Treasury 2015a, 2015b).[46] Calls for rural areas to receive similar levels of devolution as city-regions (LGA 2015) have as yet been resisted by central government.[47] Importantly, however, for decentralisation and devolution to work it is essential that any governance reorganisation does not simply lead to fragmentation and an inability to coordinate, and therefore how the decentralised and devolved parts interact and connect is crucial, both in economic terms and in governance terms (Bell 2015).

The weight of UK-wide opinion on these matters in government and policy circles has been rapidly shifting, also spurred on by the momentum for further governance changes in the devolved administrations. As part of the major push for governance devolution English cities are being offered deals on self-government but only on condition that they have elected metro-mayors,[48] in order to maximise accountability, although as yet it is not clear exactly how far in terms of tax-raising powers the city devolution plans will go.[49] However, the current momentum for UK regional and city-region governance reform which has built up in the wake of the various reports listed above, along with the aftermath of the Scottish devolution and independence debates, do not simply signal a shift from space-blind to place-based approaches. The processes is much more nuanced than this. Indeed, it would be quite wrong to see the recent UK policy shifts as simply reflecting a move away from a traditional top-down model of regional economic development to a modern decentralised and place-based model, because the UK has undergone a rather tortuous and convoluted journey towards local and regional governance and policy reform.

The origins of UK regional policy go back in various guises to the 1920s and 1930s but it was really during the post-war era between the early 1960s and the late 1970s that regional policy in the UK (Wren 1996). The policy was developed as a classic example of the traditional top-down area-based industrial policy with a primarily sectoral logic as described in Table 7.1 in the following chapter, and in this policy framework subsidies were offered by central government either for firms to locate, maintain or expand investments in various specific types of areas within the non-core regions which were facing challenges of structural change (Crafts 2012; Wren 1996).[50] This was a period during which London along with the other UK regions outside of southern England, all underwent major processes of deindustrialisation (Dixon and Thirlwall 1975; Keeble 1976; Fothergill and Gudgin 1982; Goddard and Champion 1983; Harris 1989). However, subsequently public attitudes to industrial policy changed markedly and by the early 1980s the prevailing government policies were aimed at facilitating structural change in response to market forces. Public narratives argued that previous industrial policies were partly responsible for slowing the UK's adjustment to more modern economy (Minford and Stoney 1991) and therefore the new policy settings which were introduced in the early 1980s reflected the fact that central government had no intention of inhibiting or slowing down the processes of structural change by means of industrial or regional policies. As such, the traditional model of UK regional policy, which had tended to be dominated by the concerns of the manufacturing industry, was largely dismantled during the 1980s (Minford and Stoney 1991), a period in which rapidly diverging economic fortunes, particularly between the northern and southern regions of the UK first began to appear (Brown 1989). The only form of spatial intervention policy which prevailed was a small number of new 'enterprise zone' initiatives (Tallon 2010) and urban regeneration initiatives driven by Urban Development Corporations (Hausner 1987; Parkinson *et al.* 1988), the latter of which were largely in response to public disquiet (Smith 1983; ACCUPA 1985) and social unrest regarding the declining condition of some of the UK's inner city areas. Prior to the 1980s the distinction between UK regional and urban policy had always been blurred, but during the 1980s regional policy was largely dismantled and the remnants of the overall spatial intervention policies policy remained in these largely fragmented urban policy initiatives. The motivation for these urban policy initiatives was primarily related to social issues, or what might be termed today as 'social cohesion' issues, rather than issues of economic efficiency or productivity (Lever 1987; Lawless and Brown 1986). As such these policy interventions also in part reflected various new lines of thinking within regional (Holland 1976) and urban geography (Harvey 1973: Massey and Meegan 1978; Massey 1979, 1983; Cockburn 1977) which saw cities as regions of social tension and potential conflict associated with inequalities in wealth and access to resources and assets. However, while these local initiatives had some resonance in their specific localities, in the overall panorama of 1980s and early 1990s economic policy settings, as a whole these urban redevelopment schemes had rather little impact during the 1990s, except that is for the case of the London Docklands initiative, which was primarily aimed at expanding the capacity of the London financial markets (Clark 2014) rather than rehabilitation of particular local areas of derelict urban land.

At the same time, the widespread governance centralisation in the 1980s[51] along with increasing the deregulation, privatisation and out-sourcing of many of the UK state's previous arenas of activity along with the move in some spheres towards a more 'open' form of government during the 1980s and the early 1990s (Dynes and Walker 1995; Hutton 1995; King 2015) encouraged the development of powerful London-based networks of lobbying, consulting and policy advising. As the influences on governance functions and roles became much more diffuse, diverse, tacit, informal and distributed, these myriad governance and institutional changes almost certainly enhanced the role of London's elite social, professional and political networks in shaping the development of the whole UK state at precisely the time when London was also in the vanguard of modern globalisation. In terms of economic geography, the largely deregulated environment thereby favoured London in many different governance and institutional dimensions as well as in economic dimensions.

Adopting a slightly more interventionist stance in regional matters, in 1997 the new incoming Labour administration handed responsibilities for most of the regional development activities in the UK to the newly formed regional development agencies (RDAs), working in parallel with the newly formed Regional Government Offices. The formation of the English RDAs in part followed the earlier experience of the Scottish Development Agency (SDA) and its successor agency Scottish Enterprise along with that of the Welsh development Agency (WDA). These new RDAs provided many local knowledge-related and skills-enhancement services in terms of acting as intermediaries in facilitating development actions, fostering urban regeneration initiatives, championing inward investment activities, as well as undertaking the detailed reconnaissance work necessary for brokering local development deals relating to infrastructure. The distinction between urban policy and regional policy again became rather blurred as RDAs became increasingly involved in both broader regional and more locally specific urban types of initiatives and actions. Meanwhile the arena in which RDA actions operated was also expanded to include those associated with community-based and civil society actors as well as the more traditional private and public sector actors (Imrie and Raco 2003). In the early years following their establishment these RDAs were initially organised to a large extent on a top-down model responding to instructions from central government (Healey and Newby 2014), However, over time the RDAs developed something of a character of their own, building different local capabilities differentiated according to the local and regional specifics (Healey and Newby 2014). As such, these institutions represented something of a hybrid mixture of the older and traditional top-down regional policy model and the more modern and decentralised approach to regional development.

In 2010 the demise of the RDAs in England was announced (Ward and Hardy 2012) and they were to be replaced by Local Enterprise Partnerships (LEPs). The LEPs were seen as bottom-up and locally organised groupings of actors, primarily from the private sector, which would spearhead local economic development initiatives. However, their instigation was a top-down central government decision which proved to have had little or no real long-term consideration or preparation in advance.[52] As such, individual LEPs have had to find their own roles and rationale, and while progress is being made (APPG 2012) even today there are still real questions regarding their geographical logic (NMC 2014, 2015), the resources and capabilities of many LEPs (Pike *et al.* 2015), their governance and administrative capacity and even their legal basis (Ward and Hardy 2013; Healey and Newby 2014). It is fair to say that until now, only a small number of LEPs appear to have made significant progress in developing and implementing a coherent local develop-ment agenda, and the future of LEPs will now also be heavily influenced by the devolution architecture emerging within England.

During the transition years between the 1980s dismantling of traditional regional policy and the gradual emergence of a more hybrid institutional arrangements in the years spanning the millennium which tended to display an increasing urban focus (DETR 2000), there also arose within the UK new debates and narratives concerning the current state of play of UK regional, urban and spatial policy. In particular, these debates questioned the wide-spread absence of spatial policy in the UK (Breheny and Congdon 1989; Harrison and Hart 1993) while at the same time offering new ideas regarding a more modern role for regional (Tomaney and Mawson 2002; Adams *et al.* 2003; Tomaney 2009) and urban (Boddy and Parkinson 2004; Buck *et al.* 2005) policies which explicitly incorporated matters of social cohesion and governance in their narratives.

At the time that these debates surfaced, however, they carried relatively little weight in current policy circles. Instead, the analytical advice being pro-vided to government ministers over much of the last decade since Combes *et al.* (2005, 2006) has tended to be dominated by the types of thinking emphasising agglomeration and spatial sorting effects arising from insights in new economic geography (NEG) and urban economics (Martin 2015). These lines of thinking are broadly the same lines of thinking which had largely underpinned the space-blind and top-down governance arguments offered by the 2009 World Development Report. Following the 2010 UK general elec-tion these space-blind lines of thinking also heavily influenced the movement away in UK policy circles from a primarily 'regional' narrative to a 'local' growth agenda centred around an urban and city focus (HM Government 2010, 2011). However, as we have already seen, the place-based approach has always argued that the Achilles heel of the space-blind approach is that the default outcome is de facto a range of policy settings which automati-cally tend to favour the capital city and the interests of the capital city elites (Barca *et al.* 2012). Moreover, this is the case even though such policy set-tings tend to be couched in the 'national' interest, and this is also the case irrespective of whether or not favouring the dominant city was the explicit intention of the national policy settings. In this regard, an examination of the UK's overwhelming London-centric governance settings and the burgeoning interregional inequalities across almost all areas of private and public sector productivity activity would be a case in point of the place-based critique. Today, the enormous public sector and public-private investments currently under way in London in 'productive' public investments,[53] such as transport infrastructure, education assets and economic development initiatives, continue to send strong signals to market makers and investors that London will remain the national priority locational for major funding into the foreseeable future.

Having said this, it is also possible to detect a clear shift of UK policy narratives and policy emphases since 2012 when two major reports calling for a wide-ranging shift in thinking were published (Heseltine 2012; IPPR 2012). Tentative steps in this regard were already visible at an earlier stage (Mulgan and Bury 2006; MIER 2009; Hope and Leslie 2009) but these two 2012 reports marked a real sea-change in UK policy circles. Since then a raft of independent reports and commissions have also argued for a marked shift in approach toward much more of place-based rather than space-blind thinking (IPPR 2014a, 2014b; CBI 2012; RSA 2014, 2015; Adonis 2014; HoC 2014a; ICLGF 2014, 2015; PWC and Demos 2012; ResPublica 2014, 2015; NMC 2014, 2015; LGA 2015). Each of these reports picks up on many of the governance and cohesion issues raised in the debates taking place a decade earlier (Tomaney and Mawson 2002; Adams *et al.* 2003; Boddy and Parkinson 2004; Buck *et al.* 2005; Mulgan and Bury 2006). They argue that developing more locally integrated institutional arrangements aimed at fostering innovation and entrepreneurial activities by linking for example, universities to industry, or civil society organisations to both public and private sector actors, require much greater local decision-making autonomy and much greater resources than is possible with a highly centralised and top-down governance system.

Importantly, for our purposes, however, is the fact that these various reports have all argued that a decentralised, devolved and place-based approach to governance and policy-making across the UK is in the broader *national* interest, as well as in the interests of the UK's regions, cities and localities. Cumulatively, the influence of these various reports and the private sector, public sector and civil society constituencies that they represent has become overwhelming and greater decentralisation and devolution to English city-regions was a key element of the May 2015 Queen's Speech at the opening of the new session of Parliament following the 2015 UK general election, along with very much greater powers for the Scottish Government. On the other hand, there are also real concerns that the city-region devolution process is in reality actually a highly centralised and top-down process in which Whitehall fundamentally dictates the terms of the individual City Deal which are acceptable and, as such, the processes will lead to increasing interregional governance fragmentation and rivalry (Hambleton 2014; Diamond and Carr-West 2015; O'Brien and Pike 2015).[54] There are therefore calls to restructure the whole city-region devolution process (Diamond and Carr-West 2015).

6.4.2   *Connectivity and Economic Linkage Arguments*

The second major UK policy theme aimed at addressing regional economic imbalances is that of enhancing connectivity and accessibility, both at the local city-region level and also at the interregional level. As we have seen, concern has been growing in many government, media and public policy circles regarding the apparently increasing dislocation of London and the southern regions of England from much of the rest of the UK. Indeed, as we have already seen in Chapters 2 and 3, many of the economic benefits enjoyed by London's last three decades of growing prosperity associated with modern globalisation have failed to transfer and to materialise in other UK regions, except those which are within the immediate London hinterland. The emerging UK debates and policy narratives point to two major aspects of this problem which need to be addressed in order to avoid further growth in UK interregional inequalities and national decoupling and fragmentation, and these are the issues of interregional connectivity and intra-regional connectivity. Interregional and intra-regional spillovers and linkages require interactions of people, knowledge, goods, services and money, and as we have already seen in Chapter 4, the concept of connectivity has emerged as a broad umbrella concept referring to all of these types of interactions. Numerous observers have argued that one of the major problems is that the interregional UK infrastructure is not good enough for the twenty-first century. Indeed, there is now a widespread belief in government and policy circles that one of the major reasons why UK productivity is currently so low is that "our physical infrastructure is not nearly good enough, and previous governments ducked the difficult decisions".[55] In particular there appears to be a marked gap in the quality of our infrastructure in comparison to France and other EU nations such as The Netherlands, the Nordic countries, Germany and even Spain and Italy, not to mention economies such as Japan, Korea, Canada and the USA. Many UK reports and commissions (Eddington 2006; Volterra Arup 2011; CBI 2012; Luger *et al.* 2013) have argued that infrastructure is critical for growth, and especially for enhancing the growth performance of cities (Venables 2007; PWC and the Smith Institute 2014) and city-regions via greater connectivity. However, the evidence is not equivocal, and many of the difficulties associated with measuring agglomeration effects also relate to the difficulties associated with measuring the effects of transport investments (Graham and Van Dender 2009; Venables 2007). Evidence suggests that road infrastructure has the largest impacts amongst the major categories of infrastructure investments (Melo *et al.* 2013), although the results vary significantly according to the context and the sector. There is some research which finds only limited UK economic development impacts associated with road and port infrastructure investments (Gibbons *et al.* 2012; Ball and Nanda 2014), although it is also the case that after decades of under-investment in infrastructure relative to comparator countries (Aghion *et al.* 2013) the UK now has fewer kilometres of motorways per head of population or relative to GDP than any other European country, except for some former transition economies. Indeed, the UK has only 40 per cent of the motorway infrastructure relative to either national population or national GDP than the average for the EU-15 western European countries.[56] Even increasing the scale of UK motorways by some 2.5 times would only allow the UK to reach the average for competitor European countries.

In terms of transport infrastructure, there are many reports and publications documenting the overall strategy and government thinking as well as the new pipelines[57] of investments in UK road infrastructure (HoC 2010a, 2014b: DfT 2014a, 2014b, 2014c, 2014d, 2014e), in railway infrastructure (HoC 2010b, 2015a, 2015b), and in airport infrastructure (HoC 2013). There are various issues which arise from reading these documents.

First, in terms of interregional connectivity public policy debates nowadays argue that it is necessary to find ways to generate much stronger and widespread spillovers, interactions and linkages between London and the 'south' and the 'north'. For London and the South East to genuinely act as a motor driving the wider UK economy, these types of connectivity would need to be not just widespread but almost ubiquitous, and the scale and frequency of such interactions would need to be both intense and continuous. Yet, the emerging evidence surveyed in the previous chapters suggests that this has simply not happened. As such, the fact that spillovers between London and the southern regions of England and the rest of the UK, along with a whole series of human capital, demand and fiscal linkages, all appear to be so limited calls into question the existing levels of 'north–south' interregional connectivity within the UK economy.

Second, connectivity both within and between the non-core regions also appears to be limited, and much less than what would be required in order to allow many of the non-core urban and metropolitan regions to achieve scale economies in a wide range of economic dimensions. This raises a concept often termed in the literature as 'borrowed size' and refers to the idea that the size of an individual city may not be absolutely critical in driving productivity, as is already evident in the UK data, but that polycentric networks of inter-urban interactions may allow for scale and agglomeration effects to be realised. Possible examples here are the Randstad in The Netherlands or the Ruhr in Germany (HM Government and Transport for the North 2015) where dense flows of people between smaller and medium-sized cities are widespread. Parallels have been drawn with the north of England (One North 2014) where a patchwork of small and medium-sized cities[58] are argued to face relatively limited connectivity, given their overall scale (SDG 2014; IPPR 2014c, 2015).[59] On the other hand, there are critics of these arguments whose scepticism arises out of questions of causality, in that while transport infrastructure may underpin success it cannot drive it, as other skills-related issues are also critical.[60] Yet, the infrastructure issue is still valid in as much as would London be largely the same competitive city it is today without Heathrow, the London Underground and the Channel Tunnel (Vickerman 1985)? Almost certainly not,[61] which is largely behind the thinking advocating further transport investments such as Crossrail.[62] As such, the relationship between transport infrastructure investment and the distribution of skills and employment may not be straightforward.

A complication underlying all of these debates is the fact that for many decades UK infrastructure been overly London-centric in structure, and this is the case for roads, railways, airports, and more recently also sea-ports. In a centralised state the political economy of infrastructure investments tends to favour the capital city and its hinterland, over and above questions of efficiency and equity (Albalate *et al.* 2012). However, in the case of the UK this long-standing dominance is more systemic than is the case in many other countries. The overwhelming primacy of London in the nineteenth century, as already discussed in Chapter 5, meant that UK high-speed[63] infrastructure beginning with railways (Casson 2009), originally emerged largely as a London-centric 'hub and spoke' system, which itself was highly fragmented between the radial segments developed by the different railway companies, thereby inhibiting the widespread development of transverse east–west connections. The UK highway and motorway road system also evolved along very similar lines to the railway system with the major arterial road and rail networks often being constructed immediately adjacent to each other. This 'hub and spoke' type of system is clearly observable in both the UK road and rail systems and, for many UK interregional journeys, especially those relating to international travel and international trade, it is also necessary to traverse the London economy. Indeed, the increasing trade role played by the east and south-east coast ports in the south and east of England is likely to have exacerbated this particular structure (Overman and Winters 2005, 2011), as has the Channel Tunnel rail link (Vickerman 1985).

This increasing dependency of national connectivity on the London economy is none more so evident in the case of the UK airline system, whose global and intercontinental structure is totally dominated by the London airspace. In part this is a result of the long-standing quasi-monopoly positions of both BA British Airways and BAA British Airports Authority whereby central government intentions were that London Heathrow was to be explicitly and overwhelmingly privileged as the core hub function in the UK's intercontinental airline networks followed by London Gatwick. As we have already seen in Chapter 4, the siting and choice of such intercontinental hub functions heavily determine the siting and choice of high-level corporate headquarter, decision-making and research functions (Bel and Fageda 2008). In this regard the connectivity arguments imply that the UK's hub and spoke system is likely to have heavily contributed to the growing core-periphery interregional structure from the 1980s onwards. The many decades of UK national government decisions regarding the structure of UK airline infrastructure systems means that today local decisions regarding investments in Heathrow are in effect national decisions, and this ambiguity[64] as to whether UK infrastructure investments are national or regional in nature also relates to the 2012 London Olympics.[65] Indeed, public and media discussions regarding whether Heathrow should be granted a third or even a fourth runway or discussions regarding the siting of a possible new London airport are all couched as national issues.[66] In the UK national policy for decades has been to ensure that London airspace has the dominant role, but whether in the long run this has been wise is open to question, and similar questions and issues increasingly arise regarding other forms of transport infrastructure. Decades of numerous and rather ad hoc transport investment decisions in airline, maritime, road and rail infrastructure has left the UK economy with a national and international connectivity system which has an in-built bottleneck at its core, and increasing concern regarding the long-run effects of this are at the root of today's efforts to upgrade and diversify the spatial distribution and patterns of UK infrastructure investments.

The wider considerations of the national role played by both airline and rail connectivity have been increasingly in the spotlight in recent years with the debates surrounding the efficacy of the HS2 project and also London airspace and Heathrow runway expansion options. The case for HS2 developed incrementally from one of increasing the overall transport system capacity (NAO 2013) to a potential role in reducing the UK's interregional inequalities (DfT 2014f, 2014g, 2014h; HoL 2015) by boosting opportunities for other non-core city-regions (CENTRO 2010; DfT 2011, 2012, 2014g). However, while the official government position regarding developing a national high-speed rail infrastructure is broadly very positive (DfT 2014f, 2014g, 2014h), notwithstanding the environmental considerations other analyses have cast doubt on its efficacy either regarding increasing the transport system capacity or reducing regional inequalities (Castles and Parish 2011; Aizlewood and Wellings 2011; Starkie 2013; Wellings 2014; HoC 2015a; HoL 2015). Fundamentally, it has never been made entirely clear what problem is intended to be solved by HS2; either north–south regional imbalances; or the west coast line transport capacity constraints; or a combination of the two, and clarity on these questions is essential in order to understand whether alternative options might be possible.[67] Moreover, disagreements regarding the evidence of the likely impacts and costs and benefits of the scheme as much as anything else also reflect limitations in our cost-benefit evaluation methodologies. These are broadly suitable for addressing relatively small-scale incremental changes but which are of much more limited use when it comes to considering very large-scale system-wide transitions,[68] as was evident in earlier assessments and evaluations of the likely impacts of both Heathrow Terminal 5 and the Channel Tunnel (HoC 1985). As a whole, therefore, given the questions arising regarding the intended objectives of the scheme along with challenges facing evaluation and assessment methodologies employed and also the diversity of views and evidence provided, probably the best and admittedly rather weak assessment that can currently be made is that HS2 is likely to have some regional rebalancing effect.[69] However, the scale and timing of this is uncertain and following the conclusions of the Eddington (2006) report, the size of the HS2 investment calls into question the wisdom of the scheme relative to a group of smaller interrelated projects. As such, while there is significant support for HS2 in many quarters, the economic case for HS2 as a means of regional rebalancing is not by any means clear-cut and the analytical and empirical evidence is by no means equivocal in its favour. Yet, it is also important to understand that the decisions regarding these types of national infrastructure investments are, however, framed in a much broader political economy context.

As with high-speed rail, major airport infrastructure investment decisions are also inherently framed within a broader political economy context (Niemietz 2013), which in a centralised state tends to favour infrastructure provision in and around the capital city (Albalate *et al.* 2012). However, the case for UK airport-related investments is slightly different in that this is not a question of any 'tendency' towards a capital-city logic but rather an explicit political priority. Indeed, from the perspective of the wider UK the basic economic case for expansion of the London airport capacity is barely questioned, based as it is on the assumed benefits associated with London's role as a global city (Airports Commission 2013a, 2013b, 2014a, 2015a, 2015b; CLC 2014). Yet, whether such a role has indeed fostered economic growth across other parts of the UK is hardly discussed at all, and instead is simply assumed. Indeed, increasing the capacity of the London airports in order to enhance the hub connectivity of the UK is a stated government priority rather than a matter for discussion (Airports Commission 2013a, 2014a, 2015a, 2015b). As such, only local environmental concerns and discussions regarding a possible alternative Thames Estuary airport (Airports Commission 2014b) have been the major issues challenging the options for expanding the runway capacity primarily of Heathrow Airport, and secondarily of Gatwick (Airports Commission 2014a). However, apart from these largely local London-based concerns, the national economic case for expansion of the London, and primarily Heathrow airport capacity, is largely unchallenged, and its relationship to the UK regional imbalances is hardly discussed at all, although there are serious grounds for all of these discussions to take place.[70]

The fact that wider discussions of possible alternative future network structures for the UK airport system and its links with wider UK regional issues are as yet not discussed would appear to be rather surprising, given that UK interregional inequalities have been primarily driven by modern globalisation, in which airline connectivity plays a crucial role. It may well be the case that the history of earlier UK transport investments and policy decisions automatically generates a 'lock in' or hysteresis effect in the UK which naturally favours increasing the airline hub role of London. Indeed, the UK currently has greater levels of international connectivity than any other European country (Airports Commission 2013a). Yet, observations from other countries suggest that there is no de facto reason why mono-hub systems are inherently superior to multi-hub systems. For example, because of their geography, the location of the intercontinental hubs within the USA,

Australia and Canada all allow for polycentric systems of global connectivity and therefore for spatially diverse and distributed international accessibility patterns and trade networks. Yet, even countries of a similar size and geography to the UK have very different configurations. Germany, Japan, Italy, Spain and even New Zealand all have two major global airport hubs located in very different parts of the country. The global connectivity of the UK, in contrast, is overwhelmingly dominated by the London airspace, and in terms of airline connectivity the UK is similar to the case of France and the Paris airspace. However, France has much more geographically diverse trade patterns with its major trading partners given that it borders seven different countries and none of its borders intersect with the Paris region. The majority of France's cross-border trading engagements do not involve traversing or interacting with connectivity infrastructure of the Paris economy or its hinterland. In marked contrast, in the case of the UK almost all of the UK's international commercial engagements and trade patterns are dominated by flows of both goods and people via London and the South East. In contrast, the OECD (2012b) argues that the paramount need is not just for larger international hubs and gateways, but also for much stronger 'strategic' infrastructure which links global hubs and gateways to their inland connections and the wider nationwide interregional transport system. Again, these are areas in which the UK has been heavily under-resourced.

In terms of the links between economic geography, globalisation and governance in the UK, as has become increasingly clear throughout this book, the major problem is that during the last three decades no-one foresaw that the UK would become so interregionally disconnected, fragmented and decoupled. In previous decades transport decisions regarding London's airport infrastructure were implicitly assumed to boost the whole country via a range of transport and economic linkages and as such these London-specific investment decisions were explicitly seen as being national rather than local decisions. This was very clear in the 1990s and early 2000s discussions on UK airport capacity (HoC 1996; BAA 1998: DfT 2002, 2003)[71] and reflected in the evidence submitted to the Heathrow Terminal 5 inquiry (BAA 1995a, 1995b, 1995c; Vandermeer 2001), along with the early Channel Tunnel (HoC 1985) investment discussions.[72] It is also clear from reading the associated DfT (2002) documents relating to the role of airports in each of the other UK regions which were also published in July 2002, that while there was a slow shift away from a purely London-centric debate and towards a more UK-wide agenda, the narrative still makes clear that this is only a slight shift. In contrast, however, the wide-ranging evidence presented in this book suggests that economic spillovers and linkages between London and the rest of the UK have been very limited, except in London's southern hinterland regions. The result is that today policy-makers are struggling to find ways to counter the regional decoupling, and although there have been a few attempts at a broader UK-wide discussion of the economic role of airports (CAA 2009; Hackett 2014), these still remain largely the exception.

As such, from this particular interregional perspective, in some sense many of the HS2 and Heathrow infrastructure-related cost-benefit arguments regarding the accuracy or reasonableness of different forecasting or simulation exercises (Kay 2015) miss the central point. In terms of the issues discussed in this book, today's long-term major infrastructure decisions will heavily shape future private and public sector investment decisions, which themselves will heavily shape regional fortunes. As with all such cases, the societal significance of major infrastructure investment decisions therefore means that the criteria on which these decisions are made are also shaped by broader political economy considerations. Yet, in the UK the absence of any real national transport and spatial policy planning framework[73] along with the absence of a powerful regional tier of governance and implementation or a full interregional input-output-based computable general equilibrium model of the UK economy,[74] greatly limits our ability to think in detail about these broader long-term national and regional terms.

This lack of a broader picture is reflected by the fact that many UK transport infrastructure decisions have for decades been rather ad hoc in the sense that, although there is something labelled as a 'national infrastructure plan' (HM Treasury and Infrastructure UK 2010, 2011; HM Treasury 2014), unlike in other densely populated countries such as The Netherlands (OECD 2014b), Germany,[75] Japan or Korea (OECD 2010), in the UK there is no overall long-term national infrastructure plan which is closely integrated across all forms of transportation (HoC 2015b; HoL 2015) and also with a national spatial plan. In the Netherlands this integration is built in both at the national and the local provincial level, while in Germany this integration is built in primarily at the regional level.[76] In contrast, in the UK transport and infrastructure decisions tend to be made primarily on a project-by-project and on a sector-by-sector basis, as well as on a civil service departmental basis (Hibbs 2006), with relatively little overall consideration of the long-term UK-wide outcomes of these decisions on other transport, housing or economic development arenas.

The most notable evidence of this lack of coordination and integration is reflected by the lack of data or self-awareness even on the part of public governance authorities regarding the degree to which the UK's pipeline of transport investments was regionally unbalanced in favour of London and the South East (IPPR 2011, 2013; HoC 2012a, 2012b). While there are disagreements regarding how these various regional transport infrastructure investment calculations are arrived at, the point is that the scale of the interregional differences is very large indeed and also almost entirely opaque not only to the wider public and regional stakeholders but even more importantly, to the central government decision-makers themselves. In part this is because infrastructure funding is channelled via a myriad of different pathways involving also local governments and public corporations, and therefore the opacity due to complexity and diversity of these relationships is also a major part of the story.[77] However, even allowing for the calculation disagreements and the complexity of the funding channels, it is still clear that the interregional differences between London and the South East and the rest of the UK in terms of public transportation infrastructure investment along with public-private transport infrastructure investments, are both very significant and far greater than almost anyone was aware of (IPPR 2013).[78]

As well as a missing regional tier of governance (Cheshire et al. 1992), this lack of a 'big picture' perspective incorporating economic geography and the interregional workings of the UK economy is in large part due to the fact that the UK is rather unusual among advanced economies regarding the extent to which the private sector finances and provides infrastructure (Coelho *et al.* 2014). Currently, some two-thirds of UK infrastructure investments in the pipeline are privately financed, one-fifth is publicly financed, and the rest is a mix of public-private finance. Energy projects are almost entirely privately financed, while transport projects are more or less equally publicly and privately financed (Coelho *et al.* 2014). In the UK the priority to attract private finance for infrastructure development tends to mean that investments are handled on a project-by-project basis and this mitigates many of the incentives for developing a more strategic approach to the coordination of different types of infrastructure within an integrated approach to spatial planning. This lack of a bigger perspective is also in part a cultural issue. In the UK land use decision-making and policy is primarily understood by the wider public in the sense of 'town and country' planning whereas in most of the UK's competitor OECD countries land use decision-making and policy is understood in terms of 'spatial' or 'regional and urban' planning. Whereas the original UK planning profession had very strategic perspectives, today, as we saw in Chapter 5, UK planning has become dominated by greenbelt retention and countryside protection debates. The differing nomenclature between the UK and other OECD countries is important in that the former UK terminology emphasises the primacy of very local issues and interests in land use policy-making whereas the latter OECD-wide nomenclature emphasises the larger-scale and longer-term strategic dimensions of land use decision-making and policy. At the same time the UK also has a highly centralised top-down decision-making structure, so a combination of central and local concerns dominates regional issues. The mismatch between the overwhelmingly local nature of UK land use decision-making and the wider economic benefits of many larger-scale economic development investments has already been explained by Cheshire *et al.* (1992), and this overly local and myopic approach to land use decision-making and policy also inhibits the development of a more holistic picture of regional and national economic development issues.

More fundamentally, these discussions and disagreements also raise the question as to why the observed UK interregional public investment patterns should be as they are and what precisely are the intended objectives of these highly skewed transport investment patterns? In the case of major London-based infrastructure investments, as we have already seen they are often discussed as though they are national issues and their implementation is in the national interest, whereas the evidence in this book suggests that the lack of linkages and spillovers between London and much of the UK suggests that in reality they are primarily local rather than national issues both in nature and in impacts. Crossrail is probably the best example of this, in which £5 billion of public money is partnered with £10 billion of private finance. £5 billion is a very large amount of public money for what is essentially a local development project[79] so this raises the question as to why exactly these moneys are being invested, and there are three possible responses to this question.

One answer is that these local investments are good for the London economy and public-private financial terms are efficient and effective. There is little doubt that this argument is correct (Vickerman 2013). A second argument is that the expected benefit-cost ratios incorporating private finance heavily favour the implementation of these individual infrastructure projects and provide an excellent return for the Exchequer. However, this is a weak argument. The primary job of government is not to act as a venture capitalist or an angel investor maximising public-private investment returns, but to govern for the benefit of all of its citizens. Although a particular project may generate strong returns, there are always much broader normative, philosophical and political considerations (Stiglitz *et al.* 2009) which need to be incorporated in the policy decisions regarding project or policy implementation, over and above financial and economic issues.

A third, and a much more important argument, is that these local investments are good for the London economy and therefore also for the whole UK economy. This is the same line of argument underlying the Airports Commission remit regarding why the London airport capacity should be expanded. Yet, the arguments and evidence in this book all suggest that this second case is, to use a Scottish legal term, simply 'not proven' either in the Crossrail[80] or the Heathrow investments. Other alternative considerations regarding national rail investments and national airport capacity, routing, passenger duty and taxation (IPPR 2012) and funding options may also be viable. However, unless there is a clear statement regarding exactly what specific issues are being addressed by these particular public investments, what problems they are intended to solve, and also clear statements as to exactly how the purported wider UK linkage mechanisms and induced benefits are expected to work, then it becomes impossible to assess or evaluate the rationale, viability or performance of these investments.

As Vickerman (2013) points out, in any example of infrastructure mega-projects, of which HS2, Crossrail, the Channel Tunnel and the Heathrow expansion are all examples, understanding the behavioural impacts on people and firms of these non-marginal investments is critical for evaluating the effects of these investments, and while this is relatively straightforward in small and marginal projects this is notoriously difficult in mega-projects. Indeed, as with both Crossrail and Heathrow and even the 2012 London Olympics, these same types of fundamental questions regarding precisely what are the nationwide problems intended to be addressed or solved by the projects, the precise objectives of the investments, and therefore also the various alternative systems and cost options for achieving these goals, also link very closely to one of the fundamental critiques of the HS2 scheme, namely precisely what problem is HS2 intended to address?[81] As such, many of the underlying questions regarding HS2 are actually questions which are common to many of the UK's current major infrastructure investments including the debates regarding Heathrow, Crossrail and the 2012 London Olympics. In this much broader light, the relatively lukewarm evidence favouring HS2 as much as anything else reflects difficulties in analysing the underlying workings of the UK interregional economy, our lack of clarity regarding the relationships between spatial governance and spatial strategy, and in particular reveals our lack of understanding of the reasons for the differing regional responses to modern globalisation. Moreover, it also reflects a growing awareness of the very limited ability of central government to re-shape and re-fashion future regional and interregional responses to external shocks. In particular, standard policy prescriptions relating to improvements in education have little impact on these interregional issues. This is clear from the fact that UK interregional inequalities have burgeoned over the three decades during which numerous changes in education policies have led to markedly improved overall UK educational attainment levels, while at the same time differences in interregional attainment rates and migration rates have barely budged at all. Moreover, the situation has not been helped to the extent that regional and interregional narratives were largely sidelined in favour of local and urban narratives between 2010 and 2015, a shift which tended to preclude a more holistic approach to these issues for several years.

Many of these deeper questions regarding the intended objectives of major infrastructure investments can also be raised regarding aspects of the current national and city-regional devolution and decentralisation initiatives. The potentially major changes to society implied both by these public investment projects and also by these public governance changes all raise fundamental questions about what type of society we want to be. These issues cannot be addressed simply by recourse to inspecting a list of potential public investment projects and their associated expected benefit-cost ratios, or by describing a diverse range of different city-deals. Rather, these major public investment projects and these major governance changes raise much wider societal and political economy questions regarding the future workings of the state and the future economic and social orientation of the nation. As already explained in Stiglitz *et al.* (2009), these are fundamental issues about the relationship between the polity and society about which policy-makers have to make decisions on the basis of public mandate. However, they are not purely economic questions, although economic issues inevitably will heavily shape the decisions. There are nowadays increasing calls for a constitutional debate, reflection or convention (Renwick 2014; Bogdanor 2012, 2015; Hazell 2015), and already various commentators across the political spectrum[82] have argued that the UK should change from moving towards a quasi-federal state (Travers 2015) to being a formal federal state in which English regions would also be formally represented as well as the devolved administrations, as a means both of promoting democracy and also countering the dominance of London (Brown 2014; Macwhirter 2014; Henderson and Ho 2014; Henderson 2015).

6.5 Conclusions

As we have already seen in the previous five chapters, on many dimensions the UK is nowadays one of the world's most interregionally unbalanced and unequal economies and as a whole the UK economy is becoming increasingly decoupled. At the same time, as we have seen in this chapter, on many dimensions the UK is nowadays one of the world's most highly centralised states. Yet, in the last couple of years there have been various significant movements towards the decentralisation and devolution of different governance functions to different parts of the UK. The two major national policy agendas currently aimed at responding to and addressing the UK's interregional fragmentation, dislocation and decoupling relate on the one hand to issues of governance decentralisation and devolution and on the other hand to improvements in regional and interregional connectivity. However, there is no overall uniform pattern to these movements, dictated in part as they are by complex and diverse political considerations.

In terms of governance reforms, it is clear that differing forms of governance decentralisation and devolution are nowadays becoming very much part of the UK institutional fabric. Yet, the current situation is one in which central government appears to be addressing matters of governance devolution and decentralisation in a largely ad hoc and fragmented manner. Part of the difficulty here is that Whitehall is not structured in a way that permits a broader and more systematic approach to these matters (Hazell 2015; Hope and Leslie 2009) and the agenda therefore appears increasingly to be being driven by rapidly moving political economy considerations rather than by a considered and long-term perspective. Similarly, this largely fragmented approach to governance decentralisation and devolution is also reflected in a largely fragmented and sectoral approach to infrastructure decisions. As we have seen over many decades UK infrastructure decisions in different transport sectors aimed at improving national and interregional connectivity have been rather ad hoc. Moreover, they have been largely disconnected with each other and with any broader UK land use and spatial considerations. UK transport infrastructure has typically been dominated by a London-centric hub and spoke logic, but as long as the globalisation-related benefits associated with London are diffused throughout the country via spillovers and other growth transmission effects then the national-regional hub and spoke structure is unlikely to be questioned or challenged. Yet, the evidence throughout this book suggests that these spillovers and growth-transmission effects have been largely absent for more than three decades. The experience of London and its hinterland regions in modern globalisation is both quite different and also increasingly dislocated and decoupled from that of the rest of the UK. This underlying interregional situation therefore also calls into question the ongoing London-centric hub and spoke type of thinking regarding the provision of UK transport infrastructure. If after four decades such a system has failed to provide wider and widespread benefits then why is such a system being perpetuated by further such investments? This argument applies to the expansion of Heathrow, the first phase of HS2 and to Crossrail. One argument of course is that once upgraded then this improved hub and spoke system will indeed be better able to provider wider national benefits. However, for this argument to have any basis therefore needs a clear explanation as to why these diffusion effects have not happened in previous decades, especially given the fact that the previous prevailing beliefs were so strong that such effects would indeed materialise. In reality, when it comes to infrastructure provision, today's government thinking is largely unchanged from 1980s thinking, even though that thinking entirely pre-dated modern globalisation. The world has fundamentally changed in the last three decades and so has the UK, but thinking in UK government and policy circles has barely changed at all. Infrastructure policy-making is still largely sectoral, fragmented and ad hoc and Whitehall exhibits only a very limited ability to think spatially. This continues to be the case and as such this largely fragmented approach is also likely to limit the ability of today's infrastructure investment decisions to contribute to a lessening of the UK interregional imbalances and to foster greater internal connectivity within the UK economy, except for one possibility. This possibility concerns governance devolution. If the quasi-federal UK shift (Travers 2015) associated with governance devolution to city-regions as well as the devolved administrations also leads increasingly to a re-thinking of how national infrastructure provision is decided, planned, implemented and used, then the UK will slowly move to a less mono-centric infrastructure system and one which in reality is closer to that which prevails today in countries such as the USA, Germany, Canada and Australia. The structure of governance systems and the spatial provision of public goods including infrastructure are closely interrelated agendas, and changing the former may well have implications for the latter. However, it depends on whether what is currently being labelled as 'devolution' is indeed in reality genuine devolution or simply a form of decentralisation which delegates increasing task implementation to lower and more local government tiers while in reality continuing to be fundamentally a top-down centralised governance system. This remains to be seen.

Notes

1 Stephanie Flanders, "Should Britain Let Go of London", BBC News, 26 March 2013, www.bbc.com/news/business-21934564.
2 "A real 'devolution revolution'?", www.bbc.com/news/uk-33019841.

3 "Devolution in Britain: Time for a Civic Surge", *The Economist*, 6 June 2015.

4 "Whitehall v Town Hall", BBC News, 18 December 2014, www.bbc.com/news/uk-30520065.

5 Curiously, and very much in contrast to the evidence provided in this book, Leunig *et al.* (2007) assume that the UK is so spatially represented as to draw a direct parallel with the USA, and argue that the inherent 'pork barrel' type lobbying has meant that numerous ineffective urban policy interventions have been undertaken in the UK for many years. While the latter point may well be debated the former point is simply incorrect.

6 "Cities Unshackled from Whitehall's Dead Hand", *Financial Times*, 14 May 2015.

7 Some arguments suggest that Scotland's GDP per capita would be much higher under independence once oil revenues are included. See *Scotland's Economy: The Case for Independence*, Scottish Government, Edinburgh, May 2013; *Scotland's Economic Strategy March 2015*, Scottish Government, Edinburgh, and www.gov.scot/Topics/Economy/Publications/GDP-Per-Capita. However, the long-term effects on Scotland of independence on GDP per capita are more problematic due to declining oil revenues (Deutsche Bank 2014b; McLaren *et al.* 2013; Phillips 2013; Phillips and Tetlow 2013, 2014; Citi Research 2014; Oil and Gas UK 2015) and also because the large levels of overseas ownership in Scottish industry onshore and offshore industries are likely to significantly depress GNP per capita relative to GDP per capita (McLaren *et al.* 2013, 2014), although recent data are somewhat more optimistic (Scottish Government 2015).

8 The formal Act of Union between Wales and England was in 1536 under Henry VIII and between Ireland and the rest of Britain in 1800 (which was subsequently repealed by the Republic of Ireland), although in both of these cases England had dominated these areas for centuries following earlier conquests while this had never been the case for Scotland which had always largely retained its independence.

9 At the time of the 1707 Act of Union between Scotland and the rest of Britain, Scottish investors were fully compensated by the Bank of England for their previous Darien-related losses (Schama 2001). Restoring national financial solvency is likely to have contributed to putting Scotland's economy back on a more secure long-term footing. Yet, whatever the political economy at the time of the union between Scotland and England and Wales (McLean 2008) the lack of detailed data means that there is very little conclusive evidence regarding the long-run eighteenth century economic growth effects on Scotland of entering the union (Rössner 2011). While Scotland experienced a period of intellectual enlightenment these intellectual shifts were also related to external ideas and networks well beyond Scotland (Robertson 1997) and unpicking these different influences is difficult.

10 The use of the same currency is very different to the case of an independent national currency being pegged to another currency, something which is handled by the international currency market operations of the country's central bank.

11 https://www.gov.uk/government/speeches/the-economics-of-integration.

12 The latter point is also related to the question of whether and how an independent Scotland would enter the EU. Again, there is no precedent for these issues.

13 And even pre-dating this era. See: "Free Exchange: How Long Would Scotland Keep Sterling? The Political Appeal of Currency Union and Disunion", *The Economist*, 17 September 2014.

14 www.ft.com/intl/cms/s/2/ea520ece-02c1-11e4-a68d-00144feab7de.html#axzz3fgLZHxVu.

15 Something that is expected by various commentators and sources including Pat Kane and Andrew Marr. Kane predicts a referendum by 2020 while Marr predicts that the SNP will call for another independence referendum sometime after the

Holyrood elections in 2016 and that in the not too distant future Scotland and England may go their separate ways. See: Kane, P., 2015, "The SNP Has a Hard Road Ahead", *Prospect*, 8 May; *The Andrew Marr Show* broadcast on BBC1 at 09.00–10.00 on Sunday 12 April 2015. See also "Calling the Tune", *The Economist*, 11 April 2015.

16 In terms of one of the economic geography contributions to both the optimal currency area problem and also the optimal size of a nation problem, is the fact that the UK Sterling zone provides counter-cyclical fiscal flows which counteract local and regional demand contractions, as already discussed in the previous chapter. This fiscal base is underpinned by all regions and this is beneficial to weaker regions and nations within the UK. In particular it prevents severe local monetary and fiscal contractions in the more economically vulnerable areas, which might otherwise occur under conditions of very significant fiscal devolution, as the experience of Detroit demonstrates. An integrated UK monetary and fiscal system therefore allows for the pooling of risks across nations and regions. However, on the other hand it can be argued that UK monetary policy pays most attention to the economy of England, due to its much larger size, than it does to the other UK constituent nations (Armstrong and Ebell 2015), and this asymmetry may be exacerbated by EVEL (English Votes for English Laws) (Armstrong and Ebell 2015), and therefore this might be an argument for fiscal devolution. See "The Economics of Devolution: Athens-Upon-Clyde", *The Economist*, 25 July 2015. However, the insights of this book regarding the scale of interregional inequalities within England which match those across the UK as a whole suggest that this argument is incomplete. As the findings of Deutsche Bank (2013) and the comments of Eddie George make clear, national UK monetary policy pays most attention to London, which is by far the largest regional economy within England, and not England as a whole, and therefore many of the devolution-related issues pertaining to Scotland associated with monetary, fiscal and borrowing matters are just as pertinent for all of the other non-core UK regions as they are for Scotland (Armstrong and Ebell 2014a). See also: "Why Does Government Do Less for the North East than Scotland?", BBC News, 24 September 2014, www.bbc.com/news/business-29343927.

17 The core-periphery structure of the UK economy means that maintaining regional demand levels in London and the South East which limit house price growth in these same regions via high national interest rates and therefore a strong Pound Sterling also imply even weaker demand and higher unemployment in northern regions, a point implicitly or explicitly acknowledged in 1998 by the former Governor of the Bank of England, Eddie George. See: http://news.bbc.co.uk/2/hi/business/197995.stm; www.independent.co.uk/arts-entertainment/monitor-eddie-george-on-unemployment-1180133.html; www.theguardian.com/business/1999/sep/12/interestrates.observerbusiness.

18 This type of argument assumes that central government is benevolent and as such reflects a set of arguments that are known as 'first generation' theories of fiscal federalism (Bell and Eisner 2015).

19 "Free Exchange: Goldilocks Nationalism", *The Economist*, 27 September 2014.

20 These types of arguments have even recently emerged in public debates in London. See: *BBC London News*, broadcast at 18.30–19.00 on 16 April 2015.

21 Allan Little, 2014, *Panorama: Scotland's Decision*, BBC1, 20.30–21.00, 15 September 2014.

22 In terms of political economy, it might appear to be rather naïve to assess the rise of regional–national independence movements including Scotland simply on the basis of exogenous shifts in values or preferences. Public preferences are also heavily shaped by the narratives put forward by political actors, and in this context

King (2012) argues that independence movements arise because insiders within the political system understand the weaknesses within the institutional system which yield under pressure, thereby transforming the whole system. This analysis reflects what are known as 'second generation' theories of fiscal federalism (Bell and Eisner 2015) in which political insiders take advantage of information asymmetries and objective functions which are not necessarily aligned with the common good (Bell and Eisner 2015).

23 Both Stockholm and Copenhagen are the hub airports for SAS, Amsterdam Schiphol hosts KLM and is one of Europe's largest airports, while Helsinki has become a major hub for flights between Europe and China, Korea and Japan. Indeed, by early 2014 Finnair carried more passengers to China than British Airways. See: the BBC television programme *A Very British Airline* broadcast on BBC4 at 23.00 on 14 April 2015.

24 www.scotsman.com/news/scotland-s-future-power-to-control-the-future-1-2848321; www.centreonconstitutionalchange.ac.uk/blog/would-scotland-be-wealthier-under-independence; www.centreonconstitutionalchange.ac.uk/about/people/peter-mcgregor/blog.

25 At the time of the separation process of the Czech Republic and Slovakia in the early 1990s after 45 years of communist rule, these were two regions or embryonic nations or with effectively no capital markets, few or no property rights, almost no foreign asset holdings or outward foreign direct investments, and only tiny foreign exchange and gold reserves. Moreover, there were no global contracts denominated in their existing shared common currency. Following separation GDP contracted by 2 per cent in the Czech Republic and by 4 per cent in Slovakia (Fidrmuc *et al.* 1999) and even some two years after separation, the combined output of the two countries was still only 86 per cent of the size of the Greater London regional economy. In other words, separating these two economies was a rather smaller and less complicated task than attempting to separate the London boroughs south of the River Thames from London boroughs north of the River Thames, and likely to be 'small beer' (Neil 2014) in comparison to what a break-away of Scotland from the rest of the UK would involve. Nevertheless, the separation of these two tiny and largely non-internationalised economies into the Czech Republic and Slovakia still involved 31 separate treaties and some 12,000 separate legal agreements and even then it still took more than a decade to apportion out their gold reserves. See: "Scottish Independence: Lessons from the Czech/Slovak Split", BBC Scotland News, 20 January 2013, www.bbc.com/news/uk-scotland-scotland-politics-21110521; Andrew Neil, 2014, *Scotland Votes: What's at Stake for the Rest of the UK?*, BBC2 television programme broadcast on 12 September 2014 at 21.30–22.30.

26 Fears of a break-up of Canada led to massive outflows from Quebec to primarily Ontario of both population (see: www.pch.gc.ca/eng/1359053019560/135906 1092477) and businesses (Polèse and Shearmur 2004; Semple and Green 1983) due to the effects of the uncertainty (Grady 1991) associated with the independence movement. In particular large numbers of higher order corporate functions shifted out of Montreal to Toronto (Polèse and Shearmur 2004; Semple and Green 1983). In the 1970s the two cities were largely on par economically and in terms of size, whereas subsequently Toronto surged ahead (Polèse and Shearmur 2004). Toronto's population is now some 56 per cent larger than that of Montreal (http://stats.oecd.org/Index.aspx?Datasetcode=CITIES) and in terms of productivity Toronto is almost 15 per cent higher than Montreal. (http://stats.oecd.org/Index.aspx?Datasetcode=CITIES). However, it may well be that the Quebec independence movement simply exacerbated and speeded up long-term trends given the structural differences between the cities with Montreal being

more dependent on traditional manufacturing than Toronto which was based on newer manufacturing and service industries (Polèse and Shearmur 2004). However, the cultural and political relationships between Quebec and the rest of Canada are rather more complex than the Scotland–UK case because of the different linguistic and also national state-incorporation issues (Levine 1990). See also: "Separatism in Quebec: No We Shouldn't", *The Economist*, 23 May 2015. While on the one hand there are advocates of the distinctive social and business-related features associated with Quebec's greater levels of independence (Courchene 1996; Pasquero 1997), at the same time there are also concerns that the business networks have become more introverted and less transparent. See: https://www.ceic.gouv.qc.ca/.

27 The total combined GDP of the Czech and Slovak economies in 1995 was US$220,633 in 2000 constant PPP prices, comprising the Czech Republic GDP of US$162,614 and Slovakia's GDP of US$58,019 (OECD Regional Database). For comparison purposes in 2000 constant PPP prices the UK GDP in 1995 was US$1,430,966, the GDP of Scotland was US$122,284 and the GDP of Greater London was US$255,203.

28 In comparison to the current impacts of the EU Single Market on the UK which as we have seen in Chapter 4 are of the order of 10.5 per cent of UK GDP.

29 Which of course cannot be known with any degree of certainty in advance of a break-up, and probably is contingent on the political economy and the details of the actual separation negotiations.

30 "Decentralisation: Let Them Fly", *The Economist*, 8 November 2014.

31 At the level of the OECD-TL2/EU-NUTS1 large statistical regions.

32 Basically the same argument is again made more than two decades later by Paul Cheshire for the case of the wider London economy beyond the Greater London boundaries (and consistent with the OECD urban metropolitan definitions employed in Chapter 3) in *Inside Out London*, broadcast on BBC1 at 19.30–20.00 on 2 February 2015. See also *BBC London News* broadcast on BBC1 at 18.30–19.00 on 2 February 2015.

33 Currently there have been 28 'City Deals' agreed between the UK Government, the Scottish Government and city-regional groupings in England and Scotland since 2011 (O'Brien and Pike 2015). See also: Rachel Smith and Joe Sarling, 2012, "Here's the Deal: Overview of the 'Wave 1'City Deals", Centre for Cities, London, July.

34 Note that the logic of Gibbons *et al.* (2014) runs counter to this in that they term the wage-related effects associated with migration as evidence of 'place-based' effects while all other wage-related effects not associated with migration are listed as 'people-based' effects. Following the place-based logic the confusing logic arises from the fact that these place-based and people-based effects are inherently intertwined and cannot be so neatly separated as Gibbons *et al.* (2014) claim.

35 This does not include multinational corporate relocations of personnel whereby the corporation substitutes organisational networks and ties for place-based networks and ties.

36 Obviously if a migrant remains in the destination location for a long period then new local networks and ties will be developed.

37 Typically at some £90 billion per annum. See: http://researchbriefings.files.parliament.uk/documents/SN01078/SN01078.pdf.

38 Local government expenditure on economic development in England amounts to 1.8 per cent of total local government expenditure (DCLG 2014) and at the overall UK national level economic development expenditure amounts to 0.3 per cent of UK GDP or 0.75 per cent of total public expenditure. See: https://www.gov.uk/government/uploads/system/uploads/attachment_data/file/330717/PESA_2014_-_print.pdf. In term of national funding streams for

local and regional development, the *Regional Growth Fund* provides £3.2 billion of funds 2011–2017 which are aimed at raising private sector investment for economic development amounting annually on average to some £550 million per annum. To put this into perspective, this is less than 10 per cent of the proposed funding for HS2. Meanwhile, the *Growing Places Fund* provides some £730 million to LEPs and local authorities to support local infrastructure provision, in particular related to land assembly, site clearance and related issues in order to move projects forward and to unblock local bottlenecks. https://www. gov.uk/government/publications/growing-places-fund-prospectus; https://www. gov.uk/government/uploads/system/uploads/attachment_data/file/256818/ Growing_Places_Fund_-_Programme_Report.pdf; https://www.gov.uk/government/publications/the-growing-places-fund-investing-in-infrastructure-october-2014-update; https://www.gov.uk/understanding-the-regional-growth-fund. Today government expenditure on local and regional economic development and also enterprise is currently 0.3 per cent of GDP, approximately 7 per cent of its share in its mid-1970s heyday. See: https://www.gov.uk/government/uploads/ system/uploads/attachment_data/file/330717/PESA_2014_-_print.pdf.

39 Moreover, the wisdom of arguing for the status quo may be questioned given that after numerous educational reforms over recent decades plus enormous sums of moneys invested in education, there are still huge skills shortages, widespread graduate over-skilling and skills mismatches along with one of the OECD's highest shares of unskilled workers. See: "Hiding in Plain Sight: Britain's New Underclass", *The Economist*, 22 August 2015; "Employers Warn of 'Skills Emergency' ", BBC News, 13 July 2015, www.bbc. com/news/education-33478930. As such, our knowledge of 'what works' in education and skills provision appears to be very limited, and provides weak grounds on which to base economic development policy at the national level, let alone at the local and regional level. See also: www.cipd.co.uk/binaries/ over-qualification-and-skills-mismatch-graduate-labour-market.pdf.

40 During 2000–2010 all of the activities under the remit of the RDAs typically amounted to some £3.3 billion per annum in total including the 9 billion of EU Structural Funds allocated across the period 2007–2013 (HoC 2008), or some 0.2 per cent of regional GDP. Since the abolition of the RDAs current domestic expenditure on regional economic development 2010–2014/2015 has been cut by a half relative to the RDA era to under £1 billion per annum, but is likely to increase from 2015 onwards with the introduction of the Local Growth Fund (HoC 2014c). Including EU Structural Funds total expenditure on regional economic development is currently some two-thirds of the levels pertaining in 2000–2010, or approximately 0.14 per cent of total UK regional GDP.

41 "Jim O'Neill Takes Treasury Post for Infrastructure and Devolution", *Financial Times*, 14 May 2015.

42 *Scotland in the United Kingdom: An Enduring Settlement*, Cm 8990, Cabinet Office, London, January 2015; *Powers for a Purpose: Strengthening Accountability and Empowering People*, Final Report of the Scottish Labour Devolution Commission, March 2014; *Powers for a Purpose: Strengthening Devolution*, Interim Report of the Scottish Labour Devolution Commission, March 2013. See also Silk (2012, 2014). *The Economic Implications for the United Kingdom of Scottish Independence*, House of Lords, Select Committee on Economic Affairs, 2nd Report of Session 2012–13, London, 10 April. Commission on Scottish Devolution, *Serving Scotland Better: Scotland and the United Kingdom in the 21st Century*, Final Report, June 2009. Brown, G., and Alexander, D., 1999, *New Scotland, New Britain*, The Smith Institute, London. HM Treasury, 2010, *Funding the Scottish Parliament, National Assembly for Wales and the Northern Ireland Assembly: Statement of Funding Policy*, London, October.

43 www.bbc.com/news/uk-politics-32726171;www.bbc.com/news/magazine-32720462.
44 http://webarchive.nationalarchives.gov.uk/20100202100434/www.thenorthernway.
    co.uk.
45 "Network Rail Upgrade Delayed by Government", BBC News, 25 June 2015,
    www.bbc.com/news/business-33270586. "Did the Conservatives Make False
    Rail promises to the North", BBC News, 26 June 2015, www.bbc.com/news/
    uk-politics-33286270. "Labour 'Betrayal' Claims Over Rail Upgrades Rejected",
    BBC News, 26 June 2015, www.bbc.com/news/uk-politics-33283080.
46 The current paucity of northern lateral infrastructure connections means that
    commuting between Manchester and Leeds is some 40 per cent less than it ought
    to be given their size and proximity. See: "Railways in the North: Manchester
    United", *The Economist*, 16 March 2013.
47 www.bbc.com/news/uk-politics-32873204.
48 "Osborne Offers Big Cities a Deal on Self-Rule", *Financial Times*, 14 May 2015.
49 "City Self-Rule Plan Sparks Disagreement Over Mayors", *Financial Times*,
    14 May 2015;"How to Run a City: The Wrong Trousers", *The Economist*, 20
    July 2013.
50 Between 1965 and 1972 all forms of UK regional policy assistance never amounted
    to more than 10 per cent of overall UK industrial policy assistance (Wren 1996).
    The scale of regional policy was expanded in the early 1970s such that by its hey-
    day, regional policy in 1976 accounted for 21.7 per cent of overall UK industrial
    policy. If we combine the data reported by Wren (1996, p. 81 and p. 91) with
    nominal UK GDP data at current prices and also real GDP data at 1980s prices
    it becomes evident that the scale of regional policy assistance by the early 1970s
    amounted to no more than 0.23 per cent of UK GDP and even at its peak in the
    mid-1970s amounted to just 0.43 per cent of total UK GDP. At the same time,
    total UK industrial policy assistance (including regional policy) in the forms of
    grants, tax allowances and direct subsidies to sectors such as civil aircraft and
    shipbuilding amounted to 2 per cent of UK GDP, not including agriculture or
    defence. See: www.bankofengland.co.uk/publications/.../threecenturiesofdata.xls;
    www.ons.gov.uk/ons/rel/elmr/explaining-economic-statistics/long-term-profile-of-
    gdp-in-the-uk/sty-long-term-profile-of-gdp.html. Interestingly, UK regional pol-
    icy in its heyday was typically of very similar orders of magnitude relative to the
    UK economy as was the later EU Cohesion Policy relative to the EU economy
    with its 0.34 per cent share of EU GDP (McCann 2015). In the latter EU case
    public perceptions are that this scale is relatively tiny, while in the former UK
    case public perceptions tended to perceive this historically as being relatively large
    (Crafts 2012).
51 "Devolution in Britain: Time for a Civic Surge", *The Economist*, 6 June 2015.
52 The 2010 abolition of the RDAs and the introduction of the LEPs was described
    in 2010 by the then Minister for Business, Innovation and Skills, Vince Cable, as
    'Maoist and chaotic'. See: www.theguardian.com/politics/2010/nov/12/abolition-
    regional-development-agencies-maoist-cable; www.ft.com/intl/cms/s/0/61
    1e026c-ee92-11df-9db0-00144feab49a.html#axzz3cAx4KZ6f; www.bbc.com/news/
    uk-politics-11744644.
53 As against welfare payments and health and disability-related payments.
54 "A real 'devolution revolution'?", www.bbc.com/news/uk-33019841.
55 George Osborne addressing the CBI "Osborne Faces Up To Productivity
    Challenge", 20 May 2015, www.bbc.com/news/business-32820716.
56 "Poor Governance and the Economic Development of Lagging Regions", Paper
    presented by Andres Rodriguez-Pose at the Expert Seminar on Lagging Regions,
    Berlaymont, European Commission, Brussels, 22–23 June 2015.

57 "Road Investment Strategy: Investment Plan – Commitments", Department for Transport, gisu1415j078, www.gov.uk/government/uploads/system/uploads/attachment_data/file/381496/roads-investment-strategy-summary-of-schemes.pdf.

58 www.citymetric.com/skylines/economic-history-north-england-part-3-industrial-revolution-arrives-1209.

59 The core Ruhr region of Germany comprises the major cities of Duisburg, Essen, Bochum and Dortmund along with the intervening smaller cities of Oberhausen, Recklinghausen and Gelsenkirchen and has a population of over 7 million people. The Randstad region in The Netherlands spanning the cities of Amsterdam, Rotterdam, The Hague and Utrecht along with the many intervening smaller cities is very similar in area and population to the core Ruhr region (OECD 2006). Moreover, both the Randstad and the core Ruhr region are similar in both area and population to the area spanned by Liverpool, Manchester, Sheffield and Leeds-Bradford. The wider Ruhr-Rhine region of north-west Germany ranging from Mönchengladbach and Krefeld in the west to Hamm in the east and from Recklinghausen in the north to Wuppertal, Dusseldorf and Cologne in the south is similar in both area and population (OECD 2006) to the region previously defined as the 'Northern Way' region (Northern Way 2009a, 2009b).

60 Overman, H.G, 2015, "Transport for the North and the Northern Power House", *SERC Spatial Economics Research Centre*, Blog posted 25 March. The argument offered by Overman is that spatial sorting and human capital explains most of the performance of the Randstad and the Ruhr, and that transport connectivity issues are not a primary explanatory factor in their regional performance. This argument is reflected by the fact that the Randstad does indeed have higher levels of human capital than the rest of The Netherlands while the Ruhr has relatively lower levels than many parts of Germany. However, and somewhat different to this human capital-spatial sorting argument, is the observation that the interregional productivity and income differences within The Netherlands and between the Randstad and the rest of the country are tiny relative to the UK and almost every other OECD country, and as we also see from Tables A3.1 and A3.2 the productivity levels and growth performance 2000–2010 of the Ruhr cities of Duisburg, Essen, Bochum and Dortmund have heavily out-performed not only the non-core cities of the UK but even those in southern England and Scotland. These observations suggest that indeed the superior infrastructure and connectivity of these regions may account for much of the difference with the non-core UK regions. The Netherlands as a whole has a dense road and very dense and high-frequency rail systems which crisscross the country with numerous crossing and switching points, so the national system as a whole is neither primarily a mono-hub or hub and spoke system and neither is it overly Amsterdam-centric. Indeed, none of the three largest cities of Amsterdam, Rotterdam or The Hague are the main railway hub within the national system, but rather it is Utrecht, which is also now the richest city in The Netherlands. Similarly, Schiphol airport is located at a mid-point between the four largest cities of the Randstad and is not specifically an airport for Amsterdam. The Ruhr is similar in this regard and is also very well-connected with numerous other German city-regions in all directions and well as with The Netherlands, Belgium and France. If the other cities in the vicinity of the Ruhr, namely Dusseldorf and Cologne are also included in our observations, then the productivity differences between the wider Ruhr region and the non-core UK cities become even starker. See also: "The Industrial North: Never Walk Alone", *The Economist*, 19 April 2014.

61 Although even without these assets London would in all likelihood still be very large and dominant in UK terms.

62 www.crossrail.co.uk/benefits/wider-economic-benefits/; http://volterra.co.uk/wp-content/uploads/2013/02/Economic-Benefits-of-Crossrail.pdf.

63 As against the earlier canal-based slow speed infrastructure associated with the first century of the industrial revolution (Musson 1978).

64 Indeed, this ambiguity is further highlighted by the Scottish independence debates. See: www.bbc.com/news/uk-scotland-scotland-business-35087308.

65 In 2007 The Treasury decided that expenditure on the 2012 London Olympics was UK-wide rather than being just for England or London. Yet, much of the case for the London Olympics bid was based on the local 'legacy' impacts of east London urban regeneration as well as the fact that London was the ultimate global city rather than British city. While the actual national financial benefits of the 2012 Olympics are to say the least debatable, as are the purported 'legacy' effects, the Olympics demonstrates the national-regional ambiguity which is evident in many UK infrastructure programmes. See: "The Awkward Jigsaw of England's Boundaries ", BBC News, 7 November 2014, www.bbc.com/news/magazine-29934867; "The Great Olympic Stimulus", BBC News, 19 July 2013, www.bbc.com/news/business-23377059; "London 2012 Olympics 'Have Boosted UK Economy by £9.9bn' ", BBC News, 19 July 2013, www.bbc.com/news/uk-23370270; "Tourism and the Economy: Easy Come, Easy Go", *The Economist*, 28 September 2013; Clark, R., 2014, "The Bill That Keeps on Building", *The Spectator*, 22 November 2014; "Londonism and Its Adherents: The Capital's Creed", *The Economist*, 5 February 2011.

66 "London's Airport Problem. Heathrow: Our Solution", *The Economist*, 30 March 2013; "Flight Paths for a Cloudy Future", *The Economist*, 30 March 2013.

67 See the oral evidence provided by Professor Stephen Glaister on page 298 of the transcript of the *Oral and Written Evidence to the Select Committee on Economic Affairs: The Economic Case for HS2*.

68 See the oral evidence provided by Professor Roger Vickerman and Professor Peter Mackie on pages 662–676 of the transcript of the *Oral and Written Evidence to the Select Committee on Economic Affairs: The Economic Case for HS2*. See also: https://www.gov.uk/government/uploads/system/uploads/attachment_data/file/389960/understanding-and-valuing-the-impacts-of-transport-investment-progress-report-2014.pdf.

69 See the oral evidence provided by Professor Dan Graham and Professor Tony Venables on pages 311–322 of the transcript of the *Oral and Written Evidence to the Select Committee on Economic Affairs: The Economic Case for HS2*.

70 http://westmidlandseconomicforum.co.uk/images/uploads/WMEF_Birmingham_Airport_Stimulating_Revival_September_20122.pdf.

71 Reading the associated DfT (2002) documents relating to each of the other UK regions which were also published in July 2002 it is clear that there was a slow shift away from a London-centric debate and towards a more UK-wide agenda, but the narrative still makes clear that this is only a slight shift.

72 *The Channel Link: Proceeding of The Transport Committee, First Report of the Session 1985–86: Volumes I and II*, House of Commons, HMSO, London. See also: http://discovery.nationalarchives.gov.uk/details/r/C11262362.

73 There is a National Planning Policy Framework (DCLG 2012) and also a Government Office for Science long-term Foresight programme on UK land use futures but only London has anything like a spatial plan. See: https://www.gov.uk/government/uploads/system/uploads/attachment_data/file/288843/10-631-land-use-futures.pdf; www.london.gov.uk/sites/default/files/London%20Plan%20March%202015%20%28FALP%29.pdf.

74 In spite of the fact that with the work of Kim Swales (University of Strathclyde), Jeffrey Round (University of Warwick), Peter McGregor (University of Strathclyde), Geoffrey Hewings (University of Illinois), Peter Batey (University of

Liverpool), Moss Madden (University of Liverpool), John Dewhurst (University of Dundee), Max Munday (Cardiff University) and Peter Gripaios (University of Plymouth) the UK has for more than four decades had some of the world's most experienced interregional I-O table and CGE system modellers.

75 www.bbsr.bund.de/BBSR/EN/Publications/BMVBS/SpecialPublication/2007_2009/DL_ConceptsStrategies.pdf?__blob=publicationFile&v=2; www.ub.edu/medame/PRMertins.pdf.http://shop.arl-net.de/media/direct/pdf/ssd_7.pdf; www.bbsr.bund.de/BBSR/EN/Publications/CompletedSeries/Berichte/2000_2009/DL_Berichte7.pdf?__blob=publicationFile&v=3.

76 www.plurel.net/images/D221.pdf.

77 See the letter dated 11 July 2012 by Louise Ellman MP, Chair of the House of Commons Transport Committee to Justine Greening MP, Secretary of State for Transport, along with the March 2012 Commons Scrutiny Unit Report entitled *Differences in Public Sector Transport Spending Across England*, plus the reply to Louise Ellman MP by Transport Minister Patrick McLoughlin MP dated 20 September 2012.

78 See the March 2012 Commons Scrutiny Unit Report entitled *Differences in Public Sector Transport Spending Across England*.

79 In Part 1 of the Evan Davis BBC television programme *Mind the Gap: London vs the Rest* which was broadcast on Monday 3 March 2014 on BBC2 at 21.00–22.00.

80 http://74f85f59f39b887b696f-ab656259048fb93837ecc0ecbcf0c557.r23.cf3.rack-cdn.com/assets/library/document/c/original/crossrailbusinesscasefinal300710.pdf.

81 See the oral evidence provided by Professor Stephen Glaister on page 298 of the transcript of the *Oral and Written Evidence to the Select Committee on Economic Affairs: The Economic Case for HS2*.

82 See James Forsyth, "A Voting System That's Past It", *The Spectator*, 9 May 2015; "The Great Theme of the Election is the Future of Great Britain", *New Statesman*, 7–14 May 2015.

References

ACCUPA, 1985, *Faith in the City: A Call for Action by Church and Nation*, Archbishop of Canterbury's Commission on Urban Priority Areas, Church House Publishing, London.

Adams, J., Robinson, P. and Vigor, A., 2003, *A New Regional Policy for the UK*, Institute for Public Policy Research, London.

Adonis, A., 2014, *Mending the Fractured Economy: Smarter State, Better Jobs*, Final Report of the Adonis Review, An Independent Review for the Labour Party Supported by the Policy Network, London, www.policy-network.net.

Aghion, P., Besley, T., Browne, J., Caselli, F., Lambert, R., Lomax, R., Pissarides, C., Stern, N. and Van Reenen, J., 2013, *Investing for Prosperity: Skills, Infrastructure and Innovation*, Report of the LSE Growth Commission in Partnership with the Institute for Government, Centre for Economic Performance, London.

Ahmad, E., and Brosio, G., 2015, (eds.), *Handbook of Multilevel Finance*, Edward Elgar, Cheltenham.

Airports Commission, 2013a, *Interim Report*, Woking, December.

Airports Commission, 2013b, *Interim Report. Appendix 1: Assessment of Short- and Medium-Term Options*, Woking, December.

Airports Commission, 2014a, *Consultation Document: Gatwick Airport Second Runway Heathrow Airport Extended Northern Runway Heathrow Airport North West Runway*, Woking, November.

Airports Commission, 2014b, *Inner Thames Estuary Airport: Summary and Decision Paper*, Woking, September.

Airports Commission, 2015a, *Airports Commission: Final Report*, Woking, July.

Airports Commission, 2015b, *Business Case and Sustainability Assessment – Heathrow Airport Northwest Runway*, Woking, September.

Aizlewood, K., and Wellings, R., 2011, *High Speed 2: The Next Government Project Disaster*, IEA Discussion Paper No. 36, Institute for Economic Affairs, London.

Albalate, D., Bel, G. and Fageda, X., 2012, "Beyond the Efficiency-Equity Dilemma: Centralization as a Determinant of Government Investment in Infrastructure", *Papers in Regional Science*, 91.3, 599–615.

Alesina, A., and Spolaore, E., 2005, *The Size of Nations*, MIT Press, Cambridge, MA.

APPG, 2012, *Where Next for LEPs? Report of an Inquiry into the Effectiveness to Date of Local Enterprise Partnerships*, All Party Parliamentary Group on Local Growth, Local Enterprise Partnerships and Enterprise Zones, House of Commons, London.

Armstrong, A., and Ebell, M., 2014a, *Real Devolution: The Power to Borrow*, NIESR Discussion Paper No. 437, National Institute of Economic and Social Research, London.

Armstrong, A., and Ebell, M., 2014b, "Commentary: Monetary Unions and Fiscal Constraints", *National Institute Economic Review*, 228, F4–F11.

Armstrong, A., and Ebell, M., 2014c, *Scotland's Lender of Last Resort Options*, NIESR Discussion Paper No. 434, National Institute of Economic and Social Research, London.

Armstrong, A., and Ebell, M., 2014d, *Devolution in the UK: Submission to the Smith Commission by NIESR*, National Institute of Economic and Social Research, London, 31 October.

Armstrong, A., and Ebell, M., 2014e, *Assets and Liabilities and Scottish Independence*, NIESR Discussion Paper No. 426, National Institute of Economic and Social Research, London.

Armstrong, A., and Ebell, M., 2015, "The Unintended Consequences of English Votes for English Laws", *National Institute Economic Review*, 233, R37–R44.

BAA, 1995a, *The Economic Significance of Heathrow Airport Airports Economic Impact*, BAA/1204, British Airports Authority and DTZ Pieda Consulting, Edinburgh, March.

BAA, 1995b, *Heathrow Terminal 5 Proof of Evidence: The Economic Significance of Heathrow Airport,* BAA/41, British Airports Authority and Pieda plc, Edinburgh, April.

BAA, 1995c, *Heathrow Terminal 5 Supplementary Proof of Evidence: The Economic Significance of Heathrow Airport,* BAA/43, British Airports Authority and Pieda plc, Edinburgh, June.

BAA, 1998, *UK Airports Economic Impact*, British Airports Authority and DTZ Pieda Consulting, Edinburgh.

Bailey, D., and Hildreth, P., 2013, "The Economics Behind the Move to 'Localism' in England", *Cambridge Journal of Regions, Economy and Society*, 6.2, 233–349.

Bailey, D., and Hildreth, P., 2014, "Place Based Economic Development Strategy in England: Filling the Missing Space", *Local Economy*, 29.4–5, 363–367.

Bailey, D., Hildreth, P. and de Propris, L., 2015, "Mind the Gap! What Might a Place Based Industrial and Regional Policy Look Like?", in Bailey, D., Cowling, K. and

Tomlinson, P., (eds.), *New Perspectives on Industrial Policy for a Modern Britain*, Oxford University Press, Oxford.

Ball, M., and Nanda, A., 2014, "Does Infrastructure Investment Stimulate Building Supply? The Case of the English Regions", *Regional Studies*, 48.3, 425–438.

Barber, B.R., 2013, *If Mayors Ruled the World: Dysfunctional Nations, Rising Cities*, Yale University Press, New Haven.

Barca, F., 2009, *An Agenda for A Reformed Cohesion Policy: A Place-Based Approach to Meeting European Union Challenges and Expectations*, Independent Report Prepared at the Request of the European Commissioner for Regional Policy, Danuta Hübner, European Commission, Brussels.

Barca, F., 2011, "Alternative Approaches to Development Policy: Intersections and Divergences", in *OECD Regional Outlook 2011: Building Resilient Regions for Stronger Economies,* Organisation for Economic Cooperation and Development, Paris.

Barca, F., and McCann, P., 2010, "The Place-Based Approach: A Response to Mr Gill", available at the website: www.voxeu.org/index.php?q=node/5644.

Barca, F., McCann, P. and Rodriguez-Pose, A., 2012, "The Case for Regional Development Intervention: Place-Based versus Place-Neutral Approaches", *Journal of Regional Science*, 52.1, 134–152.

Bel, G., and Fageda, X., 2008, "Getting there Fast: Globalization, Intercontinental Flights and Location of Headquarters", *Journal of Economic Geography*, 8, 471–495.

Bell, D., 2015, "The Aftermath of the Scottish Referendum: A New Fiscal Settlement for the UK?", in Bailey, D., and Budd, L., (eds.), *Devolution and the UK Economy*, Rowman and Littlefield, London.

Bell, D., and Eisner, D., 2015, "The Economic Case for Further Fiscal Decentralisation to Scotland: Theoretical and Empirical Perspectives", *National Institute Economic Review*, 233, R27–R36.

Boddy. M., and Parkinson, M., 2004, (eds.), *City Matters: Competitiveness, Cohesion and Urban Governance*, Policy Press, Bristol.

Bogdanor, V., 2012, "Mayors: Good for Britain – in the End", *Prospect*, 19 March.

Bogdanor, V., 2015, *The Crisis of the Constitution: The General Election and the Future of the United Kingdom*, The Constitution Society, London.

Bothwell, R., 2006, *The Penguin History of Canada*, Penguin Canada, Toronto.

Breheny, M., and Congdon, P., 1989, (eds.), *Growth and Change in a Core Region: The Case of South East England*, Pion, London.

Brown, G., 1989, *Where There is Greed: Margaret Thatcher and the Betrayal of Britain's Future*, Mainstream Publishing, Edinburgh.

Brown, G., 2014, *My Scotland, Our Britain: A Future Worth Sharing*, Simon & Schuster, London.

Buck, N., Gordon, I., Harding, A. and Turok, I., 2005, *Changing Cities: Rethinking Urban Competitiveness, Cohesion and Governance*, Palgrave, Basingstoke.

CAA, 2009, *International Relations: The Growth of Air Travel to Visit Friends or Relatives*, Civil Aviation Authority, London, March.

CAF, 2010, *Desarrollo Local: Hacia un Nuevo Protagonismo de las Ciudades y Regiones*, Corporación Andina de Fomento, Caracas.

Cash, D.W., Clark, W.C., Alcock, F., Dickson, N.M., Echley, N., Guston, D.H., Jäger, J. and Mitchell, R.B., 2003, "Knowledge Systems for Sustainable Development", *Proceedings of the National Academy of Sciences*, 100.14, 8086–8091.

Casson, M.C., 2009, *The World's First Railway System: Enterprise, Competition, and Regulation on the Network in Victorian Britain*, Oxford University Press, Oxford.

Castles, C., and Parish, D., 2011, *Review of the Economic Case for HS2: Economic Evaluation London-West Midlands*, RAC Foundation, London, November.

CBI, 2012, *The UK's Growth Landscape: Harnessing Private-Sector Potential Across the Country*, Confederation of British Industry, London.

CENTRO, 2010, *High Speed Rail and Supporting Investments in the West Midlands: Consequences for Employment and Economic Growth*, KPMG LLP, London, 24 June.

CfC, 2014, *Cities Outlook 2014*, Centre for Cities, London.

Cheshire, P.C., D'Arcy, E. and Guissani, B., 1992, "Purpose Built for Failure – Local, Regional and National Government in Britain", *Environment and Planning A*, 10.3, 355–369.

Citi Research, 2014, *UK-Scottish Independence: Will it Happen? What Would be the Implications?*, London, 7 March, www.citi.com.

Clark, G., 2015, *The Making of a World City: London 1991 to 2021*, Wiley Blackwell, Oxford.

CLC, 2014, *The Economic Impact of Short Term Airport Capacity Options*, City of London Corporation, London.

CLG, 2009, *Government Response to the Communities and Local Government Select Committee Report into the Balance of Power: Central and Local Government*, Cm 7712, Presented to Parliament by the Secretary of State for Communities and Local Government by Command of Her Majesty, London, September.

Cockburn, C., 1977, *The Local State: Management of Cities and People*, Pluto Press, London.

Coelho, P., Ratnoo, V. and Dellapiane, S., 2014, *The Political Economy of Infrastructure in the UK*, ESRC Institute for Government.

Colley, L., 2014, *Acts of Union and Disunion: What Has Held the UK Together – and What's Dividing It?*, Profile Books, London.

Collier, P., 2006, *The Bottom Billion: Why the Poorest Countries are Failing and What Can be Done About It*, Oxford University Press, Oxford.

Combes, P-P., Duranton, G. and Overman, H.G., 2005, "Agglomeration and the Adjustment of the Spatial Economy", *Papers in Regional Science*, 84.3, 311–349.

Combes, P-P., Duranton, G., Overman, H.G. and Venables, A.J., 2006, *Economic Linkages Across Space*, Office of the Deputy Prime Minister, London, January.

Courchene, T.J., 1996, "Corporate Governance as Ideology", *Canadian Business Law Journal*, 26, 202–210.

Cox, E., and Giovannini, A., 2015, "Northern Voices: How Far Can a Bottom-Up 'New Regionalism' Go Towards Answering the English Question?", *Juncture*, 22.1, 53–57.

Crafts, N., 2012, "Creating Competitive Advantage: Policy Lessons from History", in Greenaway, D., (ed.), *The UK in a Global World: How Can the UK Focus on Steps in Global Value Chains That Really Add Value?*, CEPR Centre for Economic Policy Research and BIS Department for Business Innovation and Skills, London.

Dahl, R.A., and Tufte, E.R., 1973, *Size and Local Democracy*, Stanford University Press, Palo Alto, CA.

DCLG, 2012, *National Planning Policy Framework*, Department of Communities and Local Government, London.

DCLG, 2014, *Local Government Financial Statistics England, No. 24*, Department for Communities and Local Government, London.

Denters, B., Goldsmith, M., Ladner, A., Mouritzen, P.E. and Rose, L.E., 2014, *Size and Local Democracy*, Edward Elgar, Cheltenham.

Derudder, B., Hoyler, M., Taylor, P.J. and Witlox, F., 2012, (eds.), *International Handbook of Globalization and World Cities*, Edward Elgar, Cheltenham.

de Serres, A., Yashiro, N. and Boulhol, H., 2014, "An International Perspective on the New Zealand Productivity Paradox", *New Zealand Productivity Commission Working Paper 2014/01*, Organisation for Economic Cooperation and Development, Paris.

DETR, 2000, *Our Towns and Cities: The Future. Delivering an Urban Renaissance*, Department of the Environment, Transport and the Regions, London.

Deutsche Bank, 2013, *London and the UK: In for a Penny, in for the Pound*, Deutsche Bank Markets Research Special Report, London, 27 November.

Deutsche Bank, 2014a, *UK Housing: London vs The Rest*, Deutsche Bank Research, London, 18 July.

Deutsche Bank, 2014b, *Scotland: Wrong Turn*, Deutsche Bank Research London, 12 September.

DfT, 2002, *The Future Development of Air Transport in the United Kingdom: South East. A National Consultation*, Department for Transport, London, July.

DfT, 2003, *Second Edition February 2003. The Future Development of Air Transport in the United Kingdom: South East. A National Consultation*, Department for Transport, London, February.

DfT, 2011, *Economic Case for HS2: The Y Network and London-West Midlands,* Department for Transport, London, February.

DfT, 2012, *Economic Case for HS2: Updated Appraisal of Transport User Benefits and Wider Economic Benefits,* Department for Transport, London, January.

DfT, 2014a, *Setting the Road Investment Strategy: Now and in The Future*, Department for Transport, London, June.

DfT, 2014b, *Road Investment Strategy: Overview,* Department for Transport, London, December.

DfT, 2014c, *Road Investment Strategy: Strategic Vision,* Department for Transport, London, December.

DfT, 2014d, *Road Investment Strategy: Investment Plan,* Department for Transport, London, December.

DfT, 2014e, *Road Investment Strategy: Performance Specification,* Department for Transport, London, December.

DfT, 2014f, *The Strategic Case for HS2,* Department for Transport, London, October.

DfT, 2014g, *HS2 Plus: A Report by David Higgins,* Department for Transport, London, October.

DfT, 2014h, *Rebalancing Britain: From HS2 Towards a National Transport Strategy,* Department for Transport, London, October.

Diamond, P., and Carr-West, J., 2015, *Devolution: A Roadmap*, Local Government Information Unit, London.

Dijkstra, L., 2013, "Why Investing More in the Capital Can Lead to Less Growth", *Cambridge Journal of Regions, Economy and Society*, 6.2, 251–268.

Dixon, R.J., and Thirlwall, A.P., 1975, *Regional Growth and Unemployment in the United Kingdom*, Macmillan, London.

Dotti, N.F., and Bubbico, R., 2014, "New Challenges for Structural Funds: The New Territorial Capital Approach in the Perspective of the Evolution of the EU Regional Policy", *European Structural and Investment Funds Journal*, 2.2, 89–100.

Dow, S.C., and Montagnoli, A., 2007, "The Regional Transmission of UK Monetary Policy", *Regional Studies*, 41.6, 797–808.

Dunleavy, P., Kippin, S. and Suss, S., 2014, *Transitioning to a New Scottish State*, London School of Economics, London. See: http://eprints.lse.ac.uk/57708/1/Transitioning-to-a-new-Scottish-state-PD-ebook.pdf.

Dynes, M., and Walker, D., 1995, *The Times Guide to the New British State: The Government Machine in the 1990s*, Times Books, London.

Eddington, R., 2006, *The Eddington Transport Study. The Case for Action: Sir Rod Eddington's Advice to Government*, HM Treasury, London, December.

Ezcurra, R., and Pasqual, P., 2008, "Fiscal Decentralization and Regional Disparities: Evidence from Several European Union Countries", *Environment and Planning A*, 40, 1185–1201.

Ezcurra, R., and Rodriguez-Pose, A., 2013, "Political Decentralization, Economic Growth and Regional Disparities in the OECD", *Regional Studies*, 47.3, 388–401.

Ezcurra, R., and Rodriguez-Pose, A., 2014, "Government Quality and Spatial Inequality: A Cross-Country Analysis", *Environment and Planning A*, 46, 1732–1753.

Fidrmuc, J., Horvath, J. and Fidrmuc, J., 1999, "The Stability of Monetary Unions: Lessons from the Breakup of Czechoslovakia", *Journal of Comparative Economics*, 27, 753–781.

Fothergill, S., and Gudgin, G., 1982, *Unequal Growth: Urban and Regional Employment Change in the UK*, Heinemann, London.

Frankel, J., and Rose, A.K., 1998, "The Endogeneity of the Optimal Currency Area Criteria", *Economic Journal*, 108.449, 1009–1025.

Garcilazo, E., J., Oliveira Martins, J. and Tompson, W., 2010, "Why Policies May Need to be Place-Based in Order to be People-Centred,", OECD Regional Development Policy Division, Paris. Available at the website: www.voxeu.org/.

Geddes, A., 2013, *Britain and the European Union*, Palgrave, Basingstoke.

Gibbons, S., Lyytikäinen, T., Overman, H.G. and Sanchis-Garnier, R., 2012, "New Road Infrastructure: The Effects on Firms", *SERC Discussion Paper 117*, Spatial Economics Research Centre, London School of Economics, London.

Gibbons, S., Overman, H.G. and Pelkonen, P., 2014, "Area Disparities in Britain: Understanding the Contribution of People vs. Place Through Variance Decompositions", *Oxford Bulletin of Economics and Statistics*, 76.5, 745–763.

Gill, I., 2010, "Regional Development Policies: Place-Based or People-Centred?" Available at the website: www.voxeu.org/index.php?q=node/5644.

Glaeser, E.L., 2008, *Cities, Agglomeration and Spatial Equilibrium*, Oxford University Press, Oxford.

Glaeser, E.L., and Gottlieb, J.D., 2008, "The Economics of Place-Making Policies", *Harvard Institute of Economic Research Discussion Paper No. 2166*, 10 November.

Goddard, J.B., and Champion, A.G., 1983, (eds.), *The Urban and Regional Transformation of Britain*, Methuen, London.

Grady, P., 1991, "The Economic Consequences of Quebec Sovereignty", *Global Economics Working Paper 1991-1*, Fraser Institute. See: https://www.fraserinstitute.org.

Graham, D.J., and Van Denden, K., 2009, "Estimating the Agglomeration Benefits of Transport Investments: Some Tests for Stability", *Discussion Paper No.2009–32*, OECD and International Transport Forum, Joint Transport Research Centre.

Hackett, P., 2014, (ed.), *Making Global Connections: The Potential of the UK's Regional Airports*, The Smith Institute, London.

Hallwood, P., and MacDonald, R., 2005, "The Economic Case for Fiscal Federalism", in Coyle, D., Alexander, W. and Ashcroft, B., *New Wealth for Old Nations: Scotland's Economic Prospects*, Princeton University Press, Princeton, NJ.

Hambleton, R., 2014, "Osborne's Devo Deals Disguise Centralisation", *Local Government Chronicle*, 18 December 2014, p. 23.

Harris, R.I.D., 1989, *The Growth and Structure of the UK Economy 1963–85*, Avebury, Aldershot.

Harrison, R.T., and Hart, M., 1993, (eds.), *Spatial Policy in a Divided Nation*, Jessica Kingsley, London.

Harvey, D., 1973, *Social Justice and The City*, Edward Arnold, London.

Hausner, V., 1987, (ed.), *Urban Economic Change: Five City Studies*, Oxford University Press, Oxford.

Hazell, R., 2015, (ed.), *Devolution and the Future of the Union*, The Constitution Unit, Department of Political Science, University College London, London, April.

Healey, J., and Newby, L., 2014, *Making Local Economies Matter: A Review of Policy Lessons from the Regional Development Agencies and Local Enterprise Partnerships*, Smith Institute, London.

Henderson, J., 2015, "The North-South Divide: Only a True Federal State Can Break the London Monopoly", *Times Higher Education*, 7 May.

Henderson, J., and Ho, S.Y., 2014, "Re-Forming the State. The Upas Tree: The Over-Development of London and the Under-Development of Britain", *Renewal: A Journal of Social Democracy*, 22.3–4, 22–41.

Heseltine, M., 2012, *No Stone Unturned*, Independent Report Submitted to HM Government, Department for Business, Innovation and Skills, London.

Hibbs, J., 2006, "Railways and the Power of Emotion: Seeking a Market Solution", in *The Railways, the Market and the Government*, Institute for Economic Affairs, London.

HM Government, 2010, *Local Growth: Realising Every Place's Potential*, London, 28 October.

HM Government, 2011, *Unlocking Growth in Cities*, London, December.

HM Government, 2015a, *Powers for a Purpose: Towards a Lasting Devolution Settlement for Wales*, Cm9020, London, February.

HM Government, 2015b, *Scotland in the United Kingdom: An Enduring Settlement*, Cm8990, London, February.

HM Government and Transport for the North, 2015, *The Northern Powerhouse: One Agenda, One Economy, One North*, Department for Transport, London, March.

HM Treasury, 2014, *National Infrastructure Plan 2014*, December.

HM Treasury, 2015a, *Fixing the Foundations: Creating a More Prosperous Nation*, Cm 9098, July.

HM Treasury, 2015b, *Spending Review and Autumn Statement 2015*, Cm 9162, November.

HM Treasury and Infrastructure UK, 2010, *National Infrastructure Plan 2010*, London, October.

HM Treasury and Infrastructure UK, 2011, *National Infrastructure Plan 2011*, London, October.

HoC, 1985, *Channel Link: Minutes of Evidence*, House of Commons Transport Committee, Session 1985–86, HMSO, London, 14 November.

HoC, 1996, *UK Airport Capacity: Volume 1 Report and Proceedings*, Second Report of Transport Committee, Session 1995–96, HMSO, London, 8 May.

HoC, 2008, *Regional Development Agencies: Written Evidence*, Business and Enterprise Select Committee, House of Commons, London.

HoC, 2009, *The Balance of Power, Central and Local Government*, HC33-1 Incorporating HC813-i-iv, Report of the House of Commons Communities and Local Government Committee, Sixth Report of the Session 2008–09, 20 May, House of Commons, London.

HoC, 2010a, *The Major Road Network*, HC5050, Report of the House of Commons Transport Select Committee, Eighth Report of the Session 2009–10, 30 March, House of Commons, London.

HoC, 2010b, *Priorities for Investment in the Railways*, HC38-11 Incorporating HC1056, Report of the House of Commons Transport Select Committee, Third Report of the Session 2009–10 Volume II, 15 February, House of Commons, London.

HoC, 2012a, *Counting the Cost: Financial Scrutiny of the Department for Transport 2011–12*, HC1560 Incorporating HC1713-i, Report of the House of Commons Transport Select Committee, Fifteenth Report of the Session 2010–12 Volume I, Report Together with Formal Minutes, Oral and Written Evidence, 7 February, House of Commons, London.

HoC, 2012b, *Regional Breakdown of Transport Spending*, Uncorrected Transcript of Oral Evidence Questions 1–68, HC776-i, House of Commons Transport Select Committee, 26 November, House of Commons, London.

HoC, 2013, *Aviation Strategy*, HC78-1 Incorporating HC765 i-vii, Report of the House of Commons Transport Select Committee, First Report of the Session 2013–14 Volume I, 15 February, House of Commons, London.

HoC, 2014a, *Devolution in England – the Case for Local Government*, HC503 Incorporating HC1018, Report of the Select Committee House of Commons Communities and Local Government Select Committee, First Report of the Session 2014–15, 9 July, House of Commons, London.

HoC, 2014b, *Better Roads: Improving England's Strategic Roads Network*, HC850, Report of the House of Commons Transport Select Committee, Fifteenth Report of the Session 2013–14, 7 May, House of Commons, London.

HoC, 2014c, *Promoting Economic Growth Locally,* Sixtieth Report of Session 2013–14, HC1110, House of Commons Public Accounts Committee, House of Commons, London, 16 May.

HoC, 2015a, *Lessons from Major Rail Infrastructure Programmes*, HC709, Report of the House of Commons Transport Select Committee, Twenty-Eighth Report of the Session 2014–15, 16 January, House of Commons, London.

HoC, 2015b, *Investing in the Railway*, HC257, Report of the House of Commons Transport Select Committee, Seventh Report of the Session 2014–15, 19 January, House of Commons, London.

HoL, 2015, *The Economics of High Speed 2*, HL Paper 134, House of Lords Economic Affairs Committee, 1st Report of Session 2014–15, House of Lords, London, 25 March.

Holland, S., 1976, *The Regional Problem*, Macmillan, London.

Hope, N., and Leslie, C., 2009, *Challenging Perspectives: Improving Whitehall's Spatial Awareness*, NLGN New Local Government Network, London.

Hutton, W., 1995, *The State We're In*, Random House, London.

Iammarino, S., and McCann, P., 2013, *Multinationals and Economic Geography: Location, Technology, and Innovation*, Edward Elgar, Cheltenham.

ICLGF, 2014, *Public Money, Local Choice*, Independent Commission on Local Government Finance, Interim Report, London.

ICLGF, 2015, *Financing English Devolution*, Independent Commission on Local Government Finance, Final Report, London.

IfG, 2013, *Civil Service Capabilities*, Kidson, M., Institute for Government, London.

IfG, 2014, *Governing After the Referendum: Future Constitutional Scenarios for Scotland and the UK*, Paun, A., Randall, J., Munro, R. and Shaddock, L., Institute for Government, London.

Imrie, R., and Raco, M., 2003, (eds.), *Urban Renaissance? New Labour, Community and Urban Policy*, Policy Press, Bristol.

IPPR, 2011, *On the Wrong Track: An Analysis of the Autumn Statement Announcements on Transport Infrastructure*, Cox, E., and Schmuecker, K., Institute for Public Policy Research North, Newcastle, December.

IPPR, 2012, *Northern Prosperity is National Prosperity: A Strategy for Revitalising the UK Economy*, Institute for Public Policy Research North, Newcastle, November.

IPPR, 2013, *Still on the Wrong Track: An Updated Analysis of Transport Infrastructure Spending*, Cox, E., and Davies, B., Institute for Public Policy Research North, Newcastle, June.

IPPR, 2014a, *Decentralisation Decade: A Plan for Economic Prosperity, Public Service Transformation and Democratic Renewal in England*, Institute for Public Policy Research North, Newcastle, September.

IPPR, 2014b, *Democracy in Britain: Essays in Honour of James Cornford*, Institute for Public Policy Research, London, February.

IPPR, 2014c, *Transformational Infrastructure for the North: Why We Need a Great North Plan*, Institute for Public Policy Research North, Newcastle, August.

IPPR, 2015, *Transport for the North: A Blueprint for Devolving and Integrating Transport Powers in England*, Institute for Public Policy Research North, Newcastle, March.

Jorgensen, D.W., and Timmer, M.P., 2011, "Structural Change in Advanced Nations: A New Set of Stylised Facts", *Scandinavian Journal of Economics*, 113.1, 1–29.

Kaletsky, A., 2015, "Britain's Greatest Problem", *Prospect*, May.

Kanbur, R., and Venables, A.J., 2013, "Spatial Inequality and Development", in Kabur, R., and Venables, A.J., (eds.), *Spatial Inequality and Development*, Oxford University Press, Oxford.

Kay, J., 2015, "No Way to Plan an Airport", *Prospect*, November.

Keeble, D., 1976, *Industrial Location and Planning in the United Kingdom*, Methuen, London.

King, A., 2015, *Who Governs Britain?*, Pelican Books, London.

King, C., 2012, "The Scottish Play: Edinburgh's Quest for Independence and the Future of Separatism", *Foreign Affairs*, September/October.

King, C., 2014, "Toil and Trouble: Scotland's Vote Created More Problems Than It Solved", *Foreign Affairs*, 19 September.

Klein, P., and Moretti, E., 2013, "Place Based Policies with Unemployment", *American Economic Review*, 103.3, 238–243.

Klein, P., and Moretti, E., 2014a, "People, Places, and Public Policy: Some Simple Welfare Economics of Local Economic Development Programs", *Annual Review of Economics*, 6, 629–662.

Klein, P., and Moretti, E., 2014b, "Local Economic Development: Agglomeration Economies, and the Big Push: 100 Years of Evidence from the Tennessee Valley Authority", *Quarterly Journal of Economics*, 129.1, 275–331.

Krugman, P., 1991, *Geography and Trade*, MIT Press, Cambridge, MA.

Krugman, P., 2015a, "This Snookered Isle", *New York Times*, 24 March.

Krugman, P., 2015b, "Seriously Bad Ideas", *New York Times*, 13th–14 June.

Krugman, P., and Venables, A.J., 1995, "Globalization and the Inequality of Nations", *Quarterly Journal of Economics*, 110.4, 857–880.

Kuhn, T., 1970a, *The Structure of Scientific Revolutions*, 2nd edition, University of Chicago Press, Chicago.

Kuhn, T., 1970b, "Logic of Discovery or Psychology of Research", in Lakatos, I., and Musgrave, A., (eds.), *Criticism and the Growth of Knowledge*, Cambridge University Press, Cambridge.

Lago-Peñas, S., and Martinez-Vazquez, J., 2013, (eds.), *The Challenge of Local Government Size: Theoretical Perspectives, International Experience and Policy Reform*, Edward Elgar, Cheltenham.

Lakatos, I., 1970, "Falsification and the Methodology of Scientific Research Programmes", in Lakatos, I., and Musgrave, A., (eds.), *Criticism and the Growth of Knowledge*, Cambridge University Press, Cambridge.

Lawless, P., and Brown, F., 1986, *Urban Growth and Change in Britain: An Introduction*, Harper & Row, London.

Leunig, T., Swaffield, J. and Hartwich, O., 2007, *Cities Unlimited*, Policy Exchange, London.

Lever, W.F., 1987, "Urban Policy", in Lever, W.F., (ed.), *Industrial Change in the United Kingdom*, Longman, London.

Levine, M., 1990, *The Conquest of Montreal: Language Policy and Social Change in a Bilingual City*, Temple University Press, Philadelphia.

LGA, 2012, *Independence from the Centre: Does Local Government's Freedom Lie in a New Constitutional Settlement*, Local Government Association, London, February.

LGA, 2015, *English Devolution: Local Solutions for a Successful Nation*, Local Government Association, London.

LGALG, 2014, *Final Report: People-Powered Public Services*, Local Government Innovation Taskforce, Local Government Association Labour Group.

Luger, M., Butler, J. and Minch, G., 2013, "Infrastructure and Manufacturing: Their Evolving Relationship", *Future of Manufacturing Project: Evidence Paper 30*, Foresight, Government Office for Science, London.

McCann, P., 2009, "Economic Geography, Globalisation and New Zealand's Productivity Paradox", *New Zealand Economic Papers*, 43.3, 279–314.

McCann, P., 2013, *Modern Urban and Regional Economics*, Oxford University Press, Oxford.

McCann, P., 2015, *The Regional and Urban Policy of the European Union: Cohesion, Results-Orientation and Smart Specialisation*, Edward Elgar, Cheltenham.

McCann, P., and Acs, Z.J., 2011, "Globalisation: Countries, Cities and Multinationals", *Regional Studies*, 45.1, 17–32.

McCann, P., and Rodriguez-Pose, A., 2011, "Why and When Development Policy Should be Place-Based", *OECD Regional Outlook 2011*, Organisation for Economic Cooperation and Development, Paris.

McLaren, J., Armstrong, J. and Gibb, K., 2013, *Measuring an Independent Scotland's Performance*, Centre for Public Policy Research Briefing Paper, University of Glasgow, 23 April.

McLaren, J., Armstrong, J. and Gibb, K., 2014, *Analysis of Scotland's Past and Future Fiscal Position: Incorporating GERS 2014 and the 2014 UK Budget*, CPPR Briefing Note, Centre for Public Policy Research, University of Glasgow, March.

McLean, I., 2008, "The Scots and the Union", *The Scottish Historical Review*, 87.2, 224, 343–345.

Macwhirter, I., 2014, *Disunited Kingdom: How Westminster Won a Referendum but Lost Scotland*, Cargo Publishing, Glasgow.

Marsh, D., 2009, *The Euro: The Politics of the New Global Currency*, Yale University Press, New Haven.

Martin, R.L., 2015, "Rebalancing the Spatial Economy: The Challenge for Regional Theory", *Territory, Politics and Governance*, Forthcoming.

Massey, D.B., 1979, "In What Sense a Regional Problem?", *Regional Studies*, 13.3, 233–243.

Massey, D.B., 1983, "Industrial Restructuring as Class Restructuring – Production Decentralization and Local Uniqueness", *Regional Studies*, 17.2, 73–89.

Massey, D.B. and Meegan, R.A., 1978, "Industrial Restructuring Versus the Cities", *Urban Studies*, 15.3, 273–288.

Melo, P., Graham. D.J. and Brage-Ardao, R., 2013, "The Productivity of Transport Infrastructure Investment: A Meta-Analysis of Empirical Evidence", *Regional Science and Urban Economics*, 43, 695–706.

MIER, 2009, *Manchester Independent Economic Review*, www.manchester-review.org.uk/index.html.

Miller, T., and Holmes, K.R., 2009, *2009 Index of Economic Freedom: The Link Between Economic Opportunity and Prosperity*, Heritage Foundation and Wall Street Journal, New York.

Minford, P., and Stoney, P., 1991, "Regional Policy and Market Forces: An Assessment", in Bowen, A., and Mayhew, K., (eds.), *Reducing Regional Inequalities*, Kogan Page, London.

Mulgan, G., and Bury, F., 2006, (eds.), *Double Devolution: The Renewal of Local Government*, Smith Institute, London.

Mundell, R.A., 1961, "A Theory of Optimal Currency Areas", *American Economic Review*, 51.4, 657–664.

Mundell, R.A., 1973, "Uncommon Arguments for Common Currencies", in Johnson, H.G., and Swoboda, A.K., (eds.), pp. 114–132, *The Economics of Common Currencies*, Allen and Unwin, London.

Musson, A.E., 1978, *The Growth of British Industry*, Batsford Academic and Educational Publishers Ltd, London.

NAO, 2013, *High Speed 2: A Review of Early Programme Preparation*, National Audit Office, London.

NESTA, 2014, *The End of The Treasury*, Wilkes, G., and Westlake, S., London.

NESTA, 2015, *Government as Impresario: Emergent Public Goods and Public Private Partnerships 2.0*, Gruen. N., London.

Niemietz, K., 2013, *Depoliticising Airport Expansion: Market-Oriented Responses to the Global and Local Externalities of Aviation*, IEA Discussion Paper No. 51, Institute for Economic Affairs, London.

NMC, 2014, *The Future of Prosperity and Public Services in Non-Metropolitan England; Interim Report*, Independent Commission on Economic Growth and the Future of Public Services in Non-Metropolitan England, March.

NMC, 2015, *Devolution to Non-Metropolitan England; Seven Steps to Growth and Prosperity: Final Report of the Non-Metropolitan Commission*, Independent

Commission on Economic Growth and the Future of Public Services in Non-Metropolitan England, March.

Northern Way, 2009a, *The Northern Way Evaluation Plan 2008–2011*, March, www.thenorthernway.co.uk.

Northern Way, 2009b, *City Relationships: Economic Linkages in Northern City-Regions*, Northern Way, Newcastle-upon-Tyne.

Northern Way, 2011, *The Northern Way Transport Compact: The Economic Case for Transport Investment in the North*, March, www.thenorthernway.co.uk.

Oates, W.E., 2011, *Fiscal Federalism*, Edward Elgar, Cheltenham, first published in 1972 by Harcourt Brace Jovanovich Inc., New York.

O'Brien, P., and Pike, A., 2015, "City Deals, Decentralisation and the Governance of Local Infrastructure Funding and Financing in the UK", *National Institute Economic Review*, 233, R14–R26.

ODPM, 2006a, *State of the English Cities, Urban Research Summary 21*, Office of the Deputy Prime Minister, London.

ODPM, 2006b, *State of the English Cities, Volume 1*, Office of the Deputy Prime Minister, London.

ODPM, 2006c, *State of the English Cities, Volume 2*, Office of the Deputy Prime Minister, London.

OECD 2006, *Competitive Cities in the Global Economy: OECD Territorial Reviews*, Organisation for Economic Cooperation and Development, Paris.

OECD 2007a, *Linking Regions and Central Government: Contracts for Regional Development*, Organisation for Economic Cooperation and Development, Paris.

OECD 2007b, *Investment Strategies and Financial Tools for Local Development*, Organisation for Economic Cooperation and Development, Paris.

OECD, 2009a, *How Regions Grow*, Paris: Organisation for Economic Growth and Development, Paris.

OECD, 2009b, *Regions Matter: Economic Recovery, Innovation and Sustainable Growth*, Organisation for Economic Growth and Development, Paris.

OECD, 2010, *Regional Development Policies in OECD Countries*, Organisation for Economic Cooperation and Development, Paris.

OECD, 2011a, *Making the Most of Public Investment in a Tight Fiscal Environment: Multi-Level Governance Lessons from the Crisis*, Organisation for Economic Cooperation and Development, Paris.

OECD, 2011b, *OECD Regional Outlook 2011: Building Resilient Regions for Stronger Economies*, Organisation for Economic Cooperation and Development, Paris.

OECD 2012a, *Reforming Fiscal Federalism and Local Government: Beyond the Zero-Sum Game*, Organisation for Economic Cooperation and Development, Paris.

OECD 2012b, *Strategic Transport Infrastructure Needs to 2030*, Organisation for Economic Cooperation and Development, Paris.

OECD, 2013a, *Regions at a Glance 2013*, Organisation for Economic Cooperation and Development, Paris.

OECD, 2013b, *Government at a Glance 2013*, Organisation for Economic Cooperation and Development, Paris.

OECD, 2013c, *Investing Together: Working Effectively Across Levels of Government*, Organisation for Economic Cooperation and Development, Paris.

OECD, 2014a, *OECD Regional Outlook 2014: Regions and Cities: Where Policies and People Meet*, Organisation for Economic Cooperation and Development, Paris.

OECD, 2014b, *The Netherlands, OECD Territorial Reviews,* Organisation for Economic Cooperation and Development, Paris.

Oil and Gas UK, 2015, *Activity Survey 2015*, Aberdeen and London, see: www.oilandgasuk.co.uk.

One North, 2014, *One North: A Proposition for An Interconnected North*, July, www.manchester.gov.uk/downloads/download/5969/one-north.

Overman, H.G., and Winters, L.A., 2005, "The Port Geography of UK International Trade", *Environment and Planning A*, 37.10, 1751–1768.

Overman, H.G., and Winters, L.A., 2011, "Trade and Economic Geography: The Impact of EEC Accession on the UK", *The Manchester School,* 79.5, 994–1017.

Parkinson, M., Foley, B. and Judd, D., 1988, (eds.), *Regenerating the Cities: The UK Crisis and the US Experience*, Manchester University Press, Manchester.

Partridge, M.D., and Rickman, D.S., 2005, "Is the U.S. an Optimal Currency Area? An Analysis of Asymmetric Shocks Using U.S. State Data." *Oxford Economic Papers*, 57, 373–397.

Partridge, M.D., Rickman, D.S., Olfert, M.R. and Tan, Y., 2015, "When Spatial Equilibrium Fails: Is Place-Based Policy Second Best?", *Regional Studies*, 49.8, 1303–1325.

Pasquero, J., 1997, "Business Ethics and Identity in Quebec: Distinctiveness and Directions", *Journal of Business Ethics*, 16, 621–633.

Paterson, L., 1994. *The Autonomy of Modern Scotland*, Edinburgh University Press, Edinburgh.

Phillips, D., 2013, *Government Spending on Benefits and State Pensions in Scotland: Current Patterns and Future Issues*, IFS Briefing Note BN139, Institute for Fiscal Studies, London.

Phillips, D., and Tetlow, G., 2013, *Taxation, Government Spending and the Public Finances of Scotland: Updating the Medium Term Outlook*, IFS Briefing Note BN148, Institute for Fiscal Studies, London.

Phillips, D., and Tetlow, G., 2014, *Policies for an Independent Scotland? Putting the Independence White Paper in its Fiscal Context*, IFS Briefing Note BN149, Institute for Fiscal Studies, London.

Pike, A., Marlow, D., McCarthy, A., O'Brien, P. and Tomaney, J., 2015, "Local Institutions and Local Economic Development; the Local Enterprise Partnerships in England, 2010-", *Cambridge Journal of Regions, Economy and Society*, Forthcoming, doi: 10.1093/cjres/rsu030.

Platt, E., 2015, "Living By Numbers", *New Statesman*, 10–16 April.

Polèse, M., and Shearmur, R., 2004, "Culture, Language and the Location of High-Order Service Functions: The Case of Montreal and Toronto", *Economic Geography*, 80.4, 329–350.

Putnam, R., 1996, *Bowling Alone: The Collapse and Revival of American Community*, Simon and Schuster, New York.

PWC and Demos, 2012, *Good Growth for Cities*, Price Waterhouse Coopers, London.

PWC and the Smith Institute, 2014, *All Change: Delivering Future City Transport*, Price Waterhouse Coopers, London.

Renwick, A., 2014, *After the Referendum: Options for a Constitutional Convention,* The Constitution Society, London.

ResPublica, 2014, *Devo-Max Devo-Manc: Place-Based Public Services*, London, September.

ResPublica, 2015, *Restoring Britain's City States: Devolution, Public Service Reform and Local Economic Growth*, London, February.

Riddell, P., 2015, "It's the Constitution, Stupid", *Prospect*, 8 May.

Riddoch, L., 2014, *Blossom: What Scotland Needs to Flourish*, Luath Press, Edinburgh.

Riddoch, L., 2015, *Wee White Blossom: What Post-Referendum Scotland Needs to Flourish*, Luath Press, Edinburgh.

Robertson, J., 1997, "The Enlightenment Above National Context: Political Economy in Eighteenth-Century Scotland and Naples", *The Historical Journal*, 40.3, 667–697.

Rodrik, D., 2007, *One Economics Many Recipes: Globalization, Institutions and Economic Growth*, Princeton University Press, Princeton.

Rodrik, D., 2011, *The Globalization Paradox: Why Global Markets, States and Democracy Can't Coexist*, Oxford University Press, Oxford.

Rössner, P.R., 2011, "The 1738–41 Harvest Crisis in Scotland", *The Scottish Historical Review*, 90.1, 229, 27–63.

RSA, 2014, *Unleashing Metro Growth: Final Recommendations of the City Growth Commission*, Royal Society of Arts, London.

RSA, 2015, *Devo Met: Charting a Path Ahead*, Royal Society of Arts, London, March.

Schama, S., 2001, *A History of Britain 2: 1603-1176 The British Wars*, BBC Books, London.

Scottish Government, 2013, *Fiscal Commission Working Group – First Report – Macroeconomic Framework*, Edinburgh, February.

Scottish Government, 2015, *Oil and Gas Analytical Bulletin*, Edinburgh, June.

SDG, 2014, *Transport Constraints and Opportunities in the North of England*, Steer Davies Gleave, London.

Semple, R.K., and Green, M.B., 1983, "Interurban Corporate Headquarters Relocations in Canada", *Cahiers de Géographie due Quebec*, 27.27, 389–406.

Silk, P., 2012, *Empowerment and Responsibility: Legislative Powers to Strengthen Wales*, Interim Report, Commission on Devolution in Wales, Cardiff, November.

Silk, P., 2014, *Empowerment and Responsibility: Legislative Powers to Strengthen Wales*, Final Report, Commission on Devolution in Wales, Cardiff, March.

Smith, A., 1983, *Passion for the Inner City*, Sheed and Ward Ltd, London.

Smith Commission, 2014, *The Smith Commission: Report of the Smith Commission for Further Devolution of Powers to the Scottish Parliament*, Edinburgh, 27 November.

SQW, 2009, *An Evaluation of the Northern Way 2004–2008: A Final Report to the Northern Way, Summary*, SQW Consulting, April.

SQW, 2011, *The Evaluation of the Northern Way 2008–11: Final Report to the Northern Way, Summary*, SQW Consulting, April.

Starkie, D., 2013, *Transport Infrastructure: Adding Value*, IEA Discussion Paper No. 50, Institute for Economic Affairs, London.

Stiglitz, J.E., Sen, A. and Fitoussi, J-P., 2009, *Report by the Commission on the Measurement of Economic and Social Progress*, see: www.stiglitz-sen-fitoussi.fr/en/index.htm.

Storper, M., 2013, *Keys to the City: How Economics, Institutions, Social Interaction, and Politics Shape Development*, Princeton University Press, Princeton, NJ.

Tallon, A., 2010, *Urban Regeneration in the UK*, Routledge, London.

Tomaney, J., 2009, (ed.), *The Future of Regional Policy*, The Smith Institute, London.

Tomaney, J., and Mawson, J., 2002, (eds.), *England: The State of the Regions*, Policy Press, Bristol.

Travers, T., 2015, "Devolving Funding and Taxation in the UK: A Unique Challenge", *National Institute Economic Review*, 233, R5–R13.

Van Den Bulcke, D., Verbeke, A. and Yuan, W., 2009, *Handbook on Small Nations in the Global Economy: The Contribution of Multinational Enterprises to National Economic Success*, Edward Elgar, Cheltenham.

Vandermeer, R., 2001, *The Heathrow Terminal Five and Associated Public Inquiries; Main Report: Chapters 1–20*, Department for Transport, Local Government and the Regions, London.

Venables, A.J., 2007, "Evaluating Urban Transport Improvements: Cost-Benefit Analysis in the Presence of Agglomeration and Income Taxation", *Journal of Transport Economics and Policy*, 41.2, 173–188.

Vickerman, R.W., 1985, "The Channel Tunnel: Consequences for Regional Growth and Development", *Regional Studies*, 21.3, 187–197.

Vickerman, R.W., 2013, "The Wider Economic Impacts of Mega-Projects in Transport", in Priemus, H., and Van Wee, B., (eds.), *International Handbook on Mega-Projects*, Edward Elgar, Cheltenham.

Volterra Arup, 2011, *Understanding the Transport Infrastructure Requirements to Deliver Growth in England's Core Cities*, Final Report to the Core Cities Group, July.

Ward, M., and Hardy, S., 2012, (eds.), *Changing Gear: Is Localism the New Regionalism?*, Smith Institute, London.

Ward, M., and Hardy, S., 2013, (eds.), *Where Next for Local Enterprise Partnerships?*, Smith Institute, London.

Wellings, B., 2012, *English Nationalism and Euroscepticism: Losing the Peace*, Peter Lang, Oxford.

Wellings, R., 2014, *Failure to Transform: High-Speed Rail and the Regeneration Myth*, IEA Current Controversies Paper No. 48, Institute for Economic Affairs, London.

Winnick, L, 1966, "Place Prosperity vs People Prosperity: Welfare Considerations in the Geographic Redistribution of Economic Activity", in *Essays in Urban Land Economics in Honor of the Sixty-Fifth Birthday of Leo Grebler*, Real Estate Research Program, University of California Press, Los Angeles.

Wren, C., 1996, *Industrial Subsidies: The UK Experience*, Macmillan, Basingstoke, Hampshire.

World Bank, 2009a, *Doing Business 2009: Comparing Regulation in 181 Economies*, Washington DC.

World Bank, 2009b, *World Development Report 2009: Reshaping Economic Geography*, World Bank, Washington DC.

World Bank, 2010, *Innovation Policy: A Guide for Developing Countries*, World Bank, Washington DC.

World Bank, 2011, *Igniting Innovation: Rethinking the Role of Government in Emerging Europe and Central Asia*, Goldberg, I., Goddard, J.G., Kuriakose, S., and Racine, J-L., World Bank, Washington DC.

Zoellick, R.F., 2012, "Why We Still Need the World Bank: Looking Beyond Aid", *Foreign Affairs*, March/April, 91.2, 66–78.

7 Issues and considerations arising from the sub-national economic policy agenda

7.1 Introduction

One of the key insights emerging from this book is the economic need for, and also the economic case for, a major reform of all of the UK city and regional institutions related to local and regional economic development. The arguments for such reforms arise specifically out of a wide-ranging and detailed exploration and analysis of all of the available data concerning the UK interregional imbalances and inequalities, the role played by modern globalisation in these imbalances, and also the problems engendered by the UK's high levels of governance centralisation. As we saw in the previous chapter, over recent years the internal pressures for reform have led to two rather distinct, but also somewhat interconnected, lines of structural reform relating to regional, urban and local development, namely increased governance devolution and decentralisation along with enhanced interregional connectivity. Yet, while the broad arguments underpinning these structural reforms have already been outlined in Chapter 6, it still remains the case that the specific details of these reforms have yet to be seriously discussed. On these points, the scale of the current mismatch between the UK's interregional performance and its institutional settings suggests that many fruitful lessons could potentially be gleaned from other countries regarding which institutional and governance arrangements could be advantageous for the UK's constituent nations, its regions and its localities. However, learning from international governance lessons is not so straightforward as it might seem, and there are both cultural and political reasons for this.

First, popular narratives in the UK media and public life frequently advocate the superiority of UK institutions over those in other countries. Moreover, narratives in the UK popular and business media also frequently stress the role of the UK as a pioneer in the vanguard of invention and innovation. These combined beliefs regarding economic dynamism and institutional set-up of the UK are therefore likely to engender resistance to regional and urban governance reforms, especially if the ideas underpinning these reforms arise to some extent from observations and experiences of other European countries. Yet, rather than leading by example, as we saw in Chapter 1, the reality of UK productivity statistics relative to other European competitors suggests that on many levels the UK potentially has far more to learn from the examples of other countries than it has to teach other countries. The only real exceptions to the UK's cultural resistance to lesson-learning from other countries are potential lessons derived from other North American or Commonwealth 'Anglo-Saxon' economies, which are felt to be relatively closer to the UK. However, in the particular case of the UK this is particularly problematic, because as we have already seen at many points in this book, when it comes to urban and regional issues it is often other European economies which offer closer comparators and therefore many of the most fruitful insights for the challenges facing the UK rather than other 'Anglo-Saxon' economies. As we saw in Chapter 6, most of the other 'Anglo-Saxon' nations reflect totally different orders of magnitude in geographical terms, most are already far more decentralised than the UK both in terms of governance and connectivity, and indeed most have a federal structure in which the nation's political and commercial capitals are separated. While on the one hand possible institutional lessons can be derived from these countries, and in particular the advantages of governance decentralisation, on the other hand in terms of detailed urban issues these countries offer very few insights. Here, the more similar geographies mean that observations of European nations are far more instructive.

Such reforms, however, are likely to face opposition on many levels. Governance reforms which attempt to deregulate land markets on the urban fringe, and in particular in greenbelt areas, will continue to face significant local opposition. Similarly, large-scale infrastructure initiatives are likely to face ongoing opposition from numerous quarters across individual regions or across several regions. In these cases the main institutional opposition to reforms will come primarily from outside of the government decision-making machine. In contrast, in the case of the further devolution of powers to the devolved administrations and also now to the city-regions, some of the opposition to these reforms is likely to emerge from within the government machine, aimed at partially countering the inevitable movement towards a quasi-federal UK state. In particular, these movements are likely to face opposition from many arms of central government and from political insiders, suspicious of the roles of lower tiers of government and fearful of relinquishing too much power. How these evolving devolution and decentralisation processes will play out exactly is not yet clear, and at the same time, drawing on lessons from other countries in order to try to map out the likely scenarios is also not necessarily always as instructive as might be expected given the fact that the UK is almost unique both in its current governance construction and also in terms of the scale of the interregional inequalities.

In contrast, the situations where institutional and governance reforms at the regional level are likely to face much less opposition are where the case for the reforms is fundamentally political and receives strong support from both central and local government. This political momentum for governance reform is now apparent both in the case of the UK's devolved administrations and now also in the case of English city-regions. Yet, such political momentum could also be problematic, because the issues being examined in this book are not fundamentally political, but economic. As such, in order for the reforms to be successful in the long run it is imperative that both the architecture of the governance reform agenda and also the relationships between the reforms and the intended objectives of the reforms are entirely consistent with the economic case, and this is the issue which this chapter will examine. As such, if there is to be a realignment of the roles of many parts of the state in the coming years it is imperative that the initial changes implemented are the best ones possible and based on the best available evidence, because once implemented unpicking the effects of bad policy decisions is much more difficult than if they had never been implemented.[1]

In this chapter we will first examine the strengths and weaknesses of likely national-regional governance and institutional transitions which the UK is currently embarking on, and will highlight the long-run opportunities and threats associated with these highest level institutional changes. Second, at a lower spatial and institutional level, in order to help identify potentially positive steps forward in the institutional design we will survey the international evidence regarding the effects of different forms of city and regional governance, and the different economic development experiences associated with different sub-national and city-region governance systems. Considering governance reforms at both the national-regional level and also regional-urban or regional-local levels is important because from economic geography we know that the economic development impacts are likely to operate at both scales. Devolution and decentralisation reforms will almost always have regional and interregional dimensions to them as well as both local and urban dimensions. As such, understanding how these governance reforms are likely to evolve both at the regional and interregional scales as well as at the local and the urban scale is essential in order to identify the likely implications and effectiveness of the reforms. Third, at the thematic and programme-specific level, it is also necessary to consider how these likely governance transitions are likely to impact on other related policies with local, urban and regional dimensions. Top-down traditional regional policies were primarily focused on employment generation whereas today much more flexible forms of local and regional development policy are aimed at addressing different types of issues including innovation, entrepreneurship, wellbeing and quality of life, as well as social and environmental sustainability. Understanding to what extent these new policy approaches will be able to dovetail with the evolving UK devolution agenda is important for identifying the evolving role of local and regional policy in the coming years. This will help us identify the areas where substantial progress can be made in policy formulation by these changes in public governance and in public investment policies and also the areas where inherent risks appear to be involved. Moreover, addressing all of these various issues across these different spatial scales and governance levels will help us to identify the remaining issues which are not presently in public debates but which need to be considered in order for the reforms to be successful. Reflecting on those regional and urban development issues which are currently not on the table is not in any way unrealistic or far-fetched given the fact that, as we have already seen, when it comes to regional and urban issues, much of what is now in mainstream UK political debates was barely mentioned even three years ago.

7.2   National–regional governance devolution and decentralisation

The UK union is an economic, social and political union (Hazell 2015). It is an asymmetric union of four nations each of which functions economically as a region, but in which 84 per cent of the union population are accounted for by England (Hazell 2015). In economic terms, the UK is an economic union with a single currency, a single integrated market, a single macroeconomic regime, and a single fiscal regime which also acts as a partial stabiliser against private sector fluctuations and imbalances (Hazell 2015). As a social union the formal role of the UK state allows for the mutual pooling of risk and guarantees equal quality and access for all citizens to the welfare state (Brown 2014; Hazell 2015). Other nationwide institutions relating to health, policing, the military, the diplomatic services, technical standards all serve to bind the peoples of the union together in different ways. In addition many other types of UK networks and institutional bindings relate variously to family and corporate ties along with the university system, and chambers of commerce also contribute to building and reinforcing ties across the union. As Hazell (2015) argues, these myriad formal and informal bindings also serve to mutually define the peoples of the UK as a common group. In terms of a political union, unionism is about the maintenance of both nationhood and autonomy and is a result of compromise, adjustment and accommodation (Hazell 2015). The central government in Westminster is sovereign and represents and provides for the whole union in matters such as defence and foreign affairs as well as the economic and social aspects of the union (Hazell 2015). However, the boundaries of sovereignty of Westminster are increasingly blurred both by internal devolved powers and also by various EU laws (Hazell 2015).

Riddell (2015) argues that today the UK Government has to consider carefully and address the links between the different forms of devolution to be offered to the three devolved administrations of Scotland, Wales and Northern Ireland as well as the differing decentralisation powers being offered to English cities and city-regions, beginning with Manchester and what is described by George Osborne as the creation of a 'Northern Powerhouse'. The importance of this consideration arises from the fact that on many levels the UK union is very much at risk, irrespective of whether or not people realise it,[2] and although public awareness of the consequences or outcomes of devolution is very low, as indeed is the awareness of these issues on the part of much of central government (Hazell 2015), it is still essential to ensure that the logic of the governance changes being introduced is as robust as possible.

Otherwise devolution which is driven primarily by short- and medium-term political motives may lead to unintended long-term consequences policy. The rise of nationalism within the UK, within England (Wellings 2012) as well as within Scotland and Wales (Colley 2014), means that a more explicitly territorial constitution may need to be established (Hazell 2015).

Devolution within the UK has so far until mid-2015 been incremental and ad hoc, and a result of fragmented bilateral deals between local governance authorities and central government (Hazell 2015). Yet, in the wake of the 2014 Scottish independence referendum and the 2015 UK general election the transfer of fundamental powers to Scotland and greater calls for powers to be transferred to the other devolved administrations as well as for parts of England (CC 2015) means that in essence the UK will drift de facto towards being rather more of a federal state in all but name (Hazell 2015). Unfortunately, until now, this drift is one in which the devolution reforms have largely taken place without any related reforms on the part of the central institutions of power in London (King 2014). Yet, the lack of any related reforms within central government and in its relations with the rest of the UK are themselves likely to weaken the very central institutions which are intended to hold the union together (King 2014). Indeed, Hazell (2015) argues that part of the problem is that Whitehall lacks the systematic capacity to think about the union, and this is exacerbated by the fact that both within Whitehall and Westminster devolution issues are dealt with in a fragmented manner by almost a dozen different bodies (Hazell 2015). This fragmented and rather piecemeal approach to devolution (Hazell 2015) and spatial and regional issues in general (Hope and Leslie 2009) reflects limited coordination between departments (IfG 2013a, 2014a) and means that there has been little or no real regard to the spillover effects of devolution on the different regions of the UK or on the UK as a whole (Hazell 2015). The UK national civil service displays a strongly federal structure (IfG 2013a, 2014a) while the UK as a whole displays no such system. Ironically, even though the individual civil service departments show varying degrees of geographical coverage (IfG 2014b, 2014c) the difficulties associated with the strongly federal structure of the civil service greatly limit the government's ability to address economic spillovers at the geographical level (NESTA 2014) and also inhibits movements towards even a weak devolved (IfG 2014d) or geographically federal governance structure for the UK. It may be that the results of the 2015 UK general election may change this situation, and that a more systematic and comprehensive approach to spillover effects of devolution will arise, although these eventualities remain to be seen. What is clear is that various alternative routes towards devolution are possible in the short to medium term, but that the actual long-term outcomes of these short-term decisions are still very unclear.

In order to help us consider the possible long-term outcomes of the short- and medium-term decisions, Hazell (2015) sets out the alternative devolution scenarios possible for Scotland, Wales, Northern Ireland and various parts of the English regions and cities, and outlines the opportunities and risks associated with each option. He defines the alternative options as *Devo More*, *Devo Even More* and *Devo Max*. The current situation is defined by Hazell (2015) as *Devo More*, given that as of mid-2015 many devolution and decentralisation commitments have already been made and set in motion such as those involving the Smith Commission in Scotland, the St David's Day process in Wales, and the various City Deals in England (CfC 2013).

Hazell (2015) argues that the impacts of *Devo More* will result in diverging social citizenship across the UK. In particular, Hazell (2015) argues that City Deals are likely to result in much more unfair funding distributions than the previous status quo as they substitute the allocation of funds on the basis of relative need with funding allocations driven primarily by bidding exercises. As such, the current process of city-region decentralisation has been argued to be a 'back door' form of centralisation (Hambleton 2014) in which the terms of decentralisation are characterised by vertical relations between Whitehall and the city-region which are dominated by The Treasury rather than by any real mutual engagement, and with little or no horizontal coordination between regions. The city-regions chosen for the decentralisation of powers, the criteria for the awarding of powers and the details of each individual City Deal will all be decided by ministers in Whitehall resulting in potentially a 'divide and rule' scenario (Hambleton 2014). Meanwhile, what Hazell (2015) defines as *Devo Even More* goes beyond the current scenario and would involve a more comprehensive devolution of spending budgets matched by greater revenue-raising powers which could, for example, include the devolution of corporation tax and employers' national insurance contributions, the decentralisation of business rates and property tax revaluations (Hazell 2015). *Devo Even More* would involve major changes and reductions in the block grant funding system in order to allow for devolved tax-raising powers. Hazell (2015) argues that under *Devo Even More* UK regional inequalities in funding would increase to levels greater than the 1930s, thereby reducing social citizenship as a means of polling and distributing risks and resources.

Finally, Hazell (2015) argues that the option defined as *Devo Max* is one which would deliver full fiscal autonomy for Scotland, whereby Scotland would raise all of its own revenues, only remitting a small portion to central government for shared UK national services. Meanwhile in England there would be devolution of health services and the introduction of local income taxes. Under this scenario the UK would retain responsibility and also bear the risks for monetary policy and the currency in the Sterling area UK market, but without authority over the fiscal policy of Scotland. Across the OECD no sub-national government raises more than half of its total revenue, a level to which Scotland is taken very close to by the Smith Commission recommendations (Hazell 2015), and it is the Smith Commission (2014) framework which is likely to largely underpin the post-2015 UK general election settlement for Scotland. Hazell (2015) argues that under *Devo Max* Scotland faces in-built financial risks in public expenditure and beyond this neither further nor full fiscal devolution are realistic options. As such, Hazell (2015) also argues that rather than being a stable solution, *Devo Max* is more likely to be a staging post to full independence.

It may well be the case that at least in the short to medium term that Scotland moves towards something like the *Devo Even More* scenario or even further towards more of a *Devo Max* situation while Wales, Northern Ireland and the English regions remain with the *Devo More* scenario or also move further to a *Devo Even More* type of settlement. How such a variegated institutional set-up might work remains to be seen, depending on what set of governance arrangements are finally agreed for different UK regions and nations. In recent years various proposals have been put forward for devolution at the local level in England aimed at giving councils or groups of local councils greater powers to integrate the delivery and financing of services (Hazell 2015), the most notable of which is the transfer of budgets and powers to the Greater Manchester Combined Authority. Indeed, there is now a widespread belief in many circles (HoC 2014; RSA 2015; Heseltine 2012) that greater fiscal devolution as part of a wider process of governance decentralisation is likely to be indirectly associated with stronger economic growth (Hazell 2015). At the same time, in the wake of the 2015 UK general election there has been increasing talk or movements towards something more like a federal set of arrangements within the UK governance set-up. On the basis of the experience of other countries such as Australia, Canada, USA and Germany, one of the governance reform options proposed by various commentators is a second upper federal chamber comprised of the nations and all of the regions of the UK (Brown 2014; Macwhirter 2014)[3] as a way of better ensuring a broader and more balanced UK system of representation across the UK, even while allowing for almost total Scottish autonomy within such a federal structure. Yet, Hazell (2015) also argues that federal reform involving an upper house will not suffice to bind the UK union together more securely because the experience of other federal countries suggests that second upper chambers tend to be party chambers first, and only federal chambers, second (Hazell 2015). On the other hand, however, quasi-federal arrangements without out a federal upper chamber, such as in Spain, have also proved to be problematic, while the current upper chamber situation in the UK hardly reflects what might be expected in an ideal national governance model.[4]

In order to help identify the most appropriate and advantageous way forward for the UK governance reforms and their links with economic geography it can be instructive to consider the experience of other countries although such comparisons need to be undertaken carefully. For example, from a UK cultural perspective it may be perceived that the most appropriate comparators are likely to be derived from other common law states. However, the only other democratic countries with common law systems which also have similar highly centralised governance frameworks similar to the UK are New Zealand and Republic of Ireland. Yet, in terms of the size of the population and the economy both of these countries are smaller in size than all but two of the UK's OECD-TL2/EU-NUTS1 large statistical regions, and only half the size of either the Greater London economy or that of the South East region. As such, governance observations from Ireland and New Zealand are of little value when discussing the emerging challenges to develop a UK governance system which is appropriate for addressing the UK's economic geography. In contrast, when it comes to governance and institutional issues, on many levels it is difficult to derive UK-relevant lessons and insights from countries such as Australia, USA and Canada. The USA, Australia and Canada all have federal structures in which the individual states or provinces are very similar in population size to the UK OECD-TL2/EU-NUTS1 large statistical regions. The average size of the individual US states is 6.4 million, of the Australian states is 3.9 million and of the Canadian provinces is 3.5 million. At the same time, and in marked contrast to most of the sub-national units within the UK, each of the US, Canadian and Australian states and provinces have very real governance and financial powers within the federal structure, whereas in the UK only three or possibly four of the OECD-TL2/ EU-NUTS1 large statistical regions have any meaningful governance roles. These federal countries exhibit much stronger bottom-up governance structures than is currently evident anywhere in the UK. Moreover, in terms of geographical size the sub-national governance units in the USA, Canada and Australia are typically similar or larger in area than England or even the whole of the UK.

The major institutional and geographical differences between the UK and the other common law democracies suggests that they provide few meaningful lessons and insights as to how the UK governance system should best evolve in the coming years to respond to the internal regional imbalances. In these terms it may well be the case that more appropriate comparator cases may therefore be derived from observations of other European nations. For the federal nation-states in Europe, the average size of the federal regions of Germany is just over 5 million people, for the federal regions in Belgium it is 3.7 million people, for the Autonomous Communities of Spain it is 2.8 million,[5] for the federal states in Austria is 930,000 and for the cantons in Switzerland is 310,000. In the large country cases within Europe, the individual sub-national federal components are more closely related in both geographical and population terms to the scale of the individual UK regions. In the small federal country cases of Austria and Switzerland the size of the regional governance units is closer to those of the UK county or local government areas while the national government arena is similar in scale to individual UK regions. Importantly, however, even in these smaller federal cases as well as in the larger federal countries, regional government plays a significant and ongoing role in determining the priorities and decision-making of the national government. Given that the UK now appears to be shifting inevitably to some sort of quasi-federal structure in response to Scottish demands, then a broader perspective on these issues suggests that some sort of UK federal arrangement containing elements of these European cases may offer some advantages over insights derived primarily from the common law comparators, especially regarding territorial and spatial issues.

However, again, insights from these comparator cases also need to be treated carefully because while the UK is currently a unitary state, most of the other common law countries such as the USA, Canada, Australia and New Zealand also all have their seats of government in different cities to their most important economic centres. Indeed, this is also true in other federal states such as Germany and Switzerland as well as in non-federal states such as Italy and de facto The Netherlands. This makes these countries significantly different to the UK on yet another governance-economic geography dimension, and therefore insights from other unitary states may also be instructive as well as from federal states. In this regard, even other large unitary states such as France[6] and Japan[7] are much more decentralised than the UK in terms of both public finances (OECD 2013) and also in terms of the strength and role of their regional meso-level governance institutions. Moreover, France in particular is also currently decentralising even further (Hazell 2015). The other main unitary states in the advanced industrialised world are almost all small countries, such as Ireland, Iceland, New Zealand, Portugal, Greece, the Baltic States, Norway, Israel, Hungary and the Czech Republic, and the UK is more centralised than any of these small countries.

The UK appears to be an outlier in its governance structures relative to other countries and also relative to its own internal economic geography. As we saw in Chapter 1, in terms of its internal economic geography the UK is more reminiscent of developing or newly industrialising economies than other advanced economies. Meanwhile, in terms of governance systems it is more reminiscent of small advanced countries rather than large advanced countries. The mismatch between the UK's interregional imbalances and its highly centralised governance system is now increasingly undermining public confidence in the efficacy of the UK. From a constitutional perspective of governance legitimacy, public officials require both the legal and democratic authorisation from the public in order for them to exercise public powers and the rules for this are normally set at a higher national level. Meanwhile, from a local public and community perspective, governance legitimacy and accountability arises from the responsiveness displayed by public officials and their levels of public engagement (Denters *et al.* 2014). If, however, there is perceived to be increasing distance between local and national levels of governance which is also associated with geographical distance from the capital city, as appears to be the case within the UK (LGA 2010), then at the local level many decisions taken nationally become increasingly perceived as being less salient, credible or legitimate (Cash *et al.* 2003) for the local public than those which could be taken more locally. This increasing disconnection between national decisions and local decisions challenges the local relevance of national government and is now at the heart of UK public debates regarding devolution. The result of the increasing public awareness of these mismatches is that the current UK trend towards some form of devolution and decentralisation now appears to be inevitable. Yet, the current city-region devolution arrangements being negotiated are at much smaller scales than the highest levels of sub-national government in most federal states, and in particular at a much smaller scale than the highest levels of sub-national government in other large country federal states. A possible problem, therefore, is that there will be an in-built dysfunctionality in the evolving UK sub-national governance system due to there being too much of a size imbalance between central government, a devolved London governance structure (LFC 2013), and the devolved governance arrangements across the rest of England.

Such imbalances may also arise not just in terms of the size of governance structures, but also the size-distribution and the power-distribution of the sub-national governance structures. Whatever devolution or decentralisation arrangements actually materialise within the UK in the coming years, the rather ad hoc and differing approaches to devolution currently being discussed are likely to lead to an asymmetric pattern of devolution and decentralisation which is a long way from the logic underpinning the fully federal systems in countries such as Germany, USA (Riddell 2015), Australia or most of Canada (Bell 2015). What Scotland is currently being offered is close to the level of federal autonomy enjoyed by Canadian provinces or Swiss cantons[8] while what the other devolved administrations and city-regions are being offered differ significantly. Riddell (2015) therefore suggests that the evolving UK governance system is likely to be much closer in reality to either the special arrangements in Quebec or the quasi-federal arrangements linking the autonomous communities in Spain OECD (2012b).[9] Indeed, the unbalanced population size and economic size of the components of the likely UK sub-national governance pattern reflected by a devolved Scotland, new devolved powers for Wales[10] and Northern Ireland plus the different city-deals (HM Treasury 2015a) looks remarkably similar to the unbalanced structure of Spanish sub-national governance. At the same time, the arguments in this book also suggest that the current relationship between the economics of the different parts of the UK and the national governance system of the UK is already highly dysfunctional due to the enormous mismatches between the economic and institutional arenas, and an increasing awareness of these mismatches is itself driving much of the devolution agenda. Therefore, if the inherent movement towards a quasi-federal system is not to lead to even greater long-run mismatches within the UK it is essential that the underlying internal economic logic of the UK also heavily shapes the logic of the governance reforms. As yet, however, there is little evidence that the devolution agenda, or rather devolution agendas, currently under way in the UK have any coherent logic to them designed to address the complex fiscal and constitutional implications which will automatically arise in the long run from their implementation (Bell 2015).

The arguments and evidence in this book suggest that at best the highly centralised and top-down London-centric UK governance system has wholly failed to help steer the wider UK economy though the surging currents of modern globalisation and to counter or respond to the growing internal imbalances within the UK over the last three or four decades. At worst, the policy-making frameworks and approaches associated with this top-down and London-centric UK governance system have actually contributed to these internal imbalances and inequalities. Therefore, while on the one hand there are currently valid concerns not to move towards an increasingly dysfunctional UK governance system in the coming years, there is also the very real concern not to continue with largely the same system, which in terms of local and regional economic development has at best proved to be non-functioning and at worst is already heavily dysfunctional.

From this broader perspective which links governance to economic development, the evidence and arguments put forward in this book also suggest that the current steps towards enshrining 'English Votes for English Laws' (EVEL)[11] will barely scratch the surface of the underlying economic issues[12] and in the long run these steps could even be counter-productive if in effect these issues are in the short term swept under the carpet of an English proto-parliament. This would be particularly the case if the issues concerning the enormous regional disparities within England are not accompanied by some form of real representation for English regions in national decision-making, such as for example via new meso-level institutions (Cox and Jeffery 2014) or via more formal federal-types of arrangements. This is essential in order to overcome both existing governance anomalies which are now becoming uncovered by the current debates as well avoiding further anomalies, because even within England there are national-regional mismatches in representation and governance which are similar in nature to those associated with the West-Lothian question. These West-Lothian-type anomalies arise from the fact that so many London-specific issues are perceived as being synonymous with national issues. For example, London MPs are able to vote on transport issues in other parts of England but the reverse is not true,[13] and this asymmetry is particularly important given the transport infrastructure disparities between English regions discussed in Chapter 6. If clarity is to be provided and West-Lothian-style anomalies are to be resolved by EVEL, then clarity needs to be provided regarding whether in reality many London-specific investments are indeed fundamentally national or local in nature. As well as transport investments, these issues also apply to many heritage, theatre and educational investments. The test of whether local infrastructure assets or investments are indeed national in nature depends crucially on the scale of the interregional linkages and spillovers associated with these investments. In a top-down highly centralised governance system these questions are all in effect swept under the carpet by being subsumed into the structure of what is ostensibly national polity. If, however, these questions are now again being raised regarding the relationships between Scotland and the rest of the UK, then at least as many similar such questions also arise regarding the relationships between London and the rest of UK. The current ad hoc devolution arrangements have so far failed to address these deeper questions but as devolution and decentralisation proceed, these issues will increasingly emerge. In other words, devolution to English city-regions also means that in the long run resolving many of the governance and interconnection problems within England will become just as important and challenging as addressing the differing issues arising between the administrations in the three devolved regions and central government. Moreover, these interconnections need to be understood not just in terms of infrastructure but also in terms of institutional and fiscal linkages. Devolution may well have profound and greatly differing financial implications for different areas depending on the specifics of the individual devolution agreements and the various city deals. These long-term public finance impacts and implications will depend on the local long-term demographic changes and the local long-term productivity influences, as well as the long-term interregional fiscal agreements which are put in place. As yet, these complex multi-level governance financial issues are hardly being discussed at all in the media, except regarding the case of Scotland. Devolution always involves profound changes in the nature, logic and mechanisms of the institutional connectivity between regions and between the sub-national and national levels of governance. It is therefore essential that an apparently differentiated, nuanced and tailored approach to devolution is in reality not simply a short-term and ad hoc process, and this is ensured if these long-term connectivity issues are considered at all levels and at all stages in the devolution process and negotiations.

7.3   City–region governance: form, function and geography

Until now, almost all of our discussions of devolution have essentially been about top-down trends, involving power moving downwards from national government to sub-national units, whereas there is also potentially a bottom-up agenda to devolution which will be discussed here shortly. However, in terms of space-blind arguments, there are few or no real justifications for such a UK devolution agenda, whereas in terms of the place-based arguments, one major justification for the primarily city-region devolution agenda within the UK is that the UK already has a very heavily urbanised population. As such, both the economic and social challenges facing the UK as well as the economic and social opportunities evident in the UK tend to be heavily concentrated in cities. If governance innovations associated with devolution are able to improve the local and regional economic development environment then the overall scale of these improvements is likely to be much higher if they are focused in these urban contexts. The logic here is that if such initiatives have positive impacts, then within the UK these devolved efforts to engender local institutional re-alignment, to build stronger local and regional policy complementarities, and to enhance local and regional knowledge spillovers and network effects, are likely to have much stronger effects in an urban setting than if they are scattered over wider urban and rural spaces. From a national perspective, a UK urban-centric devolution agenda (CfC 2014a) therefore makes sense on many different levels, such as providing for the concentration of resources, avoiding governance fragmentation and facilitating policy coordination.

At the same time, there are also major arguments for devolution-related actions and systems at the broader regional level. As we have seen throughout this book, the interregional inequalities and the productivity weaknesses within the UK display a very strong core-periphery regional structure. Coordination between city-regions is likely to be critical in arenas such as transport and energy. While some transport and energy-related issues such as commuter transport infrastructure and the energy use of buildings may be regarded as primarily local issues, many transport and energy issues are not in any way confined to specific individual urban arenas. Inter-regional and inter-city connectivity and national and regional energy provision are examples of this. Similarly, major foreign investments in many manufacturing or engineering sectors do not consider individual urban areas as the appropriate domain with respect to which their location and investment decisions are made. While a functional urban area may make sense for certain types of policy decision-making, relating for example to commuter transport facilities and services, for many other policy decisions a functional urban area makes little sense for policy-making. In addition, exactly how the devolution-related efforts to foster large-city growth can spill over to the UK's large number of mid-sized cities (Bolton and Hildreth 2013) as well as some of the economically weaker small towns and suburbs[14] is as yet unclear.

These different spatial logics still pose real challenges for the optimal design of a more devolved UK institutional and governance system and, as we have seen above, it is still not clear exactly how the overall UK-wide devolution agenda will evolve. Yet, given that greater city-region devolution appears to be definitely on the UK political agenda it is useful to consider the international evidence on metropolitan urban governance and to use this evidence to throw light on what the likely optimal city-region governance arrangements for the UK will be, given the specifics of the UK's existing spatial and institutional arrangements. As well as devolving power downwards from Whitehall to the individual city-region the current English city-region devolution agenda as well as the Welsh governance challenges[15] also involve the upward pooling of power and resources from local authorities to combined city-region governance bodies. As such, devolution in the UK also involves a trend towards greater meso-level governance arrangements rather than simply a move towards localism. Jessop (2000) argues that these meso-level governance arrangements need to be flexible and adaptive across different geographies, jurisdictions and political relations (Jones 2009) for different agendas, what he terms 'meta-governance'. As we have seen, it is in terms of these meso-level governance arrangements that the UK has been severely lacking in comparison to other advanced countries. The worldwide evidence on the characteristics and efficacy of these types of top-down and bottom-up governance integration processes comes from the recent OECD (2015a) survey on the nature and forms of metropolitan urban governance across OECD cities and countries, and the following sections draw heavily on this material. This material is very pertinent to the UK case in which city-regions are increasingly seen as an important scale at which devolution is likely to operate on various dimensions.

In terms of bottom-up governance coordination, the OECD (2015a) evidence shows that city governance coordination between intra-urban municipalities is essential on many levels because the decisions in one municipality will often have spillover impacts in other municipalities (OECD 2015a). Similarly, coordination helps to ensure that decisions are made at the right scale. The result is that statistically, greater urban fragmentation is associated with lower urban productivity. A doubling of the number of municipalities within a city reduces productivity by 6 per cent, and in some cases the adverse effects of fragmentation associated with misaligned incentives and coordination failures (Cheshire and Gordon 1996; Cheshire and Magrini 2009) are sufficiently severe as to fully offset any potential agglomeration-related productivity gains (Ahrend *et al.* 2014a). On the other hand a city-wide governance body can reduce this penalty by up to one-half (Ahrend *et al.* 2014a; OECD 2015a). In other words, bottom-up governance coordination from the lowest levels upwards is essential in many cases to realise the efficiency and effectiveness benefits of the provision of public goods.

Adjusting governance systems is also essential over time as the spatial and economic context evolves. As cities grow they tend to naturally become more administratively fragmented because new municipalities and localities develop and as new flows of commuting emerge (OECD 2015a). Yet, the types of governance fragmentation which are typically observed across the OECD reflect not only the geographical fragmentation which is associated with different bodies being responsible for policy decisions in different intra-urban spatial areas, but also to different sectoral areas of policy or service provision. Moreover, the challenges associated with fragmentation are further complicated by the fact that the spatial and sectoral dimensions of governance rarely map neatly onto each other. In other words, different services or areas of decision-making often display a different geographical logic regarding the spatial areas concerned. Overlapping and lack of alignment are therefore common features of fragmentation, with multiple actors and decision-makers responsible for often uncoordinated areas of responsibility. The scale of these trends means that nowadays, across the OECD countries, there is a widespread and almost systematic mismatch between urban socio-economic areas and administrative jurisdictions (OECD 2015a). Moreover, these mismatches and overlaps are endemic even in the case of countries which are typically ranked as displaying the highest quality institutional and governance systems.

Generally speaking, the larger is the city the larger is the number of intra-urban municipalities, intra-urban decision-making bodies and institutional actors, all defending their interests, with cities such as Chicago and Paris displaying well over a thousand different policy-making bodies, actors and institutions (OECD 2015a). The number of actors involved and the typical lack of sectoral-spatial alignment of their roles makes administrative reorganisation for better urban governance all the more difficult, and requires public vision and political will. As such, while the need to develop coordinated urban governance systems operating at the right level with the right levers of power is always there from an economic point of view but its success often depends on the willingness and support of central government (OECD 2015a). This issue is currently very pertinent in the UK with the move towards 'city deals'. Devolution downwards from the Westminster to the city-region will also involve addressing lower level institutional fragmentation within the city-region domain and highlights the importance of building new bottom-up coordination systems. A difficulty here, however, is that to move towards a genuine devolution setting will require that the bottom-up coordination agenda will need to address the inherited overlapping fragmentation and the fact that the existing governance systems will not easily map onto each other. In other words top-down devolution also involves the bottom-up harmonising, simplifying, rationalising of myriad different local governance and institutional systems.

There have been, and are, many ongoing attempts in all OECD countries to try to improve urban governance systems. The 1960s and 1970s was a period when many OECD countries implemented urban governance reforms, and the UK followed this pattern with the creation of several new metropolitan counties. The 1980s was a period of few or no governance reforms across OECD economies, while greater efforts at governance reforms were again evident from the 1990s onwards. In particular, since the millennium there have been more urban governance reforms across OECD countries than in any earlier era (OECD 2014a, 2015a). In some cases these involve redefining administrative boundaries by merging municipalities, while in most cases they involve allowing existing municipalities to partner for certain purposes within an existing institutionalised set-up (OECD 2015a). However, the result is that at present out of the 263 OECD metropolitan urban areas of over 500,000 some 31 per cent of OECD urban metropolitan areas have no metropolitan governance body at all, 51 per cent have a metropolitan governance body without any regulatory powers, and only 18 per cent have a metropolitan governance body with regulatory powers (Ahrend *et al.* 2014b; OECD 2015a). Moreover, for those areas which do have metropolitan governance bodies of any sort, the three areas in which metropolitan governance bodies are most closely active are regional economic development, transport and spatial planning (OECD 2014a, 2015a) with 70–80 per cent of metropolitan governance bodies actively engaging in these fields. On a much smaller level between 25 per cent and 35 per cent of metropolitan governance bodies are involved in arenas such as waste disposal, water provision, sewerage provision, culture, leisure and tourism, while only 15 per cent are involved with energy provision (OECD 2014a, 2015a).

These observations are insightful for the current UK city-region devolution debates. The major arguments advocating city-region devolution in the

UK are almost all related to economic development including transport and spatial planning. City-region devolution in England in particular is not being advocated by either central or local government primarily for reasons related to waste disposal, water and sewerage management, energy provision or even leisure and tourism. Such issues are of course important, but they are sub-sumed within the broader overall economic development agenda, and this is an arena in which cross-jurisdictional metropolitan-wide governance bodies are most common amongst OECD countries. As we have seen in Chapters 3, 4 and 5, it is clear that the UK's cities are rather different to each, or at the very least there are different groups of cities within the UK. The movement towards differentiated and tailored 'city deals' may therefore suggest that different metropolitan-wide and city-region-wide governance arrangements with different roles and responsibilities may evolve in different city-regions, depending on the geography, the major challenges being addressed, and the existing lower level institutional fragmentation to be overcome. Again, obser-vation of the OECD-wide evidence on these matters is instructive.

The OECD (2014a, 2015a) classifies metropolitan-wide governance bod-ies into four major types according to how stringent they are in institutional terms. The least stringent type is characterised by informal or 'soft' coord-ination based on information sharing and consultation activities, but with little or no actual enforcement tools and with limited engagement with citi-zens (OECD 2014a, 2015a). Across the OECD these bodies account for some 52 per cent of metropolitan governance arrangements (Ahrend *et al.* 2014b; OECD 2015a). The second least stringent type is the *inter-municipal body*, which is often established in order to share the costs and responsibilities for a single purpose or a small number of purposes. Some of these inter-municipal bodies may also include arrangements for involving other sectoral bodies or higher levels of government (OECD 2014a, 2015a). Across the OECD these bodies account for some 24 per cent of metropolitan governance arrange-ments and cities displaying these systems typically have populations of the order of 2 million people (Ahrend *et al.* 2014b; OECD 2015a). The second most highly stringent form of metropolitan governance comprises the for-mation of a *supra-municipal authority* which is a layer of governance above the individual urban municipalities. This can be created either via a directly elected metropolitan government or by higher levels of government setting down a non-elected structure, and the average size of the cities which have a supra-municipal authority is 2.5 million people (OECD 2014a, 2015a). The success of these supra-municipal authority arrangements typically depends on the extent of municipal involvement and the financial capacity of the body (OECD 2014a, 2015a). Across the OECD these bodies account for some 16 per cent of metropolitan governance arrangements (Ahrend *et al.* 2014b; OECD 2015a). Finally, the most stringent form of metropolitan gov-ernance is that where a city is granted a special status of a *metropolitan city* giving them the same status as the next upper level of government (OECD 2014a, 2015a). Across the OECD these bodies account for only 8 per cent of metropolitan governance arrangements and the average size of a metropolitan city is just under 4 million people (Ahrend *et al.* 2014b; OECD 2015a). Meanwhile, across the OECD the cities which display no metropolitan governance arrangements are typically smaller cities of the order of 1.5 million people (Ahrend *et al.* 2014b; OECD 2015a).

Informal and 'soft' metropolitan governance arrangements including supra-municipal authorities generally involve the very modest financial commitments. Across the OECD informal and 'soft' institutional arrangements typically display budgets of just US$3 per metropolitan area inhabitant. The OECD evidence suggests that the very modest budgets associated with the loosest forms of metropolitan governance can be either an attractive or debilitating feature (OECD 2015a). On the one hand, the potential attractiveness associated with governance reforms with small budgets is that stakeholders will have fewer fears that their own budgets will be significantly and adversely affected, and as such they may be willing to participate in the new governance arrangements. On the other hand, the small budgets may lead to an inability to effect any substantial economic or social changes, and as such these concerns will tend to limit serious engagement on the part of key stakeholders. In contrast, much higher budgets tend to be evident in the case of inter-municipal authorities. Across the OECD, inter-municipal authorities, which tend to be tasked with one or a small number of specific roles, typically exhibit budgets of US$184 per inhabitant. Budgets are in part related to tasks and roles and as such are not simply related to level of stringency of the governance arrangements. Even the second most stringent form of metropolitan governance arrangement, the supra-municipal authorities, typically only display budgets of US$14 per urban inhabitant (OECD 2015a). However, all three of these types of governance and coordination arrangements are dwarfed by the budgets of metropolitan cities, which across the OECD average some US$2759 per urban inhabitant (OECD 2015a).

In the case of the UK, the current city-region devolution agenda, which is primarily evident in England, most closely reflects the metropolitan city logic, which is the most stringent form of city governance evident across the OECD. However, a major difference between the UK and the OECD-wide evidence is that the size of the individual 'city deals' in the UK relates to much smaller population units than the average for the OECD. Across the OECD metropolitan cities with significantly devolved powers that are equivalent to the next higher tier of sub-national government are typically of the order of 4 million people, which is much closer in population size to the individual UK OECD-TL2/EU-NUTS1 regions, than it is to the city-region areas which are currently involved in 'city deal' discussions with The Treasury. Apart from London, the next two largest city-regions of Manchester and Birmingham are of the order of half of the average OECD size for these types of sub-national governance arrangements, while the rest of the UK city-regions are no larger than one-third or even one-quarter of the typical OECD size. Indeed, within the UK the size of the city-regions which are being offered 'city deals' are typically of the size of OECD cities which tend to have no metropolitan governance arrangements at all.

Again these observations raise the question as to whether city-region devolution within England is currently taking place at the appropriate spatial and institutional level. Within England at least, the proposed city-regions offered individual 'city deals' are intended to be the highest level of UK sub-national government below national government, although many parts of England are as yet not being offered such deals. As such, apart from London the largest of the proposed English city-regions being offered 'city deals' are smaller than the average size of the individual Spanish autonomous communities while the majority of the proposed UK city-region governance units are similar in size to the individual federal areas of Austria. Of all the large population OECD countries Spain has the smallest average population size of the top tier of sub-national governance units, while Austria has the second smallest top tier governance units within the OECD. These are the two federal-type country comparators most closely reflecting the population governance-geography institutional structure that is currently evolving within England at least. Meanwhile, in population terms the average size of the UK's three devolved regions is slightly smaller than the average size of the individual federal areas of Canada, Belgium and Australia and somewhat larger than the individual autonomous communities of Spain. Even amongst the other large unitary OECD states, which are already far more decentralised than the UK, the top tier sub-national governance units are on average much larger than most of the individual city-regions discussing 'city deals'. These various OECD-wide observations of metropolitan urban areas, federal areas and governance systems raises the spectre of an inbuilt national-regional governance dysfunctionality emerging within the UK due to imbalances in population size and representation at the national levels. The size of the UK's three devolved administrations generally reflects what from international experience appears to be broadly a workable size while the population size of the individual English city-regions currently being offered devolution appears from the international evidence to be far too small.

This issue of the appropriate size of the highest tier of sub-national governance unit is also related to the specific economic development role to be played by this particular tier of governance. As Clark *et al.* (2010) point out, local government fulfils broadly four distinct roles, namely: the representation of citizens in the actions of the elected officials; the provision and delivery of household, personal and amenity-related activities and services; the regulation activities associated with the provision and enforcement of guidelines necessary for maintaining social order and community wellbeing; and finally, the fostering or development and investment activities. Clark *et al.* (2010) argue that the fourth role of sub-national government, namely the stimulation of development and investment, is fundamentally a 'market facing' role which is quite different in nature to the other three roles which are primarily 'citizen facing' in nature. Whereas the three 'citizen facing' roles operate within a defined sub-national government geographical area, which is sometimes at the level of city and sometimes at a sub-urban municipality level, the economic development and investment activities operate with different markets, geographies, time frames, partners, financing, stakeholders, tools and audiences (Clark *et al*. 2010). As a result these more complex and varied activities require different structures and organisational arrangements from the other three roles (Clark *et al*. 2010), often involving different vertical and horizontal governance relationships (OECD 2010) which extend well beyond simply the individual urban area, and undertaken with regard to very different time frames.

At present, the importance of organising the devolution of governance and public-goods delivery activities at the level of a functional urban regional (FUR) scale has become something of a mantra in UK policy circles. Yet, there is a large and long-standing operations research-based literature on the optimal siting of urban public facilities (ReVelle 1987) and nowhere in this literature is there a theorem or even a principle that FUR is necessarily the most appropriate spatial scale at which to implement public investments. The reason is that it depends on the problem at hand. For example, urban employment-commuting patterns may be the best spatial guide for organising intra-urban transportation systems but they are not necessarily a good guide as to the optimal travel behaviour of hospital patients or of care workers. Nor are they likely to be of much use when discussing many energy-related issues. Moreover, these issues become most complex when economic development questions are being addressed. In particular, the question of what are the most appropriate institutional and governance structures for promoting economic development and investment in the UK's city-regions is further complicated by the fact that the geography of the individual UK city-regions is rarely self-contained. While a small number of UK city-regions such as London and Bristol can be considered to be primarily monocentric spatial systems, the cities in the regions of the North West, North East, Yorkshire and Humberside, West Midlands and East Midlands together form city-systems which are largely polycentric. Yet, in terms of governance structures for different economic development and investment activities and purposes, this creates significant challenges.[16]

The insights from the OECD-wide evidence suggest that in such polycentric contexts the most common form of institutional arrangements is actually the least stringent type of governance characterised by informal or 'soft' coordination based on information sharing and consultation activities, but with little or no actual enforcement tools and with limited engagement with citizens (OECD 2015a). In the UK case this poses a major challenge within these polycentric regional settings because while the imperative for stringent long-term coordination and cooperation processes across jurisdictions is critical in areas such as transport, energy and inward investment, the requisite governance and institutional settings involved in city deals are far more suited to the largely self-contained challenges typically facing a single monocentric city context. While individual city deals are being implemented it is therefore unclear exactly how agendas such as a 'Northern Powerhouse' are to be undertaken unless some form of supra-municipal body is also to be set up to coordinate the economic development and investment agendas of the individual city-regions. Most Local Enterprise Partnerships (LEPs) are largely incapable of playing such a role as their institutional capacity is far too limited (Pike *et al.* 2015) and also because they do not neatly map onto the requisite geographical areas. As such, exactly what form such inter-municipal or supra-municipal bodies will take in each regional context and regarding each specific issue remains an open question. Moreover, exactly how citizens' participation and engagement is to be facilitated in such cases in order to ensure public accountability in this cross-jurisdictional inter-urban context is also as yet undefined.

One possible response to these complex economic development and investment issues is that the current individual city-region 'city deals' are in reality primarily focused only on upgrading the first three 'citizen facing' roles of sub-national government,[17] including the provision of health and social care services (IPPR 2014a), crime prevention, education, local transport (LGG 2010) and amenities services (LGA 2013a). If this is indeed the case, then the institutional and governance arrangements framing the 'market facing' economic development and investment roles of sub-national government still remain an open question. This is particularly so following the replacement of the regional development agencies (RDAs) with LEPs. Indeed, the lack of clarity on these matters, and particularly as they relate to the inter-urban and region-wide coordination and connectivity challenges associated with transport, energy and inward investment, remains a serious concern. If, in reality, the types of economic development and investment activities discussed here still remain largely the prerogative of central government, then this reopens the question as to what exact purpose is being served by the forms of English devolution being pursued?

As well as the issue of size of the top tier of sub-national governance and also the particular economic development and investment roles to be played by this governance tier, there are also important questions for the evolution of the current UK institutional set-up which are related to the varied nature of the sub-national governance arrangements being implemented. As the OECD (2015a) makes clear, identifying the most appropriate urban and regional governance arrangements is ultimately a political and social choice which is also very much dependent on the existing institutional, economic, geographical and political context (OECD 2015a). However, there are three common challenges which must always be addressed in these choices, namely: the challenge to be able to coordinate policy horizontally and vertically across different tiers and jurisdictions of government; the challenge to act institutionally and financially in terms of staff budgets, financing structure and power; and the challenge to be perceived as legitimate and to develop trust and credibility with citizens, with the private sector, civil society and with other levels, tiers and arenas of government (OECD 2015a). These three challenges reflect the potential objectives to be met and the possible tools to be used to meet these objectives. At the same time, these three challenges also reflect the perceptions by citizens (OECD 2015a) of the salience, credibility and legitimacy (Cash *et al.* 2003) of the proposed institutional and governance responses. Building trust and engagement on the part of citizens is generally regarded as being critical in order for governance reforms to be successful (OECD 2001a, 2001b, 2009c, 2011c), but as well as accountability and transparency, this also implies that the objectives of the institutional reforms are regarded as being both realistic and that the proposed governance systems are appropriate for the challenges to be addressed. Evidence suggest that citizens are often happier where governance coordination works well. For example, both urban sprawl tends to be lower and citizens' satisfaction with urban transport systems tends to be higher in cities with a metropolitan governance body in comparison with those that do not have such bodies (OECD 2015a).[18] Yet, the OECD-wide experience suggests that even if coordination is indeed in the public interest, the need for coordination between municipalities and different governance bodies can be undermined by local free riding, misaligned incentives, asymmetric information and local principal-agent problems. In the UK not all interested parties are automatically on board with the devolution processes (Carter 2015) and finding ways to overcome such resistance will be essential if city-region devolution processes are to be successful.

Resistance to the devolution agenda may arise from within the very local arena due to the fact that the scaling-up and merging of powers to a combined meso-level of governance implies responsibility and jurisdictional changes which may change the local political composition and control and also reduce power at the very local level (IfG 2014d). Resistance from the public arises from general scepticism about politicians, issues of local identity and control, and also a lack of awareness of the potential benefits of devolution (IfG 2014d). Therefore, in order to overcome these barriers the devolution agenda has to be sufficiently large, comprehensive, at an appropriate spatial scale, it must allow for the strengthening of local governance accountability and competences, and it must engage the citizens in major choices (IfG 2014d). At present, however, there is a sense of urgency[19] for the overall architecture of the individual city-region governance devolution packages to be aligned with the 2015 spending review (HM Treasury 2015b). Yet, while speed can be an important element in building momentum into the institutional reforms process, it is essential that speed does not mean haste. On the one hand, the devolution agenda will be undermined if the public perceive that it is being primarily used for implementing nationally determined top-down public sector funding cutbacks[20] rather than genuinely facilitating local development possibilities and increasing accountability in response to local citizens' preferences. Indeed, there are real fears in some quarters that devolution is simply being used as a means to implement cuts more effectively without central government facing all of the blame.[21] On the other hand, the evidence throughout this book suggests that superficial critiques[22] of the 'Northern Powerhouse' agenda which argue that these initiatives will simply be an expensive waste of resources because it is fundamentally educational and entrepreneurial inequalities which cause the north–south divide wholly misunderstand the depth and complexity of the factors leading to interregional differences. In general, most interested observers believe that the city-region devolution agenda and the Northern Powerhouse agenda do indeed offer real economic development possibilities if they are properly funded, focused on long-term investments, and delivered with real local and regional autonomy in mind.

While the governance devolution agenda has received widespread private sector as well as public sector backing it will still face different forms of resistance from various quarters. In terms of trust and public participation, evidence from across the OECD suggests that metropolitan governance reforms often face public resistance from residents who fear losing out from the reforms (OECD 2015a). Indeed, across the OECD trust in local government is much higher in small cities of below 0.5 million people than it is for cities of between 0.5 million and 2 million people (OECD 2015b), with the European rankings of citizens' perceptions of quality of life in cities being dominated by small cities. On the other hand, above 2 million people trust in local government falls markedly (OECD 2015b). Curiously, many of the new city-region governance devolution arrangements emerging in the UK are being implemented at scales where public trust is seen to be the lowest, and this is likely to engender resistance. There are also differences in the level of citizen satisfaction and trust across various urban governance dimensions. London has the highest level of citizens' satisfaction with urban transportation facilities of any large UK city (European Union 2013), whereas it has the lowest levels of healthcare satisfaction (European Union 2013). In contrast, Newcastle has the highest local healthcare satisfaction with the lowest levels of satisfaction with transportation systems (European Union 2013). If citizens' satisfaction with the status quo is high then there may well be different forms of resistance to different reforms on the grounds that the system does not need to be reformed. Devolutionary reforms to Newcastle's transport system or to London's healthcare system may make much more sense in terms of priorities than reforms across the board.

Birmingham is argued to have suffered from over-centralisation and poor management[23] while Manchester ranks in the top 10 per cent of European cities in terms of the public satisfaction with its administrative services (European Union 2013). Such trust gives good grounds for Manchester to take on much higher level governance roles for its citizens. Yet, why exactly the integration of health and care services should be a cornerstone of the Manchester devolution settlement is not at all clear. Rather surprisingly to most analysts, commentators and observers of the governance debates, the headlines about devolution arrangements in Greater Manchester are currently dominated by health and social care, rather than about economic development.[24] While better integration of such services often makes sense at a city-region level

(OECD 2015c),[25] the impetus for UK devolution and governance reforms has been overwhelmingly driven by concerns regarding economic development[26] rather than by healthcare issues. The major risks of governance devolution reforms being spearheaded by healthcare reforms are twofold. First, health and social care are politically charged agendas and the reality of politics and the 24-hour media society that we live in implies a tendency for these issues to overshadow much longer-term but at least as important matters relating to transport and economic development. Second, whether devolution of health and social care is fiscally viable in the long run depends on the relationship between demographic shifts, and in particular the local rate of societal ageing, and productivity growth of the local working age population. However, as yet these issues seem to be largely absent in the current devolution debates.

Societal ageing has major long-term fiscal consequences on devolved governance administrations due to the increasing long-run demands for health and social care services associated with an ageing society (OECD 2012a, 2015c). The ability of the local economy to provide for such services also depends on the long-run demographics and productivity of the working age population. In regions facing the in-migration of older, wealthier and higher income groups primarily for reasons of leisure and amenities, the cost of providing services for the elderly are mitigated by the fact that to a large extent the in-migrants are able to access these services in the private or quasi-private sectors. In contrast, in regions facing large outflows of young people seeking work elsewhere, these outflows will mean that such localities are not only ageing relatively more rapidly than other regions but also the growth in size and productivity of the local workforce will be hampered. For the long-run provision of health and social care services this is a toxic combination. In contrast, cities enjoying large inflows of young and highly skilled workers will exhibit a population which is ageing relatively slowly and a local workforce whose size and productivity growth will be consistently stronger. This relatively benign combination allows a city to better respond to its own health and social care needs. These critical issues and the implications of differential demographic shifts for the long-term viability of devolved city-region governance arrangements have been barely discussed at all in the current UK city-region arrangements and debates. This is all the more surprising because the differential population growth and ageing trajectories across UK cities and towns have been discussed in detail for more than a decade (ODPM 2006a, 2006b, 2006c). In particular, as we have seen in Chapters 2 and 3, the population and demographic shifts are relatively more adverse for large cities outside of the south of England than for either smaller towns or large cities in southern England (ODPM 2006a, 2006b, 2006c). Although many northern regions and cities again started to enjoy population growth in the last 15 years due primarily to immigration, it is unlikely that the UK will again experience such a surge in immigrant inflows. The long-term demographic prognosis for these cities is still much weaker than southern cities and regions and therefore in these northern city-regions the overwhelming priority for devolution arrangements should be regarding economic development, and not health and social care activities. For southern cities and regions including London, healthcare would indeed appear to be a possible priority for devolution deals.

At the same time, resistance to governance devolution reforms is also possible from central government actors who also fear such losses. Resistance to devolution from the centre arises from the fact that central government lacks trust in sub-national government competence or accountability (IfG 2014d), persuading other ministers to cede power is very difficult, and central government can always reorganise local government and re-centralise at whim. As a result of such top-down resistance central government departments may be tempted to hive off managerially difficult or politically toxic portfolios while keeping centralised less problematic portfolios. In reality, in a highly centralised country such as the UK any movement towards devolved power will always be primarily a top-down process, with HM Treasury in the position to decide exactly what form and mode of devolution is acceptable in each case. In other words the default case remains a centralised top-down governance system and local city-regional government bodies have to propose and argue the competence grounds on which power should be devolved. Yet, although realpolitik means that such a suggestion is entirely unrealistic, an alternative negotiation approach would be for the default case for devolution competence to be that of devolution, and for the Treasury to have to argue the case to maintain centralised control (Diamond and Carr-West 2015). Although this is politically infeasible it actually raises a very fundamental point. If the primary objective of city-region governance devolution is the long-run enhancement of local economic development then as we have seen throughout this book the Treasury's performance on this issue with regard to the cities and regions outside of London and its hinterland regions has been at best very poor, and more likely extremely poor. A few moments of reflection serve to demonstrate that if the default position of devolution negotiations were indeed devolution, then it would be very difficult to think of any cases where the Treasury could successfully argue for continued centralisation, except in the case of southern cities and regions. Fear of this very point is also likely to be a reason why the devolutionary negotiations will in the end be more top-down rather than bottom-up, and such a top-down process will therefore engender different forms of resistance to devolution than bottom-up resistance.

As well as both bottom-up and top-down resistance to governance reforms, there will also be resistance from those who have concerns about losses of political accountability and governance legitimacy (Cash *et al.* 2003; OECD 2015a), not to mention fears of increased 'red tape' and bureaucracy. In order to counter such fears, citizen and civic participation is often encouraged in these types of bodies. Therefore, in order to ensure both accountability and institutional fitness for purpose the role of elected officials is often seen as being critical (Barber 2013; Bogdanor 2012). However, the interaction between democratic processes and the institutional-governance interface is not always smooth, and the UK is no exception here.[27] Across the OECD some 55 per cent of metropolitan governance bodies are comprised of elected officials such as mayors, although only 11 per cent are directly elected themselves, and these typically correspond to the most stringent forms of governance such as supra-municipal authorities or metropolitan cities (OECD 2015a). In terms of civic society, however, across the OECD only 9 per cent of metropolitan governance bodies involve any formal representation on the part of the private sector or civil society, and where such representation is evident it tends to be in those bodies with the fewest responsibilities (OECD 2015a).

Ironically as such, while the more stringent forms of city governance are associated with direct democratic representation, at the same time, the governance bodies with the greatest responsibilities tend to display the lowest levels of private sector, civil society and citizen representation. In other words, although modern theories of governance tend to emphasise the importance of stakeholder engagement and citizen participation in ensuring the success of local, urban and regional policy-making, the more that powers and responsibility are devolved downwards, the less widespread and varied is the citizen and stakeholder engagement and the more that these responsibilities remain within the public sector and political arenas. Overcoming these trade-offs between responsibility, engagement and accountability is likely to be difficult and finding the right balance in the new devolved arrangements will be a challenge. In order to overcome these various problems and to foster cooperation and coordination at the right levels the two major approaches which have been advocated on the basis of both analyses and widespread international development experience are the use of contractual arrangements and financial transfers (OECD 2004, 2007, 2008, 2015a). However, OECD-wide evidence also suggests that the use of contractual arrangements and financial transfers is most successful if also carried out in conjunction with responding to five key needs: the need to identify concrete metropolitan projects to foster cooperation; the need to build a sense of ownership on the part of all stakeholders; the need to ensure reliable sources of financing; the need to provide incentives and finance for compromises; the need to implement monitoring and evaluation mechanisms. In the case of the UK each of these key needs will be evident in the city-region devolution challenges facing each combined metropolitan urban authority seeking a tailored city deal.

More importantly, however, raising these issues makes it clear that in the UK context many of the key questions currently remain largely unanswered and many issues remain unresolved regarding the nature, form and purpose of city-region devolution. Indeed, in the case of the UK devolution arrangements, even beyond the questions of scale and structure discussed above, there are still questions remaining such as whether city-region and mayoral devolution deals should be subject to local referenda, whether more or less power should be vested in city-regions, and whether some forms of fiscal devolution is possible or advisable (Harrison 2015). The draft bill allowing for city-region devolution in England and Wales[28] which is currently progressing through the House of Commons[29] makes it very clear that while city-region devolution is an individually negotiated process ultimately city-region devolution is still primarily a top-down process. If this is the case, and city deals are also meant to be tailored to local context, then it becomes difficult at this stage to identify the likely themes which will be common to all city deals and those themes which are likely to differ. The small size of the city-regions seeking city deals also suggests that their relative bargaining power regarding the specific terms of the individual city deal is likely to be very limited. In particular, in the end it is likely to be Whitehall which primarily decides on the size and purpose of the devolved budgets.

The structure of this negotiation logic also raises another long-term issue. We also know from the discussions above and in the previous chapter that widespread shifts towards devolution will also change the overall governance structure and logic of the UK. In particular, any movement towards city-region fiscal devolution is likely to change the role and relative scale of interregional transfers. Following the insights of Chapter 5 and Chapter 6, it may be the case that calls for more fiscal autonomy for London (LFC 2013), if granted, may adversely affect the overall budgets available for other city-regions. For example, possible local revenue and fiscal schemes aimed at incentivising local development such as the retention of business rates,[30] 'earn back' or TIF (tax incremental financing) systems (LFC 2013) are being considered in various arenas. Yet, the efficacy of such schemes also depends on the negotiated baseline budgets and targets, so the overall impacts of such initiatives, if and where they are implemented, on the national system of interregional transfers which currently operates are as yet unknown. Trench (2013) argues that even with devolved revenue raising powers block grants from central to devolved administrations still need to be based on needs rather than on fiscal equalisation. Yet, the unknown effects of devolution on these fiscal transfers become even more significant if the range of city deals actually implemented are heterogeneous, as looks likely.

Again, these issues bring us to the regional questions raised in Chapter 2 and also in Chapters 5 and 6. The economic geography problem of the UK is a core-periphery issue of which the varying urban performance is simply the most obvious manifestation. However, as has already been discussed throughout this book, the problem is a regional and interregional one, and not simply an urban issue. At the interregional level, an insight from Spain is that the national governance system comes under severe internal pressure if the financial relationships between the national and the sub-national governance units vary too much. The UK's governance system as it currently appears to be evolving is moving towards an institutional set-up in which there is a fully devolved autonomous region (Scotland), two quite different but heavily devolved regions (Wales and Northern Ireland), numerous small town and rural areas with no devolution, plus various heterogeneous city-regions each with limited devolution and with differentiated degrees of decentralisation over specific arenas. Of these, one such city-region, namely London, already has enormous economic advantages over all other UK city-regions, not least of which is scale, so any interregional economic imbalances may be further exacerbated by greater city-region fiscal devolution. Finally, there is as yet little or no indication regarding how the larger city-regions or city-region corridors (Grant Thornton 2014) or devolved administrations (Shaw *et al.* 2013; Henderson *et al.* 2015) are to relate to the smaller second and third tier towns and cities (ResPublica 2015) in their hinterlands (ICA 2015), areas which across Europe are nowadays playing an increasingly important economic role (Dijkstra *et al.* 2013, 2016; SGPTD 2013). Part of the issue here is that the precise objectives of city deals are not entirely clear, and in particular, the role played by city deals in fostering economic development. Overall, therefore, the long-term financial and fiscal implications of the current UK-wide devolution trends including the current city-regional arrangements are hard to predict, although some institutional and fiscal imbalances inadvertently already appear to be being built into the UK's governance system. As such, it is difficult to see how some rather dysfunctional governance relationships limiting inter-urban and region-wide cooperation and coordination can be avoided, unless some additional region-wide governance arrangements are also put in place.

This takes us back to earlier discussions. As has been the case for most of the last three decades, a major weakness in the UK's evolving institutional system appears to be a lack of any real national-regional governance coordination system which encourages core-periphery economic linkages and spillovers. While bottom-up local cooperation and coordination appear to be improving with the advent of combined authorities which are seeking city-region deals, the inter-urban cooperation at the regional levels appears to be largely absent, except where the regional level of governance already exists, as is the case in the three devolved administrations plus to some extent Greater London. The potential to build scale and synergies in many different economic development arenas would appear to be critical for northern cities, as reflected in the 'Northern Powerhouse' agenda. However, such an agenda requires coordination and financing systems at a pan-regional level linking different metropolitan urban regions. Many of the same cooperation, coordination, transparency and accountability challenges facing individual metropolitan and city-regions described above will also be evident at the inter-urban and regional levels. Yet, given heterogeneous city deals along with the movement towards individual city-region mayors in which political accountability is framed at the city-region level, it becomes difficult to see how inter-urban region-wide cooperation and coordination will work in practice. Even more importantly, it becomes entirely unclear how inter-urban region-wide cooperation and coordination with national government will take place.

As already mentioned, individually negotiated city deals are likely to be primarily top-down affairs. However, in the type of quasi-federal system to which the UK is currently drifting, primarily top-down relations between central government and any possible coordinated inter-urban and region-wide actions make little or no sense in the long run. In federal systems the governance and institutional arrangements are genuinely two-way with the state-level entities having significant power to facilitate intra-state or inter-state coordination and cooperation initiatives. Given the core-periphery structure of the UK economy the need to develop such region-wide actions and initiatives as well as urban actions within the context of an overall re-framed interregional set-up requires that in the long run more genuinely federal types of governance arrangements are likely to be required. Otherwise, it is hard to see how in the long run the evolving governance system will avoid coming under constant internal pressures leading to systemic institutional dysfunctionality.

The current UK-wide devolution agenda amongst the four constituent nations is one in which there are significant governance imbalances across the system while the city-region devolution agenda within England and Wales is focused on sub-national governance units which are very small by OECD standards. At the same time, the rationale for English city-region devolution is still largely unclear when discussed in the light of the various inter-urban or interregional connectivity issues. In particular, this lack of clarity is very marked in terms of the links between local governance devolution and the broader range of economic development and investment activities which extend beyond individual city-region jurisdictions such as transport, energy and inward investment. International evidence suggests that city governance and city-region governance are typically quite different issues and some form of regional governance authority is still required (Slack and Coté 2014). Greater city-region devolution alongside increasing devolution in the three devolved administrations may help to provide a better balance between the governance trajectories across all parts of the UK and to maintain the union, albeit in a very different form from the current one (Hutton 2015), but the inter-urban coordination and cooperation activities which the governments in the three devolved regions provide still appear to have no real parallels in England beyond the remit of central government.

7.4 Governance changes and local economic development and innovation policies

The final part of the evolving institutional and governance jigsaw which we need to address is the question of exactly how local and regional development policy, and in particular its links with innovation policy, in the current context are also expected to relate to the governance changes. As well as responding to heterogeneous preferences and fostering public accountability, one of the major driving forces underpinning the current UK governance devolution agenda relates to the fostering of innovation, entrepreneurship and the enhancing of local economic development. This is very clear both from the policy statements of the Scottish[31] and Welsh governments and also from the various reports and commissions advocating city-region devolution within England and Wales (RSA 2014a, b, 2015). The underlying argument here is fundamentally a place-based argument. This posits that on many levels innovation is fundamentally a local phenomenon (Moretti 2012; Hughes 2012) and therefore that more devolved and local policy-making which allows for greater autonomy and flexibility in the design and delivery innovation policies will allow innovation opportunities to be more easily tapped into by public interventions. This is not to say that all innovation is local in nature. Indeed, many of the recent innovation and productivity evidence-based reviews[32] demonstrate that innovation is both a local and a global phenomenon (Wright 2014). However, the view that many of the most appropriate and effective innovation and entrepreneurship-related policy actions and interventions are undertaken at the local or regional level (Wright 2014) now reflects something of a widespread international consensus supported both by a range of international development institutions (World Bank 2010, 2011; OECD 2011a; McCann 2015) and also a large international academic literature which argues for a place-based logic to innovation and entrepreneurship policies (McCann and Ortega-Argilés 2013a; Audretsch *et al.* 2015).

In the specific case of the UK, however, these international views are especially pertinent in that recent thinking (Heseltine 2012; IPPR 2012) has shifted towards the view that the overly centralised and top-down nature of public policy has limited the efficacy of innovation-related policies by failing to build on local capabilities. City-regions and local areas are now being proposed by various commentators and bodies as the most appropriate spatial and institutional arenas in which to drive UK growth (CfC 2014b) by fostering different types of innovations and innovative actions, including university-business (Lambert 2003; Witty 2013; Hughes and Kitson 2013) and university-city linkages and spillovers (Abreu *et al.* 2008; RSA 2014c; LGA 2013b),[33] entrepreneurship and SME-focused policies (CfC 2014c), housing policies (IPPR 2014b; Falk 2014; Heywood 2015) as well as efforts aimed at fostering skills (RSA 2014d; JRF 2014). This shift in thinking reflects a widespread acknowledgement that innovation is not purely a private sector concern, but is also heavily shaped by both the public sector (Mazzucato 2013) and also even civil society actors. In addition, following on from calls for fundamental innovation in the provision of public and social services (NESTA 2011, 2012a, 2013a, 2013b, 2014, 2015; IfG 2013b), in the light of the devolution debates, the governance reforms associated with cities are now being advocated as the ideal settings for fostering both public-sector (CfC 2014d) and social innovation (NESTA 2012b; McInroy and Jackson 2015) and indeed many such initiatives are now being undertaken.[34] These local linkages, spillovers and innovation-enhancing initiatives also reflect a broader understanding of local connectivity which is intrinsically related to devolution and which go beyond transportation issues. Indeed, the fact that governance devolution and a range of innovation-related issues are now understood as being interconnected, and also the importance which is given to these interconnections, is reflected by the fact that the UK ministerial portfolio for communities and local government with responsibility for cities and localities was combined with the portfolio business, innovation and skills with responsibility for universities.[35] Moreover, this pooling of ministerial responsibilities continues beyond 2015.

In the case of the UK these current ideas regarding governance and policy heavily reflect international thinking, and they also represent something of a fundamental shift in our UK-based understanding of the relationship between governance, place and innovation. Traditionally, UK policy on innovation has had little or no real geographical, regional or local institutional underpinnings. Official UK government views about entrepreneurship and innovation-related policies have traditionally largely displayed an implicit space-blind type of logic with much of the focus placed on the role played by national productivity, skills and educational policies and settings.[36] However, in the years following the turn of the millennium there were the first hints of a shift in thinking by central government with Treasury papers published in 2001 and 2003 (HM Treasury 2001, 2003) discussing the regional and local dimensions of UK productivity,[37] the links with clusters (DTI 2001), and the links between geography and innovation (DTI 2006a). These reports suggested an increased emphasis on policies at the local and regional levels (HMT, DTI and ODPM 2003) leading possibly to significantly greater devolution of powers away from London (Pilch 2004). However, beyond the interests of the three devolved administrations plus to a lesser extent London, this potentially place-based shift in national government thinking was neither long-lasting nor fundamental and was soon superseded by a broadly space-blind narrative (Combes *et al.* 2006) in which devolved governance largely disappeared from mainstream political debates. This was also manifested in an almost total lack of central government support or impetus provided for the contemporaneous Northern Way initiative or the North East devolution agenda.[38] Furthermore, within a few years all UK national discussions regarding productivity and economic performance were totally overtaken by the impacts of the 2008 global economic crisis, so tentative discussions about the links between local and regional issues and productivity were totally sidelined by national debates.

This remained largely the case until the issues were again raised in two far-reaching and influential reports (Heseltine 2012; IPPR 2012), which as we have already seen have since been followed by numerous other reports and arguments (Bailey and Hildreth 2013, 2014; CfC and MC 2014; Bailey *et al.* 2015) following similar lines of argument. The importance of these reports was that they reflected major and growing doubts about the efficacy of the UK's top-down, nationally directed and primarily space-blind policy settings, particularly in the light of the experience of other countries. In particular, concerns over the impacts of the UK's traditional policy approaches have started to emerge over recent years because although the UK's inter-regional educational differences have become so tiny as a result of national policies, the UK has simultaneously experienced both a growing 'valley of death' (HoC 2013) problem along with burgeoning interregional inequalities. These ideas and concerns have now again been reflected in recent Treasury thinking and policy (HM Treasury 2015a) which again has started to adopt various place-based lines of argumentation. However, in order to make these workable, the City Growth Commission (RSA 2014a) argues that a successful city-region devolution agenda requires reforms of both local government finances and taxes, constitutional reforms of central government, and demonstration of the commitment on the part of the metropolitan city-regions to competence and capability. Furthermore, multi-year financial settlements will be required, the freedom to spend grants without ring-fencing and greater borrowing flexibilities, and finally the ability to retain the proceeds of growth through outcomes-focused finance models (RSA 2014a). Yet, one of the key challenges in England will be to find ways to ensure that LEPs perform as well as possible (IPPR 2015) in conjunction with devolved city-regions in the UK. The larger and more densely populated LEP areas are likely to enjoy productivity advantages over other LEP areas (Harris and Moffat 2013) while in the long run those located in the southern core regions have generally out-performed those located in the northern non-core regions (ONS 2015). However, the current UK governance system of local, city and regional spatial matters is a complex and rather messy patchwork of numerous overlapping roles and jurisdictions[39] which greatly inhibits effective planning (Wong *et al.* 2015). The LEPs do not coincide with the devolved city-regions and while both bodies are being encouraged to coordinate and interact, they are also being encouraged to interact even more with the 'Catapult' network programme both as places to undertake research and to develop innovations (BIS 2014). Encouragement is one thing, but substantive action is quite another thing, and this depends on resources, decision-making autonomy, and also the legal basis for action. The current patchwork of agencies and jurisdictions, far from simplifying the economic development landscape, has made it far more fragmented and disjointed. Indeed, one of the major advantages of the previous RDA system was that they had a single pot of money from which to draw, enabling the scale and concentration of resources, and wide-ranging autonomy in terms of how to deploy these resources (Healey and Newby 2014), whereas Crowley *et al.* (2012) argue that the current ongoing changes are likely to exacerbate existing regional inequalities.

Yet, even if devolutionary shifts are indeed under way there still remain immense challenges to be overcome in order to realise a more genuinely place-based approach to local and regional development. As we have already seen in Chapter 6, the primarily space-blind logic is still by far the dominant central government governance orthodoxy within HM Treasury and Whitehall in general. The UK government and institutional architecture is strongly federal in terms of its space-blind civil service structure (IfG 2013a) but almost entirely unitary, top-down and non-federal in geographical terms, except recently for the three devolved administrations. In marked contrast countries such as the USA, Canada, Australia and Germany are all strongly

Table 7.1 Traditional and modern regional policy

	Traditional Regional Policy	*Modern Regional Policy*
Objectives	Compensating temporarily for location disadvantages of lagging regions	Tapping into under-utilised potential in all regions to enhance development in all regions
Unit of Intervention	Administrative units	Functional economic areas
Strategies	Sectoral approach	Integrated development projects
Tools	Subsidies and state aids	Mix of hard capital (infrastructure) and 'soft' capital (business support, credit availability, networking systems)
Actors	Central government	Multi-level governance involving different tiers or levels of local, regional and national government working in partnership and alongside the private and civil society sectors
Objectives	Employment	Various diverse objectives
Performance Assessment	Employment	Use of outcome indicators, monitoring and evaluation systems

Source: OECD (2009a); McCann (2015).

federal geographically and therefore inherently more place-based in terms of policy. Ironically, as we have seen throughout this book the UK is the country which is interregionally one of the most unbalanced in the industrialised world and yet has a governance and institutional system which is one of the least able to respond to these issues. Moreover, although there is now a widespread awareness of the importance of such reforms as well as significant political and public momentum for reforms, in reality reforming the UK governance system in a way which better allows it to respond to these issues is in many ways more of a challenge for the UK than for almost any other country. In order to see this it is useful to consider how mainstream thinking about regional development policy across the international arena has changed over recent decades.

Traditional regional policy was almost entirely a top-down and sectoral matter, and traditional UK regional policy as implemented during the post-war era until the late 1970s was a classic reflection of this traditional thinking. As we see in Table 7.1, the approach was top-down, as was natural in such a highly centralised state, with central government allocating grants on the basis of administrative areas to specific types of industries and firms largely on a sectoral basis.[40] At the time the economic thinking underlying the 1960s and 1970s regional policy approach in the UK reflected the prevailing understanding of the workings of regional economies both in the UK (Armstrong and Taylor 1985) and also in the North American and international literatures (Isard *et al.* 1959; Isard 1960; OEEC 1961; Meyer *et al.* 1965; McKee *et al.* 1970; Friedmann and Alonso 1964, 1975).

On the other hand, the governance and devolution evidence presented in the last two chapters strongly suggests that the UK is seeking to move towards a more modern approach to local, city and regional policy. More modern approaches derive from widespread international evidence and experience (Rodrik 1999, 2007; McCann and Ortega-Argilés 2013b, 2013c; Foray *et al.* 2012) and the lessons from numerous examples suggest that policy should not be focused on specific sectors, but on various types of activities and initiatives in which the private sector takes on as much of the leading roles as possible in conjunction with the public and or civil society sectors.

As we see in Table 7.1, the aim of the modern approaches is to tap into unrealised local potential and to build on the knowledge and possibilities perceived by local actors and stakeholders. This also requires a broad and flexible multi-level governance framework in which different actors can take on different roles on different issues and in different circumstances. Building local cooperation, coordination and empowerment are the key features of the approach and different objectives and goals may be pursued as required. The intended outcomes relating to, for example, innovation, will be very different from those aimed at enhancing environmental sustainability, which in turn will be different from those relating to the fostering of social cohesion or those focused on promoting wellbeing (OECD 2014b). In each case it is essential to have clarity regarding the intended outcomes and the expected theory of change according to which these outcomes are perceived to be realised and it is necessary for these issues all to be publicly discussed and agreed in advance. A 'theory of change' approach to policy design and policy evaluation is often very powerful in examining complex social systems and identifying areas for improvement (DCLG 2010, 2011). This also ensures that all stakeholders and interested parties understand what the policy intentions are and the likely mechanisms by which these intended outcomes will be achieved, while still allowing for the possibility that unexpected influences may hinder or even thwart the realisation of the desired outcomes. Any such unexpected influences and events will be uncovered in the subsequent monitoring and evaluation exercises and lessons can be learned as appropriate.

Experimentalism (CST 2007; Hughes 2012) is essential in such approaches as this fosters a process of self-discovery (Hausmann and Rodrik 2003), as is always the case with any forms of innovation. Moreover, innovation in the public sector also implies experimentalism. In order to facilitate this a small number of appropriate and carefully considered outcome indicators (Barca and McCann 2011) need to be chosen for each specific activity and all activities need to be monitored and evaluated as a routine part of the policy cycle and policy process. Outcome indicators are not chosen because the outcomes are known in advance but for precisely the opposite reason, namely that the outcomes are not known in advance (Rodrik 2004). Rather, outcome indicators, monitoring and evaluation are all needed in order to help track the progress towards the intended outcomes of the project. In order to assess policy progress in the light of the theory of change increasingly the setting of policy goals is also associated with building an evidence base and data amenable to policy monitoring and evaluation (OECD 2008, 2009b). Baseline data on all issues must therefore be gathered ex ante in order to help both with the choice of priorities and also in order to help track progress.[41] Moreover, evaluation must include both quantitative and qualitative techniques (Fabling *et al.* 2012) wherever possible, otherwise evaluations will always be biased (Jaffe 2015). There is now a large literature on evaluation (Davies *et al.* 2000; Pawson 2006; Gault 2013; Link and Vonortas 2013), but the aim of evaluation is not to engender a league-table culture of winners and losers but rather to help improve government and policy-making (Bryson *et al.* 2012; Glennerster 2012; NESTA 2013c) by instilling a culture in which the intended outcomes of a policy and the various roles and responsibilities being undertaken by different parties are all made clear and transparent from the outset. Evaluation is not simply an econometric exercise, but rather a means of capacity building (NESTA 2013d), as long as any failure to achieve expected goals does not imply sanctions. Otherwise actors will not take risks and innovation will be stymied. Failure or less-than-expected performance outcomes must be allowed for as they are a natural part of innovation processes and are essential in order to identify actually what works (WWN 2014) and in which context and why. Lessons from other countries and regions can also be instructive in this regard in order to help interpret local evidence (GHK and CURDS 2006).

The relationships between stakeholders can be contractual or incentive based (OECD 2001a, 2001b, 2004, 2005, 2007, 2008, 2009a, 2009b, 2009c) but as with monitoring and evaluation activities the primary purpose of these relationships is to build institutional capacity, governance capabilities and to foster trust between diverse actors and constituencies as well as different jurisdictions and level of governance (OECD 2009c, 2011b, 2011c). Functional economic areas are the appropriate spatial setting for these policy approaches, although as we have already seen, such economic areas will differ according to the issues being addressed, and could be at the level of cities or wider regions (OECD 2014a).

While it is clear that there is widespread enthusiasm and momentum within the UK to move towards more modern policy settings, it still remains the case, however, that the UK's governance and institutional set-up is itself, and already has been, a major obstacle to such a movement. The prevailing institutional settings mean that the UK has not enjoyed as smooth a transition from the old policy model to the new policy model as many other countries. Regional policy in the UK was largely dismantled in the 1980s and 1990s, except for the use of EU regional development funds (McCann

2015) and also the activities of various urban development corporations (UDCs) most of which were top-down centrally controlled bodies, alongside a range of much smaller urban policy initiatives. This led to something of a 20-year hiatus in UK spatial policy thinking and policy learning. It was not until the establishment of the English Regional Development Agencies (RDAs) in 1999 and 2000 alongside the Government Offices for the Regions that institutional changes heralded the first steps towards a more modern UK regional policy approach. These agencies and government bodies were established on a model which reflected the earlier and largely successful experience of the Scottish Development Agency (SDA) and its successor organisation Scottish Enterprise (SE), as well as that of the Welsh Development Agency (WDA).[42] RDAs were intended to provide a new institutional layer better capable of delivering integrated development packages while also being large enough to adopt a more long-term strategic approach to economic development policy (CLG and BERR 2008; Benneworth 2001). Yet, as we have seen, the progress made by the RDAs was curtailed by their abolition in 2010 and the establishment of the system of LEPs. Indeed, since 2010 the movement away from the RDAs towards centrally managed competitive funding streams again reflects something of a further shift towards a top-down governance logic.

These periodic changes of direction, ad hoc reconfigurations of institutional settings, and even the dismantling of many policy-settings, has limited the policy-learning possibilities in the UK, and weakened its ability to self-adjust to a better institutional framework. These institutional weaknesses are critical, because it is clear from the international evidence that getting the institutional settings right is by far the most important determinant of a successful regional policy (OECD 2012a). In particular, well-functioning multi-level governance systems are essential for good regional policy and this is precisely the arena where the UK is at its weakest, because local government has been hollowed out and undermined by central government for decades, as have been many of the UK's regional development institutions. The quality of UK sub-national government at the level of EU-NUTS2 regions is more or less the same as in France and Northern Spain, but below much of Germany, Austria, the Low Countries and the Nordic Countries (European Union 2014). As such, in the UK the movement from a traditional regional policy approach to a more modern approach to local and regional policy-making is in many ways a more difficult and longer journey than in almost any other country. As such, UK city-region devolution or increased powers for the devolved administrations are of themselves no guarantee at all of economic development success unless these are also accompanied by a whole host of other elements, including institutional capacity-building, outcome-oriented policy-making, a widespread culture of policy-monitoring and evaluation, and a public sector with the freedom to experiment and innovate alongside the private and civil society sectors without the fear of sanctions from central government.

The signs of potential UK success across these various dimensions are not auspicious, however. During their decade or more of operations most evaluations of the activities of the RDAs were largely favourable and supportive of what the RDAs were doing and how they were developing their remits (HoC 2008; Arup 2000; ODPM 2004; DTI 2006b; BERR 2008a, 2008b, 2009a, 2009b; BIS 2009; NAO 2003, 2005, 2010a, 2010b). However, these evaluations were based primarily on their job creation and safeguarding activities as well as their engagement with different local, national and international stakeholders (HoC 2008). Yet, there are always problems with evaluations where results are self-reported because of subjectivity (BIS 2012). Indeed, the National Audit Office (NAO 2010a) review of RDAs found it difficult to accurately evaluate their impacts due to limited data and weak evaluation methodologies. At the same time, the RDAs' work was also limited by the fact that many expenditure lines were controlled by central government, making integrated development approaches very difficult. However, the NAO did find evidence of an important coordination role played by RDAs between numerous other agencies. Yet, while many of the earlier employment-related assessments were subject to criticism regarding their lack of counter-factual frameworks, various analyses involving more advanced econometric techniques have also found favourable employment, output, productivity and survival impacts of these types of schemes (Hart and Scott 1994; Hart *et al.* 2008a, 2008b; Harris and Robinson 2004; Harris and Trainor 2005; Criscuolo and Martin 2008a, 2008b; Criscuolo *et al.* 2012; Crafts 2012; Moffat 2013, 2014).[43] The use of counter-factual types of approaches has long been advocated in regional policy (Moore and Rhodes 1973; Swales 1997) and econometric techniques can partly deal with such issues (Gibbons *et al.* 2014; Overman 2012), as have simulation exercises.[44] In particular, evaluations over longer time spans and incorporating both quantitative and qualitative evidence can be very powerful. Yet, such evaluations also depend crucially on the extent to which the intended objectives of a policy, against which the policy is being evaluated, are themselves realistic and meaningful.[45] In 2007 the previously more broadly and loosely defined objectives for RDAs were superseded by the requirement to promote regional growth faster than the previous trend cycle, to promote interregional convergence by reducing regional disparities (HoC 2008), and since 2009 they were required to report progress against GVA, rather than just jobs created as had previously been the case (NAO 2010a, 2010b). In hindsight, these latter objectives were utterly absurd, given the tiny levels of funding made available to RDAs in comparison to the size of their regional economies[46] and the bigger issues discussed throughout this book. In reality these latter objectives should never have been advocated, as they overwhelmed and distracted RDAs from operating according to more sensible and meaningful objectives while also allowing for mistaken political critiques of their activities. Indeed, Crowley *et al.* (2012) argue that many of the criticisms raised against the previous local development and regeneration policies, and in particular RDAs and NDCs (New Deal for Communities), were unfounded in that they tended to exaggerate the amounts of money actually spent, and also because they were evaluated against unrealistic benchmarks, such as GDP or GVA.

The previous weaknesses and difficulties in evaluating the performance of the RDAs still largely remain under the current economic development arrangements.[47] In its evaluation of the Regional Growth Fund (Ward 2014) the National Audit Office (NAO 2012) found that its granting allocations were in line with its remit which was designed to increase private sector jobs in economically weaker areas which were more reliant on public sector jobs. However, it was too early at that stage to robustly evaluate the impacts of the programme itself, and a follow-up evaluation (NAO 2014) found that insufficient resources had been allocated to live projects and also that no long-term evaluation plans of the impacts of the programme itself had been developed. Indeed, these evaluation difficulties are not specific to economic development issues, but to UK government in general. In 2013 the National Audit Office found it impossible to identify current levels of UK central government departmental spending on evaluation (MC and IfG 2014) because either Whitehall departments did not have this information or because it would apparently be too costly to produce it. In Canada, by contrast, having such information is mandatory. This suggests that another important aspect of the assessment of policy impacts is also somewhat lacking in the UK when it comes to regional policy-type questions, namely civil service impact assessments. Across the OECD and EU governments and civil service-type institutions often undertake 'impact assessments', but of a very different type to the econometric and policy evaluation activities discussed above. Civil service impact assessments examine the effects of a new policy or policy approach on the institutional settings and on the service-delivery performance criteria affecting the governance institutions. These impact assessments are primarily legal in nature and examine issues relating to control and management, legal liability, interactions and potential conflicts with other policy arenas, decision-making data availability, and other such matters. One would assume and hope that the emerging combined authorities in the current city-region devolution negotiations have all undertaken such internal impact assessments. However, even if they have, the fact that the UK Government itself is unable to identify exactly how much it invests itself in evaluation, then such central government impacts assessments, if they exist, are likely to have been rather limited in nature and are unlikely to provide a strong basis for promoting a culture of public sector innovation and experimentalism, alongside outcome-orientated policy-making and evaluation. Any criticisms which could potentially be pointed at UK regional policy and its evaluation or at the institutional capacity of city-regions or devolved administrations could also more generally be pointed at UK government as a whole. Indeed, the evidence in this book suggests that national UK government policy has wholly failed many of the UK's regions, at least in terms of promoting their long-run economic development, and that a big part of the problem is a complete lack of knowledge on the part of central government as to what to do, or how to reform government to improve its own performance in this arena. For many of the issues discussed throughout this book involving complex interactions between economic geography, globalisation and governance, there is simply no counter-factual which can be employed using econometric evaluation techniques. Rather, observations, insights and lessons from other countries are the only realistic counterpoint against which the UK experience can be considered, and in this light the UK's performance as a whole regarding regional issues is not something to be proud of.

7.5 Conclusions

This chapter has outlined some of the issues arising from the current direction of UK policy regarding cities and regions with its focus both on governance devolution and the enhancement of connectivity. As we see, the devolution issues regarding the city-regions and the devolved administrations are complex and intertwined and at present there are real risks that the is UK drifting towards an unbalanced and potentially dysfunctional quasi-federal governance system in which the underlying economic tensions straining the unity of the state fail to be properly addressed. Moving away somewhat from an overly top-down and centralised state the UK is shifting towards an institutional system where the highest level of sub-national governance is very small by the standards of other large OECD economies and also highly unequal in terms of autonomy. At the same time, the governance changes being sought have still made very little headway regarding the coordination possibilities between the different devolved areas. These changes may well lead to an additional set of future governance challenges arising in the not-too-distant future, in particular regarding the promotion of interregional connectivity. At the same time, the devolved city-regions areas are also large in terms of the areas typically best-suited for fostering trust, and this also may well put pressure on the public's confidence in the new arrangements as the new policy arena unfolds. It will be necessary to build different institutional arrangements that can coordinate actions and initiatives between city-regions on different issues. But again these types tend to have only limited public support and awareness and very limited finding, and such matters are unlikely to be resolved simply by means of elected mayors of combined authorities. Outside of the devolved administrations there is still a much-needed higher level of formal representation and engagement with central government which is lacking in the current devolution proposals. This lack of representation and coordination is also problematic given the change of culture required to move away from a traditional and top-down view of local and regional policy to a modern approach one which is also bottom-up. The multi-level governance settings which are required to foster innovation and experimentalism within an outcome-oriented policy environment are extremely difficult to introduce in such an overly top-down and London-centric national governance system, and the past performance of central government itself in this regard offers little encouragement as to likely future success of these developments.

Notes

1 The IFS (Institute for Fiscal Studies) has argued that more than 60 per cent of the planned expenditure cuts proposed from 2010 onwards are still to be realised in the 2015–2020 parliament, and that the scale of these cuts may amount to "a fundamental reimagining of the role of the state". See: www.bbc.com/news/business-31126283; www.bbc.com/news/business-30327717.

2 www.theguardian.com/commentisfree/2015/may/06/union-is-at-risk-constitution-unit-devolution-election-scots.

3 With an optimal membership size of approximately 70 representatives. See Hanretty, C., 2015, "Cut the Commons: to 400 MPs", *Prospect*, October.

4 "Bagehot: A Democratic Embarrassment", *The Economist*, 13 June 2015.

5 Although Spain is not strictly speaking a federal nation-state the nature of the roles and responsibilities and constitutional basis of the Spanish Autonomous Communities (OECD 2012b) means that for analytical purposes the OECD treats them as being effectively federal states (OECD 2013).

6 Mainland France plus Corsica previously had 22 administrative regions, which are due to be reduced to 13 as of 1 January 2016. In addition there are five overseas regions. See: "New Kids on the Block", *The Economist*, 9 May 2015. Each of these regions levies their own taxes and also receives direct financial support from central government. The regions have significant powers over investments in infrastructure, education, universities, research and business support. There are directly elected regional representatives, although the regions lack any separate legislative basis. The average population of France's regions in 2015 was 2.45 million, increasing to 3.66 million in 2016. The regions are then subdivided into departments, whose size and roles largely reflect those of local government areas in the UK. At the lowest governance levels below that of the departments France is extremely fragmented with more than 36,000 municipalities (OECD 2015a). http://en.wikipedia.org/wiki/Regions_of_France.

7 Japan has 47 prefectures with an average population of 2.7 million people. Each prefecture has a directly elected governor and directly elected members of the prefecture assembly. Each prefecture is subdivided into cities and districts which again approximately reflect the size and roles of UK local government. http://en.wikipedia.org/wiki/Prefectures_of_Japan.

8 See: "Separatism in Quebec: No We Shouldn't", *The Economist*, 23 May 2015.

9 A system which Hazell (2015, p. 13) describes as "remarkably dysfunctional".

10 "Welsh Devolution: The Reluctant Dragon", *The Economist*, 24 November 2012.

11 "Bagehot: England's Sensible Slumber", *The Economist*, 20 June 2015.

12 Moreover, defining which categories of public expenditure are UK-wide or just English or just region-specific is in many cases extremely difficult and certainly much less straightforward and far more complex than the simple political narratives imply. See: "What is an English Law?", BBC News, 16 December 2014, www.bbc.com/news/uk-30497707.

13 Comment by Ed Miliband on the BBC1 *Andrew Marr Show*, 10.00–11.00, Sunday 21 September 2014.

14 "The Trials of Life in Tilbury", *The Economist*, 16 August 2014; "Suburban London: Trouble in Metroland", *The Economist*, 24 August 2013; "Social Ills: Trouble Spreads Out", *The Economist*, 17 May 2014.

15 www.lgcplus.com/Journals/2014/01/21/d/r/x/Commission-on-Public-Service-Governance-and-Delivery-Wales.pdf.

16 For example, in the case of Jaguar-Land Rover (JLR), one of the most important economic actors in the Midlands, JLR spent £3 billion on components in the auto supply chain in the West Midlands in 2013. However, the West Midlands now has six LEPs instead of one 'old' RDA Advantage West Midlands. In terms of regional operations JLR crosses three LEPs and two separate city-regions: it has facilities at the i54 engine plant (Black Country LEP); the Castle Bromwich and Solihull assembly plants (both Greater Birmingham and Solihull LEP); and the Whitley and Gaydon engineering and R&D centres (Coventry and Warwickshire LEP). While LEPs are seeking to coordinate some activities it still remains the case that for UK local and regional development policy public-private coordination has been greatly complicated and in many cases weakened on many levels by moving to such fragmented institutional settings as LEPs and this will also be the case even for city-regions. Similar arguments can be made regarding the supply chains of Nissan in the North East, Rolls Royce and Airbus, or for that matter numerous inward FDI investments along with the vast majority of logistics and distribution systems. See: http://centreofenterprise.com/wp-content/uploads/2014/03/GBS-SEP-Appendix-C.pdf.

17 Although the Sheffield city-region deal suggests that this argument is not necessarily correct. See: www.bbc.com/news/uk-england-south-yorkshire-34414584.

18 "The OECD Recommendations on the Governance of Public Investment", Paper presented by Joaquim Oliveira-Martins, Head of the OECD Regional Development Department, at the Expert Seminar on Lagging Regions, Berlaymont, European Commission, Brussels, 22–23 June 2015.

19 www.chroniclelive.co.uk/news/north-east-news/next-six-weeks-vital-north-9710576.

20 In various north of England media and policy circles the 'Northern Powerhouse' agenda is variously referred to as the 'northern poorhouse' or the 'northern powercut' agenda. See: http://speri.dept.shef.ac.uk/2015/04/07/devo-manc-northern-powerhouse-northern-poorhouse/.

21 www.theguardian.com/business/2015/jul/04/powerhouse-poorhouse-north-east-fears-devolution-wont-help; www.theguardian.com/commentisfree/2015/jul/06/wally-believing-talk-northern-powerhouse.

22 www.iea.org.uk/blog/re-heating-regional-policy-flaws-in-the-%E2%80%98northern-powerhouse%E2%80%99.

23 "Birmingham: Second City, Second Class", *The Economist*, 10 November 2012.

24 www.bbc.co.uk/news/uk-england-manchester-33477953; www.bbc.co.uk/news/uk-england-manchester-31656313; www.bbc.co.uk/news/uk-england-manchester-31615218; www.bbc.co.uk/news/business-31629396; www.bbc.co.uk/news/health-31590885.

25 "Decentralising Healthcare: Control Yourself", *The Economist*, 28 February 2015.

26 www.bbc.co.uk/news/uk-england-manchester-29876939; "Manchester: UK's New Order?", *Financial Times*, 20 February 2015.

27 "City Self-Rule Plan Sparks Disagreement Over Mayors", *Financial Times*, 14 May 2015; www.bbc.com/news/uk-england-manchester-29876939; www.bbc.com/news/uk-england-manchester-29879148.

28 www.centreforcities.org/blog/a-snapshot-of-the-city-and-local-government-devolution-bill-2015/.

29 http://services.parliament.uk/bills/2015-16/citiesandlocalgovernmentdevolution.html.

30 "George Osborne: Councils to Keep £26bn Business Rates", www.bbc.com/news/business-34445311; "Partial Reversal of Thatcher's Local Government Castration", www.bbc.com/news/business-34449708.

31 *Scotland's Economic Strategy*, Scottish Government, Edinburgh, March, and *An Economic Strategy for Wales?*, IWA Institute of Welsh Affairs, Cardiff.
32 https://www.gov.uk/government/publications/future-of-manufacturing.
33 https://www.gov.uk/government/publications/universities-and-growth-government-response-to-the-witty-review; https://www.nesta.org.uk/sites/default/files/reinventing_the_civic_university.pdf; www.ippr.org/files/images/media/files/publication/2012/02/beyond-bricks-mortar-boards_Feb2012_8659.pdf?noredirect=1.
34 "Radical Local Government: Political Petri Dishes", *The Economist*, 22 September 2012; "Innovation in Local Government: Britain's Local Labs", *The Economist*, 22 September 2012.
35 See: "A Portfolio Career", *Times Higher Education*, 17 July 2014; "All in This Together", *Times Higher Education*, 24 July 2014; "Government Sees That Growth is Already in the University Mission", *Times Higher Education*, 24 July 2014; "The Engines of Regional Prosperity?", *Times Higher Education*, 27 November 2014; "Centre Sparks", *Times Higher Education*, 27 November 2014;
36 Almost all of the Economics Papers, Occasional Papers, Research Papers, Strategy Documents and Reports published by the DTI (Department of Trade and Industry), BERR (the Department of Business Enterprise and Regulatory Reform) and BIS (the Department for Business Innovation and Skills) between 2007 and 2015 are entirely sectoral and space-blind in construction with no regional or geographical dimension whatsoever.
37 http://webarchive.nationalarchives.gov.uk/+/http:/www.hm-treasury.gov.uk/ent_prod_index.htm.
38 www.thejournal.co.uk/north-east-analysis/north-east-wants-devolution-says-8023063.
39 "The Awkward Jigsaw of England's Boundaries ", BBC News, 7 November 2014. See: www.bbc.com/news/magazine-29934867.
40 As we have seen in Chapter 6, at its zenith in the late 1970s total UK regional policy expenditure was just over 0.43 per cent of UK GDP, while for most years it was closer to 0.3 per cent of GDP.
41 See *Evidence of Impact: Making the Case*, NESTA, London, www.nesta.org.uk.
42 The SDA was established in 1975 and the WDA was established in 1976. Both the SDA and the WDA were subsequently either wound up or transformed into another type of institution. The SDA was reorganised into Scottish Enterprise (SE) in 1991 with a two-tier system comprising an umbrella organisation (SE) overseeing a series of Local Enterprise Companies (LECs) which are fully integrated into SE and are responsible for local development initiatives. SE is now part of the Scottish Government and works alongside its much smaller sister organisation, Highlands and Islands Enterprise. Meanwhile the WDA was abolished in 2006 and its activities were transferred to the Welsh Government.
43 See also: http://gov.wales/docs/caecd/research/081106-analysis-regional-selective-assistance-scheme-stage-one-en.pdf.
44 https://pure.strath.ac.uk/portal/files/14546878/strathprints007267.pdf.
45 A useful set of debates on these matters is contained in Lawless *et al.* (2011).
46 Which were in total typically some £3.3 billion per annum in total including the 9 billion of EU Structural Funds allocated across the period 2007–2013 (HoC 2008), or some 0.2 per cent of regional GDP.
47 Current domestic expenditure on regional economic development 2010–2014/2015 has been cut by a half relative to the RDA era to under £1 billion per annum, but is likely to increase from 2015 onwards with the introduction of the Local Growth Fund (HoC 2014). Including EU Structural Funds total expenditure on regional economic development is currently some two-thirds of the levels pertaining in 2000–2010, or approximately 0.14 per cent of total UK regional GDP.

References

Abreu, M., Grinevich, V., Hughes, A., Kitson, M. and Ternout, P., 2008, *Universities, Business and Knowledge Exchange*, Council for Industry and Higher Education and Centre for Business Research, Cambridge.

Ahrend, R., Farchy, E., Kaplanis, I. and Lembcke, A., 2014a, "What Makes Cities More Productive? Evidence on the Role of Urban Governance from Five OECD Countries", *OECD Regional Development Working Papers 2014/05*, Organisation for Economic Cooperation and Development, Paris.

Ahrend, R., Gamper, C. and Schumann, A., 2014b, "Approaches to Metropolitan Area Governance: A Country Overview", *OECD Regional Development Working Papers 2014/03*, Organisation for Economic Cooperation and Development, Paris.

Armstrong, H.W., and Taylor, J., 1985, *Regional Economics and Policy*, Philip Allan, Oxford.

Arup, 2000, *Evaluation of Regional Selective Assistance 1991–1995*, Arup Economics and Planning, London.

Audretsch, D.B., Link, A. and Walshok, M., 2015, (eds.), *Oxford Handbook of Local Competitiveness*, Oxford University Press, Oxford.

Bailey, D., and Hildreth, P., 2013, "The Economics Behind the Move to 'Localism' in England", *Cambridge Journal of Regions, Economy and Society*, 6.2, 233–349.

Bailey, D., and Hildreth, P., 2014, "Place Based Economic Development Strategy in England: Filling the Missing Space", *Local Economy*, 29.4–5, 363–367.

Bailey, D., Hildreth, P. and de Propris, L., 2015, "Mind the Gap! What Might a Place Based Industrial and Regional Policy Look Like?", in Bailey, D., Cowling, K. and Tomlinson, P., (eds.), *New Perspectives on Industrial Policy for a Modern Britain*, Oxford University Press, Oxford.

Barber, B.R., 2013, *If Mayors Ruled the World: Dysfunctional Nations, Rising Cities*, Yale University Press, New Haven.

Barca, F., and McCann, P., 2011, *Methodological Note: Outcome Indicators and Targets – Towards a Performance Oriented EU Cohesion Policy* and examples of such indicators are contained in the two complementary notes on outcome indicators for EU2020 entitled *Meeting climate change and energy objectives* and *Improving the conditions for innovation, research and development*. See: http://ec.europa.eu/regional_policy/sources/docgener/evaluation/performance_en.htm.

Bell, D., 2015, "The Aftermath of the Scottish Referendum: A New Fiscal Settlement for the UK?", in Bailey, D., and Budd, L., (eds.), *Devolution and the UK Economy*, Rowman and Littlefield, London.

Benneworth, P., 2001, *Regional Development Agencies: The Early Years*, Regional Studies Association, Seaford.

BERR, 2008a, *Evaluation of Regional Selective Assistance (RSA) and Its Successor, Selective Finance for Investment in England (SIFE)*, BERR Occasional Paper No. 2, Department for Business, Enterprise and Regulatory Reform, London, March.

BERR, 2008b, *Appendices for 'Evaluation of Regional Selective Assistance (RSA) and Its Successor, Selective Finance for Investment in England (SIFE)*, BERR Occasional Paper No. 2, Department for Business, Enterprise and Regulatory Reform, London, March.

BERR, 2009a, *Impact of RDA Spending – National Report – Volume 1 – Main Report*, Department for Business, Enterprise and Regulatory Reform, London, March.

BERR, 2009b, *Impact of RDA Spending – National Report – Volume 2 – Regional Annexes*, Department for Business, Enterprise and Regulatory Reform, London, March.

BIS, 2009, *RDA Evaluation: Practical Guidance on Implementing the Impact Evaluation Framework*, Department for Business, Innovation and Skills, London, December.

BIS, 2012, *Feasibility Study: Exploring the Long-Term Impacts of Business Improvement Services*, Hart, M., and Drews, C-C., Department for Business, Innovation and Skills, London.

BIS, 2014, *Review of the Catapult Network: Recommendations on the Future Shape, Scope and Ambition of the Programme, Hauser, H.*, Department for Business, Innovation and Skills, London.

Bogdanor, V., 2012, "Mayors: Good for Britain – in the End", *Prospect*, 19 March.

Bolton, T., and Hildreth, P., 2013, *Mid-Sized Cities: Their Role in England's Economy*, Centre for Cities, London, June.

Brown, G., 2014, *My Scotland, Our Britain: A Future Worth Sharing*, Simon & Schuster, London.

Bryson, A., Dorsett, R. and Portes, J., 2012, "Policy Evaluation in a Time of Austerity: Introduction", *National Institute Economic Review*, 219, R1–R3.

Carter, A., 2015, *Hopelessly Devo-Ted?*, Centre for Cities, 4 June, www.centreforcities.org.

Cash, D.W., Clark, W.C., Alcock, F., Dickson, N.M., Echley, N., Guston, D.H., Jäger, J. and Mitchell, R.B., 2003, "Knowledge Systems for Sustainable Development", *Proceedings of the National Academy of Sciences*, 100.14, 8086–8091.

CC, 2015, *Devolution Declaration: A Modern State for a Stronger Britain*, Core Cities Declaration for Devolution, 14 May, www.corecities.com.

CfC, 2013, *City Deals: Insights from the Core Cities*, Centre for Cities, London, February.

CfC, 2014a, *Cities Outlook 2014a*, Centre for Cities, London.

CfC, 2014b, *Economic Growth Through Devolution: Towards a Plan for Cities and Counties Across England*, Centre for Cities, London.

CfC, 2014c, *Small Business Outlook 2014*, Centre for Cities, London.

CfC, 2014d, *Linking Economic Growth to Public Sector Reform*, Centre for Cities, London.

CfC and MC, 2014, *Industrial Revolutions: Capturing the Growth Potential*, Centre for Cities and McKinsey & Company, London.

Cheshire, P.C., and Gordon, I.R., 1996, "Territorial Competition and the Predictability of Collective (In)Action", *International Journal of Urban and Regional Research*, 20.3, 383–399.

Cheshire, P.C., and Magrini, S., 2009, "Urban Growth Drivers in a Europe of Sticky People and Implicit Boundaries", *Journal of Economic Geography*, 9.1, 85–115.

Clark, G., Huxley, J. and Mountford, D., 2010, *Organising Local Economic Development: The Role of Development Agencies and Companies*, Organisation for Economic Growth and Development, Paris.

CLG and BERR, 2008, *Prosperous Place: Taking Forward the Review of Sub-National Economic Development and Regeneration*, Department for Communities and Local Government and Department for Business Enterprise and Regulatory Reform, London, 31 March.

Colley, L., 2014, *Acts of Union and Disunion: What Has Held the UK Together – and What's Dividing It?*, Profile Books, London.

Combes, P-P., Duranton, G., Overman, H.G. and Venables, A.J., 2006, *Economic Linkages Across Space*, Office of the Deputy Prime Minister, London, January.

Cox, E., and Jeffery, C., 2014, *The Future of England: The Local Dimension*, Institute for Public Policy Research North, Newcastle, April.

Crafts, N., 2012, "Creating Competitive Advantage: Policy Lessons from History", in Greenaway, D., (ed.), *The UK in a Global World: How Can the UK Focus on Steps in Global Value Chains That Really Add Value?*, CEPR Centre for Economic Policy Research and BIS Department for Business Innovation and Skills, London.

Criscuolo, C., and Martin, R., 2008a, "Longitudinal Micro Data Study of Regional Selective Assistance in Wales: Report", CEP Centre for Economic Performance, London.

Criscuolo, C., and Martin, R., 2008b, "Longitudinal Micro Data Study of Regional Selective Assistance in Wales: Final Report Stage 2", CEP Centre for Economic Performance, London.

Criscuolo, C., Martin, R., Overman, H.G. and Van Reenen, J., 2012, "The Causal Effects of an Industrial Policy", *CEP Discussion Paper 1113*, Centre for Economic Policy, London, January.

Crowley, L., Balaram, B. and Lee, N., 2012, *People or Place? Urban Policy in an Age of Austerity*, The Work Foundation, London, September.

CST, 2007, "Strategic Decision-Making for Technology Policy", UK Council for Science and Technology, November. See: http://webarchive.nationalarchives.gov.uk/+/www2.cst.gov.uk/cst/reports/#Strategic.

Davies, H.T.O., Nutley, S.M. and Smith, P.C., 2000, *What Works? Evidence-Based Policy and Practice in Public Services*, Policy Press, Bristol.

DCLG, 2010, *Research Into Multi-Area Agreements: Long-Term Evaluation of LAAs and LSPs*, Department for Communities and Local Government, London.

DCLG, 2011, *Long Term Evaluation of Local Area Agreements and Local Strategic Partnerships 2007–2010: Final Report*, Depart for Communities and Local Government, London.

Denters, B., Goldsmith, M., Ladner, A., Mouritzen, P.E. and Rose, L.E., 2014, *Size and Local Democracy*, Edward Elgar, Cheltenham.

Diamond, P., and Carr-West, J., 2015, *Devolution: A Roadmap*, Local Government Information Unit, London.

Dijkstra, L., Garcilazo, E. and McCann, P., 2013, "The Economic Performance of European Cities and City-Regions: Myths and Realities", *European Planning Studies*, 21.3, 334–354.

Dijkstra, L., Garcilazo, E. and McCann, P., 2016, "The Effects of the Global Financial Crisis on European Regions and Cities: Insights from OECD and European Data", *Journal of Economic Geography*, Forthcoming.

DTI, 2001, *Business Clusters in the UK: A First Assessment. Volume 1: Main Report; Volume 2: Regional Annexes; Volume 3: Technical Annexes*, Department of Trade and Industry, London.

DTI, 2006a, *Innovation in the UK: Indicators and Insights*, DTI Occasional Paper No. 6, Department of Trade and Industry, London.

DTI, 2006b, *Evaluating the Impact of England's Regional Development Agencies: Developing a Methodology and Evaluation Framework*, DTI Occasional Paper No. 2, Department of Trade and Industry, London.

European Union, 2013, *Quality of Life in Cities: Perception Survey in 79 European Cities*, Publications Office, Brussels.

European Union, 2014, *Investment for Jobs and Growth: Promoting Development and Good Governance in EU Regions and Cities*, Sixth Report on Economic, Social and Territorial Cohesion, Publications Office, Brussels, July.

Fabling, R., Grimes, A. and Stevens, P., 2012, "The Relatives Are Fine: Use of Qualitative Firm Data in Economic Analysis", *Applied Economics Letters*, 19.7, 615–618.

Falk, N., 2014, *Funding Housing and Local Growth: How a British Investment Bank Can Help*, The Smith Institute, London.

Foray, D., Goddard, J., Goenaga, X., Landabaso, M., McCann, P., Morgan, K., Nauwelaers, C., Ortega-Argilés, R. and Mulatero, F., 2012, *RIS3 GUIDE*, European Commission Directorate General for Regional Policy and Institute for Prospective Technological Studies, Joint Research Centre, Smart Specialisation Platform, Seville.

Friedmann, J., and Alonso, W., 1964, (eds.), *Regional Development and Planning: A Reader*, MIT Press, Cambridge, MA.

Friedmann, J., and Alonso, W., 1975, (eds.), *Regional Policy: Readings in Theory and Applications*, MIT Press, Cambridge, MA.

Gault, F., 2013, (ed.), *Handbook of Innovation Indicators and Measurement*, Edward Elgar, Cheltenham.

GHK and CURDS, 2006, *What Works in Regional Economic Development: Learning from International Best Practice*, GHK Birmingham and CURDS Newcastle University, August.

Gibbons, S. Nathan, M. and Overman, H.G., 2014, "Viewpoint: Evaluating Spatial Policies", *Town Planning Review*, 85.4, 427–432.

Glennerster, R., 2012, "The Power of Evidence: Improving the Effectiveness of Government by Investing in More Rigorous Evaluation", *National Institute Economic Review*, 219, R4–R14.

Grant Thornton, 2014, *Where Growth Happens: The High Growth Index of Places*, Autumn, www.grant-thornton.co.uk.

Hambleton, R., 2014, "Osborne's Devo Deals Disguise Centralisation", *Local Government Chronicle*, 18 December, p. 23.

Harris, R.I.D., and Moffat, J., 2013, "Total Factor Productivity Growth in Local Enterprise Partnership Regions in Britain, 1997–2008", *Regional Studies*, see: http://dx.doi.org/10.1080/00343404.2013.799770.

Harris, R.I.D., and Robinson, C., 2004, "Impact of Regional Selective Assistance on Sources of Productivity Growth: Plant-Level Evidence from UK Manufacturing", *Regional Studies*, 39, 751–765.

Harris, R.I.D., and Trainor, M., 2005, "Capital Subsidies and Their Impact on Total Factor Productivity: Firm-Level Evidence from Northern Ireland", *Journal of Regional Science*, 45, 49–74.

Harrison, B., 2015, *The Big Debates Emerging Around the Cities Devolution Bill*, Centre for Cities Blog, 26 June, www.centreforcities.org.

Hart, M., and Scott, R., 1994, "Measuring the Effectiveness of Small Firm Policy: Some Lessons from Northern Ireland", *Regional Studies*, 28, 849–858.

Hart, M., Driffield, N., Roper, S. and Mole, K., 2008a, *Evaluation of Regional Selective Assistance (RSA) Selective Finance for Investment in England (SFIE)*, BERR Occasional Paper No. 2, Department for Business Enterprise and Regulatory Reform, London, March.

Hart, M., Driffield, N., Roper, S. and Mole, K., 2008b, *Evaluation of Regional Selective Assistance (RSA) in Scotland 2000–2004*, Scottish Executive Social Research, Scottish Government, Edinburgh, www.scotland.gov.uk/socialresearch.

Hausmann, R., and Rodrik, D., 2003, "Economic Development as Self-Discovery", *Journal of Development Economics*, 72.2, 603–633.

Hazell, R., 2015, (ed.), *Devolution and the Future of the Union*, The Constitution Unit, Department of Political Science, University College London, London, April.

Healey, J., and Newby, L., 2014, *Making Local Economies Matter: A Review of Policy Lessons from the Regional Development Agencies and Local Enterprise Partnerships*, The Smith Institute, London.

Henderson, G., Lodge, G., Raikes, L. and Trench, A., 2015, *Borderland West: Assessing the Implications of a Stronger Wales for the West of England*, IPPR Institute for Public Policy Research North, Newcastle, February.

Heseltine, M., 2012, *No Stone Unturned*, Independent Report Submitted to HM Government, Department for Business, Innovation and Skills, London.

Heywood, A., 2015, *Working Together – Thinking Alike: What Do Councils and Local Enterprise Partnerships Expect from Housing Associations?*, Smith Institute, London.

HM Treasury, 2001, *Productivity in the UK: 3 The Regional Dimension*, HM Treasury, London.

HM Treasury, 2003, *Productivity in the UK: 4 The Regional Dimension*, HM Treasury, London.

HM Treasury, 2015a, *Fixing the Foundations: Creating a More Prosperous Nation*, Cm9098, London, July.

HM Treasury, 2015b, *A Country That Lives Within Its Means: Spending Review 2015*, Cm9112, London, July.

HMT, DTI and ODPM, 2003, *A Modern Regional Policy for the United Kingdom*, HM Treasury, Department of Trade and Industry and Office of the Deputy Prime Minister, London.

HoC, 2008, *Regional Development Agencies: Written Evidence*, Business and Enterprise Select Committee, House of Commons, London.

HoC, 2013, *Bridging the Valley of Death: Improving the Commercialisation of Research*, Eighth Report of Session 2012–13, HC348 Incorporating HC1936-I and ii, Session 2010–12, House of Commons, London, 13 March.

HoC, 2014, *Promoting Economic Growth Locally*, Sixtieth Report of Session 2013–14, HC1110, House of Commons Public Accounts Committee, House of Commons, London, 16 May.

Hope, N., and Leslie, C., 2009, *Challenging Perspectives: Improving Whitehall's Spatial Awareness*, NLGN New Local Government Network, London.

Hughes, A., 2012, "Choosing Races and Placing Bets: UK National Innovation Policy and the Globalisation of Innovation Systems", in Greenaway, D., (ed.), *The UK in a Global World. How Can the UK Focus on Steps in Global Value Chains That Really Add Value?*, BIS e-book, CEPR and Department for Business, Innovation and Skills. See: www.cepr.org/pubs/books/cepr/BIS_eBook.pdf.

Hughes, A., and Kitson, M., 2013, *Connecting with the Ivory Tower: Business Perspectives on Knowledge Exchange in the UK*, UK-IRS UK Innovation Research Centre, Cambridge.

Hutton, W., 2015, *How Good Can We Be: Ending the Mercenary Society and Building a Great Country*, Little Brown, London.

ICA, 2015, *Growth Beyond Big Cities: The Role of Britain's Industrial Towns in Delivering Jobs and Prosperity*, Industrial Communities Alliance, Barnsley.

IfG, 2013a, *Civil Service Capabilities*, Kidson, M., Institute for Government, London.

IfG, 2013b, *Connecting People with Practice: People Powered Change: Insights from the Connecting Policy with Practice Programme in 2013*, Hughes, N., Institute for Government, London.

IfG, 2014a, *Civil Service Reform: One Year On*, Thomas, P., Kidson, M. and Wright, W., Institute for Government, London.

IfG, 2014b, *The Civil Service in Territorial Perspective: A Data-Driven Analysis of Whitehall and the Devolved Administrations*, Paun, A., and Munro, R., with Whitehall Monitor, Institute for Government, London.

IfG, 2014c, *Whitehall Monitor 2014: A Data-Driven Analysis of the Size, Shape and Performance of Whitehall*, Freeguard, G., Bouchal, P., Munro, R., Nimmo, C., and McCrae, J., Institute for Government, London.

IfG, 2014d, *Achieving Political Decentralisation: Lessons from 30 years of Attempting to Devolve Power in the UK*, Gash, T., Randall, J. and Sims, S., Institute for Government, London.

IPPR, 2012, *Northern Prosperity is National Prosperity: A Strategy for Revitalising the UK Economy*, Institute for Public Policy Research North, Newcastle, November.

IPPR, 2014a, *Devo More and Welfare: Devolving Benefits and Policy for a Stronger Union*, Institute for Public Policy Research, London, March.

IPPR, 2014b, *Home Economics: The Role of Housing in Rebalancing the Economy*, Institute for Public Policy Research North, Newcastle, July.

IPPR, 2015, *Developing Resilient Local Economies: Good Practice Among Local Enterprise Partnerships*, Institute for Public Policy Research North, Newcastle, February.

Isard, W., 1960, *Methods of Regional Analysis: An Introduction to Regional Science*, The Technology Press and Wiley, New York.

Isard, W., Schooler, E.W. and Vietorisz, T., 1959, *Industrial Complex Analysis and Regional Development*, John Wiley and Sons, New York.

Jaffe, A.B., 2015, A Framework for Evaluating the Beneficial Impacts of Publicly-Funded Research, Motu Note No. 15, Motu Economic and Public Policy Research, Wellington, New Zealand.

Jessop, B., 2000, "Governance Failure", in Stoker, G., (ed.), *The New Politics of British Local Government*, Macmillan, Basingstoke.

Jones, M., 2009, "Phase Space: Geography, Relational Thinking, and Beyond", *Progress in Human Geography*, 33.4, 487–506.

JRF, 2014, *How Can Local Skills Strategies Help Low Earners?*, Sissons, P., and Jones, K., Joseph Rowntree Foundation, York.

King, C., 2014, "Toil and Trouble: Scotland's Vote Created More Problems Than It Solved", *Foreign Affairs*, 19 September.

Lambert, R., 2003, *Lambert Review of Business-University Collaboration: Final Report*, Report to the Chancellor of the Exchequer, London.

Lawless, P., Overman, H.G. and Tyler, P., 2011, *Strategies for Underperforming Places*, SERC Policy Paper 6, Spatial Economics Research Centre, London.

LFC, 2013, *Raising the Capital: The Report of the London Finance Commission*, London Finance Commission, London.

LGA, 2010, *Who's In Charge? Decision Miles*, Local Government Association, London.

LGA, 2013a, *Modelling Devolution: Working Together to Deliver Local Services*, Local Government Association, London.

LGA, 2013b, *Higher Education and Local Government: Collaborating for Growth*, Local Government Association, London.

LGG, 2010, *Funding and Planning for Infrastructure*, Local Government Group, London, September.

Link, A.N., and Vonortas, N.S, 2013, (eds.), *Handbook on the Theory and Practice of Program Evaluation*, Edward Elgar, Cheltenham.

McCann, P., 2015, *The Regional and Urban Policy of the European Union: Cohesion, Results-Orientation and Smart Specialisation*, Edward Elgar, Cheltenham.

McCann, P., and Ortega-Argilés, R., 2013a, "Modern Regional Innovation Policy", *Cambridge Journal of Regions, Economy and Society*, 6.2, 187–216.

McCann, P., and Ortega-Argilés, R., 2013b, "Redesigning and Reforming European Regional Policy: The Reasons, the Logic and the Outcomes", *International Regional Science Review*, 36.3, 424–445.

McCann, P., and Ortega-Argilés, R., 2013c, "Transforming European Regional Policy: A Results-Driven Agenda and Smart Specialisation", *Oxford Review of Economic Policy*, 29.2, 405–431.

McInroy, N., and Jackson, M., 2015, *The Local Double Dividend: Securing Economic and Social Success*, The Smith Institute, London.

McKee, D.L., Dean, R.D. and Leahy, W.H., 1970, (eds.), *Regional Economics*, Free Press, New York.

Macwhirter, I., 2014, *Disunited Kingdom: How Westminster Won a Referendum but Lost Scotland*, Cargo Publishing, Glasgow.

Mazzucato, M., 2013, *The Entrepreneurial State: Debunking Public vs Private Sector Myths*, Anthem Books, London.

MC and IfG, 2014, *International Delivery: Centres of Government and the Drive for Better Policy Implementation*, Mowat Centre and Institute for Government, Toronto and London.

Meyer, J.R., Kain, J.F. and Wohl, M., 1965, *The Urban Transportation Problem*, Harvard University Press, Cambridge, MA.

Moffat, J., 2013, "Regional Selective Assistance (RSA) in Scotland: Does It Make a Difference to Plant Survival?", *Regional Studies*. See: http://dx.doi.org/10.1080/003 43404.2013.786826.

Moffat, J., 2014, "Regional Selective Assistance in Scotland: Does It Make a Difference to Plant Productivity?", *Urban Studies*, 51.12, 2555–2571.

Moore, B., and Rhodes, J., 1973, "Evaluating the Effects of British Regional Economic Policy", *Economic Journal*, 83, 87–110.

Moretti, E., 2012, *The New Geography of Jobs*, Houghton Mifflin Harcourt, New York.

NAO, 2003, *Regional Grants in England*, Report by the Comptroller and Auditor General, HC702, Session 2002–2003, London, 17 June.

NAO, 2005, *Guidance on Independent Performance Assessment of the Regional Development Agencies*, National Audit Office, London.

NAO, 2010a, *Regenerating the English Regions: Regional Development Agencies' Support to Physical regeneration Projects*, Report by the Comptroller and Auditor General HC214, Session 2009–10, National Audit Office, London, 30 March.

NAO, 2010b, Independent Supplementary Reviews of the Regional Development Agencies, National Audit Office London, June.

NAO, 2012, *The Regional Growth Fund*, Report by the Comptroller and Auditor General HC17, Session 2012–13, National Audit Office, London, 11 May.

NAO, 2014, *Progress Report on the Regional Growth Fund*, Report by the Comptroller and Auditor General, National Audit Office, London, 20 February.

NESTA, 2011, *Innovation in the Public Sector Organisations: A Pilot Survey for Measuring Innovation Across the Public Sector*, Hughes, A., Moore, K. and Kataria, N., London.

NESTA, 2012a, *Innovation in Policy: Allowing for Creativity, Social Complexity and Uncertainty in Public Governance*, Christiansen, J., and Bunt, L., London.

NESTA, 2012b, *Neighbourhood Challenge: Learning from Innovative Communities*, London.

NESTA, 2013a, *State of Innovation: Welsh Public Services and the Challenge of Change*, Gatehouse, M., and Price, A., London.

NESTA, 2013b, *Innovation in the Public Sector: How Can Public Organisations Better Create, Improve and Adapt?*, Mulgan, G., London.

NESTA, 2013c, *Making Evidence Useful: The Case for New Institutions*, Mulgan, G., and Puttick, R., London.

NESTA, 2013d, *What Should the 'What Works Network' Do?*, Puttick, R., and Mulgan, G., London.

NESTA, 2014, *The End of the Treasury*, Wilkes, G., and Westlake, S., London.

NESTA, 2015, *Government as Impresario: Emergent Public Goods and Public Private Partnerships 2.0*, Gruen. N., London.

ODPM, 2004, *Assessing the Impacts of Spatial Interventions: Regeneration, Renewal and Regional Development. The 3Rs Guidance*, Office of the Deputy Prime Minister, London.

ODPM, 2006a, *State of the English Cites, Urban Research Summary 21*, Office of the Deputy Prime Minister, London.

ODPM, 2006b, *State of the English Cites, Volume 1*, Office of the Deputy Prime Minister, London.

ODPM, 2006c, *State of the English Cites, Volume 2*, Office of the Deputy Prime Minister, London.

OECD, 2001a, *Cities for Citizens: Improving Metropolitan Governance*, Organisation for Economic Cooperation and Development, Paris.

OECD, 2001b, *Citizens as Partners: OECD Handbook on Information, Consultation and Public Participation in Policy-Making*, Organisation for Economic Cooperation and Development, Paris.

OECD, 2004, *New Forms of Governance for Economic Development*, Organisation for Economic Cooperation and Development, Paris.

OECD, 2005, *Building Competitive Regions: Strategies and Governance*, Organisation for Economic Cooperation and Development, Paris.

OECD, 2007, *Linking Regions and Central Government: Contracts for Regional Development*, Organisation for Economic Cooperation and Development, Paris.

OECD, 2008, *Making Local Strategies Work: Building the Evidence Base*, Organisation for Economic Cooperation and Development, Paris.

OECD, 2009a, *Regions Matter: Economic Recovery, Innovation and Sustainable Growth*, Organisation for Economic Growth and Development, Paris.

OECD, 2009b, *Governing Regional Development Policy: The Use of Performance Indicators*, Organisation for Economic Growth and Development, Paris.

OECD, 2009c, *Community Capacity Building: Creating a Better Future Together*, Organisation for Economic Cooperation and Development, Paris.

OECD, 2010, *Regional Development Policies in OECD Countries*, Organisation for Economic Growth and Development, Paris.

OECD, 2011a, *Regions and Innovation Policy*, Organisation for Economic Growth and Development, Paris.

OECD, 2011b, *OECD Regional Outlook 2011: Building Resilient Regions for Stronger Economies*, Organisation for Economic Cooperation and Development, Paris.

OECD, 2011c, *Together for Better Public Services: Partnering with Citizens and Civil Society*, Organisation for Economic Cooperation and Development, Paris.

OECD, 2012a, *Promoting Growth in All Regions*, Organisation for Economic Cooperation and Development, Paris.

OECD, 2012b, *Reforming Fiscal Federalism and Local Government: Beyond the Zero-Sum Game*, Organisation for Economic Cooperation and Development, Paris.

OECD, 2013, *Government at a Glance 2013*, Organisation for Economic Growth and Development, Paris.

OECD, 2014a, *OECD Regional Outlook; Regions and Cities – Where Policies and People Meet*, Organisation for Economic Cooperation and Development, Paris.

OECD, 2014b, *How's Life in Your Region? Measuring Regional and Local Well-Being for Policy Making*, Organisation for Economic Cooperation and Development, Paris.

OECD, 2015a, *Governing the City*, Organisation for Economic Growth and Development, Paris.

OECD, 2015b, *The Metropolitan Century: Understanding Urbanisation and Its Consequences*, Organisation for Economic Growth and Development, Paris.

OECD, 2015c, *Ageing in Cities*, Organisation for Economic Cooperation and Development, Paris.

OEEC, 1961, *Regional Economic Planning: Techniques of Analysis for Less Developed Areas*, Organisation for European Economic Cooperation, Paris.

ONS, 2015, *GVA for Local Enterprise Partnerships, 1997–2013*, Prothero, R., Office for National Statistics, 19 February.

Overman, H.G., 2012, "Geographical Economics and Policy", in Fischer, M.M., and Nijkamp, P., (eds.), *Handbook of Regional Science*, Springer, Heidelberg.

Pawson, R., 2006, *Evidence-Based Policy: A Realist Perspective*, Sage, London.

Pike, A., Marlow, D., McCarthy, A., O'Brien, P. and Tomaney, J., 2015, "Local Institutions and Local Economic Development: The Local Enterprise Partnerships (LEPs) in England, 2010–", *Cambridge Journal of Regions, Economy and Society*, Forthcoming.

Pilch, A., 2004, (ed.), *Towards a Modern Regional Policy*, The Smith Institute, London.

ResPublica, 2015, *The Missing Multipliers: Devolution to Britain's Key Cities*, London, October.

ReVelle, C., 1987, "Urban Public Facility Location", in Mills, E.S., (ed.), *Handbook of Regional and Urban Economics Volume 2: Urban Economics*, North-Holland, Amsterdam.

Riddell, P., 2015, "It's the Constitution, Stupid", *Prospect*, 8 May.

Rodrik, D., 1999, "Institutions for High Quality Growth: What They Are and How to Acquire Them", Lecture Presented at the IMF Conference on Second Generation Reforms. See: www.imf.org/external/pubs/ft/seminar/1999/reforms/rodrik.htm and published as Rodrik, D., 2000, *NBER Working Paper 7540* and in Roy, K.C. and Sideras, J., 2006, (eds.) *Institutions, Globalisation and Empowerment*, Edward Elgar, Cheltenham UK and Northampton, MA.

Rodrik, D., 2004, "Industrial Policy for the Twenty-First Century", Working Paper, Kennedy School of Government, Harvard University, Cambridge, MA.

Rodrik, D., 2007, *One Economics Many Recipes: Globalization, Institutions and Economic Growth*, Princeton University Press, Princeton.

RSA, 2014a, *Powers to Grow: City Finance and Governance*, City Growth Commission, October. See: https://www.thersa.org/discover/publications-and-articles/reports/ unleashing-metro-growth-final-recommendations/.

RSA, 2014b, *Unleashing Metro Growth: Final Recommendation*, Royal Society of Arts, City Growth Commission, London, October. See: www.thersa.org/ discover/publications-and-articles/reports/unleashing-metro-growth-final-recommendations/.

RSA, 2014c, *UniverCities: The Knowledge to Power UK Metros*, Royal Society of Arts, City Growth Commission, London, October. See: https://www.thersa.org/discover/ publications-and-articles/reports/univercities-the-knowledge-to-power-uk-metros/.

RSA, 2014d, *Human Capitals: Driving UK Metro Growth Through Workforce Investment*, Royal Society of Arts, City Growth Commission, London, July. See: https:// www.thersa.org/discover/publications-and-articles/reports/human-capitals-driving-uk-metro-growth-through-workforce-investment/.

RSA, 2015, *Devo Met: Charting a Path Ahead*, Royal Society of Arts, City Growth Commission, London, March. See: https://www.thersa.org/discover/ publications-and-articles/reports/devo-met-charting-a-path-ahead/.

SGPTD, 2013, *Second Tier Cities and Territorial Development in Europe: Performance, Policies and Prospects*, Applied Research 2013/1/11, ESPON, Luxembourg.

Shaw, K., Blackie, J., Robinson, F. and Henderson, G., 2013, *Borderlands: Can North East and Cumbria Benefit from Greater Scottish Autonomy?*, Association of North East Councils and Institute for Public Policy Research North, Newcastle, July.

Slack, E., and Coté, A., 2014, *Comparative Urban Governance*, Government Office for Science, Future of Cities Working Paper, London.

Smith Commission, 2014, *The Smith Commission: Report of the Smith Commission for Further Devolution of Powers to the Scottish Parliament*, Edinburgh, 27 November.

Swales, J.K., 1997, "A Cost-Benefit Approach to the Evaluation of Regional Selective Assistance", *Fiscal Studies*, 18.1, 73–85.

Trench, A., 2013, *Funding Devo More: Fiscal Options for Strengthening the Union*, Institute for Public Policy Research, London, January.

Ward, M., 2014, "Regional Growth Fund", *Standard Note SN/EP/5874, Economic and Policy Statistics*, House of Commons Library, London.

Wellings, B., 2012, *English Nationalism and Euroscepticism: Losing the Peace*, Peter Lang, Oxford.

Witty, A., 2013, *Encouraging a British Invention Revolution: Sir Andrew Witty's Review of Universities and Growth: Final Report and Recommendations*, Department for Business, Innovation and Skills, London. See: https://www.gov.uk/government/ uploads/system/uploads/attachment_data/file/249720/bis-13-1241-encourag ing-a-british-invention-revolution-andrew-witty-review-R1.pdf.

Wong, C., Webb, B., Schulze-Baing, A., Baker, M. and Hincks, S., 2015, "Monitoring Government Policies and Programmes in England", in Woltjer, J., Alexander, E., Hull, A. and Ruth, M., (eds.), *Place-Based Evaluation for Infrastructure and Spatial Projects*, Ashgate, Farnham.

World Bank, 2010, *Innovation Policy: A Guide for Developing Countries*, World Bank, Washington DC.

World Bank, 2011, *Igniting Innovation: Rethinking the Role of Government in Emerging Europe and Central Asia*, Goldberg, I., Goddard, J.G., Kuriakose, S. and Racine, J-L., World Bank, Washington DC.

Wright, M., 2014, *Making the UK a Globally Competitive Investment Environment, The Wright Review of Advanced Manufacturing in the UK and Its Supply Chain.* See: www.thewrightreport.net.

WWN, 2014, *What Works? Evidence for Decision Makers*, What Works Network, London.

Postscript

Rodrik (2011) has argued that in the face of modern globalisation modern states cannot continue to co-exist in their current (pre-modern globalisation) form with democracy, because so many fundamental influences on the economy are external to the decision-making power of the state and also beyond the state's ability to respond to the democratic wishes of its citizens. The UK is a case in point. The influence of modern globalisation on the UK has been so enormous, as to effectively tear the country into certainly two, and possibly three largely separate economies. This is reality which the highly centralised UK state has been largely unable to influence, to shape or to respond to, and in some sense, the highly centralised state has inadvertently exacerbated the problem. As we have examined in detail throughout this book the fortunes of the UK economy have indeed increasingly 'gone south' (Elliot and Atkinson 2012) in a manner which was largely unexpected and unintentional and a result of modern globalisation, and only partly intentional and planned due to the UK's top-down institutional, governance and policy-settings. However, the consequences of this are that, in spite of the fact that London has become one of the world's most globalised cities, the UK as a whole in real terms has barely progressed in almost half a century relative to other EU and OECD countries. Relative to the other advanced economies throughout the OECD and the EU, the long-run productivity gains associated with London and the southern regions of England are largely cancelled out by the poor productivity performance of the non-core regions of the UK. In reality there are no real beneficial economic spillovers from the core regions to the non-core regions, except possibly for the case of Scotland, and the result is that the UK as a whole has effectively made no real progress over more than four decades relative to our competitors. Moreover, simply promoting further things that the UK apparently does well in such as higher education, international finance, the Queen and the BBC[1] along with Heathrow Airport and even London as a whole, will not improve the national situation in the long run, because the issues are too deep and wide-ranging in nature. The UK is characterised by long-standing strengths and structural weaknesses which are fundamentally geographical and regional in nature. They are heavily intertwined with the UK's global relationships, but most importantly with its relationships with the

EU, which in economic terms are far larger than most observers realise, and which impact on the UK's different regions in very different ways. Moreover, as a result of the differential geographical impacts of modern globalisation, the weaknesses of the UK's non-core regions relative to the core regions have become even more serious over recent decades. The UK is now at a point where the national governance and institutional system is not only largely incapable of responding to these deep-seated weaknesses, but to a large extent is now also a contributor to the ongoing structural weaknesses.

However, this book has not argued that the economic geography of UK regional development patterns is either solely or even primarily a result of institutional or governance questions. On the contrary, the book has argued that the various spatial market mechanisms reflect the impacts of extraordinarily powerful globalisation forces and processes, which ultimately drive the observed patterns of economic geography. While they are useful in describing some specific mechanisms and responses, models of new economic geography and urban economics as a whole tell us very little about the internal workings of the UK economy, Instead, a broader regional economics and regional science approach with some urban economic elements included provides a far more instructive and appropriate analytical framework for understanding the economic geography of the UK economy. At the same time, governance and institutional issues do shape to various degrees the possible responses to, and outcomes of, market forces, and in many cases the institutional-shaping of market outcomes is non-trivial (IfG 2014, 2015). Indeed, as has also been explained at various points in the book, within the UK the increasing disengagement, dislocation and decoupling of the 'south' and the 'north' demonstrates that the highly centralised UK governance systems and the associated primacy of London in UK economic policy-making has proved in hindsight to have been both overly centralised and far too narrowly framed. A simple test of this contention is to consider whether UK political parties would have campaigned in favour of the current landscape and whether the UK electorate would have voted for this scenario some 30 years ago, if they had known in advance that these outcomes were to transpire. In all likelihood the answer would have been a resounding no, except possibly for the most libertarian-minded voters. Obviously, none of today's outcomes could have been foreseen, and indeed none of them were. But this is not the point. The point is that the actual outcomes are largely unintended and unexpected and the UK governance system has proven to be not only largely impotent in responding to these interregional problems, but to varying extents appears unwittingly to have exacerbated them. This is one of the reasons why there has been such a widespread backlash against governance centralisation and top-down institutional arrangements across all parts of England as well as across the four devolved nations of the UK.

The evidence and arguments in this book derived from more than two thousand different sources and from worldwide comparative evidence suggest that there are profound arguments suggesting that fundamental devolutionary shifts are in the interests of the UK state as a whole, as long as they are implemented at the right spatial scales and with the appropriate governance tools and representation. In particular, finding ways to increase the prosperity of the UK's second and third tier cities in line with the experience of so many other countries which are richer than the UK (Dijkstra *et al.* 2013; LJMU 2012) ought to be a serious priority. However, such devolution and decentralisation trends face serious obstacles precisely because of the structure and culture of the central UK government and civil service. The current UK city-region devolution arrangements are at much smaller scales than most of the highest levels of sub-national government in large federal countries and at the same time at a scale which is consistent with the lowest levels of public trust in city governments. The extent to which these devolutionary changes can respond to the UK's burgeoning interregional inequalities and imbalances remains to be seen, although there are serious challenges ahead. In particular, the devolutionary trends currently in motion also point to the creation of a highly skewed and unbalanced quasi-federal structure with little underlying consideration to the long-run fiscal implications (Bell 2015), and which may well lead in the long run to further fundamental governance problems.

A final issue which also colours all of these discussions concerns the ongoing attempts to eradicate the public sector deficit. The opportunities associated with governance devolution will be undermined if the public perceives devolution as being an easy means by which central government is able to implement public sector cutbacks while attempting to avoid much of the blame. In the popular media the purported need for the UK's widespread public sector cutbacks is based on the argument that the economic problems faced by Britain in the aftermath of the 2008 global economic crisis were largely due to debt-addiction (Kaletsky 2015a), overly high public expenditure and excessive public borrowing. The subsequent 2010 'emergency' Budget aimed at stabilising the public finances therefore supposedly saved the UK from bankruptcy (Kaletsky 2015a) and in the long run has led to a recent recovery of demand. While there are still debates regarding the actual growth figures,[2] many of these public debt and deficit-related arguments are regarded as being largely bogus both by a wide range of serious academic economists across different analytical schools (Krugman 2015; Martin and Rowthorn 2012)[3] and also on practical grounds by those who manage public finances (Kaletsky 2015a, 2015b). In 2007, immediately prior to the 2008 crisis, UK government debt to GDP ratio was close to its lowest level in a century while the budget deficit was also quite small and inflation was low (Krugman 2015; Kaletsky 2015c). Many argue that the 2010 Budget quashed a recovery which had already begun (Krugman 2015) and directly led to a four-year slump (Keegan 2014). The deteriorating public finances were thus primarily a result of stagnant output growth (Krugman 2015), which as Keynes had explained is an entirely unsurprising outcome when deficit-reduction policies are introduced at a time when interest rates are close to zero (Kaletsky 2015a; Keegan 2014). Furthermore, the ongoing discussions in the UK media about long-term fiscal plans and the likely timing of the balancing of the UK's public finances are in reality also largely meaningless given that public deficits represent a small difference between two huge numbers, namely public spending and taxation, either of which can be affected by many unpredictable factors (Kaletsky 2015a). Yet, irrespective of the veracity or otherwise of these arguments, the political economy reality that the UK will have to live with for the coming decade is one of public sector retrenchment. However, whereas UK political debates in the last six years have been dominated by discussions of deficits, there has been almost no discussion of the UK's weak productivity performance. In the coming years these issues will return with a vengeance in political debates because in the end the economic welfare and societal well-being of the country depend crucially on its productivity performance. The productivity collapse of much of the UK is overwhelmingly borne by the non-core regions of the UK, and it is these same regions which are also facing the sharpest public sector retrenchment. The idea that governance devolution should also be associated with fiscal neutrality and that cuts in interregional transfers are likely to proceed further does nothing to address the underlying economic problems regarding the non-core regions. The problems of the UK's non-core regions are not just self-contained local problems. Rather, they are problems regarding the economic and governance relationships between the core regions and the non-core regions or, more accurately, the almost total absence of such relationships. The UK's long-run growth and productivity problem is as much as anything else a regional problem, a problem of economic geography, and one which is compounded by an overly centralised governance structure. The greater is the extent to which the UK maintains primarily a space-blind, top-down and sectoral logic to its governance and policy-making processes the less it will be able to successfully respond to these issues. However, a more interventionist shift in UK policy-making can currently be detected in which the government plays more of a role in shaping the economic and social decisions affecting productivity, and the governance devolution and the regional agenda are central to this shift (Kaletsky 2015c). As we have already seen, in the case of the UK the urban economic arguments favouring the policy prioritisation of cities are generally very weak, in that the performance of most UK cities does not reflect simple textbook-type models. On purely positive grounds, therefore, the logic of city-focused policy prioritisation is rather limited, and the positive justification based on existing performance is largely restricted to the more prosperous regions of the UK. On the other hand, given the existing scale of UK urbanisation, the majority of the UK's economic and social problems as well as the majority of the UK's economic and social possibilities are also to be found in cities. As such, the current logic of city-focused policy prioritisation can be strongly justified on normative grounds, with policy aiming to shift the workings and productivity performance of UK cities much closer to that which would be expected from a textbook-type model. As such, this is a place-based argument based on realising the untapped economic potential of the cities, given their assets and institutions. If successful, improving city productivity in our under-performing cities and regions will significantly contribute to improving overall UK productivity and the city-region governance reforms are intended to help achieve this. However, whether the current devolutionary trends and institutional reforms can indeed help the UK to overcome its deep-seated productivity problems in the long run still remains to be seen (NEF/CC 2015), and as this book has explained, there are still major challenges and risks ahead.[4] Moreover, these challenges are magnified by ambiguities regarding the links between devolution and the intended societal objectives which devolution is designed to achieve (NEF/CC 2015). Yet, it may also be the case that the current city-region devolution agenda is the key idea (Rodrik 2014) which helps to build consensus and to overcome much of the natural resistance to institutional changes. If so, this may help to foster a long overdue process of national governance reforms and productivity improvements based on a broader understanding of the regional underpinnings of UK prosperity.

Notes

1 See: Elliot and Atkinson (2012) and the review of their book *A Black and White View of Britain's Economy* in the *Financial Times* on 18 June 2012 by Lord Andrew Adonis and also the book review "Relegation for Albion" in *The Economist* on 28 July 2012.
2 "Perhaps Austerity Didn't Choke Off UK Recovery", www.bbc.com/news/business-34402234.
3 "Osborne's Plan Has No Basis in Economics", *The Guardian*, 12 June 2015.
4 www.theguardian.com/business/2015/dec/10/north-south-divide-set-to-widen-over-next-three-years-study-shows?CMP=Share_iOSApp_Other. See: Cities Outlook 2016, Centre for Cities, London http://www.centreforcities.org/wp-content/uploads/2016/01/Cities-Outlook-2016.pdf. http://www.theguardian.com/business/2016/jan/25/north-heads-list-of-low-wage-high-welfare-cities. Townsend, A., and Champion, T., 2014, "The Impact of the Recession on City Regions: The British Experience", Local Economy, 29, 38–51. "While London Rides the Crossrail Gravy Train, the North is Stuck in Reverse", The Guardian, 25 February 2016. https://www.jrf.org.uk/report/uneven-growth-tackling-city-decline. Regional GDP, Eurostat News Release, 39/2016, 26 February 2016, Eurostat, European Commission, Luxembourg.

References

Bell, D., 2015, "The Aftermath of the Scottish Referendum: A New Fiscal Settlement for the UK?", in Bailey, D., and Budd, L., (eds.), *Devolution and the UK Economy*, Rowman and Littlefield, London.

Dijkstra, L., Garcilazo, E. and McCann, P., 2013, "The Economic Performance of European Cities and City-Regions: Myths and Realities", *European Planning Studies*, 21.3, 334–354.

Elliot, L., and Atkinson, D., 2012, *Going South: Why Britain Will Have a Third World Economy by 2014*, Palgrave Macmillan, Basingstoke.

IfG, 2014, *Political Economy of Infrastructure in the UK*, Coelho, M., Ratnoo, V. and Dellapiane, S., Institute for Government, London.

IfG, 2015, *Political Economy of Growth and Reform*, Coelho, M., Institute for Government, London.

Kaletsky, A., 2015a, "Getting Credit for Everything: The Chancellor's Cunning Plan", *Prospect*, April.

Kaletsky, A., 2015b, "Britain's Greatest Problem", *Prospect*, May.

Kaletsky, A., 2015c, "Osborne Has Rejected Thatcher", *Prospect*, August.

Keegan, W., 2014, *Mr Osborne's Economic Experiment: Austerity 1945–51 and 2010–*, Searching Finance, London.

Krugman, P., 2015, "This Snookered Isle", *New York Times*, 24 March.

LJMU, 2012, *Second Tier Cities in Europe: In an Age of Austerity Why Invest Beyond the Capitals?*, European Institute for Urban Affairs, Liverpool John Moores University and ESPON, Liverpool.

Martin, W., and Rowthorn, R., 2012, *Is the British Economy Supply Constrained II? A Renewed Critique of Productivity Pessimism*, UK-IRC UK Innovation Research Centre, Cambridge.

NEF/CC, 2015, *Democracy: The Missing Link in the Devolution Debate*, Lyall, S., Wood, M. and Bailey, D., Report Presented at the Symposium England's Dreaming: The New Devolution Debate, New Economics Foundation and the Crick Centre, London and Sheffield, 3 December.

Rodrik, D., 2011, *The Globalization Paradox: Why Global Markets, States and Democracy Can't Coexist*, Oxford University Press, Oxford.

Rodrik, D., 2014, "When Ideas Trump Interests: Preferences, Worldviews, and Policy Innovations", *Journal of Economic Perspectives*, 28.1, 189–208.

Index

References to illustrations are given in *italics*.

Taylor & Francis eBooks

Helping you to choose the right eBooks for your Library

Add Routledge titles to your library's digital collection today. Taylor and Francis ebooks contains over 50,000 titles in the Humanities, Social Sciences, Behavioural Sciences, Built Environment and Law.

Choose from a range of subject packages or create your own!

Benefits for you

>> Free MARC records
>> COUNTER-compliant usage statistics
>> Flexible purchase and pricing options
>> All titles DRM-free.

REQUEST YOUR **FREE** INSTITUTIONAL TRIAL TODAY

Free Trials Available
We offer free trials to qualifying academic, corporate and government customers.

Benefits for your user

>> Off-site, anytime access via Athens or referring URL
>> Print or copy pages or chapters
>> Full content search
>> Bookmark, highlight and annotate text
>> Access to thousands of pages of quality research at the click of a button.

eCollections – Choose from over 30 subject eCollections, including:

Archaeology	Language Learning
Architecture	Law
Asian Studies	Literature
Business & Management	Media & Communication
Classical Studies	Middle East Studies
Construction	Music
Creative & Media Arts	Philosophy
Criminology & Criminal Justice	Planning
Economics	Politics
Education	Psychology & Mental Health
Energy	Religion
Engineering	Security
English Language & Linguistics	Social Work
Environment & Sustainability	Sociology
Geography	Sport
Health Studies	Theatre & Performance
History	Tourism, Hospitality & Events

For more information, pricing enquiries or to order a free trial, please contact your local sales team:
www.tandfebooks.com/page/sales

 Routledge
Taylor & Francis Group

The home of
Routledge books

www.tandfebooks.com